D0376322

EARLY AMERICAN
ARCHITECTURE

Bell-tower of the mission church. San Diego de Alcalá, California (*Floyd Ray*)

EARLY AMERICAN ARCHITECTURE

FROM THE FIRST

COLONIAL SETTLEMENTS

TO THE NATIONAL PERIOD

BY HUGH MORRISON

Dover Publications, Inc.
New York

NOTE TO THE DOVER EDITION, 1987

The following titles listed in the "Reading Suggestions" at the ends of chapters in the present volume have been reprinted by Dover Publications:

Architects' Emergency Committee, *Great Georgian Houses of America* (Dover 0-486-22491-0 and 22492-9).

J. Frederick Kelly, *The Early Domestic Architecture of Connecticut* (Dover 0-486-21136-3).

Russell Hawes Kettell, ed., *Early American Rooms, 1650–1858* (Dover 0-486-21633-0).

Alfred Easton Poor, *Colonial Architecture of Cape Cod, Nantucket and Martha's Vineyard* (Dover 0-486-22375-2).

Published in Canada by General Publishing Company, Ltd., 30 Lesmill Road, Don Mills, Toronto, Ontario.
Published in the United Kingdom by Constable and Company, Ltd.

This Dover edition, first published in 1987, is an unabridged, unaltered republication of the third printing (1966) of the work originally published by Oxford University Press, New York, in 1952. The present edition is published by special arrangement with Oxford University Press, 200 Madison Avenue, New York, N.Y. 10016.

Manufactured in the United States of America
Dover Publications, Inc., 31 East 2nd Street, Mineola, N.Y. 11501

Library of Congress Cataloging-in-Publication Data

Morrison, Hugh, 1905–
  Early American architecture.

  Originally published: New York : Oxford University Press, 1952.
  Bibliography: p.
  Includes indexes.
  1. Architecture, Colonial—United States. 2. Neoclassicism (Architecture)—United States. 3. Architecture, Modern—19th century—United States. 4. Architecture—United States. I. Title.
NA707.M63 1987   720′973   87-6745
ISBN 0-486-25492-5 (pbk.)

Table of Contents

Part Two. Spanish and French Colonial Architecture

Part Three. Georgian Architecture: 1700–1780

CONTENTS

Foreword

*'Upon these considerations, we have been induced to undertake the present
extensive work: the purpose of which is to instruct rather than to amuse; in
which nothing will be omitted that is elegant or great; but the principal regard
will be shown to what is necessary and useful.'* — ISAAC WARE (1756)

MY PURPOSE in writing this book has been quite as grimly didactic
as was that of Isaac Ware, and if any entertainment or amusement
has crept in, it is purely coincidental. Like his, mine has been an extensive task: a comprehensive account in one volume of architecture in the
American colonies from St. Augustine in 1565 to San Francisco in 1848.

One might justifiably question the need for such a work, for writings
on this field are legion. Frank J. Roos in his invaluable bibliography,
Writings on Early American Architecture, lists nearly three thousand
items — books, monographs, periodical articles, and so on — on architecture in the eastern half of the United States before 1860, and scores more
have been published since that list was compiled in 1943.

But no one book, hitherto, has attempted to deal with *all* types of
buildings — houses, churches, forts, log cabins, markets, mills, public
buildings, colleges, and the like — as these developed over several generations in *all* the colonies — English, Dutch, Swedish, French, and Spanish —
over the widespread regions of the present-day United States. Such a book,
it seemed, might be useful.

My effort, accordingly, has been to present an organized history of architecture in the American colonies, gathering together as well as might
be the essential contributions of scores of books on special building types
and on the architecture of various states and regions, as well as the dis-
closures of hundreds of periodical articles on special research problems.
No one volume, of course, can do full justice to so large a subject, and it
is necessary at once to acknowledge that many scores of buildings of fine
quality and considerable historical interest have received no mention —
despite the almost irresistible temptation to include them.

Since complete inclusiveness was impossible, the effort has been to make
a revealing selection from the mass of available material, in the interest of
clarity and meaningful interpretation. There is, to be sure, a substantial
framework of facts, technical terms, names, and dates. But the chief aim
has been to give a clearly organized and extensive body of information
in a form and in terms that the layman without previous knowledge of
architectural history may readily understand.

The primary emphasis of the book is on the character and development of the many styles in early American architecture, and the conditions and influences that produced them. I have chosen, for reasons given in the first chapter of the text, to apply the term 'Colonial,' as a stylistic designation, to the styles of the seventeenth century, and the term 'Georgian' to that of the eighteenth century. In order to make the several styles clear, each one has been presented, both in text and illustrations, by a selection of typical or 'classical' examples, by monuments of unusual historical importance, and particularly by buildings that are dated with reasonable certainty. This selective method has its limitations. Actually, in traveling about the country, we seldom encounter 'classics'; most buildings are stylistic mixtures, or so simple in form and decoration as to escape stylistic classification. Even so, many are of excellent architectural quality, and a few such 'hybrid' or 'minor' structures are included. But on the whole it has seemed wisest to reveal stylistic norms; the reader, with increasing experience, will discover for himself that architecture is an art of almost infinite variety.

There is more to architecture, of course, than mere style. I have devoted much attention to what is 'necessary and useful' in buildings: matters of structure and of plan, materials and methods of building, and even such practical problems as heating, lighting, and sanitation, though information on these matters is gravely inadequate. Likewise some account of the people of the colonial period, the kind of life they led, the tools and furniture they used, the carpenters and masons who built their houses and churches and taverns, forms part of the broad picture I have attempted to draw.

I have been particularly interested in regionalism in American architecture. While endeavoring to avoid romantic references to 'picturesque' New Orleans, 'quaint' Cape Cod, or 'glamorous' Santa Barbara, I have tried to bring out the distinctive quality and color of architecture in the many different regions of the country, and occasionally to picture its setting in the plantations, villages, and towns of the colonial era.

It will be seen that illustrations play a large part in this book. It has always seemed to me that in studying architecture we should learn to read buildings themselves, rather than mere words about them. For this purpose, almost every building referred to in the text is illustrated, and many not only by exterior views but by plans, interior views, and details, so that they may be known inside and out. The text is shaped directly to the illustrations and refers to them constantly. Many of the plans, maps, and charts have been especially drawn, and the photographs are the best a long search could discover. For greater usefulness, each illustration is listed in the index, under the name of the building, location, or appropriate technical term. Speaking of technical terms, I have defined or made clear the meaning of such where they first appear in the text, and have also listed them in the index with reference to appropriate text passages or pictures; the index thus serves as an illustrated glossary of technical terms.

Reference notes — giving the source of a quotation or of information —

are relegated to the back of the book, where they are numbered in sequence by chapters. But 'content' notes, which elaborate or qualify the text, appear at the foot of the appropriate page.

The bibliography at the end of each chapter is a selected list of the best books on the field of that chapter, but makes no attempt at completeness or, particularly, reference to articles in periodicals. Additional bibliographical information may easily be found in the book by Roos mentioned above, and in the *Art Index* to periodical literature.

For the convenience of teachers and scholars who may wish to obtain original prints of photographs used in this book, the reference matter contains an index of institutions and individuals from whom photographs were obtained and their addresses at time of publication.

Hanover, New Hampshire   *Hugh Morrison*
October 1951

Acknowledgments

FOR AID in making this book, first tribute is owed to Philip Aylwin White of Springfield, Vermont, who made more than forty drawings of plans, structural details, and maps. For his conscientious and skilful help and his faithful friendship throughout the progress of the work, I extend my warmest thanks.

To the Guggenheim Foundation I am grateful for award of a fellowship in the year 1948–9, during which the major portion of the text was completed.

My greatest debt is to the men and women whose scholarship over the past two generations has built up the increasingly solid structure of American architectural history. To most of them I can accord only the passing salute of a reference note at the back of the book, small recognition indeed for valuable work on which I have leaned heavily.

But I would pay special tribute to the men to whom I owe most: to Fiske Kimball, whose *Domestic Architecture of the American Colonies and of the Early Republic* established a generation ago a scholarly basis for subsequent study of early American architecture, and who read most of the typescript and helped the project in many ways; to Thomas Tileston Waterman, architect and outstanding author whose recent death has been a great blow to scholarship in this field; and to Professor Talbot Hamlin of Columbia, whose careful checking of the typescript gave me many valuable suggestions.

I would also acknowledge the great value to me of the work of the following: John Mead Howells on New Hampshire; Martin Shaw Briggs on Massachusetts and East Anglia; John Frederick Kelly on Connecticut; Harold J. Shurtleff and Samuel Eliot Morison on the log cabin and other special fields; Antoinette Forrester Downing on Rhode Island; Helen Reynolds and Rosalie Fellows Bailey on the Dutch Colonial; Thomas Jefferson Wertenbaker on the middle colonies; Henry Chandlee Forman on Maryland and the South; Samuel Gaillard Stoney and Beatrice St. Julien Ravenel on South Carolina; Carl Bridenbaugh on the cities of the eastern seaboard and on the architect Peter Harrison; Charles E. Peterson and Samuel Wilson on the architecture of the Mississippi valley; George Kubler on New Mexico; and Rexford Newcomb and John A. Berger on California and the Southwest.

As for colleagues and friends at Dartmouth College, I extend cordial thanks to Professor Arthur Jensen for editorial help; to Professor Van H. English for his work on maps; to Miss Maude French of the Carpenter Art Library and Miss Mildred Morse of the Department of Art for their unfailing helpfulness at every stage of the work; and to Miss Virginia L. Close of the Reference Department of the Baker Library.

With only one exception, my requests to publishers for permissions to reproduce illustrative material or quote passages from books were generously granted. My many obligations in this respect are indicated by the credit lines and the reference notes, but I would make especial mention of the generous help of the University of North Carolina Press, the Harvard University Press, and the Yale University Press.

Obtaining photographs for this work entailed hundreds of letters to museums, historical societies, and photographers in all parts of the United States. Again, my obligations are so numerous that they can be suggested only by the credit lines, but I am especially indebted for the generous and intelligent assistance given by Colonial Williamsburg, Inc.; the Essex Institute at Salem; the Historic American Buildings Survey at the Library of Congress; the Holland Society of New York; and the Mount Vernon Ladies Association of the Union.

To the many photographers whose work is represented in this book I am most grateful for permission to reproduce pictures. I wish to express especial thanks for generous co-operation to Wayne Andrews of the New-York Historical Society; Samuel Chamberlain of Marblehead; Mr. and Mrs. Reginald G. Esden of Hanover; Donald R. Hannaford of San Francisco; Laura Gilpin of Santa Fe; Cortlandt Van Dyke Hubbard of Philadelphia; and Frances Benjamin Johnston of Washington.

The entire group of photographs was purchased for the collection of the Department of Art and Archaeology at Dartmouth College, and I wish to express warm appreciation to Dartmouth College for permitting these photographs to be used in the production of the book.

Mrs. George Maurice Morris and Mr. Charles Scarlett, Jr. helped me generously with both information and photographs of their beautiful homes, The Lindens in Washington and Whitehall near Annapolis. Warm thanks are due to Shepard Vogelgesang and Stevenson Flemer for contributing drawings.

And, of course, for long-suffering, generous, and intelligent help from start to finish, my wife Elizabeth Newman Morrison deserves the biggest and most grateful credit line of all.

Dartmouth College   H. M.

Part One

COLONIAL ARCHITECTURE

THE SEVENTEENTH CENTURY

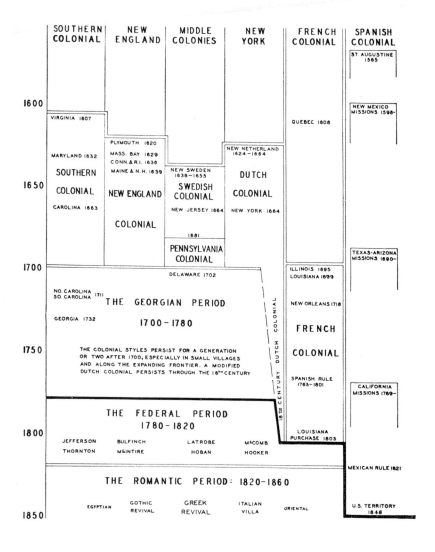

	SOUTHERN COLONIAL	NEW ENGLAND	MIDDLE COLONIES	NEW YORK	FRENCH COLONIAL	SPANISH COLONIAL
						ST AUGUSTINE 1565
1600	VIRGINIA 1607				QUEBEC 1608	NEW MEXICO MISSIONS 1598-
	MARYLAND 1632	PLYMOUTH 1620 MASS. BAY 1629 CONN. & R.I. 1636		NEW NETHERLAND 1624—1664		
	SOUTHERN	MAINE & N.H. 1639 NEW ENGLAND	NEW SWEDEN 1638—1655 SWEDISH	DUTCH		
1650	COLONIAL		COLONIAL	COLONIAL		
	CAROLINA 1663	COLONIAL	NEW JERSEY 1664	NEW YORK 1664		TEXAS-ARIZONA MISSIONS 1690-
			1681 PENNSYLVANIA COLONIAL			
1700	NO. CAROLINA SO. CAROLINA 1711	DELAWARE 1702 THE GEORGIAN PERIOD 1700-1780			ILLINOIS 1695 LOUISIANA 1699 NEW ORLEANS 1718 FRENCH	
	GEORGIA 1732					
1750	THE COLONIAL STYLES PERSIST FOR A GENERATION OR TWO AFTER 1700, ESPECIALLY IN SMALL VILLAGES AND ALONG THE EXPANDING FRONTIER. A MODIFIED DUTCH COLONIAL PERSISTS THROUGH THE 18TH CENTURY			18TH CENTURY DUTCH COLONIAL	COLONIAL SPANISH RULE 1763-1801	CALIFORNIA MISSIONS 1769-
1800	THE FEDERAL PERIOD 1780-1820 JEFFERSON THORNTON	BULFINCH McINTIRE	LATROBE HOBAN	McCOMB HOOKER	LOUISIANA PURCHASE 1803	
						MEXICAN RULE 1821
1850	THE ROMANTIC PERIOD: 1820-1860 EGYPTIAN	GOTHIC REVIVAL	GREEK REVIVAL	ITALIAN VILLA	ORIENTAL	U.S. TERRITORY 1848

1. Chart of the chief periods and styles of American architecture to 1860 (Philip White)

1

The Colonial Styles

THE ARCHITECTURE of colonial America spanned more than two centuries of time and most of a continent in space. From the crude shelters of the first settlers it developed first to the medieval style of the seventeenth century and then to the Renaissance formalities of the eighteenth. It extended through regions as disparate as New England and California, Florida and the Midwest, the Atlantic seaboard and the deep South. In each region and in each generation, architecture reflected prevalent conditions of climate, materials, building techniques, and social organization, but even more was it influenced by the historic national traditions of the peoples settling the new continent, and by the ebb and flow of the architectural tides originating in Europe.

This book is a history of the Colonial and Georgian styles in America, and of the conditions and influences that produced them. The story is not a simple one, and to give the reader an over-all perspective we may introduce it by a chart of the main periods and styles of American architecture to 1860 (fig. 1). Our chronological limits are indicated by the solid black line on the chart: to the Revolutionary War in the colonies of the Atlantic seaboard; to 1803 in French Louisiana; and to 1848 in the Spanish colonies. The vertical divisions indicate the chief regional styles. The only important horizontal division within the colonial period is that which separates the seventeenth and eighteenth centuries in the eastern colonies; this line marks a profound and important change of style, and introduces an inevitable problem of terminology. Just what do we mean by the term ' Colonial '?

' Colonial ' and ' Georgian '

Quite arbitrarily, we shall in this book use the term ' Colonial ' to apply to those styles that flourished in the eastern colonies in the seventeenth century, and the word ' Georgian ' for the style that flourished in the eighteenth century in the English colonies of the Atlantic seaboard. The fact that the eastern provinces remained colonies of England until the Revolution may make such a distinction seem slightly illogical — as indeed it is from the standpoint of political history. There are three reasons, however, why it may be helpful in discussing architectural history.

First, it points up the immense difference between the seventeenth- and eighteenth-century styles rather more forcefully than do the corresponding terms ' Early Colonial ' and ' Late Colonial.' Secondly, it avoids a certain confusion in discussing the evolution of each of these styles; the author, quite candidly, has always been befuddled by terms such as ' The Late Early Colonial Style ' or ' The Early Late Colonial Style,' and prefers the relative lucidity of ' Late Colonial ' and ' Early Georgian.'

The third reason for adopting terms as defined above is that the evolution of usage seems to justify it. During the 1870's and 1880's, when early American architecture first began to be studied, almost everything from the hypothetical log cabins of the Pilgrims to the white-columned mansions of the pre-Civil War era was termed, with fine indiscrimination, ' Colonial.' From the 1890's onward, the buildings of the last century and a half of that era were singled out as ' Georgian.' Still later, as scholarship progressed, the post-Revolutionary styles were further distinguished from the Georgian as ' Federal ' and ' Greek Revival.' By this time the word ' Colonial,' robbed of much of its former broad scope, had no precise significance as a stylistic term. But in recent years it has increasingly been applied to ' all that was left ' — the styles of the seventeenth century. We are content to use it in this latest sense. The confusion with political history is in any case a minor one, and it is minimized by the custom, adopted in this book, of capitalizing the word ' Colonial ' when referring to architectural style rather than to a political era. Since the field of American architectural history has not yet achieved a universally accepted terminology of periods and styles, it is perhaps better to be arbitrary in choosing and defining terms than to compound the confusions of the past.

With this apology, then, we shall refer to the first three major chronological divisions of American architectural history as the Colonial period, to 1700; the Georgian period, from 1700 to 1780; and the Federal period, from 1780 to 1820. It goes without saying that the evolution of architectural style is a continuous flow, like time itself, and any division by dates is arbitrary. Transitions from one style to another do not occur overnight, but as a gradual process occupying a decade or two; and such transitions occur at different times in different places. While it is true, for example, that in cities such as Boston, Newport, Philadelphia, Williamsburg, or Charleston, the Colonial style developed into the Georgian as early as 1700, or the Georgian in turn gave way to the Federal style shortly after the Revolution, it is also true that in northern New England, across the Alleghenies, and in the Old West similar transitions occurred from one to three generations later. The sequence of styles in American architecture is geographic as well as chronological; it is a sequence that repeats itself, belatedly and variously, along the ever-expanding frontier.

Colonial styles of the eastern regions

The distinctive qualities of architecture in different regions seem of particular importance and interest in a country of such great geographic size and such variety in climate and available building materials. The great differences in the Colonial styles of the several regions of America were due in part to such physical factors, but even more largely to the diverse nationalities of the first settlers. The Southern Colonial style of Maryland and Virginia and the New England Colonial style were most nearly akin, since they were both imported from England, but there were characteristic differences between them, due partly to climate and partly to the different economic developments of the two regions. The Dutch Colonial of New York and northern New Jersey originated in Holland and Flanders and developed as a distinctive style of great tenacity; even after the Georgian was victorious in most of the English colonies, Dutch Colonial persisted in its own course until well after the Revolution.

New Sweden was founded in 1638 in the Delaware region, and Swedes are credited with introducing the log cabin to this country; but the colony lasted only a generation and its architectural influence was minor. More important was the Pennsylvania Colonial style, but settlement in that region began so late in the seventeenth century (Philadelphia was founded in 1682), and architecture developed so rapidly into a full-fledged Georgian style that the Pennsylvania Colonial tradition is discussed in Part III of this book as but a prelude to the Georgian architecture of that region. The strong impress of the German settlers in Pennsylvania on architecture and crafts continued, however, well into the eighteenth century.

These regional styles, needless to say, were not so neatly bordered and defined as our maps and pictures may suggest. Architectural borders, like climatic ones, blur into bands; rarely are they as clean-cut as the line through the middle of Long Island that once separated New England and Dutch Colonial styles; more often they reveal fascinating mixtures and blends. But regional differences did exist and, once established, continued to manifest themselves to some degree throughout the Georgian and Federal periods.

Medieval character of the seventeenth-century styles

All the Colonial styles, except the Spanish, were medieval; their origins were in the late Gothic styles of western Europe. Nothing in the New World, of course, approached the architectural magnificence of the great cathedrals, the rich guild halls, or the splendid manor houses of Gothic Europe; no pioneer society could afford buildings of such size or elaboration. But the emigrants to the colonies could aspire to equal the farmhouses and barns of the rural towns whence most of them came, and the Colonial buildings of New England and Virginia are transplanted replicas of the humbler structures of England's Gothic villages, just as the Dutch Colonial style owes its form and motives to the late medieval houses of Flanders and Holland.

When America was first settled, the Gothic style was already outmoded in the countries of western Europe; all the largest and finest edifices were being built in the new manner of the Renaissance (fig. 2). By the year 1600, Italy had long since forgotten the Gothic; France had built its lovely chateaux on the Loire, and the great palaces of the Louvre and Fontainebleau were growing; Spain had adopted the 'Cold Classic' of Philip II; and Holland was experimenting with the new classic vocabulary. In the very year that the Pilgrims landed at Plymouth, Londoners could see rising over the throngs of traffic in Whitehall the towering walls of a new palace designed for James I in the severely formal manner of the Italian Renaissance.

But these great stone palaces, though ' advanced ' in style, were few in number; the new mode was still the prerogative of aristocracy. Perhaps few of the men who emigrated to the colonies had seen them, and those who did, we may imagine, were not favorably impressed. Architectural taste, for the common man, is not established by seeing, as a visitor, one or two fashionable new buildings in a fast metropolis of dubious moral repute; it is established by the buildings and the streets that surrounded

ITALY	FRANCE	SPAIN	ENGLAND	AMERICA
1420 EARLY RENAISSANCE		GOTHIC PERIOD		
1500 HIGH RENAISSANCE	EARLY RENAISSANCE	PLATERESQUE		1500
DEVELOPED RENAISSANCE	DEVELOPED	ELIZABETHAN	1570	
1600	RENAISSANCE	JACOBEAN	1600	
BAROQUE	RENAISSANCE PERIOD			COLONIAL
	LOUIS XIV	ANGLO-CLASSIC (STUART)		
1700	CHURRIGUERESQUE			1700
	LOUIS XV (ROCOCO)	(BAROQUE)	GEORGIAN	GEORGIAN
	LOUIS XVI			
1780 NEOCLASSIC	EMPIRE	NEOCLASSIC	NEOCLASSIC	1780 FEDERAL
	MODERN PERIOD			

2. Chart of major European styles of the Renaissance period (Philip White)

him as he grew up, that he lived in and loved as home. If the hardy Essex villager who ventured a trip to London chanced to glimpse Whitehall Palace, Greenwich Palace, or Bedford Square, we may guess that he preferred the old brick and half-timbered Gothic buildings that lined London's streets until the Great Fire of 1666, and that he liked best of all the thatch-roofed cottages of his native village.

Thus it is easy to understand that when the colonists came to settle in a wilderness, they not only lacked the time, the skill, the architectural knowledge, the materials, and the money to duplicate the great Renaissance mansions of the aristocracy; they lacked even the desire to do so. It took nearly a century to evolve the economic means, the building skills, and the social ambitions for an aristocratic architecture, and when these arrived, the Georgian style was born. Thus the curious fact that, though the Renaissance in architecture began in England as early as 1570, it did not begin in America until 1700. The lag of 130 years is no mere aesthetic accident; it measures the gap between the economic and social conditions of Europe and those of pioneer America.

Simplicity and practicality were the keynotes of the Colonial styles. Building was a direct outgrowth of urgent practical necessities; there was little time or money for elaboration or adornment, and Colonial houses had very little ornament. Exteriors were a frank and honest statement of interior uses and structural necessities. The houses have an indigenous flavor, a native quality, that make them seem genuine and permanent rather than period pieces. In contrast to the later Georgian, the Colonial styles were entirely unpretentious; they were the expression of a pioneer society, whereas the Georgian, with its formal symmetry and its finer materials and delicately executed ornament, was the expression of a wealthy and polite society.

The Spanish Colonial style

The Spanish Colonial architecture of Florida and the Southwest, and the less-known French Colonial architecture of New Orleans and the Mississippi valley, are both so different from the Colonial styles of the Atlantic seaboard, so remote from them geographically, and of such different chronological span, that they deserve separate treatment. They are therefore taken up in Part II. It will be observed in the chart (fig. 1) that the history of Spanish Colonial architecture, over a period of nearly 300 years, embraces a span of time nearly as long as the whole history of American architecture in other regions. The Spanish also differs from all other Colonial styles in its complete departure from the medieval. Spain's earliest Renaissance style (the Plateresque) had begun seventy years earlier than England's Elizabethan and by 1600 had evolved through the correct classic formalities of the developed Renaissance into the extravagant and exciting corruptions of the Baroque.

These styles, like all Renaissance styles, were primarily the creation and the expression of absolutism and aristocracy. Moreover, Spain's colonization of the New World originated, not in the grass roots of religious rebellion or economic escape, but in the halls of the Escorial. Spain's conquest was imposed from the top: she wanted gold for the King and souls for the Faith. Her soldiers and *comandantes* were trained in the royal army, and her missionary padres in the Franciscan and Jesuit orders. The style they imported to the New World was the newer, official style of Church and State — the Spanish Baroque. Brought four thousand miles across sea and trackless desert, simplified by the crude hands of Indian laborers, muted by wind-blown sands, it gave its unmistakable accent and grace to the golden missions of the Southwest.

By the time the Mexican flag was run down at Monterey in 1846, the eastern seaboard had passed through a new architectural era, the Federal period, marked by a new influence — the wave of Neoclassicism that swept over all western Europe at the end of the eighteenth century. Thomas Jefferson's Capitol at Richmond demonstrated that by 1785 we had finally caught up with the vanguard of European architectural fashions. Impelled by a new national self-consciousness and led by our first great individual architects, men such as Bulfinch and McIntire, Jefferson and Latrobe, the United States entered a great period of building and achieved one of its finest styles.

But in the period of Romanticism which followed, the promising augury of a single national, and American, style disintegrated into aesthetic confusion. The Greek Revival and Gothic Revival were twin spearheads of a romantic eclecticism that garnished the land with Greek temples and Gothic castles, Egyptian pylons and Italian villas, Romanesque churches and Islamic mosques. The ideal of *style* as the fit and comely expression in form of necessary plan and structure gave way to the ideal of styles as optional envelopes, and the more exotic the better. Architecture, as Lewis Mumford has put it, became more scenery than solid.

The nadir of this decline was reached in the period following the Civil War. But out of the awkward shapes and vulgar details, the ostentatious display and aesthetic bankruptcy of these dismal decades, arose the foundations of a valid modern architecture in the work and thinking of the great American triumvirate, Richardson, Sullivan, and Wright. On these foundations has been built the achievement of the twentieth century: a developing modern American architecture which may yet become one of the great styles of architectural history.

No period is, of course, uniform within itself or has a monopoly on merit; in every period and in every region of American architecture we can find much not only of interest but of fine quality, and through it all the impressive panorama of the growth of civilization on a new continent.

Primitive shelters of the first settlers

That growth had crude beginnings indeed. When the colonists first landed, they had neither time nor facilities to build substantial frame or brick houses such as they knew in the mother countries. So in all the colonies — Plymouth, Massachusetts Bay, Rhode Island, Connecticut, New Netherland, Maryland, Virginia — for the first few years they built but crude shelters to house themselves that they might survive.

In 1620 the *Mayflower* did not drop anchor in Plymouth Harbor until 16 December. Under gray skies, with cold winds and snow flurries, fifty-three adult men faced the task of providing food, shelter, and protection against a winter that had already begun. Groups of men went on shore every day to fell and carry timber, returning at night to sleep on the boat. By Christmas Day they began erecting their first building, a storehouse some twenty feet square. In that first winter they built seven ' cottages ' to live in, a meeting-house, and two more storehouses. Seven dwellings for 102 men, women, and children would have meant an insupportable congestion except that, in Governor Bradford's words, ' that which was most sadd and lamentable was, that in .2. or .3. moneths time halfe of their company dyed, espetialy in Jan: and February, being the depth of winter, and wanting houses and other comforts. . .' [1]

The landing at Jamestown in 1607 had been on 14 May, a more clement season, and the men began straightway to build a fort and some flimsy and inadequate shelters against sun and rain. Speaking of the September of that year, Captain John Smith wrote: ' As yet we had no houses to cover us, our Tents were rotten, and our Cabbins worse than nought. . .' [2] The relief ships which arrived in January 1608 found the survivors 'utterly destitute of howses, not one as yet built, so that they lodged in cabbins and holes within the grounde. . .' [3]

Much the same was true at New Amsterdam. Cornelis Van Tienhoven, Secretary of New Netherland, described the dugouts used by the first families:

Those in New Netherland and especially in New England who have no means to build farmhouses at first according to their wishes, dig a square pit in the ground, cellar fashion, six or seven feet deep, as long and as broad as they think proper; case the earth all round the wall with timber, which they line with the bark of trees or something else to prevent the caving-in of the earth; floor this cellar with plank, and wainscot it overhead for a ceiling; raise a roof of spars clear up, and cover the spars with bark or green sods so that they can live dry and warm in these houses with their entire families for two, three or four years, it being understood that partitions are run through these cellars, which are adapted to the size of the family. [4]

From a number of such early descriptions, it is possible to define four types of temporary shelters built by the first colonists. None of them was newly invented. The wigwam was borrowed from the Indians; the others were based on the crude huts and cabins of shepherds, charcoal burners, and peat diggers on the moors and meadows of England.

Dugouts. Most primitive were dugouts, such as those described by Van Tienhoven. They were pits dug in the ground and roofed over by poles and bark. Sometimes they were only half-excavated, to a depth of about three feet, with an upper wall built of sods.

Cabins. 'Cabin' meant a much more flimsy structure in the seventeenth century than it does today. Usually its walls were made of vertical stakes driven into the ground, with wattles (willow or hazel withes) woven between them and daubed with clay. Forked sticks (' crotchets ') supported a short ridgepole, which carried a roof of poles and turf or thatch.

Wigwams. The prevailing type of Indian wigwam, from Quebec to the Carolinas, was not the conical tepee of the western plains Indians, but a round-roof structure of oblong plan. It was usually about twice as long as it was wide. The structure consisted of a framework of slender poles, the butt ends stuck into the ground and the tops bent over and lashed together to form a semi-cylindrical roof. This framework was covered by Indian woven mats or pressed bark or skins. A square hole in the middle of the roof let out the smoke of the fire. The Indians also built smaller wigwams, round in plan and covered by a dome-shaped roof, like a beehive.

The Indian wigwam was clearly easier to build, more weatherproof, and more spacious than the primitive dugouts and cabins, and the colonists adopted both the structure and the name. The English improved the Indian model by constructing fireplaces and crude wooden chimneys, and providing doors hung by wooden hinges to hewn door frames (fig. 3).

Cottages. 'Cottages' were built within the first year of settlement at Plymouth, Salem, Jamestown, and elsewhere. The word sometimes meant, in the seventeenth century, a temporary shelter such as a cabin, but more

3. An 'English wigwam' reconstructed at Pioneer Village, Salem, Mass. (Paul J. Weber)

often it seems to have meant a more permanent structure, built like a frame house but of ruder construction and inferior finish. The colonists brought with them axes, adzes, and other tools for rendering timber, and we know that by 1608 at Jamestown and by 1621 at Plymouth, clapboards were being exported to England. There are also early references to 'hewn

4. Leyden Street, Plymouth, in 1627 (Samuel Chamberlain etching from Harold R. Shurtleff, *The Log Cabin Myth*, Harvard University Press)

planks.' It seems probable, from all available evidence, that cottages were built with frames of hewn planks or squared timbers, covered by broad boards laid flush, or smaller lapped clapboards.

Some may have had wattle-and-daub walls, as in England; both Bradford and Winslow refer to the fact that in 1621 a storm 'caused much daubing of our houses to fall down.' But more likely the wattle-and-daub was used as a filling between exterior clapboards and an interior wainscot of matched boards. Or the filling may have consisted simply of clay and chopped straw, a mixture that was sometimes formed into rolls called 'cats' and used as an insulating material.

Perhaps the seven cottages at Plymouth, recorded as completed by the fall of 1622, were of this type. A drawing of Leyden Street restored as it may have appeared in 1627 (fig. 4) shows two clapboard cottages, one story with garret, plain batten doors, small shuttered windows, and thatched roofs. The chimneys were made of hewn timbers connected by crosspieces and filled with wattle-and-daub. The ground floor inside was probably beaten earth. The flimsy chimney construction and inflammable thatched roofs caused the Plymouth Colony to pass a law in 1626 stipulating that new houses should not be thatched, but roofed 'with either board, or pale and the like.'

On the hill in the distance is the fort built in the summer of 1622 to guard the settlement. It was made with a strong frame of hewn oak timbers, walled by planks heavy enough to stop arrows. These were mortised into the corner posts, and there were girts and summer beams to support the flat roof. Governor Bradford wrote that it was

5. English cottages reconstructed at Pioneer Village, Salem (Paul J. Weber)

both strong and comly . . . of good defence, made with a flate rofe and batll-
ments, on which their ordnance were mounted, and wher they kepte constante
watch, espetially in time of danger. It served them allso for a meeting house and
was fitted accordingly for that use.[5]

The Pioneer Village at Salem (fig. 5), built for the Massachusetts Bay
Tercentenary celebration in 1930, is a careful reconstruction of Salem village as it may have appeared in the first years of settlement. There are several cottages of a type similar to that at Plymouth, except that here the
walls are of broad boards nailed flush on the frame, and some of the chimneys are of small logs laid cob-fashion, plastered inside with clay. Plain
batten doors, small shuttered windows, and thatched roofs are also evident. The photograph shows, in the background, a round-roof ' English
wigwam.'

The log-cabin myth

For the past hundred years it has commonly been supposed that the
' cabins ' built by the early settlers were log cabins. This legend has been

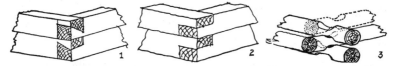

6. Types of log construction: (1) hewn logs with half-dovetail joints, blockhouse
type; (2) hewn logs with lapped joints, blockhouse type; (3) round logs with saddle-
notched joints, log-cabin type (Harold R. Shurtleff, *The Log Cabin Myth*, Harvard
University Press)

thoroughly studied by Shurtleff in his extremely valuable book, *The Log
Cabin Myth*.[6]

By ' log cabin ' we mean a dwelling built of round logs, laid horizontally one on another, with notched corners and protruding ends. A detail
of the corner construction is seen in figure 6; each log has a curved notch
cut on both top and bottom to permit a close interlock. Spaces between
logs, if any, are chinked with moss, clay, or oak chips. As defined above,
the log cabin did not exist in any of the English colonies in the seventeenth century and was used very little throughout most of the eighteenth
century. Neither did the Dutch use it in New Netherland, nor the French
in Canada. It was a form of construction unknown in England, France,
Holland, and southern Europe generally; it was likewise unknown to the
American Indian.

The log cabin is a very superior form of construction for a pioneer society. The technique of building it is not difficult; it can be constructed
quickly by a group of neighbors out of pine and spruce logs readily available in most wilderness regions; it requires no tool but an axe; most important it requires no nails or other hardware, virtually impossible to procure in a frontier land. It is strong, durable, and reasonably weatherproof.
It is tempting to believe that our early ancestors, gifted with ingenuity as

well as courage, invented such an admirable solution to their urgent problem of quick and durable shelter.

Apparently they did not. The English colonists did build blockhouses and prisons using logs hewn square and notched at the corners for either lapped or dovetailed joints (fig. 6). This is indeed a superior type of construction, but it requires many tools and much skill and more time. The log cabin, if it had been known, would have supplanted the flimsy dugouts and cabins and wigwams the pioneer settlers actually built.

True log-cabin construction is thought to have been introduced into this country by the Swedes when they settled Delaware in 1638. Log cabins were widely prevalent in Scandinavia in the early seventeenth century, particularly in Sweden. There are several literary records of ' log houses ' built in Delaware in the seventeenth century, and a Dutch traveler named Danckaerts saw one in 1679 which he described as having notched corners and protruding ends. In the eighteenth century, German settlers in Pennsylvania built large numbers of log houses, using both squared-log and round-log construction. Since most of the Germans entered the country by way of the Delaware valley, they may have acquired the technique from the Swedes, though log construction was known in Switzerland and in parts of Germany, and they may have introduced it independently.

English colonists were reluctant to use the log cabin for dwelling purposes, even in the eighteenth century, and it was the Scotch-Irish who did most to popularize its use. Coming from a land of inferior housing conditions, they found it highly practical and satisfactory. Penetrating to the frontier of Maine and New Hampshire, pushing westward across the Alleghenies and southward into Virginia and North Carolina, the Scotch-Irish made the log cabin a symbol of the American pioneer. The form became common by the mid-eighteenth century, and the name ' log cabin ' in its modern sense was first used in an Irish community in the valley of Virginia in 1770.

How did it happen that the modern ' log-cabin myth ' grew up? It is indeed, as Shurtleff has said, a comedy of errors. It all started in the famous ' log cabin and hard cider ' presidential campaign of 1840. A Democratic orator, impugning the rival candidate's refinement, said that the White House was too good for him; William Henry Harrison would be content, he orated, with a log cabin and a jug of hard cider. The Whigs took up this golden opportunity with alacrity. William Henry Harrison, they averred, was the kind of American who would be *proud* to live in a log cabin; the log cabin became a symbol of courage, simplicity, honesty, ruggedness, and plain democratic homely Americanism. They passed out log-cabin badges, sang log-cabin songs, and celebrated with plenty of hard cider. Daniel Webster, in a moving speech at Saratoga, pictured his old family log cabin ' amid the snowdrifts of New Hampshire ' as the home and hearth of all the toil, sacrifice, indomitable courage, and domestic virtue that had been wrought into the fabric of this great land. Harrison won the election, and for the rest of the century the log cabin became a valuable political asset.

The next year (1841), the Reverend Alexander Young, a Whig, published his *Chronicles of the Pilgrim Fathers* and, in an innocent footnote to the first year at Plymouth, stated that the Pilgrims' houses ' were probably log-huts, thatched, and the interstices filled with clay.' Before many years, other historians accepted and developed the log-cabin myth. In speeches, articles, journals, and learned histories, it snowballed. In historical pageants, Puritans garbed in sober black and white — which they never wore — prayed to God and killed Indians before the doors of reconstructed log cabins — which they never lived in. School textbooks came out with convincing illustrations of pioneer Plymouth and Jamestown, of Miles Standish or of John Alden and Priscilla, all before log-cabin settings. Serious historians accepted the myth as a matter of course, and even found much evidence in early chronicles to support it. Small wonder: building records of the early seventeenth century are scanty, and their terminology obscure with forgotten words about unknown techniques. It was easy to misinterpret them. But with the publication in 1939 of Shurtleff's book, a model of exacting scholarship, there can no longer be any doubt in our minds about the log-cabin myth.

The first frame houses

As soon as they were able, the early settlers replaced their flimsy and temporary dugouts, cabins, and wigwams with ' fayre houses ' — in other words substantial and well-finished houses such as they had lived in in the mother country. Within a year or two, in most settlements, timber-framed houses were under construction. Saw pits were dug, brick kilns were set up, and there was a hum of activity. In the words of Robert Johnson, describing the life at Henrico, Virginia, in 1612:

Being thus invited, here they pitch, the spade men fell to digging, the brickmen burnt their bricks, the company cut down wood, the Carpenters fell to squaring out, the Sawyers to sawing, the Souldier to fortifying, and every man to somewhat. And to answer the first objection for holesome lodging, here they have built competent and decent houses, the first storie all of bricks, that every man may have his lodging and dwelling place apart by himselfe, with a sufficient quantitie of ground alotted thereto for his orchard and garden to plant at his pleasure, and for his own use.[7]

Probably most temporary shelters were replaced by permanent structures within a decade after settlement in each colony. And though the former remained characteristic of new settlements on the advancing frontier of each succeeding period, they were soon but a memory in the old established colonies. By the middle of the seventeenth century the pious and garrulous Edward Johnson could write of Massachusetts Bay:

. . . the Lord hath been pleased to turn all the wigwams, huts, and hovels the English dwelt in at their first coming, into orderly, fair, and well-built houses, well furnished many of them, together with Orchards filled with goodly fruit trees, and gardens with variety of flowers. . .[8]

The houses they built are almost identical in structure and in style to **those they had left at home in England, and it would be hard to cite a** more striking instance of the tenacity of the craft traditions of an old culture, persisting under new conditions and in a new environment, than the extraordinary similarity between the Colonial houses of New England and the late medieval houses of Old England.

The English architectural background

The majority of the early settlers of New England were hard-working, thrifty, English middle-class folk. And until the outbreak of the civil war in England in 1642, almost all of them came to America to seek religious freedom rather than wealth. They came, most of them, from the farming and fishing villages of the southeastern counties of England: Norfolk, Suffolk, Essex, Cambridge, Hertford, Middlesex, Surrey, and Kent; small towns and crossroads villages such as Haverhill, Sudbury, Ipswich, Dedham, Toppesfield, Wethersfield, Braintree, Hadham, Maldon, Billericay, Wickford, Canterbury — to name only a few that are familiar to New Englanders today.

In the early seventeenth century the architecture of these English towns was still entirely medieval. Houses were predominantly timber-framed structures; building stone was lacking in the whole region and was imported only for the most expensive buildings. ' Solid ' brick houses were built in Norfolk; but in Suffolk, Essex, and Kent brick was used for big manor houses and churches rather than for ordinary houses. And in Hertford, Middlesex, and Surrey it was hardly used at all; the timber-framed house was all but universal in this region.

The timber frame was a massive affair of hewn oak posts and beams, pegged at the intricate joints; its construction, followed in the seventeenth-century houses of New England, will be treated in detail in the following chapter.

The wall itself, supported by the timber frame (a kind of embryonic skyscraper construction), was composed of two general types of filling or insulation. The most primitive of these, used in the cheaper houses, was wattle-and-daub, a basketwork of willow or hazel withes set into the interstices of the frame and daubed with clay or plaster inside and out. Clay was cheaper than plaster but could not be left exposed to the weather; a hard plaster was accordingly preferred. Made of sand and lime thoroughly mixed, with cow hair and dung kneaded in as a binder, it was generally white in color and very durable. In the second type of filling, brick masonry (' nogging ') was built within the interstices of the frame. If protected by plaster or boards, the cheaper ' soft ' or unburned bricks could be employed; if exposed to the weather, hard burned bricks were used, laid in horizontal courses or sometimes in decorative herringbone patterns.

The wall filling, either of wattle-and-daub or of brick nogging, was sometimes left exposed but was generally protected by an exterior surface of plaster, clapboards, or slates. Several combinations of structure and material were thus possible, and the houses of an English medieval village presented a rich variety of pattern, color, and texture. Five of the most common architectural effects are illustrated in figure 7, an imaginary reconstruction of a row of medieval houses. The first is timber-framed with both frame and brick nogging exposed to the weather, affording a warm color combination of dark brown and orange-red. The second has both frame and filling covered by an exterior coat of hard white plaster. The third, which might have a wall filling of either soft brick or clay, is protected by an outer layer of clapboards. The English call these ' weatherboards '; they are usually wider than the clapboards used in colonial America (6 to 8 inches instead of 5), and are either flat or tapered to a thin edge. In the seventeenth century, weatherboarding was used only in the southeastern counties of England. The fourth house in the row has an exposed frame, and the panels of wall filling are covered by plaster. The color contrast of age-darkened oak framing timbers and white plaster

7. Five types of architectural treatment in English houses of the Gothic period (H. C. Forman, *The Architecture of the Old South,* Harvard University Press)

panels suggested the common English term ' black-and-white work ' for this treatment; in America, the term ' half-timber ' construction is more commonly used and is applied either to this or to the first type shown. The fifth house is covered by tiles or slates attached, like shingles, to a series of horizontal slats or battens nailed to the house frame. The English would call this a ' tile-hung ' house.

Of the five types of wall treatment, only the third became at all common in the English colonies. It is believed that half-timber houses with exposed frames may have been built in the earliest years, but no documentary evidence or remaining edifice affords positive proof. Lime was so scarce that the second type was used but very rarely, and the tile-hung house was also extremely rare, though contemporary descriptions reveal that it existed. The clapboard-covered frame house, then, was all but universal in the English colonies of the seventeenth century.

Architectural features and ornament were far simpler in late medieval English houses than in contemporary manor houses, churches, or guild halls. Framing timbers were wrought into decorative patterns, and sometimes their projecting ends or surfaces were carved. Overhanging upper stories, patterned brickwork, leaded casements, and shaped chimneys gave a certain richness of form and texture, but no ordinary house boasted such Gothic decorative details as flying buttresses, pointed-arch windows and doorways, pinnacles, or carved gargoyles. Most farmhouses were very simple. A seventeenth-century house at Kingsbury Green in Middlesex, for example, reveals no decoration at all, unless the tile chimney pots are

counted as ornaments (fig. 9). But with its clapboarded walls, front overhang, steep roof, and central chimney, it bears a remarkable similarity to
such Colonial buildings as the McIntyre garrison house at Scotland,
Maine (fig. 60).

The Master Weaver's House at Dedham in Essex (fig. 8), dating from
the late fifteenth or early sixteenth century, has a combination of plastered walls and a clapboarded gable end, with overhangs at both upper
stories. Its end-to-the-road arrangement, fine Tudor chimney with sloped
offsets, and the unusual location of the chimney at the side of the house
rather than in the middle or at one end are all features echoed in the ear-

8, 9. Master Weaver's House at Dedham, Essex, England. House at Kingsbury Green,
Middlesex, England (Martin S. Briggs, *Homes of the Pilgrim Fathers*, Oxford University Press)

liest houses of Jamestown. Figure 10 shows a characteristic English yeoman's house of the seventeenth century, in the village of Brenchley in
Kent. The house illustrates a variety of wall construction: brick for the
ground story, a tile-hung second story, and weatherboarding for the gable
ends. Slant-roofed sheds, added at the ends, accentuate the picturesque
grouping of the masses. The windows are in groups of three, the side
units fixed, the center one a hinged casement swinging outward, with the
glass cut in diamond-shaped panes and set in a lead lattice. Steep roofs,
overhang, and sheds give this house an extraordinary similarity to the
Richard Jackson House, built in Portsmouth, New Hampshire, in 1664
(Fig. 11). Indoors, the heavy-timbered ceilings, the simple batten doors,
the huge fireplaces, and the heavy furniture of these Gothic houses of
southeastern England make immediately evident the precise origin of the
New England Colonial style in all its details.

READING SUGGESTIONS

The bibliography at the end of each chapter is a selected list of the best
books on the field of that chapter. In connection with this first introduc-
tory chapter, it may be well to mention three outstanding books in the field
of Colonial and Georgian architecture as a whole. These are all confined

10. English yeoman's house of the seventeenth century, Brenchley, Kent (Samuel Chamberlain)

11. Richard Jackson House, Portsmouth, New Hampshire, 1664 (Samuel Chamber lain)

to domestic architecture and, except for the third, have no treatment of French and Spanish Colonial architecture; but within its field each is invaluable.

Fiske Kimball, *Domestic Architecture of the American Colonies and of the Early Republic,* Scribner's, New York, 1922. Though published a generation ago and now long out of print, this remains the most comprehensive and scholarly treatment of the development of architectural style in the eastern United States in the Colonial, Georgian, and Federal periods.

Thomas T. Waterman, *The Dwellings of Colonial America,* University of North Carolina Press, Chapel Hill, 1950. This is the most up-to-date scholarly account of the styles of the colonies of the Atlantic seaboard, lavishly illustrated.

Richard Pratt, *A Treasury of Early American Homes,* Whittlesey House, New York, 1949. Selected houses from the early Colonial period through the Greek Revival of the nineteenth century. The brief sections of text and extended captions are competent and interesting, but it is the 250 large color photographs that make this the most beautiful picture book on American architecture yet produced.

With more immediate reference to the subject matter of this chapter, Harold R. Shurtleff's *The Log Cabin Myth* (Harvard University Press, 1939) is not only an authoritative discussion of the log cabin and its history, but an excellent account of the building methods of the earliest colonists from Newfoundland to North Carolina.

Two-thirds of Martin Shaw Briggs' *Homes of the Pilgrim Fathers in England and America,* 1620–1685 (Oxford University Press, New York, 1932) deals with the houses of the Pilgrims in England and in Holland; the remainder of the book contains the best brief account of New England Colonial houses.

2

The Colonial House in New England

A COMBINATION of circumstances — cold climate, solid construction, and a long-persistent village economy — has preserved in New England a larger number of seventeenth-century buildings than exists in any other region of the United States today. We know that there were many frame houses in seventeenth-century Virginia, but not one surviving example may with certainty be dated before 1700. In New England, however, the number of known seventeenth-century frame houses approaches some four score. Many of these buildings, and the documents that shed light upon them, have been thoroughly studied, and some have been carefully restored. For these reasons the early houses of New England afford the greatest single source of knowledge about American architecture of the seventeenth century, and particularly about details of plan and construction, doors, windows, hardware, furniture, and the like.

These details of plan, structure, and style in New England seventeenth-century houses form the subject of this chapter. In analyzing them it is necessary to use a technical vocabulary, which, though extensive, is applicable to houses of other regions and periods and is therefore basic to an understanding of all architecture in the American colonies — and indeed that of the present as well, for most of the terms are still used by carpenters and masons today.

COLONIAL HOUSE PLANS

There was considerable variety in the plans of seventeenth-century houses. Each house, naturally, was shaped by circumstances of family need, available means, site, and the accidents of time. It is nonetheless possible to define the three most common — almost ' standard ' — plan-types in New England, and even to suggest how these probably succeeded one another in an evolutionary sequence. The three types of plans are shown in figure 12.

The *one-room plan* was the simplest and the earliest type. It was used in the early cottages at Plymouth and Salem (figs. 4 and 5), and remained common in smaller and poorer dwellings throughout the century. The front door opened into a small vestibule, in those days called the ' porch,' with a steep staircase crowded up against an immense chimney. The main room was a combination living-dining-cooking room of ample size, usually about 16 by 18 feet, called the ' keeping-room ' or more often the ' hall ' —

both are terms descended from medieval England.* The fireplace, of cavernous size, was set into the huge chimney mass. The staircase led to one large sleeping room upstairs, which was either under sloping rafters in a story-and-a-half house, or in a full height second story.

The *two-room plan* was simply the one-room plan with a parlor added at the other side of the chimney and porch, giving two fireplaces back to back. Several instances are known in which the parlor was actually added as a second unit to a previously built one-room house, but more com-

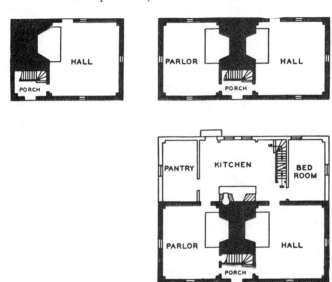

12. Typical plans of New England Colonial houses (Philip White)

monly, when families could afford it, both units were built at once. Upstairs there were two sleeping rooms invariably called, after the room below each, the ' hall chamber ' and the ' parlor chamber.' A variant of this plan had a large projecting porch, 8 or 10 feet square, in front of the house, and the room over it was called the ' porch chamber.'

The *added lean-to plan* was the result of an addition at the back of the house, with roof rafters ' leaning ' from one-story eaves at the back against the top of the wall of the main house (see section, fig. 18). As an addition, the lean-to seldom had the same roof pitch as the main house. The added space was used for a separate kitchen. The cooking was done in a fireplace added to the back of the central chimney mass. Though the customary location of the bake-oven was within the fireplace (at one side of the back), it was easier in the case of such an added fireplace (usually made of brick) to build the bake-oven outside the fireplace, to one side, rather

---

* The words ' porch ' and ' hall ' both have different meanings today. When they are used in Part 1 of this book it will be in the seventeenth-century sense.

than to cut into the earlier masonry. On the cold side of the kitchen was a pantry, and on the warm side, facing the southern sun, a downstairs sleeping room — the only one in the Colonial house known as a ' bedroom.' The space under the lean-to roof was used as a garret or for one or two small bedrooms (' lean-to chambers ') reached by a stairway from the kitchen.

An *original lean-to* house was identical in plan, except that, as the term implies, the back rooms were built at the same time as the main house instead of being added later. This permitted the builders to use continuous rafters in the rear roof slope, giving a uniform pitch from ridge to eaves. The kitchen fireplace could also be built directly into the main chimney stack.

Lean-tos, either added or original, are very common in New England, and houses with the characteristic short roof pitch in front and a long pitch sweeping close to the ground in back are called ' saltboxes,' from their resemblance to the shape of old salt boxes — though ' candle box ' would have done as well, for they were of the same shape, though longer.

These plan-types form a logical evolutionary sequence. One authority says that in Connecticut the two-room plan prevailed up to 1650; that from 1650 to 1675 it shared honors with the added lean-to type; and that from 1675 to 1700 the original lean-to became general.[1] But a one-room house might have been built at any time in the century, and it is wisest not to regard any plan-type as a chronological determinant.

THE HOUSE FRAME

Made of massive oak timbers, hewn with axe and adze and jointed with amazing skill, the frame of the house is a delight to anyone with craftsman's blood in his veins. Oak was used because it was sturdy and lasting; the timbers were of huge size because they had to carry a heavy load of clay or brick nogging within the walls, and the cutting away of so much wood at the notched joints required added thickness.

Framing timbers were always hand-hewn. This was true long after sawmills were introduced; indeed it remained true in many localities well into the nineteenth century. It has been suggested that the long persistence of the more laborious method was due to the fact that the carriages of the early sawmills were too short to take long framing timbers, or that the blades could not be trusted to cut the heavier beams.[2] This does not seem plausible when we realize that framing timbers were still hand-hewn for many years after the advent of the long-carriaged, steam-powered circular saw in 1814. The real reason, probably, was that transporting an oak log to the sawmill and bringing back the heavy beam was too much work; a good axeman could hew out a sizeable beam *in situ* in an hour or two. He stood with the log at his left side and, following chalk lines snapped to mark the square baulk of timber, hewed one side flat at a time, using a broadaxe (fig. 13). First he made ' back-cuts ' at frequent intervals — side strokes across the grain, which left deeply scored cuts on the finished timber, at right angles to its length. Then he worked quickly down the length, the long chips, already cut off at the base of the stroke, flying clear. A broadaxed beam was rough-surfaced — the scored back-cuts may still be seen in many an attic rafter — and if it were to be used in any exposed position, as for example spanning the hall or parlor, its surfaces were care-

13. Use of the broadaxe (Bernard Chapman)

fully smoothed with an adze. Like a hatchet with its blade at right angles to a short handle, and razor-sharp, the adze was used to dress down surfaces to a smoothness hardly surpassed by machine-sawing.

Most of the joints in a Colonial frame are varieties of the mortise-and-tenon, cut into the timbers with auger, chisel, and mallet (fig. 14). The

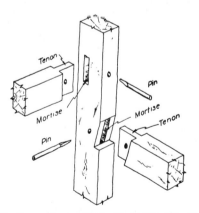

14. Mortise-and-tenon joints (Stevenson Flemer)

tenon, or flange, fits into the mortise, or socket; a hole is bored through the whole joint and a round wooden pin, known as a treenail (pronounced 'trunnel'), run through the joint to secure it. These joints show more than skill; they show the pride of craftsmanship.

Cellar and foundation

Cellars were seldom used in England, but in New England almost always. Sometimes the cellar extended under the whole house, more often only under the hall, from which a steep stair descended to it; there was never a cellar under a lean-to addition. Cellar space, in other words, was not regarded as a means of keeping the floor warm, but only as a storage place for vegetables and other bulk foods. It was naturally cool in summer, and to keep it above freezing through the winter the foundation was

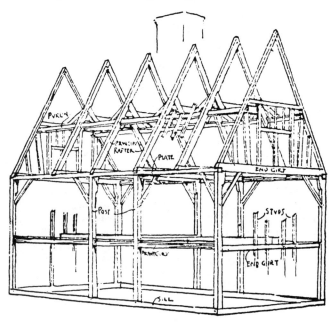

15. Frame of the Fairbanks House, Dedham, Mass. (Norman M. Isham, *Early American Houses*, The Walpole Society)

banked outside with dead leaves every autumn. The cellar was low, with dirt floor, and the wall was invariably of fieldstones, laid up dry or with clay mortar (lime mortar was rare and expensive in the early days). On the outside the foundation was hardly visible, since the house sat low on the ground.

Framing timbers

Ten kinds of framing timbers were employed in the Colonial house, and since their particular uses and names have remained standard in frame construction for more than two centuries, knowledge of their functions and terminology is essential to an understanding of the basic structure of most American buildings. Even after the advent, in the 1840's, of the lighter timbers used in the modern ' balloon ' frame, the ancient terms persisted and are still in use today. These framing timbers are here described beginning with the foundation and building up to the ridgepole.

Sills. The sills rested on top of the foundation walls and carried the rest of the frame. They were good-sized beams, jointed securely at the corners (figs. 15 and 19).

Posts. The posts were the main vertical supports. There were usually eight of them, those near the chimney being called ' chimney posts,' the others ' corner posts.' In houses without an overhang, the posts were two

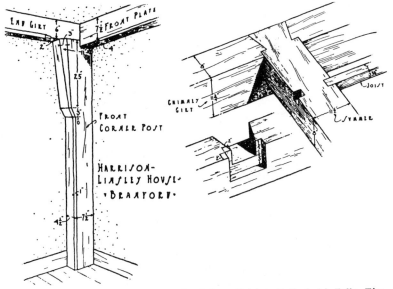

16, 17. ' Musket-stock ' post and shouldered dovetail joint (J. Frederick Kelly, *The Early Domestic Architecture of Connecticut,* Yale University Press)

stories high. They were widened at the top to afford a bearing for the crosswise girts. This widening was accomplished in two ways: hewing the beam to a gradually greater width, producing what is known as a ' flared ' or ' splayed ' post (figs. 28, 20C); or hewing it to a musket-stock shape, called a ' shouldered ' post (fig. 16). The upward expansion of size in flared and shouldered posts is always visible from the inside, except where posts have been later cased in by boards, as they often were in the eighteenth century.

Girts. The girts were main horizontal supports carrying the second floor. They were mortised into the posts, and known, according to location, as ' front girts,' ' rear girts,' and ' end girts.' Those connecting the chimney posts from front to back were called ' chimney girts.'

Summer beams. The summer was a heavy beam spanning the middle of a large room, usually from end girt to chimney girt, and it served as an intermediate support for the floor joists of the story above (figs. 19 and 26). Carrying a heavy load and spanning 16 to 20 feet, it was one of the biggest beams in the house, often 8 by 12 inches, sometimes 10 by 14. It was laid flatwise, with regularly spaced notches cut into the upper corners to take the ends of the floor joists. The joint of summer and girt was a particularly beautiful piece of workmanship. Known as a shouldered dovetail (fig. 17) it was so cut that the summer could not be pulled or pushed out of its socket in the girt. The summer was dropped into place and its sheer weight was sufficient to keep it in place; this was the only joint in the house not pinned by treenails. There were four summer beams in an ordinary house, spanning hall and parlor downstairs, and the two main chambers upstairs.

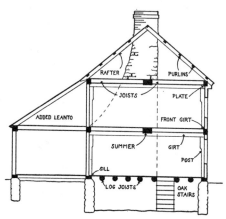

18. Section of a lean-to house showing framing members (Philip White)

Joists. Joists were small beams that carried the floor boards. They ran across the house in two spans: from front girt to summer beam, and from summer beam to rear girt. Their ends rested in notches so that the top surfaces of all timbers were flush to take the floor boards. Joists were small timbers — 3 by 4 inches or less — spaced about 20 inches apart. Being visible from the room below they were carefully formed: sawed out, or split from larger timbers and planed smooth. Ground-floor joists, being out of sight in the cellar, were often mere logs, bark left on, slightly flattened at the top (fig. 18).

Plates. The plates were horizontal timbers at the top of the wall on which the rafters rested (figs. 15 and 18). The four main crosswise timbers at the third-floor level were called upper end girts and upper chimney girts, and they served as ties to hold the front and back walls together against the outward push of the slanting rafters.

Rafters. The slanting beams supporting the pitched roof were of two types: principal rafters, heavy timbers generally rising over posts in the lower frame; and common rafters, lighter timbers spaced between principal rafters.

Purlins. Purlins were horizontal beams set between principal rafters at one or more levels between plate and ridgepole. In figure 18 four purlins on each side of the roof are shown, but the number varied in different types of roof framing. They were always supported by the principal rafters.

Ridgepole. In Colonial construction there was often no ridgepole at all (see figs. 15 and 19). The rafters met each other in lapped joints. Sometimes short lengths of ridgepole were framed between these rafter joints. This is in contrast to modern frame construction where a continuous ridgepole is used.

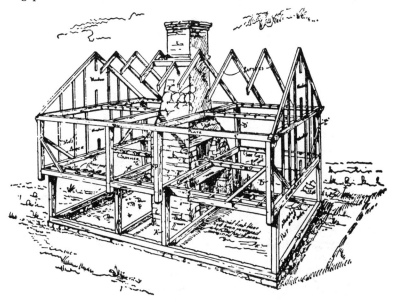

19. Frame of the Gleason House, Farmington, Conn. (Norman M. Isham, *Glossary of Colonial Architectural Terms*, The Walpole Society)

Braces. Diagonal braces against wind pressures were often employed. They spanned upper or lower corners (figs. 15 and 19), and the small wall studs were cut to fit them.

Collars. A collar was a crossbeam in the garret, usually just over a man's head, tying two rafters together at that level and serving to brace them.

Raising bees

Oak is very heavy. The erection of a house frame was far beyond the capacity of a single family, so it became a community social occasion known as a ' raising.' For some weeks in advance, preparations were made: the men dug the cellar, laid the foundations and sills, cut and notched every piece of timber required in the frame, and whittled dozens of hardwood treenails. The women prepared quantities of food, for the men who did the work were fortified by food and liberal quantities of flip or grog.

On the day of the ' raisin',' the entire front and rear wall frames were assembled flat on the ground: posts, studs, girts, plates, and braces, fitted together and pegged into single 'broadsides.' Standing shoulder to shoulder the men lifted, and, as the plate came shoulder-high, brought pikes into play to push it higher. These were metal-tipped poles some sixteen feet long. As the broadside neared the vertical, other men with pikes steadied it from the opposite side. The other broadside was next raised. The crucial moment came when other gangs of men raised the two end girts into the air; then the two broadsides were given the final push which slipped tenon into mortise, the pins were driven, locking corner posts and end girts together, and the frame stood. From then on, it was easy to place and secure the remaining girts, summer beams, braces, et cetera. The rafters usually went up after an interval for refreshment. The skeleton frame then stood complete, ready for its layers of floor boards, wall boards, and roof boards.

The overhang

One of the most common features of New England Colonial architecture was the overhanging second story, or 'jetty' as it was called. The overhang usually ran across the front of the house, sometimes at the ends, rarely at both front and ends, almost never at the back. Three buildings (apart from blockhouses) are known to have had overhangs on all four sides, but all are now destroyed. A gable-end overhang at the third-story level was fairly common, especially in Connecticut (fig. 36).

Overhangs called for a different method of framing the wall. In figure 19 it will be observed that the four main crosswise girts of the second floor projected beyond the tops of the four posts that supported them. To the projecting ends of these girts were fastened the four vertical posts of the second story. The bottoms of these posts extended below the joints, and in many houses they were carved into pendants, or 'pendills' as the colonists called them (fig. 20 left). Between these hanging posts, and framed into them, was an extra set of front girts called 'upper front girts' as they were a foot or two in front of, and slightly above, the regular front girts. On this framework the second-story wall was carried. This type of overhang is known as a 'framed overhang' and is distinguished by its bold projection.

Another type was the hewn, or false, overhang. This was not framed by separate timbers at all, but simply hewn into a two-story front post (fig. 20). The lower part of the post was cut away so that its face was a few inches behind that of the upper part, and the transition between the two was effected by what appears from outside to be a carved bracket. The hewn overhang was never more than six inches, and usually only three or four; it commonly is found on both ends as well as on the front of a house. It appeared only in the last third of the seventeenth century, particularly in Connecticut. After 1700 it dwindled to little more than an inch in projection, persisting, however, until the last quarter of the eighteenth century, when it disappeared altogether.

The origin and purpose of the overhanging upper story remains uncertain. But one popular legend can be dispensed with immediately. That it was a feature introduced by the colonists for defense against the Indians is impossible for three reasons. First, the overhang almost never occurred on all four sides of a house, and the Indians were hardly polite enough to attack only the ' guarded ' side. Secondly, the overhang was not equipped with machicolations (trap doors), and thus would have offered more protection to the attackers than to the defenders. Thirdly, it was a feature that certainly originated in medieval England, where there were no In-

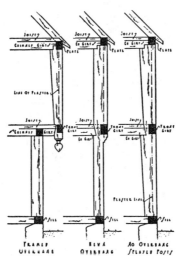

20. Main posts in three types of Colonial frames (J. Frederick Kelly, *The Early Domestic Architecture of Connecticut*, Yale University Press)

dians. Confusion on this point has probably arisen because of a failure to distinguish between houses and blockhouses: the latter *were* intended for security against the Indians, and they had a defensive overhang on all four sides.

The overhang certainly came to the colonies from England, but why it was used there is not definitely known. One school holds that it served as a protection from rain to the ground-story shops with their open fronts — but there were plenty of shops not so protected. Another school holds that along the crowded medieval streets land values became very high and overhanging upper stories increased usable space over a given site — but the overhang occurs just as frequently in small villages and isolated farmhouses as it does in medieval cities. A third school holds that it was a technical matter of framing: separate posts for the two stories were stronger than one long post weakened at the middle by a triple joint for the insertion of the necessary three horizontal girts. A fourth school holds that the overhang is purely aesthetic in origin: the medieval people liked its looks. The last two theories seem the most plausible but the matter re-

mains unsettled. Certain it is that the overhang gives a marked architectural character to New England Colonial houses.

WALL CONSTRUCTION

The house frame served as a massive skeleton for support of the enclosing walls and roof. The exterior wall surface, or ‘ siding,’ was almost invariably made of clapboards. But hidden beneath these was a core of studs
and filling. The studs were vertical timbers, spaced about two feet on centers, and framed into the sill below and the girt above; clapboards were
nailed onto them. Since they carried a light load they were small (about
$2\frac{1}{2}$ by 3 inches) and were usually sawed rather than hewn.

Filling

Between the studs was the filling of the wall, which served as insulation.
It was of several types, all similar to English prototypes. The most primitive consisted of clay and chopped straw formed into rolls or ‘ cats ’ and
laid up between the studs. The English type of wattle-and-daub was employed, except that at first lime was so scarce that the ‘ daub ’ was simply
a mixture of clay and straw instead of hard lime plaster. Brick nogging
was used, as in England, but due to the expense of kiln-burned brick a
crude kind of sun-dried brick made of clay pressed in molds was employed. These ‘ soft bricks ’ were large and were set on edge between the
studs. By the end of the century, kiln-burned bricks were used and continued to be into the eighteenth century.

The filling, of whatever type, was the chief element in the thickness and
weight of the wall. All evidence suggests that in the earliest days it may
have been exposed on the exterior, with the framing members showing
as in English half-timber work. But it must be admitted that no example
of this survives in New England, and no documentary evidence proves it
beyond doubt. If indeed exposed half-timber construction was used, there
is little doubt that almost immediately such walls were protected by an
exterior covering of clapboards. The New England climate, with its driving rains and extremes of temperature, would have disintegrated exposed
clay daubing in a short while. Since clapboards were exported to England
from Plymouth within the first year, it is reasonable to suppose they would
have been used for local building.

Clapboard siding

Colonial clapboards (a name probably derived from the German *Klap-
holz*, meaning barrel stave) were thin, wedge-shaped boards, about 5
inches wide and only 4 to 6 feet long — enough to cross three or four studs.
Each end was beveled so that adjacent ones overlapped at the stud (fig.
21). They were invariably split or ‘ riven,’ rather than sawed, by means of
a special tool called a ‘ froe ’ or ‘ frow.’ It resembled a butcher's cleaver,
with a heavy broad blade about 15 inches long, and a handle turned up
at right angles to the blade. A log of 10 or 12 inches’ diameter was stood

on end and split in half by pounding the back of the blade with a wooden mallet called a ' froe club.' Each half was again split in half, and then into quarters, eighths, and so on, producing a number of wedge-shaped pieces about half an inch thick tapering to a thin or ' feather ' edge.

Oak was commonly used in Rhode Island and Connecticut, as well as in the middle and southern colonies; cedar was preferred in Massachusetts, with pine a second choice. Oak was the most durable, but the short lengths had a tendency to warp and lift their nails. Clapboards were fastened to the studs by hand-forged nails with large flat heads. The overlap was about an inch, leaving a ' weather,' or exposed surface, of about four inches.

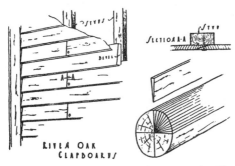

21. Riven oak ' feather-edged ' clapboards (J. Frederick Kelly, *The Early Domestic Architecture of Connecticut*, Yale University Press)

Flat or ' parallel ' boards, usually sawed out of pine, were used in several seventeenth-century houses, beginning as early as 1637. Being more regular to start with than hand-riven clapboards, their outer surfaces were often planed smooth, and in some cases finished at the lower corner with a bead. In certain parts of Connecticut and Rhode Island ' flush siding ' rather than lapped clapboards was used. This consisted of rather wide boards of white pine nailed flat against the studs, corners beveled so that the edge of the upper board overlapped the lower.

Sheathing

' Sheathing ' is a layer of boards just underneath an outer covering, as for example under clapboard siding, or on roofs, underneath shingles.

Sheathing was not used under clapboards during most of the seventeenth century. This seems curious, as it would have made a tighter wall and excellent insulation, and cheap mill-sawed boards were available in many localities by the mid-century. Perhaps the colonists clung to the heavy and clumsy filling of clay or brick simply because it was the English tradition. Authorities differ about when wall sheathing was first introduced, but Isham says:

About 1700, and perhaps a little earlier, boards were put on the walls and to these the clapboards were nailed. These boards were horizontal and were often bevelled along their joints to keep out the weather. Shingles could be nailed to these boards . . . as they evidently could not be nailed directly to the studs.[3]

This early sheathing was apparently the same as the flush siding de-scribed above, and may well have developed from it. It seems logical to suppose that sheathing was first used for shingled walls, where it was es-sential as a nailing base, and that the superior tightness of such a double layer led to the general adoption of sheathing under clapboards about 1700. At any rate wall sheathing became general in the eighteenth cen-tury, and gradually the old-fashioned filling of clay or brick was aban-doned.

Shingles

Shingles were hand-riven with a froe from a squared baulk of white pine, oak, chestnut, or cedar. They were of various dimensions, crude and thick compared to modern mill-cut shingles. They ranged in length from 14 inches up to 3 feet, and were attached with a weather varying from 8 inches in the short shingles to 16 in the long ones. The heavy butts and the rough split along the grain gave a shingled wall or roof an attractive texture.

There seems considerable doubt about when shingles were first used as a wall covering in New England. They were probably used on the roof of the Plymouth Company's Aptucxet Trading Post as early as 1627, and they were certainly being made in Connecticut by 1640, as their sizes and prices are discussed in the New Haven Court Records of that year. Although there are today about a dozen seventeenth-century New England houses with walls covered by shingles, it would be risky to assume that these are original rather than later replacements of clapboard siding. The English used overlapping slates, hung in a manner similar to shingles, but they did not use wooden shingles for a wall covering.

The earliest known shingled houses in this country are those built by the Dutch on Long Island in the middle of the seventeenth century, and it appears that the earliest ones in New England are in near-by Connecti-cut. The Gleason House in Farmington, built between 1650 and 1660, is shingled, and the Lyon House in Greenwich, built perhaps a decade later, has very long hand-hewn shingles with rounded ends, such as were used by the Dutch on the Wyckoff House at Flatlands, Brooklyn, in about 1640. This may justify a tentative hypothesis that shingles as a wall covering were introduced in New Netherland, and spread first to Connecticut and later to Massachusetts. In any event, they were used in Boston by 1679, for Jasper Danckaerts, describing the city in that year, says: 'All the houses are made of thin, small cedar shingles, nailed against frames, and then filled in with brick and other stuff; and so are their churches.' [4]

'All the houses' is doubtless hyperbole, for we know there were some frame houses with an exterior covering of plaster. Plaster surfacing was common enough in England, but scarcity of lime and the fact that plaster does not withstand a severe climate account for its comparatively rare use in New England. When employed, it was sometimes in the form known as 'roughcast,' containing an aggregate of pebbles to give it a rough texture. This was doubtless the type of surfacing referred to as 'the rough cast of the outsyde of the new house' in a Boston contract dating from 1638.[5] The plastered front of the old Feather Store in Boston, built in 1680, was adorned with molded plaster reliefs.

Sawing lumber

Mention has been made of the fact that all sorts of boards and planks — such as those used for walls, roof sheathing, floors, and wainscot — and smaller beams such as studs and joists, were sawed rather than hand-hewn. This was done from the founding of the several colonies; ' sawyers ' are recorded among the first settlers.

They used small handsaws for most purposes, but for ripping long boards and planks they used a two-man saw with a long flexible blade stretched in a frame, known as a ' whip-saw.' A pit was dug in the earth and a long timber, previously squared by a broadaxe, was placed over it. One man, the ' sawyer ' or ' top-sawyer,' stood on top and guided the cut along the timber from end to end; the other, standing below and known as the ' pitman,' provided the main motive power on the down-stroke, and got most of the sawdust in his eyes. As early as 1630, because of the demand for houses and the shortage of labor, Massachusetts regulated the pay of the building trades: ' It is ordered that sawyers shall not take above *12d* a scoore for saweing oake boards, and *10d* a scoore for pyne boards, if they have their wood felled and squared for them.' [6]

But the laborious pit-sawing was so costly of time and labor that water-power sawmills were soon erected. Sawmills were common in Europe from the middle of the fifteenth century but were not used in England. According to Defebaugh, ' the first one erected in England was supposed to have been built in 1663, at which time hundreds of them were in use in New England, but this mill was torn down to gratify a popular prejudice which insisted that such an institution would take bread out of the mouths of the working people.' [7] Fears of similar trouble prevented the erection of another sawmill in 1700, and as late as 1767 one was destroyed by a mob.[8]

But in New England labor was scarce and dear, and big proprietors such as Gorges in Maine and Mason in New Hampshire had no need to worry about technological unemployment. Gorges requested the construction of a sawmill for his colony at York, Maine, as early as 1623; another was built on the Salmon Falls River, near Portsmouth, New Hampshire, in 1633. The number increased rapidly in later decades.*

The first ' sash ' sawmills were modified pit-saws — cumbersome up-and-down affairs, driven by a connecting-rod from a crank on the shaft of a water wheel. For generations this bar which applied the motive power continued to be called a ' pitman.' An improvement was the introduction of several parallel saws in a frame, to saw many boards at once, a device known as a gang-saw; it was first used in Berwick, Maine, in 1650. No further major improvement in mill-sawing occurred until the introduction of steam power and the perfection of the circular saw in the nineteenth century. Both sash and gang saws left parallel scoring on the boards

---

* For some further account of the early history of sawmills, see page 92.

they produced, and whether produced by man power or water power, boards to be used for finish were always planed smooth by hand.

COLONIAL WINDOWS

The windows of the earliest houses were few and very small; those in the cottages at Plymouth and Salem (figs. 4 and 5) were about a foot or a foot and a half square. The small size has been attributed to danger from Indian attacks, but more probably the reason was the scarcity and high cost of glass. Early seventeenth-century houses frequently had no glazed windows; oiled paper or sliding board shutters were used instead. Window glass was imported from England; even there it was too expensive for use in the poorer sort of dwelling, and its export to the colonies was heavily taxed. Many letters to England instruct emigrants to bring glass and lead for windows; indeed leaded glass was so cherished that it was sometimes bequeathed in wills as something separate from the house.

Most of the English glass was called ' Newcastle glass '; it was extremely thin — about one-sixteenth of an inch — and the remnants of it that survive today are easily distinguished by their irregular surface and an amber and violet iridescence caused by metallic impurities such as manganese.

An attempt to start glass manufacture in New England was made in 1639, but it was unsuccessful. According to Kelly, further attempts were few, the glass was of poor quality, and local glass manufacture was not successfully established on a commercial basis in the colonies until as late as 1792.

But from 1650 on, glazed windows were universal in the better houses, and their size tended to increase as the century advanced. Colonial windows were invariably of the casement or hinged type, the outward-swinging sash being made either of iron or thin wood bars. Diamond-shaped panes of glass (' quarrels ') were set in lead bars (' calmes '). Because of the flexibility of the leading the glazed light was attached to rigid bars, serving as stiffeners. Sometimes these ran transversely (' saddle bars ') ; sometimes they were upright pieces of wood (' guard bars ') set into holes in the head and sill of the window.

The diagonal pattern of leaded quarrels was a survival of English medieval windows, which were fitted with a diagonal lattice of interlaced wattles or bars before the introduction of glazing. Small rectangular panes were easier to produce, and were widely used in England in the middle and late seventeenth century, but seldom in the colonies. Notable examples are a single casement sash formerly in the William Coddington House at Newport, Rhode Island (1641), now preserved in the Rhode Island Historical Society, and the restored windows of the Parson Capen House at Topsfield, Massachusetts (1683).

Though the units or ' lights ' were small in size, they were often combined in groups of two, three, and even four to give a wide horizontal window. The interior aspect of a three-light window may be seen in figure 26. The heavy vertical bars separating the lights are called ' mullions.' A contract of 1657 specified that windows in the chambers were to be

' three lights of two foote long and one foot broad; the lower rooms, the two windows are to be four lights, two feet in length.' ⁹ Frequently the windows were divided into upper and lower lights by horizontal transom bars, as in the Whitman House at Farmington (fig. 36), another factor that tended to keep individual lights of a very small size.

It is not generally realized that a large proportion of Colonial windows were stationary. Bedroom windows commonly were fixed units instead of swinging casements, since people believed that the night air was noxious. Hall and parlor windows in groups of two or more lights usually had one or more fixed units and one casement. A typical arrangement is that of the Abraham Browne House in Watertown: a three-light window has two fixed lights at the sides and a hinged casement in the middle; this window is reproduced in the American Wing of the Metropolitan Museum.

The structural setting of Colonial windows was simplicity itself. Wall studs served as the side jambs, and the head and sill were mortised into the studs at appropriate heights. Since the lights were only about 2 feet high, the sill came about 4 feet above the floor, and the head at 6 feet or a little over. Fixed windows did not even have a separate sash: the leaded glass fitted into grooves in the frame, and the guard bars, sprung into holes in head and sill, stiffened the glazing.

The modern type of double-hung sash window is definitely of Georgian or later date in the colonies. Indeed, many medieval leaded windows must have survived until the Revolution, as several instances are recorded of their being removed at that time to afford lead for bullets. But during the eighteenth and nineteenth centuries all Colonial casement windows were replaced by double-hung sash; they appear in Colonial houses today only as modern restorations.

COLONIAL ROOFS

Roof coverings

Thatched roofs were used in the first years of settlement and were common in New England through the first three-quarters of the seventeenth century. Thatch was employed not only on cottages, but on ' fair houses ' and even on churches. The thatcher's craft was especially well developed in southeastern England, whence the majority of the Pilgrims came. Numerous horizontal poles were laid across the principal rafters, and tightly bound bundles of reeds and straw fastened to them, beginning at the eaves and working the rows upward toward the ridge. Tightly jammed together, a year's weathering packed the thatch into a dense and fairly waterproof covering. But it leaked in prolonged rains, in dry weather it was a fire menace as the colonists found out, and its normal life was little more than a generation, after which it had to be rethatched.

The colonists early turned to hand-riven wood shingles to form a durable and waterproof roof. These were of large size, and in a few houses they were attached directly to a series of horizontal purlins — a carry-over of thatch poles. Usually, however, the rafters were sheathed by a layer of boards to afford a better nailing base for shingles. Boards containing too many defects for flooring were used for 'roofers.'

Roof-framing

The direction of these boards determined the two different methods of roof-framing. At first they ran vertically: the principal rafters carried a number of rather small purlins, closely spaced like thatch poles, on which the roofing boards were nailed, running from ridge to eaves. This is known as a 'purlin roof' (see fig. 22A). In the later system, groups of common rafters were set between each pair of principal rafters, and the roofing boards nailed across these running lengthwise of the house. An in-

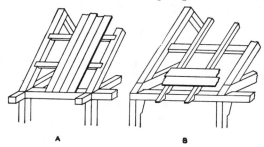

```
        A                              B
```

22. Types of Colonial roof-framing (Philip White)
(A) 'purlin roof' with vertical sheathing boards
(B) 'rafter roof' with horizontal sheathing boards

teresting change in the function of the purlins thus occurred. At first they carried roof boards and in turn were supported by rafters. Later, the common rafters carried the roof boards, and in turn were supported by the purlins, which ran *under* them to be framed into principal rafters. Since they served merely as an intermediate support to the common rafters, their number could be reduced to only one or two sets on each side of the roof. There is thus a consistent and logical evolution from a structural system designed for thatch to a structural system designed for sheathing and shingles. But it was not a strictly chronological evolution, since examples of the later type can be found early in the century (notably the Fairbanks House, fig. 15), and some purlin roofs are found in houses constructed late in the century.

Slate was used as a roof covering in Boston as early as 1654, but it did not become at all common in the seventeenth century. There is frequent mention of tiles and tile makers in early records, and burned tiles were used before the end of the century, but tile roofs were certainly as rare in New England as they were common in New Netherland.

The gabled or pitched roof

Almost all New England houses had gabled or pitched roofs. Following the English medieval tradition, the roof pitch was very steep — as much as 60° in the early houses. This steep pitch was advantageous for thatched roofs, but even after these disappeared it lingered for some time. As the tradition died out the roof pitch became less steep, finally becoming stabilized at about 45°.

There were no gutters. The roof came down to slightly projecting eaves, formed by the rafter ends with their covering sheathing and shingles. Toward the end of the century the eaves were boxed in by a ' fascia ' or face board, with a ' plancer ' or soffit board forming the flat under surface; these, together with a simple bed molding at juncture of plancer and wall, formed a rudimentary ' cornice.' But it was not until the eighteenth century that moldings, brackets, dentils, and other details were added to form the full classical cornice of the Georgian style.

The gambrel roof

The gambrel roof has two slopes on each side, a short upper slope of low pitch and a long lower slope of steep pitch (see fig. 32). The name may have come from the resemblance of the angle thus formed to the gambrel, or hock of a horse's hind leg, though it more possibly derives from the old French *gamberel,* a crooked stick used by butchers. In the *Boston Gazette* as late as 1737 we find advertised, ' To be Sold at publick Vendue, by Capt. Daniel Goffe . . . One Tenement two Stories upright, with a Gambering Roof. . .' [10]

The gambrel roof was long supposed to have been introduced to America by the Dutch, but it did not appear on Dutch houses until the eighteenth century, and since it was used long before that in both New England and Maryland, in these regions, at least, it may certainly be counted an English feature. Henry VIII used it over the Great Hall of his Hampton Court Palace in 1530–32, and Briggs shows it to have been fairly common in Essex farmhouses of the seventeenth century.[11] Its origin was doubtless due to a desire for economy: Gothic gabled roofs, with their extremely steep pitches and extravagant heights, may have been ' clipped off ' at the top to save material and to use shorter rafter lengths.

The introduction of the gambrel roof in the English colonies may date back to about 1640, but there is so much doubt about the dates of early gambrel-roofed houses and, indeed, whether their roofs are original, that the matter requires further study.* The earliest example the date of which

---

* There are, or were, gambrel roofs on the following houses reported to have been built before 1680. The dates given are from the authorities referred to. All evidence with regard to date and subsequent history, to determine whether roofs were later remodeled, should be carefully reviewed before accepting these as authentic original examples.

1. Sergeant Henry Bull House, Newport, R.I. 1638. Downing: *Early Homes of Rhode Island,* p. 22.
2. Walter Fyler House, Windsor, Conn. 1640. Chamberlain: *Open House in New England,* p. 44.
3. East wing of the Fairbanks House, Dedham, Mass., 1641 (?). Alvin Lincoln Jones: *Old Colonial Homes* (1894).
4. Cross Manor, Maryland. *c.*1643. Forman: *Early Manor and Plantation Houses of Maryland,* p. 32.
5. John Ward House, Haverhill, Mass. ante 1645. Chamberlain, op.cit. p. 46.
6. Old Gaol, York, Maine. 1653. Chamberlain, op.cit. p. 55.

is certain is that of Harvard Hall, Cambridge, built 1674–7. That of the Peter Tufts House at Medford, Massachusetts, was built in 1675, and there were other examples in New England in the following decades. The gambrel roof became very common in eighteenth-century New England.

The hipped roof

The hipped roof is shaped like a gabled roof with the corners cut off, forming triangles at the ends and trapezoids at the sides (see fig. 282). It is almost universally an eighteenth-century type. The earliest known examples in the colonies are those of the Court House, Talbot County, Maryland (1680–81), and the Wren Building at Williamsburg (1695–1702). A simpler type of hipped or pyramidal roof was used in New England meeting-houses of the seventeenth century, but never, so far as is known, on New England houses of the seventeenth century.

The rainbow roof

This unusual type of roof occurred in a few New England seacoast communities, such as those of Cape Cod, Nantucket, and Martha's Vineyard. It was like a pitched roof, but with each slope forming a light convex curve (fig. 52). Little is known of its history and it is perhaps chiefly an eighteenth-century rather than a seventeenth-century type. There is no reasonable structural explanation for its use. Very possibly such roofs were built by shipwrights who were accustomed to the difficult process of steaming and curving ships' ribs and treated their roof rafters in the same way out of sentiment; perhaps they liked to have their houses as 'ship-shape' as possible. In any event the effect of the subtly curved roof is most graceful, and its construction a triumph of neat workmanship.

Dormer windows

Dormer windows were very rare in seventeenth-century New England. The word 'dormer' was defined in 1703 as 'a window made in the roof of a house, it standing upon the rafters.' [12] Most of the dormer windows that appear today on New England Colonial houses are almost certainly additions made in the eighteenth or nineteenth century. Garret rooms were lighted, in the seventeenth century, by windows in the gable ends, or quite frequently broad cross gables were introduced to permit windows on

7. West wing of Fairbanks House, Dedham, Mass. 1654 (?). Alvin Lincoln Jones: *Old Colonial Homes*.

8. Mt. Airy, Maryland. c.1660. Forman, op.cit. p. 88.

9. Saulsbury House, Maryland. c.1663. Forman, op.cit. p. 183.

10. Otwell, Maryland. c.1670. Forman, op.cit. p. 178.

11. Cherry Grove, Maryland. c.1670. Forman, op.cit. p. 241.

12. Sueton Grant House, Newport, R.I. c.1670. Downing: op.cit. pp. 23, 25.

13. Harvard Hall, Cambridge, Mass. 1674–7. Morison: *Harvard College in the Seventeenth Century*, vol. II, p. 423.

14. Peter Tufts House, Medford, Mass. 1675. William Sumner Appleton: *Old Time New England*, vol. 28, no. 1 (July 1937), p. 17.

15. Troth's Fortune, Maryland. c.1676. Forman, op.cit. p. 189.

16. Harlow House, Plymouth, Mass. 1677. Chamberlain: op.cit. p. 69.

Concerning the half-dozen Maryland examples cited above, see footnote, page 164.

the front side, as in the John Ward House at Salem (fig. 44). These were called 'lucome' windows by the colonists — a word perhaps derived from the French *lucarne*. They were superior to the narrow dormer window in providing more interior space, and in giving a bolder and more positive architectural effect. Indeed, one of the major architectural virtues of Colonial houses is the simplicity of their roof surfaces, uncluttered by the narrow and nervously perched dormers of a later era.

THE CHIMNEY

Perhaps the most striking feature of a Colonial house was its massive central chimney. The common house of lean-to plan had five separate fireplaces, and all were built into a central stack which often measured as much as 10 by 12 feet. The foundations in the cellar were made of stone, often reinforced and tied together by embedded timbers. Just under the floor, on either side, the stonework was corbeled out to support the big stone slabs that served as hearthstones for the rooms above.

The earliest chimneys were built of wood and clay, as we have seen. Though they frequently caught fire, or had to be re-daubed, these crude chimneys continued long in use especially in the poorer sort of house. But in 'fair' houses, solid stacks of stone were built, and they became practically universal in the seventeenth century. Since lime was expensive for many years the rough fieldstones were laid with clay mortar up to the point where the stack emerged through the roof. From here up, lime mortar was employed.

The lack of lime in many regions was a serious obstacle. Limestone was uncommon in Massachusetts and almost wholly lacking in Connecticut; Rhode Island, however, had good quarries and exported lime to neighboring colonies after the mid-century. Seacoast towns made an inferior sort of lime by burning oyster and mussel shells; sometimes these were incompletely calcined and bits of shell are visible in the mortar.

Kiln-burned brick was rare in the early days, but as it became available it was used in combination with stone for chimneys. Frequently, for example, stone was used to the underside of the roof and the chimney was 'topped out' with brick; or a brick top replaced an earlier stone one. The lean-to kitchen fireplace and its bake-oven were frequently added in brick to an earlier stone chimney. Sometimes the extra flue was led into the main flue at the garret level; sometimes it continued independently through the roof behind the old top, giving the visible part of the chimney an L- or T-shaped cross section.

The flues from the separate fireplaces emerged into a common flue in the upper part of the chimney, though sometimes this was divided into halves by a 'withe' of thin stone slabs, set on edge. No form of flue lining was employed. Incidentally, to the early colonist, the word 'chimney' referred to what we call a flue, and the whole thing was called a 'stack.' In the garret, particularly in the larger houses, there was sometimes a smoke chamber in the upper part of the main flue — an enlarged space with cross bars, reached through a sheet-iron door, for hanging and curing meats.

The stack diminished in size as it rose (fig. 19), usually emerging through the roof behind the main ridge. Though the chimney top might be L- or T-shaped, it was usually a simple rectangle, perhaps with one or two over-sailing courses of brick or stone to form a simple cap. Several of the larger houses in Massachusetts and Rhode Island had more elaborate chimneys of pilastered form (figs. 35, 49), derived from English prototypes.

Colonial documents make many references to the office of 'chimney-viewer.' Chimney-viewers were appointed to inspect the chimneys of all

23. Colonial 'porch' or entry (Antoinette F. Downing. *Early Homes of Rhode Island,* Garrett and Massie)

houses, every three months during the summer and every six weeks in winter, to see that they were kept clean, well daubed with clay, or the masonry sound. It was an important function in the early days of wood-and-clay chimneys and thatched roofs, as the safety of the community depended largely on this form of fire prevention.

THE FRONT DOOR AND PORCH

The house was entered through a heavy front door made of two thick-nesses of boards, the outer layer running vertically, the inner layer hori-zontally, the whole liberally studded with large-headed hand-forged nails driven through both layers and clenched on the inside. The door was car-ried on long wrought-iron 'strap' hinges — a length of two feet was not uncommon — with a small ring at the butt end hung upon a shouldered peg, or 'pintle,' driven into the door frame. The strap hinge remained the common type for outside doors until the late eighteenth century. The earliest latches were of wood, with a leather string to raise the latch passed through a hole in the door to the outside. Later, wrought-iron latches with thumb-pieces and boldly designed handles were fastened to the door, and wrought-iron knockers appeared. All outside doors were fastened at night by a strong wooden bar placed across the inside, and even after iron shot-bolts were introduced the wooden bar continued long in use as added security. Iron locks of the modern type were not made until after the Revolution.

The stair

Once within the small porch, one came directly to a steep winding stair-case, crowded in front of the huge chimney (fig. 23). It had three or four 'winders' (diagonal treads) framed into a stout newel post around which they ascended, then a short straight run of steep pitch, and more winders at the top to bring the flight into the small upper hall. The earliest stair-

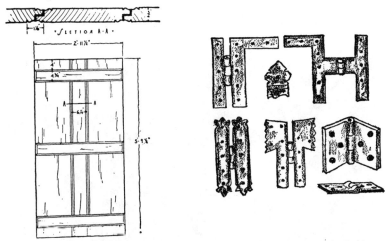

24. Typical Colonial batten door (J. Frederick Kelly, *The Early Domestic Architecture of Connecticut,* Yale University Press)
25. HL, H, hatchet, and butt hinges (*Old American Houses and How to Restore Them,* Doubleday and Company, copyright 1946 by Henry Lionel Williams and Ottalie K. Williams)

cases were enclosed by vertical wainscot running from floor to ceiling, but this was soon superseded by a more open construction with handrail and balusters.

In later houses such as the Capen House at Topsfield (fig. 38) the newel post rose only shoulder-high and was topped by a four-sided knob similar to the exterior pendants. The handrail, usually of oak, came into the newel at a steep slant. Balusters of simple form and short, stumpy curves were lathe-turned out of hard pine, though in Rhode Island we occasion-ally find a 'false' baluster sawed out of a flat board (detail at left in fig. 23). All seventeenth-century staircases were of the 'closed string' type: that is, a wide slanting board concealed the ends of the treads and risers. Below this, vertical wainscot ran to the floor.

Batten doors

Doors on either side of the porch led into the hall and parlor. Like all interior doors, they were light and thin, consisting of a single thickness of

vertical boards fastened together by three or four horizontal battens on
the exterior side (fig. 24). Long strap hinges were not necessary to support these light doors, and before the end of the period the familiar types
of H and H-and-L hinges had come into use (fig. 25). 'Butterfly' hinges,
such as may be seen in figure 28, were also used. The back, or batten, side
of the door usually faced the porch so that from within the hall or parlor the vertical boards, rebated together and molded at the joints, matched
the vertical wainscot of the fireplace wall.

THE HALL

The hall was the main room of the Colonial house. In early days it
served as living room, dining room, kitchen, and workroom. After the

26. Typical New England Colonial 'hall,' Concord Antiquarian Society, Concord,
Mass. (Samuel Chamberlain)

introduction of the lean-to, all of the cooking and much of the sewing,
candle-making, spinning, and weaving were removed to the kitchen, but
the hall still remained the center of family life. It was a room of generous
size — about 16 by 18 feet — but low-studded so that the ceiling beams
barely cleared a tall man's head.

The floor generally had a double layer of boards, for the cellar was not
heated. The subfloor was made of 'slitwork' — irregular boards only half
an inch thick — and the finish floor consisted of one-inch oak boards of

good width, rarely less than a foot. Instances have been found of a layer of fine sand between subfloor and finish floor, probably used for insulating purposes. In the last part of the century hard pine — broad boards 16 to 20 inches wide — succeeded oak. Occasionally there was only one layer of heavy planks, lapped at the joints and pegged through to the joists.

Much of the sturdy architectural character of the interior was due to the exposed framing. The flared or shouldered posts strengthened the corners, and sometimes projected from the middle of a wall to support the big summer beam (fig. 26). Girts were visible in the upper corners of the room, and the ceiling consisted of joists with their covering floor boards

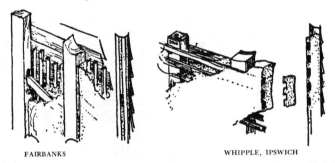

FAIRBANKS   WHIPPLE, IPSWICH

27. Primitive lath and plaster, Fairbanks and Whipple Houses (Norman M. Isham, *Early American Houses,* The Walpole Society)

crossing the room in two spans over the summer beam. One of the few purely decorative treatments of the Colonial house is the ' chamfering ' of these main structural timbers. Carpenters, using an adze, hewed the corners of posts, girts, and summers to a simple bevel, or used special planes to form a bevel edged by round corner beads. The ends of these chamfers were ' stopped ' by ornamental cuts.

Within this framework of timbers that boxed the room, the wall surfaces were covered either by plaster or by wainscot. The early ' plaster ' consisted merely of fine white clay, bound by hay or straw, and troweled to a smooth surface. When lime was available the wall was finished with fine lime plaster. In the very early Fairbanks House at Dedham the wall filling (fig. 27) consisted of small sticks of riven oak, held in place by a crosspiece sprung into grooves in the studs, the whole liberally daubed with a whitish clay — a primitive kind of lath and plaster. In the Whipple House at Ipswich (fig. 27) oak laths nailed across the face of the studs served as a base for the rough plaster, which thus concealed the studs. When brick nogging was used, plaster surfaced the brick and was also carried over the face of the studs and braces, which were hacked or scored to provide a bond for it.

Wainscot, or interior wooden surfacing, was used from very early in the seventeenth century. The broad pine boards, with beveled or molded edges, covered the studs but left the posts and girts exposed (fig. 28). Generally, wainscot boards ran horizontally on exterior walls, where it was easy to nail them across the vertical studs, and vertically on interior walls, where they extended from floor to ceiling to form a thin partition. The fireplace wall thus almost invariably had vertical wainscot, a treatment that continued in favor well into the eighteenth century. The wainscot on exterior walls sometimes covered from floor to ceiling, but more often was reduced to a dado from floor to chair rail (or ' wainscot cap ' as it was often called), with plastered walls above.

In the closing years of the seventeenth century, strips and molded pieces were attached over the wainscot to form the earliest paneled walls. Old pine wainscot, where it has fortunately escaped painting, has weathered

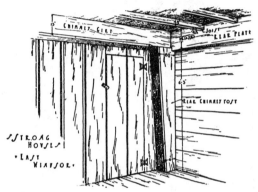

28. Room in the Strong House, East Windsor, Conn. (J. Frederick Kelly, *The Early Domestic Architecture of Connecticut,* Yale University Press)

to a russet brown tone and satin-like sheen. There is no evidence that wainscot or other interior woodwork was painted before the end of the seventeenth century, though furniture was painted much earlier.

The fireplace

The architectural and domestic focus of a Colonial hall was the great fireplace. Like the chimney stack, it was made of fieldstone, or of brick when the latter became available. In Connecticut and Rhode Island, stone prevailed through most of the century; an example is the impressive kitchen fireplace in the Ogden House at Fairfield, Connecticut (fig. 29); in Massachusetts brick was more common.

The size of the fireplace was considerably larger than that of today for several reasons: the fireplace was a heating unit, and a fire of big oak logs was kept burning all the time in cold weather; it was a cooking unit, and both because of the large families and the relatively large amount of meat consumed, needed to have plenty of room for roasting spits, stewpots, and the like. Briggs cites four fireplaces that are, on the average, 8 feet wide and over 4 feet high.[13]

The ' mantel tree ' or lintel across the fireplace opening was often of stone but in the biggest fireplaces was a squared timber of oak as much as 10 by 18 inches in section. Its height above the hearth was sufficient to keep it from burning, though it often became charred.

The equipment of the earliest fireplaces consisted of a green wood lug pole bisecting the chimney flue 6 or 8 feet above the hearth; from it hung the pot chains and 'trammels' (pot hooks of adjustable length). When iron was available, an iron rod, usually lower, took the place of the wooden trammel bar. Later, the familiar swinging iron crane, fastened by

29. Lean-to kitchen, Ogden House, Fairfield, Conn. (Samuel Chamberlain)

eyes set into the masonry at one side, served as a support for hooks and trammels — an obvious improvement as the pots could now swing forward away from the blaze for inspection during cooking. In brick fireplaces, the section back of the fire was occasionally laid in a herringbone pattern; sometimes a cast-iron fire-back protected the bricks. The earliest supports for the logs were simple iron dogs; the more graceful and elaborate andirons of wrought iron or polished brass are generally of eighteenth-century date. Naturally, the parlor and chamber fireplaces were smaller and had no trammel bars or cranes, since no cooking was done in these rooms.

Furniture

The hall was the focus of family activities in a Colonial house, and its furniture was, to say the least, miscellaneous. All indoor activities, including carding, spinning, weaving, sewing, reading, and sometimes even corn-husking, took place here. Neighbors or chance travelers were received in the hall, and here the children played and the young folks courted, sitting rather primly, we may imagine, on the straight high-backed benches at opposite sides of the fireplace.

The furniture was simple and solid. The heavier pieces were made of oak, others were chiefly of pine and maple. Unlike most modern replicas, these pieces were usually painted. The colonists mixed powdered colored clays with sour milk — not unlike the casein paint of today — and usually applied such colors to pine and maple, and sometimes even to oak.[14] The table was usually of the medieval stretcher type, though the handier circular table with swinging gate-legs to support drop-leaves was coming in, as was the similar butterfly table. Backless benches and stools, both low and high, were numerous. The 'joint stool' with mortised and tenoned joints was the most common; even simpler was the three- or four-legged stool with legs housed in a solid top.

Around the table were usually found one or two slat-backed armchairs, at the ends, and several side chairs with uncompromising straight backs and horizontal slats. Lathe-turned legs for tables and chairs were common. Elaborate high-backed chairs with fine hand-carved decoration (fig. 26) were likely to be imported pieces, valued highly enough to be worth the precious space they occupied on shipboard. Such were the fine Cromwellian chairs, leather or cloth upholstered, and the beautifully carved Flemish chairs. Most of the furniture, however, was simple and sturdy homemade stuff. Upholstery was scarce, hard wooden seats or woven rush seats being the rule. In addition to the tables and chairs, there were chests for linen and bedding, heavy cupboards for clothes, and tall dressers for pewter and wooden dishes. Almost always near the fireplace was a long settle, enclosed at the bottom to keep drafts off the backs of legs, and with high straight back and side-pieces curved out to form arms.

The lighting arrangements were completely inadequate. Windows were small and, as the light faded, only small grease lamps and sputtering candles dipped or molded of home-rendered tallow or bayberry wax mitigated the gloom. The 'Betty lamp,' which fed grease from an iron reservoir to a wick, was a poor illuminator. Ingenious holders on the backs of chairs (which were often scorched) were contrived to bring candles closer to the delicate handwork or fine print which the mistress and master of the house might pursue of an evening. There were also stands of wood or iron with adjustable bracket arms, and lamp holders to set on the table. There were no whale-oil or kerosene lamps, as yet, and a chandelier blazing with candles for general illumination was an extravagance reserved for very rare occasions, or very wealthy people.

There were many boxes. Large boxes and small boxes, boxes for long-stemmed churchwarden clay pipes, salt boxes, tobacco boxes, and candle boxes to keep the rats from eating up the winter's supply. A special box, usually with a slanting top, rested on a chest or stand and was known as the 'Bible box.'

Window and bed curtains were of homespun, dyed brown, red, or blue, more rarely green or yellow. Rugs were called 'floor-cloths' and were quite rare; the 'Turkey carpettes' occasionally encountered in seventeenth century documents were far too valuable to walk on — a ' carpet ' then meant a luxurious covering for a table. ' Rugs ' in seventeenth-century parlance were something to put on beds. In general the more re-fined products, such as looking-glasses, silverware, fine fabrics, china, books, and the finer furniture and wearing apparel, were imported niceties and consequently rare.

OTHER ROOMS

The parlor was the ' best room ' of the house. Considering its size, its functions were extremely limited. While friends and neighbors were re-ceived in the hall, ' important ' guests such as the minister or comparative strangers were received into the parlor. Consequently it held the best of the family furniture — any imported chairs or chests the family might be lucky enough to own, the most treasured possessions, and the best bed. For it was also a guest room, accommodating the more honored visitors. Pri-marily, however, the parlor was the ceremonial room for family gather-ings, on Sundays, at times of weddings, funerals, and other important occa-sions.

The parlor was not usually as large as the hall. It had the same depth — 16 to 18 feet commonly — but was somewhat narrower. This disparity in size is a direct reflection of the fact that the room served fewer functions; it is also good evidence that the Colonial builders cared little for exact symmetry, since the resultant façade composition was bound to be slightly irregular.

The kitchen, when it existed as a separate room in the lean-to, was lo-cated so that its fireplace might be built onto the central chimney stack. The kitchen fireplace, of course, was very large and equipped with the usual trammel bar or crane. The bake-oven was an important adjunct. Raised two or three feet above the floor, its sides and top consisted of a circular or oval-shaped dome, neatly constructed of brick. The floor was made of brick, or of a single slab of stone. The oven was heated by glow-ing wood embers, the coals then raked out and the loaves put in and the opening closed by an iron door. Hot stones were similarly used. Essen-tially, it was a ' fireless cooker.'

The kitchen usually served for eating as well as cooking, and its furni-ture included a trestle table, benches, and one or two chairs. It was also a workroom and contained such articles as a wash-bench (there were no sinks with running water), powdering tubs for the salted meats, meal chests, a cheese press, a spinning wheel, and often a loom. A pallet bed in the corner was used, perhaps, by an indentured servant or apprentice.

The kitchen stairway was partitioned off by vertical wainscot from floor to ceiling, molded at the joints. Beyond it was the downstairs bedroom, and at the opposite end, the door to the small pantry. This room was at first called, variously, the ' buttery,' ' butlery,' or ' bottlery,' a place where bottled goods — chiefly ale and beer — were stored. But the word ' pantry ' (from the French *pain*), meaning a place for bread and dry provisions, became the more common term in the seventeenth century. Vegetables, of course, were stored in the cold cellar, but the kitchen ceiling joists were liberally hung with hams, sides of bacon, onions, and the like.

The chambers, or upstairs bedrooms, were rather congested. The house of two-room plan had only two chambers; the lean-to house might have two more in the lean-to garret. ' It was no uncommon thing,' Eberlein says, ' for two or three children or young persons to sleep in one bed and there was often more than one bedstead in a room. Truckle or trundle beds for children were frequently put in the bedchambers of their elders. . .' [15] Servants and apprentices, if not put in the kitchen, occupied the frigid reaches under the slanting rafters of the garret. Indeed the garret often served — especially in houses on the main highroad – as a sort of dormitory for wayfarers. Its dim and dusty spaces, complicated by all manner of rafters, purlins, and collar beams, and by the great chimney rising in its midst to the lofty ridge, doubtless served in the seventeenth century, as in all ages since, for a miscellany of chests, barrels, broken-down furniture, spinning wheels in need of repair, and other household debris.

Reading Suggestions

For general historical and descriptive works on New England Colonial architecture see bibliography, Chapter 3. The following books are particularly recommended for their treatment of the plan, structure, and interiors of the New England Colonial house.

J. Frederick Kelly, *The Early Domestic Architecture of Connecticut,* Yale University Press, New Haven, 1924. One of the classics in the literature of American architectural history, this book is unrivaled in its discussion and illustration of plans and structural details.

Norman M. Isham, *Early American Houses,* The Walpole Society, Boston, 1928. A brief but authoritative treatment of structural and stylistic features.

Norman M. Isham, *Glossary of Colonial Architectural Terms,* The Walpole Society, Boston, 1939. An illustrated glossary of structural and technical terms.

Russell Hawes Kettell, ed., *Early American Rooms,* 1650–1858, Southworth-Anthoensen Press, Portland, Maine, 1936. A group of famous Colonial rooms, with accounts of day-to-day colonial life, beautifully published.

Samuel Chamberlain, *Beyond New England Thresholds,* Hastings House, New York, 1937. The finest collection of photographs yet published of the interiors of New England Colonial houses.

Henry Chapman Mercer, *Ancient Carpenters' Tools,* Bucks County Historical Association, Doylestown, Pa., 1929. Authoritative work on Colonial tools and carpentry.

Meyric R. Rogers, *American Interior Design,* W. W. Norton, New York, 1947. Best general survey of the history of American furniture, accessories, and domestic implements; well-illustrated.

Esther Stevens Brazer, *Early American Decoration,* Pond-Ekberg Co., Springfield, Mass., 1940. Early American decoration of furniture, walls, tinware, etc.

3

New England Colonial Architecture

IT IS NOT necessary to tell here of the first rigorous years of the New England colonies: the religious zeal that animated most of the settlers; their arduous work at clearing the forests, planting fields, fishing, hunting for food and furs; or the constant danger from the Indians. Suffice it to recall that less than two decades saw the foundation of the seven New England colonies: Plymouth, 1620 (merged with Massachusetts in 1691); Massachusetts Bay, 1628; Rhode Island, 1636; Connecticut, 1636; New Haven, 1638 (merged with Connecticut in 1662); Maine, a proprietorship to Sir Ferdinando Gorges, 1639 (merged with Massachusetts, 1677–1820); and New Hampshire, a proprietorship to Captain John Mason, 1639 (merged with Massachusetts, 1641–79). A map of these colonies as they existed in 1650 appears in figure 30.

The Massachusetts Bay Colony was throughout the seventeenth century populous and successful, the focus of English colonial life, and the mother of the other New England colonies. The Bay Company sent over a preliminary group of settlers under Governor John Endecott, who founded Salem, the first capital, in 1628; the town was augmented by about 350 more colonists during the following year. But in 1629 the Company was reorganized and came under the control of the Puritans, who determined to use it for the founding of a Puritan Commonwealth. Great preparations were made and in 1630 John Winthrop's fleet of 17 ships, bearing 2,000 colonists, arrived. A sizeable contingent had come from Boston in Lincolnshire, after which the new capital of the colony was named. Within the decade, some 18,000 more settlers arrived.

Boston started out shabbily enough. In 1630 the land was bare and tree-less; wigwams, mud-walled huts, and tents of dilapidated sails mingled on the shores of the bay with gaunt frame houses still the raw color of the new-cut lumber. In 1634 a mud-walled 'fort' was built on Castle Island, overlooking the harbor, to be replaced ten years later by a structure of 'pine trees' and earth. Building was active, streets were taking form — often congested by heaps of lumber, stones, clay, and other debris piled in them by the builders. 'His Majestie's Commissioners,' describing the condition of Massachusetts in 1665, reported to their sovereign:

Boſton is ye cheif Towne in it, ſeated upon a Peninſule, in the bottom of a Bay, which is a good Harbour, and full of fiſh; it was fortified this yeare 1665 with two Blockhouſes; They had before a Caſtle upon an Iſland in the roade, where ſhipps muſt paſs, about five or six miles from the Towne; Their Houſes are generally Woodden, their ſtreets crooked, with little decency & no uniformity, & there neither dayes, months, ſeaſons of the yeare, Churches, nor Inns are known by their Engliſh Names. At Cambridg they have a Wooden Colledg . . . it may be feared that this Colledge may afford as many Schiſmaticks to ye Church, & ye Corporation as many Rebells to the King, as formerly they have done, if not timely prevented. . .[1]

As Boston grew, it threw off a crescent of towns around it: Newtowne (Cambridge), Charlestown, Dorchester, Watertown, Lexington, Concord, Gloucester, Roxbury, Ipswich, Reading, Braintree, and others.

30. New England settlements about 1650 (Van H. English)

THE NEW ENGLAND COMMUNITY

These towns and villages of the seventeenth century were closely knit units of religious, economic, and social life. For an account of the settlement of a typical New England community we may turn to the pages of Edward Johnson's *Historie of New England* (1653), describing the Massachusetts of the mid-seventeenth century, and particularly the town of Woburn:

This Town, as all others, had its bounds fixed by the General Court, to the contenese [contents] of four miles square . . . the grant is to seven men of good and honest report, upon condition, that within two year they erect houses for habitation thereon, and so go to make a Town thereof . . . these seven men have power to give and grant out lands unto any persons who are willing to take up their dwellings within the said precinct . . . [they] ordered and disposed of the streets of the Town, as might be best for improvement of the Land . . . and were helpful to the poorest sort, in building their houses. Thus was this Town populated, to the number of sixty families, or thereabout, and after this manner are the Towns of New England peopled.[2]

The chief aim was compactness, both for proximity to the meeting-house and for protection against the Indians. It was necessary to forbid farmers from settling far out in the countryside; thus, for example, the General Court of Massachusetts decreed in 1635 that no dwelling should be built more than half a mile from the meeting-house in any new village. Expansion of population was taken care of by increasing the number of new communities rather than the size of existing ones. Groups split off from established centers to form new centers. Thus Charlestown split off from Boston and in turn threw off Woburn; Lynn colonized Nahant; Dedham came out of Boston and in turn founded Medfield. This kind of 'hen-and-chickens' growth meant small, well-knit towns and insured a coherent community life.

When a township grant was made to a group of founders, the village site was chosen and a stretch of common land (the village 'common') reserved, with the place for the meeting-house facing it. Plots of land around the common were granted to individuals in freehold. They were roughly equal, but varied somewhat in size and shape according to topography and need; in Dedham, for example, married men received lots of twelve acres, bachelors only eight acres. The largest plot would go to the minister, and on it was erected the best house in town. Land outside the village — meadowland, upland, marsh, or woodlot — was equitably divided. Various controls over land transfers and land inheritance made the development of large estates difficult, and New England became a region of small land parcels and compact settlements, very different from the feudal patroonships of the Dutch along the Hudson or the lordly plantations of Virginia and Maryland.

Village forms were as varied as the topography they grew on, but all centered on the meeting-house and the fenced-in common, with the houses clustered around it. In regions near the frontier the whole was surrounded by a stockade; in more established areas, houses stretched a little further out along the highroad to the next town. Houses were built close to the road; often they had a rail fence around the yard, with a stepping-stone and hitching-post in front. The elms the settlers planted grew to stately shade trees. So accustomed are we to the gleaming white houses of New England villages that it is hard to picture them otherwise, but paint was not used until after 1700, and in the seventeenth century houses weathered to silvery grays in the seacoast towns and to rich chocolate browns in interior villages, certainly a mellow foil to the russets and brilliant yellows of the autumn oaks and maples.

FRAME HOUSES IN NEW ENGLAND

Brick and stone houses were rare indeed in New England; only eight houses of brick and four of stone are known to have been built before

1700; doubtless there were others, but the total number must have been comparatively small. Many hundreds of frame houses were built, and of the several score remaining today we shall examine ten that are of unusual architectural quality and interest. Each, built for a particular family and on a special site, was individual in form and subject to its own kind of growth, and yet each illustrates features characteristic of the New England Colonial style.

Fairbanks House, Dedham, Massachusetts. c.1637

This is probably the oldest frame house standing in the United States. With its rambling additions and varied collection of roofs, it is also one of the best examples of the ' growing house ' of Colonial times (figs. 31, 32). Jonathan Fayerbanke moved from Boston, whither he had arrived from Yorkshire in 1633, to the new town of Dedham on the occasion of its founding on 10 September 1636. He was granted twelve acres of land, including ' upland in his grant for an house Lott,' as well as four acres of ' Swampe ' land. The oldest part of the house, in the center of the picturesque group, was probably built in 1637 or 1638. Facing south, with its back to the road, the steep-roofed mass with its burly chimney sits close to the ground with an air of comfortable solidity. Walls weathered to a rich brown, sagging roofs, and age-darkened timbers bespeak its three centuries of use. Windows have been changed, perhaps many times, but a fragment of leaded diamond-pane sash found in the hall chamber suggests their original appearance, and perhaps the two tiny upstairs windows indicate their original size.* The sturdy oak frame (fig. 15) with its eight two-story posts is of the ' upright ' type, without overhang. Principal rafters are jointed together at the ridge, but there is no ridgepole, and only one purlin on each side.

The original house had only the small porch and two main rooms downstairs, and of these the hall was at first larger than the parlor (fig. 33). Later the parlor was lengthened to the east by 6 feet and the chamber over it correspondingly enlarged; this addition is the small hipped-roof section visible in figure 31. The massive brick chimney measures 8 by 10 feet. The interiors were over the years much changed by repairs, added plaster, wallpaper, and paint, but there is still some very old wainscot in the hall that may be original: it is made of wide boards with beaded edges, laid horizontally and overlapped, like clapboards. On the west wall of the chamber overhead, too, one may see remains of the old clay filling, daubed on split oak laths between the heavy studs (fig. 27).

Jonathan Fayerbanke must have prospered: he took an active part on committees and at town meetings from the start; he received additional land in grants dated 1637, 1642, 1644, and 1656; and as his acres grew, so did his house. A lean-to containing two rooms was added at the back; the long roof reaches very close to the ground on the north side, and sagging rafters have warped its surface. A new wing, virtually a separate house, was added at the east (at right, fig. 31); tradition has it that this was

* One measures 20 by 28 inches, the other only 17 by 22.

31. Fairbanks House, Dedham, Mass., *c.*1637, from the southeast (courtesy Dartmouth College)

32. Fairbanks House from the northwest, showing lean-to addition and added wings (courtesy Fairbanks Family in America)

built for the oldest son John and his bride in 1641. Entered by a curious little porch tucked into the angle, this wing contains two rooms, each with a corner fireplace, and a large chamber above reached by a winding stair. The west wing, supposedly built about 1654, though connected with the hall by a door and step, also stands as a separate house. It never had fireplaces or chimney, and the rooms are believed to have been used as chambers by the hired men. Both these wings have gambrel roofs of a typical New England profile, and, if their dates can be trusted, are very early examples of this form. It is well to caution that dates based on family tradition are often unreliable, and Chandler was of the opinion that the wings were not completed until 1680; but it seems probable that the two

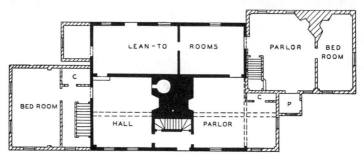

33. Plan of the Fairbanks House (Philip White)

references in Jonathan Fayerbanke's will to ‘ all my houses ’ were intended to mean the three units forming this group. They were bequeathed to his eldest son John on Jonathan's death in 1668. For more than 300 years the house has remained in the ownership of the Fairbanks family.

Whipple House, Ipswich, Massachusetts. 1639

This fine old house grew in size as did the generations of Whipple families that lived in it. The oldest part of the house, at the west (left, in fig. 34) , was of the one-room plan type, with entrance door, stairway, and huge chimney at one end. The rooms were of great size, and it is possible that the large chamber above the hall was divided by a wooden partition to form two sleeping rooms. This first unit was certainly built before 1650, possibly as early as 1638.* Captain John Whipple, the second of the family to own the house, was prosperous in business affairs. He had received a license in 1662 ‘ to still strong water for a year and retail not less than a quart at a time and none to be drunk in his house.’ He made a large addition in 1670†, more than doubling the size of the house. This gives it, from the outside, the familiar central-chimney appearance, though the

* A document of 10 October 1650 confirms that the house was ‘ formerly sould ’ to John Whipple by one John Fawn. Fawn owned the land from c.1634 to 1638 and may have built the house at that time. See Thomas F. Waters, *The John Whipple House*, *Publications of the Ipswich Historical Society*, no. xx, 1915, pp. 1–6.

† The year after his father's death — not documented, however, until his will of 2 August 1683.

façade is actually asymmetrical. The rooms of the new addition were unusually fine, containing triple-light windows, fine molded framing timbers, and one structural rarity: summer beams crossed at right angles. The diagonal lattices of the windows have unfortunately been restored in wood rather than with lead calmes.

Though the front of the house has no overhang, Captain Whipple evidently fancied the motive, and, at the east end where he was free of the lines of the older house, built two overhangs — one to each story — and

34. Whipple House, Ipswich, Mass., from the northwest (HABS)

what is more remarkable, both are hewn rather than framed overhangs. The hewn or false overhang, rare at any period in Massachusetts, usually dated from late in the century in Connecticut. It is a question whether, divorced from its original structural significance, it had not become purely a matter of aesthetic fashion, a rarity indeed in Colonial architecture. The next owner, a Major John Whipple, added a lean-to of considerable size at the back of the house to complete its present-day form.

Scotch-Boardman House, Saugus, Massachusetts. 1651

This classic example of the New England saltbox house (fig. 35) was built in 1651 by the owners of the Saugus Ironworks company, to house Scotch prisoners captured by Cromwell in the Battle of Dunbar and sent to America as indentured servants. After serving their indenture, they were absorbed as estimable members of the community, and the house was bought by the Boardman family in 1687.

The house has not yet been restored to its original condition; there is evidence in the framing that it once boasted a projecting front porch, two large cross gables, and possibly a third gable over the porch. In this form it would have strongly resembled two other houses with projecting porches and three gables: the Henry Bridgham House in Boston, built in 1670, and the Jonathan Corwin or ' Witch ' House in Salem, completed in 1675. We know also that the original windows were triple casements in front and double casements on the ends.[3] But as it stands, it is typical of a large number of seventeenth-century houses with unbroken roof slopes. The simple and symmetrical facade composition is made dynamic by the bold

35. Scotch-Boardman House, Saugus, Mass., 1651 (Wayne Andrews)

framed overhang and is climaxed by an unusually vigorous chimney shaped by pilasters on front and back. The rear roof has a long downward slope of slightly broken pitch, as was common on houses with added lean-tos. Many of the interior features — wainscot, batten doors, unplastered ceilings in the second story, garret stairway, and chimney — are original. Few examples of the typical New England house remain so unmarred.

Whitman House, Farmington, Connecticut. 1664

The Whitman House, carefully restored in 1934 (fig. 36), is another classic example of the New England style.[4] Like many Connecticut houses it has a six-inch gabled overhang at the ends, while the front juts more boldly — a foot and a half in this instance. The lower ends of the four second-story posts project below the overhang and are carved into pendants, their square section revealing the shape of the timbers. The diamond-pane windows are very small and divided by vertical mullions and horizontal transoms into four lights each. The big lean-to at the rear was added sometime after 1700. In order to give the rear roof a uniform pitch, the original rafters of the main roof were shortened and its pitch lowered. At the same time the chimney was cut off correspondingly and rebuilt: under the roof it is of well-selected flat fieldstones laid in a mortar of clay mixed with hay, but above the roof it is made of small blocks of red sandstone, laid in good lime mortar. Since brick was commonly available after

36. Whitman House, Farmington, Conn., 1664 (Samuel Chamberlain)

1700, the kitchen fireplace in the lean-to was made of brick, and its separate flue carried up in back of the old stone stack.

Every detail of the interior — batten doors with iron strap hinges, wide floor boards and wainscot, chamfered beams and joists — is typical of the period, and the great stone fireplace in the hall measures 7 feet in width and 3½ in height. A brick bake-oven built into the stonework of the hall fireplace demonstrates its use for cooking before the lean-to kitchen was added.

Capen House, Topsfield, Massachusetts. 1683

The parsonage built for the Reverend Joseph Capen at Topsfield, Massachusetts, is perhaps the most perfect of New England Colonial houses (fig. 37). Little altered from the time of the raising bee on ' JUN Ye 8, 1683,' as inscribed in two places on the heavy oak frame, the house was acquired by the Topsfield Historical Society in 1913, restored with great care, furnished in the seventeenth-century manner, and is now, properly maintained and open to the public, a mecca for students of Colonial architecture.[5] Its unusually large hall, with fireplace, ceiling beams, and furniture, has been reproduced in the American Wing of the Metropolitan Museum of Art.

The Capen House appears very English; indeed, it would sit as naturally in the rolling countryside of the hamlet of Toppesfield, in Essex, as it does on its knoll in the Massachusetts village. Strong overhangs in front and at gable ends emphasize its quiet horizontal lines, repeated by the fine shadows of the dark brown clapboards and weather-beaten shingles. The pilastered chimney bespeaks a Tudor heritage, as do the small

37. Parson Capen House, Topsfield, Mass., 1683 (Wayne Andrews)

square-pane leaded casements. Carved pendants decorate the overhangs, varied by bold brackets under the gable ends and flanking the front door.

Inside the porch, the steep staircase, with knobbed newel and turned oak balusters primly decorating it (fig. 38), winds up before the chimney. Hand-forged nails stud the heavy front door, while battens secure the board doors to hall and parlor. The hall (and by this time the documents speak frequently of it as the 'kitchen') is a study in wood: wide wooden floor boards, sanded smooth; wainscoted walls; wooden ceiling beams; stools, tubs, boxes, and other utensils made of wood. A fireplace of ample breadth (fig. 39), spanned by an oak mantel tree 16 inches square, is flanked by high-backed settle and weaving frame. Perhaps because this was a minister's house, the parlor (fig. 40) is the larger of the two rooms. Indeed its ample size, $17\frac{1}{2}$ by 19 feet, demanded two heavy summer beams to carry the weight of the second floor (see plan, fig. 41). Gate-leg table and slat-backed Carver armchairs, though humbler than the graceful and polished Chippendale of a later century, nonetheless suggest the room's importance. Every detail of this house proclaims the frugality and yet the dignity of the Puritan divine, the respect in which he held himself and which the community accorded to him.

38. View across porch to parlor, Capen House (Samuel Chamberlain)

*Paul Revere House, Boston. c.*1676

In the seventeenth century historic North Square was only a block in-land from the docks and wharves of the waterfront. A neat island of re-spectable little houses and shops, it was permeated by the pungent smell of tar, oak chips, and hemp, and through it walked ship's carpenters, riggers,

39. Fireplace in the hall, Capen House (Samuel Chamberlain)

40. Parlor of the Capen House (Samuel Chamberlain)

sail makers, and caulkers, for North Boston was the heart of the ship-building trade.

On the west side of the triangle was a narrow plot of land owned by one John Jeffs, who is thought to have built, about 1676, the small house made famous a century later by Paul Revere. At the time Revere lived in it, from 1770 to 1800, it had already grown to a full three-story height, and later in the nineteenth century it deteriorated into a ramshackle tenement. In 1908 it was carefully studied and restored to its seventeenth-century form.

Even by the 1670's, Boston had started on its patchwork development of

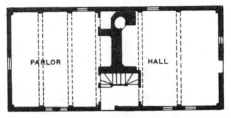

41. Plan of the Capen House (Philip White, after Millar)

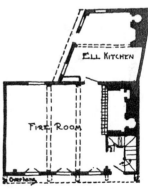

42. Paul Revere House, Boston, c.1676 (Detroit Publishing Co.)
43. Plan of the Paul Revere House (Joseph E. Chandler, *The Colonial House,* R. M. McBride and Co.)

curving streets and crooked lots, for the house, occupying almost the full
width of its lot, bends its ell to a crooked line (fig. 43). Doubtless at first
the house was of the familiar one-room plan, for the deeply recessed fireplace in the hall has a bake-oven. The small porch and winding stair are
in front of the chimney, and the large room is spanned by two summer
beams. But the kitchen in the crooked ell must have been added early, for
above its door the kitchen chamber overhangs boldly. It was through this

44. John Ward House, Salem, Mass., 1684 (Frank Cousins, The Essex Institute)

back door that Paul Revere left quietly (for the square was full of soldiers) for his famous ride on the 18th of April in '75.

The façade (fig. 42) has an overhang supported by the three main crosswise timbers — the chimney girt and two summers. Wall studs are covered
by 'parallel' rather than feather-edged clapboards, beaded at the lower
corners. The pendants, quarreled windows with shutters, front door, and
roof shingles have been restored in the seventeenth-century style, as has
the hall. But the second-story chamber is fully plastered, cased, paneled
and painted as it might have been in Revere's day.

John Ward House, Salem, Massachusetts. 1684

Salem is a town of many gables, and one of its most impressive gabled
edifices is the John Ward House, which stands as a colonial museum in
the grounds of the Essex Institute (fig. 44). John Ward bought the lot on
which the house originally stood on 13 November 1684 and built his first
small house immediately after. It included only the west half of the present

house: the parlor and its chamber above, the big chimney, porch, and stair (fig. 45). There were few houses in that day that boasted an over-hang at both front and end, an arrangement that gave much added space to the chamber in the second story. To enlarge and light the garret, a wide cross gable was introduced on the front side.

In this first stage, the house must have strongly resembled the near-by Benjamin Hooper (Hathaway) House in Salem, built only two years be-fore (fig. 46). Hooper's house had a front overhang and a bold cross gable,

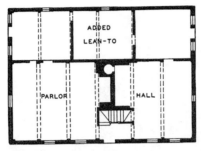

45. Plan of the John Ward House (Philip White, after Essex Institute)

though it lacked an end overhang. The asymmetrical placement of the windows of the façade is noteworthy: arranged on a diagonal, and with changed emphasis of size, they suggest the dynamic verticals of Gothic rather than the flat symmetries of the Renaissance. The massive off center chimney completes this subtle balance.

46. Restored elevations of the Benjamin Hooper (Hathaway) House, Salem, 1682 (Joseph E. Chandler, *The Colonial House*, R. M. McBride and Co.)

At some later date, John Ward added the eastern half of his house, with its summer-beamed hall and enormous fireplace. The overhang he carried across the front but not around the east end, and he framed the new addi-tion in pine rather than oak. At some time before his death in 1732 he added the long lean-to across the back of the house. As in most added lean-tos, the roof breaks pitch with the original one.

The subtleties of the Hooper House recur in the finished Ward façade. Symmetrical to a casual glance it is far from regular. As the hall is narrower than the parlor, both door and chimney are off-center; the gables differ in width and in roof pitch; the windows in the east gable are off-center to its axis; the middle window is not over the ' central ' door. No house better illustrates that the Colonial builder cared nought for symmetry: he accepted it if the plan called for it, but he never regarded it as an aesthetic necessity as did his Georgian successors. He doubtless did not consciously strive for, but he may unconsciously have remembered, the moving surfaces and shifting accents, the dynamic silhouettes and vertical aspirations of Gothic England.

47. Turner ('Seven Gables') House, Salem (Mary H. Northend)

The Turner House, Salem. c.1670

Even more ' Gothic,' more picturesque and complex, is the rambling, much-remodeled Turner House in Salem, original of Hawthorne's ' House of Seven Gables.' [6] During the centuries of its existence, wings, walls, ells, gables, and even chimneys have been added, torn down, and again rebuilt, and it is no wonder that Hawthorne did not know that in its heyday it was a house of eight gables. John Turner, Salem mariner, bought the land in 1668 and probably within a year or two built the house, facing it south on Salem harbor. At first it was of two-room plan, with two cross gables in front; later a lean-to was added. At this stage it must have looked very much as the John Ward House now does. The end of this first house, with one cross gable and the central chimney, may be seen at the right in figure 47.

Captain Turner soon became master of a fleet and a fortune, with his ketches the *Prosperous*, the *John & Thomas*, and the *Willing Mind* which brought rich cargoes to his own wharf on the harbor. About 1678, we may suppose, he added the large south wing (at left, fig. 47), and a two-story porch in the angle between it and the old house. Together, they largely concealed the former façade. The wing contained a new parlor, a chamber, and a garret lighted by three gables. It was on a larger and more elaborate scale than the old house, with a new chimney, higher-studded

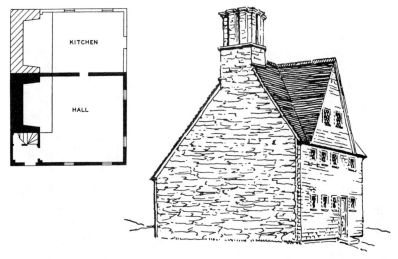

48. Plan of Rhode Island house with lean-to addition, forming a 'stone-ender' (Philip White)
49. Early form of the Eleazer Arnold House, Lincoln, R.I., 1687 (Antoinette F. Downing, *Early Homes of Rhode Island*, Garrett and Massie)

rooms, double casement windows, and overhangs with carved pendants on both porch and wing. Captain Turner died in 1680 at the age of thirty-six, leaving a nine-year-old son and four daughters.

In 1692 John Turner II reached the age of 21 and was appointed administrator of his father's estate. This was the tragic year of Salem's witch-craft madness, and it may be assumed that he sought to make a secret hiding place for the protection of his sisters. A new kitchen addition, back of the old lean-to, had made the original central chimney unnecessary, and the famous ' secret staircase ' within this chimney from second floor to garret may have been built in that year.[7] The last major change in the old house probably occurred about 1720, when Turner remodeled the interiors of the forty-year-old south wing, replacing all the small case-ment windows with their leaded panes by larger sliding-sash windows, casing in the old structural posts and beams, and adding the fine Georgian paneling in the parlor. During his lifetime the house had fourteen rooms and eight gables, a rambling and picturesque collection of wings and roofs looking out across the harbor. By the middle of the nineteenth century many minor changes had occurred; gables had been removed, and over-hangs cased in. But Hawthorne visited the house frequently in these years, and though he always averred that any similarity to the *House of Seven Gables* was purely coincidental, there seems little doubt that it inspired the setting of his novel published in 1852. The house was rescued from semi-ruin in 1908 and carefully restored in succeeding years.

Eleazer Arnold House, Lincoln, Rhode Island. 1687

Even within New England, there were minor regional variations in the Colonial style: differences in materials, in ways of framing a house, or of

50. Hall of the Eleazer Arnold House (HABS)

adding to it. Rhode Island, unlike Massachusetts and Connecticut, had a plentiful supply of building stone and lime for mortaring it. Conse-quently, a common local form was the 'stone-ender' house. This arose from a characteristic local method of enlargement. Starting with a one-room house (fig. 48), with fireplace at the end, the first addition was com-monly a rear lean-to instead of another room at the opposite side of the chimney. The lean-to room served as a kitchen. Its fireplace was built be-side that of the hall, and the combined chimneys of the two were so wide that they covered virtually the whole end of the house. A later addition, at the opposite end, was sometimes made to accommodate bedrooms.

The Eleazer Arnold House is a notable example of the stone-ender. As originally built (fig. 49), it had a clapboarded front wall two stories high, a high-peaked front gable, and a long rear roof over the kitchen lean-to. The chimneys of hall and kitchen combine to form a stone end wall of imposing breadth and height. The chimney top, shaped by many pilasters, is one of the most elaborate in New England. The fireplace in the hall (fig. 50) is one of the largest: 10 feet 8 inches wide, 5 feet 3 inches high, and 3 feet 10 inches deep. Its great oak mantel tree is over 12 feet long and together with the heavy ceiling timbers presents a dramatic picture of the massive construction of a Colonial house.

51. Jethro Coffin House, Nantucket, Mass., 1686 (Samuel Chamberlain)

The 'Cape Cod house'

The phrase 'New England Colonial' most commonly evokes a mental image of the typical 'Cape Cod house,' with its low one-story eaves, white clapboarded or shingled walls, gabled roof, and big central chimney. It was a type that became all but universal in small houses of the eighteenth century in the New England colonies. Though the type doubtless originated earlier, surprisingly few authentically dated seventeenth-century examples remain today, and in most of these, eighteenth-century windows, door casings, and cornice trim alter the original effect.

Perhaps the nearest approach to an authentic seventeenth-century 'Cape Codder' surviving today is the Jethro Coffin House, built on Nantucket Island about 1686 (fig. 51). It is a saltbox with long rear roof slope, very small windows of the medieval type, and a big central chimney with four large fireplaces. The chimney top is ornamented by an inverted horseshoe, a unique decorative feature which, it is conjectured,[8] must have been an anti-witch device, since it is well known that witches do not fly down flues protected in this fashion. The house was thoroughly restored in 1927 under direction of the Society for the Preservation of New England Antiquities, and though little original work remained, surviving fragments indicated shouldered oak posts, and summer beams of pine. The original bricks of the chimney were of large size ($2\frac{1}{2}$ by $4\frac{1}{4}$ by 10 inches) laid in clam-shell mortar. It is not known whether the walls were originally covered by shingles, but they have been restored with hand-split shakes. The house lacks the snug lowness usually associated with the Cape Cod style, because the front wall is posted about a story and a half high before the rafters begin to pitch.

More in accord with the conventional picture of the Cape Cod house is the Jabez Wilder House at South Hingham, Massachusetts (fig. 52). The main house is believed to have been built in 1690, the miniature wing probably in the eighteenth century. The graceful rainbow roof on the house is a rarity, the straight-pitched gable of the ell being the common type. The paneled and framed front doors, sliding-sash windows, quoined corners, and white painted walls must, of course, be later changes, but the house nonetheless retains a Colonial simplicity and informality of great charm.

52. Jabez Wilder House, South Hingham, Mass., 1690? (Samuel Chamberlain)

STONE HOUSES IN NEW ENGLAND

New England has a great abundance of stone: ledge outcrops, underlying strata of sandstone, granite, and some limestone; and such an abundance of glacial boulders that the stone walls separating fields have become a characteristic part of the landscape. In the circumstances, it may seem strange that stone houses were so extremely rare in the seventeenth century and even in the eighteenth. But several reasons account for the almost universal use of wood. In the first place, wood was easier to shape into a suitable building material, and hence cheaper. In the second place, glacial boulders and fieldstones could not be laid in a durable wall without lime mortar, and lime was so scarce and expensive in the seventeenth century that this was not practicable in most regions. Kimball cites the unhappy experience of Goveror Winthrop, who tried to build a stone house near Boston in 1631, but ' there came so violent a storm of rain . . . (it not being finished, and laid with clay for want of lime) two sides of it were washed down to the ground.' [9] A third reason, doubtless, was the general unfamiliarity of the colonists with stone building. Most of them came from southeastern England, a region in which there is an almost complete

53. Henry Whitfield House, Guilford, Conn., 1639-40 (Wayne Andrews)

dearth of good building stone; even such great medieval cathedrals as Canterbury and Westminster Abbey had to be built largely of Caen stone imported from France. And finally, either stone or brick, unless laid in very thick walls, is subject to damp-penetration and is a very poor insulator. Though Jefferson greatly deplored, as late as 1784, Americans' ' unhappy prejudice ' against building in stone or brick, the prejudice was well founded from a practical point of view.

A very few stone houses, however, were built. The most notable of these was the Henry Whitfield House at Guilford, Connecticut, overlooking Long Island Sound (fig. 53). As the minister's house and the town's first fort and meeting-house, it was a structure of unusual size and importance. Reverend Whitfield and his party of colonists, numbering some forty men, bought the town site from the Indians on 29 September 1639, and probably occupied temporary shelters that winter. Tradition asserts that the stone house was begun in the fall of 1639, so it may have been completed during the following year. Whitfield left it to return to his native England in 1650, and during the next two and a half centuries so many changes and remodelings occurred that only a small part of the present building consists of original work. Bought by the State of Connecticut in 1900, successive restorations culminating in a very thorough rebuilding in 1936 have restored the imposing building to something very much like its original condition.[10]

The observer is at once struck by its thoroughly English Gothic appearance. Thick walls, small casement windows, massive chimneys, and steep roof make it easy to picture the house in an English village of the

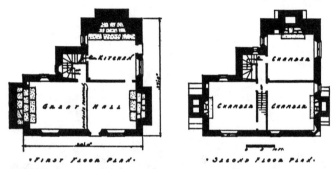

54. Plans of the Whitfield House (J. Frederick Kelly, *Old Time New England*)

Tudor period. The local ledge stones are laid in a mortar of clay and pulverized oyster shells to a two-foot thickness, and the deep jambs inside the leaded casements are splayed to a 30° angle to admit more light. Door and windows of the west façade are asymmetrically arranged. The extremely steep roof (60° pitch) is penetrated by small dormer windows; such features, though extremely rare in Colonial architecture, are not unknown, and their presence here may be inferred from the complete lack of windows in the gable ends.

The masonry of the great north chimney is entirely original. It is easy, in a stone house, to incorporate fireplaces and chimneys in the walls, and this doubtless accounts for the end chimneys with sloped offsets, a feature as rare in New England as it is common in Virginia. The end chimneys permitted two adjacent rooms on the first floor (fig. 54), and since the building was at first used as a meeting-house, it is believed that these two rooms were thrown together by raising to the ceiling a wainscot partition, hung on strap hinges — a feature found in some other early Connecticut houses. The interior walls are of bare whitewashed stone and — adjacent to the kitchen — broad wainscot boards. The main fireplace is over 10 feet in width, and spanned by a 14-by-16-inch oak lintel. The kitchen wing, with its own huge fireplace, was probably added after the original construction, but there is no evidence to show whether or not the stair tower in the angle of the ell is original; if it is, the plan of the first house might have resembled that of certain Virginia houses of the seventeenth century, which had a projecting stair tower at the back, as well as end chimneys.

Interiors have been restored with adzed oak framing members, oak and hard-pine floor boards, and pine and whitewood wainscot, finished only with several coats of paste beeswax rubbed into the wood. Upstairs are three chambers and a steep stair leading to the lofty garret. The southwest chamber has a small corner window; though otherwise unknown in Colonial architecture, this feature was restored on the basis of references in Palfrey's *History of New England* and Smith's *History of Guilford*.

There are documentary references to two other stone houses: John Smith's ' Old Stone Castle ' at Warwick, Rhode Island, built in 1649; and the John Winthrop house built in New London, Connecticut, before 1657, but both of these have disappeared. The one-story stone cottage at Gloucester, Massachusetts, called James Babson's ' Cooperage Shop,' from its use about 1700, is credited with a date of 1659. The Spencer-Pierce-Little House in Newburyport was probably built in the seventeenth century; at least it is known to have been in existence in 1701. Stone-enders were built in Rhode Island, and in Connecticut there were a few houses with ends of stone and clapboarded front and rear walls, such as the Pardee-Morris House, built about 1680–85 in New Haven. But on the whole, stone houses in seventeenth-century New England were rare indeed.

BRICK HOUSES IN NEW ENGLAND

Brick houses were almost as rare as those of stone in the seventeenth century, and for much the same reason. Bricks were plentiful enough: clay was everywhere available, brickmakers came over with the earliest settlers, kilns could be built and plenty of fuel cut for them, and there are records to show that bricks were being made from the very early years in several New England towns.* But lime for mortar to lay them in was another matter, and so also was the general prejudice in favor of frame construction. Although in East Anglia brick construction was more common than stone, it was confined to churches and expensive manor houses, and it is safe to say that most of the emigrants to the colonies had lived in frame houses.

Brick was undoubtedly earliest used in New England for chimney construction, to supplant the primitive clay-daubed wooden chimneys which were in such constant need of repair. The chimney of the Fairbanks House (*c*.1637) at Dedham is of brick, and bricks were found in the ruins of the Plymouth Company's trading post at Aptucxet, built as early as 1627. Crudely molded brick, burned to varying degrees of hardness and laid in clay mortar, was also used as nogging for walls throughout the seventeenth century, as we have seen. The earliest documentary reference to brick houses in New England is in Edward Johnson's description of Boston in 1652:

* Salem, 1629; Chelsea, 1630; Hartford, 1638; New Haven, 1640; Plymouth, 1643.

. . . the chief Edifice of this City-like Towne is crowded on the Sea-bankes, and wharfed out with great industry and cost, the buildings beautifull and large, some fairly set forth with Brick, Tile, Stone, and Slate, and orderly placed with comly streets, whose continuall inlargement presages some sumptuous City.[11]

One of the principal brick-making centers in Massachusetts was Medford; its kilns were set up early, and after the Revolution it produced about four million bricks annually.

We have definite knowledge of only eleven brick buildings in seventeenth-century New England; nearly half of them were built in Medford, and all but one date from the last quarter of the century.* It is safe to as-

55. Peter Tufts (Cradock) House, Medford, Mass., 1675 (Society for the Preservation of New England Antiquities)

sume that there were others, for most of the ' known ' examples have disappeared today. Several of them showed advances in plan or decorative detail toward the eighteenth-century style.

Notable is the Peter Tufts House at Medford (fig. 55), a large house of Georgian plan-type with central hallway and two rooms on either side in each story. Its construction in 1675 is attested by the court testimony of a mechanic working on it in that year.[12] The brick walls are 18 inches thick, and the end chimneys, unusual in New England, were presumably incorporated in them for economy. The separate flues are brought together in the gables. The steep main roof slope (51°) is truncated at the top to form one of the earliest-known gambrel roofs. Near the ends of the house, in each story of the façade, were small oval ' port-holes ' or windows, 16 by

* The Indian College at Harvard (1654–6); Harvard Hall (1674–7); **Peter Tufts House at Medford** (1675); Usher House at Medford (1677?); Peter Sergeant (Province) House, Boston (1676–9); John Foster (Hutchinson) House, Boston (c.1688); Joseph Peaslee Garrison, East Haverhill (1675?); Richard Hazen House, Haverhill (c.1694); Jonathan Wade House, Medford (1690's); **Nathaniel Wade House, Medford** (1690's); and Stoughton Hall, Harvard (1699).

20 inches, of unexplained origin. There were originally two more in each end gable, making a total of eight. They were bricked up in 1872, but some of them were reopened in a remodeling of 1890. These openings were impracticable for gunfire, and it is believed they may have been purely decorative.[13]

The interior contains superb oak summers and girts, with chamfered edges and elaborate stops, and an original stairway to the second floor, but many parts of the fabric date from the remodeling of 1890. A brick entrance porch was added and dormer windows inserted, and the original groups of casement windows set under shallow relieving arches were replaced by sliding sash.[14]

56. Peter Sergeant House, Boston, 1676–9. Conjectural restoration of north end (rendering by R. E. Collins in Thomas T. Waterman, *The Dwellings of Colonial America*, University of North Carolina Press)

The original Usher House at Medford (1677?) was also a full two and a half stories in height, with a central hallway and end chimneys, but only one room in depth. The old Hazen House in Haverhill (c.1694) was restored in 1915 with latticed and transomed casement windows under segmental-arched heads and thus it appears more medieval, but like the Tufts House it has a belt course between stories.

Undoubtedly the most famous brick house in seventeenth-century New England was that built for Peter Sergeant in Boston. Sergeant, who had come to Boston in 1667, became a wealthy merchant and later served as a judge and a member of the Governor's Council. The land he bought on 21 October 1676, a large tract extending halfway from Washington to Tremont Street, included a fine garden and orchard, stable, and coach house. The big house which he built, with brick walls about 2 feet thick, was completed by 1679. These walls, incorporated in a later business building, were demolished in 1922 and revealed evidence of the original appearance of the building.[15] A conjectural restoration of the north end (fig. 56) gives the probable appearance of the house in its seventeenth-century form.

The ruined walls revealed massive end chimneys, projecting four feet

from the wall and containing two fireplaces on each floor. Setbacks at the
sides gave the chimneys a tapered mass similar to that of Virginia chimneys of the seventeenth century, and, like them, the upper part of the
stack stood detached from the gable wall. Each stack was topped by detached chimney shafts, set diagonally. The end walls had copings, probably shaped to curved Flemish gables. The finding of a large number of
curved molded bricks suggests that there were three smaller Flemish
gables adorning the main façade. Such clustered chimneys and Flemish
gables were used on English manor houses of the Elizabethan period, but
they were very rare in the colonies. The only similar features surviving
today are to be found on the much smaller Bacon's Castle, Virginia, built

57. The Sergeant House as remodeled in 1728 to serve as the Province House of
Massachusetts (S. A. Drake, *Landmarks and Historic Personages of Boston*)

about a generation earlier than the Sergeant house. The windows were
topped by segmental arches. Exceptionally large, they were probably divided by mullions into several small lights, and these were undoubtedly
fitted with leaded glass of the medieval type.

The Sergeant House was early accustomed to viceregal society. Governor and Lady Bellomont visited it for several months in 1697, and Sergeant's third wife, whom he married in 1707, was Lady Phips, widow of
the former Governor Sir William Phips. After Sergeant's death in 1714
the mansion was purchased by the province (in 1716) to serve as a residence for the royal governors.[16] It was thenceforth known as the Province House.

The provincial annals reveal various small expenditures for repairs and
maintenance in succeeding years, but the major alterations which transformed it from a medieval house to a Georgian mansion (fig. 57) were
probably made in 1728. On 26 December 1727 it was

Ordered . . . that the Province House be forthwith repaired, and put into a
suitable Condition for the reception of His Excellency and His Family, which He
hath signified to His Honour the Lieutenant Governor will be very acceptable to
him.[17]

A sum of £2,299 was duly paid in the following December, and this would certainly account for major changes.[18] The medieval roof and gables were removed, a third story added under a new gabled roof, and the old leaded casements replaced by sash windows. The stone steps were 'handsomely railed with an Iron rail fence' in 1734–5,[19] and, since the payment was £447, possibly the columned entrance portico was also added at this time. In its iron railing was interwoven '16 PS 79' in commemoration of the original builder. Perhaps also at this time was added the huge cupola. Perched atop it was a famous weathervane made by Deacon Shem Drowne in the form of a pot-bellied Indian with gleaming glass eyes and outsized bow-and-arrow pointing the wind. The Indian figure was doubtless derived from the great seal of the province. The exterior appearance of the Province House after these extensive remodelings is known from an old print.[20] The interiors were doubtless also lavishly remodeled: Hawthorne's description of the house as it appeared in 1840 mentions wall paneling, Dutch-tiled fireplaces, and an elaborate stairway with twisted balusters.

But the great house of the province fared ill after the Revolution. Devoted to a succession of State and business uses, its interiors were gutted by fire in 1864, and its remaining walls incorporated in a brick business structure; this in turn was demolished in 1922, thus revealing the last remnants of Peter Sergeant's ambitious mansion of two and a half centuries earlier.

Even more remarkable than Sergeant's house was the three-story brick residence built by John Foster in Boston about 1688, and later occupied by Governor Hutchinson. Probably planned by an English architect, in the mature style of the English Renaissance, this house may be counted the first Georgian building in the American colonies; its history is accordingly discussed in a later chapter.

Undoubtedly the number of brick houses in Boston increased rapidly during the 1680's and 1690's, as it did in New York and Philadelphia in the same decades. The disastrous fire of 1679, which destroyed an estimated 150 buildings, led to a town order that all new houses be built of 'stone or bricke, & covered with slate or tyle.'[21] It was evidently impossible to enforce this ordinance at the time because of materials shortages, but another bad fire in 1691 led to a new regulation requiring masonry construction. This was more stringently enforced, especially after a third fire in 1711 (the worst in Boston's colonial history), and by 1715 no more frame dwellings were being built. In 1722, Boston was a very substantial city containing, if we may believe the somewhat sanguine legend on Captain John Bonner's map:

| Streets 42 | Lanes 36 | Alleys 22 | Houses near 3000 |
| 1000 Brick | rest Timber | | Near 12000 people |

GARRISONS AND BLOCKHOUSES

Community life in the seventeenth century was by no means secure. Indians lurked around the fringes of settlements, even near the seacoast, and

frontier towns were never safe from raids. One of the first buildings the
Pilgrims erected was the fort on the hill at Plymouth, as we have seen, and
many towns girt themselves with stockades. Universal compulsory military
service existed from the earliest days. The union of Massachusetts, Plymouth, Connecticut, and New Haven colonies in 1643 to form the New
England Confederation was primarily for protection against the Indians.
The confederation had a standing ' army ' of 300 men.

Random skirmishes with French and Indians continued for generations,
and in King Philip's War (1675–7) fierce hostilities laid waste many Massachusetts and Rhode Island towns. It was at this time that Governor
Andros issued an order requiring all towns and villages ' forthwith without

58. Fort Halifax, Winslow, Maine, 1754 (HABS)

Delay, to Fortify and make compleat, in some convenient Place, a block or
palizadoed House, or Place for a Retreat to Women and Children, etc.'
Indian raids instigated by the French continued intermittently from 1689
until the Treaty of Paris in 1763. Among the more famous raids was the
Deerfield Massacre, in 1704, when the western Massachusetts town was
burned, forty-eight persons killed, and a hundred taken prisoner to Canada.

The colonists seem to have used the term ' blockhouse ' and ' garrison '
more or less interchangeably, but more usually applied the former term
to a square fort with overhangs, the latter term to a structure similar to an
ordinary house but with thick protective walls.

Blockhouses or ' commaunders ' were usually square in plan, with the
second story overhanging the first on all four sides. A good example is
Fort Halifax at Winslow, Maine (fig. 58). Though built in 1754, it probably represents an early type, with heavy square-hewn timbers dovetailed
at the corners, a pyramidal roof, very small windows with heavy shutters,
and an occasional loophole for firing. Fort McClary, at Kittery Point,
Maine, was built about 1715. Photographs taken before the modern restoration show that it had an unusual pentagonal plan, stone walls below
and wood above, and a ladder, hinged at the sill of the door in the upper
story, which could be pulled up like a drawbridge.

59. William Damme garrison house, Dover, N.H., c.1675 (*Old Time New England*)

Garrisons, or fortified houses, were built in almost all New England towns, and they were particularly common in the frontier towns of Maine and New Hampshire. Gilmanton, New Hampshire, had four garrisons, one at each corner of the town. Like an ordinary house in plan and appearance, garrisons were used in times of peace as one-family dwellings, but were strongly built and capable of protecting a number of families in times of danger. Isolated families frequently built garrisons on their own land, for their own protection.[22]

Representative of the type is the William Damme garrison at Dover, New Hampshire (fig. 59), built about 1675. With two rooms and a central chimney, the house lacks defensive overhangs but the walls are made of hewn oak logs, some of them over 20 feet long, fitted with lapped joints at the corners. The original windows were very small but have since been enlarged and fitted with sliding sash. The Doe garrison (1648) at Newmarket is more elaborate and of different construction: two and a half stories high and with hewn overhangs on all four sides, the walls consist of 3-inch-thick oak planks, set vertically and rebated into the horizontal framing members at top and bottom. But hewn-log construction with lapped or dovetailed corner joints was the more common type, as in the Bunker garrison (1652) at Dover and the Gilman garrison (1656) at Exeter.

Where brick was available, as near the Medford and Haverhill kilns in Massachusetts, masonry-walled garrisons were built because of their obvious safety against fire attacks. Such, for example, were the Peaslee garrison (1675?) at East Haverhill and the Hazen garrison (c.1694) at Haverhill. As log-cabin construction with round logs came to be known in New England in the eighteenth century, this was probably used increasingly for frontier garrisons in Maine and New Hampshire. The two-story Bridgeman garrison (1746) at Vernon, Vermont, appears in an old drawing to have been of this type.

The Micum McIntyre garrison at Scotland (near York), Maine, is an impressive early structure (fig. 60). If indeed built between 1640 and 1645, as claimed, it may share with the Lower Log House on Darby Creek, Pennsylvania, the distinction of being the oldest log structure in America.[23] The 8-inch-thick pine and oak timbers are square-hewn and half-dovetailed at the corners, and there is a 14-inch overhang on all four sides. As was often the case, clapboard siding and sash windows were added later, giving an appearance differing little from that of an ordinary house in New England, or indeed, in old England (cf. fig. 9). In a surprise attack by French and Indians on the night of 5 February 1692, the McIntyre garrison was the only building in the village of York and its vicinity not destroyed.

There is at North Edgecomb, Maine, a rare example of an octagonal blockhouse, with second-story overhang on all eight sides and a cupola or lookout over the roof. Heavy shutters close all windows, and an extra-thick nail-studded door bars the single entrance. This was built as late as 1808. In the early days of the Maine frontier, when isolated settlers were constantly raided by French and Indians, between 1690 and 1745, a ma-

60. Micum McIntyre garrison house, Scotland, Maine, 1640–45? (HABS)

jority of the ordinary dwelling houses were built with square-hewn log walls fitted with loopholes.

NEW ENGLAND COLONIAL MEETING–HOUSES

The Puritan meeting-house of the seventeenth century, though an extremely plain and barn-like edifice, was an original architectural form. Nothing quite like it was known in England or in the other colonies. In Virginia the Anglican Church was established, and it was considered proper there to build churches following the Gothic tradition of the mother country. But Gothic architecture was anathema to the Puritans: its cruciform churches, its sculptured saints, its shadowed vaults and lofty spires savored too much of ' Popery,' and carved choir stalls, capitals, and stained-glass windows were nought but vain distractions to eye and mind which should be absorbed in prayer or sermon; '. . . the setting of these places off with a theatrical gaudiness does not savor of the spirit of a true Christian society,' declared Cotton Mather. Even the word ' church ' was eschewed; a house for worship was nothing more, in itself, than any other meeting place. Indeed for several generations it was used for town meetings and other gatherings of the community: ' a house for the town ' was what the people of Northampton called it.

The Puritans had no architectural precedent for such a building. The Dissenters in England had met in any house or hall that would accommodate them: usually a guild hall, sometimes a tavern, even a barn. In New England few such buildings were available, and it became the first business of new settlers to make a meeting-house for congregation and community. The first ones were crude indeed: frame buildings, say 20 by 30 feet in plan, usually with thatched roof, and without tower, spire, cross, or other embellishment. The congregation sat on aggressively uncomfortable benches with narrow seats and a single timber as a support for the shoulder blades, men and women primly separated, on one side and the other.

The traditional orientation was also rejected. Gothic churches had an altar at the end, with the seats (if any) facing it, and a pulpit at the middle of the long side. But with the abandonment of the altar, the side pulpit became the focus of the service, benches were arranged facing it (i.e., lengthwise of the church), and the main entrance door in back of them opened in the middle of the long side. This placement of benches and entrance remained typical of New England meeting-houses until well into the eighteenth century — it is found, for example, in the Old South in Boston as late as 1729.

With such an interior arrangement there was little point in an oblong floor plan, and perhaps by mid-century a square floor plan was adopted. This ' four-square ' New England meeting-house became the familiar type. The interior might be 40 to 45 feet square. An aisle down the middle separated men and women; the pulpit or table was opposite the door. There might be a gallery. Instead of a gable roof these square churches had hipped or pyramidal roofs, with a little square platform at the top carrying a belfry. The bell rope hung down to the middle of the aisle below and must have been a temptation to the irreverent.

Just such was the Old Ship Meeting-House at Hingham, Massachusetts (fig. 61).[24] This was built in 1681; it is the oldest surviving church built in the English colonies, and the only one in New England dating from the seventeenth century. By vote of the town, its dimensions were fixed at 45 by 55 feet, and the height of the posts at 20. We can imagine that all

61. Old Ship Meeting-House, Hingham, Mass., 1681 (Wayne Andrews)

were interested, for the building cost £430 and was paid for by direct taxation of the 143 members of the congregation. The lofty interior is supported by an exposed frame, like some of the great Gothic halls of England. Three main trusses (fig. 62) span the narrow dimension. Resting on the side posts, each has a 45-foot tie beam, holding the lower ends of the principal rafters together, a vertical king post, and long side struts curved to a pointed arch, meeting near the top of the king post. By means of short connecting pieces, these struts brace the main rafters. This was a hall of considerable size — wider than the nave of any English Gothic cathedral. Alleged to have been built by ships' carpenters, it sufficiently resembles an inverted ship's hull to justify the traditional name of the meeting-house.

In 1731, the church was widened 14 feet on the northeast side (at right, fig. 63), and a balancing addition at the southwest was made in 1755. At the same time the old oak benches were replaced by pews, a gallery added on three sides, the old leaded-glass medieval windows replaced by wooden sliding sash, and two porches with Georgian decorative detail added. The congregation also voted to hang a flat ceiling under the tie beams, thus concealing the magnificent roof-framing, but this was removed in the restoration of 1930.

The exterior, with its plain clapboarded walls, hipped roof, and railed platform, betrays no taint of the idolatrous Gothic. Originally the roof was varied by a small gable over the middle of each side, but during the

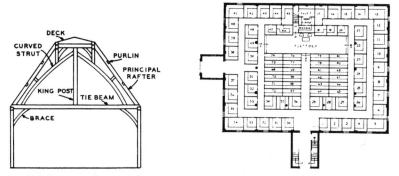

62. Roof truss of the Old Ship Meeting House (Philip White, after Murray P. Corse)
63. Plan of the Old Ship Meeting-House (Murray P. Corse, *Old Time New England*)

eighteenth-century enlargements these were eliminated and the new roof extended over the side additions; the belfry was rebuilt at the same time.

Though other churches have gone, we know that very similar were the first (1640) and second (1670) meeting-houses at New Haven, and those at Salem (1670), Woburn (1672), and Bristol (1684). In the meeting-houses at Lynn, Hatfield, and West Springfield the hipped roof was varied by gables on all four sides. The meeting-house at West Springfield was built in 1702, and is here shown (fig. 64) restored with its two rows of

64. Meeting-house, West Springfield, Mass., 1702 (Antoinette F. Downing, *Early Homes of Rhode Island*, Garrett and Massie)

leaded windows, the four gables above the sides, and a lofty cupola carrying the belfry. Forthright and severe, like the Puritan divines who preached within it, this high, square church has a quaint and prim propriety.

As the eighteenth century opened, even the Puritans became less averse to the idea of the sanctity of the house of God; the word 'church' appears more and more frequently, and they seemed ready for a more dignified, though not an ornate architecture. The new pattern came from the churches that Sir Christopher Wren had built in London in the generation following the Great Fire of 1666. Once followed in Christ Church (the Old North) in Boston, built in 1723, Wren's style was almost universally adopted and became the source of the Georgian church architecture of the eighteenth century.

OTHER COLONIAL BUILDINGS

Of the many other types of buildings found in New England towns and villages during the seventeenth century we know very little. Schools, town halls, colleges, stores, mills, and taverns are known only by a few references in ancient chronicles or one or two surviving examples. It is thus impossible to say with certainty what was typical of the architecture of these buildings, but such account as may be given of them may round out our picture of the Colonial style.

Schools

Church annals are full of instances of enlargement or rebuilding of the meeting-house. Not infrequently the old building was moved or rebuilt or altered for use as a school or town-house. ' In this way,' reports Wertenbaker, ' the four-square type of architecture in time became identified with the town-house and the school, and when the old building fell into decay, or burned, the structure which replaced it frequently was planned in a similar mold.' [25] Thus the old town-house at Lenox, with hipped roof, platform, and cupola, was a descendant of the seventeenth-century four-square meeting-house, and so also were the original buildings of some of the academies. Boston led the way in establishing free public schools. Famous ' Boston Latin ' was founded in 1643, and two more public schools were founded before the end of the century, but unfortunately we know nothing of their architectural appearance.

The ' Old College' at Harvard. 1638–42

Harvard (1636) and William and Mary (1693) were the only colleges founded in the seventeenth century. The first building for William and Mary, designated by Christopher Wren in the Georgian style, is a part of the Williamsburg Restoration. The first Harvard building was demolished in 1678, but from account books and building records, and particularly from study of English collegiate architecture of that era, it has been possible to recreate, with considerable certainty, its probable plan and appearance.[26] The conjectural restoration, done with the aid of the architects of the Williamsburg Restoration, is shown in figures 65 and 66.

The Old College at Harvard was begun in 1638 and completed in time for the first commencement in 1642; by that fall it housed the entire student body. Poorly built, with only a partial cellar, and sills laid direct on the ground, it soon deteriorated. President Dunster complained in 1655 that it was ' in a very ruinous condition, being not fitt for Scholars long

65. The Old College at Harvard, 1638–42 (Harold R. Shurtleff, *Old Time New England*)

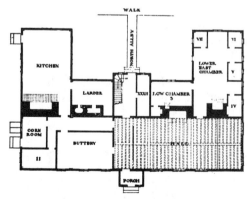

66. Plan of first floor, the Old College at Harvard (Harold R. Shurtleff, *Old Time New England*)

to abide in,' and indeed it had to be demolished a generation later. Yet there is little doubt that during its short existence it was the most ambitious building in New England. The construction was similar to that of a frame house, with oak frame, clapboard siding, wooden floors and wainscot, and a shingled roof. The four large chimneys were of brick, with separate flues for the many fireplaces, and the medieval casement windows were, according to building accounts, made of iron. Undoubtedly there were steep roofs, cross gables, and overhanging stories. There was a cupola atop the roof, and a college bell, probably at the gable peak over the main stair tower.

The plan must have been E-shaped. Only such an arrangement would have permitted the large number of studies, each with window, described in the records; it was, moreover, a favorite type of plan in Tudor manor houses. The first floor (fig. 66) had as its chief room the long Hall, with beamed ceiling, ample window area, and big fireplace. This served as living and dining room for the sixty students, as well as a place for lectures, prayers, and 'disputations.' Separated from it by a 'Screen' was the passageway between the entrances, the main traffic artery. On its west wall were the 'buttery tables' or student bulletin boards. The buttery itself contained great stores of beer barrels, crocks of butter, cheeses, and loaves of bread. The door to the passage was a Dutch door, the lower half forming a counter, over which light lunches, called 'bevers,' were dispensed. Twice a day students came to this 'buttery hatch' to get their bevers of bread and beer.

The kitchen was large, and evidently an impressive sight to visitors, with its panoply of racks, spits, tongs, kettles and skillets, and full supply of wooden and pewter dishes — but not one of china or pottery. The larder was for food storage, and the 'corn room,' in particular, for the large stores of corn, wheat, and rye, in which many students paid their college bills. Other rooms on the first floor were devoted to chambers and studies.

On the second floor was the Long Chamber, a sort of dormitory for a dozen or fifteen students, supervised by the Senior Fellow, who was assigned the largest and finest study in the College, as well as the porch study for his batman. In the southeast corner was the Harvard College Library, containing some 2000 volumes, which, so far as is known, and contrary to English custom, were left unchained. For the rest, both second and third stories contained chambers and studies. Three or four students shared each chamber, usually sleeping two to a bed. Opening from the chamber were the small private studies, where each student kept his books and did his work — by daylight from one small window, for there were no lights at night. Chamber-mates were called *camerarii*, a term soon shortened in collegiate slang to 'chums.' The Old College fell into such ruinous condition that in 1676 the College kitchen, commons, and library were transferred to the new Harvard Hall then under construction, and the building was demolished in 1678.

Harvard Hall, Cambridge. 1674–7

The 'New College' was a four-story brick building, undoubtedly the most imposing structure in the English colonies at the time. Money and materials, subscribed by several Massachusetts towns, were collected as early as 1672, but the frame was not raised until 7 August 1674, on which occasion one John Francis broke his leg, submitting therefor a lengthy

67. The Burgis print of Harvard College in 1726. Left: Harvard Hall (1677); middle: Stoughton (1699); right: Massachusetts (1720) (courtesy Harvard University News Office)

bill for 'wines and other nesisitys' of convalescence. The master builder was Samuel Andrew of Cambridge, a man 'well skilled in the mathematics.' Owing to delays occasioned by the Indian wars, the building was not substantially completed until 1677.

William Burgis's *Prospect of the Colleges* shows Harvard Hall as it appeared in 1726 (fig. 67). Rectangular rather than E-shaped in plan, the building measured 42 feet in breadth and 97 in length and, with its steep-pitched roof and six cross gables on each side, was thoroughly medieval in appearance. Windows were divided by mullions and transom bars to form four lights each on the first story and six on the second. Extraordinary for the period were the cornices over the first-story windows, presumably shaped in molded brick, and ornamented with little ball finials and pendants. The two string courses angled up a foot or so to give a curiously awkward decorative motive to the main (south) façade (fig. 68), and the two entrance doors were flanked by pilaster-like strips topped by ball finials. The windows, equipped with leaded diamond-pane casements of the conventional type, were topped by flat arches below and segmental arches — generally favored in the seventeenth century — in the second story.

Harvard Hall had a gambrel roof. Though there were probably earlier examples (see p. 37), this is the first in the colonies the date of which is

68. Restored south elevation of Harvard Hall (Harold R. Shurtleff drawing from S. E. Morison, *Harvard College in the Seventeenth Century*, Harvard University Press)

reasonably certain, for it was undoubtedly framed in at the time of the raising. In profile it is almost identical to the gambrel roof of the Peter Tufts House (1675) at near-by Medford, but its greater width and height permitted two stories in the attic. The upper slopes, ' guarded with Ballisters ' in 1691, were surmounted by a meeting-house type of belfry and two massive clusters of chimneys.

From the Burgis print and from records of the College, it has been possible to make conjectural restorations of the façade and floor plans.[27] The central room on the ground floor (fig. 69) was the great Hall, which, like its predecessor in the Old College, served for meals, chapel, lectures, and disputations. The ' screen,' arranged parallel to the front wall, formed a corridor between the two entrance halls. The tables in the Hall were probably arranged with the head table for the Fellows near a fireplace; another balancing it for Masters and Bachelors; and long tables at the sides for the undergraduates. There were doubtless chairs at the head tables and long backless benches at the others, as in English colleges today. Doubtless, too, the buttery tables, where students found their seating rank in order of seniority, were located in the hall next to the buttery. Timothy Pickering describes in his memoirs how

Every scholar carried to the dining-table his own knife and fork, and, when he had dined, wiped them on the tablecloth. . . The standing dish was fresh beef baked, — now and then a plain, hard, Indian-meal pudding, — and a baked plum pudding once a quarter . . . The scholars residing in the college provided their own breakfast in their chambers, and their tea in the afternoon.[28]

They could buy bread, butter, eggs, and other supplies from the butler at the buttery hatch. The kitchen, with an outside door, and the buttery,

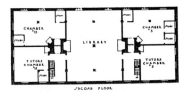

69. Conjectural floor plans of Harvard Hall (Harold R. Shurtleff drawing from S. E. Morison, *Harvard College in the Seventeenth Century*, Harvard University Press)

with its barrels of beer, racks of bottles, and stores of food, were located at the east end of the building, and there were two chambers with small private studies at the opposite end.

Two stairways reached, on the second floor, the library, two tutors' chambers, and two students' chambers, which were reached by vaulted passages through the chimney stacks. The third floor contained six chambers and eighteen studies, and there were three more chambers under the low slanting roofs of the fourth floor. Harvard Hall was destroyed by fire in January 1764, along with most of its library of 5000 volumes, the largest in the colonies to that time. It was replaced by its present-day successor, ' New ' Harvard Hall, in 1765–6.

The ' Indian College,' Harvard. 1654–6

Even earlier than old Harvard Hall was the short-lived Indian College. Supported by English funds ' for the Conveniencye of six hopfull Indian youthes,' the effort to train Indian scholars as ministers and missionaries proved unsuccessful here as it did later at Williamsburg and Dartmouth, but Harvard gained from the abortive enterprise a sizeable brick building, big enough to accommodate a score of students and the College's printing press.[29] The building was completed in 1656 but lasted only two generations, being torn down in 1698.

Stoughton Hall, Harvard. 1698–9

The last of Harvard's seventeenth-century buildings was given by Lieutenant Governor William Stoughton and named in his honor. Bricks from the demolished Indian College were used in its construction; in return for this, one chamber and study were reserved gratis for an Indian scholar — but so far as is known none showed up to claim the privilege. Arranged with Harvard Hall and the later Massachusetts Hall to form three sides of a quadrangle open to the west, Stoughton is the middle building shown in the Burgis Print (fig. 67). Devoted entirely to dormitory purposes, it was as long as Harvard Hall but only half as deep (23 feet), giving cross-ventilation in all of its spacious chambers. The four chambers on each floor were arranged on either side of the entrances and stair halls; each chamber had a fireplace and small private studies (lighted by the narrow windows shown in the first, seventh, eighth, and fourteenth bays of the façade) — an ideal arrangement for a college dormitory at any period.

But except for its medieval windows, Stoughton was early Georgian in style. Angle quoins marked the corners, entrances were flanked by pilasters and topped by segmental pediments, and the whole façade was symmetrically composed. The Stoughton coat of arms carved in stone adorned the center of the façade. The building was badly damaged during the Revolution and was torn down in 1781.

First Town-House, Boston. 1657–8

The first town hall, built in the seventeenth century, stood on the site of Boston's Old State House. A sum of £300 which Robert Keayne set aside in his will for the construction of a market place and town-house was more than doubled by subscriptions from ' Townesmen,' and on 1 August 1657 a contract was signed with Messrs. Thomas Joy and Bartholomew Bernad for the construction. It was to be

a very substantiall and Comely building . . . sixty six foot in Length, and thirty six foot in Breadth from outside to outside, set upon twenty one Pillers of full ten foot high . . . the wholl Building to Jetty over three foot without the Pillers everie way . . . according to A modell or draught presented to us, by the sd. Tho. Joy, & Barth. Bernad. The time wch Payment shall be as followeth viz: one Hund. Pound at the Bringing of the Timber to the Place, A second Hund. at the raysing, a third Hund. at the inclosure & Covering, a fourth at the finishing and Compleating . . .[30]

The building was completed and occupied in 1658, and, though it was destroyed by fire in 1711, it has been possible to make a conjectural restoration (fig. 70) based on the original specifications. This shows an open-walled public market — a traditional medieval form — on the ground floor. Three rows of seven stout posts supported the upper stories, which were walled by broad planks three inches thick, ' well grooved into one another ' and planed smooth on both sides. The roof was of the meeting-house type: hipped, with a ' walke upon the top fourteen or 15 foote wide with two turrets, & turned Balasters and railes, round about the walke.' Third-story rooms were lighted by three cross gables on each side. The three-foot overhang ' everie way,' a very rare feature in non-military architecture, was braced by diagonal struts from the posts and ornamented by corner pendants. A steep stairway, hitched to one end of the building like an inelegant afterthought, clambered to the upper rooms. These consisted of Boston's first public library, a gift of Robert Keayne; a large

70. First Town-House, Boston, 1657-8. Conjectural restoration by Charles A. Lawrence (The Bostonian Society)

room ' for the courts to meete in both in Winter & Sumer, & so for the Townesmen & commissioners of the Towne '; a room for an Armory (Keayne had organized the Ancient & Honorable Artillery Company of Massachusetts and become its first commander) ; and ' a gallery or some other handsome roome for the Elders to meete in.' [31] Crude though this building was in comparison to its fine Georgian successor, Boston's first Town-House deserves a place of honor as the first of a long series of buildings that sheltered the growth of American democracy; it seems especially significant that in this earliest forerunner the functions of democratic government and public library were united.

Commercial architecture

The first building erected by the Pilgrims at Plymouth was a storehouse ' for common use to receive them and their goods.' [32] Begun late in the fall of 1620, by parties of men who returned each night to sleep on the boat, it was finished at Christmas time. It was about 20 feet square, with a thatched roof. But only three weeks later, on 14 January 1621, it caught fire and burned. Storehouses were among the first constructions in all the colonies, but descriptions of them in early documents are so brief that it is not possible to picture them in detail.

The Pilgrims were active traders, at first with the Indians, later with the Dutch. In the March of 1627 they received letters of greeting from Isaack de Rasières, Governor of Manhattan, with the suggestion that trade between the two colonies might be mutually advantageous. Readily acceding to the suggestion, the Plymouth Plantation built in that same year

71. The Aptucxet Trading Post, Bourne, Mass., 1627, as reconstructed in 1930 (Samuel Chamberlain)

the Aptucxet Trading Post, some twenty miles from Plymouth on the south side of Cape Cod. Fifteen miles of the distance across the Cape could be covered by creeks and streams; goods were then portaged five miles to the terminus near the mouth of the Manamet River. This short cut eliminated the long voyage around the Cape and greatly facilitated trade with the Dutch.

The Aptucxet Trading Post (fig. 71) was rebuilt on its ancient foundations in 1930. It consisted of two rooms on the ground floor, the main one about 23 feet square, the other a small ell. A large chimney between the two contained fireplaces back to back. Foundation stones were laid in a mortar made of sand and oyster-shell lime, and fireplaces and chimney were of brick. The structure of frame, oak clapboards, and interior pine wainscot beaded along one edge is inferred from various evidence.[33] The reconstructed roof is steep and covered with 3-foot pine shingles, laid 18 inches to the weather. Fragments found in the ruins indicate leaded glass windows, but these were probably very small. The main room contained a fireplace nearly 7 feet wide, with brick-enclosed brewing ' copper ' at one side. Between the exterior clapboards and the horizontal pine wainscot was laid a filling of plaster made from white sand and oyster-shell lime, mixed with salt-marsh grass as an insulator. The restoration of the Aptucxet Trading Post, though conjectural in many details, was based on careful research and is important as giving the probable appearance and construction of a building erected at least ten years earlier than the oldest surviving New England house.

The Aptucxet venture seems to have been successful, for in 1628 the Plymouth colonists built a second trading post on the site of Augusta, Maine, and in 1633 a third on the Connecticut River, at the site of Windsor. The latter was a 'prefabricated' job, the frame and clapboards being cut in Plymouth and sent to the site by ship. 'Comming to their place,' as Governor Bradford reports, 'they clapt up their house quickly, and landed their provissions, and left the companie appoynted, and sent their barke home, and afterwards palisadoed their house aboute, and fortified them selves better.' [34] This last venture was not accomplished without some difficulty from both Indians and Dutch.

One of the most frequented buildings of the New England community was the village tavern or 'ordinary.' Taverns were usually authorized by the town fathers or commissioners. Thus we learn from the Cambridge town records for 20 September 1648 that 'It is ordered, that there shall be an eight peny ordinary piovided, for the Townsmen'; and that the Selectmen of Hingham in 1702 gave Landlord Andrews permission to sell 'Strong Waters on Broad Cove Lane' provided that he saw that his customers could keep their legs and get home at a reasonable hour; or that in Cambridge 'the Townsmen do grant liberty to Andrew Belcher to sell bears and bread for entertainment of strangers & the good of the Towne.' [35]

The ordinary was a respectable and much-used place for the discussion of both town and church affairs. Meetings of town officials were frequently held in taverns, the good cheer consumed in the line of duty being covered by the taxpayers: 'Ordered the clerk to pass a bill to the Town Treasurer for 2 pounds 4 shillings 7 pence to pay Mr. John Muzzey for entertaining the selectmen in 1724.' [36] The ordinary was apt to be particularly busy on Sundays, for there was a long church service in the forenoon and another in the afternoon. During the noon hour, particularly in winter when the meeting-house was unbearably cold, townspeople repaired to the ordinary to be warmed and fortified, the ladies usually retiring to a large bedroom beyond earshot of the barroom. Near the barroom was the taproom with its bulk stores of rum, wine, ale, and beer, in various kegs and bottles, and on the shelves all manner of glasses, mugs, and tankards.

Boston abounded in taverns, inns, and grogshops. We may gain some idea of better-class inns from the inventory published when the King's Arms was sold in 1650. It reveals ground-floor accommodations consisting of a bar, a public room near it, a small parlor, a large 'Chamber called the Exchange,' and, of course, a kitchen and larder. Upstairs were three large chambers, each one named, for the 'better sort' of guests, and in the garret three smaller unnamed chambers for ordinary folk. The inn yard contained stables, pigsties, the necessary brewing house, a pump, and ' one house of office ' or privy.[37]

On the whole, we know little about the architecture of the early inns. We may assume that the first ones were like houses, and that as business developed, lean-tos and ells were added for the accommodation of wayfarers, and sheds and stables for the horses and coaches. Such early inns as the Old Ordinary at Hingham, perhaps built in 1650, and the Munroe Tavern at Lexington, built in 1695, were later so much added to and remodeled that their original character is obscured. The Red Horse Inn at South Sudbury, made famous as Longfellow's ' Wayside Inn,' was probably built in 1686 but later completely changed. Purchased by Henry Ford, it has been restored as an old-time inn with a miscellany of seventeenth-, eighteenth-, and nineteenth-century furnishings and accoutrements.

Industrial architecture

Little is known of seventeenth-century mills, except that they existed from the very earliest times in the New England settlements. Almost every town history records a gristmill erected within the first year or two of settlement, although there are few descriptions of how the mill was built or what it looked like.

Along the seacoast there were a good many tide mills.[38] Tidewater creeks and salt marshes were dammed, sluiceways built, and gates hung on stout wooden dowels. The pressure of the incoming tide swung the gates open; on the ebb they would automatically close to impound a reservoir with an eight- or ten-foot head of water. An undershot wheel turned the milling stones. Probably the oldest tide mill was that at Hingham, Massachusetts, a gristmill built in 1643. An old shingled structure with ancient-looking mechanisms still stands at the mouth of a tidal basin near the harbor's head, but it is impossible to state how old the present building is. A tide-powered sawmill was built at Manchester, Massachusetts, in 1644 ' upon the river near the meeting-house,' but it was demolished in 1826. Beverly had a gristmill built in 1649; Danversport another of later date; Chelsea's Slade Spice Mill was built in 1721 and until recently was still operating. Other tide mills dotted the Maine coast. Inland, of course, running streams provided power for gristmills. Operated by either overshot or undershot water wheels, the power was transmitted by shaft and gear mechanism to turn the top millstone (in a horizontal plane) over the stationary nether millstone.

Sawmills, also operated by water power, were known in New England from 1623 on (see p. 33). Mason's sawmill on the Salmon Falls River may have been built by Danes, for the New Hampshire Provincial Papers reveal that in the very early years ' Captain Mason sent into this country eight Danes to build mills, to saw timber and tend them. . .' [39] Many other early sawmills are listed by Bolles and Defebaugh.[40]

The Dutch in Holland were operating sawmills by wind power in the opening years of the seventeenth century, and by 1633 there were three wind-driven sawmills on Manhattan Island. The earliest known windmill in New England was erected at Watertown, Massachusetts, before 1632, for in the latter year it was moved and re-erected on Copp's Hill in Boston. John Humphrey built a windmill at Lynn in 1636, and another at Plymouth was mentioned in 1637. In later years they became common, and until a few years ago no less than a dozen could still be seen on Cape Cod. Almost all were 'smock' mills, following the English pattern, rather than the 'post' mill favored by the Dutch.[41] Windmills changed little in form during the eighteenth century, and the famous Old Mill at Nantucket may be selected as a typical example (fig. 72).

The Old Mill is the only survivor of a magnificent row of four giant

72. The Old Mill, Nantucket, Mass., 1746 (courtesy Churchill P. Lathrop)

mills that formerly crowned Windmill Hill on Nantucket Island. Built in 1746 by Nathan Wilbur, a Nantucket sailor, it is preserved today by the local Historical Association. An octagonal tower, covered with white-oak shingles, encloses three stories connected by steep stairs. At the top is the 'cap,' pent-roofed and resting on a curb so that the entire top can be revolved to present the sails to the wind. This is accomplished by means of a long 'tail pole' which serves also as a wind brace. A big cart wheel attached to the lower end of the tail pole permits the entire cap to be rotated by a horse, or by a man working with tackle. Windmill sails range from 45 to 60 feet in diameter, and each sail is from 5 to 7 feet wide. They turn a heavy wooden 'windshaft,' in this case 16 inches through, which is tilted slightly upward to keep the sails out from the bottom of the tower. A 10-foot oak 'brake wheel,' with iron cogs pegged onto it in sections, actuates the vertical shaft, and the shaft in turn rotates the stone. The granite millstones measure 5 feet in diameter and 1 foot thick. This mill had a grinding capacity of 10 bushels an hour in a good breeze, and it was worked at least occasionally up to the time of World War II.

Rye, corn, and wheat were ground, and it was customary to take a toll of the product in payment for milling.

The first windmill set up on Copp's Hill in Boston excited the awe of the Indians. Writing of the year 1634, William Wood remarks that

They doe much extoll and wonder at the English for their strange Inventions, especially for a Windmill, which in their esteeme was little less than the worlds wonder, for the strangeness of his whisking motion, and the sharpe teethe biting the corne into such small peeces; they were loath at the first to come neere to his long armes, or to abide in so tottering a tabernacle, though now they dare goe anywhere so farre as they have an English guide.[42]

Rhode Island windmills usually had a circular or domed top — a feature peculiar to East Anglia — and the cap was rotated by a big chain wheel and gear mechanism instead of a tail pole. The first windmill there was built at Newport by Peter Easton in 1663, but it was blown down on 23 August 1675.

Newport Tower

Much more famous is the Old Stone Mill at Newport (fig. 73), a most unusual structure. Eight crudely made piers and arches form an open arcade supporting an approximately circular tower of about 23 feet exterior diameter and 18 feet interior diameter. The masonry, of local stones laid in a mortar composed of sand and lime (whether shell lime or burned limestone it is impossible to say), is of a type found in Rhode Island chimneys of the last half of the seventeenth century. The wall may originally have been two or three feet higher than it now is. Such, in brief, is the physical form of a building that has aroused more controversy than any other in the history of American architecture. Some seventy periodical articles, written by scholars of many nationalities, and two recent books [43] have dealt with the problem of who built this edifice, for what, and when.

The earliest certain fact in its history is that Governor Benedict Arnold mentioned it in his will in 1677 as ' my stone built wind-miln.' Two other documents of 1677 and 1678 also refer to it, but no earlier document of Rhode Island history, from the founding of Newport, does. There are two major theories for the origin of the tower. The first is that Governor Arnold built it as a windmill, perhaps about 1665, and that its unusual architectural form may have been inspired by a very similar observatory erected in 1632, from designs by Inigo Jones, on the estate of Sir Edward Peyto at Chesterton in England; the observatory was later (c.1730) converted into a windmill.[44] The other theory is that the Newport Tower was built as a ' fortified church ' by some Norsemen and Swedes who might have made an expedition to Newport in the years 1355–64,[45] and that Governor Arnold found its ruins handy to remodel into a mill.

If the windmill was indeed in existence when Newport was founded in 1639, it would seem strange that no document before 1677 mentions it, for such a mysterious relic of antiquity would have excited much curiosity. But this is no place to marshal all the hundreds of arguments — historical, archaeological, cultural, and architectural — which the embattled ' Arnoldeans ' and ' Norsians ' have flung at each other. Like the Shakespearians and Oxfordians, each side has an answer to every ' fact ' or argument advanced by the other. Excavations undertaken during the summer of 1948 afforded no positive evidence whatever in favor of either theory. The only fact not well canvassed by the partisans is that circular stone ' tower mills ' of similar form, though without the arcade below, were built by the French along the St. Lawrence, and as far west as St. Louis — and

73. Newport Tower, Newport, R.I. (HABS)

a number of them still stand. But to date we can only conclude that there can be no incontrovertible proof of either theory until more evidence is found. In the meantime, readers who enjoy the spectacle of an invincible force attacking an immovable body will enjoy the literature: the Quixotes tilting at the windmill theory have made an admirable assault. Apart from its intrinsic interest as a puzzle, however, the Newport Tower has little significance in the history of Colonial architecture. Nothing quite like it had been built before, or was ever built afterward until two freak imitations sprang up in the nineteenth century.

THE COLONIAL STYLE

The Colonial architecture of New England has sometimes been viewed as a remarkable new achievement in a new world. It has been assumed that the colonists gradually adapted the tradition of the mother country to new conditions, evolved new forms, and achieved an architectural style that was essentially American. Nothing could be further from the true picture. So far as we can determine, no single new building technique

was invented, and no new architectural form evolved in the English colonies in the seventeenth century. Not even the log cabin, which every
circumstance of opportunity and urgent need conspired to call forth, was
invented in the New World. The most that can be said is that the sawmill was more widely used in the colonies than in the mother country,
and that the four-square church adapted old forms to a novel plan.

In truth Colonial architecture was entirely traditional, and almost entirely unprogressive. Structurally and aesthetically, it was late English
Gothic transplanted to a new and different climate. We have seen how
every feature of construction — oak frame, wall filling, clapboard siding,
wainscot, fireplace, chimney — came straight from the homeland; and how
every architectural form, such as the leaded casement window, the overhang, the steep roof, finds its prototype in medieval England. We can see
little stylistic evolution in these features during the course of the century.
It has sometimes been thought that the overhang, as a traditional feature,
gradually declined in popularity, but this seems unlikely: the largest number of surviving examples date from the 1680's. Minor changes did occur:
roof pitches declined, the gambrel roof gained in favor late in the century, shingled walls became more common. But no major change in style
occurred.

This is not surprising; the Gothic style in England itself, based on a
slowly developed tradition rather than on aesthetic convictions, was
equally slow to change. In that era there was, indeed, no consciousness of
' style ' at all: people built, as they spoke, in a language of which
they were largely unconscious, and certainly with no idea that some other
language might be better. The Renaissance architect, by contrast, *was* con-
scious of style: he regarded ' beauty ' as an absolute which might be
rationally calculated, reduced to rules of proportion and detail, and imposed upon any building of whatever purpose or structural arrangement.

This is not to say that the Gothic craftsman did not strive for beauty.
Though he did not bother to analyze its nature or the means of achieving it, he did, after all, carve his posts into pendants; he edged his beams
with all manner of chamfers and stops; he planed his wainscot boards to
fine moldings — none of which was necessary from a practical point of
view. Gothic ornament was derived from the materials and the structural
system employed rather than arbitrarily imposed upon them; it was integral rather than applied. It was multiplex and diverse, the product of
the fancy and skill of the individual workman; we might almost say that
Gothic ornamentation was a form of play. The English house, and especially the manor house of the Tudor period, was extraordinarily rich in
this hand-wrought ornament. The carpenter shaped his framing timbers to decorative patterns, the joiner carved projecting beam ends
into grotesque heads or foliate patterns, the mason laid his bricks in all
manner of herringbones and diapers, and the glazier cut his glass and
shaped his leading into some of the most intricate and beautiful windows
in all architectural history.

The Colonial style is the most deficient, when compared to its English
prototype, in its relative paucity of ornament, and this shortcoming was

due, of course, to the pioneer conditions of the New World. The Colonial builder's primary concern was with the need to be filled, the materials to be used, and the shaping of them into a sound and workmanlike structure. Thus modern critics have sometimes called the Colonial a 'functionalist' style. Provided we keep in mind that the Colonial builder had no doctrine or dogma of 'functionalism' in mind, the word is not inappropriate. On the whole, he built naturally. He shaped his rooms according to need, he hewed and jointed his frame with a great sense for strength and durability, he fitted his doors or sheathed his walls with respect for good and proper workmanship. He let structure express itself, he used his materials frankly as they came. But his few touches of ornament show that he desired to enhance and express the nature of structure and materials, and his English backgrounds show that he would have gone further in this direction if he could have afforded to do so.

Similarly, his conception of function was far from sheer materialism. Today, it seems inconceivable to some that so much space in so small a house could be devoted to the pious pretenses of the parlor. This is only another way of saying, however, that function is now and always has been a psychological or spiritual matter as well as a physiological one – and fashions in these matters change. Piety was no pretense in the Puritan Commonwealth of the seventeenth century. The austere Puritan religion required a place for Bible readings and family ceremonies, and only in a semi-sacrosanct place could spiritual and formal social occasions find a suitable setting. The Puritan parlor nourished the transplanted culture of Europe in a wilderness; from it grew the religious and literary tradition of New England that has been so seminal in the shaping of American culture.

In a more practical way, the Colonial house was unfunctional in several respects. In an extremely cold climate, it was a poor thermal mechanism. The colonists did not learn for a century that an extra layer of sheathing boards would have been a better insulator than the clumsy and heavy filling of clay or bricks. They did not find out that a huge chimney flue is a great thief of warm air, and that for all but cooking, they would have done better to build the small, shallow fireplaces and the small chimney flues of the eighteenth and early nineteenth centuries. Their interior illumination was atrociously bad; but here at least they had the excuse of the high cost of window glass and the fact that good wick lamps had not been invented.

The enormous oak house frames, so laboriously hewn and jointed, are a monument to conservatism and lack of inventiveness. Mill-sawed framing members, small and light, with lapped and spiked joints, would have been far quicker and easier to produce and build; the sawmill was there and presumably the necessary nails could have been wrought. It must always remain a cause for amazement that the modern balloon frame was not invented until 1833.

But new inventions and new ways of doing things come slowly in man's slow history. It is perhaps less remarkable that the first colonists did not build better, than that they built as well as they did. Confronted by the myriad urgencies and difficulties of a pioneer existence, it was more than enough to equal the standard set by their forebears in a settled society and a secure existence. Civilization has always advanced in established societies, not on their pioneer fringes. Edward Eggleston's aphorism that ' men can with difficulty originate, even in a new hemisphere' should be amended to read ' *especially* in a new hemisphere.'

READING SUGGESTIONS

Books on the early history, plan, structure, and interiors of New England Colonial houses are referred to in the bibliographies for Chapters 1 and 2. No single book deals adequately with New England churches or public buildings of the Colonial period. On regional or local fields the following are recommended:

Connecticut:

J. Frederick Kelly, *The Early Domestic Architecture of Connecticut*, Yale University Press, New Haven, 1924.

—, *Early Connecticut Meetinghouses* (2 vols.) , Columbia University Press, New York, 1948.

New Hampshire:

John Mead Howells, *The Architectural Heritage of the Piscataqua*, Architectural Book Publishing Co., New York, 1938.

—, *The Architectural Heritage of the Merrimack*, Architectural Book Publishing Co., New York, 1941.

Rhode Island:

Antoinette Forrester Downing, *Early Homes of Rhode Island*, Garrett and Massie, Richmond, 1937.

Vermont:

Herbert Wheaton Congdon, *Old Vermont Houses*, Stephen Daye Press, Brattleboro, 1940.

Primarily pictures:

Samuel Chamberlain, *Open House in New England*, Stephen Daye Press, Brattleboro, 1937. (Samuel Chamberlain's other picture books, on Cape Cod, Lexington, Cambridge, Salem, Nantucket, are all excellent.)

Alfred Easton Poor, *Colonial Architecture of Cape Cod, Nantucket and Martha's Vineyard*, William Helburn, New York, 1932.

See also bibliography for Chapter 14.

4

Dutch Colonial Architecture, 1624–1820

THE HUDSON RIVER VALLEY, the west half of Long Island, and the northern part of New Jersey were settled largely by the Dutch in the early 1600's (fig. 74). Though they governed the region less than fifty years, they impressed on it a distinctive and long-persistent architectural style — a style brought from the quaint streets of Amsterdam, Leyden, and Utrecht, and from the rich farms of the Dutch and Flemish lowlands. Transplanted to the New World, it grew and developed over a period of two hundred years into something distinctly American, yet it never quite lost the flavor of its Dutch and Flemish origin.

Henry Hudson sailed up the river in 1609, reaching a point near Albany before he gave up this third attempt to find a northwest passage. From 1610 on, Dutch explorers and fur traders penetrated the region, despite the fact that James I of England had in 1606 granted it to the Plymouth Company. To protect and encourage this trade, the Dutch West India Company was founded in Amsterdam in 1621, and christened the new colony ' New Netherland.'

Plans were already under way for the settlement of ' New Amsterdam ' and the building of a fort at the mouth of the Hudson. It would appear that the Dutch East India Company (before formation of the West India Company) had requested the famous English architect Inigo Jones to design a proper fort, for there exists in Ireland a letter from Jones to the Company, written in 1620, giving detailed advice. ' To build with timbers with a palizad about with boards,' he cautions, ' may be expedient for the time, but to build in stone and lime will be more lasting.' He describes how earth from a moat 20 feet wide and 10 feet deep may be utilized, and recommends that the ' Bawne ' (wall or rampart) should be:

bulded in drest stone and robble back to 20 foot high and 6 foot thick att base to 4 foot at Parapat with open Embrazures as will be seen in the fare drawing. Good fresh lime can be carryed beyond the seas in tight casks and this to four measures of sand is a sufficient mix. The military artificer can so arrang the quarters within the Bawne as he may think best fitt, when timbers can be used. My carvings and ornaments in the stone and to the gate and the arche are made clear to scale and to the mason.[1]

Some years passed, however, before the expedition under Kryn Fredericks arrived, in 1625, with forty-two immigrants and quantities of seed, farming implements, swine, sheep, and cattle. Peter Minuit, first Director

General of New Netherland, arrived on 4 May of the following year, and that summer purchased the island of 'Manhattes' from the Indians for the legendary small sum of 60 guilders.

Kryn Fredericks brought with him detailed instructions for founding the new community. The design of the fort was minutely specified, and so also was the layout of the village, with a market place in the center, houses around it for the members of the Council and other notables, a schoolhouse, hospital, and church all under one roof, and living quarters

74. Map of New Netherland, about 1650 (Philip White)

for unmarried persons, ships' crews, and other employees of the Company. The number of houses to be built for farmers and the extent of lands to be allotted to them were specified. Help in construction was to be obtained from Indians at Fort Orange, for wages of two *stivers* (about four cents) a day.[2]

But Fredericks found labor and materials scarce, and the best he could build was little more than a blockhouse, palisaded by red-cedar logs and some earthworks. Thus Fort Amsterdam was first completed in 1626. His own 'First View' (fig. 75), supposedly showing the condition of the colony in 1626–8, is somewhat glorified; perhaps it shows the fort not as it actually was but as the Company intended it, for it is depicted as having the sloping walls and projecting artillery emplacements (Vauban bastions) of a fully developed fort. The bastions might be the 'flankers' mentioned in Inigo Jones's letter, but it is not possible to discern any close correspondence between Jones's design and Fredericks's picture.

Fort Amsterdam was rebuilt in 1633–5, however, on a sturdier basis, with a quadrangle of walls enclosing an area some 250 by 300 feet and with bastions at the four corners. But only the northwest bastion was faced by stone, and the other earth walls soon disintegrated into sodded inclines used chiefly as a lounging place for the village hogs. Within the fort arose a cluster of buildings: a guardhouse, barracks, three windmills, the governor's house, and — in 1642 — a large church with double-gabled roof. Congested and ill-built, Fort Amsterdam was indefensible and twice

75. The 'First View' of New Amsterdam, perhaps drawn by Kryn Fredericks, reversed to show proper topographic relations (The New-York Historical Society)

during its history surrendered without firing a shot. It was finally demolished in 1789.

By the end of 1626, the Dutch had erected 'thirty bark-covered houses' at New Amsterdam. Many of the families lived in dugouts such as those described by Cornelis Van Tienhoven. But that they built better houses as soon as they could is revealed by the Reverend Jonas Michaelius, who wrote in 1628: 'they are therefore beginning to build new houses in place of the hovels and holes in which heretofore they huddled rather than dwelt.' [3]

MATERIALS AND CONSTRUCTION

The new houses of the Dutch settlers were built of wood, brick, or stone, the favorite material differing according to locality and date; often all three materials were used in one house, the settlers striving consciously for a pleasing effect through variety of texture and color.

Although very few frame houses dating from the seventeenth century survive today, it is safe to assume that at first they were numerous. Dutch-men certainly were familiar with wood construction, and, as Wertenbaker writes: 'we may imagine them, broad axe in hand, felling trees, squaring the great beams, setting up the framework, covering with crude boards, erecting wooden chimneys. When the West India Company, wishing to develop an export trade in timber and clapboards, set up great windmills for sawing timber, planks and perhaps even small beams became abun-dant.' [4]

Framing and wall construction were much the same as in New Eng-land, with heavy posts, smaller studs, and a framework of laths holding a filling of clay bound by chopped straw or horsehair. This was protected by exterior siding, most commonly wide clapboards rather than the verti-cal plank siding of north Holland. But shingles were widely used, espe-cially in Long Island and New Jersey. The Flemish and Walloon settlers favored very long hand-hewn shingles laid as much as fourteen inches to the weather, and attached to horizontal strips nailed to the studs. The New England system of heavy summer beam, lighter floor joists, and floor boards was less favored than a series of very heavy joists — almost as heavy as summer beams — spanning the house from front to back, spaced about four feet apart, and carrying a plank floor. Such heavy transverse ceiling beams may be seen in figure 86.

Plans, specifications, and contracts in seventeenth-century New Amster-dam were simple, not to say slipshod, as is illustrated in a contract dated 6 May 1642, between one Jan Janse Schepmoes and Thomas Chambers, an English carpenter (who later prospered to become first lord of Fox Hall Manor), for the building of a house 'twenty by thirty feet':

It shall be enclosed all around and overhead with clapboards tight against the rain, inside even as the mason's house, one partition, one bedstead and pantry, two doors, one double and one single transome window. The carpenter shall de-liver 500 clapboards for the house; Schepmoes shall furnish the nails and the food for the carpenter during construction, which commences this day, and for eight weeks, when the house, accidents excepted, must be ready, and when the whole shall be duly completed, Schepmoes shall pay to Thomas Chambers in addition to board, the sum of one hundred and sixteen guilders . . . provided the car-penter shall hew the timber to the best of his ability. [5]

Stone houses are very common in the Hudson valley and in New Jersey. In the earliest work, stones of convenient size were picked up in the fields or broken from ledges and laid in a rough, irregular rubble, the joints filled with clay bound by straw or hair. As soon as lime was obtainable — from the oyster shells of the Atlantic coast or the limestone ridges of the Hudson — the more durable lime mortar was used. Gradually the masonry improved: more regular stones, more carefully laid in random-width courses, succeeded the unpatterned rubble, and eventually tooled blocks, carefully smoothed and fitted, formed even-coursed walls. Walls were very heavy, ranging from one and a half to three feet thick. [6] A large smooth stone was usually laid as a cornerstone or lintel and marked with the date of erection of the house or the initials of the owner.

But from the first, the Dutch burghers of New Amsterdam and the farmers of the Hudson valley must have looked forward to building in brick. Brick was the traditional material of the mother country, and Dutchmen were the most skilled bricklayers in Europe. They used a variety of shapes, colors, and bonds — deep reds and salmon pinks, bright yellows and oranges, and purples ranging to glazed blacks, with many curious patterns and inset glazed tiles to enliven their walls.

Skilled brickmakers were among the early settlers of New Netherland, and, according to Jameson's *Narratives,* brick kilns were operating in New Amsterdam as early as 1628.[7] The patroon of Rensselaerswyck, below Al-

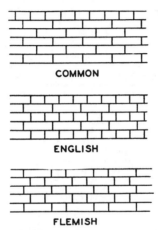

COMMON

ENGLISH

FLEMISH

76. The three chief types of brick bonds (Philip White)

bany, established brick kilns soon after the settlement of the colony in 1630, and his account books show that yellow brick produced there between 1630 and 1646 sold for 15 florins the thousand.[8] Indeed brickmaking became a leading industry of this region, and brick was exported from Fort Orange to the Dutch settlement on the Delaware River.

It is wise to view with skepticism claims that many of the old houses were built of brick 'imported from Holland.' In all the colonies, there were standard measurements for two types of brick: the larger size, measuring about $2\frac{1}{2}$ inches in thickness, was termed 'English brick,' the smaller size, about an inch thinner, was termed 'Holland brick.' References in early documents to Holland brick, accordingly, almost certainly refer to size rather than geographic origin. Furthermore, as in Virginia, there is no doubt that after the first few years brick could be made locally far more cheaply than it could be imported.

Brick bonds, like other architectural details, were imported from the mother country. In Flanders, 'Flemish bond' (see fig. 76) was common, and the Flemish and Walloon settlers presumably brought it with them. In Holland, 'English bond' was common, but in the fifteenth and sixteenth centuries a variant now known as 'Dutch cross bond' was used: it is similar to English bond except that the stretchers in the alternate courses break joints with each other (fig. 77). The effect from a distance is of continuous diagonal lines, producing several kinds of diaper or cross patterns by judicious variation of the color or thickness of the mortar joints. It is one of the most attractive bonds in all brick masonry and lends itself to a wide variety of decorative patterns.

Brick houses were dated either by large iron figures on the walls or gable ends, or by figures inlaid with bricks of a contrasting color.[9] The red and yellow bricks, together with glazed tiles and lozenges set into walls

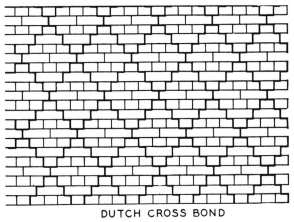

DUTCH CROSS BOND
77. Dutch-cross-bond brickwork (Philip White)

or window arches, and the strong reds and blacks of the pantiles, which soon supplanted the early thatch for roof covering, made the brick houses of New Netherland a vivid contrast to the sober-sided houses of the New England Puritans, Madam Knight, describing New York about the close of the seventeenth century says:

The Buildings are Brick Generally, very stately and high, though not altogether like ours in Boston. The Bricks in some of the Houses are of divers Coullers and laid in Checkers, being glazed, look very agreeable. The inside of them is neat to admiration; the wooden work, for only the walls are plaster'd, and the Sumers and Gist [girts] are planed and kept very white scour'd, as so is all the partitions if made of Bords.[10]

THE DUTCH COLONIAL STYLE

A generation ago it was supposed that 'Dutch Colonial' meant one definite kind of house — the kind with wide clapboards, a broad gambrel roof with flaring eaves, and fieldstone masonry to taste — and this fixed type was standardized in the streets of America's suburbs. No such uniformity existed in the New Netherland of the seventeenth century or in the New York and New Jersey of the eighteenth.

Professor Wertenbaker's valuable researches show that there were really two European styles from which the architecture of New Netherland sprang: that of Holland, which prevailed in New Amsterdam and the Hudson valley; and that of Flanders, which prevailed in New Jersey and parts of Long Island.[11] Moreover, the ' Flemish ' style of Long Island, which evolved early in the seventeenth century and was executed largely in wood, differed markedly from that of New Jersey, which was pre-dominantly an eighteenth-century development, with stone the favorite material. The name ' Dutch Colonial ' is really a misnomer for the New Jersey type, for as Bailey points out, ' it came into existence after the fall of the New Netherland government and reached its greatest height in the half century after the American Revolution.' [12]

But since the term ' Dutch Colonial ' has been applied to the architec-ture of all these regions and periods for some generations, it is probably fruitless to abandon the label, and it does serve as a useful generic term. We may clarify the actual picture if we examine and define three distinct phases of the style: the true Dutch Colonial of New Amsterdam and the Hudson valley; the Flemish Colonial of the seventeenth century, best seen in the houses of Long Island; and the Flemish Colonial of the eighteenth century, as exemplified in the houses of northern New Jersey.

Early New Amsterdam

Early in its history New Amsterdam became a cosmopolitan town: Dutchmen, Swedes, English, Flemings, French, Germans, and Walloons mingled in its streets; a Jesuit missionary from Canada, passing through in 1643, found eighteen languages spoken.[13] But the Dutch were predomi-nant, and architecturally the town was a replica in miniature of Amster-dam. ' There were the same curving streets lined with quaint houses, the same use of every open space for gardens or orchards, the same canals run-ning through the heart of town, the same sky-line with its tiled roofs, church tower and picturesque windmill, the same waterfront with its wharves and slips, and protecting batteries.' [14]

On Winckel Street, five stone buildings housed the Company's indus-tries: workshops of the carpenter, the blacksmith, the cooper, the armorer, the tailor, the shoemaker, and the hatter. A wooden church and a small parsonage were built on Pearl Street in 1633, and a second larger church with a steep-pitch twin-gabled roof was built within the fort in 1642. The town was growing northward from the fort; it stretched along the East River with its slips and wharves and reached the wooden stockade cutting across the island at what is now Wall Street (fig. 78). In 1641-2, near the eastern waterfront was built the fine stone City Tavern, four full stories high with a spacious garret under the steep roof, which was covered by red pantiles and topped by a belfry (fig. 79). Governor Kieft felicitated himself ' that he now had a fine inn, built of stone, in order to accom-modate the English who daily passed with their vessels from New England to Virginia . . . and who might now lodge in the tavern.' [15] In 1654 the Company turned the tavern over to the use of the municipal authorities and it was thenceforth the *Stadthuys* or Town-House.

The houses were mostly two and a half or three and a half stories high;

several such might have been seen at the intersection of Broad Street and
Exchange Place (fig. 80). The chief architectural feature was the stepped
gable, with a series of ' corbie-steps ' (crow steps) rising to a chimney or
some sort of ornamental finial at the apex. These crow steps had been
used in the medieval architecture of the Low Countries and Germany for
generations; they are said to have been built to enable the chimney sweeps
to climb up the steep gables, though the real explanation may be that in

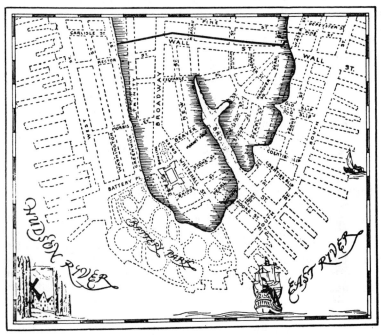

78. Plan of New Amsterdam in the middle of the seventeenth century. Broken lines
show streets and piers of present waterfront (courtesy Dartmouth College)

brick they were easier to build than were raking gables. Often, as in Holland, there were doors in one or more upper stories, for block-and-tackle
entrance of heavy goods (fig. 81).

Windows had small panes and usually hinged outward; the larger ones
were divided by heavy transoms into upper and lower sections (the
' double transome window ' of Schepmoes' contract). They were made
sprightly with shallow arches built of stone or brick, with the space beneath sometimes filled in with a wooden plank or adorned by gay inset
tiles. Though yellow and red bricks prevailed, these were often relieved
by patterns in headers burnt to a blue-black. Straight-sided gables or even
concave-curved gables, like those in Holland, often replaced the stepped
gable.

Peter Stuyvesant arrived as Director of New Netherland in 1647, and during his stormy administration the Dutch captured New Sweden, on the Delaware (1655). Their own villages continued to expand in size and number up the Hudson. Albany was formally organized as Beverwyck in 1652; Kingston (Wiltwyck) was founded in 1653, and Schenectady and Hurley (Nieuw Dorp) in 1662. By this time New Amsterdam had grown to the impressive population of 1600 souls. But the Dutch rule was to be short-lived. In 1664 Charles II granted to his brother the Duke of York

79. City Tavern, New Amsterdam, 1641-2, used as the *Stadthuys* or Town-House, 1654-99 (from a print of 1679)

all the territory between the Connecticut River and Delaware Bay. Colonel Richard Nicolls sailed into New Amsterdam harbor with a fleet of four ships, and Stuyvesant surrendered the fort and town on 8 September 1664. Thus New Netherland came to an end and New York began.

But for several generations the city remained predominantly Dutch in population, customs, and architecture. By 1664 the Renaissance movement was in full swing in Dutch architecture, and the influences coming overseas from Holland merged with those imposed by the English administrators and governors to effect a gradual transformation of the Dutch Colonial, after 1700, to a more formal, more classical style. New York must have remained largely Dutch in appearance, however, until the great fire of 1776 destroyed most of the old city. And since what was spared by the fire has long-since fallen victim to commerce, the best surviving examples of early Dutch Colonial houses are to be found in the up-river towns.

The Albany region

As early as 1614 fur traders built a stockaded post at Albany, and in 1623 thirty families of Walloons settled there. Fort Orange was completed the next year, so the Albany region was really settled earlier than New Amsterdam. For generations it was dominated by the great manor of Rensselaerswyck.

Despite much romancing about the 'lordly manors of the Hudson,' the architectural remains today are on the whole unimpressive. Princely in acreage and affluence indeed they were (Rensselaerswyck included over a thousand square miles of land), but their manor houses, never palatial,

80. Dutch houses at Broad and Garden Streets, New York, in 1700 (Samuel Hollyer engraving, The New-York Historical Society)

have suffered sadly with the passage of the years. Two patroonships, Rensselaerswyck and Colen Donck, were established under Dutch rule, and nine great manors were erected by the English: Fordham in 1671; Fox Hall, at Kingston, in 1672; Rensselaerswyck in 1685; Livingston, with its lordly 160,000 acres, in 1686; Pelham in 1687; Philipsborough in 1693; Morrisania in 1697; Cortlandt in 1697; and Scarsdale in 1701.

Of all these great estates, today only two possess buildings of any considerable architectural interest. Other manor houses remain but have been cluttered or defaced by additions or subtractions; several have simply disappeared. As a social and economic institution, the manors were more than equivalent to the holdings of the landed aristocracy of Virginia, but it is unfortunately true that the Hudson valley today holds nothing to be compared, architecturally, with the great Georgian houses of Virginia.

The earliest, and the only successful, patroonship was Rensselaerswyck, founded in 1630 by Kiliaen Van Rensselaer, a director of the West India Company. The colony, and the English manor which followed it, eventually included a domain extending some 24 miles along the Hudson — on both sides — and numbered several thousand tenants. Although Kiliaen Van Rensselaer watched over the infant enterprise with every solicitude — purchasing and sending supplies, choosing tenants, checking accounts, ordering a church to be made at one time and concerning himself about a brandy distillery at another — he never saw Rensselaerswyck. Sitting in his counting-house in remote Amsterdam, he managed every detail of the vast patroonship with shrewd foresight until his death in 1647.

One of the three remaining manor buildings is Fort Crailo at Rensselaer, opposite Albany (fig. 82). This was the administrative center of the eastern branch of the patroonship, and Kiliaen ordered it built; there is even record that in 1642 he sent a ship laden with stone, brick, and tile for building, and it is reasonable to suppose that Fort Crailo (named after a Van Rensselaer estate in Holland) was its intended destination. At any rate a smooth stone in the cellar wall bears the inscription ' K.V.R. 1642

81. Dutch house in William Street, New Amsterdam, 1648 (*Valentine's Manual*)

ANNO DOMINI.' This may be, then, one of the rare instances of a house made of imported brick.* It was solidly built to serve as a fortress, with loopholes in the wall of the ground floor. Large additions were made in 1740 — much of the interior woodwork is probably of the later date — but the massive exterior remains an excellent example of the Dutch style.

The gables are straight-lined, with ' elbows ' at the lower corners, and are finished by courses of brick set at right angles to the steep edge of the gable, these courses joining the horizontal ones in a saw-tooth line (see fig. 83). Known as ' mouse-tooth ' finish (from the Dutch *muisetanden*), the arrangement made the exposed copings more weatherproof than continuous horizontal courses would have been. Mouse-tooth finish is found in the medieval houses of Flanders, from which it spread not only to New Netherland but to those parts of England subject to Flemish influence, notably the region around Great Yarmouth. There was much shipping to Yarmouth across the North Sea from the ports of the Low Countries, and in the sixteenth and seventeenth centuries many Flemish bricklayers

* Waterman believes that this house was built at an unknown later date, and the inscribed stone re-used. See *Dwellings of Colonial America*, p. 209.

worked in Norfolk County. They brought with them these 'tumbled in' brick gables, as the English call them. The example illustrated in figure 83 is a brick cottage at Potter Heigham, northwest of Yarmouth. But the motive undoubtedly came to the Hudson valley via Holland rather than England, for many Flemings fled from their homeland at the time of the Spanish occupation in the 1620's, going first to Holland and then emigrating to New Netherland.

82. Fort Crailo, Rensselaer, N.Y., 1642? (Cortlandt V. D. Hubbard)

The wall of Fort Crailo is laid in Dutch cross bond, giving a diaper-patterned surface. Solid batten-type shutters are carried on wrought-iron hinges, and the roof is of red pantiles. The building is now owned by the state, and the modern restoration has been carried out in the medieval style. The parlor has huge widely spaced floor joists carrying, from wall to wall, a floor of wide heavy planks. Walls and chimney-breast are wainscoted with vertical pine boarding, molded at the joints. Furniture is uncarved, except for a chair and chests which might have been imported. The windows are divided by mullions into two or four lights with diamond-pane casements, a type that probably prevailed in early New Netherland as it did in New England.

Urban Albany had its step-gabled houses as did New Amsterdam. None remains today, but it is clear from the precise delineations of the painter James Eights that many still existed in the early nineteenth century. In an oil painting of 1805, he showed the fine brick house of the Domine

Schaets, built in 1657, with two full stories and a stepped gable concealing two more stories in the steep-roofed attic. Three more houses with medieval stepped gables were then visible on Pearl Street. The Harmanus Wendell House of 1716 and the Beekman-Vanderheyden House of 1725 also had stepped gables.

But straight-lined gables prevailed in the rural architecture of the northern countries: Albany, Schenectady, Rensselaer, and Columbia. A fine typical example is the Hendrick Bries House at East Greenbush, built in 1723 (fig. 84). Although in dilapidated condition today, it reveals the straight-line plan — two or three rooms in a row — the steep roof with end

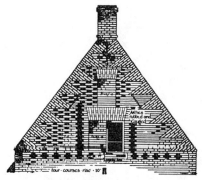

83. ' Mouse-tooth ' finish of brick gables, cottage in Norfolk County, England (drawing by John S. Corder, courtesy B. T. Batsford, Ltd.)

84. Hendrick Bries House, East Greenbush, N.Y., 1723 (HABS)

chimneys, and fine cross-bond brickwork with sharp mouse-tooth finish along the gable edges. The masonry was secured to the interior wooden frame by 'beam anchors' of wrought iron, and the Dutch always made a virtue of necessity by shaping these into a variety of fascinating decorative spots: hearts, trefoils, fleur-de-lys, and — here — daggers. The Adam Van Alen House near Kinderhook (1737) and the Arendt Bradt House in

85. Gable end of Leendert Bronck House, West Coxsackie, N.Y., c.1738 (Cortlandt V. D. Hubbard)

Schenectady (c.1715) are other fine examples of the plain, solid Dutch Colonial.

At West Coxsackie, New York, is a pair of houses built by the Bronck family. An ancestor named Jonas Bronck had settled north of Manhattan in 1639, giving his name to the region now known as the Bronx. Pieter Bronck, a stepson, bought land from the Indians in the upper valley and built a stone house in 1663. To this was added, about 1738, by Leendert Bronck, a larger brick house, connected to the earlier one by a passageway. Both houses were little altered in later years and are now carefully preserved by the Greene County Historical Society. Figure 85 shows the gable end of the later house, with elbows at bottom and top, mouse-tooth brick triangles ornamenting the gable edge, and Dutch-cross-bond brickwork. The shutters for the two windows are of the heavy batten type, unpaneled, and above these is a shuttered granary door. The living room (fig. 86) is spanned by heavy joists resting on curved knees, as in ship construction — a feature that occurs in several farmhouses on both sides of the upper

86. Living room of the Leendert Bronck House (Cortlandt V. D. Hubbard)

Hudson. The steep open stairway, floor of wide heavy planks, and divided front door with iron strap hinges are typical of the period.

The interiors of these houses, both in New Amsterdam and the Hudson valley, were typically Dutch in their cheerful colors. Walls were white-washed or wainscoted, and the window openings enlivened by yellow or blue curtains. Sometimes kitchen floors were paved with warm red brick. Fireplaces were framed by charming blue Delftware tiles. Beds were built-in like steamer bunks, with draw-curtains or shutters to close them off. Furniture, except for some carved and painted chest or ' best ' chair imported from Holland, was of the simplest. All the smaller household objects could be stowed away in cupboards, and there was a neat economy of space as befits a maritime people. All the ironwork is interesting — the hinges and locks, the fireplace fixtures and kitchen utensils — wrought in bold black shapes against white walls. An eighteenth-century traveler from Maryland admired the neatness of the Albany houses:

87. Senate House, Kingston-on-Hudson, N.Y., 1676–95 (HABS)

Their chamber floors are generally laid with rough plank, which in time by constant rubbing and scrubbing becomes as smooth as if it had been planed . . . They have their beds generally in alcoves so that you may go thro' all the rooms . . . and never see a bed. They affect pictures much, particularly Scripture history, with which they adorn their rooms. They set out their cabinets and buffets much with china. Their kitchens are likewise very clean, and there they hang earthen or Delft plates and dishes all around the walls.[16]

The middle counties

Further down the Hudson valley, in Ulster and Dutchess counties, stone rather than brick was the primary building material and remained so through the eighteenth century. Though so much admired today that ' old stone houses ' has become almost one word, the Dutchmen themselves doubtless would have preferred brick; but they were an adaptable people and took what came to hand.

There are many stone houses in Wiltwyck (Kingston, founded in 1653), but perhaps most famous is the Senate House (fig. 87), so-called because the first sessions of the New York State Legislature were held in it for a few weeks in the autumn of 1777. Wessel Wesselse ten Broek built the house sometime between 1676 and 1695; he laid the walls in rough-faced stones of fairly regular size, carrying them up on the end gable above the garret windows. In plan, like many of the Dutch houses, it was only one room deep with three rooms strung out in a row, two of them with outside doors. The gabled roofs were of lower pitch than in the northern counties. The interior woodwork and roof were burned by the British in 1777, but the rebuilt roof with its row of sloping dormers is of the early style.

New Paltz was founded in 1677 and boasts several good examples of the

88. Freer House, New Paltz, N.Y., 1720 (Wayne Andrews)

early Dutch Colonial style. The same stone walls, the gabled roof with sloping shed dormers, the strung-out plan with two doors and three chimneys that we have seen in the Senate House are echoed in the Abraham Hasbrouck House, built about 1717. The contemporary Freer House in New Paltz (fig. 88) has in addition the clapboarded gable ends, solid shutters, and divided door with sheltering hood that are so often seen in the Dutch style. There is also the lean-to at the back, often added to Dutch houses to contain narrow bedrooms back of the main front rooms.

Hurley, in Ulster County, is almost completely a Dutch town. Its houses line the street of the village, farm lands stretching back of them. Long and narrow, with thick stone walls for the ground story, gable ends shingled or clapboarded, they have an air of repose. Roof pitches are moderate, and occasional dormers light the capacious attics. Windows are small and arranged without regard to symmetry; the houses sit low on the ground and are without decoration or pretension.

Dutchess County, stretching eastward from the Hudson to the Connecticut boundary, has some frame houses and other signs of New England influence, but for the most part its stone houses are like those of its sister county across the river. From the middle of the eighteenth century onward, however, a combination of brick and stone was fairly frequent and it is amusing that the latter was considered the humbler material, being relegated to rear walls, while brick — the Dutchman's true love — was boasted on the front and end walls.

89. The 'Old Stone House at Gowanus,' Brooklyn, N.Y., 1699, as re-erected in Brooklyn Park, 1934 (HABS)

Throughout the Hudson valley, in the seventeenth century, houses were one and a half stories high (except in Albany), and had gabled roofs of greater or less pitch. The two-story house was an eighteenth-century innovation, and so was the gambrel roof. A gambrel roof was built as early as 1705 (on the Salisbury House at Leeds), but the shape did not become popular until 1725; after that it became increasingly common in all the river counties.

Further down the Hudson, in Westchester County, was the great Philipsborough Manor, chartered by the English in 1693. Though part of the foundations of the present Philipse Manor Hall at Yonkers may have been built by Frederick Philipse as early as 1682, the superstructure was erected after 1700 in the Georgian style. The history of this important building is accordingly reserved for a later chapter.

Although most of the Colonial houses of Long Island belong to the Flemish style, there is one remarkably good example of the true Dutch Colonial type, the 'Old Stone House at Gowanus' (fig. 89). It was built in 1699, as indicated by large wrought-iron figures at both gable ends, by

Nicholas Vechte, an enterprising and ingenious farmer of the Gowanus section of Brooklyn.[17] Thinking perhaps to protect himself from the pirates who frequented Gowanus Bay, he built his house with walls full two stories high of solid stone 'several feet thick,'[18] little realizing that these walls were to sustain heavy musket and cannon fire in the fierce battle of Long Island that eddied around them on 27 August 1776.

Above the stone walls, he completed his steep gables in fine brickwork, adorned by a diaper pattern of black headers and the favorite triangular insets. A later occupant, one Jacques Cortelyou, added his initials in iron letters high on the gable end. Nicholas Vechte dug canals from the bay to his farm, so that he could float his barges full of produce to the New York market; he is even reported to have locked a tidal reservoir which, by a series of canal gates, insured him of access to the bay even at low tide. His house was demolished in 1897, but a replica was built in 1934 and stands today as a museum of the Dutch Colonial past.

Dutch Colonial churches

Before the seventeenth century began, Dutchmen in the motherland had given up the centuries-old Gothic tradition in ecclesiastical architecture, associated as it was with Catholic beliefs and ritual. To the Calvinists, mystery and ritual were corruptions of faith, and Calvin himself had warned against ornateness or ' beauty ' in church edifices. With the Protestant emphasis on preaching rather than on the Mass, the pulpit replaced the altar as the focal point of the church. Toward the end of the sixteenth century a new form of Protestant church arose in Holland, based on an octagonal plan, with the pulpit opposite the door and an octagonal roof rising to a belfry. Such was the first Protestant church in Holland, built at Willemstad in 1595.

This fashion came to New Netherland in the seventeenth century. In 1641 Kiliaen Van Rensselaer ordered made a wooden model for a small octagonal church, which he sent to his overseer at Rensselaerswyck. We do not know whether it was built, but many others like it were erected in succeeding years, such as the churches at Bergen (fig. 90) and Hackensack in New Jersey, and at Jamaica, Brooklyn, and New Utrecht on Long Island. All were small octagons, topped by extravagantly steep octagonal roofs shaped like candle snuffers.

The interiors were very plain and arranged so that all eyes focused on the pulpit opposite the door. The pulpit at Albany is described as ' octagonal in form, as usual raised upon a pedestal and reached by a flight of narrow steps, the trimmings and mouldings were of oak, beside the minister's hand was a small bracket for the hour-glass.'[19] In the church at Claverack ' the men were ranged around the walls and the women in orderly rows in the center. Above their heads is a wooden ceiling with prodigious rafters. The walls are plastered and meant to be white; the woodwork is painted blue.'[20]

The Sleepy Hollow Church at Tarrytown, built by Frederick and Catherine Philipse of Philipsborough Manor in 1699, is larger, and nearly rectangular in plan (fig. 91). Its high rubble-stone walls have a barn-like severity, and they are pierced by a door and a few large windows framed in brick and shaped to a pointed arch — the result of a remodeling in 1837. The roof is a typical Flemish gambrel, like a flared bell with curving sides. On top of it perch an open octagonal belfry, with a bell cast in Holland in 1685, and a wrought-iron weathervane, given by Frederick Philipse and cut with his initials.

During the eighteenth century several churches were built on a square plan, with a steep-pitched roof and belfry very similar to the New England seventeenth-century type. But as congregations grew larger and more

90. Octagonal Dutch Church, Bergen, N.J., 1680 (Thomas Jefferson Wertenbaker, *The Founding of American Civilization; The Middle Colonies,* Charles Scribner's Sons)

wealthy and English influences pervaded eighteenth-century New York, bigger buildings, modeled after the Georgian churches of New York, Boston, and Philadelphia prevailed, and the distinctive little Dutch octagons gradually crumbled and disappeared.

91. Sleepy Hollow Church, Tarrytown, N.Y., 1699 (The Holland Society of New York)

FLEMISH COLONIAL HOUSES: SEVENTEENTH CENTURY

The Colonial houses of Long Island, southern New York, and northern New Jersey are quite unlike the houses of New Amsterdam and the Hudson valley. Sheathed by wide clapboards or shingles, or solidly built of New Jersey sandstone, their distinctive architectural feature is a roof projecting two feet or more, in front and in back, and gracefully curved or flared at the eaves. Until a decade ago there seemed no satisfactory explanation for the origin of the flared eaves. Prototypes in Dutch architecture of the seventeenth century were sought without success, and it has been suggested that perhaps the projecting roof was devised locally to keep the clay-and-straw mortar from washing out of masonry joints. But if this were true, why is the projecting roof not found in the upper Hudson valley where the same crude mortar walls were used, or why, indeed, was it used on the clapboard and shingled houses of Long Island where no mortar was exposed at all?

The only possible explanation seemed that it was a stylistic innovation, originating in New Netherland. ' Gradually there arose,' wrote one of its most thorough historians,[21] ' a native style which had no prototype in Europe. . . It is a distinctive architecture and our only indigenous form until the coming of the modern skyscraper.' But just as Shurtleff and Morison demonstrated that the Puritans did not invent the log cabin, Wertenbaker has shown that the projecting curved eaves of the ' Dutch ' Colonial are in reality of Flemish origin, and America seems to have lost its last claim to stylistic originality in Colonial architecture.

In that maritime region of Flanders, which was comprised of what is now southern Holland, western Belgium, and the northern tip of France, there may be found farmhouses whose low walls are built of clay mixed with lime and straw. Most of them are story-and-a-half structures, with two or three rooms in line and narrow bedrooms opening back of these. To protect the clay walls from rain, flared eaves project two feet or more. ' When the roof is thatched,' says Wertenbaker, ' the projection is usually formed by several rows of red tiles to constitute what the Flemings call a " flying gutter "; if tiles are used, the sweep of the curved roof is uninterrupted.' [22]

Many of the Flemings and Walloons of this region fled to Holland at the time of the Spanish occupation in the 1620's. Skilled artisans found employment and permanent residence in Dutch cities, but Dutch farm lands were already overcrowded, so many of the displaced farmers continued overseas to New Netherland. There they settled in farming areas, not in cities. It is difficult to say how large a proportion of the population they constituted — one writer [23] estimates two-thirds — but undoubtedly certain counties were predominantly Flemish, particularly those of northern New Jersey, while Flemings, Walloons, and French were scattered widely elsewhere in southern New Netherland.

As early as the mid-seventeenth century the characteristic Flemish projecting curved eaves appeared on Long Island houses. They may, at first, have consisted of a few rows of tiles or shingles forming the overhang, with a thatched roof above. But later, with the abandonment of thatching, the overhang became integral with the main roof structure, and it was boarded in to form a boxed cornice, 5 or 6 inches deep at the outer edge.

As durable lime mortar was introduced in stone-walled houses, the overhanging roof might well have been abandoned — as far as its original function goes — but the curve gave a graceful fillip to the roof line and the overhang a welcome sense of shelter. And instead of disappearing, the projection grew deeper until, in the late eighteenth century, posts were added under it and a full-width front porch was born. Thus old-country forms brought to the New World because of tradition found new meanings and uses and over many generations were modified and themselves became new traditions.

Besides the flared eaves, Flemish Colonial houses were marked by an especially attractive version of the gambrel roof, but this was not used until the eighteenth century and was the distinctive feature of the later Flemish Colonial style.

Long Island

The Flemish style of the seventeenth century is best represented on Long Island. Five towns were settled on western Long Island during the Dutch rule: Nieuw Amersfoort (Flatlands), Breuckelen (Brooklyn), Vlakkebos (Flatbush), Nieuw Utrecht, and Boswijck (Bushwick, later Woodtown). They were peopled by a mixture of Dutch, Flemish, Walloon, and French Huguenot farmers. Long Island was well wooded, but stone was rare, and the houses were built mostly of frame construction, with walls filled with clay and straw and covered by clapboards or shingles. Brick houses were rare; it has been stated that there were only three all-brick houses (outside of New Amsterdam, of course) in the whole region of southern New Netherland.[24] Beyond the Dutch settlements were the English villages of eastern Long Island — neat, clustered, white under the elm trees, every line and shadow of house and barn and village common bespeaking their New England ancestry. Until the Dutch farms were largely destroyed by the advance of the commuters' specials, no clearer dividing line between architectural regions existed anywhere in the United States than this split up the middle of Long Island.

One of the earliest of the Dutch farmhouses was the Pieter Wyckoff House in Flatlands (fig. 92). This may have been built as early as 1639–41; certain it is that, like most of the old houses, different sections were built at different times.* Study of the floor and attic beams reveals that at first the house was only three-fifths of its present depth, and it probably had the steep roof favored in the earliest years. At an unknown later date the house was deepened and would have received at that time the lower-pitch gabled roof with curved projecting eaves at front and back. The wing was added still later, perhaps in 1784. The oldest shingles,

---

* The HABS date of c.1739 is probably too late. See data cited in Bailey, *Pre-Revolutionary Dutch Houses and Families*, pp. 88–91, 111.

on the southeast side, are hand-hewn cypress shakes 3½ feet long, with rounded ends, and laid 14 inches to the weather. On the other sides these have been replaced by shorter square-cut cedar shingles. The typical Dutch door and shutters are paneled, and there is the characteristic pair of end chimneys.

How the Wyckoff House might have become still larger is illustrated by the very similar Bergen House in Flatlands (fig. 93). The central part, built about 1680, was originally square — it was lengthened to the west, or near side in the photo, in 1819 — but was so much deeper than the Wyckoff house that its gabled roof was lofty enough to enclose a second story, and

92. Pieter Wyckoff House, Flatlands, Brooklyn, 1639–41? (Frank Cousins, The Essex Institute)

even a garret above that lighted by little windows beside the end chimney. The pitch and flare of the roof, the shingled siding, the Dutch door and paneled shutters are all similar in style to those of the Wyckoff House, but the obtrusive gabled dormer windows are a much later addition. A record shows that in 1796 the house of Johannes Bergen, measuring 34 by 34 feet, was in good condition, valued at $350. In 1801 he added a kitchen wing and chimney on the east side, and in 1824 his son Cornelius Bergen added the small west wing, shown in the photo. Both wings were in the style of the original house. Houses like these, almost without exception, had cellars reached from the outside by a hatch and a short flight of stone steps; the hatch doors are here visible at the front corner.

Most of the old houses of Staten Island were built of irregular field-stones, laid in a rough rubble wall. One of the earliest was the Hendrickson House at Rossville (fig. 94). A stone marked ' 1696 I.H.' recalls that the house was built in that year by one Ian Hendrickson. The left portion of the house had fieldstone walls mortared with mud and oyster-shell lime. There was no cellar under this section but ' it had one of the rare early primitive fireplaces built out into the room, with a hole in the garret floor for the smoke to escape through and a short chimney to conduct the smoke from the garret outside.' [25]

Such fireplaces were built on a dirt or stone hearth, adjacent to the
wall, which was protected by brick backing, and the hole in the garret
floor led into a large hood, built of clay-daubed wood, which passed up
through the garret and roof to a small chimney. These 'hood' fireplaces
may still be seen in ancient peasant structures in Europe and were probably used in all the colonies. Forman describes a crude story-and-a-half
frame hut in Virginia with just such an arrangement: the hearth is of dirt,
the gable-end wall is protected by an iron fireback and clay-daubed lath
strips, and the lath-and-plaster hood in the garret tapers to a small

93. Bergen House, Flatlands, Brooklyn, c.1680 (Frank Cousins, The Essex Institute)

boarded flue which emerges through the roof.[26] Hood fireplaces were
probably common in early Dutch Colonial houses, though the only one
that has survived in its original form is in the Hasbrouck House in New-
burgh, New York, famous for its use as Washington's headquarters in
1782–3.

The frame extension at the right end of the Hendrickson house was

94. Hendrickson House, Rossville, Staten Island, 1696 (The Holland Society of New
York)

added after the Revolution. Very likely it was at this time that the sloping dormers and the deep overhanging eaves were added, since study of the timbers shows them not to be original. This interesting house was demolished a generation ago to make way for a Standard Oil plant.

FLEMISH COLONIAL HOUSES: EIGHTEENTH CENTURY

The distinguishing feature of the later Flemish Colonial house is the gambrel roof. It appears in this region in the early years of the eighteenth century — that of the Ackerman House at Hackensack (1704) is the earliest certainly dated example. The 'Dutch gambrel,' as it is often called, has a distinctive shape. As shown in figure 95, the typical New England gambrel of the eighteenth century has a generous and full contour, the upper and lower slopes of almost equal length, and the lower slope quite

95. Types of gambrel roofs: (A) New England; (B) 'Dutch'; (C) 'Swedish' (Philip White)

steep — about 60°. The Dutch gambrel, however, has the break higher up, giving a short upper slope of about 22°, and a long sweeping lower slope of about 45° pitch. Combined with the curved overhang, the Dutch gambrel is shaped like a wide-flaring bell, and it is certainly the most beautiful of the many varieties of gambrel roof.

Its architectural heritage is not certainly known. There seems general agreement, however, that it was not Dutch in origin. Gambrel roofs are exceedingly rare in Holland, and there seems doubt that they were used at all in the seventeenth century. It is possible that the English type of gambrel roof, which appeared in New England in the 1670's and perhaps earlier, spread first to the easterly half of Long Island, which was settled by people from Connecticut, and thence to the Dutch regions. Bailey states that the New England shape of gambrel was used by the Dutch colonists, ' especially at first.' [27] Waterman, stressing the importance of the French Huguenot component of the population of the region (especially in northern New Jersey), argues the probability that the Dutch gambrel is in reality a Huguenot contribution, and that it was doubtless derived from the French mansard roof.[28] The gambrel is, however, radically different in shape and is always associated with folk rather than formal architecture. The more probable explanation seems to be that this particular roof profile originated in the same region as the projecting flared eave — the Flemish area of southern Holland, western Belgium, and northern France — though this has not yet been established.

A third type of gambrel roof shown in figure 95 is more like the New England than the Dutch type, but its lower pitch is the steepest of the three. It is most common in Delaware and Pennsylvania and may be of Swedish origin, as will be shown in a later chapter.

The Jan Ditmars House, formerly in Flatlands, was built at some time before 1700, though the exact date is not certainly known. If the gambrel roof shown (fig. 96) is original it may be the earliest example in this region, but one should notice that already it has the characteristic Flemish shape. This house is deep enough to accommodate a full second story

96. Jan Ditmars House, Flatlands, Brooklyn, c.1700 (Frank Cousins, The Essex Institute)

and garret under the roof, and in other respects — wide shingles, boxed overhangs, and end chimneys — it is almost a twin to the Bergen House. The Dutch never built exterior chimneys, like those in Virginia, but kept the chimney stack within the wall, covering it up, in wooden houses, with clapboards or shingles. But there was almost always a bake-oven at the back of the kitchen fireplace, protruding outside the house as a round-topped brick or stone vault. In later years most of these were demolished; undoubtedly all that remained of the bake-oven of the Ditmars House when the photograph was taken was the blanked-up opening visible on the end wall.

The earliest Dutch barns had clay floors and thatched roofs, but as time went on floors were planked in oak or hickory, and roofs shingled. Until the late 1920's a huge old Dutch barn (fig. 97) stood on the Ditmars property. It had very low side walls, but its tremendous width carried the gabled roof to a goodly height, as was typical of Dutch barns throughout southern New Netherland. Peter Kalm, the Swedish naturalist, made a trip through the colonies in 1748–9 and described the barns in the New Brunswick region:

The barns had a peculiar kind of construction hereabouts, which I will give a concise description of. The whole building was very great, so as almost to equal a small church; the roof was pretty high, covered with wooden shingles, declining on both sides, but not steep: the walls which support it were not much higher than a full-grown man; but on the other hand the breadth of the building was the more considerable: in the middle was the threshing floor, and above it, or in the loft or garret, they put the corn which was not yet threshed, the straw, or anything else, according to season: on one side were stables for the horses, and on the other for the cows, and the smaller cattle had likewise their particular

97. Ditmars barn (Maud Esther Dilliard)

stables or styes; on both ends of the buildings were great gates, so that one could come in with a cart and horses through one of them and go out at the other: here was therefore under one roof the threshing floor, the barn, the stables, the hay loft, the coach house, etc. This kind of building is chiefly made use of by the Dutch and Germans . . .[29]

At one end of the Ditmars barn was a ' hovel,' a shed with an open front for pigs and for storing farm implements. Wertenbaker has traced this Dutch type of barn to the combined house and barn of the peasants of Lower Saxony; it is found in modified form all over central and southern Holland. Even the Flemish farmers seem to have preferred it to their native type, for they brought it with them from Holland to the banks of the Hudson and the Raritan.

The finest examples of the Flemish Colonial style are in northern New Jersey, particularly in Bergen County. Almost all of the surviving examples are eighteenth century, and a large proportion of them are of stone construction. It is interesting that stone was so much favored, for excellent forest timber was readily available and wood construction of course would have been cheaper. Bailey speculates [30] that the work of quarrying, dressing, and transporting the stones would have been impossible but for the abundant supply of slave labor. From an early time, the Proprietors had granted seventy-five acres of land for every slave brought into the colony.

The classic example of the style is the Abraham Ackerman House at Hackensack (fig. 98). Born in Holland, Ackerman was brought to New Amsterdam at the age of three, lived for a time in Bergen, where he was married to Aeltye Van Laer, and bought land in Hackensack in 1689. The original house was a small wing to the west of the present edifice, probably built in 1695–6. This wing was removed in 1865, but one of its foun-

98. Abraham Ackerman House, Hackensack, N.J., 1704, east end (R. Merritt Lacey, HABS)

dation stones bears the date 1696. During the next ten years, his family grew from six to twelve living children, and the need for an extensive addition to the house must have been urgent. This, the present main house, was completed in 1704. A stone at the east end is inscribed ' A.A.M.: G.A.M.: D.A.M.: 1704'; the initials refer to the three builders, Abraham Acker Man and his two eldest sons, Gerret and David.

They built well. The house is of red New Jersey sandstone, with remnants of the original clay-and-hair mortar still visible. On the front (fig. 99), the stones are smoothly dressed and fitted in regular courses, but side and rear walls are rougher, with courses of varying heights and stones of different lengths. The free pattern and rough texture thus obtained are rather better looking than the smooth ashlar of the front, and modern repointing of the masonry with white lime mortar, instead of the old red New Jersey clay, has made the masonry pattern more visible — to its advantage. Even when side and rear walls were of rough masonry, in most New Jersey stone houses the corners were strengthened by large well-finished stones, as may be seen in the northeast corner of this house. The fieldstone is carried a foot above the line of the eaves; above it the gambrel end is shingled. The chimney, as usual, is within the wall, and a very small arched window beside it lights the peak of the garret. The roof overhang, slightly greater in front than in back, is unsupported except for two quite unnecessary round posts flanking the front entrance, added about 1900. The window sash are replacements dating from about 1800.

The plan and interior arrangement of the Ackerman House conform to the standard Dutch practice for a house of its size (fig. 100). Plan evolu-

99. Abraham Ackerman House from the south   (R. Merritt Lacey, HABS)

tion in Dutch Colonial houses was not unlike that of New England houses. The first stage generally consisted of a single large room, serving as kitchen-dining-living room, with big fireplace and chimney at one end, and a garret reached by a ladder and trapdoor. Perhaps Abraham Ackerman's first house was of this type. A second stage had two large rooms downstairs, each with its outside door.* Bedrooms, if any, were narrow and at the back, and opened directly into the main front rooms, thus eliminating the need for a central hall. The rear rooms generally lacked fireplaces. The third plan-type — that of the Ackerman House — had a central hall from front to back, each end equipped with a Dutch door for light and air. Two rooms opened from it on either side, though sometimes the narrow back rooms were entered only from the front rooms rather than from the hall.† In such a house, one large room was used as a

* Like the gambrel roof, Waterman attributes this two-room plan to French Huguenot influence, but it is commonly found in farmhouses in Flanders. See *Dwellings of Colonial America*, p. 199.

† The thick stone partition to the left of the hall in the Ackerman House is an unexplained and fascinating peculiarity. Was it originally an outside wall? Was the main house perhaps built in two sections, the first one sometime after 1696, to be completed

kitchen-dining-living room and the other as a best bedroom-parlor, as in New England.

The interiors of the early houses reveal heavy framing beams, hand-hewn and occasionally chamfered or molded at the corners. Walls are usually plastered, or wainscoted to the height of the chair rail and plastered above. The kitchen fireplace, with its bake-oven door at the back, was often large enough to contain seats at the sides, and it was spanned by an immense wooden lintel above. Other fireplaces were smaller and framed by glazed blue Delftware tiles showing scriptural scenes. In the eighteenth century the fireplace wall was usually paneled and equipped

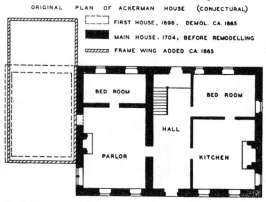

100. Probable original plan of the Ackerman House (Philip White)

with an abundance of cupboards with doors hung on hand-wrought iron hinges. There was very little carved woodwork until the Revolutionary period.

In front of the entrance door was the typical Dutch *stoep,* a low platform with a bench at either side. Peter Kalm later wrote:

before each door there was an elevation, to which you ascend by some steps from the street; it resembled a small balcony, and had some benches on both sides on which the people sat in the evenings, in order to enjoy the fresh air, and have the pleasure of viewing those who passed by.[31]

From the front hall, usually, a stairway rose to the garret, and in the early days the stair was boxed in, with a door at the foot, as in the Ackerman House, to prevent any of the heat from rising into the attic and being wasted. Later, in the mid-eighteenth century, the stair might be open, with simple balusters and handrail. The garret itself was originally unfinished and unpartitioned, serving as workshop, storage loft, and children's sleeping quarters. In the Ackerman House the big wool wheels and looms for weaving blankets were stored in the great open garret as late as the 1840's; after that, as happened in most houses, the upstairs bedrooms

by the hall and east rooms in 1704? Though the files of the Historic American Buildings Survey contain measured drawings of this important house and an unusually complete collection of documents concerning it, they offer no clue to the solution of this puzzle.

were partitioned off from the attic, one by one, and the dormers added as required. These dormers, it will be observed, are fortunately of the early sloping type, following the upper roof pitch, and harmonizing much better with the roof mass than do gabled ones.

A near-by contemporary of the Ackerman House is the Terheun House, overlooking the banks of the Hackensack River (fig. 101). The house was built, probably before 1709 but certainly not as early as 1670 as often stated, by a French Huguenot family which had come to New Jersey, via

101. Terheun House, Hackensack, c.1709 (Robert W. Tebbs)

Holland, in the seventeenth century. The thick walls are of rough-hewn stone, now whitewashed, and above the low-ceilinged first story the construction is of wood, with a wide-spreading gambrel roof sheltering the two stories contained within it. This roof projects in front to form a full-width porch, with four posts supporting the eaves, but the porch, like the dormer windows, was a nineteenth-century addition. The frame wing at the right was also added to the house about the year 1800.

Fully as charming as the Ackerman House is that erected by Jacobus Demarest at River Edge, New Jersey, before 1720. Built of rough-cut stone, stuccoed and whitewashed on the front, the house sits low and comfortably on the ground and seems amply sheltered by its flared gambrel roof, unsullied by dormers of any kind. The windows, pleasantly crooked, are of the standard eighteenth-century type: a large twelve-light sash above with an eight-light sash below, which can be raised and fastened by pegs. The house has paneled shutters and a divided Dutch door, the upper portion of which is pierced by tilted oval bull's eyes of thick bottle glass. Except for a modern brick bay window on an old wing, and the textureless modern composition roofing, the Demarest House is a well-nigh perfect example of the style.

One factor that adds variety and interest to Flemish Colonial houses is the interplay between small wings and large central masses. In New Jersey the small wing is likely to be the earlier portion of the house, as in the Ackerman and Demarest Houses. After a larger house was built beside it, the wing might be converted into a kitchen, with slave quarters in

102. Roelof Westervelt House, Tenafly, N.J. (The Holland Society of New York)

the garret. Such was the history of the Roelof Westervelt House at Tenafly (fig. 102). The small wing, built about 1745, had one large room with an immense fireplace, behind which was a ladder leading to the slaves' quarters. The main house was not built until 1798 and is a fine example of the style, with smoothly dressed regular masonry and a broad gambrel roof, which contrasts interestingly with the gabled roof of the little wing.

Frequently another wing would be added at the other end of the main house, perhaps for a married son, or for grandparents, and rarely would it balance the first too slavishly in placement, size, or detail. Not until the nineteenth century did it become customary to build one or two small wings at the same time as the main building.

Entrance doors were frequently topped by simple rectangular transom windows — usually four or five panes in a row; the wing door of the Westervelt House is unique in its row of eight miniature panes. Occasionally, as over the front door of the Ackerman House, there is a transom with a simple fan of tracery fitted within its wide low rectangle. Other interesting windows will be found in gambrel ends. Most usually garrets were lighted by two or three sash windows near the floor level, and an additional small window high up near the roof: rectangular at first, then, in the eighteenth century, a semicircular lunette, finally two quarter-circle windows.

Toward the latter part of the eighteenth century one final development in the Flemish Colonial style took place. The projecting roof, having proved a welcome shelter to those sitting on the *stoep* of an evening to

103. Dyckman House, Broadway and 204th Street, New York City, *c.*1783 (HABS)

' have the pleasure of viewing those who passed by,' was projected still more, the overhang supported on a series of square pillars, and the *stoep* extended the full width of the house, thus forming a wide front porch which could easily be surrounded by a rail. The old Lefferts House in Flatbush, a late seventeenth-century structure partly burned in 1776, was rebuilt during or after the war in this fashion.

The Dyckman House, built about 1783, at Broadway and 204th Street, New York City, is a picturesque example of this last phase of Flemish Colonial (fig. 103). The gambrel roof has a splendid sweep over the generous porch. Attractive also is the pleasant combination of whitewashed masonry and wide clapboards, and the variation in level between the main house and the small gabled wing. James Thacher, a surgeon's mate, had seen houses like this five years before when his regiment marched from King's Ferry across the Hudson and into New Jersey. In his *Military Journal* he wrote: ' These towns are inhabited chiefly by Dutch people . . . there is a peculiar neatness in the appearance of their dwellings, having an airy piazza supported by pillars in front, and their kitchens connected at the ends in the form of wings.' [32]

Houses of this type continued to be built until as late as 1835. One of the late examples is the Vreeland House, in Leonia Borough, near Englewood, New Jersey (fig. 104). The small stone wing may have been built about 1786; the main house, of frame construction with clapboard siding, was built in 1818. The main house is of considerable size and, like late Georgian houses, has two chimneys at each end. By this date the Georgian style had flowered and faded and the Federal period was near

104. Vreeland House, Leonia Borough, Englewood, N.J., wing c.1786, main house 1818 (HABS)

its end; yet the only trace of these newer influences are a doorway with a delicate classical enframement and elliptical fanlight, and some interior carved woodwork. A little later than this the Greek Revival was to take the stage, and in the last Flemish Colonial houses the simple square porch posts were replaced by classical columns.

Taken as a whole, however, the Dutch and Flemish houses maintained a remarkable isolation from the ebb and flow of eastern architectural styles, preserving their own character and quality with remarkable tenacity for 200 years. The Spanish Colonial style of the Southwest persisted even longer, but it was separated from the active architectural centers of the eastern seaboard by at least 2000 miles of wilderness. The only explanation for the longevity of the Dutch Colonial style seems to be the extraordinary insularity of the Dutch people themselves. The observant Peter Kalm, speaking of New Brunswick, New Jersey, had this to say:

One of the streets is almost entirely inhabited by Dutchmen who came hither from Albany, and for that reason they call it Albany Street. The Dutch only keep company among themselves, and seldom or ever go amongst the other inhabitants, living as it were quite separate from them.[33]

If there was this much isolation between High Dutch and Low Dutch living together in one community, who can wonder that neither one would much esteem the robust Georgian forms of Independence Hall, a-building when Peter Kalm wrote; or, fifty years later, the Adam delicacy and chastity of the post-Revolutionary period; or, forty years later than that, the marble majesty of the Greek Revival? They conserved the old, as a farming people will; they abided in quiet contentment with an architecture that belonged peculiarly to them.

READING SUGGESTIONS

The best brief treatment is found in Thomas Jefferson Wertenbaker's *The Founding of American Civilization: The Middle Colonies* (Scribner's, New York, 1938) , pp. 40–81.

The two standard and invaluable reference volumes are Helen Wilkinson Reynolds's *Dutch Houses in the Hudson Valley Before 1776* (157 illus.) , publ. for the Holland Society of New York by Payson and Clarke, New York, 1929; and Rosalie Fellows Bailey's *Pre-Revolutionary Dutch Houses and Families in Northern New Jersey and Southern New York* (180 illus.) , publ. for the Holland Society of New York by William Morrow and Co., New York, 1936

Historic Houses of the Hudson Valley, by Harold Donaldson Eberlein and Cortlandt Van Dyke Hubbard (Architectural Book Publishing Co., New York, 1942) , has 200 excellent illustrations; a large number of them, however, are of Georgian, Federal, and Greek Revival buildings.

Earlier books, of value primarily for family histories and genealogy, historical lore and legend are: Harold Donaldson Eberlein, *The Manors and Historic Homes of the Hudson Valley,* J. B. Lippincott, Philadelphia, 1924; Eberlein, *Manor Houses and Historic Homes of Long Island and Staten Island,* J. B. Lippincott, Philadelphia, 1928; Rowland C. Ellis, *Colonial Dutch Houses in New Jersey,* Carteret Book Club, New York, 1933; and Maud Esther Dilliard, *Old Dutch Houses of Brooklyn,* Richard R. Smith, New York, 1945.

5

Southern Colonial Architecture

FIVE HUNDRED miles along the Atlantic, from Delaware Bay to the Savannah River, from coastal Tidewater to the rolling uplands of the Piedmont, the Old South spread its plantations. Tobacco and turpentine, rice and indigo, cotton and southern pine came slowly down its great rivers; white men and black pushed back upstream bearing furniture and mirrors, linen and snuff, axes and the long rifles: they moved inland up the hills, through the gaps in the long Blue Ridge; they met other streams of pioneers flowing down the great valley of Virginia from the north.

In this great region Southern Colonial architecture developed, from crude shelters and frame and brick farmhouses in the seventeenth century to the sophisticated Georgian mansions of the eighteenth. The settlers of the Old South were predominantly English, and their architecture betrays its debt to the mother country no less than does that of New England; yet the two regional styles differ in many respects. The people came for different reasons, and to different lands.

The Englishmen who settled Virginia had no quarrel with the Anglican Church or with the King; they were loyal to the institutions and beliefs of the mother country. As Shurtleff has pointed out, ' the Virginia parish was a transplanted parish of the Church of England; the Virginia House of Burgesses, from its first meeting in 1619, imitated the forms and procedure of the House of Commons.' [1] Unlike the New Englanders, who came largely from East Anglia, Virginians came from many regions: Devon, Kent, East Anglia, Surrey, Middlesex, the Cotswold Hills.

They were also of diverse social origins: there were brothers or younger sons of peers, county squires, merchants and professional men, as well as a large group of artisans and indentured servants — who, after serving out their bond of four or five years, became yeomen farmers and even prosperous planters. Virginia became a Crown colony in 1624, with a royal governor appointed by the king. At the time of the Civil War of 1642, she remained loyal to the Crown, and the many Royalists who sought refuge there added to the aristocratic traditions of the colony.

The South, more than New England, was oriented to the ocean. One after the other the great rivers came down to the sea: the Susquehanna and Potomac; the James, York, and Rappahannock; the Chowan, the Tar, and the Santee; Charleston's Cooper and Ashley; the swampy Edisto and broad Savannah. Inland travel north and south was virtually impossible; the rivers were the only means of communication in the early days, and along them grew the great plantations. Such roads as existed were frequently impassable except to saddle horses, and this meant a certain iso'ation: each plantation of necessity formed a self-contained unit, many miles away from its nearest neighbor. Compared to New England, it was a land without towns and villages. With its one-crop economy, huge land holdings, and the introduction of slave labor, the South was destined to develop an aristocratic society and an aristocratic architecture.

Yet in another sense the South was less 'isolated' and provincial than New England. The ship that collected the tobacco casks from the small dock almost at the back door would next berth at the teeming quays below London Bridge, and it would return just as directly with a box of coats and dresses cut to order in the latest mode of the Court. Thus it was easy, in fashions, manners, and in architecture, to keep in close touch with the mother country. And it was also easy to take the light boat from the same small dock and go a-visiting: to the neighbor a few miles along the river, or around the point and up the next river; thus members of the southern aristocracy visited and entertained each other with lavish hospitality, intermarried wealth and position with position and wealth, achieved a hereditary elite and an elite architecture.

Early Jamestown

But all this took two centuries. Neither life nor architecture was aristocratic in the harsh days of the early settlement. The ill-fated colony that Sir Walter Raleigh planted on Roanoke Island in 1585 disappeared in mystery in 1587; the rescue expedition three years later found a high palisade on the site, but no houses, and no people. Very likely the doomed village consisted of a fort and some crude huts, such as were built at Jamestown a generation later; we may assume that the collection of log cabins produced for the Roanoke Pageant of 1938 was the last flowering of the log-cabin myth.

Sir Christopher Newport's fleet, the *Sarah Constant,* the *Goodspeed,* and the *Discovery,* brought about a hundred colonists to Jamestown in 1607. They sheltered themselves at first in flimsy 'cabbins and holes within the grounde.' The infant colony suffered from poor government and lack of industry, and only 60 out of some 400 souls survived the disastrous winter of 1609–10. But a new fleet arrived in 1610, and from then on conditions improved. There was sufficient building so that by 1615 Jamestown

is reduced into a hansome forme, and hath in it two faire rowes of howses, all of framed Timber, two stories, and an upper Garret, or Corne loft high, besides three large, and substantiall Storehowses . . . and this town hath been lately newly, and strongly impaled, and a faire platforme for Ornance in the West Bulworke raised . . .[2]

The town of Henrico was founded further up the James River, and so energetically did Sir Thomas Gates (Governor 1611–14) push forward the building there that Ralph Hamor was able to describe the town in 1615 as follows:

There is in the town 3 streets of well framed howses, a hansom Church, and the foundation of a more stately one laid, of Brick . . . beside Store houses, watch houses, and such like: there are also . . . five faire Block houses, or commaunders, wherein live the honester sort of people, as in Farmes in *England,* and there keepe continuall centinell for the townes security . . .[3]

It appears from early accounts that within a decade, three different types of 'permanent' building had been employed in Virginia. There were frame houses, with hewn-timber frames covered by clapboards, and wooden chimneys plastered with clay. There were brick buildings; as early as 1611, Robert Johnson reported 'competent and decent houses, the first storie all of bricks' at Henrico,[4] and an ambitious brick church

105. Conjectural restoration of the First State House, Jamestown, Va., *c.*1635 (H. C. Forman, *The Architecture of the Old South,* Harvard University Press)

had been started there. Blockhouses were also built, undoubtedly of hewn-log construction with flat sides and notched joints, like those built later in New England.

Though little but foundations and fragments of hardware remain on the site of Jamestown today, excavations and researches have made possible a fairly detailed picture of the early architecture of this first English community in Virginia.[5] The palisaded James Fort, which was the first concern of the settlers, was a large triangle 420 feet on the south side and 300 feet on the other two sides. Stout posts and planks, standing 14 feet high and embedded 4 feet in the ground, formed the 'curtains,' and the three corners were reinforced by blockhouses made of great hewn timbers; their roofs served as artillery platforms. Within the fort were the 'two faire rowes of houses,' numbering perhaps some 34 small dwellings, each about 16 feet square, a church, and the storehouses.

The row houses of Jamestown are of particular interest as revealing an architectural type common in medieval Europe. It doubtless existed elsewhere in the colonies, notably in early Boston and New Amsterdam, but only at Jamestown have the actual foundations been preserved for study. One such group was the First State House, a group of three houses standing by the river bank (fig. 105). The first two were erected before 1635, the third before 1655. They were built of brick, laid in English bond, two and a half stories high, with central chimneys and pantiled roofs. The pitched roofs ran transverse to the long axis of the row, thus presenting gables, side by side, along the façades. This arrangement, while picturesque, would have been impractical in regions with heavy snowfalls.

The plan of each unit (fig. 106) was of a type illustrated for row houses in England in Moxon's *Mechanick Exercises,* and distinctly unlike the typical Virginia farmhouse plan. Between the solid party walls, each unit consisted of a lateral corridor with a recessed staircase, and back-to-back

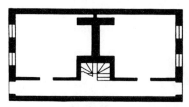

106. Unit plan of the First State House, Jamestown (Philip White, after Forman)

fireplaces between front and back rooms. Windows were of leaded quarrels set in wrought-iron casements — one found in the ruins was only a foot and a half wide — and the iron handles and latch bars were wrought in ornamental shapes. Other hardware included rim locks, large keys, strap hinges, H-hinges, elaborate cock's head hinges, and keyhole escutcheons, all of markedly English pattern (fig. 107).

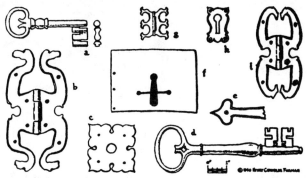

107. Medieval door and furniture hardware from Jamestown (H. C. Forman, *The Architecture of the Old South,* Harvard University Press)

Another row-house group at Jamestown consisted of five buildings, four probably erected in the 1660's and the fifth in 1685. This last served as the Fourth State House. These buildings had a continuous longitudinal gabled roof instead of a series of cross gables. Some had projecting porches, and the State House had a stair tower projecting from the rear façade, like the ' cross-plan ' houses discussed later. The row of houses, as illustrated by Forman,[6] was very medieval in appearance. The series of disastrous fires that Jamestown suffered culminated in the destruction of the State House in 1698 and led to the transfer of the capital to Williamsburg in the following year.

Seventeenth-century frame houses in Virginia

Probably frame houses outnumbered brick houses in seventeenth-century Virginia. The fact that no example of certain date survives today is owing partly to the deterioration of wood construction in the Virginia climate, and partly to the fact that the smaller farmhouses of the early period were often taken over later on for slave quarters and allowed to fall into ruin. But documents give considerable evidence about the construction of the early frame houses, and their appearance may be conjec-

108. Kitchen of Market Square Tavern, Williamsburg, as reconstructed (Richard Garrison photo, Colonial Williamsburg)

tured from their brick contemporaries that still survive, or from the simple wooden houses of the eighteenth century that continued the early style. Such for example are the kitchens of the Market Square Tavern (fig. 108) and the Orr House at Williamsburg.

There was an abundant supply of wood: pine, cedar, oak, hickory, chestnut, cypress, ash, and elm were to be had for the cutting. Framing timbers were hewn square with the broadaxe, smoothed with an adze, and the notched joints cut with chisel, mallet, and auger. Clapboards were riven with froe and club, as in New England, and we know that they were produced during the first winter at Jamestown, for the ships carried a return cargo of oak clapboards in the spring of 1608. Clapboards used for exterior siding were — and still are — called 'weatherboards' in Virginia, as in England. Floor boards, sheathing, and wainscot were cut in the saw pits with long whip-saws; every large plantation had two or more sawyers constantly at work. The earliest mention of a sawmill in Virginia was in

1625; a few years later they became more numerous, and sawed timber was easier to obtain. A book published in London in 1650 illustrated a ' Sawmill for Virginia ' with a water wheel and crank actuating a gang-saw of three parallel blades, cutting a squared baulk of timber into four planks.[7] Carpenters' tools, imported from England, were much the same as those of today.*

House construction was undoubtedly much the same as in New England. Clay bound with straw, and possibly salt-marsh grass, was used as a wall filling, and a number of houses in Williamsburg had brick nogging.[8] Since the colonists were familiar with English half-timber houses, it has been supposed that they may have been built with exposed nogging in early Virginia,[9] but there is absolutely no evidence, material or documentary to prove this quite logical supposition. For the most part, at least, we may assume that frame and filling were covered with weatherboards. Not until the early eighteenth century did it become the usual practice to paint weatherboarding with white lead and oil.[10] Roofs were thatched, at first, and later shingled. The windows were small, of the medieval casement type with leaded diamond panes; so far as is known the first windows of the sliding-sash type in Virginia were those ordered for the Capitol in Williamsburg in 1699.

The most striking feature of Virginia farmhouses was the great exterior chimney, wide enough at the bottom to enclose the great kitchen fireplace, and narrowed by sloped offsets at the sides to a straight stack at the top. As a fire-protection measure, the chimney frequently stood a few inches free of the wooden gable end. The gabled roof was all but universal in the seventeenth century: the hipped roof does not appear in Virginia until after 1700, and the gambrel roof probably at about the same time.† This simple type of weatherboard farmhouse continued popular throughout much of the eighteenth century in minor structures such as the detached kitchens, offices, and outbuildings of the big mansions. Many examples may be seen in the Williamsburg restoration.

Brick houses of the seventeenth century

Skilled brickmakers were among the first settlers, clay was abundant, and lime could be obtained from oyster shells. We have seen that as early as 1611 brick was being made at Henrico, and soon it became the favored material. Indeed the prejudice of the English authorities in favor of brick construction is revealed in an order of 1637 requiring every man owning a hundred acres to build ' a dwelling house of brick, to be twenty-

---

* The Henrico County Records inventoried the tools of one John Cumber as follows: a jack plane, four ' plow ' planes, a smoothing plane, a keyhole saw, several gouges, two augers, two joiners' heading chisels, a pair of compasses, a square, two pocket rules, two broadaxes, three adzes, two chisels, two handsaws, two hammers, a whip-saw.[11]

† The hipped roof of the Ball Room Wing at Fairfield is assumed to be an early eighteenth-century addition. One of the oldest gambrel roofs in Virginia, according to Forman (p. 91) dates from about 1700. When the gambrel roof is more widely adopted in Virginia, during the first quarter of the eighteenth century, it is commonly of the ' Maryland ' profile, with a short and very steep lower slope. Examples are the Moore House, Yorktown and the Nightengale and Travis Houses at Williamsburg.

four feet in length and sixteen feet in breadth, with a cellar attached ' [12] —
a bureaucratic impertinence more honored in the breach than the ob-
servance. But by 1638 Secretary Richard Kemp had built an all-brick
house at Jamestown, and the first two units of the State House had already been completed — in general brick construction became far more
widespread in seventeenth-century Virginia than it did in New England.
The reason for this may be sought, perhaps, in the fact that the settlers of
New England were predominantly from the southeastern counties of England, where there was very little brick building, whereas the settlers of
Virginia came from all parts of England, including regions where brick
was a favored material.

There have been the usual traditions, in Virginia as elsewhere, that
brick for some of the old houses was ' imported from England.' While it
may occasionally have been brought in as ballast to a light cargo, brick
was not an import material. Indeed, from an early time brick was being
exported to Bermuda in exchange for limestone, and in the latter half of
the seventeenth century it was considerably more expensive in England
than it was in Virginia.[13]

Brick laid in English bond was favored in seventeenth-century buildings, whereas in the eighteenth century the more attractive Flemish bond
prevailed. It is tempting to postulate a stylistic evolution of this nature,
but since one wall of the earliest extant brick building in Virginia (the
Thoroughgood House) is laid in Flemish bond, such theories had best
wait the discovery of more evidence.

Seventeenth-century house plans

Seventeenth-century Virginia houses exhibit four plan-types, ranging
from simple to complex. They form a logical sequence of evolution, but
as in New England this cannot be taken as strictly chronological.

The simplest and in general the earliest type was the *one-room plan*
with end chimney. The ' House on Isaac Watson's Land ' in Jamestown,
built about 1644, may represent the type (fig. 109A). The one main
room, about 20 feet square, had a brick floor, front and back doors, and
small windows. At one end of the room was a fireplace, big enough to
take an 8-foot log, a small chimney closet, a bake-oven beside the fireplace, and in front of it the base for a brewing ' copper.' The loft was
probably reached by a ladder.

The *two-room plan,* boasting a hall and parlor, is exemplified by the
Wishart House at Norfolk, built about 1680 (fig. 109B). The hall was
the larger of the two rooms; the front door opened into it, and in the rear
corner was a steep stairway, partitioned off by vertical wainscot. The distinctive difference between New England and Virginia houses of two-room
plan was in the location of the chimneys: in New England, a central chimney contained two fireplaces, back to back; in Virginia there were two
chimneys, at the ends. These chimneys either projected outside the end
walls or were built within them.

The *central-hall plan* (fig. 109C) took full advantage of the cross-ventilation gained by locating chimneys at the ends. The hallway, with doors

at front and back and a stair to the garret, was at first a narrow passage separated from the main room merely by a screen or parclose; later it became a spacious room, much used for summer living.

The *cross plan* (fig. 109D), most elaborate and apparently latest in date, is represented by a group of seven known examples in Virginia. The buildings of this group had a two-story projection in front, containing a vestibule or porch below, and a porch chamber above. From the porch one entered a central hallway, if there was one, or directly into the main room. At the back was a projecting stair tower, with a stairway of the open-well type, the runs ascending around the sides of the tower. Sometimes the stair was located in the central hallway and the rear projection

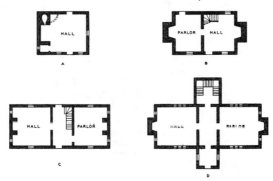

109. Types of seventeenth-century house plans in Virginia (Philip White)

used for a parlor, as at Malvern Hill; sometimes the rear projection was omitted altogether, as at Foster's Castle. The Jamestown State House had fireplaces in the middle of the long sides of the main rooms; these side fireplaces were common enough in England, but the exception in Virginia. All other houses of this group had chimneys at the ends.

The cross plan is peculiar to the Colonial architecture of the South. Examples of it are found in Maryland and Bermuda as well as Virginia, but not elsewhere. The projecting porch with porch chamber above was fairly common in New England Colonial houses, and the Whitfield House at Guilford, Connecticut, may at one time have had a projecting stair tower at the back; but nowhere except in the South do both features occur to form a full cruciform plan. Since a religious motive for the adoption of this type of plan does not seem plausible, a satisfactory explanation of its origin remains to be sought in English medieval domestic architecture.

In the opening years of the eighteenth century there was one further development of plan: narrow rooms or ' cells ' were added back of the two main rooms, as in the lean-to additions of New England houses. The resultant roof shape, with a longer slope at the rear than in front, is in Virginia, however, called a ' catslide ' instead of a ' saltbox.' [14] This type of plan was transitional to the spacious double file of rooms on either side of a fine central hallway that characterizes the Georgian mansions.

These typical Virginia Colonial houses, in frame or brick, rectangular in plan or with projecting porch, seem to have had no single regional source in England. The Virginia settlers came from many parts of the mother country, and the architectural traditions that they brought are correspondingly varied. The projecting porch is especially common in Sussex, whereas the two-room plan-type may be found in Norfolk, Suffolk, Cambridgeshire, and even in Essex, that mother county of New Englanders. A house at St. Osyth, Essex, for example (fig. 110) bears a strong resemblance to the typical Virginia frame farmhouse with its story-and-a-half elevation, steep-gabled roof, and exterior end chimneys.

A picture of the High Street in Billericay, Essex (fig. 111), shows one house with a somewhat unusual roof, which might be described as a gable

110. House at St. Osyth, Essex, England (Martin S. Briggs, *Homes of the Pilgrim Fathers,* Oxford University Press)

111. The High Street, Billericay, Essex, England (Martin S. Briggs, *Homes of the Pilgrim Fathers,* Oxford University Press)

with the top corner sliced off. This is known as a ' jerkin-head ' roof, or alternatively as a ' clipped gable,' and it appears sporadically in Southern Colonial architecture from Maryland to South Carolina. The old term for this construction was ' a roof hipped above the wind-beams ' — the ' wind-beams ' being the horizontal collars tying the rafters together across the middle or upper part of the attic.

Jerkin-head roofs were fairly common in the houses and barns of Kent and Surrey, especially of the period 1580–1620, but their origin is obscure. They were used on thatch-roofed houses and may have originated in the medieval period as a partial protection of gable-end walls built of wattle-and-daub. The form would seem to have no practical advantage in weatherboard houses, but in brick houses it would simplify construction of gable ends by reducing the number of bricks cut to the slant of the raking cornices.

Little seems to be known of the history of this form in the colonies; perhaps the earliest example was that of the Thomas Sessions (Shield) House in Yorktown, built about 1693. There were several others in the early eighteenth century,* and practically all of these were brick buildings.

Of Virginia houses of the seventeenth century, six examples may be selected as representing the character and range of the style. Four of these survive today; the two largest and most elaborate have been demolished.

Adam Thoroughgood House, Princess Anne County. c.1636–40

The Adam Thoroughgood House, near Norfolk, is the oldest house not only in Virginia but perhaps in the English-speaking colonies.† Thoroughgood came to Virginia as an indentured servant in 1621, worked off his bond, became a man of position, and sat as a burgess in 1629. He bought a tract of land on Lynnhaven Bay in 1636. When he died in 1640, he willed a house on this land to his widow, Sarah Offley. The house (fig. 112) must have been built, accordingly, between these latter two dates. The walls are solidly built of brick, laid in English bond on three sides and in Flemish bond on front. In plan and style it stands as the archetype of the small Virginia farmhouse of the seventeenth century. Fortunately evidence of subsequent remodelings can be traced in the walls, and thorough study [15] has made possible a picture of its probable original appearance (fig. 113).

Like the wooden farmhouses, it was a low-eaved, story-and-a-half house with steep-gabled roof. The roof was originally unbroken by dormers, the two upstairs rooms being lighted only by tiny windows in the end walls. In place of sliding-sash windows there were medieval cross-mullioned windows, the fixed transom lights above and the hinged casements below being glazed with leaded diamond panes. Windows were topped by low

---

* St. James' Church, Goose Creek, S.C., 1711; Mulberry Castle, S.C., 1714; the Lower Chapel of Middlesex County, Va., 1714–17; the south dependencies at Stratford, Va., c.1725; the Old Stone Church, Augusta, Va., 1749.

† The Fairbanks House at Dedham, Massachusetts (c.1637) may antedate it.

segmental arches and framed by a pattern of glazed headers. The front door was built up of two layers of boards — vertical outside, horizontal inside — secured by closely spaced wrought-iron nails. Of the two end chimneys, one was set within the wall and the other projected as an imposing mass, 11 feet wide at the base, its sloped weatherings protected by special brick and tile patterns. Above the roof both chimneys were

112. Adam Thoroughgood House, Princess Anne County, Va., 1636–40, south end (HABS)

113. Restored south and east elevations, Adam Thoroughgood House (H. C. Forman, *The Architecture of the Old South*, Harvard University Press)

T-shaped in plan. The sloping cornices of the gables were adorned by lines of glazed header bricks. The interior was of the simple hall-and-parlor plan, similar to that illustrated in figure 109B. Different as this house was from its early contemporaries in New England, it shared with them qualities of strength and simplicity and many details from a common ancestry in medieval England.

Warburton House, James City County. c.1680

Though smaller in size than the Thoroughgood House, the Warburton House (Pinewoods), built a generation later, reveals the more advanced central-hallway plan (cf. fig. 109C). Otherwise its architectural features were almost identical – the steep roof (50°), the arched windows and door, and the T-shaped chimney stacks (fig. 114). But the walls were

114. Warburton House, James City County, Va., c.1680 (H. C. Forman, *The Architecture of the Old South*, Harvard University Press)

built of Flemish-bond brick masonry, and the headers glazed to throw a dark checkerboard pattern across the wall. The original woodwork of the interior has been burned out, but the elements of the plan, with its central hall, two rooms, and small closets built beside the interior chimneys, were typical of the period. In the contemporary Wishart House at Norfolk (plan, fig. 109B) there were two great exterior chimneys, like the south chimney of the Thoroughgood House, and one stylistic detail which became more common in the latter half of the century: flat-arch windows instead of segmental-arched ones.

Greenspring, James City County. c.1646

The largest and most imposing house of seventeenth-century Virginia, and ancestor of the mansions to come, was built by Sir William Berkeley, Royal Governor from 1642 to 1677. His mansion Greenspring, near Jamestown, was probably built soon after his appointment in 1642. Unfortunately only the foundations remain, but these reveal an L-shaped plan (fig. 115) with the main block nearly 100 feet in length. The front door opened upon a spacious entrance hall; at the left beyond a huge double fireplace was the dining room, with the kitchen in an ell behind it. The stairway had its own hall, and beyond it was a living room with a projecting fireplace. The servants' quarters were probably in detached buildings.

The architect Latrobe visited Greenspring in 1796 and left a sketch showing a one-story building with a high roof pierced by dormer windows, a projecting entrance porch topped by a curvilinear gable, and windows divided by mullions and filled with leaded casements; fragments of the latter were found in the rubbish of the foundations.[16] The brick walls were laid in English bond. The rich interiors we can only conjecture, but they were probably wainscoted in oak. Since remains of polychromed decorative plaster work have been found in two other Virginia houses: beautifully modeled foliage, masques, and heraldic devices, colored in blue, pink, and green and perhaps used for overmantels or ceilings,[17] it may be surmised that the Royal Governor's rooms were no less

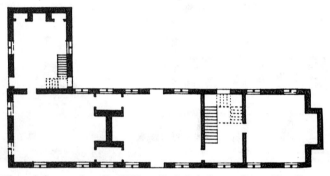

115. Plan of Greenspring, Sir William Berkeley's house, James City County, Va., c.1646 (Thomas T. Waterman, *The Mansions of Virginia*, University of North Carolina Press)

ornate. In them, the autocratic Berkeley entertained the refugee Royalists and the aristocracy of Virginia with extravagant hospitality. Latrobe, accustomed to the sophisticated style of the Federal period, found Greenspring unimpressive; he tells in his diary of his visit in July 1796:

On the 28th I went in the stage to Williamsburg, where I found horses that carried me to . . . Greenspring about six miles SW of the city . . . The principal part of Greenspring house was erected by Sir William Berkeley . . . It is a brick building of great solidity, but no attempt at grandeur . . . Many of the first Virginia assemblies were held in the very room in which I was plotting the death of Muskitoes . . .[18]

His historical interest was not sufficient to prevent his ordering the demolition of the old house when he built a new mansion near the same site for William Ludwell Lee.

Bacon's Castle, Surry County. c.1655

Famous Bacon's Castle is no less a reminder of the ruthless Berkeley. The house (fig. 116), two full stories high, was built by Arthur Allen soon after his arrival in the colony in 1649, possibly about the year 1655.[19] This is the earliest of the Virginia cross-plan houses, and one of the most remarkable architectural monuments of the Colonial period. Windows and interior trim were later changed, but careful study of the fabric has made possible a restoration of its original appearance (fig. 117).

The brick walls were laid in English bond and adorned by several decorative features. Over the door a battlemented motive enclosed a triangular pediment executed in molded brick — an embryonic classical feature unique in the colonies at this time. The line between first and second stories was marked by a projecting belt course of semicircular profile, composed of two courses of molded brick. While the first-story windows were topped by segmental arches, those in the second story had flat arches and brick enframements. The windows themselves were divided by cross

116. Bacon's Castle, Surry County, Va., c.1655, west end (Wayne Andrews)

mullions to form casements below and transom lights above, glazed in the medieval style.

Even more remarkable were the decorative end gables, unique among surviving Colonial houses. Each end wall was shaped at the top to form a Flemish gable, springing from corbeled parapets above the eaves and rising through bold curves and steps to a rectilinear finial at the top. Standing a few inches free of these gables were triple chimneys, set diagonally and joined only at the caps; they rose from a straight stack 10 feet in width and nearly 4 feet in depth. Clustered chimneys such as these are known to have been used on two other Virginia houses, and Flemish gables were rarely used elsewhere in the colonies*; together, they are today unique in American Colonial architecture.

* Triple chimneys were used at Winona, Northampton County, Virginia (c.1700?) and on the Ball Room Wing (early 1700's) at Fairfield in Gloucester County. A Flemish

The origin of these motives, as of all other architectural forms in the Colonial style, is to be sought in medieval England. Clustered chimneys, stepped gables, and curved Flemish gables may be found on Tudor Gothic manor houses of the periods of Henry VIII and Elizabeth; the gable motive was probably brought to England from the Low Countries by Dutch or Flemish workmen who were numerous in England, especially during the reign of Elizabeth. They are, then, features of the English Tudor Gothic style and the term ' Jacobean,' so often applied to Bacon's Castle, is not particularly appropriate.*

The plan of Bacon's Castle (fig. 118) was cruciform, with a projecting

117. Restored south façade of Bacon's Castle (H. C. Forman, *The Architecture of the Old South,* Harvard University Press)

gable may have been used on the second Bruton Parish Church (1683) at Williamsburg. Both clustered chimneys and Flemish gables were used on the Peter Sergeant House (1676–9) in Boston.

* The term ' Jacobean,' as a stylistic designation, is ambiguous. It is meant to apply to the style of buildings erected during the reign of James I (1603–25). During this period two entirely different styles were current, and toward the end of it a third was born. Most buildings erected in England during the reign of James I were belated examples of the medieval style and may appropriately be called ' Tudor Gothic,' this being the last style-phase of England's Gothic. A substantial minority, especially large palaces and manor houses, were in the new style of the early Renaissance. Inaugurated in England by Kirby Hall (1570) and other great houses of Elizabeth's period, the new style developed during the period of James I. Clustered chimneys and Flemish gables continued in use but they are not definitive of the style; far more distinctive is the first introduction of classical decorative detail, as witness the lavish interiors of Knole House (1603) or Aston Hall (1618). This style, since it originated in her reign, may appropriately be called ' Elizabethan.' But this immature style of the early Renaissance was succeeded by the very different and much more competent classicism of Inigo Jones during the last years of James I's reign. Thus as a stylistic term, ' Jacobean ' should be qualified as ' Jacobean I ' or ' Jacobean II ' or ' Jacobean III,' or preferably not used at all because of its ambiguity. American historians most often intend the first or second meaning, but fail to state which. The author prefers to use the less equivocal terms ' Tudor Gothic,' ' Elizabethan,' and ' Early Stuart ' for the three styles. But *chacun à son goût.*

porch about 10 feet square in front and a somewhat larger stair tower behind. From the porch an arched doorway led directly into the hall, 22 by 25 feet, and another arched door opened to the stair tower. Little of the original woodwork remains except the large crossed summer beams, chamfered and molded, which span the hall and parlor. The open-well staircase led to a large cellar containing milk room, storeroom, kitchen, and a fireplace 8 feet in width. The cellar windows were unglazed, being set with horizontal wooden guard bars, square in section and placed diagonally in the frame. There were two large bedrooms on the second floor and three more in the lofty garret.

The old brick house received the name of Bacon's Castle at the time of the rebellion in 1676. Corrupt Governor Berkeley was profiting too

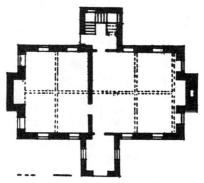

118. Plan of Bacon's Castle (Thomas T. Waterman, *The Mansions of Virginia,* University of North Carolina Press)

largely from fur trading with the Susquehanna Indians to wish to punish them for their raids on the upper settlements. Refusing to take action himself, he even refused to authorize Nathaniel Bacon, a popular planter who had seen one of his own overseers murdered, to undertake an expedition. Bacon with 300 volunteers marched anyway, put down the Indians, and was rewarded by having a price set on his head as a rebel. In the civil war that followed, the Arthur Allen House was seized and garrisoned by Bacon's men, but he died at the moment of victory, of fever or perhaps by poison. Berkeley pursued Bacon's followers with vindictiveness until even the English authorities were sickened by the spilling of blood. Berkeley was recalled the following year, and his ' old and rotten ' House of Burgesses was dissolved.

Foster's Castle, New Kent County. 1685–90?

The house of Colonel Joseph Foster, built probably between 1685 and 1690, was less elaborate than Bacon's Castle (fig. 119). A story and a half high, with single chimneys built within the end walls, it boasted a large projecting porch but lacked the balancing stair tower behind. This gave it a T-shaped plan (fig. 120) with a central hallway; the two main rooms had closets flanking the interior chimneys. The façade presented three

features of architectural interest: the wide three-light windows, distinctly
unusual in Virginia; the round window in the front gable, almost unique
in the seventeenth century; and a belt course around the porch, raised
over the front door to form a ' battlement ' motive.

Another cross-plan house of very similar form was Christ's Cross (called
' Criss-Cross '), in New Kent County, built by George Poindexter about
1690.

Fairfield, Gloucester County. 1692 and later

One of the larger Virginia houses of the seventeenth century was Fairfield, the Lewis Burwell house on Carter's Creek, a tributary of the York
River. Begun in 1692, this house represented the transition from Colonial

119. Foster's Castle, New Kent County, Va., 1685–90? (H. C. Forman, *The Architecture of the Old South,* Harvard University Press)

to Georgian style, from the farmhouses of the seventeenth century to the
mansions of the eighteenth. Fairfield was burned about 1897, and the
foundations together with a few old photographs and a drawing do not
make its architectural history entirely clear. But there was certainly a
long, two-and-a-half-story main building of medieval style (fig. 121). To
this was added, probably in the early years of the eighteenth century, the
one-and-a-half-story Ball Room Wing at the east (right) end of the original house.

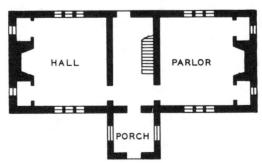

120. Plan of Foster's Castle (Philip White, after Forman)

The old wing may have originated, as Forman believes, in a two-story hall-and-parlor house which was soon after doubled in length.[20] The presumptive casement windows and twin chimneys in pairs were medieval in style; medieval, too, was a heavy plank door with wrought-iron nails, found in the ruins. As Wertenbaker points out, ' the thick walls, the tiny panes of the narrow windows, the towering Tudor chimney stacks, the massive cellar arches, the linen-fold paneling of the hall carved to represent drapery, link this old house with the England of the sixteenth century.' [21] The great chimney on the Ball Room Wing, with its triple shafts set diagonally and linked at the caps, recalls Bacon's Castle and Tudor Gothic manor houses. But the hipped roof and modillioned cornice were

121. Conjectural south elevation of Fairfield, Lewis Burwell House, Carter's Creek, Va., 1692, right wing later (Thomas T. Waterman and John A. Barrows, *Domestic Colonial Architecture of Tidewater Virginia*, Charles Scribner's Sons)

Georgian features; one wonders if Lewis Burwell was impressed by the new style of the College at near-by Williamsburg, or whether he was following the pattern set by the Governor's Palace there. Inside the wing was an impressive ball room, and references to it speak of carved paneling and a great marble mantel [22]; perhaps the fragment of a marble architrave found in the tree-covered ruins is a relic of this vanished splendor.

Three years after Fairfield was begun, the cornerstone of the Wren Building at the College of William and Mary was laid, and in 1699 the colonial capital was transferred from Jamestown to Williamsburg. Virginia at the end of the century was ready to turn from the old to the new: from the medieval tradition of England in the sixteenth century to the classical fashion of Sir Christopher Wren in the seventeenth; the Georgian style in the colonies was about to be born.

Colonial churches in Virginia

Virginia churches of the seventeenth century have suffered severely with the years: only one complete edifice and the ruined tower of a second remain standing today. Yet exhaustive study of ancient records [23] shows that no fewer than four-score churches and chapels were built during the

1600's. Practically all of these were of the Church of England, built and maintained by public taxation. After the Revolution, the Anglican Church was disestablished, and with no more public revenue and a general decline of religion many churches were abandoned. Ruin begun by the elements, fire, and vandalism was completed by the surging armies of the Civil War.

But in the seventeenth century every county had its parish churches and tributary ' chapels of ease,' scattered over the thinly settled area. The early ones were usually located for accessibility by water, but later, as dirt roads and bridle paths netted the Tidewater wilderness, people could come by carriage and horseback, and the church was located at a fork or crossroads. A convenient supply of drinking water was often a primary consideration. These churches stood alone — or perhaps with a small courthouse near by — rather than as the focal point of a tightly knit village community, as in New England.

Usually they were small frame structures, rectangular in plan, with one aisle and pews at the sides, and utterly plain; for the most part they lacked even a tower. The first two churches at Jamestown, built in 1607 and 1608, were no more than flimsy huts of turf, spars, and thatch. Captain John Smith later wrote of how they were built:

I well remember wee did hang an awning . . . to three or foure trees to shadow us from the Sunne, our walles were rales of wood, our seats unhewed trees till we cut plankes, our Pulpit a bar of wood nailed to two neighboring trees . . . This was our Church, till wee built a homely thing like a barne, set upon Cratchets,* covered with rafts, sedge, and earth; so was also the walls . . .[24]

The third church, built in 1610, was a framed structure of sawed lumber, of good size — 24 by 60 feet — and ' with fair broad windowes, to shut and open ' and ' two Bels at the West end.' Despite its bare simplicity, considerable ceremony was observed at service:

Every Sunday, when the Lord Governour and Captaine Generall goeth to Church, he is accompanied with all the Counsailors, Captaines, other Officers and all the Gentlemen, and with a Guard of Holberdiers in his Lordship's livery, faire red cloaks, to the number of fifty, both on each side and behinde him: and being in the Church, his Lordship hath his seate in the Quier, in a green Velvet Chaire, with a Cloath, with a Velvet Cushion spread on a Table before him, on which he kneeleth, and on each side sit the Counsell, Captaines, and Officers, each in their place, and when he returneth home againe, he is waited on to his house in the same manner.[25]

All of which sounds singularly like Saint-Simon's descriptions of the home life of Louis XIV at Versailles some sixty years later.

---

* ' Cratchets ' were upright poles with natural forks at the top, used to support a ridgepole. S. E. Morison and Forman believe that in writing of ' cratchets,' John Smith was thinking of ' crucks.' But since the latter term was then current, presumably Captain Smith said what he meant. It seems unnecessary to suppose that the English construction employing a framework of ' crucks,' or curved tree trunks, was ever employed in the colonies. There is no other material or documentary evidence that it was. But see Shurtleff, *Log Cabin Myth*, p. 138, note 25, and H. C. Forman, *Architecture of the Old South*, pp. 13-15.

But this church was replaced as early as 1617 by another frame structure, and even that soon deteriorated, so that the first permanent church
at Jamestown, built in 1639–44, was actually the town's fifth edifice. With
brick walls over 2½ feet thick, the church was a simple rectangle, 22 by
56 feet in its interior dimensions (fig. 122). Along the sides were Gothic
wall buttresses, and the windows were of leaded glass; it must have resembled a small medieval parish church in England. When Jamestown
was burned in Bacon's Rebellion of 1676, the church lost its interior fittings and roof, but was rebuilt within the old walls in 1680. It was at this
time, probably, that a brick pavement was laid in the nave, and the massive tower added in front. This tower, with walls 3 feet thick at the base,
is the only part of the old church still standing. Its walls were of English-

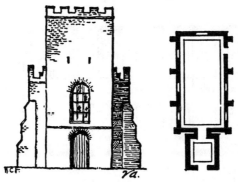

122. Façade and plan of the church at Jamestown (H. C. Forman, *The Architecture
of the Old South*, Harvard University Press)

bond brickwork. A round-arch door penetrated the front wall; over it was
a round-arch window in the second story, and a belfry occupied the third
story.

After the transfer of the colonial government to Williamsburg the
church became less important, and it was eventually closed in 1758.
Within half a century it had fallen into complete ruin, its walls torn
down, and only the tower left standing; the present structure on the site
is a replica built for the Jamestown tercentenary in 1907.

Though Lynnhaven Parish Church in Princess Anne County was built
in the eighteenth century, its plan (fig. 123) was probably more typical
of the small seventeenth-century church than was the Gothic plan of the
church at Jamestown. The west doors opened to the main aisle, and at
the back of the church were stairways leading to a gallery across the end.
The floor was divided by box pews, the large ones at the front assigned
to magistrates, vestrymen, and important families of the parish. In this
church the second pew in front of the pulpit was assigned to the Thoroughgood family, ' as their Privilege from the gift of the Glebe.' During
the course of growth it was frequently necessary to add ' hanging pews '
or galleries for more people. These were usually located along the sides
of the church, toward the back, and there were also pews in the corners

flanking the communion table. Almost invariably there was a door at the
south, and the pulpit, reached by a steep flight of steps and topped by a
sounding board, stood at the opposite side. Such small, simple churches
had no wall buttresses, and no projecting tower at the front.

Just such a plan is exemplified in little Merchant's Hope Church in
Prince George County. Documents place the construction of the building
at 1657, but it is hard to believe that the present exterior, with its round-
arch, sliding-sash windows, and its flared eaves with modillioned cornice,
is of seventeenth- rather than eighteenth-century date, for the style is
indubitably Georgian.

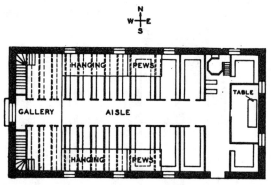

123. Plan of Lynnhaven Parish Church, Princess Anne County (Philip White, after
George C. Mason)

At Smithfield, in Isle of Wight County, stands the most complete and
authentic of Virginia churches of the seventeenth century: the 'Old
Brick' or Newport Parish Church (fig. 124). According to well-founded
tradition it was built in 1682* by Charles and Thomas Driver, master
masons, under the direction of Colonel Joseph Bridger. Though it lacks
flying buttresses, pinnacles, and spires, Old Brick is the most convincingly
Gothic church of the Colonial period, its every detail speaking of the
small parish churches of the late medieval period in England. Down the
side were deep wall buttresses with sloping set-offs and round-arch windows equipped with crude tracery in brick forming pointed lancets.

The walls, over 2 feet thick, were laid in rough Flemish bond, and at
the west end (fig. 125) was a massive tower, 20 feet square, rising in three
stages to the belfry. The base of the tower was probably left open as a
porch (fig. 126), and over the round-arch opening was a curious triangle,
a sort of embryo pediment, originally a panel of white plaster but now a
marble tablet commemorating the church's restoration.

* A date of 1632 has long been claimed. This is based chiefly on an inscribed brick
removed from one wall (and now set in the chancel woodwork) alleged to read '1632,'
but the '3' is vague and is more probably an '8.' Modern scholarship, weighing a great
deal of other evidence, places the date at 1682. See G. C. Mason, op.cit. pp. 192–7;
Thomas T. Waterman: 'The Bruton Church and Two Contemporaries,' *Journal of the
American Society of Architectural Historians*, vol. IV, nos. 3–4, July–Oct. 1944, pp. 43–6.

124. Newport Parish (Old Brick) Church, Smithfield, Va., 1682, from the southeast (John O. Brostrup, HABS)

125. Newport Parish Church from the southwest (John O. Brostrup, HABS)

The original interior features have completely disappeared, but there seems to have been a rear gallery supported by a massive beam. In size, the church was similar to that at Jamestown. The restored wine-glass pulpit and sounding board are of the colonial period.

This building was used for Anglican services for 150 years. In 1828 a young deacon renamed it ' St. Luke's,' but since this name was never validated by consecration or action of the vestry and the church was closed only four years later, the old name seems the more proper one. After its abandonment in 1832 the church fell into ruin, climaxed by the collapse of the roof and a part of the east gable on a stormy night in 1886. But this disaster resulted in a rebuilding and restoration of the church in the early

126. Plan of Newport Parish Church (Philip White)

'nineties, and it is maintained as a public monument by the Association for the Preservation of Virginia Antiquities.

One other seventeenth-century church seems to have been of the Gothic type. Excavations recently completed at Williamsburg show the close similarity of the second Bruton Parish Church, built in 1683, to the Old Brick Church at Smithfield. It was of the same size, there were the same wall buttresses, and quite possibly it was directly influenced by the church completed the preceding year. A crude sketch of the building made in 1701 by the Swiss traveler Francis Louis Michel shows that the end gables, instead of being crow stepped, were of the Flemish-gable shape used on Bacon's Castle. Only the foundations of this church now remain: after the colonial capital was transferred to Williamsburg in 1699 a much larger church was needed, and the present Bruton Parish Church, a fine Georgian structure, was completed in 1715.

Maryland in the seventeenth century

The seventeenth-century Colonial architecture of Maryland is very similar to that of Virginia. Spread along the Tidewater bays and deep inlets of Chesapeake Bay, and reaching inland along the Patuxent River, a miniature Potomac, are the same story-and-a-half brick houses, the same steep-pitched roofs, the same end chimneys and simple interiors that we have seen along the lower reaches of the James and the York. However, a few distinguishing features mark the Maryland style with a character of its own. Great double chimneys at the ends with little pent-roofed closets built between them, the popularity of the gambrel roof, and an especial delight in glazed brick patterns on the walls give the Maryland Colonial a sprightly individuality.

Indeed the Marylanders seem to have met the rigors of colonial life with a sense of humor. They took pride, to be sure, in their feudal estates such as Tudor Hall, My Lady Sewall's Manor, or Rose Hill, but they also gave to their houses such vigorous and candid names as Hard Bargain, Bachelor's Hope, Thrumcapped, Want Water, Dear Bought, and Peddy Coat's Wish. When William Parrott built himself a small two-room cottage, soon after 1652, it was promptly dubbed Parrott's Cage, and after the dozens of Prospects, Woodlawns, and Cedar Parks in the colonies, it is indeed refreshing to encounter a Maryland plantation named Aha, the Cow Pasture!

Charles I granted the Maryland charter to George Calvert, Lord Baltimore, in 1632, but on Calvert's premature death the settlement of the new colony fell to the second lord, Cecil Calvert, who sent out an expedition in 1634. The ships *Ark* and *Dove* landed on 27 March at a Yoacomico Indian village on the banks of the St. Mary's River, a tributary of the Potomac at tidewater. Instead of ' falling first upon their knees and then upon the aborigines,' the colonists courteously bought the village for certain axes, hatchets, and bolts of cloth, and occupied the long wigwams of the departing Indians as their first houses, converting one of them for use as a chapel.

The village was named St. Mary's. A fort was erected, ' a Pallizado 120 yards square with four flankes,' and a town was laid out in accordance with Lord Baltimore's solicitous instructions. The first houses were undoubtedly wood and thatch cottages such as those at Plymouth and Jamestown. Father Andrew White in his *Relation of Maryland,* published in London in 1635, mentions that excellent bricks were being made, but masonry construction was hampered by the lack of lime for mortar. The difficulty was soon overcome, however, for a letter of 1638 describes the construction of a story-and-a-half frame house with brick foundations and chimneys, and the big brick Governor's Castle was built the next year.

There is some evidence of log construction in Maryland in the seventeenth century. The Assembly enacted in 1669 ' that there be a Logg house Prison Twenty Foot Square Built at Augustine Harmans in Batlemore County.' [26] This was probably a hewn-log structure similar to the blockhouses built in all the colonies. Cabin Neck (after 1650), Cherry Grove (*c*.1670), and Walnut Grove (*c*.1683) all have hewn-log walls covered by hand-riven shingles or clapboards.

Standard frame-and-clapboard construction, with brick nogging, was frequently employed in Maryland, and Forman in his *Early Manor and Plantation Houses of Maryland,* 1634–1800 illustrates several surviving examples. Marylanders frequently used a combination of frame construction in front and rear walls with brick masonry at the ends, as at Clocker's Fancy (*c*.1658) in St. Mary's City. Indeed one brick-ended house has an interesting type of board-and-batten construction in front and rear walls: vertical planks of random widths are covered at the joints by narrow battens with beveled corners. If original, these walls are extremely unusual in the Colonial period. The nearest equivalent is a type of vertical plank siding used in Rhode Island,[27] and it is interesting to know that the house in question, called ' The Ending of Controversie,' was built by one Wenlocke Christison, a Quaker fugitive from the Puritan intolerance of Plymouth to the religious freedom of the Maryland colony. He built his house in Talbot County about 1670, and possibly derived the structural system from New England. But just as likely it came from a similar English form of ' muntin-and-plank ' partition.[28]

But in Maryland as in Virginia the brick house was the ideal. About

127. Make Peace, Somerset County, Md., c.1663 (H. C. Forman, *The Architecture of the Old South,* Harvard University Press)

90 per cent of the brick houses have Flemish-bond masonry; a scattered few use the English or common bond; a very few indeed have an all-header bond, peculiar to Maryland. Particularly characteristic of the Maryland Colonial style is the delight in decorative patterns of glazed bricks. On fully half of the brick houses of the colony there are wall patterns made with burned headers whose glass-like brilliance sparkles when reflecting the sun's rays. Most common is the all-over diamond or diaper pattern, but single or interlocking diamonds, hearts, zigzags, or initials and dates are employed. A notable example is Make Peace (c.1663) in Somerset County (fig. 127), with chevrons or inverted V's on one gable and extensive diamond patterns on both end walls. The English called such work ' black diapering.' This decorative fashion found particular favor along the Eastern Shore, where it is probably a sign of influence from southern New Jersey.

One of the earliest buildings at St. Mary's City was the house erected by Thomas Cornwaleys about 1639. It was the largest house of its time in the colonies and was later (after 1664) the residence of Chancellor Philip Calvert, then of Charles Calvert, third Lord Baltimore, and of the colonial governors. The building was of brick, and the recently excavated foundations reveal an unusual plan, 54 feet square. But the explosion of the governor's arsenal, which included seventeen barrels of gunpowder in the basement, sent the building sky-high in October 1694, and its original architectural form cannot be ascertained.*

The Old State House at St. Mary's was erected for the Provincial Assembly in 1676. This also was destroyed (in 1829), but a reconstruction was made for the Maryland Tercentenary celebration in 1934. The original building, erected by Captain John Quigley 'at a cost of 300,000 pounds of tobacco and cask,' was of brick and built on the cross plan (fig. 128), like Bacon's Castle. It had an open porch some 16 feet square in front, and a balancing stair tower in back with a rear door for access to the garden. The interior contained a single large Assembly Room, 26

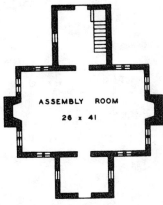

ASSEMBLY ROOM

26 x 41

128. Plan of the Old State House, St. Mary's, Md., 1676 (Philip White, after Forman)

by 41 feet. At each end was a big arched fireplace, and huge 12- by 16-inch beams spanned the ceiling (fig. 129). It should be noticed that the wrought-iron casement windows had leaded rectangular panes, rather than diamond-shaped ones, as did the nearly contemporary Capen House at Topsfield, Massachusetts. Old bricks were used in the restoration, and the interior is furnished and decorated in the seventeenth-century manner.

At the time the State House was built, St. Mary's remained quite bucolic. Charles Calvert described the village of 1678 in his report to the

* The restorations of the building published by Forman, who excavated the foundations, are highly conjectural. With a steep-hipped roof, for which no authority is cited, a balustraded roof deck, and twin chimneys, the building as pictured does indeed resemble the restored Governor's Palace at Williamsburg. But on Forman's evidence, from 1694 to 1836, 'a long time elapsed during which we know exactly nothing about the building.' The restoration of the roof, deck, and cupola is based on fragmentary descriptions in a novel published in 1836. It is hardly necessary to point out that the original roof was probably blown up or burned off in 1694, and that whatever appeared in its place in 1836 could have been the result of eighteenth- or even nineteenth-century reconstruction. A hipped roof in 1639 seems quite incredible. See H. C. Forman, 'The St. Mary's City "Castle," Predecessor of the Williamsburg "Palace,"' *William and Mary Quarterly*, 2nd Series, vol. 22, no. 2 (April 1942), pp. 136–43; and *Architecture of the Old South*, 108–12 and footnote 9, p. 96.

Lords of the Committee of Trade and Plantation as follows: ' There are not above Thirty houses and those at considerable distances from each other, and the buildings, as in other parts of the Provynce, very meane and Little, and generally after the manner of the meanest farm houses in England.' [29] A little later, indeed, St. Mary's was abandoned when Annapolis was laid out as the new capital in 1694. Its buildings quickly vanished and hardly a trace remained until the modern restoration.

129. Assembly Room of the Old State House, St. Mary's, as reconstructed in 1934 (Enoch Pratt Free Library, Baltimore)

The most remarkable seventeenth-century house in Maryland was Bond Castle, in Calvert County (fig. 130). It was built on land granted by Cecil Calvert to Sir John Bond in 1649; the date of the house is not known but is presumed to be within the last quarter of the century. Photographs taken before the demolition of the house reveal it to have been a picturesque and rambling structure, with many gables and wings, as medieval-looking as the House of Seven Gables in Salem. It had a heavy hand-hewn frame, clapboard siding, and steep roofs of various pitches. We may assume that originally the windows were leaded casements, and that there were no dormer windows. The house was of the cross plan, the main block only a story and a half high, but the porches two and a half stories.

Three features of these porches are of exceptional interest. The east porch (shown in fig. 130) had a second-story overhang on two sides, and the west porch one on three sides; there were also gable-end overhangs at the third-floor levels. Such overhangs, common in New England, are all but unknown in the South.* The door to the east porch was topped by a curvilinear head (fig. 131) of a type unknown elsewhere in the colonies, though clearly derived from English Gothic prototypes. The porch itself, with its built-in seats below and porch chamber above, was a feature known elsewhere as we have seen, but its high openings on three

130. Bond Castle, Calvert County, Md., from the southeast (H. C. Forman, *The Architecture of the Old South*, Harvard University Press)

sides screened by turned wooden spindles was, so far as is known, unique in the American colonies, though it was a common and attractive feature of English Gothic houses.

The plan of Bond Castle (fig. 132) shows a central hallway 9 feet wide, with a steep stair in one corner, and two main rooms. The one on the

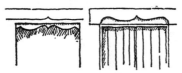

131. Doorheads, east porch of Bond Castle, Md., and Pitchford Hall, England (H. C. Forman, *The Architecture of the Old South*, Harvard University Press)

left, with a fireplace big enough to take 6-foot logs, was doubtless the kitchen-dining room. The two end wings, of different widths and heights, were added later, one to serve as a separate kitchen, the other as a bedroom. The chimneys were probably rebuilt at this time, for they stood further out from the main gables than usual. They had an unusual early decoration: inset double arches such as occur on certain Tudor chimneys

---

* The Cupola House at Edenton, North Carolina (*c.*1715), had a second-story overhang across the front only.

in England. Unique in many of its details, vigorous in its picturesque whole, Bond Castle was an outstanding example of Colonial architecture. It was torn down, only a few years ago, to make room for a farm structure.

Most Maryland houses of the seventeenth century were of the same architectural style and underwent the same type of plan evolution as the farmhouses of Virginia. Representative was Resurrection Manor, in St. Mary's County. When first built, about 1660, this was a one-room house with a steep stair climbing up beside the chimney to the garret (plan,

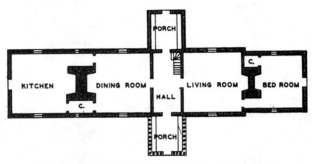

132. Plan of Bond Castle (Philip White, after Forman)

fig. 133). Later a second room was added to form a hall-and-parlor plan, and the line of the addition may still be seen in the brick masonry of the façade (fig. 134). Except for its off-center door and the rectangular (rather than T-shaped) chimneys, Resurrection Manor appears almost a replica of Virginia's Warburton House.

The persistence of this simple architectural type into the eighteenth century is illustrated by Carthagena, built about 1711 in St. Mary's County. The front and end walls of this house were of brick, and the rear wall of frame construction. More advanced in plan than Resurrection Manor, it had a central hall separating the two main rooms, and very

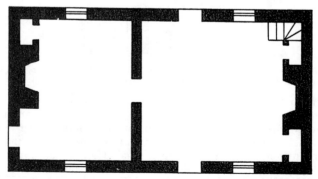

133. Plan of Resurrection Manor, St. Mary's County, Md. (Philip White, after Forman)

narrow back rooms or 'cells' along the rear of the house. Carthagena was torn down in 1934 to provide old brick for the State House restoration.

The rear cells developed to full-sized rooms in the early eighteenth century, to produce a plan like a hall-and-parlor house doubled in depth (fig. 135). This called for two fireplaces at each end of the house. Frequently the chimneys projected outside the end wall, and between them was built a 'chimney-pent,' a very common feature of Maryland

134. Resurrection Manor (H. C. Forman, *The Architecture of the Old South*, Harvard University Press)

Colonial houses. The chimney-pent takes many forms. Most commonly it is a small closet with a shed or pent roof set between the chimneys (fig. 136A). The wall may be built of brick or of wood, and it may be flush with the chimney face or project beyond it. The chimney-pent in effect added to the interior space and, at the same time, buttressed the chimneys and added to the massive appearance of the end wall. Chimney-pents occur outside of chimneys as well as between them (fig. 136B) and in some houses are two stories high, affording closets in each story. The

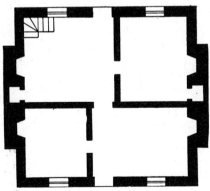

135. Type of four-room plan in early eighteenth-century Maryland houses (Philip White)

chimney-pent is by no means confined to Maryland, occurring in all the southern colonies, and in both the seventeenth and eighteenth centuries; like all other Colonial features, it finds its counterpart in the ' ingle recess ' of English Gothic houses.

The gambrel roof was more popular in Maryland than in any other southern colony. The Maryland gambrel has a distinctive profile, more like the New England than the Flemish type, but with a steeper bottom pitch than either. The earliest example in Maryland may date back to

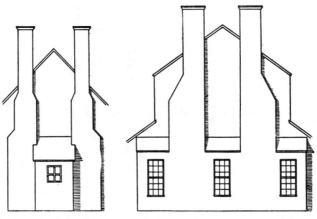

136. Single and triple chimney-pents, St. Mary's County (Philip White, after Forman)

1683,* but the form did not achieve its greatest popularity until the eighteenth century.

Only two of Maryland's seventeenth-century churches survive. One of the vanished churches, however, has a particular interest. The Calverts were of the Catholic faith, and at St. Mary's City was erected, at some time between 1634 and 1638, the first Roman Catholic church built by Englishmen in the New World.[30] Excavations in 1938 revealed the foundations in a Latin cross plan of this brick Chapel of St. Mary, but there was little other evidence from which to conjecture its appearance. In Dorchester County ancient Trinity Church still stands. Built in the late seventeenth century, it is a plain brick edifice with pointed-arch windows, some wall buttresses, and a round apse of almost Romanesque severity. Another survivor of the seventeenth century is the Third Haven Friends' Meeting-House at Easton, built in 1682. It is of wood construction, like its contemporary the Old Ship Church in Hingham, Massachusetts, and

* In *Early Manor and Plantation Houses of Maryland* (1934), Forman illustrated half a dozen gambrel-roofed houses supposedly dating from 1643 to 1676, but since the dates of all of these were uncertain, it seems wise to accept his more cautious inference, in *The Architecture of the Old South* (1948), that the first Maryland gambrel roof is that of Larkin's Hills in Anne Arundel County, which may date as early as 1683 (see p. 151).

in the main room the exposed construction of posts, girts, and beams has a medieval quality.

One of the few cross-plan buildings in Maryland was the Talbot County Court House, built in 1680–81. In a restoration (fig. 137) based on the original specifications for the building in the *Maryland Archives*,[31] we may see the characteristic porch, windows, and end chimneys of the medieval style, but one feature is entirely new: what was called an ' Italian ' or ' hip't ' roof covered the building. If authentic, it was the first hipped roof in the English colonies, forerunner of the favorite roof form of the Georgian style.

137. Conjectural restoration of Talbot County Court House, Md., 1680–81 (H. C. Forman, *The Architecture of the Old South*, Harvard University Press)
138. Newbold-White House, Harvey's Neck, N.C. (Frances Benjamin Johnston)

The Carolinas

A distinctive form of Southern Colonial architecture grew up in the colorful streets of Charleston and its near-by river plantations before the end of the seventeenth century. It was in 1663 that Charles II granted ' Carolina,' a huge tract of land between the Virginia border and Spanish Florida, to ' eight noblemen ' of his court. The first settlers in the Charleston region came under the patronage of Anthony Ashley-Cooper in 1669. Somewhat earlier, squatters from across the Virginia border settled the region of the Chowan River, 300 miles to the north. These widely separated settlements gradually developed into North and South Carolina. Though the distinction in name was used as early as 1691, it was not until 1711 that the colony was officially divided and provided with separate royal governors.

The earliest settlement in what is now North Carolina was made in the region between Albemarle Sound and the Virginia border. A company of men from Jamestown traveled overland to the vicinity of Edenton as early as 1622, and thereafter the region was gradually settled by Virginians: for the most part young men and recently freed indentured servants. By 1665 the entire region was thinly settled. Probably no houses of the seventeenth century remain, but there is record that Governor Yardley of Virginia ordered a frame house of the English type to be built as a compliment to the chief of the Roanoke Indians in 1654.

There is no doubt that other farmhouses were of the Virginia type, built at first of frame, later of brick. One of the earliest surviving examples is the Newbold-White House at Harvey's Neck (fig. 138), built in the early eighteenth century. A story-and-a-half house with steep-gabled roof, Flemish-bond brickwork with glazed headers, central hall and interior end-chimney plan, and small segmental-arched windows, it looks very much like the Warburton House in Virginia. Most of these early houses in North Carolina were destroyed at the time of the Tuscarora War, which almost forced the abandonment of the colony in 1713.

An unusually large number of log cabins survive from the pioneer days

139. Gregg log cabin, Caldwell County, N.C. (Frances Benjamin Johnston)

of North Carolina. These have been well studied and photographed by
Waterman and Johnston [32] and provide us with an exceptionally complete picture of this type of building. After its introduction by the Swedes
in Delaware and — possibly separately — by the Germans in Pennsylvania,
the log cabin became the favorite pioneer dwelling along the expanding
frontier in the eighteenth century. It was especially favored by the re-
sourceful and adaptable Scotch-Irish pioneers who built their farms in the
Piedmont uplands and the valley of Virginia. Thence, as Scotch-Irish,
German, and Quaker settlers pushed down the great valley, they brought
the log cabin to North Carolina.

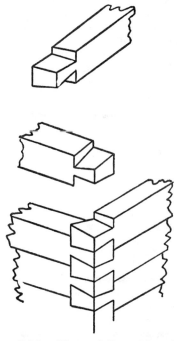

140. Self-draining dovetail joint (Thomas Jefferson Wertenbaker, *The Founding of
American Civilization; The Middle Colonies,* Charles Scribner's Sons)

No very early examples of round-log construction in North Carolina can
be ascertained, but this simple type, requiring little more than an axe and
some skill, was probably the first, temporary, stage of building. William
Byrd of Westover surveyed the Virginia-North Carolina border in 1728
and reported that ' Most of the Houses in this Part of the Country are
Log Houses, covered* with Pine or Cypress Shingles, 3 feet long and one
broad. They are hung upon Laths with Peggs, and their doors to turn
upon Wooden Hinges, and have wooden Locks to secure them, so that the
building is finisht without nails or other Iron-work.' [33]

  * ' Covered ' always meant ' roofed ' in the early accounts.

But round-log construction was soon supplanted by square-hewn beams, and the crude saddle-notched joints, which collected water and eventually rotted, by tighter dovetailed corner joints. Interstices between logs were chinked by stone spalls or wood chips, daubed with clay-and-straw or, in the Moravian buildings at Winston-Salem, clay-and-flax. Chimneys, at first made of wood plastered with clay, were later built of stone and brick. An example dating from about 1726 is the McIntyre Cabin in Mecklenburg County, with wide joints caulked with clay, no windows, and a ladder beside the interior chimney to reach the loft.

The Gregg House in Caldwell County (fig. 139) shows how, somewhat later, the logs were hewn thinner — indeed almost like wide, thick planks — and so carefully dovetailed at the corners that no chinking was needed between them. The topmost logs at the ends of the cabin were projected to carry the wall plate forward, thus offering a modicum of protection from rain to the lower wall. Rain could still gather in an ordinary dovetailed joint, and builders soon evolved an ingenious form of dovetail in which all jointed surfaces sloped outward, thus draining any water that might penetrate the joint (fig. 140).

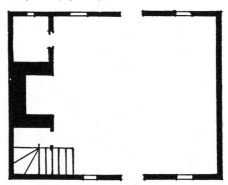

141. One-room log-cabin plan (Thomas T. Waterman, *The Early Architecture of North Carolina*, University of North Carolina Press)

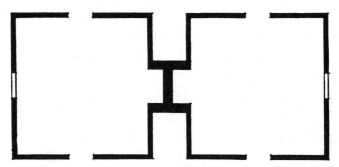

142. ' Saddle-bag ' log-cabin plan (Thomas T. Waterman, *The Early Architecture of North Carolina*, University of North Carolina Press)

The early log cabins were one-room affairs (fig. 141), usually with front and back doors, dirt floors, and small unglazed windows equipped with shutters. Beside the large interior chimney there might be a ladder or stair to the loft and a storage closet on the other side. As more space was

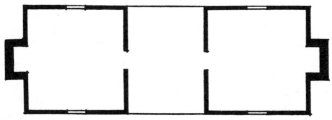

143. 'Dog-run' or 'possum-trot' log-cabin plan (Thomas T. Waterman, *The Early Architecture of North Carolina*, University of North Carolina Press)

needed, this unit was doubled in a back-to-back arrangement, one chim-ney stack serving both halves of the house. In this 'saddle-bag' plan (fig. 142), the units or 'pens' rarely exceeded 24 feet in maximum dimen-sion, this being the practicable limit for finding straight logs without too much taper and for handling them in building. A further step produced a house of two pens, each with its own chimney, and a breezeway between,

144. Typical 'dog-run' cabin, Green River Plantation, Polk County, N.C. (Frances Benjamin Johnston)

the whole covered by the roof (fig. 143). This ' dog-run ' or ' possum-trot ' house plan, probably originating in Virginia, found wide use throughout the South, the breezeway being very convenient for eating and sitting in warm weather, and for curing pelts, storing traps, and sheltering the dogs in winter. When the roof projected amply to shelter walls and even chimneys (fig. 144), the whole formed a very practical and pleasant dwelling.

Far to the South, the Charleston region was settled by a mixture of peoples: English, Irish, Welsh, Scotsmen, Dutchmen from Holland and

145. Early houses of Charleston, S.C. (HABS)

also from New York, migrant New Englanders, and Negroes from Barbados and the West Indies. Perhaps the three dominant strains were the English who first came in 1669, and who were later strongly reinforced by the emigration of Dissenters fearing James II's Catholicism; French Huguenots who fled France at the Revocation of the Edict of Nantes in 1685; and the shrewd and experienced planters who migrated to Carolina from Barbados and became a dominant factor in the infant colony, greatly encouraging its trade with the West Indies in barrel staves, timber, salt meat, and corn, in return for sugar and molasses. Both cotton and indigo were planted in the first year of Charleston's settlement.

It is hard to speak of a ' typical ' early architecture in Charleston, for successive fires have left scarcely a town house built before 1740.[34] But we know that in the earliest years frame construction predominated. It was generally (and correctly) held that frame houses were cooler than those of brick. In 1682, Thomas Newe saw in Charleston about a hundred houses ' wholly built of wood, though there is excellent Brick made, but little of it.' [35] After a disastrous fire in 1740 the Assembly required that all buildings should be constructed of brick and stone, with roofs of slate or tile. It was probably the French Huguenot love of color that gave to these brick houses a stucco coating in many tints of yellow, pink, green, or blue, topped by the red or deep purple of the convex roof tiles. Their simple and straightforward pre-Georgian style was long continued and may still be seen in many of the older streets of Charleston (fig. 145).

West Indian influence may account for the typical house plan: end to the street; rooms strung out in a line, one room deep so as to afford cross-ventilation; and piazzas shading the long side (generally the south or west) and overlooking a small enclosed garden. This Charleston single-

146. Medway, S.C., 1686. Restoration of the original house (H. C. Forman, *The Architecture of the Old South,* Harvard University Press)
147. Original plan of Medway (Samuel G. Stoney, *Plantations of the Carolina Low Country,* Carolina Art Association)

house plan was the best achieved anywhere in the entire South for withstanding a hot climate and, together with the town's sea breezes and relative freedom from malaria-bearing mosquitoes, accounts for the fact that most of the plantation folk took refuge here for the summer.

The piazza may have been introduced from the West Indies, but it developed as a characteristic Charleston form. Those of the colonial period were almost always of one story and were made of wood; the fine iron balconies and rails were a nineteenth-century development. The word ' piazza ' first appears in local documents in 1700, and with increasing frequency after 1750. But definite reference to the two-story piazza does not occur until the end of the eighteenth century.[36]

The cosmopolitan character of Charleston is evident also in the plantation houses along the shores of the Cooper River: of the three earliest, one was built by a Dutchman, one by a French Huguenot, and one by an Englishman. Medway, the oldest recorded house in South Carolina, was built in 1686 by Jan Van Arrsens and, with its crow-stepped gables, is unmistakably Dutch. The original house (figs. 146, 147), now encysted in later additions, already showed the plan destined to become typical in the next century for plantation houses facing a river prospect on one side and a main approach on the land side: doors of equal importance in front and rear, opening into a great entrance hall usurping the larger part of the first floor. The house was originally a story and a half high, with stepped gables at the ends. The locally burned brick, poor in quality, was covered by stucco.

Middleburg, built by Benjamin Simons, a French Huguenot, in 1699, is probably the oldest frame house in South Carolina. The single line of rooms, permitting cross-ventilation, with shading piazzas on both sides, is the basic plan of the Charleston single house (fig. 148). The exterior

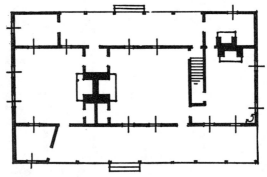

148. Plan of Middleburg, S.C., 1699 (Samuel G. Stoney, *Plantations of the Carolina Low Country,* Carolina Art Association)

is utterly simple, with clapboarded walls and a hipped roof. The porch posts, square to the height of the rail and round above that, do not as yet betray an ambition to be classical columns. Inside, the rooms are plastered on exterior walls, but partitions are sheathed with vertical boarding, and the heavy corner posts and girts project into the room in true Colonial style.

Mulberry, built in 1714, is one of the most provocative houses of the colonial period (fig. 149). Tradition says that Thomas Broughton, planter, politician, and Englishman, modeled his home after Seaton Delaval, the family estate in England designed by the heavy-handed Sir John Vanbrugh. If true, Broughton showed singular prescience, for Seaton was not built until 1718–28. The house was built in the reign of Queen Anne and has been labeled ' Queen Anne,' ' Jacobean,' ' Baroque,' and ' Georgian.' But Mulberry defies this feverish attempt to find a word for it: it seems a sort of melting pot of architectural forms, as diverse in origin as the population of the colony.

The central block, laid up in English-bond brickwork, is straightforward enough: Virginian in flavor, with its gambrel roof ' hipped above the wind-beams.' But what about the flared eaves: were these Flemish in origin, and the iron beam anchors Dutch? Had some Dutchman from New York brought these ideas to Carolina? Even more puzzling are the four almost-detached corner pavilions topped by hipped roofs and bell-shaped turrets. Turrets very similar to these had been used in seventeenth-century France; are they here the memory of some Huguenot emigré? Classical aspirations there are too: modest modillions under eaves, and square porch posts channeled and molded with columnar pretensions. A more practical ambition is blazoned on the awkward pediment: in these

149. Mulberry, S.C., 1714 (Wayne Andrews)

days there was hope of developing silk culture in Carolina — a neighboring plantation was even named Silk Hope — and carved on this pediment is a sprightly sprig of mulberry, framed by a horseshoe! The figures ' 1714 ' pierce the pennons of the fine iron weathervanes surmounting the corner pavilions.

The plan of the main floor (fig. 150) is as distinctive as the exterior.

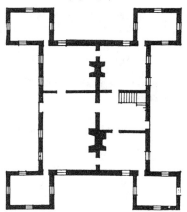

150. Plan of Mulberry (Thomas T. Waterman, *The Dwellings of Colonial America,* University of North Carolina Press)

With single rooms in the corner pavilions and a formal stair hall on axis, it approaches the perfect axial symmetry of Georgian planning, but the reception hall occupies the major portion of the entrance front, permitting only smaller rooms in the other three corners. Waterman attributes this plan, and a few others like it, to French Huguenot influence, and cites a parallel to Francis I's shooting lodge Chalvau, near Fontainebleau; [37] but the corner pavilions and certain other features are also found in Wollaton Hall (1580–88) and Bolsover Castle (1613) in England, and one would have expected Broughton to follow English precedents rather than French. The house commands fine views of the rice fields and the west branch of the Cooper River. The main interior rooms were redecorated about 1800 and are handsome examples of the then-popular Adam style.

Mulberry seems to reveal the transition from Colonial architecture, with its diversity of ethnic traditions, to the unified formality of the eighteenth-century Georgian style. Already the church of St. James at Goose Creek (1711) had revealed the unmistakable influence of Sir Christopher Wren, and the full tide of English Renaissance influence was about to set in. And as though to welcome it, undreamed-of prosperity entered the Carolina Low Country with the developing rice trade. Rice culture is said to have begun in 1686, and within ten years the crop was large enough to tax all available shipping. Rice prosperity, based on slave labor, built an aristocracy of wealth and soon studded the shores of the Ashley and Cooper with fine plantation houses and the streets of Charleston with elegant city residences. South Carolina was made a Crown colony in 1719, and, with secure frontiers and certain wealth, entered its first golden age of architecture in the third and fourth decades of the eighteenth century.

READING SUGGESTIONS

The best single book on Southern Colonial architecture is Henry Chandlee Forman's *The Architecture of the Old South: The Medieval Style,* 1585–1850 (Harvard University Press, Cambridge, 1948). Though many details of text and illustrations are conjectural, the book as a whole is a convincing demonstration of the medieval character of the Colonial style in Maryland, Virginia, the Carolinas, and Bermuda. The best publications on the various colonies are:

Maryland:

   Henry Chandlee Forman, *Early Manor and Plantation Houses of Maryland,* 1634–1800, Easton, Md. 1934.

   Katherine Scarborough, *Homes of the Cavaliers,* Macmillan, New York, 1930.

   Henry Chandlee Forman, *Jamestown and St. Mary's: Buried Cities of Romance,* Johns Hopkins Press, Baltimore, 1938.

Virginia:

   T. T. Waterman and J. A. Barrows, *Domestic Colonial Architecture of Tidewater Virginia,* Scribner's, New York, 1932.

T. T. Waterman, *The Mansions of Virginia, 1706–1776*, University of North Carolina Press, Chapel Hill, 1946. Chapter 2 surveys the seventeenth century.

George Carrington Mason, *Colonial Churches of Tidewater Virginia*, Whittet and Shepperson, Richmond, 1945.

Henry Irving Brock, *Colonial Churches in Virginia*, Dale Press, Richmond, 1930. With photographs by Frances Benjamin Johnston.

North Carolina:

T. T. Waterman (text) and F. B. Johnston (photos), *The Early Architecture of North Carolina*, University of North Carolina Press, Chapel Hill, 1941.

South Carolina:

Samuel Gaillard Stoney, *Plantations of the Carolina Low Country*, Carolina Art Association, Charleston, 1938.

Beatrice St. Julien Ravenel, *Architects of Charleston*, Carolina Art Association, Charleston, 1945.

Albert Simons and Samuel Lapham, *Charleston, South Carolina*, American Institute of Architects, Washington, 1927.

Part Two

SPANISH AND FRENCH

COLONIAL ARCHITECTURE

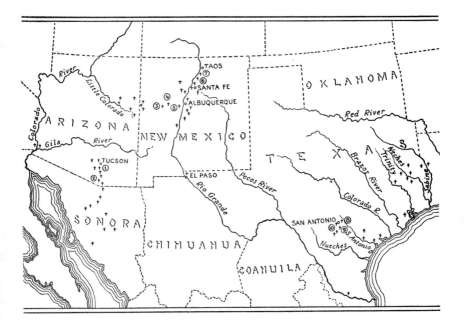

151. Spanish missions of the Southwest. Locations of the more important **missions** and visitás founded before the mid-eighteenth century are shown by crosses. **Several** are now in ruins; those of major architectural importance are numbered as follows:

(1) San Xavier del Bac, Ariz.
(2) San José de Tumacácori, **Ariz.**
(3) San Estevan, Ácoma, N.M.
(4) San José, Laguna, N.M.
(5) San Augustín, Isleta, N.M.
(6) Santo Tomás, Trampas, N.M.
(7) Ranchos de Taos, N.M.
(8) The Álamo, San Antonio, Tex.
(9) San José, San Antonio, Tex.
(10) Purísima Concepción, San **Antonio**

(Van H. English)

6

Florida and the Spanish Southwest

A SCANT TWO YEARS after the English sailed into Jamestown
harbor, 1600 miles away to the west Don Pedro de Peralta, newly
appointed Governor, was building La Villa Real de Santa Fe de San Francisco, capital of the province of New Mexico. Over thousands of miles of
sea and desert, Spanish *comandantes* with the sword and Spanish padres
with the cross were achieving an empire for King and Faith. An immense
gulf separated the forested shores of the Atlantic seaboard from the deso-
late wastes of the Southwest: a gulf of wilderness, inhabited only by Indians; and a gulf of beliefs, customs, and architectural traditions which
the newly arriving colonists were bringing. Spanish Colonial architecture,
as it developed over a period of two and a half centuries and through
thousands of miles of territory, stands entirely apart from the Colonial
and Georgian styles of the eastern seaboard, an exotic and fascinating
chapter in American architectural history.

Long before St. Augustine was founded in 1565, Spanish explorers had
charted almost the entire extent of their future vast empire. In 1535–6
Cabeza da Vaca had penetrated the unknown Rio Grande wilderness to
the region of El Paso, and continued in a wide-sweeping arc through
southern Arizona and western Mexico to Culiacán. Pánfilo de Narváez
had landed at Tampa Bay and marched inland in 1528, and the rash
De Soto with 600 men left Tampa Bay in 1539 to make a three-year overland expedition of thousands of miles through what is now Florida,
Georgia, the Carolinas, Tennessee, Alabama, across the Mississippi and
up it nearly to the Ohio, westward into what was to become Arkansas and
Oklahoma, thence floating down the Arkansas to the Mississippi again,
where he died in 1542. A remnant of his party perished on the plains of
Texas, but another remnant reached Mexico by boat in 1543 to tell of his
fantastic Odyssey.

In the meantime the great Coronado, in search of the legendary seven
golden cities of Cíbola, traversed the mountains and plains of Arizona,
New Mexico, Colorado, and Kansas, and in 1542 Cabrillo sailed up the
Pacific coast beyond San Francisco. By 1543, Mexico, which Cortez had
captured only a generation before, was settled to a line about 200 miles
north of Mexico City, and already over 150 Franciscan and Dominican
friars had arrived to spread the faith. These friars were the real founders
of Spanish Colonial architecture in the United States, as it may be seen
today in the five great ' mission fields ': Florida, New Mexico, Arizona,
Texas, and California.

Florida

On 3 April 1513, Ponce de León landed near St. Augustine and claimed for the King of Spain a vast and ill-defined region which he named ' Florida.' His colony lasted only five months because of illness, lack of food, and troubles with the Indians, and no successful settlements were made by the numerous other Spanish explorers of the next half century. But in 1564 three shiploads of French Huguenots, seeking refuge from religious persecution, settled north of St. Augustine and built a triangular fort which they named Fort Caroline. Philip II of Spain could ignore Frenchmen, but he could not endure Protestants; furthermore, the raids of English corsairs on the Spanish treasure fleets passing through the Bahama Channel along the Florida coast were becoming intolerable. In 1565, accordingly, Pedro Menéndez de Avilés, Captain General of the Spanish treasure fleets, equipped a large expedition to establish a defense outpost. Among the 2000 persons embarked on 19 vessels, he brought 26 priests and friars. On 8 September 1565, Menéndez founded St. Augustine. By deceit and trickery he gained the surrender of the French garrison of Fort Caroline, bound the men with ropes, and then, as he was ' directed by the grace of God,' had them stabbed to death.

Menéndez built a crude fort of earth and logs, which he named San Juan de Pinos. Twenty years later, when Sir Francis Drake occupied the fort during a night attack in 1586, one of his officers, Lieutenant Cates, wrote:

When the day appeared, we found it built all of timber, the walles being none other but whole Mastes or bodies of trees set upright and close together in manner of a pale, without any ditch as yet made, but wholly intended with some more time . . . The platforme whereon the ordinance lay, was whole bodies of long pine trees, whereof there is great plentie, layd acrosse one on another, and some little earth amongst. There were in it thirteen or fourteene great peeces of Brasse ordinance, and a chest unbroken up, having in it the value of some two thousand pounds sterling . . .[1]

Drake sacked and burned the fort and town, but after his departure for Roanoke Island the inhabitants came back from the woods and rebuilt.

In 1593 12 Franciscan friars arrived, and over a period of years the Spanish founded some 40 missions, stretching along the east coast from St. Catherine's Island to Miami, and along a westerly trail from St. Augustine to the Gulf. Only one Spanish priest lived at each mission, teaching the Indians cattle raising and agriculture as well as Christian doctrine. A catechism in the Indian language was printed. One of the most important missions was on the island of Guale, some 50 miles north of St. Augustine, but there were others at Tolomato, Topquini, and New Smyrna. The missions were built of stone and wood, but, except for the ruined walls of the mission at New Smyrna, virtually nothing of the Florida mission buildings remains today.

Indian attacks and pirate raids on St. Augustine continued through the first century of its history, and it is reported that nine different forts of wood and earth were built. The raid of Captain John Davis, an English buccaneer, in 1668, and the founding of Charleston by the English in 1670 conspired to convince the King of Spain that a stronger fort was needed, and in 1672 a great stone fort was started.

The Castillo de San Marcos at St. Augustine, one of the most impressive monuments of Spanish architecture in the United States, was started on 2 October 1672. By 1675 three walls were completed and a wooden palisade enclosed the fourth side, but it was not until 1756 that the bastions, moat, and outworks as we see them today were finally completed.

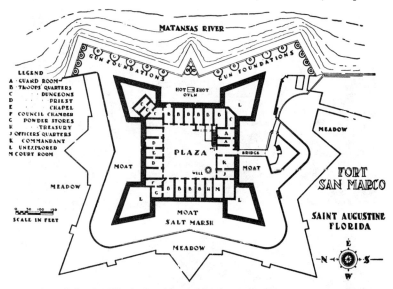

152. Plan of the Castillo de San Marcos, St. Augustine, Fla., 1672–1756 (Rexford Newcomb, *Spanish Colonial Architecture in the United States*, J. J. Augustin)

Built by Indians, slaves, soldiers, and townspeople, the fortress is massively constructed of blocks of coquina limestone, a soft gray-white stone quarried on near-by Anastasia Island, cemented with an oyster-lime mortar. The plan (fig. 152) shows an open courtyard or plaza about a hundred feet square, surrounded by casemates with heavy vaulted ceilings to support the artillery platforms above. In these rooms were located a chapel, barracks, magazines, officers' quarters, a council chamber, storerooms, and several gloomy dungeons. The outer walls or 'curtains' were 25 feet high and 12 feet thick at the base, sloping to 7 feet thick at the top.

In one corner of the courtyard was a wide ramp, now converted to a flight of steps, up which artillery was drawn to the top (fig. 153). The platform or *terreplein,* 40 feet wide, was surrounded by a parapet pierced for 64 guns. At the four corners were triangular shaped bastions with sloping sides to deflect cannon balls, and around the whole was a moat 40 feet wide (fig. 154). The only entrance, through the south wall, was protected by a barbican, drawbridge, and portcullis, and above the latter

may be seen a hole about 5 inches in diameter through which melted lead
could be poured on the heads of attackers.

The Castillo de San Marcos is the best surviving example in the United
States of the European type of fortress that was developed after the advent
of gunpowder in the late Middle Ages. Retaining many medieval features, it has the lower, sloping walls and projecting bastions developed to
counter artillery fire, and popularized in the seventeenth century by the

153. Plaza and stairway to the *terreplein,* Castillo de San Marcos (J. Carver Harris
photo, courtesy National Park Service)

French military engineer Marshall Vauban after whom they were named
' Vauban bastions.' The cost of the fort was some 30 million dollars, a sum
which is said to have caused the King of Spain to remark that ' its curtains and bastions must be made of solid silver.' Nonetheless the fortress
served him well, withstanding attacks by the English in 1702, 1728, and
1740.

The Spanish built other forts in Florida, but none so large or formidable. Fifteen miles south of St. Augustine stand the ruins of Fort Matanzas,
built of stone in 1736. It is medieval in plan, with a keep, and is a most
impressive sight rising out of its lonely marshes. Fort San Carlos was built
in Pensacola in 1698 of pine logs, but it was rebuilt of brick in 1783.

The only church building in Florida surviving from the Spanish period is the Catholic Cathedral in St. Augustine, built in 1793–7, very near
the end of the Spanish regime. A serious fire in 1887 left little but the

coquina limestone walls, and the subsequent restoration, with added tran-sept, tower, and pierced gable belfry, hardly gives an authentic picture of the original edifice. We can imagine how it must have looked, however, for many drawings of the cathedral exist, and the architect's name is known.

The ' Oldest House ' in St. Augustine is probably typical of the Spanish domestic architecture of the eighteenth century. Sometimes alleged to have

154. Air view of the Castillo de San Marcos (J. Carver Harris photo, courtesy National Park Service)

been built in 1564, it was more probably built in 1763; at least there is an unbroken chain of titles since that date. It is a simple two-story struc-ture, the thick lower wall built of coquina limestone, the second story of frame construction with clapboard siding. A hipped roof covers second-story porches at each end. Interiors have low ceilings, hand-hewn cedar beams, and large fireplaces.

Florida passed to Britain in 1763, was receded to Spain in 1783, and then remained Spanish until the American occupation in 1821. But com-paratively few early buildings survived and the Spanish architectural tra-dition virtually died out in Florida until its revival as an eclectic fashion in the late nineteenth and twentieth centuries.

New Mexico

The Spanish Colonial architecture of New Mexico is markedly differ-ent from that of the other mission fields. Less magnificent than the ba-

roque architecture of Texas or Arizona, simpler and more primitive than
the missions of California, the unique character of the New Mexican missions resides in their almost perfect blend of Indian and Spanish influences. The churches are Spanish in plan and general form, but they owe
much of their construction and decorative detail to the traditions of the
Pueblo Indians.

The Indian pueblos are of great antiquity, many of them dating back
to the great period A.D. 900–1200. The Indians, agricultural rather than
nomadic, built huge communal edifices of stone and adobe, locating them

155. San Geronimo de Taos, Taos, N.M., c.1540? (Wayne Andrews)

near their fields and filling them well with stores of food. Defense
against the savage Apache and other nomadic warriors was the prime factor in determining the plan and form of the pueblo building. The dwellings were built in receding terraces, four and five stories high, with the
inner and lower rooms used for storage, and the outer ones for living
quarters (fig. 155). There were in ancient times no doors in the lowest
story, access to the roof being by ladders which could be drawn up for
defense, and thence by other ladders or flights of steps to the various
levels.

Where ledge stone was available, flat slabs were laid in adobe mortar,
sometimes chinked by stone wedges or spalls. But more usually the walls
were of adobe — clay heaped up and molded into shape in stratified layers
and dried by the sun. Surfaces were hand-smoothed by a coating of adobe
plaster, made of wetter, thinner clay, and walls were often coated with
white gypsum.

The tops of the walls were spanned by round logs, called *vigas,* carrying smaller poles across them and a layer of rushes or branches or closely
spaced split sticks on which to rest the thick layer of clay that formed the
flat roof. Since the *vigas* were cut laboriously with primitive stone axes

and often brought from considerable distances, they were not lightly discarded, and old logs were often re-used in new construction. If they happened to be too long, the ends were simply allowed to project outside the wall, thus producing a characteristic, if accidental, feature of the pueblo style.

Roof surfaces sloped gradually to provide drainage, the water being carried by water spouts (*canales*) outside the wall. Windows were small, few, unframed, and unglazed; a pit in the floor with a smoke hole in the roof served as fireplace, and there were only hides or blankets to close doorways. Such were the Indian pueblos that the arriving Spanish found at Ácoma and Isleta, Quarai, Taos, Pecos, Zia, and elsewhere in New Mexico.

Coronado had come to the region as early as 1540, but it was more than half a century before the Spanish attempted a permanent settlement. In 1598 Don Juan de Oñate, wealthy mine owner of Zacatecas, equipped an expedition of some 400 soldiers and settlers, 83 wagons and carts, and about 7000 head of stock. On 11 July he established the first Spanish settlement in New Mexico at a Tewa Indian village on the west bank of the Rio Grande about 30 miles north of Santa Fe. Oñate named it San Juan de los Caballeros, and a church named San Juan Bautista was dedicated on 8 September. The province was divided into seven mission districts, under the direction of eight Franciscan friars. While governor, Oñate made exploratory trips — one as far east as the present Wichita, Kansas, and another westward to the Gulf of California. Secret accusations launched against him in Mexico City and faraway Madrid caused his resignation in 1607. The Viceroy in Mexico appointed Don Pedro de Peralta Governor in 1609.

Peralta, acting on instructions, founded a new capital at Santa Fe in the winter of 1609–10, and between 1610 and 1614 he built the Governor's Palace, the oldest surviving non-Indian building in the United States. The palace was the most important unit in the presidio, a rectangular walled enclosure measuring some 400 by 800 feet and containing barracks, chapel, offices, magazines, and prisons. The palace itself (fig. 156) was a long, low structure facing an open plaza at the south, fronted by a *portal* (covered porch) supported on wooden posts. The building was done by Indians, but already the white men had introduced an improvement on the prehistoric method of building: the clay was precast in wooden boxes to form large sun-dried adobe bricks. The *portal* with its bracket capitals was a Spanish feature; so also was the central enclosed *patio* (plan, fig. 157) and the framing of doors and windows with wood, but the flat roof and projecting *vigas* were of Indian origin. After 1692 twenty-eight successive Spanish governors lived here; after them, Mexican governors, and then American territorial governors from 1846 to 1907. The building was restored in 1909 to house the Museum of New Mexico.

The Spanish authorities were soon disappointed in New Mexico as a source of gold, and the province became primarily a venture in missionary work and frontier protection. By 1626 43 churches had been built and some 34,000 Indians converted to Christianity. The Franciscan padres trudged hundreds of miles across the desert, establishing mission outposts eastward as far as Pecos, north along the Rio Grande to Taos, westward to Zuni and the Hopi pueblos in northern Arizona, and southward to El Paso del Norte (fig. 151). They introduced new crops and livestock, instructed the Indians in agriculture, crafts, and music. The seventeenth century was the great era of mission building.

156. Palace of the Governor, Santa Fe, N.M., 1610–14 (Wayne Andrews)

But while the friars taught Christian love and brotherhood, the Spanish governors and soldiers levied tribute, forced labor, and imposed cruel punishments and imprisonment. Indian resentment culminated in the widespread and well-organized Pueblo Revolt of 10 August 1680. Some

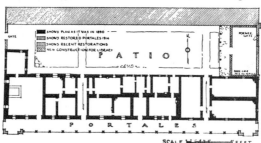

157. Plan of the Governor's Palace, Santa Fe (Rexford Newcomb, *Spanish Colonial Architecture in the United States,* J. J. Augustin)

400 Spaniards, including 22 padres, were killed; a band of about a thousand survivors, men, women, and children, besieged in the presidio at Santa Fe, broke out on 21 August, and fled 400 miles southward to El Paso. For thirteen years there were no Spaniards in New Mexico; the mis-

sions were destroyed or allowed to fall into ruin, the haciendas were sacked. It was not until 1692 that de Vargas, with 300 men, reconquered the province. Most of the missions were re-established by 1695, and gradually their ruins were rebuilt. The eighteenth century was an era of renewed and more intensive Spanish colonization.

The New Mexican mission churches of the seventeenth and eighteenth centuries were built by Indians. The Franciscan padres who directed their labors must have had recollections of the baroque architecture of Spain with its great vaulted and domed churches, and its ornate and colorful carving in stone and wood, but they were confronted by unskilled and ignorant laborers and had, perforce, to modify their architectural ambitions to the abilities of the workmen and the materials which they could procure. It is striking that no arches, vaults, or domes were used in the mission churches of New Mexico.* It was probably thought safer to avoid arched construction in so easily weathered a material as adobe, and, in churches built of stone, arches were perhaps not used because the Indians did not know how to cut and trim stones into the precise shapes of voussoirs. The remoteness and scarcity of lumber and the difficulty of shaping it into arched centering probably also account in some measure for the simple post-and-lintel structural system employed.

On the other hand, it is known that the Spaniards brought iron tools with them: a contract made in Mexico City in 1621 provided ' that there should be given each friar, the first time that he went to the province, a quantity of tools and materials for building his church. These included . . . ten axes, three adzes, three spades, ten hoes, one medium-sized saw, one chisel, two augers, and one plane. A large latch for the church door, two small locks, a dozen hinges, some small latches, and 6,000 nails of various sizes. . .' [2] The introduction of axes and adzes had important effects, for *vigas* could now be hewn square, corbels and capitals cut in more elaborate forms, and window and door frames made of wood. In general, women and children built the adobe walls, as they had in the pueblos; the men considered this beneath their dignity but took readily to carpentry and woodwork, and we can imagine how delighted they must have been with the new axes and other tools.

Building a mission church was a laborious undertaking (fig. 158). Each friar directed the enterprise as best he could, choosing the site, laying out the plan, and superintending the construction and decoration. The church with its high walls and large interior space was a more difficult building problem than any Indian pueblo, and the friars had to be ingenious in working out methods of construction. There is no evidence that block and tackle were available, and in order to raise the heavy logs for the roof structure one wall of the church was usually built thicker than the other, to serve as a working platform and possibly as a fulcrum for levering the *vigas* into place. The walls rose often to a height of 35 feet. Consequently they had to be much thicker than the walls of the pueblos. At Ácoma one

* Kubler cites one or two arched doorways but believes they are late in date and probably the result of remodelings. *The Religious Architecture of New Mexico*, pp. 38, 48.

wall was over 7 feet thick, the other almost 5. They tapered upward, diminishing as much as 30 inches in thickness to the top, giving a characteristic slanting or ' battered ' exterior silhouette.

The Indian women kneaded the clay with hoes and bare feet, mixing it with straw or manure as a binder, in the form boxes or *adoberos*. The adobe bricks thus formed were large — about 10 by 18 inches, and 5 inches thick, each one weighing 50 or 60 pounds. After drying a day or two in the sun they were turned out of the forms, and later stacked in piles. When stone was used, as at Laguna, Abo, Giusewa, and in the foundations and lower courses at Ácoma, it was in broken flat fragments, laid in the manner of the prehistoric pueblos.

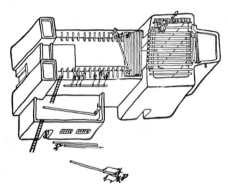

158. Building a New Mexican mission in the seventeenth century (George Kubler, *Religious Architecture in New Mexico*, The Taylor Museum)

At the top of the wall, heavy brackets or corbels were set into the adobe to act as bearing surfaces for the transverse *vigas*; they were usually cut in elaborate scrolled forms (see fig. 165) and painted in strong colors. The *vigas* spanning the nave were well over 30 feet long — at Ácoma one 42 feet long has been found — and they were sometimes brought from great distances. Sometimes they were left in the round, as at Ácoma, Laguna, and Trampas; for other churches the Indian axemen hewed them square and painted the sides with floral or geometric ornament. The *vigas* were spaced a few feet apart and across them were laid ceiling boards — roughhewn planks sometimes painted on the nether side — or cedar poles (*savinos*) laid in a herringbone pattern. On these rested the adobe roof, 6 inches to a foot thick and weighing many tons. The roof was surrounded by a parapet several feet high, and in the seventeenth century this was often crenelated, adding to the fortress-like appearance of the massive nave. The roof surface was pitched slightly, and drained by *canales* projecting through the parapet. When a roof began to leak, more adobe was piled on.

The characteristic features of plan, exterior, and interior of the New Mexican mission churches may best be seen in particular examples, and of these the most impressive is the great church of San Estevan at Ácoma.

' Sky-crowned Ácoma,' an ancient pueblo built in the dangerous days of nomadic invasions, crowns a rugged flat-topped mesa rising 350 feet above the surrounding desert. For centuries the Ácoma Indians lived here, tilling their crops on the plain below, and carrying all fuel and food by a tortuous path — punctuated by steps and ladders — to the refuge in the sky. Coronado visited it in 1540, and in 1629 Padre Juan Ramírez, trudging on foot and alone for scores of miles, came to the mesa to found a mission.

The church, a-building for many years, was perhaps completed in 1642, and it must have been a herculean task, for all materials were carried on

159. The *convento* and church from the northeast, San Estevan, Ácoma, N.M. (Laura Gilpin)

the backs of Indians up the steep trail, and another longer one, El Camino del Padre, which Ramírez built. Timbers for the roof, 14 inches square and some 40 feet long, are said to have been brought from the San Mateo mountains 30 miles away. Soil for a burial ground, and for the padre's garden in the patio — beautifully described in Willa Cather's *Death Comes for the Archbishop* — was brought up from the valley.

The church faces east, and its façade (fig. 159) consists of a bare wall penetrated only by the entrance door and a window to light the choir loft. The square flanking towers project boldly from the side walls and rise to belfries with rectilinear openings, reached by a winding stairway in a circular shaft in the south tower. On the north side of the church is the domicile or *convento,* with enclosed patio, living rooms, workrooms, storerooms, and balcony (fig. 160).

In New Mexico in the seventeenth century, [Kubler reports] the *conventos* were inhabited by one friar and in exceptionally large pueblos, such as Ácoma and Giusewa, by two . . . The persons employed in the service of the establishment varied between six and twelve, usually including a bell ringer, a cook, two or three sacristans, a porter, two boys for the service of the friars' cells, two or three women to grind corn, and occasionally a gardener. These were of course all Indians, and a few of them lived in the *convento* itself.[3]

The church at Ácoma presents an imposing sight from the southwest with its lofty, battered walls, strong towers, and the *vigas* projecting in a random pattern to throw slanting shadows across its pitted walls. Patches of adobe plaster have crumbled away to reveal the rough fieldstones of the foundation and lower wall and the large adobe bricks above. The plan (fig. 161) is coffin-shaped, with a long nave narrowed at the west end

160. Balcony of the *convento*, San Estevan (HABS)

to a polygonal sanctuary. There are no transepts, but the patio of the *convento* is surrounded by a covered walk — an unaccustomed luxury in New Mexico. Over the front entrance is a choir loft, with a great transverse beam resting on decorated corbels and supported by two posts with bracket capitals.

Inside, the nave is cool, dim, and spacious, the walls whitened with

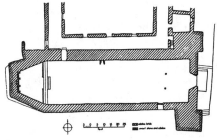

161. Plan of San Estevan (George Kubler, *Religious Architecture in New Mexico*, The Taylor Museum)

gypsum (figs. 162, 163). Almost always in New Mexican churches there are few windows, and these high up and usually on the side of the *convento,* but here they are in the opposite wall (section, fig. 164). The corbels are cut in vigorous, heavy curves and painted to give a barbaric splendor to the roof. The Pueblo Indians, who had made mural paintings in black, white, blue-green, yellow, and red for their prehistoric *kivas* or ceremonial chambers, were sometimes allowed by the padres to project their ancestral art on the walls of a Christian mission. Typical painted corbels may be

162. Interior toward the sanctuary, San Estevan (Mitchell Wilder photo, courtesy The Taylor Museum)

seen in figure 165, and at Ácoma the end wall of the sanctuary is adorned by a great painting, simulating in crude and vigorous forms the carved and painted reredos over the altar in Spanish baroque churches.

One of the most remarkable features of the New Mexican churches is a transverse clerestory window located so that, though invisible from the nave, it throws a mysterious light on the sanctuary and altar. Figure 158 shows how, in a typical church, the transept roof was raised a few feet higher than the nave roof. This permitted the introduction of a low horizontal window over the nave roof, light from which would flood the sanctuary. Such clerestory windows are unknown elsewhere in Spanish Colonial architecture, or indeed in Christian architecture anywhere in the world, and they seem to have been an invention of the Franciscan padres of New Mexico. Perhaps they were thinking of the great domes, ringed with windows, that crowned the crossings of Spanish baroque churches and flooded the transepts and choir with light. Unable to achieve so difficult a structural feat, their substitute was simple and ingenious, and perhaps more impressive to the Indian congregation in the nave of the church because of its very mysteriousness. Ácoma originally had such a transverse clerestory window, but it was damaged in the Pueblo Revolt of 1680 and was probably eliminated in repairs to the roof made after the reconquest in 1692.

These clerestory windows account for the unconventional orientation of the New Mexican churches. In most of them, the façade faces the east

163. Corbels and *vigas,* San Estevan (HABS)

and the sanctuary and altar are at the west, a reversal of the customary Catholic practice. A typical day at the mission began with early morning services, and who can doubt that the padres, with their Spanish sense for the dramatic, had planned the whole church edifice so that through the concealed overhead window the whole altar and sanctuary would be mys-

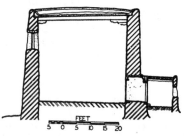

164. Cross section of the nave, San Estevan (George Kubler, *Religious Architecture in New Mexico,* The Taylor Museum)

teriously illumined by the light of the morning sun? The handling of light as an active element in architectural effect was a prime interest in the baroque churches of Italy and Spain.

So also was the construction of walls or colonnades converging slightly to enhance the perspective illusion of depth. There are New Mexican churches with nave walls that are not parallel to each other, and occasionally the rear wall of the sanctuary is skewed away from the right angle to the main axis, notably in the churches at Laguna and Ranchos de Taos. Floors also slant upward — or downward — toward the altar. It is possible that these curious divergences from the normal rectilinear plan were an attempt to play with perspective effects, but the reason is not certainly known.

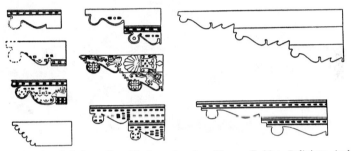

165. Painted corbels from New Mexican churches (George Kubler, *Religious Architecture in New Mexico,* The Taylor Museum)

Mission San José at Laguna was founded in 1699, by Governor Cubero, and the church was completed in 1706. It is named for a former lake, some miles west of Albuquerque. The walls are of coarse stones laid in thick adobe mortar, surfaced by fine adobe plaster. The façade (fig. 166) is of the simplest New Mexican type: a plain wall, with entrance doors and a window to the choir loft, and a shaped parapet at the top pierced for two bells. In front is a walled forecourt or *atrio,* used for outdoor mass on Sundays and feast days. The low buildings of the *convento* (plan, fig. 167) may be seen at the left of the façade, and at the right is a one-story baptistery — a small room, entered by double doors from the front end of the church, and containing an adobe baptismal font. Some of the smaller New Mexican mission churches had a balconied façade: the floor joists of the interior choir loft projected through the façade to support an exterior balcony, which may have been used for the outdoor services.

On entering the church at Laguna (fig. 168) one sees immediately overhead the choir loft, supported by its massive crossbeam resting on carved corbels, and above the log joists, cedar poles laid herringbone fashion — a survival of prehistoric ways. The nave has only three windows, high up on the left side, and is roofed by the usual *vigas* resting on carved corbels. Laguna has also the most remarkable mural paintings of any of the New Mexican missions. Along the nave walls, at dado height, are crude but vigorous motives from Pueblo Indian mythology: sun, rain, and

thunder symbols. The sanctuary (fig. 169) with converging walls, as at
Ácoma, is completely covered by floral arabesques, panels of saints and of
the Trinity, symbols of the sun and moon, great scrolls and spirally
twisted columns, an extraordinary and skilful blend of Indian and Spanish baroque motives. It resembles a painted replica of the great carved

166. San José, Laguna, N.M., 1699–1706, façade and *atrio* (Laura Gilpin)

stone altar screens of Spain, though the immediate models were doubtless
Mexican churches of the seventeenth century.

The Indians' love of color and symbolism was satisfied also by numerous pictures and carvings. Some European originals were doubtless
brought over, but soon, working under the direction of the missionaries,
the Indians made primitive copies and, as time went on, they relied more

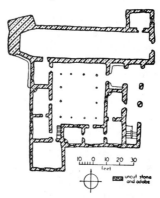

167. Plan of church and *convento*, San José (George Kubler, *Religious Architecture
in New Mexico*, The Taylor Museum)

168. San José, the nave, with choir loft over entrance (Laura Gilpin)

169. The sanctuary and altar, San José (Laura Gilpin)

and more on their own conceptions. Images of the saints, called *bultos,* were carved of soft wood, coated with gesso, and painted. Painted images, called *santos,* were made on smooth wood panels covered with gesso, on canvas, or even on skins or tin, in the earth colors and vegetable dyes used by the Indians since prehistory.

Mission Santo Tomás at Trampas, though small, has a more complex plan than the churches at Ácoma and Laguna. The façade has no towers,

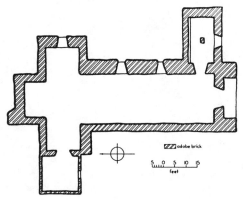

170. Plan of Santo Tomás, Trampas, N.M. (George Kubler, *Religious Architecture in New Mexico,* The Taylor Museum)

but projecting buttresses at the sides enclose a recess containing an outdoor balcony at the choir-loft level. The plan (fig. 170) shows one thick nave wall and one thin one, and a baptistery opening from the front end of the nave. The church has transepts separating the nave from the sanctuary, and beside one transept a small sacristy, a not uncommon feature in the New Mexican missions. It is usually a small room, containing a cupboard and rack for church vessels and vestments, a small altar, and sometimes a fireplace.

The interior (fig. 171) has a floor of hand-hewn wooden slabs in place of the more common adobe. Otherwise, it is very typical of the mission churches, with its gypsum-whitened walls, few windows, choir loft, and the heavy carved corbels at the ceiling. Where mural paintings were lacking, carved and painted woodwork constituted the chief decoration. Doors were often the simple batten type, of heavy planks, but sometimes they were paneled, carved, or set with spindles. Since iron hinges were rare, doors were pivoted on round wooden pins that fitted into sockets in the sill and lintel. Windows, never glazed in the early days, were often barred by wooden spindles, between which sheets of mica or talc were set; there might be wooden shutters on the inside. There were also carved capitals topping the posts that supported choir loft or *portal,* brilliantly painted chancel screens, and choir balustrades.

The church at Ranchos de Taos (figs. 172, 173) was built as late as 1772. With its boldly projecting transepts and massive buttress at the west end, the windowless walls of the sanctuary, and the soft-contoured irregularities of the adobe wall, it is almost like a piece of abstract sculpture. Buttresses were often added to the seventeenth-century churches as a reinforcement to disintegrating adobe walls, but they were commonly built *de novo* in the eighteenth century.

Comparatively little is known about the Spanish Colonial domestic architecture of New Mexico, but judging from nineteenth-century survivals the houses were usually built around a central patio, which afforded communication from room to room, and which might be sur-

171. Santo Tomás, the nave toward entrance and choir loft, c.1760 (Laura Gilpin)

rounded by a covered *portal*. Fireplaces were often built into the corners of rooms. *Vigas* spanning the ceiling were carved or painted in the finer houses. There were many carved and paneled chests (*cajas*) for clothes and food, and high carved cupboards (*trasteros*) with grilled or paneled doors. Poorer households might have only one handsome chair, reserved for the infrequent visits of the priest and handed down from father to son. Homes of the wealthy *hacendados* in the valley of the Rio Grande were naturally bigger and finer, sometimes of two stories, but they shared with all other architecture of New Mexico the rectangular masses, the flat roofs, soft contours, and the projecting *vigas* shadowing white, lively surfaced walls under the southwestern sun.

In the late eighteenth century New Mexico began to lose its two-century-old isolation. A trail from Santa Fe to San Antonio was traced in 1787, and in 1792 a French frontiersman made the first round trip to St.

172. Façade of church, Ranchos de Taos, N.M., 1772 (Wayne Andrews)

173. Church, Ranchos de Taos, from the west (Wayne Andrews)

Louis over what later became the famed Santa Fe trail. Mexico achieved its independence from Spain in 1821, and, revolting against Church as well as King, withdrew all support from the missions. By 1832 a visitor to New Mexico could report that the churches were ' almost destroyed, and most of them are surely unworthy of being called the temples of God.' [4] In 1834 the Mexican government secularized all the missions, and they gradually fell into disrepair and complete ruin. In the twentieth century, some have been carefully restored, but many others, such as those at Quarai, Abo, and Giusewa, thrust crumbled piles of stone and adobe, as ancient-looking as the cyclopean walls of long-deserted Tiryns and Mycenae, into the lonely sky.

Texas

The vast region which the Spanish called *Tejas* had been visited by explorers many times in the sixteenth and seventeenth centuries, but it was remote — 700 miles from Santa Fe — inhabited by hostile Indians, and considered by the viceregal government in Mexico City an unprofitable ground for missionary work. Spurred by LaSalle's descent of the Mississippi and his building of a French fort on Matagorda Bay in 1685, the Spanish sent an expedition to establish several missions in eastern Texas. The first of these, and the easternmost Spanish outpost, was San Francisco de la Tejas, founded in 1690 at an Indian village some distance south of the present Nacogdoches. In later years, five other East Texan missions were established, between the Trinity and the Sabine Rivers, but they were not successful. Their growth impeded by the hostility of the Indians and intermittent fights with the French, they were ultimately abandoned. The mission buildings, of wood, have long since disappeared.

In the meantime, missionary and colonizing activity continued in the safer southern and central sections of the province. A dozen missions, ranging from San Saba (near Abilene) in the north to the mouth of the Rio Grande, over 400 miles south, were established by 1731 (map, fig. 151). Seven of these, widely scattered, have disappeared completely; the remaining five are all in the vicinity of San Antonio, which has sometimes been called the ' mission capital of Texas ' (or ' of the world ' by some Texans).

The Texan missions, like those of New Mexico and California, were founded by Franciscan friars. Outstanding among these was Fray Antonio Margil, a man of exceptional energy and administrative ability. He had founded the Franciscan College at Zacatecas, Mexico, and served two terms as its president. He then became *padre presidente* of the Texan mission field and between 1716 and 1722 founded, or re-established after temporary abandonment, a total of nine missions. Hallenbeck says of him: ' In ability, industry, and intellectual calibre Margil deserves to rank next to Junípero Serra of the California field.' [5] He died in 1726, and his ashes repose in the Cathedral of Mexico City.

San Antonio and its most famous mission, the Álamo, were founded in 1718 when Don Martín de Alarcón, Spanish Governor of the province of Texas, arrived with 72 soldiers, friars, and settlers, and almost 2000 head of livestock. He was accompanied by Fray Antonio Olivares, who founded the mission of San Antonio de Valero, named in honor of the Marquis de Valero, Viceroy of Mexico, but later called San Antonio de los Álamos because of a group of cottonwood trees in the vicinity. To Americans it is more famous simply as ' the Alamo,' scene of the last desperate fight of 150 Texans, including Davy Crockett and Colonel James Bowie, in the Texan War of Independence in 1836.

The Álamo mission was primarily an Indian school, and it had an extensive enclosure for shops, dwellings, storehouses, et cetera. The mission

174. The Álamo, San Antonio, 1744–57 (Wayne Andrews)

church was begun in 1744 and finished in 1757; during its five short years of existence, it must have seemed a transplanting of European magnificence into the wilds. Its elaborately carved stone portal, with arched doorway flanked by niches and two pairs of spirally fluted columns, may still be seen (fig. 174). Flanking the façade were twin towers, and the nave was covered by a tunnel vault and a fine dome. But the towers, nave vault, and dome collapsed in 1762 and the church was never repaired. It was a roofless ruin, filled with debris, during the siege of 1836. Since then the walls have been restored, a new wooden roof added, and the façade with its present arched top rebuilt, but the Alamo can hardly claim the architectural distinction of some of its neighboring missions.

San José was begun in 1720 and when it was finished in 1731 was the finest of all Spanish Colonial missions. On the very day of its completion three more missions were begun: San Francisco de la Espada, San Juan Capistrano, and La Purísima Concepción. The year 1731 marked the beginning of real growth at San Antonio: a *presidio*, or military stronghold, was established to protect the new mission town, and additional families of colonists arrived. San Antonio became the seat of civil government and the largest settlement in Texas.

The Palace of the Governor (fig. 175) was built 140 years later than its counterpart at Santa Fe and is correspondingly finer in construction. The wall is built of stone rather than adobe mud. Over the magnificent paneled and carved entrance door is a keystone bearing the arms of the Hapsburgs and the date 1749. Wrought-iron grilles bar the windows, and projecting *canales* carry the drain water from the flat roof. The interior has

175. Palace of the Governor, San Antonio, 1749 (Claude B. Aniol)

ten rooms and a large covered *portal* overlooking the patio with its old stone well. Of interest are the two hooded fireplaces in corners of the *Salon de Baile* (ball room), and the handsome reception room with door and windows giving onto the patio. The *comedor* (dining room, fig. 176), with its hooded fireplace, white walls, heavy roof structure, and rough furniture, has a primitive charm. The building was restored in the 1930's and is maintained by the city of San Antonio.

It is probable that the five famous missions of San Antonio were designed by professional builders rather than amateur friars, and that the building was done by skilled artisans. To be sure, Indian neophytes doubtless helped, and we know that they dug the excellent irrigation canals that watered the orchards, gardens, and vineyards, but we also know that some of the beautiful sculptured decorations of San José were done by a Mexican artist, and it seems likely that no friar designed the vaults and domes of San José and the Purísima Concepción. The Texan missions attempt a certain grandeur and opulence rivaled elsewhere in Spanish Colonial architecture only by San Xavier at Tucson. They are closer to Spanish models than the simpler and humbler missions of New Mexico and California.

Spain's architecture throughout the seventeenth century had been dominated by the baroque — a style in which the cold and correct classicism of Philip II had exploded into a riot of disrupted and corrupted classical

176. Dining room, Governor's Palace, San Antonio (Claude B. Aniol)

forms. Columns, entablatures, and pediments were broken into pieces and recombined in novel and forceful ways; façades were swept into swirls and silhouettes made dynamic by reverse curves and spirals. In its drama and in its vivid appeal to the senses, the baroque style was the architectural expression of that Catholic Reaction which was striving through every means to regain some of the ground lost to the Protestant Reformation. Extravagant forms, garish color, brilliant lighting effects, and flickering mural paintings fused with music, incense, and gorgeous ritual to produce a powerful emotional impact. The baroque style was grand opera in architecture.

The latest phase of the style was so remarkably exemplified in the work of one Spanish architect, Manuel Churriguera, that it has received his name and is called the Churrigueresque. This final paroxysm of the early eighteenth century has all the complexity, color, and ornateness of the baroque but is particularly marked by smaller, endlessly interweaving forms and glistening highlighted bits and tips, like the contents of a bait box petrified in stone.

Nowhere in the world — even in Spain or Italy itself — was the baroque

177. San José y San Miguel de Aguayo, San Antonio, 1720–31 (Wayne Andrews)

better done than in Mexico, and from Mexico its influence was felt — in diminishing waves — in the Spanish Southwest. Imperfectly remembered, transmuted by crude materials and unskilled workmanship, it reveals itself in New Mexico only in such details as clerestory lighting or the painted sanctuaries of Ácoma and Laguna. In California it is apparent in a larger number of doorways, altars, windows, and façades. But Spanish influence reached its greatest heights in the missions of Texas and Arizona.

Mission San José y San Miguel de Aguayo at San Antonio was begun in 1720, under the direction of Fray Antonio Margil, with the patronage of the Marquis de Aguayo. It stands four miles south of the Álamo, in Mission Valley. When completed in 1731 it was the most ambitious of the Spanish architectural monuments north of the Mexican border, and in time it became one of the most prosperous missions, though in later years it was surpassed by several in California.

The church (fig. 177) is a solid structure built of *tufa*, a porous limestone, with a surface coat of stucco, and architectural details in brown sandstone. The wide façade is dominated by a massive belfry with arched

204 COLONIAL ARCHITECTURE

openings and pyramidal roof, reached by a spiral stairway of live-oak steps. Perhaps a balancing belfry over the north tower was originally planned. The chief architectural motive of the façade is the central carved enframement of the door and circular window (fig. 178) done by the Mexican sculptor Pedro Huizar. Taken by itself, the ornamentation of

178. Sculptured main portal of San José, by Pedro Huizar (HABS)

scrolls, niches, sculptured saints, shells, foliage, and other Churrigueresque details is over-profuse and nervous, but in its place, between the simple massive walls at the sides, it is a superb accent, a jeweled sunburst that is the more telling for the simplicity of its setting. In total composition and in detail, this is the finest Spanish Colonial façade in the United States.

The nave (plan, fig. 179) is roofed by three groin vaults, supported at the point of thrust by exterior wall buttresses, and by a hemispherical dome rising 60 feet in height over the fourth bay of the nave; beyond this

is a tunnel-vaulted sanctuary, raised two steps. There are no transepts. On
the south side of the church is a chapel which serves also as a baptistery.
It is roofed by three saucer-shaped domes resting on crude pendentives,
and in the middle of the south side is a particularly elaborate window,
with profuse carvings by Pedro Huizar (fig. 180), perhaps the most beautiful single feature in all Spanish Colonial architecture.

Extending eastward from the back of the church are the living rooms,
kitchen, storeroom, bedrooms, et cetera, of the *convento,* and, facing the
patio on the south, a cloister two stories in height, with superimposed
arcades. The mission complex also included an area of eight acres, surrounded by a high stone wall with fortified towers, containing barracks
for soldiers, offices, storerooms, shops, a gristmill, an outdoor oven, a

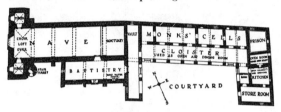

179. Plan of San José (Rexford Newcomb, *Spanish Colonial Architecture in the
United States,* J. J. Augustin)

water-supply system led through the walls in handmade tiles, and an Indian pueblo of 84 compartments.

Mission San José, along with the other Texan missions, was secularized
in 1794. Its lands were divided up among Spaniards and Indians, and the
church fell into ruin. In 1868 the north wall and nave vaults fell in, and
the great dome collapsed on Christmas Eve, 1874. Other damage was suffered from vandalism and the elements. But fortunately San José was
completely restored in 1933, under the careful direction of the architect
Harvey P. Smith, who also restored the Governor's Palace, and it may
now be seen in something closely similar to its original condition.

Mission Nuestra Señora de la Purísima Concepción de Acuña was originally founded in 1716 in the East Texan field, but fights with the French
and the Indians caused its tranfer to the San Antonio area in 1731. The
new church (fig. 181) begun in that year is almost as monumental as San
José but lacks its fine sculptured decorations. The façade has massive twin
bell towers and a satisfying breadth but is marred by an inept pediment
over the main door. The small rooms at the base of the towers are used as
baptistery and bell room. As in all the Texan missions, the orientation is
the conventional one, with façade to the west and sanctuary at the east.
The nave is roofed by a tunnel vault with transverse reinforcing ribs, expressed outside by heavy wall buttresses. Over the entrance is a choir loft.
The Purísima Concepción has a full cruciform plan (fig. 182), with altars
in the north and south transepts as well as in the sanctuary, and over the
crossing rises a dome and lantern. The construction is very solid, with
tufa walls nearly 4 feet thick. The buildings of the *convento,* with heavy

stone arches and tunnel vaults, extend to the south of the façade. The
church was repaired in 1850 and is the best preserved of the Texan missions.

Two other missions in the San Antonio area were built in 1731: San
Juan Capistrano and San Francisco de la Espada. Both had been founded
in East Texas in earlier years. San Juan is largely in ruins but from its
walls may be traced an exceptionally large mission complex, with various
dwellings, storerooms, shops, offices, dormitories, kitchens, and refectories.
St. Francis of the Sword also had a large mission complex. The church
built in 1731 was torn down and rebuilt in 1845, except for the façade,

180. The baptistery window, San José, carved by Pedro Huizar (Wayne Andrews)

but the latter still stands and is of unusual charm (fig. 183). Built of rough blocks of stone and some brick, it lacks the flanking towers of the larger churches, having instead a lofty central parapet pierced by three arches to form a belfry or *campanario*. Most striking is the polylobed horseshoe arch of the main door, undoubtedly a relic of the days when the Moors occupied most of Spain. Beside the door is a wooden cross, thank-offering for a saving rain that fell in response to prayers after a long drought.

181. Nuestra Señora de la Purísima Concepción de Acuña, San Antonio, 1731 (Wayne Andrews)

During the late eighteenth century the Texan missions declined. The Indian population had been greatly reduced by diseases and epidemics, secular authorities were often in conflict with the missionaries, new white settlers were pouring in, and there was a general decline of religious faith. Finally the missions were secularized in 1794 and their brief career brought to an end.

Arizona

The history of the Arizona missions is a stormy one. Of some dozen or more founded in the seventeenth and eighteenth centuries, only one remains intact today, but that one is often regarded as the finest mission in the United States. The 'Arizona field' was in the southern part of the present state, around Nogales and Tucson, a region inhabited by the gentle and peaceful Papago Indians. But it was surrounded by more ferocious tribes: the Yuma, Maricopa, Navaho, and Apache, and not a single mission escaped their fierce attacks.

The earliest missions in Arizona, actually, were five establishments scattered among the Zuni and Hopi pueblos of the northeastern part of the state. Founded early in the seventeenth century from Santa Fe, they

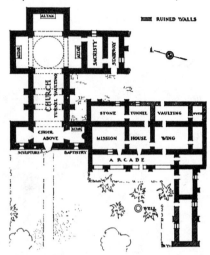

182. Plan of church and *convento*, La Purísima Concepción (Rexford Newcomb, *Spanish Colonial Architecture in the United States*, J. J. Augustin)

really belonged to the New Mexican group. Probably no large buildings were built; in any event they were destroyed in the Pueblo Revolt of 1680, never rebuilt, and not even their sites are known for certain today.

Another abortive effort was made, much later, along the Colorado River, where it forms the boundary between Arizona and California. Two missions were founded in 1780 near Yuma, to serve as halfway stations between the southern Arizona and California fields. The very next year the murderous Yuma Indians massacred the 46 white men at the two missions and carried the women away into slavery. The buildings were destroyed, and no attempt ever made to rebuild them.

The main mission field in southern Arizona (fig. 151) was more successful. Its history may be divided into two phases: Jesuit and Franciscan. The early missions were of Jesuit foundation, the only such in the Spanish Colonial provinces of present-day United States. The founder was Eusebio Francisco Kino, a Spaniard who had come to Mexico City in 1681 as royal cosmographer and who turned to missionary work in 1687. From his headquarters at Mission Nuestra Señora de los Dolores near the Mexican town of Magdalena, in Sonora, he made journeys and established missions. In those days there was no boundary between Sonora and Arizona, and the whole mission field was known as Pimeria Alta. During twenty-four years of service, Padre Kino established 24 missions in Pimeria Alta, 7 of them within the present limits of Arizona.

But the Jesuit missions were ill-fated. The earliest, San Gabriel de Guevavi, was founded in 1692 but it was sacked by the Indians in 1782, the padres were killed, and the mission was never rebuilt. Nothing remains of it today but a few fragments of walls and traces of orchards and gardens. San José at Tumacácori, about ten miles north of Nogales, was

183. San Francisco de la Espada, San Antonio, 1731 (Rexford Newcomb, *The Old Mission Churches and Historic Houses of California*, J. B. Lippincott)

founded in 1697, but in that early period it was only a small *visitá* or chapel which the padres from near-by Guevavi visited for occasional services. San Xavier del Bac was founded in 1700, but the Jesuits never built more than a poor adobe church there, and even this was destroyed by Indians and rebuilt several times. The Jesuits established several more *visitás*, but they were little more than adobe huts and have entirely disappeared. Only three of the missions are known to have been in full operation at the time of Father Kino's death in 1711, and after this time missionary work almost ceased.

During the eighteenth century there was increasing dissatisfaction with the Jesuits in Spain, and in 1767 King Carlos III ordered the removal of all Jesuits from the Spanish dominions. They were transported as virtual prisoners to the island of Corsica. The Jesuits in Pimeria Alta destroyed or carried away most of their records, thus leaving many uncertainties in the early history of this region.

The Viceroy in Mexico City asked the Franciscan friars to take over the Jesuit missions of Pimeria Alta. With characteristic energy they did so. Within five years they reported 200 parishioners at the adobe church of San Xavier mission, 86 at Guevavi, 93 at Tumacácori, and 200 at a new *visitá* which they had built, San José del Tucson. In 1776 they caused the establishment of a presidio at Tucson. A young friar, Francisco

Garcés, affectionately known by the Indians as the ' Old Man,' was responsible for the Franciscan achievements of this period of reorganization.

The old *visitá* at Tumacácori was promoted to mission status, and an imposing new church was begun in 1785 and completed early in 1800. The walls are built of adobe, 6 feet thick at the base, diminishing to 3 feet at the top; the copings are of burned brick, the better to withstand weathering. The façade, with a semicircular gable at the top and superimposed columns surmounted by a species of steep pediment, seems to have been more severely classical in treatment than its neighbor San Xavier. The single bell tower at the south side is extremely wide and three full stories high, with walls nearly 10 feet thick. Tumacácori had an excellent system of irrigation and extensive vineyards, orchards, and gardens. But the church was attacked by Indians in 1840 — after it had been abandoned as a mission — and the interior woodwork and roof were burned; the building has remained ever since in a semi-ruined condition. But it has at least been protected as a National Monument since 1908, and there is hope that someday it will be restored.

Nine miles south of Tucson, on a low hill facing south over the broad Santa Cruz valley, stands San Xavier del Bac, sole intact survivor of the Arizona missions. Founded by Father Kino in 1700, the present church was begun by the Franciscans in 1784 and consecrated in 1797. Architecturally, it is the most ambitious of all the Spanish Colonial churches (fig. 184).

The wide façade is flanked by massive tower divisions. The walls are built entirely of burned brick, covered with a layer of lime stucco, their whiteness relieved only by the window openings and dark wooden balconies. Above a balustrade at the top of the façade there is a terraced setback to the octagonal towers. These rise in two stories of arched openings, with the west tower crowned by a small dome and lantern. Most striking are the square corner piers connected to the octagonal towers by flying buttresses topped with scrolls like gargantuan snails — a motive familiar in the baroque architecture of Italy and Spain, and probably transmitted hither via Mexico. Indeed the tower design at San Xavier is strikingly similar to that of the late seventeenth-century mission at Caborca, in Sonora, another mission founded by Father Kino.

The central third of the façade dominates the composition, not only by its profusion of carved and molded ornament in the Churrigueresque style, but by the soft red color of its brick masonry. The gable, with its great scrolls, curved top, and interlaced arabesque reliefs, climaxes a fairly rectilinear composition of pilasters, cornices, and niched statues of saints flanking the central openings. The choir-loft window has a projecting curved balcony in dark wood, and is topped by a large shell, symbol of the Franciscan Order.

The plan (fig. 185) shows a fully developed cruciform church. One of the small rooms at the base of the towers serves as a baptistery, with an old baptismal font and walls covered by murals. Above is a choir vestry, adjacent to the choir loft. The nave, transepts, and apse are covered by five low domes made of brick, invisible on the exterior. The high dome over the crossing rests on an octagonal drum, and this in turn is supported over the square space below by four flat triangular panels built out from the corners.

The interior of San Xavier (fig. 186) is lavishly ornamented in the baroque style with carved stone, molded plaster, woodwork, and mural paintings. An immense altar screen, framing images of the Virgin and

184. San Xavier del Bac, Tucson, Arizona, 1784–97 (Museum of Modern Art)

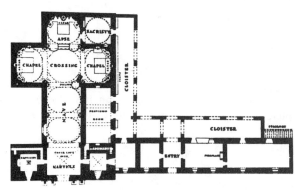

185. Plan of church and *convento,* San Xavier del Bac (Rexford Newcomb, *Spanish Colonial Architecture in the United States,* J. J. Augustin)

San Xavier, occupies the whole end wall over the altar, richly painted in gilt and polychrome. Each transept serves as a chapel, containing two altars and a profusion of decoration. Beside the sanctuary is a domed sacristy, and this in turn opens to the long arched corridor of the cloister. The buildings of the *convento,* the patio, and the walled forecourt in front of the church are part of a modern restoration and depart from the original plan.

San Xavier was abandoned as a mission in 1823, but services were re-

186. Interior of the mission church, San Xavier del Bac (HABS)

sumed in 1859, and the modern restoration was undertaken by Bishop Granjon in 1906. Standing isolated among the cacti and sagebrush of a desert, it seems like a shining mirage, and it is indeed one of the most impressive of all Spanish Colonial buildings; Hallenbeck calls it ' first of all the missions established in the New World.' [6] Yet perhaps because of its very ornateness, the confusion of its planes and surfaces, it must stand second as an architectural composition to San José at San Antonio, and as a complete establishment it was far surpassed by several of the great missions of California.

READING SUGGESTIONS

The newest and most interesting narrative account is Trent Sanford's *Architecture of the Southwest* (W. W. Norton, New York, 1950) . Another comprehensive popular treatment is Cleve Hallenbeck's *Spanish Missions of the Old South-*

west (Doubleday, Page and Co., New York, 1926). A valuable summary, in outline form and with admirable illustrations, is Rexford Newcomb's *Spanish-Colonial Architecture in the United States* (J. J. Augustin, New York, 1937).

By all odds the most authoritative and complete discussion of a single mission field is George Kubler's *Religious Architecture of New Mexico* (The Taylor Museum, Colorado Springs, 1940).

L. B. Prince's *Spanish Mission Churches of New Mexico* (Torch Press, Cedar Rapids, 1915) and E. R. Forrest's *Missions and Pueblos of the Old Southwest* (A. H. Clark, Cleveland, 1929) stress general history rather than architectural style.

Two recent publications, Charles M. Brooks's *Texas Missions, Their Romance and Architecture* (Dealey and Lowe, Dallas, 1936) and E. L. Hewett and R. G. Fisher's *Mission Monuments of New Mexico* (University of New Mexico Press, 1943) are disappointingly superficial.

7

Missions and Ranch Houses of Alta California

CALIFORNIA possesses a larger number of well-preserved missions
than any other of the former Spanish mission fields in the United
States, and many examples of Spanish and Mexican domestic architecture
of great interest. The mission chain, begun in 1769 and completed in
1823, is the latest in date of the five groups, coming over 200 years later
than the founding of St. Augustine and 170 years later than the first New
Mexican mission. All told, there were 21 missions, extending along more
than 500 miles of the old Camino Real (the royal road or ' King's highway,' see fig. 187) from San Diego in the South to Sonoma, north of San
Francisco Bay.

California was known to Spaniards, English, and Russians long before
its settlement. Cabrillo had skirted the coast as far north as Oregon in
1542-3, and Vizcaíno visited San Diego and Monterey harbors in 1602.
After a voyage up the west coast in 1578-9, Sir Francis Drake proposed to
Queen Elizabeth the foundation in California of an English colony, ' New
Albion,' a generation before the landing at Jamestown, but it came to
naught. Baja (Lower) California was first settled in 1697 by the Jesuits,
who founded a chain of fourteen missions along the lower peninsula, now
a part of Mexico. On the expulsion of the Jesuits in 1767, their missions
were put in charge of the Franciscans. At this time the Spanish feared
Russian expansion down the Pacific coast from Alaska, and, to forestall it,
decided on colonizing Alta (Upper) California. José de Gálvez, *visitador-
general* of King Carlos III in Mexico, determined on the immediate
foundation of presidios and missions at San Diego and Monterey, and a
third mission at a point halfway between. He chose Gaspar de Portolá as
Governor of the new province, and Junípero Serra, a Franciscan friar, to
head the missionary work.

Father Serra (1713-84), a man of ardent belief and great executive
ability, was one of the great men of colonial history on this continent.
Trained in a Franciscan convent and the Lullian University on the Island
of Majorca, he went to Mexico City in 1749. After missionary and teaching service on the northeastern frontier and at the College of San Fernando in Mexico City for a number of years, he was appointed *padre
presidente* of the California mission field, beginning at the age of 56
what would be a lifetime's work to most men.

A man of indomitable courage, Serra walked the 400 rugged miles from
Loreto to San Diego despite an ulcerated leg. Arriving on the first of July,

he founded his first mission, San Diego de Alcalá, on 16 July 1769. His small party was nearly wiped out by disease and starvation, surviving the first winter on little more than spiritual fervor alone. Relieved by the arrival of supplies near the end of the following March, Portolá and Serra traveled northward, by both sea and overland routes, to Monterey Bay. When the Spaniards arrived they erected a wooden cross on the shore, hung a bell on the branch of an aged oak tree, and said the first Mass

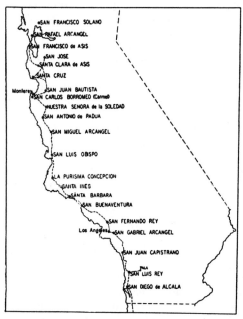

187. Franciscan missions of California and their locations on the Camino Real (Philip White)

amidst the incomparable beauty of the Monterey peninsula. The second mission, dedicated to San Carlos Borromeo, was founded on 3 June 1770, and on the same day the Spanish flag was unfurled over the new presidio. Thus was founded Monterey, destined to be the capital of California under Spanish, Mexican, and American rule for three-quarters of a century. When Portolá returned homeward to tell of his achievements, the Viceroy in Mexico City ordered flags flown, the church bells rung, and a special High Mass to be celebrated: Alta California was finally occupied.

The indomitable Serra then drove himself and his followers to the task of establishing missions along the whole 400-mile line from San Diego to Monterey in order that he might ' reap the souls ' of the thousands of Indians along this fertile and scenic coast. Not only physical difficulties and dangers frustrated him. Spanish soldiers in the presidios, who raped Indian women and killed Indian men, made even more vexing the problem of converting the Indian to the white man's religion. To ease his task and make clear the separation between the spiritual and the secular, Serra moved the Monterey mission five miles away from the presidio to the beautiful valley of the Carmelo River, and on 9 July 1771 rededicated it as San Carlos at Carmel. This was to be his ' home ' mission and the administrative capital of the mission chain until 1803. For similar reasons the mission at San Diego was moved in 1774 to a site six miles northwest of the presidio.

Within five days after re-establishing San Carlos, Serra marched southward 75 miles into the Santa Lucía mountains and planted the cross of Mission San Antonio de Padua. A few weeks later, he founded Mission San Gabriel, a hundred miles north of San Diego in the Los Angeles wilderness. San Luis Obispo, named for St. Louis, Bishop of Toulouse, was founded on 1 September 1772, completing the first ' spurt ' of founding; the next four years were devoted to consolidating gains.

In the early years crops were poor, conversions were slow, and Serra encountered administrative difficulties with the new Governor Fages. In the winter of 1772–3 he journeyed 2000 miles to Mexico City to seek more support. He covered 1200 miles of this journey on foot, alone but for the company of one Monterey Indian. Support was promised by the new Viceroy, Antonio Bucareli, and the promises were kept. An overland route from Sonora through southern Arizona to San Gabriel was opened, and over it, in the autumn of 1775, came 240 colonists – men, women, and children – a thousand head of livestock, and much heavy agricultural equipment, as well as baptismal fonts, church bells, holy images, and sacred vestments and utensils.

Serra's dream of a mission at the Golden Gate, as a northern outpost of Spanish civilization, was realized on 29 June 1776, just five days before the independence of the thirteen English colonies on the Atlantic coast was declared at Philadelphia. The mission was named San Francisco de Asís in honor of the founder and patron saint of the Franciscan Order. The establishment of the presidio on 17 September was celebrated by a huge barbecue, ringing bells, booming cannon, and muskets, somewhat to the amazement and terror of the Indian guests. Father Serra completed his work with the foundation of San Juan Capistrano in the fall of 1776; Santa Clara de Asís in 1777; and – at the age of 69 – San Buenaventura in 1782.

Two years later, after a farewell visit to each of the nine missions he had founded, Father Serra died. He was buried in the sanctuary at San Carlos, and the Indians brought armloads of wild flowers to cover his grave. In fifteen years, Father Serra had not only established the missions and made over 6000 Indian converts; he had taught them agriculture, irrigation, stock raising, innumerable trades and crafts, and a peaceful and ordered community life. It is fitting that his image should stand in Statuary Hall in the Capitol at Washington as one of the two greatest Californians. Steps are now being taken to canonize Father Serra as a saint of the Roman Catholic Church.

Serra's successor, the aged Fermín de Lasuén, was hardly less able; perhaps a less ardent and inflamed enthusiast, he excelled as an able and tactful administrator. Under his leadership as *padre presidente* (1785–1803), nine new missions were founded, and all grew greatly in agricultural and industrial wealth, in numbers of converts, and particularly in architectural splendor and extent. Lasuén first carried out a scheme long dear to Serra by founding the missions of Santa Barbara and La Purísima Concepción along the Santa Barbara Channel. Gaps in the northern part of the chain were filled by Santa Cruz and Soledad, both founded in 1791.

There followed a decade of building and rebuilding at the older missions, including splendid new churches at Carmel, San Buenaventura, the Presidio Chapel at Monterey, San Juan Capistrano, and San Luis Obispo. Lasuén capped his career by the extraordinary feat of founding in one year — his seventy-seventh — five new missions: San José, San Juan Bautista, San Miguel Arcángel, San Fernando Rey, and San Luis Rey. He retained his faculties and worked actively until his eighty-third year. Lasuén died on 26 June 1803 and was buried beside Serra near the altar at San Carlos.

Father Lasuén was followed by Estevan Tapis as *presidente* from 1803 to 1812, and he in turn by several other padres for the next score of years. But although some of the missions increased in population, wealth, and architectural impressiveness during this era, the days of decline were at hand. The founding of Santa Inés in 1804 completed the chain of nineteen missions between San Diego and San Francisco; the missions at San Rafael Arcángel (1817) and San Francisco Solano (1823), both in the region north of San Francisco Bay, came as postscripts to the whole venture, and neither was ever successful.

From 1810 onward, the rumblings of revolution in Mexico, with the attendant uncertainties about the fate of the mission program, caused dissidence among Indian converts. There were serious epidemics of disease, especially white men's diseases to which the Indians had little resistance. After 1812, at 16 of the 19 missions, the number of deaths annually exceeded the number of births, and it was only by new conversions that the populations were maintained at all. In 1813 the Spanish Cortés ordered the secularization of all American missions over ten years old. The decree was not enforced in California, but its presence on the books gave grasping secular authorities and private ranch owners a new weapon in their unremitting attempts to bring the mission lands under their control.

When in 1821 Mexico declared its independence from Spain, the missions lost all government support; and when the final order to secularize came in 1834, they had completely lost their original vitality. Ten missions were turned over to the secular authorities in 1834, six more in 1835, and the remaining five in 1836. Legally the Indian converts got one-half the property, but in a few short years shrewd whites were able to dispossess them, selling off the herds of cattle for quick cash, and distributing the rich lands to relatives and friends. Within a decade the missions were not only depopulated and stripped of their property but falling into complete ruin, except for those buildings which were put to use as hay barns, stores, saloons, stables, and taverns. Santa Barbara, alone of all the missions, remained throughout in Franciscan hands.

The last *padre-presidente*, Narciso Durán, died in 1846, and in the same year the Americans entered Monterey to claim California. Presidents Buchanan and Lincoln made praiseworthy efforts to invalidate Mexican sales contracts and restore small amounts of land to the missions, but this feeble stimulant did not suffice to revive them. It was not until the twentieth century that their crumbled ruins were once more restored, and then only as impressive relics of a romantic early history.

Life at the missions

The degree of success achieved by the Franciscan friars in civilizing the Indians was remarkable considering the extraordinarily low culture from which they started. Of small stature and repulsive appearance, the California Indians were ignorant, lazy, and cowardly. They had little or no communal life, no agriculture, no domestic animals, and were but indifferent hunters. They ate little meat because it was too much work to catch it, except for frogs, lizards, snakes, rats, and an occasional skunk or unwary coyote. Along the coast they netted fish, and a dead whale drifted ashore was occasion for a banquet. But for the most part they subsisted on acorns, piñon nuts, mesquite beans, and various roots and berries. In the summer the men wore nothing. In winter, in the San Francisco region, they donned a coat of mud to keep warm overnight, washing it off the next morning. The women wore grass aprons, and sometimes skin capes over the shoulders. They were filthy in their personal habits, living in vermin-infested wigwams of poles and grass. There were perhaps 70,000 of these Indians living in the mission area. The largest number to come under missionary influence at any one time was 21,066, in 1824.

The typical mission was founded by the *padre presidente*, accompanied by two other friars, one to superintend spiritual matters, the other temporal affairs; anywhere from three to a dozen soldiers; and — after the first hard years — two or three dozen Christianized Indians from other missions to help with the labor. A cross was raised, a bell hung on a tree branch, Mass said, and the mission was founded. Whites and Indians together then set to work to build temporary shelters of poles and *tule* grass, similar in construction to the Indian wigwams. Within a year or two, more substantial adobe structures were built, with roofs of poles thatched with *tule*. The near-by Indians were easily tempted into baptism by gifts of food, trinkets, and clothes, and helped readily enough in building the necessary chapel, dwelling rooms for padres and soldiers, shops, storerooms, stables, and corrals. It was only after the whole was enclosed by a stockade or quadrangle of buildings that they realized they were in a sort of prison of their own making. Unbaptized Indians might come and go as they pleased, but the neophyte lived under strict discipline. Sometimes he escaped to the woods, but invariably he was pursued by padres and soldiers and retrieved — if necessary by use of the frightening noise-sticks.

But as time went on, most neophytes preferred the security of the mission to their former life; food was far better, clothes were an interesting accessory, and the many tools and crafts of the Spaniards delighted them. The padres were also wise enough to overlook many of the pagan traditions and superstitions, and to indulge the Indians' love of pageantry by making the many *fiestas* a combination of religious ceremony, chanting and music, athletic events, bullfights, traditional Indian games, and in the evening, pagan dances under torchlight.

The typical day began at sunrise with the Angelus and morning prayers and Mass. After breakfast the morning was taken up by instruction or work in the fields or shops, then dinner at noon and a siesta until two. Work was resumed for the afternoon until an hour before sunset, when the Angelus called to prayers and rosary. After supper the Indians were free for their own amusements until bedtime.

The religious instruction was in Bible and catechism, praying and singing, without too much of doctrinal matters. The padres taught and encouraged the use of Spanish, but only the exceptional Indian learned to read or write.

From the first, stock raising became the most important economic activity of the missions. Herds of cattle, horses, goats, and sheep were imported and over the years grew to great size. San Gabriel in 1826 had 15,300 cattle, 725 horses, 91 mules, 215 hogs, 10,000 sheep, and 38 goats. The final inventory at San Diego in 1832 lists 4,500 cattle, 13,500 sheep, 150 goats, 220 horses, and 80 mules. San Buenaventura boasted 41,000 head of stock in 1816; and San Luis Rey 50,000 in 1826. At San Juan, one of the small missions, 50 head of cattle a week were slaughtered for meat. The Indians became skilled herdsmen and ranchers, and built corrals and stables. Hides were tanned and the men made excellent leatherwork, especially saddles. Shoes and tallow were manufactured in quantity.

Agriculture and husbandry were also of great importance. The missions owned the richest lands, and as the fields were plowed, sown, and tilled, great harvests of corn, wheat, hemp, flax, and cane were reaped. San Luis Rey produced 67,116 bushels of grain in 1810, but such a crop was often surpassed by the most productive of the missions, San Gabriel in the south and San José and Santa Clara in the north. Most of the missions produced more food than they required, and sold large amounts to feed the soldiers at the presidios. Irrigation was developed to a high point. Dams, aqueducts, and reservoirs, made of stone and tile, brought water from considerable distances. In the early years, meal was ground by the Indian women with stone *metates* (mortars), but a water-powered gristmill was built at San Gabriel in 1810, and the first sawmill powered by water was built there in 1819.

In the truck gardens all manner of vegetables were grown: beans, beets, peas, lentils, onions, carrots, pimentos, corn, potatoes, squash, cucumbers, and melons; and in the orchards and vineyards pears, peaches, pomegranates, apples, oranges, lemons, apricots, plums, cherries, grapes, and figs flourished in the benign climate. Olives were pressed for oil, and grapes for wine.

Perhaps the most remarkable achievement of the missions was the teaching of a great variety of arts and crafts, some highly skilled. At first only the padres were the teachers but later skilled artisans were sent from Mexico, to travel from mission to mission teaching their crafts. Looms were brought or built, and the Indian women wove wool, cotton, and flax into textiles for blankets, clothes, and furnishings. The men made shoes, hats, soap, candles, harnesses, and saddles. They were skilled in cabinet-making and woodcarving, as the mission tables, chairs, benches, cupboards, chests, doors, pulpits, and altars attest; and at the smithies they made wrought-iron locks, keys, hinges, spurs, scissors, and cattle brands for the mission herds.

The resident population of neophytes at a mission ranged from a few hundred to a maximum of 2,869 at San Luis Rey in 1826, though of course it varied from year to year. In the banner year of 1824, the total population of the twenty-one missions was 21,066, an average of just over a thousand Indians per mission. Over the whole mission period, the five largest establishments, in order, were San Luis Rey, San José, San Diego, Santa Barbara, and San Gabriel. The missions also reached the widely scattered populations of the Indian *rancherías* in the interior. The padres erected chapels at these settlements, often 30 or 40 miles distant from the mother mission. Such chapels were called *asistencias* (contributing chapels) and *visitás* (visited chapels), and regular services were conducted by padres sent out from the mission.

The mission buildings

The word 'mission,' of course, applies not to the church alone but to a whole community and its complex of buildings. These were built, added to, rebuilt, and restored over the years. The precise layout differs at every mission, but the eventual plan was in most cases a large quadrangle of buildings surrounding an open patio. The nearest approach to the ' ideal ' type is seen in the plan of Santa Inés (fig. 188). The church was the largest and loftiest of the buildings, usually forming one side, or a part of one side, of the patio. The California churches are not oriented: the façade may face west, but as often east; San Diego faces southwest, San Carlos northeast, Santa Barbara south. Beside the church extended a long arcaded corridor fronting a series of rooms. Since these opened onto the highway, they were usually used by white men. Nearest the church was the *convento:* a living room, kitchen, and cells for the two padres of the mission. There was usually an office for the major-domo, or overseer, who kept business records, and two or three rooms for the few soldiers forming the resident guard. Other rooms were reserved for guests, since the missions were hospitable inns for all travelers along the Camino Real.

Facing inward toward the enclosed patio were the rooms or dormitories of the resident neophytes, fronted by an arcaded corridor. Unmarried Indian youths and girls were segregated in dormitories within the mission compound and these rooms were locked up at night. The residential quarters are often referred to as the 'monastic' buildings, a term that in strict usage refers only to a monastery, such as those of the regular Benedictine or Augustinian monks; the Franciscan mission was hardly a true monastery.

The other sides of the patio consisted of kitchen, refectory, shops, and storerooms of all sorts, and sometimes an infirmary. The plan of San Juan Capistrano (fig. 197) shows rooms around the patio used for wine-pressing, weaving, soap-making, olive-pressing, carpentry, a candle shop, hat shop, smithy, wine cellar, pantry, and powder magazine. Usually outside the mission compound there would be other buildings such as a granary, gristmill, pottery, tannery, hay barn, stable, and corral. The

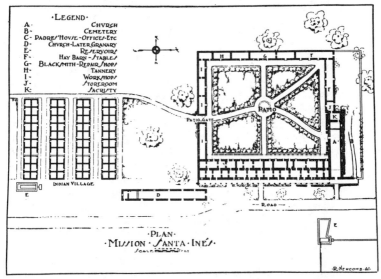

188. Plan of a typical California mission showing church, monastic buildings, patio, shops, and Indian dwellings (Rexford Newcomb, *The Old Mission Churches and Historic Houses of California*, J. B. Lippincott)

enclosed patio itself was beautifully planted with shrubs and flowers, with gravel paths and a central fountain of running water. Sometimes in the larger missions there was a small private patio for the padres. The mission cemetery was behind or beside the church. At some distance was the *rancheria* or Indian village, where the married families lived, either in disordered collections of pole-and-thatch wigwams, as at San Luis Rey and San Francisco, or in neat row houses of adobe and tile, as at Santa Inés and Santa Barbara.

Materials, structure, and style

The California missions exhibit a far wider variety of materials and structural systems than do those of New Mexico. The chief material, of course, was adobe. The clay, sand, and water were mixed in large basins to a thick soupy consistency, sometimes with straw as a binder, and poured into molds to dry in the sun. The large blocks thus formed were laid with mud-mortar joints or, in finer construction, lime mortar. A well-made adobe wall has considerable load-bearing strength, but since church walls were sometimes as high as 30 feet, they were usually made 5 or 6 feet thick for lateral stability and given massive exterior buttresses for additional strength. Even in lower structures, adobe walls were seldom less than 3 feet thick.

To prevent erosion of the walls by the winter rains, they were almost invariably covered by a coat of lime-and-sand stucco, the lime being obtained by burning limestone or sea shells, of which there was a plentiful supply. The stucco was finally brushed with a lime whitewash, inside and out.

Kiln-burned bricks were widely used in the California missions, particularly for the square piers supporting the arcades, or to reinforce arches and frame openings in adobe walls. The bricks were about 10 inches square and $1\frac{1}{2}$ to 2 inches thick, rather soft, and of a strong red color. They were used for fireplaces and chimneys, arches, vaults, and domes, pavements of corridors and rooms, and occasionally to face a wall with an adobe core, as at San Luis Rey.

Roofs at first were covered by *tule* thatch, but this was inflammable. Hostile Indians burned the mission at San Diego in 1775, and on two occasions set fire to the roofs at San Luis Obispo with flaming arrows. The first fireproof red tiles for roofing were produced at San Luis Obispo in 1786, and in a few years they became universal in all the major mission buildings. Each tile was a tapered half-cylinder, about 12 inches in diameter at the large end and 8 inches at the small end, and about 2 feet long. It was formed on a half-round, tapered wood mold, the clay then dried and kiln-baked. Laid in overlapping rows, the tiles made an indestructible roof, of a handsome red color and rich texture.

The ambition of the padres was to build eventually in stone. Limestone and a rather soft yellow sandstone were available, but the great labor of cutting and dressing stone blocks prevented their frequent use. The church at San Gabriel, begun in 1791 and laid with stone walls to the window-sill level, was the first stone structure, and only five others were built: San Carlos at Carmel, the Presidio Chapel at Monterey, San Buenaventura, San Juan Capistrano, and Santa Barbara. Stone was extensively used, however, for the dams and aqueducts of irrigation systems. Stone walls, being of indifferent workmanship, were usually covered by stucco.

A species of 'concrete' was used in certain walls, domes, and aqueducts. Newcomb speaks of it as 'lime and sand mortar combined with stones and pieces of brick and tile' — in other words, a coarse rubble bound together by mortar, not to be confused with the much superior Portland cement concrete evolved in the later nineteenth century.

Roof construction was almost invariably of wooden beams, rafters, and sheathing, and wood was of course used for doors, furniture, corbels, window grilles, and other details. Redwood, pine, and oak were plentiful in the north, and oak and sycamore in the south, but big timbers were hard to cut and transport, and it required great labor to saw them into planks and boards. Adobe was accordingly favored wherever it could be used. These Spanish builders did not know the principle of the truss: consequently the width of their churches was limited by the length and strength of single beams, which accounts for the comparatively long and narrow naves of the mission churches.

The basic structural unit was the pier and arch, usually made of burned brick and covered with stucco. Repeated endlessly in the long arcades, it is the major architectural motive of the missions. Vault forms, however, were seldom ventured. San Carlos at Carmel had a curious tunnel vault of parabolic shape over the nave, but it was made of wood. San Gabriel had a segmental-arched tunnel vault in stone over the nave, but it was so badly cracked in the earthquake of 1803 that it had to be removed the following year. A small tunnel vault in stone remains, however, over the sacristy, and the baptistery has a small hemispherical dome. There were small domes, made of brick, over the Mortuary Chapel at San Luis Rey, and small domes of stone or ' concrete ' top several of the bell towers. The vaulted church *par excellence* was San Juan Capistrano, with both domes and groined vaults in stone, but these were destroyed in the earthquake of 1812. In a region plagued by earthquakes, it was well that most of the padres contented themselves with simple beamed and raftered roofs resting on solid adobe walls.

Architecturally, the California missions lie between the primitive charm of the New Mexican pueblo missions and the baroque splendors of Texas and Arizona. Nowhere is there a façade so majestically organized as that of San José at San Antonio, a portal of such baroque intricacy as that at San Xavier, or decorative sculptures to rival those of Pedro Huizar. On the other hand, the California missions boast a few arches, vaults, and domes that the New Mexican padres and Pueblo Indians never ventured, and occasional portals, bell towers, patio fountains, and altar screens betray baroque ambitions.

On the whole, it was a simple craftsman's architecture, without much striving for ' high style,' but with a good sense for straightforward building and the organic expression of the structural system employed. All buildings had massive and solid walls with softly modeled stucco surfaces, opened by few doors and windows. Low-pitched roofs with red tiles and broad projecting eaves sheltered the walls against rain, and shaded patios and arcaded corridors gave protection from the California sunlight. *Campanarios* or bell towers afforded the chief architectural accents, in the form of pierced walls and gables, each arch holding a bell, or in the form of a terraced and domed tower flanking the façade. Almost as important were the long arcaded corridors, fronting the mission compound or surrounding its patio, giving architectural unity with the repeated rhythm of the arch to what might otherwise have been a monotonous and straggling extent. These arches always rested on substantial square piers rather than on round columns, and they frequently showed variations in span and shape, as though measured by guess and by eye rather than by rule, thus producing a not unpleasing irregularity. Patios are not always strictly rectilinear, and façades are rarely symmetrical. With their soft, simple surfaces, warm colors, varied bell towers, and long cool arcaded corridors, the California missions have a restfulness and charm scarcely equaled in the missions of other regions.

A table giving the name, date, and location of all the missions, in the order of their founding, with the date of erection of the present mission church, is given on page 250. Of the 21 missions, 4 have disappeared or stand in ruins: Santa Cruz, Soledad, San José, and San Rafael. Three others have been ' restored' out of all semblance to the original: San Luis Obispo, San Francisco, and Santa Clara. But the remaining 14, standing in various degrees of preservation, constitute the most impressive group of Spanish Colonial architectural monuments in present-day United States. To describe each mission with its church, patio, and compound would be beyond the scope of this chapter, but an examination of the five ' best,' architecturally, will reveal the characteristic features of the California style, as well as its outstanding monuments. These are, in order of their founding, San Diego, San Carlos Borromeo, San Juan Capistrano, Santa Barbara, and San Luis Rey.

San Diego de Alcalá

The first of the missions was founded on 16 July 1769. The buildings erected on Presidio Hill that year were crude sheds of poles roofed with *tule* grass, surrounded by a stockade. After the removal to Mission Valley in 1774 better buildings were undertaken: Serra's report for the year indicates a wooden church, an adobe *convento,* a granary, smithy, and fourteen wooden houses for the neophytes. These buildings were burned in an attack by 800 Indians in November 1775, but two years later a second church, 14 feet wide and 56 long, with adobe walls and a thatched roof, had been completed. As the mission grew, a larger church, 15 by 84 feet, was built in 1780, with shops and dwellings around three sides of a patio enclosed on the fourth by an adobe wall 11 feet high. This sequence of growth and improvement of buildings was characteristic of all the missions.

The present church was built in 1808–13. Fortunately it was not damaged by the earthquakes of 1812, but the mission was abandoned and it became a roofless ruin after secularization in 1834. The restoration of 1931 is perhaps unauthentic in details, but in general feeling it gives a good picture of the simpler type of mission architecture.

The façade (fig. 189) is without flanking towers, and its soft-textured whitewashed brick is broken only by coarse moldings surrounding door and window, with a curved parapet at the top. The dominant architectural feature is a four-story *campanario* standing almost free of the side wall of the church. Restored on the basis of a sketch made by Major Churchill during the Mexican War, its rough base, tapered silhouette, and tiered arches for the five bells are of unusual charm (see frontispiece).

The timber-roofed nave (fig. 190) is quite typical of most simple mission churches. The plan is a long narrow rectangle, 26 by 159 feet, with no transepts and no architectural distinction, other than a low chancel rail, between nave and sanctuary. The floor is of square red tiles, a traditional feature, but the fixed pews are wholly modern; in Spanish days the floor was empty and the Indians stood or knelt during service. The thick walls are unbroken except by a door at the right, leading to the patio, and the high windows, with their splayed reveals and plank shutters. The original roof timbers, over 30 feet long, were brought, according to legend, from the inland sierras 60 miles distant. Stations of the Cross

189. San Diego de Alcalá, façade and *campanario*, 1808–13, restored 1931 (Josef Muench)

adorn the nave walls. The altar is flanked by arched niches with statues of saints, and above it hangs a picture supposedly of the Murillo school, preserved from the fire of 1775. To the left of the front entrance is a small baptistery, and over the entrance is the customary choir loft. This cool, white interior, so simple in every detail, is typical of the smaller churches of the mission chain.

Little remains of the monastic buildings at San Diego, but a typical arcaded corridor (fig. 191) has been restored, with its tiled floor, beamed ceiling, and row of simple arches resting on square piers. Adobe ruins reveal the location and extent of the original patio, and a fine stone dam three miles above the mission indicates the highly developed irrigation system that the mission employed during the days of its prosperity. In 1797 San Diego had a population of 1,405 Indians, largest of the chain in that year.

San Carlos Borromeo

San Carlos at Carmel, like San Diego, fell into complete ruin during the nineteenth century and only the church and the rooms of the *convento* have been restored today. But as the 'home' mission of Fathers Serra and Lasuén, and as the administrative center of the whole mission enterprise for over thirty years, it must always remain the first of the missions in historical importance. San Carlos Borromeo, named after a sixteenth-century archbishop of Milan, was founded at Monterey on 3 June 1770, but the mission was moved five miles to the beautiful valley of the Carmelo River on 9 July 1771. During his fifteen years as *padre presidente*, Junípero Serra was too busy with the problems of establishing civ-

190, 191. Nave of the mission church and corridor on the patio, San Diego (Floyd Ray)

ilization in a wilderness to devote much time or attention to architectural amenities. He built as best he could, in wood, adobe, and thatch. At Carmel, until Lasuén's time, the mission consisted of rather disreputable adobe structures.

Lasuén, the great builder, devoted his first eight years as *presidente* to founding and building other missions, but in 1793 he began a splendid new church at Carmel. He determined to build it of stone and obtained the services of a master stonemason, Manuel Estevan Ruiz, who came from Monterey to Carmel during the winter of 1792–3 to instruct the Indians in cutting and laying masonry. The cornerstone of the new church was laid on 7 July 1793, and the completed edifice dedicated in September 1797.

Captain George Vancouver visited Carmel in the November of 1794 and has left a description of the work in progress:

Some of them [the Indians] were at the time engaged under the direction of the fathers in building a church with stone and mortar. The former material . . . is of a light straw color, and presents a very rich and elegant appearance, in proportion to the labor that is bestowed on it. It is found in abundance at no great

depth from the surface of the earth; the quarries are easily worked, and it is, I
believe, the only stone the Spaniards have hitherto made use of in building . . .
The lime they use is made from sea-shells, principally the ear-shell [abalone],
which is of a large size and in great abundance on the shores . . .[1]

Master mason Ruiz was probably an amateur architect who had traveled in Mexico. He certainly had a bold invention; architecturally, San

192. San Carlos Borromeo, Carmel, Calif., 1793-7 (Josef Muench)

Carlos was without doubt the most ambitious church built in California
up to that time.

The broad façade (fig. 192) has plain surfaces of tawny-colored stucco
as a foil to the richly carved masonry. The round-arch main portal, framed
by pilasters and entablature, is somewhat conventional and pedestrian,
as though taken from an architectural handbook, but the interlaced star-
and-quatrefoil window above, with its distinctly Moorish flavor, shows
imaginative flair. The flanking towers, set forward a few inches for emphasis, are dissimilar. The south tower, with two arched openings on the
front and one on the south side was doubtless intended as the bell tower
and thus emphasized by greater size and richness. Baroque finials crown
its four corners, and a set-back octagonal drum carries eight pinnacles
and the curious dome, circular in plan and half-egg-shaped in section.
Surmounted by its ancient wrought-iron cross, this dome certainly owes
its exotic silhouette to the Moorish tradition in Spain. Access to the
belfry is gained from the patio by a flight of stone steps. The north tower,

of smaller size and with single arched openings and simpler treatment, was probably intended as a foil to the superior importance and richness of the bell tower. Like many other California façade compositions, it illustrates that the padres dared to depart from an obvious and trite symmetry. Some of the seven bells of the church are now hung in this north tower.

It is unfortunate that so fine a unit as the south tower is partially obscured at the base by the *convento* building extending in front of it. This included a large *sala* or reception room, kitchen, dining room, cells for the padres, and a library — unusually important because San Carlos housed the mission records and a collection of some 2500 volumes. One of the rooms is now restored as Father Serra's cell, furnished only with a plank table, a rush chair, rawhide bed, the little Bible from which he

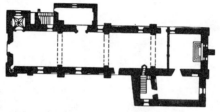

193. Plan of the church, San Carlos (Philip White, after Newcomb)

read, a stone with which he beat his chest, and a chain of metal to scourge his back.

The interior of San Carlos is unique among the missions in its wooden tunnel vault, shaped in a parabolic arch. Spanning a width of 29 feet, the planks forming this vault are supported by three transverse stone ribs carried on pairs of pilasters projecting from the wall (two of these ribs may be seen in the sketch of the ruins before restoration, fig. 194). Though the stone walls are 5 feet thick, the point of thrust of these arched ribs is met by exterior wall buttresses — unnecessary, perhaps, but a logical and organic expression of the structural system. Even more remarkable is the interior wall treatment, with pilasters and the wall itself curving inward to the impost of the main vault, the wall reaching a thickness of 7 feet at this level. This surely reveals a designer who, although architecturally naive, was a bold engineer with a keen sense, in his articulation of ribs, pilasters, and buttresses, for structural logic. One wonders whether Estevan Ruiz knew anything of the wooden tunnel vaults, shaped to a pointed arch, in French Gothic structures. The vault stood securely for fifteen years but was damaged in the earthquake of 1812 and had to be removed the following year.[2] The modern restoration, begun in 1882, was at first incorrect, but the vaulted roof has been correctly restored in recent years.

The plan of the church (fig. 193) shows the customary choir loft over the entrance; it was reached by a small spiral stairway in the north tower. At the base of the south tower is a small baptistery, with engaged 'Doric' columns at the corners carrying a stone ribbed ceiling in the form of a

Gothic tierceron vault. The baptistery still contains an ancient bronze
holy-water font brought from Spain. Midway on the left side of the nave
is an elaborately carved doorway leading to a small lateral chapel added
in 1817. Steps rise to the sanctuary, and beneath stone slabs in the floor,
before the altar, lie the bodies of Father Crespi, Father Serra, Father
Lasuén, and Father López. A low arched doorway leads from sanctuary to
sacristy, on the north side, and beyond this is the cemetery, with the
bodies of nearly 3000 Indians.

When Father Serra moved Mission San Carlos to Carmel, the first mission church at Monterey became the chapel of the presidio, La Capilla

194. Walls and arches of the nave before restoration, San Carlos (Rexford Newcomb,
The Old Mission Churches and Historic Houses of California, J. B. Lippincott)

Real, and it served as an *asistencia* to San Carlos until 1834. As the place
of worship of the Spanish and Mexican governors of California, this was
the most important church, politically, in the province. The first adobe
church was replaced by a stone chapel in 1794, as big as many of the mission churches, and better preserved today than most (fig. 195).

The façade is the most elaborate and ornate of any of the California
churches. The two-story composition of pilasters and entablatures looks
as though it might have been taken from some architectural handbook,
but its inept placing on the wall and such meaningless details as the
'floating' pediment over the window reveal the enthusiastic amateur
rather than the trained architect. The topmost frame, enclosing a relief
figure of the Virgin of Guadalupe beneath a large scallop shell, is flanked
by spiral scrolls of baroque character, but they are small, tight, and timid,
and the whole façade is dry and academic in comparison with the dynamic efflorescence of San José in Texas. The delicately wrought moldings and details, however, are so similar to those at Carmel that we may
suppose Estevan Ruiz and his Indian craftsmen worked on both buildings. The nave was lengthened to 150 feet, and a new main altar and
transepts with fine side portals added in 1858, but otherwise the building
has been little changed.

San Juan Capistrano

The most ambitious of all the mission churches was that at San Juan Capistrano. Though the great church was shattered in the earthquake of 1812 and the workshops of the large patio have largely crumbled, enough remains of the ivy-covered ruins to enable us to reconstruct the buildings where once lived more than 1300 neophyte Indians.

195. Capilla Real, Monterey, Calif., 1794 (HABS)

San Juan, named for a Franciscan theologian born in Capistrano, Italy, and canonized by the church in 1690, was founded by Serra on 1 November 1776, the seventh of the missions. The first of its buildings was a little adobe chapel located on the east side of the patio (at A in the restored plan surveyed and drawn by Rexford Newcomb, fig. 197). Only 17 feet wide and roofed with timber and thatch, the chapel was completed in 1777 and has survived earthquake and wear to become California's oldest building, and the only church now standing in which Father Serra actually conducted services.

In front of the old chapel, as time went on, were added a refectory and reception hall, the *convento* of the padres across the south front, and the long wing projecting beside the front plaza, which housed the guard, major-domo, and guests. Eventually a series of workshops and storehouses extended around a large patio with a fountain in the center. Though the stucco-covered brick arcades have sixteen arches each, no two sides are parallel or of the same length, and the spans of the arches vary as though their spacing had to be modified to fit the approach to unexpected corners. At some distance from the patio was the *ranchería* of Indian dwellings, made of whitewashed brick with tiled roofs and arranged in neat rows.

In 1797, under the presidency of Lasuén, a large new church was begun. At the time it was the only mission church to have a full cruciform plan, the only one to be built entirely of stone, and the only one to be roofed by domes (fig. 196). At its consecration on 7 September 1806 were held the most elaborate ceremonies in the history of the province. The new church was designed by Isidoro Aguilar, a master stonemason of Culiacán

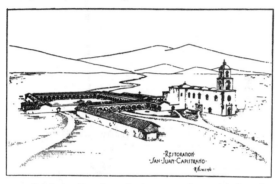

196. Restoration of Mission San Juan Capistrano as it stood before the earthquake of 1812 (Rexford Newcomb, *The Franciscan Mission Architecture of Alta California,* Architectural Book Publishing Company)

in Mexico; he himself carved many of the fine details, but died in 1803 before its completion. The church was built of fine-grained yellow sandstone, quarried six miles away, with architectural trim in a blue-gray sandstone. Lime for the mortar was obtained by burning limestone quarried ten miles to the north. In front was a single bell tower, standing on the main axis; its terraced and arcaded upper stories were topped by a small dome and cross rising to the great height of 120 feet.

The nave was 30 feet wide, and the transepts projected about 20 feet to east and west (plan, fig. 197). Over the three bays of nave and crossing were shallow saucer-shaped domes supported on arches spanning the nave. Cutting the curved, wedge-sided blocks of stone for these domes must have been the most difficult feat in stone masonry ever attempted in Spanish California; it is not certainly known whether the domes were visible outside or covered by a low-pitch gabled roof. The transepts and sanctuary were roofed by domical groined vaults. The sanctuary vault remains standing (fig. 198); with its polygonal plan and five wall arches, it is reminiscent of a Gothic chevet vault, though the structural system is, of course, quite different.

Aguilar undoubtedly detailed the beautiful moldings, far bolder and richer than in any other California mission; especially noteworthy are the fluted pilasters with complex base and cap moldings, the three great arches of transepts and sanctuary, the triple-molded wall arches in the nave, and the fine door leading from the sanctuary to the adjacent vaulted sacristy. Many of the details of the lost church must remain conjectural, and it is a pity that this, the most ambitious architectural effort of the California missions, should have been destroyed only six years after its completion. On 8 December 1812, Indians were attending the sunrise mass of the Feast of the Immaculate Conception when an earthquake

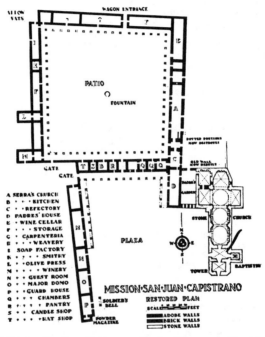

197. Plan of Mission San Juan Capistrano (Rexford Newcomb, *Spanish Colonial Architecture in the United States*, J. J. Augustin)

cracked open the domes of the nave, and a second shock brought down the great tower. Forty were crushed by the tons of falling masonry, and only five Indians and the padre escaped alive. Services were resumed in Father Serra's old chapel, and the stone church was never rebuilt. But solicitous care has been given to the remaining structures and grounds. The cool corridors, ivy-covered ruins, and trees and shrubs of the plaza, alive with swallows and doves, make it today the most picturesque and romantic of the old missions.

Santa Barbara

Of all the chain, Santa Barbara perhaps best deserves the title queen of the California missions, for here one not only sees the largest and one of the finest of mission churches and the best-maintained group of monastic buildings, but also senses the quality of the life for which it was built, for Santa Barbara has never been out of the hands of the Franciscan Order, and the brown-robed friars still work and pray in its quiet seclusion.

The mission was founded on 4 December 1786, tenth in the chain, and the first to be founded by Lasuén. The third church, built of adobe and

198. Sanctuary of the ruined church, San Juan Capistrano (Floyd Ray)

tile in 1794, was completely destroyed in the earthquake of 1812, and the present structure was erected in 1815–20. Santa Barbara is the only one of the major mission churches with a symmetrical façade (fig. 199). Of great width, since the towers stand outside the nave walls, and rising from imposing steps to superb towers, the façade has unusual monumentality. The bare walls at the sides concentrate attention on the central temple

199. Façade, Mission Santa Barbara, 1815–20 (HABS)

motive. More strictly classical than the façade of any other mission, this motive of six engaged columns carrying a crowning pediment undoubtedly reflects the reaction from baroque extravagance to a more severe classical taste, evident throughout Europe during the last half of the eighteenth century.

Father Ripoll, who designed the church, took as his immediate pattern a Roman Ionic temple façade of four columns, with a Greek fret pattern adorning the architrave, published as Plate x in a Spanish edition of Vitruvius still preserved in the mission archives. Evidently deeming four columns insufficient for so broad a façade, he elected to use six, blandly separating the middle pair to admit the main doorway and round window over it. And to ' reach to the top ' he attenuated the columns to completely non-classical proportions and perched them on pedestals to gain even more height. The detail, notably in the Ionic capitals, is clumsy and oversized, and the stepped gable over the pediment is an unfortunate addition. On the whole, the effort of the good padre and his untutored Indians to apply some ' architecture ' of the fashionable new mode to an otherwise traditional and dignified façade was a failure.

But the more credit to him for the superb towers (fig. 200) ; based on a long tradition in Mexico, and before that in Spain, they are handled with a vigor and authority that far eclipse the treatment of the similar towers at San Xavier, completed a generation earlier. They are massive, some 20 feet square, and simply treated with single arch openings on each side and slightly splayed corners. Much of their effect of stability is gained by the slight reduction in area of the top stories. The crowning domes, which might have been featureless, gain structural character by the spurred ribs and small crowning cupolas. The west tower is climbed by a steep spiral stair and affords a splendid view over the modern city of Santa Barbara.

The nave of the church measures 39 by 176 feet (see plan, fig. 201) and the 6-foot-thick sandstone walls are pierced by high windows and adorned by seven pairs of giant pilasters. Roof timbers over 40 feet long were brought from the Santa Cruz islands, but these are unfortunately concealed by a hung board ceiling. The so-called ' thunder-bird ' ornaments of painted cedar on this ceiling were carved by the Indians, who modified a winged-distaff decoration pictured in the copy of Vitruvius mentioned above. Doors in the nave lead, on the right, to a walled cemetery containing the bodies of some 4000 Indians, and on the left, to the patio. This with its central fountain, rare plants, and semi-tropical trees, forms a secluded retreat for the Franciscan friars — one to which women, except reigning queens and the wives of American Presidents, are not admitted.

At some distance to the south of the mission stood an unusually well-ordered Indian village. About 250 dwellings were arranged in rows, back to back, each with its private entrance and a room measuring 12 by 19 feet. Built of adobe, stuccoed and whitewashed, the village was surrounded on three sides by an adobe wall, but was open on the fourth to a fine plaza fronting the mission.

In 1806 a creek was dammed a mile and a half above the mission and water brought by an open stone aqueduct to a stone reservoir 110 feet square and 7 feet deep, located on the hillside above the mission. From here, water flowed to a beautiful octagonal fountain in the front plaza, built in 1808, and from the fountain through a carved stone bear-head spout to a long laundry basin where the Indian women washed the clothes. There was also a water-powered gristmill, a granary, pottery, tannery, weaving mill, and the usual orchards, vegetable gardens, and stables. At its peak, Santa Barbara mission had a resident population of 1,792 Indians.

200. East bell tower of the mission church, Santa Barbara (Will Connell)

The mission suffered the usual reverses during the period of secularization, but was never completely abandoned. In 1853 the four remaining friars founded a Franciscan missionary college, which still functions today. Additional space was provided in 1865 by adding a second story to the monastery buildings, and some minor alterations were made later. After severe damage in the earthquake of 1925 the church was beautifully restored and reinforced with steel and concrete, and it is hoped that its appearance of over a century and a quarter ago may thus be lastingly preserved.

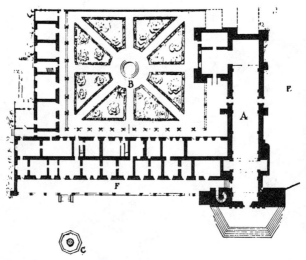

201. Plan of Mission Santa Barbara (Rexford Newcomb, *Spanish Colonial Architecture in the United States,* J. J. Augustin)

San Luis Rey

One of the last gaps in the mission chain, between San Diego and San Juan Capistrano, was filled by the founding of San Luis Rey de Francia, in 1798. This was the last of Lasuén's foundations and was destined to become the largest and most prosperous of all missions in the Western hemisphere. In its banner year, 1826, San Luis Rey had a resident population of 2,869, almost a thousand larger than its next nearest rival, and it boasted 50,000 head of livestock.

Situated in a fertile valley 35 miles north of San Diego, the mission was named in honor of St. Louis IX, King of France in the thirteenth century. Lasuén left in charge the able and energetic Father Antonio Peyri, who served here for thirty-three years before returning home to Spain at the end of the mission era.

Within a few weeks of the founding the Indians had cut 175 wooden beams and prepared 8000 adobe bricks, and a herd of 900 cattle, sheep, and horses was donated by the near-by older missions. An adobe, tile-roofed church of considerable size was completed in 1802, but the mission prospered so phenomenally that in less than a decade Father Peyri determined on a larger and finer church. This, the present structure, was built 1811–15, and other buildings were added later to complete a patio measuring 500 feet square. Father Peyri is reputed to have been trained as an architect; this seems unlikely in view of the typical Franciscan schooling in Spain and Mexico, but he undoubtedly took a leading hand in the design of the new church.

The broad façade (fig. 202), with its towers projecting outside the

202. San Luis Rey de Francia, the mission church, 1811–15 (HABS)

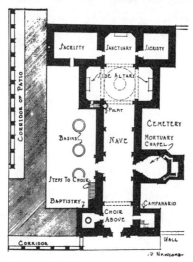

203. Plan of the mission church, San Luis Rey (Rexford Newcomb, *The Old Mission Churches and Historic Houses of California*, J. B. Lippincott)

nave walls, is handled with more architectural assurance than that of
Santa Barbara. The tripartite division by façade buttresses clarifies the
composition of the whole. The central bay, with a simple rectilinear
frame for the portal, flanking statue niches, round window, and curved
gable at the top, is securely composed. The bell tower, one of the finest,
is similar to those at Santa Barbara but has a broader bevel at the corners
to form an irregular octagon; this is echoed in the shape of the dome. A
more formal effect would have been gained by twin bell towers, but as it
stands the asymmetric grouping of façade and monastery is interesting and
unified. An unusual feature is the delicate latticed parapet over the

204. Interior of the mission church, San Luis Rey (HABS)

monastery corridor; it is ingeniously built of flat red tiles laid in a diaper
pattern. The brick masonry of San Luis Rey is of exceptionally good
workmanship. All architectural trim of the façade — moldings, cornices,
niches — is made of molded brick, so smooth that it resembles terra cotta.
The color contrast with the white stucco seems a little harsh, and one wonders whether this trim was not originally coated with stucco.

The church is a large structure with full cruciform plan (fig. 203). The
walls, 6 feet thick, have an adobe core faced by burned brick and stucco.
Beneath the left tower is a small baptistery, containing a soapstone font
carved by the Indians. A stairway in the right tower leads to the choir
loft, over the entrance, and on up to the belfry; there is also an exterior
stairway to the choir loft, as at San Gabriel.

An unusual feature is the little mortuary chapel on the right side of the
nave. Octagonal in plan, and with a rectangular altar space opening from
it, this chapel is roofed by a brick dome resting on engaged columns at the
angles below. The altar, with paired Corinthian columns and a broken
segmental pediment above, is a thoroughly sophisticated baroque composition. All the detail of this little chapel is of fine molded brick covered by stucco. Doors beside the altar open to little stairways and passages within the wall, which command a high outlook over altar and

chapel, a feature believed to have permitted the Indians to view and mourn the remains of the dead.

The nave (fig. 204), 28 feet in width and 30 in height, is divided into five bays by brick pilasters against the wall, with stucco surfacing crudely painted to simulate black marble. The open ceiling beams resting on corbels have been restored. Near the crossing is a paneled and painted wood pulpit, made in the local *carpenteria;* it can be reached from a door in the transept by a ' secret ' stairway within the thickness of the wall.

Since it is the only surviving mission church of cruciform plan, the treatment of the crossing at San Luis Rey has particular interest. Tran-

205. *Asistencia* of San Antonio de Pala, 1815–16 (HABS)

septs project 15 feet at the sides and the sanctuary, with the high altar, projects at the back. Rising at the corners of the square crossing thus formed are massive pilasters carrying four arches of 24-foot span, all built of brick. Above these, flat triangular ' pendentives,' such as were used at San Xavier, convert the square to an octagonal base on which rests the dome. The dome is of wood, octagonal in shape and crowned by a lantern which admits a flood of light through its eight windows. As restored, this lantern corresponds to a description of the one completed in 1829; it is a feature unique among the missions.

Flanking the sanctuary and entered from it are two large sacristies; the one at the left completes the enclosure of a small patio for the private use of the padres. Since 1893, San Luis Rey has been used as a Franciscan missionary college, and at present about forty friars receive training and administer to the outlying Indian chapels.

At one time, San Luis Rey served no less than six *asistencias* at outlying Indian villages. The only one that survives today is the small chapel of San Antonio de Pala, located about 25 miles northeast of the mission in a mountain-enclosed valley. Indians of this valley had helped in the construction of the new mission church, and on the day of its dedication, the Feast of St. Francis, 4 October 1815, they were rewarded by the foundation of an *asistencia* as a chapel in their home valley. A simple church was built within a year, and in another year a thousand converts were worshipping in it. The chapel, well restored today, is a simple rectangle 27 by 144 feet, with adobe walls stuccoed and whitewashed (fig. 205). Sycamore beams and rafters support the red-tiled roof, and the walls are painted with architectural decorations in dull reddish brown, yellow, and black. Although larger than most, Pala suggests for us the primitive charm of the many *asistencias* that once formed part of the mission chain. In its cemetery stands a particularly beautiful *campanario* with arched openings for two bells, copied from the tower of the church at Juarez, Mexico; this is the only original detached *campanario* of the mission chain. The Franciscans returned in 1893 to take up their work with the Pala Indians, and today the chapel serves some 250 devout members of the Indian reservation in the valley.

While San Diego, San Carlos, San Juan Capistrano, Santa Barbara, and San Luis Rey are of outstanding architectural interest, it is with regret that one omits reference to the many ' lesser ' missions, for each has its own distinctive charm. Notable, for example, are the great buttressed walls and lovely *campanario* of fortress-like San Gabriel Arcángel, one of the oldest and most prosperous of all the missions. The single bell tower of San Buenaventura rivals those of Santa Barbara and San Luis Rey; San Miguel Arcángel has the most remarkable of all Indian mural paintings in the nave of its serene church; San Juan Bautista is the only mission to boast a five-aisled church; La Purísima Concepción, with the most nearly perfect of all modern restorations, speaks eloquently of the simple materials and homely craft of its Indian builders. The missions will always fascinate historians of architecture, but the Spanish in California had an interesting military and domestic architecture which also merits attention.

Presidios and pueblos

If it was the function of the missions to convert and civilize the Indians, it was the function of the presidios to house the *comandantes* and soldiers who guarded the mission chain and administered the civil laws made in Spain and Mexico. It must always remain a matter for wonderment that a few hundred white men, scattered along a 500-mile strip of coast, could be protected against scores of thousands of Indians by a mere handful of soldiers: even after ten years of occupation, the total military force in Alta California numbered only eighty men.

There were four presidios in all: San Diego, established in 1769; Monterey, 1770; San Francisco, 1776; and Santa Barbara, 1782. Almost nothing remains of the buildings, partly because of their adobe construction, but primarily because their sites have since become the centers of populous cities.

At first the presidios, like the missions, were crude pole and thatch structures surrounded by wooden stockades. Within a few years more sub-stantial forts, usually of adobe around an open plaza, were built. We know that the presidio at Monterey had such a plaza, surrounded by a

10-foot wide corridor with redwood posts to support the tiled roof; the presidio chapel on the south side of the plaza is all that remains today. At the time of Vancouver's visit in 1792, the San Francisco presidio was notoriously weak, and the Spanish hastily erected a new fort in 1794. But as Berger reports, ' even the Castillo de San Joaquín proved a dismal failure. Every time a cannon was fired, the shock crumbled the adobe walls.' [3] And at San Diego, the Spanish engineer Córdoba reported in 1796 that the presidio defenses had ' no other merit than that the enemy would perhaps be ignorant of their weakness.'

The best built and best maintained of the presidios was that at Santa

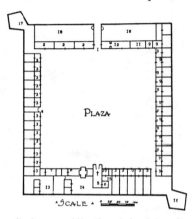

206. Plan of the Santa Barbara presidio (founded 1782) as it was in 1788 (Rexford Newcomb, *The Old Mission Churches and Historic Houses of California*. J. B. Lippincott)

Barbara. It was located on the site of four city blocks of the modern business district. A report by the *comandante* to Governor Fages in 1788 enables us to reconstruct its appearance fairly acurately (fig. 206). The entire presidio was surrounded by an outer wall of adobe 7 feet thick and 12 high. Bastions at the east and west corners mounted small cannon. Within the wall were corrals for cattle and horses, and an inner rectangle of one-story adobe buildings, plastered and whitewashed. The main gate, 20 feet wide, was flanked by a guardroom on one side and storerooms on the other. On either side of the plaza, 320 feet square, were soldiers' quarters, and the side opposite the gate contained the most important buildings: a chapel in the center, chaplain's rooms to one side of it, and the suites of the commanding officer and ensign on the other. Vancouver, who visited the place in 1793, reported that ' the presidio excels all others in neatness, cleanliness, and other smaller though essential comforts. . .'

It was the duty of the governor of Alta California to encourage secular as well as religious colonization, and to this end three *pueblos* or civilian towns were founded. They were not very successful. Governor Neve established the first one, San José, in November 1777, on the eastern bank of the Guadalupe River, about four miles distant from the newly founded

Mission Santa Clara. There were sixty-six colonists, including several ex-soldiers, Mexican peons, and their families. Each was allotted a piece of land for planting, and each built a crude log-and-mud dwelling. The settlers were an unruly lot and for years scandalized the near-by padres by their dissolute life and impious behavior. As they refused to attend services at the mission, the saintly Father Catalá built a road from the pueblo to the mission door and planted along it three rows of black willow trees, forerunner of the modern Alameda connecting the towns of San José and Santa Clara. Even this shady encouragement failed to work, and eventually the undiscouraged padres built an *asistencia* at San José, whither they trudged in search of souls to save.

207. José Antonio Aguirre House, San Diego, 1825–30 (reproduced with permission from *Sunset Western Ranch Houses*)

Seeking to improve over the dubious moral tone of San José, Governor Neve requested the Mexican viceroy to send farming families for his second pueblo. But when the party finally arrived, it was a motley crowd of farmers, Negroes, Indians, mulattoes, and ex-convicts. This was the group that established, on 4 September 1781, *La Reina de los Ángeles,* nucleus of modern Los Angeles, a safe ten miles west of Mission San Gabriel. Within a decade the population of 139 assorted souls had built adobe houses, barracks, granaries, and a public hall, and was producing more grain than any of the missions except neighboring San Gabriel. The local church, Nuestra Señora de los Ángeles, was reconstructed as the modern Plaza Church in 1861. The third pueblo, Branciforte, was established on the site of modern Santa Cruz.

Domestic architecture

Most of the surviving ' Spanish Colonial ' houses of California date from the Mexican and American eras. After the revolution of 1821, the Mexican government frowned on the great holdings of the missions and encouraged instead the development of private farming and stock raising by making huge land grants. Great herds of cattle and sheep roamed the inland ranges, and at the seacoast ports hides and tallow were traded with Yankee skippers for luxury manufactures from the East brought around the Horn. The decades of the 1830's and 1840's saw a golden era of prosperity, and the towns of Monterey, Santa Barbara, and San Diego were centers of a charming and active social life.

The farmhouse was known as a *casa de campo,* and its grounds might be distinguished as a *hacienda* if devoted to agriculture, or *rancho* if devoted to stock raising. A house in town was called a *casa de pueblo.* Materials and construction of the houses were fundamentally the same as in the missions — adobe, wood, and tile prevailing — but the houses were simpler architecturally. The typical arrangement of the larger residence

208. Casa Estudillo, San Diego, 1825–6 (reproduced with permission from *Sunset Western Ranch Houses*)

is illustrated in the house built by José Antonio Aguirre (fig. 207) at San Diego between 1825 and 1830. Three wings embraced a patio open on the fourth side. The *corredor* or veranda facing the patio was invariably supported by wooden posts or brick piers, not by the heavy arcades of the

209. Santiago Arguëllo House, San Diego, 1833 (reproduced with permission from *Sunset Western Ranch Houses*)

missions. The *corredor* served as a shady lounging place beside the patio and was much used for outdoor living; it also served as access to all the rooms opening on it. In the Monterey region patios are likely to face south, to gain warmth in the winter months, but in southern California the reverse orientation is frequent. Sometimes, as in the Aguirre House, the main rooms were fronted by *corredors* on both sides. Simple shed roofs covered the three wings.

Another fine house of the same period is the Casa Estudillo in the Old Town at San Diego (fig. 208). Built in 1825–6, its dozen rooms enclose a

210. The patio, de la Guerra House, Santa Barbara, 1819–26 (HABS)

large patio. The thick adobe walls carry heavy roof timbers bound together by rawhide thongs. The shed roofs of the wings pitch away from the patio, as in the Aguirre House, giving a very low exterior wall, adorned only by paneled exterior shutters. The appearance of the patio of such a house is illustrated in figure 209, the Santiago Arguëllo House at San Diego, built in 1833. Widely spaced wooden posts support the low-piched roof where it overhangs the *corredor*. The simple structural detail and long low lines give an impression of smallness, yet the house contains fourteen rooms within its solid adobe walls.

Typical of the finer *casa de pueblo* is the de la Guerra House at Santa Barbara (figs. 210, 211). Captain José Antonio de la Guerra was *comandante* of the presidio from 1815 to 1842, and he built his house between 1819 and 1826. As owner of 200,000 acres of land, producer of over $100,-000 worth of cattle annually, and an important figure in the military and political life of the province, de la Guerra was a lavish entertainer. The complete simplicity and modesty of his house are the more surprising, though we are left in no doubt with regard to its comfort and hospitality. The house surrounds its patio on three sides, with a broad *corredor* offering welcome shade. Square wooden posts support the projecting eaves of the tile-covered roof. Walls are of adobe plastered and whitewashed inside and out, though at one time wooden siding was added to protect them from weathering. The captain kept not only a well-stocked wine cellar (*bodega*) but one of the few private libraries in the province. The gardens, once famous, have now been engulfed by business structures.

211. The *corredor*, de la Guerra House (HABS)

212. South (entrance) façade of Rancho Camulos, Ventura County, Calif. (Rexford Newcomb)

Rancho Camulos, famous as the locale of Mrs. Helen Hunt Jackson's novel *Ramona*, was the center of a vast estate granted in 1839 to Lieutenant Antonio del Valle and comprising much of the area of five modern townships in Ventura and Los Angeles counties. The old wing of the house (at the bottom in the plan, fig. 213) was built in 1839, the new wing ten years later. The main rooms face north, for coolness, on the long veranda and open patio with its gravel walks and clipped rose and cypress hedges. A separate building on the north side houses the kitchen (*cocina*) and service rooms, and there is a detached chapel approached by a lat-

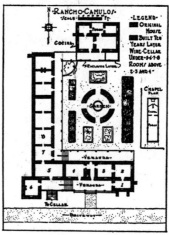

213. Plan of Rancho Camulos (Rexford Newcomb, *The Old Mission Churches and Historic Houses of California*, J. B. Lippincott)

ticed shelter. The south façade (fig. 212) is very simple, with typical veranda posts, beveled at the corners through part of their height, supporting a thin-edged roof. Walls are of whitewashed adobe, and roofs covered by hand-riven shingles or 'shakes.'

Further north in Ventura County is Rancho Olivos, one of the most beautiful of all Spanish-California houses (fig. 214). It is of a type less common in southern California than in the north, where many close parallels may be found in such towns as Monterey, San Juan, or Sonoma. These houses are of two stories rather than one, with long verandas below and balconies above, the supporting posts running in two stories to the roof. The ground story contains the living room, dining room, kitchen, and service rooms, and an exterior stairway leads to the balcony from which the bedrooms are reached. Usually the ends of veranda and balcony are closed by wide vertical boarding or lattice work, to give privacy and a partial protection from the wind; at Rancho Olivos the purpose is served by projecting rooms at the ends. Light balcony railings add the only touch of decoration to an otherwise very simple exterior. The low-pitched gable roof, covered with shingles, is hipped at both ends. Such houses, with all rooms in a straight-line plan, do not need projecting ells or wings, and the patio is enclosed merely by high adobe walls. The patio at Rancho Olivos is entered through a charming gateway, opposite the house, bearing a pierced gable and bell over the simple round-arch entrance. Both front and rear façades have the two-story verandas.

214. Rancho Olivos, Ventura (Donald R. Hannaford)

Monterey is especially rich in old adobe houses. It saw its greatest prosperity in the 1830's and 1840's, and many fine *casas de pueblo* were built in this era. Despite the prevalence of good redwood, pine, and oak in northern California, adobe remained the favorite building material; it was warm in winter and cool in summer, and required less labor than hand-sawing and hewing the necessary timbers and boards. Limestone was available in Monterey, but only one house of the period was built entirely of this material. The adobe walls averaged about 3 feet in thickness for ground-story walls, 2 feet for second-story walls, the offset being on the interior, since this gave additional space to the bedrooms. The adobe blocks were laid with mud-mortar joints about an inch thick and surfaced by a smooth-textured mud plaster. The surface was whitewashed every year to harden it against rain. In later years, as mill-sawed lumber became common, the adobe was frequently covered by wood siding — horizontal clapboards, or vertical board-and-batten being used.

The classic example of the Monterey type is the house built in 1834 by Thomas Larkin, the first American consul to Alta California. It is surrounded on three sides by a two-story balcony (fig. 215); the fourth side faces a walled patio. A low-pitch hipped roof affords a comfortable sense of shelter. Some of the old small-pane sash windows remain; these are set at the outer surface of the thick wall, forming deep window seats within. The interior reveals are splayed and paneled in such a way that the shutters fold back to become a part of the paneling. Interior walls are whitewashed, and the wide hand-hewn planks of the second floor, carried on heavy hewn joists, form the ceilings of the lower rooms. Second-story rooms usually had ceilings of wide pine boards, beaded at the joints. Despite the solidity of construction, the exterior effect of the Larkin House is one of airy lightness, produced by the slender porch posts, light balcony rail, and thin cornice. There is no ornament whatever, except for the delicate tracery of climbing roses and bougainvillaea.

215. Thomas Larkin House, Monterey, 1834 (Donald R. Hannaford)

Similar fine examples of the northern Californian *casa de pueblo* may be seen in the Soberanes House at Monterey (1829), the José Castro House at San Juan (1830), the Blue Wing Tavern at Sonoma (1834), the Vallejo House at Sonoma (1836), and the McKinley House at Monterey.

An interesting variant of the type has a cantilevered balcony for the second story, with slender posts running from balcony floor to projecting eaves. One façade of the Castro House at San Juan is treated in this manner, and another example is the Old Whaling Station at Monterey (fig. 216). This was built by Captain Davenport, a Cape Cod whaler who came to Monterey in 1854 to organize the Monterey Whaling Company. Despite its late date (the house was completed in 1855), it has many features typical of the Monterey style: thick adobe walls, a main entrance with a pair of narrow doors, small-pane windows (24 light over 24 light sash), and the long balcony.

But New England ideas had come with the Yankee traders, and by this time might be found on Pacific shores the familiar New England 'saltbox' house, with lean-to and long roof slope at the rear, and a certain compact propriety of shape that contrasts sharply with the spread-out one-story *ranchos* of California. Yankee influence may account also for the introduction of tidy and proper interior staircases, which evidently proved so acceptable that the picturesque exterior staircases to balconies were abandoned and are rarely seen now.

But the one-story house always remained popular; there were several in Monterey. With their long low lines and utter simplicity of surface and detail, they were a strong influence on the development of the modern California style in the 1930's and 1940's.

216. Old Whaling Station, Monterey, 1855 (Donald R. Hannaford)

Roofs always count for much in California houses. Where redwood was abundant, hand-split shakes were used and they give a rich color and texture to the broad low surfaces. But red tiles were always favored by those who could afford them, for they gave a dramatic color and texture to the exterior. Sometimes, as families came on poorer days, tiles were sold and replaced by shingles. An interesting variant is the roof covered by tiles to the line of the wall, with shingles on that portion of the roof projecting over the balcony. It may be that this originated in an effort to save weight on the cantilevered balconies, but if so it was also sometimes adopted in houses with supporting posts running clear to the ground.

Adobe houses were not necessarily a monotonous white. The ' whitewash ' applied to the walls and to balcony woodwork was often tinted to an off-white color or even a delicate pink, warm gray, or soft green. Exterior doors, shutters, and window trim were painted in more solid tones of gray, green, and brown. Combined with the color and texture of roof surfaces and the luxuriant shrubs and flowering vines of a semi-tropical climate, the houses of Alta California, so extremely simple in architectural form and detail, achieved a richness of color and texture that might well have been envied by the weather-beaten skippers from far-off Portsmouth, Salem, and Nantucket.

The Custom House at Monterey, a rambling red-tiled adobe structure in three wings, seems to epitomize the early history of California, for its first wing was built in 1814 under Spanish rule, the one-story middle section was built in 1822 by Mexican authorities, and the third portion was erected after the American occupation. It was on the flagstaff of this building that Commodore Sloat unfurled the Stars and Stripes on 7 July 1846, thus bringing to an end a period of Spanish and Mexican rule that had begun almost 300 years before at St. Augustine.

Spanish Colonial architecture might have persisted for many more decades, for it takes more than a change in government to change an architectural style. But that more profound revolution was soon forthcoming when frantic prospectors from Sutter's Creek poured into the claims offices with the magic cry of ' Gold! Gold! ' Within a year the harbor of San Francisco was bristling with masts and the passes from the East were a seething torrent of men, teams, and hopes. By the end of '49 San Francisco's population had leaped to 25,000, and by the end of '50 her quiet *casas de pueblo* were lost amidst a welter of rooming houses, taverns, dance halls, prospectors' supply stores, breweries, assay offices, and gambling dens. The quiet patio gave way to the false front and the honky-tonk, and an architectural era was over.

THE FRANCISCAN MISSIONS OF CALIFORNIA

IN THE ORDER OF THEIR FOUNDING

Name	Date	Under	Erection of present church	Location
1. San Diego de Alacalá	16 July 1769	Padre Serra	1808–13	Moved in 1774 to Mission Valley, 6 miles northwest of San Diego
2. San Carlos Borromeo	3 June 1770	Padre Serra	1793–7	Moved to Carmel, 5 miles from Monterey, on 9 July 1771
Presidio Chapel, Monterey	3 June 1770	Padre Serra	1794	Monterey. Nave lengthened and transepts added, 1859
3. San Antonio de Padua	14 July 1771	Padre Serra	1810–13	6 miles from Jolon
4. San Gabriel Arcángel	8 Sept. 1771	Padre Serra	1794–1806	10 miles E of Los Angeles
Nuestra Señora de los Ángeles	4 Sept. 1781	Padre Serra	1822	Los Angeles, as an *asistencia* to San Gabriel. Reconstructed as the Plaza Church in 1861

Name	Date	Under	Erection of present church	Location
5. San Luis Obispo de Tolosa	1 Sept. 1772	Padre Serra	c. 1799	San Luis Obispo
6. San Francisco de Asís	29 June 1776	Padre Serra	1782–91	San Francisco. Called 'Mission Dolores'
7. San Juan Capistrano	1 Nov. 1776	Padre Serra	1797–1806	San Juan Capistrano
8. Santa Clara de Asís	12 Jan. 1777	Padre Serra	1818–22	Santa Clara
9. San Buenaventura	31 March 1782	Padre Serra	1794–1809	Ventura. Rebuilt 1812–15
10. Santa Barbara	4 Dec. 1786	Padre Lasuén	1815–20	Santa Barbara. Reconstructed 1926–7
11. La Purísima Concepción	8 Dec. 1787	Padre Lasuén	1813–18	5 miles N of Lompoc. Reconstructed 1935–40
12. Santa Cruz	28 Aug. 1791	Padre Lasuén	1799 (only ruins left)	Santa Cruz. Church 'reproduced' 1931
13. Nuestra Señora de la Soledad	9 Oct. 1791	Padre Lasuén	1831 (only ruins left)	2 miles from Soledad
14. San José de Guadalupe	11 June 1797	Padre Lasuén	c. 1806	15 miles N of San José. Destroyed 1868
15. San Juan Bautista	24 June 1797	Padre Lasuén	1803–12	San Juan Bautista
16. San Miguel Arcángel	25 July 1797	Padre Lasuén	1816–18	10 miles N of Paso Robles
17. San Fernando Rey de España	8 Sept. 1797	Padre Lasuén	1804–6	Near San Fernando
18. San Luis Rey de Francia	13 June 1798	Padre Lasuén	1811–15	5 miles E of Oceanside
San Antonio de Pala	4 Oct. 1815		1815–18	21 miles from San Luis Rey, to which it was an *asistencia*
19. Santa Inés Virgen y Mártir	17 Sept. 1804	Estevan Tapis	1817	3 miles E of Buellton. Restored 1911–17.

Name	Date	Erection of Under present church		Location
20. San Rafael Arcángel	14 Dec. 1817	Mariano Payeras	1817 (gone)	An *asistencia* of San Francisco until 1823, then a mission
21. San Francisco Solano	4 July 1823	Padre José Altamira	1823–4	Sonoma. Under presidency of José Señan

READING SUGGESTIONS

Of a vast literature on Spanish California, the acknowledged standard on architectural history is Rexford Newcomb's *Old Mission Churches and Historic Houses of California* (J. B. Lippincott, Philadelphia, 1925). Newcomb's surveys and measured drawings in *The Franciscan Mission Architecture of Alta California* (Architectural Book Publishing Co., New York, 1916) and his pictorial survey in *Spanish-Colonial Architecture in the United States* (J. J. Augustin, New York, 1937) are also useful.

The best general history of the missions, without particular stress on architectural style and details, is John A. Berger's *Franciscan Missions of California* (G. P. Putnam's Sons, New York, 1941). A briefer but interesting narrative is given in Part v of Trent Sanford's *Architecture of the Southwest* (W. W. Norton, New York, 1950).

Residential architecture is well treated in D. R. Hannaford and R. Edwards's *Spanish Colonial or Adobe Architecture of California, 1800–1850* (Architectural Book Publishing Co., New York, 1931).

Admirable collections of photographs of the missions are found in two small books: *The Missions of California,* by Will Connell (Hastings House, New York, 1941) and *California Missions,* by Karl F. Brown with photographs by Floyd Ray (Garden City Publishing Co., New York, 1939).

8

French Colonial Architecture of the Mississippi Valley

THAT THE FRENCH is the least known of the Colonial styles may seem strange in view of the immense size of the French colonial empire in North America: in the late seventeenth and early eighteenth centuries it was even greater in extent than the Spanish holdings, extending from the Alleghenies to the Rocky Mountains and from the Gulf of Mexico to Labrador and Hudson's Bay (fig. 217). But in all this vast region there were few towns: the French established forts and traded with the Indians for furs, but comparatively few permanent settlers migrated to the new territory. By the middle of the eighteenth century, except for plantations along the lower river and small settlements clustered around military posts scattered throughout the vast area, the Mississippi valley remained a lonely wilderness. The meagre revenues from commerce hardly balanced the costs of military and political administration, and with the loss of French Canada to England after the Seven Years' War (1756–63) France readily relinquished the unprofitable colony of Louisiana to England and Spain.

Time has dealt harshly with the few remains of French Colonial building: pioneer relics have long since been obliterated in big cities such as Detroit and St. Louis; small towns in the Mississippi bottoms have been destroyed by floods; and French New Orleans was largely wiped out by the disastrous fires of 1788 and 1794. But patient study of documents and of the few remaining buildings has revealed a Colonial style of uniquely French character.

Historical background

The architectural style, like the earliest settlement, seems to have come up the St. Lawrence and down the Mississippi valleys. During the whole of the seventeenth century French explorers, trappers, missionaries, and settlers worked inland. Tadoussac on the St. Lawrence was established in 1600, Quebec in 1608, and Montreal in 1611. The Great Lakes offered a highway of water, and the French dotted the shores at strategic points with forts: Sault Ste. Marie in 1668; Frontenac, 1673; Duluth and Fort des Miamis in 1679. Already in 1673 Marquette and Jolliet had descended the Mississippi as far as its junction with the Arkansas, and in 1679 strategic Fort Crèvecœur was built halfway down the Illinois River. The way was prepared for LaSalle to lead his epoch-making expedition: striking out from new Fort Crèvecœur with some fifty men, he descended the Mississippi to the Gulf and on 9 April 1682, set up a cross and a column bearing the arms of France on the bank of the river, claiming the entire territory and tributary system of the Mississippi for the King of France and naming it, in honor of him, Louisiana.

LaSalle's reports went back to Versailles and, in due season, to Madrid. The Spanish, who had completely neglected the lower Mississippi since

217. Map of French North America to the middle of the eighteenth century (Van H. English)

De Soto's discovery a century and a half before, hastily established forts and mission outposts in East Texas, but it was too late: the French formally annexed Louisiana as a Crown colony in 1699, making Biloxi the first capital. Other settlements were made at Mobile, Fort Toulouse, Natchez, and Natchitoches in the early eighteenth century. *Voyageurs* and Jesuit missionaries came in from the upper valley, and *coureurs de bois* traded with the Indians and brought in pelts. But it was not primarily

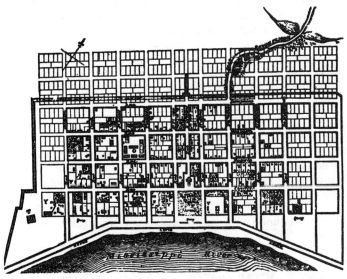

218. Plan of the Vieux Carré, New Orleans, laid out by LeBlond de la Tour and Adrien de Pauger, 1721 (Harvard University Department of Landscape Architecture)

a colonizing effort: the aging Louis XIV was more interested in reaping gold and silver than in planting communities and farms.

Early in the reign of Louis XIV's great grandson, the infant Louis XV, feverish financial speculations in Louisiana land led to the establishment of a new trading center. An expedition under Jean Baptiste LeMoyne, Sieur de Bienville, founded a new town in 1718, about a hundred miles from the Gulf, and named it *Nouvelle Orléans,* in honor of the regent Philippe, Duc d'Orléans. New Orleans was one of the early planned towns in America.* In 1721, fifty men, under the direction of the engineers LeBlond de la Tour and Adrien de Pauger, plotted a city on the familiar gridiron plan, with some eighty rectilinear blocks (fig. 218). A town square, the Place d'Armes, faced the broad sweep of the river and was surrounded by church, school, and governor's palace. Such street names as the Rue Chartres, Rue St. Louis, Rue Dauphine, Rue Bourbon, Rue Bienville are eloquent reminders today of the French origin of this

* Charleston (1680), Philadelphia (1682), Annapolis (1694), and Williamsburg (1699) preceded it.

old portion of town, now called the Vieux Carré. In 1723, New Orleans superseded Biloxi as the capital of Louisiana.

Other towns grew up 500 miles northward, in what was then called the Illinois Country, after the Indian nation of that name. Kaskaskia (1695) and Cahokia (1700) were on the Illinois side, and Vincennes (1735) was on the Wabash, in what is now Indiana. St. Louis was founded in 1764, and Ste. Geneviève, Missouri, in 1785. A dozen or more other small towns farmed the river bottomlands or worked the lead mines of Missouri. In the early eighteenth century these were oriented chiefly to Quebec and French Canada, but as New Orleans grew in size, its influence, politically and commercially, gradually predominated.

When France lost Louisiana in the Treaty of Paris in 1763, all territory east of the river was ceded to England, all territory west of the river (but including New Orleans) went to Spain. However, the transfer meant little in the Illinois Country, which remained culturally French until the American westward movement. Even in New Orleans, where the Spanish regime was of more force, French traditions remained dominant and were even reinforced by the immigration and settlement, between 1760 and 1790, of several thousand French Acadians, expelled from Nova Scotia by the British. The ' 'Cajuns ' settled largely in the bayou districts of southern Louisiana. New Orleans grew as a cosmopolitan city, a kind of *bouillabaisse* of French, Spanish, Canary Islanders, Germans, Acadians, and — increasingly — American traders and flatboatmen from faraway Pittsburgh and the Ohio Country. It is not surprising that the city's architecture reveals a fascinating blend of influences. Unhappily, a large part of eighteenth-century New Orleans was destroyed by fires: in 1788 a fire destroyed more than 800 houses; and a second fire leveled over 200 buildings in 1794. In a sense, New Orleans was ' wiped clean ' in preparation for the American era, which began with a ceremony on 20 December 1803, marking the purchase of the Louisiana Territory by the United States. The Place d'Armes was to become Jackson Square, and French and Spanish architectural influences were to give way to the Federal and Greek Revival styles of the new nation.

French Colonial materials and construction

French Colonial houses in the Mississippi valley were usually of half-timber construction, but with framing differing markedly from English half-timber houses, and a variety of different materials for the wall filling. Most primitive and most common was the *poteaux-en-terre* house, meaning, literally, ' posts in the earth.' Heavy upright logs, usually of cedar in the Illinois Country and of cypress in Louisiana, were hewn flat on two or four faces and set several feet deep in the ground. They were spaced only a few inches apart. The spaces between were filled by a variety of materials. Simplest and cheapest was *bouzillage*, a mixture of clay and grass or, in the South, clay and Spanish moss. The Williams House in Natchitoches (1776) had clay filling bound by deer hair instead of moss. Such walls were at first left exposed, so that the structural frame was visible. The filling was easily eroded, and the posts tended to rot in the ground, so the construction was not very durable. Sometimes the wall spaces were filled with rubble stones set in clay, a filling known as *pierrotage*.

The origin of the *poteaux-en-terre* house is obscure. Brackenridge supposed that the construction may have come from Santo Domingo, but it seems more likely to have come down from the north. It is said to have been used extensively in the first buildings of Detroit (founded 1702), and there are several early examples in Ste. Geneviève, Missouri. In essence, it is similar to the log-palisade construction of the Iroquois and Huron Indians, which the French Canadians knew well. Although Peterson states that it 'seems to be unknown in Canada,' [1] the close architectural relationship between the Illinois Country and the St. Lawrence valley suggests that a Canadian origin will be found.

In order to prevent the rotting of logs in the ground, an improved type of construction employed a stone foundation topped by a timber 'sole' or sill, with the upright logs resting upon it. The wall filling in this *poteaux-sur-sole* construction was of the same type as before. In Louisiana spaces between log uprights and diagonal braces were often filled with bricks (*briqueté-entre-poteaux*), but since the bricks were soft and porous they were always covered by a coat of lime plaster, a surfacing which is almost universal in New Orleans today.

Stone houses were less common than those of half-timber construction, but the 'first' building in St. Louis, a large fur-trading depot erected in 1764, was of stone, and in general so were the finer and more expensive houses. The tradition of stone building was of course familiar to anyone who had passed through the St. Lawrence valley. Log-cabin construction of the familiar horizontal round-log type was unknown to the French, and apparently the first true log cabin in St. Louis was built by one John Coons, a Philadelphia carpenter, as late as the time of the Revolutionary War.

One-story houses

The typical French pioneer house was of one story, containing three or more rooms placed in line, with stone chimney in the center or at the end, the whole surrounded by a *galerie* which gave access to the rooms. An end room might be halved to form two small bedrooms or *cabinets*. Such a house was pictured by General Victor Collot in his *Journey in North America* after a visit to the Illinois Country in 1796 (fig. 219). It is evidently of *poteaux-en-terre* construction, with a railed *galerie*, and slender posts supporting the eaves. The roof shape is entirely characteristic of the French Colonial style: a steep-pitch hipped roof rises over the house proper while a lower-pitched roof covers the *galerie*.

The oldest extant house in the Midwest, at Cahokia, Illinois, was built for an *habitant* of unknown identity, probably about 1737 (fig. 220). In 1763 Captain Saucier, a French military engineer, bought it, and his son François sold it in 1793 for use as a county courthouse and jail. It has since been known as Cahokia Courthouse. After peregrinations to the St. Louis Fair in 1904 and to Jackson Park, Chicago, the house was returned in 1939 to its original foundations, where it reigns in restored glory as a historic monument.

The Cahokia Courthouse is of the superior *poteaux-sur-sole* construction, with fine stone chimneys at the ends. The surrounding *galerie* and double-pitch hipped roof are typical of the style, but the house is of unusual size with its four rooms and spacious attic. Windows are glazed casements, with wood shutters *(contrevents)*, and other refinements in-

219. *Habitant* house in the Illinois Country, as pictured by General Victor Collot in his *Journey in North America*, 1796 (courtesy Charles E. Peterson)

clude beaded ceiling beams, handsome wrought-iron hardware, and interior walls plastered on split lath. The building shares the qualities of unadorned simplicity and frank rugged structure of the typical New England Colonial house, yet belongs to a completely different architectural tradition.

Quite similar to it, though smaller in size, were the early Bienvenue

220. Cahokia Courthouse, Cahokia, Ill., *c.*1737, as re-erected in 1939 (HABS)

House in St. Louis, three or four of the old houses at Ste. Geneviève,[2] and the Manuel Lisa House in St. Louis, which Professor Ramsay Traquair of McGill University has asserted to be identical in style with early houses along the Ottawa River. This basic form remained unchanged throughout the eighteenth century, as is shown by the Jean Baptiste Vallé House built in Ste. Geneviève in 1785. The upright log walls of the house are covered with white plaster, protected by the wide *galerie*. Though the

221. 'Madam John's Legacy,' New Orleans, *c.*1727 (Louisiana State Museum)

region had been ceded to Spain a generation before, and the household was listed in the 1787 census as belonging to Don Juan Bautista Vallé, the Illinois Country still remained essentially French in customs, speech, costume, and architecture. Even the year before the Louisiana Purchase, a fine French Colonial house was built by Pierre Ménard on the river bluff below Fort Kaskaskia, its low-pitch hipped roof spreading wide over a thin-posted *galerie* of airy lightness.

A few French Colonial houses still stand in the close-packed streets of New Orleans' Vieux Carré. Of these the oldest is ' Madam John's Legacy ' on Dumaine Street (fig. 221). It was built by Jean Pascal, a sea captain who came to New Orleans in 1726 and probably completed his house within the next year or two. Many of the early houses, especially in the bottomlands, were raised 6 or 8 feet above the ground on brick piers as a precaution against floods. Later, when this safety factor was found unnecessary, the ' raised cottage ' style, as it came to be called, persisted as a popular mode of construction. The basement, housing office and service rooms, was closed in by a brick wall. A staircase rising to the open *galerie* at the main-floor level served as a means of communication to the rooms. Slender cypress colonets supported the hipped roof, which has the characteristic double pitch. The narrow dormers with arched windows were doubtless added later to make use of the attic space.

Lafitte's Blacksmith Shop (fig. 222) was built between 1772 and 1791 by Jean and Pierre Lafitte, illicit dealers in black ivory who, according to

222. Lafitte's Blacksmith Shop, New Orleans, 1772–91 (Kosti Ruohomaa from Black Star, © Time, Inc.)

tradition, posed as blacksmiths to mask their nefarious trade. The house is of *briqueté-entre-poteaux* construction, as may be seen where the plaster has crumbled away to expose the soft brick laid between framing timbers of cypress. Nearly square in plan, the house originally had four rooms of equal size. There was no *galerie* so the double-pitch roof was no longer needed, but the tradition was remembered in a graceful flare of the roof at the eaves. The tile roof recalls the fact that in the earliest days roofs thatched with palmetto leaves, or shingled with split cypress shakes, were common, but after the fire of 1794 the Governor, Baron de Carondelet, offered builders a premium for the use of tile to reduce the fire hazard. Both the Spanish type of tapered half-cylinder and the French type of flat pantile were used extensively. The warm reds of the tiled roofs and the pastel tones of stuccoed walls formed a perfect background for the flowering vines and tubs of camellias and hydrangeas which adorned the intimate little courtyards.

The Ursuline Convent at New Orleans

Much valuable source material on the early history of public and institutional buildings in New Orleans was brought to light in the summer of 1938 by Samuel Wilson. Working in the Archives Nationales in Paris, he found many documents and more than a hundred architectural drawings done by official French architects in New Orleans for barracks, hospitals, storehouses, and other structures. Of these the most interesting was the Convent of the Ursuline Nuns.[3] As early as 1726 it was arranged that

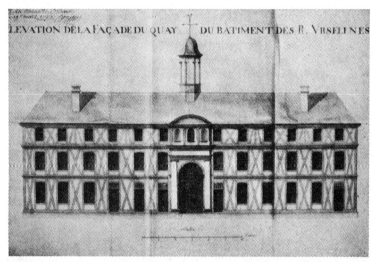

LEVATION DE LA FAÇADE DU QUAY   DU BATIMENT DES R. VRSELINES

223. Ursuline Convent, New Orleans, first building, 1734. Architect's elevation of the façade (Archives Nationales, Paris, courtesy Samuel Wilson)

a group of Ursuline nuns from Rouen should go to New Orleans ' to relieve the poor sick and provide at the same time for the education of young girls.'

Arriving at New Orleans in October 1727, the Ursulines were temporarily housed in what must have been a large residence for those early days. In a letter to her father, Sister Madelaine Hachard reported:

Our residence . . . is in the most beautiful house in the city, it is of two stories & above, a mansard, we have there all the apartments necessary, six doors to enter the apartments below, there are all around large windows, however there is no glass, but the windows are stretched with fine and clear cloth, which gives as much daylight as glass.[4]

Meantime a convent was under construction, but administrative conflicts and shortages of materials and labor delayed its completion until 1734. Its final form probably followed drawings made by the architect de Batz and approved by the chief engineer of the colony, Broutin, on 19 March 1733 (fig. 223). The building was three stories high, of half-timber (*columbage*) construction, with the diagonal bracing of the frame forming a series of X's and the interstices filled with bricks. This type of construction was common in medieval France and was widely used in early Louisiana. The design, however, with its axial symmetry, regularly spaced windows, central pavilion bearing a large segmental pediment, and crowning cupola, showed a Renaissance formality. The steep-pitch hipped roof was covered by tiles. A one-story wing of brick, with angle quoins, stucco cornice, and steep hipped roof, served as a military hospital, and a few years later other wings were added to serve as kitchen and hospital laboratory.

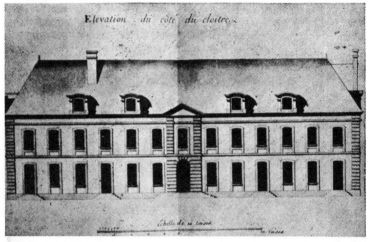

224. Ursuline Convent, second building, 1748–52. Architect's elevation of the façade (Archives Nationales, Paris, courtesy Samuel Wilson)

The main convent building, however, was short-lived. The framing timbers, exposed for many months during construction, soon began to rot and within a dozen years the building was ready to collapse. Drawings for a new and more permanent edifice were done by de Batz and Broutin, dated 10 November 1745, and construction followed in 1748–52. Built of stucco-covered brick, the new building was pure Louis XV in style (fig. 224). Formally and spaciously composed, it reveals the traits of its particular generation in France: the abandonment of applied orders of pilasters or columns, the slightly arched windows, broad hipped roof with small dormers, the narrow central pavilion (such as may be seen in Courtonne's Hotel de Matignon, 1721, in Paris) and particularly the delight in rusticated quoins, familiar in Jean Aubert's Hotel Biron (1728) on the Rue de Varennes, Paris. The ground floor was used largely for the dormitory, classrooms, refectory, and infirmary of the orphanage maintained by the Ursuline sisters; the second floor contained the nuns' chambers, library, infirmary, and storerooms. The Ursulines built a new convent in 1823–4, and the old building and its land were presented as a gift to the Bishop of New Orleans. Many remodelings and repairs since that,

date have altered the original architectural character, but the old building on Chartres Street, now known as the Archbishopric, still stands.

The plantation houses

The plantation houses of the lower parishes in Louisiana were mostly
of two stories. Typical is the eighteenth-century house in Acadia Parish
pictured in figure 225. An evolution of the ' raised cottage ' style, the

225. Typical plantation house of the Louisiana bayou country. Acadia Parish (Shepard Vogelgesang)

plantation houses usually had stucco-covered brick walls and columns
below, and wood construction above. The *galerie* extended only across
the front (see plan B, fig. 226), or across both front and back, giving
cross-ventilation to a single line of rooms (plan A, fig. 226). The brick
supporting posts were shaped as classic columns, but the second-story supports were almost invariably smaller wooden colonets. An exterior stair
case served for access to the *galerie* and second-story rooms.

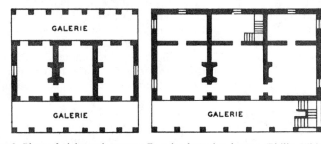

226. Plans of eighteenth-century French plantation houses (Philip White)

The larger plantation houses had a *galerie* extending around all four
sides. Such was Parlange at New Roads in Pointe Coupée Parish (fig.
227). The house was built in 1750 [5] by the Marquis Vincent de Ternant,
whose widow married Charles Parlange, a French naval officer. The plantation is still owned by descendants of the Parlange family. The house is
in every respect a classic example of the French Colonial style as it developed in the lower valley. Ground-story walls, columns, and floor are of

brick, upper-story walls of cypress timbers *bouzillé* with clay and Spanish moss. The *galerie* circles the house, and slender wooden colonets support the sheltering hipped roof, which is covered by cypress shakes worn to a silvery gray. French doors, fitted with outer blinds and surmounted by ornamental fan transoms, open from living rooms to the *galerie*. A wide stairway on the main front descends to the grounds studded with live oaks and pecans. A cedar-lined driveway flanked by octagonal brick *pigeonniers*, painted white, leads to the river.

227. Parlange, Pointe Coupée Parish, La., 1750 (HABS)

Equally fine are Darby on Bayou Tèche, built by François St. Marr Darby in the late eighteenth century, and the Keller Plantation in St. Charles Parish, built for the Fortier family at about the same time. The Keller Mansion (Homeplace Plantation) has a small interior stair connecting lower and upper service halls, but the main stairs are at opposite corners of the surrounding *galerie* (fig. 228). Ground-story walls are of brick, and the pillars supporting the *galerie* floor are of brick covered with stucco, shaped to a curious square capital as at Parlange. The upper *galerie* is of wood with exposed beams and wide cypress floor and ceiling planking. The light balustrade is surmounted by slender wooden colonets of typical profile. The lower story (plan, fig. 229), with its thick walls and brick floors, is devoted to servants' rooms, a large dining room with fireplace, a serving pantry, and wine rooms. The kitchen was in a detached building 50 feet from the house. The two wine rooms have great platforms for barrels and hogsheads and racks for several thousand bottles; their floors are of alternating green and white marble squares.

The main floor has a reception room and several chambers of various sizes whose intercommunicating doors suggest that cross-ventilation was more to be desired than privacy. The interiors are simple, with wide cypress floor boards, simple wood trim, plastered and papered walls, and

wooden mantelpieces. There are none of the plaster moldings or cornices
or carved marble mantels that adorn the later Greek Revival mansions.
Furniture, draperies, wallpaper, and the original roofing slates (now replaced by a metal roof) were all imported from France. The Keller
Plantation and Parlange, two of the largest French Colonial houses surviving today, are so similar in plan and in detail that it can be surmised
they were built by the same master builder.

228. Keller Mansion (Homeplace Plantation), Hahnville, St. Charles Parish, La.,
c.1801 (HABS)

Natchez, Mississippi, some 200 miles up the river from New Orleans,
is particularly rich in fine houses of ante-bellum days, but almost all of
these date from the Federal and Greek Revival eras. The one important
relic of the French Colonial style is famous Connelly's Tavern on Ellicott
Hill (fig. 230). It stands near the spot where Andrew Ellicott, a surveyor
appointed by President Washington to determine the line of demarca-

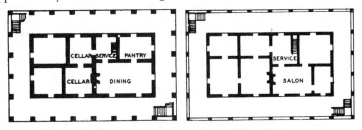

229. Plans of the Keller Mansion (Philip White)

tion between American and Spanish territory, first raised the American
flag in the lower Mississippi valley, on 29 February 1797, as reported in
his *Journal*. The house was probably built between 1796 and 1799, when
Patrick Connelly is known to have operated a tavern on this site.

Built of brick in the lower story and of wood above, it has the familiar
exterior staircase at one corner of the *galeries* which front both stories.
There are slender wooden posts at both levels, and the roof between the

230. Connelly's Tavern, Natchez. Miss., before 1800 (Natchez Garden Club)

two interior chimneys is raised to form a gable-on-hip, with a broken
pitch. Cypress framing timbers and heavy plank floors formed part of the
original construction. Some details, such as the elliptical fanlight, interior
door casings, and mantelpieces, are restored in the Federal style. Connelly's Tavern, after a half-century of deterioration as a mill tenement,
was bought by the Natchez Garden Club in 1935, restored and furnished,
and now serves as headquarters of the club, which has set a national
standard in making available to the public the houses and gardens of a
city unusually rich in fine architecture.

The extraordinary similarity between Connelly's Tavern and the
Larkin House at Monterey (fig. 215) has led to the supposition that
Spanish architectural influences during the period of Spanish rule, 1763–
1801, determined the style of the Louisiana plantation houses. But it is
quite evident that the style was part of a long-continuing French tradition, fully formed in Parlange, which was built a dozen years before the

Spanish acquired Louisiana. The strong similarity between certain buildings of the French and Spanish Colonial styles may be viewed as the result of similar needs, in similar climates, and of similar methods of building.

These French plantation houses, with their circling *galeries,* also bear a resemblance to the great houses of a generation later in the ' Plantation Greek ' style. But the latter probably developed by almost insensible steps out of the former; certain it is that the great houses of the 1830's and

231. The Cabildo, New Orleans. 1795 (Louisiana State Museum)

1840's have a much more complete vocabulary of Greek Revival decorative detail, and especially a single giant order of classical columns rather than the superposed orders of houses like Parlange.

The most markedly Spanish influence in Louisiana is to be seen in the Cabildo in New Orleans (fig. 231) erected in 1795. Facing the old Place d'Armes, it was built to house the Cabildo, a legislative and administrative council composed of Spanish officialdom. Weightily composed with a full panoply of Renaissance architectural forms, the design very probably came from Mexico. Indeed in its two lower stories, the building seems almost a copy of the Casas Reales built in Antequera in 1781.[6] The steep-sided mansard roof forming the third story was an addition of the 1850's.

Although France regained all of Louisiana west of the Mississippi by the Treaty of San Ildefonso in 1801, Napoleon sold the whole territory to the United States on 30 April 1803. It was not until six months later that the dual transfer was celebrated in ceremonies in the Place d'Armes at New Orleans. On 30 November, the Spanish turned over control to the

French, and on 20 December, the French transferred authority to the Americans. The effects of American enterprise were soon apparent. The first steamboat to navigate the Mississippi arrived at New Orleans in 1812, and the city began its mushroom growth. Steamboat arrivals in 1814 numbered 21, and freight received totaled 67,000 tons. By 1840, the traffic had grown enormously: steamboat arrivals in that year numbered 1,573, and freight totaled over 537,000 tons. Cotton was king; New Orleans was the fourth largest city in the nation and the second largest port. Enormous wealth poured into the city and its surrounding plantations, and the era of the great plantation houses was at hand.

READING SUGGESTIONS

Published books afford only very fragmentary accounts of French Colonial architecture in the Mississippi valley; there is need for a comprehensive volume on the subject. The best brief account of French Colonial architecture in Louisiana is in the American Guide Series (Federal Writers' Project), *Louisiana* (Hastings House, New York, 1941). Important source material is contained in the following periodical articles:

Samuel Wilson, ' An Architectural History of the Royal Hospital and the Ursuline Convent of New Orleans,' *Louisiana Historical Quarterly,* vol. 29, no. 3 (July 1946), pp. 559–659.

Charles E. Peterson, 'French Houses of the Illinois Country,' *Missouriana,* vol. I, no. 4 (August–September 1938), pp. 9–12; ' Old Ste. Genevieve and its Architecture,' *Missouri Historical Review,* vol. 35, no. 2 (January 1941), pp. 207–32; ' Notes on Old Cahokia,' *French American Review,* vol. I, no. 3 (July–September 1948), pp. 184–225; and *Colonial St. Louis: Building a Creole Capital,* Missouri Historical Society, St. Louis, 1949.

Scattered accounts of various individual buildings may be found in the following books:

John Drury, *Historic Midwest Houses,* University of Minnesota Press, Minneapolis, 1947.

Nola Nance Oliver, *Natchez, Symbol of the Old South,* Hastings House, New York, 1940.

Italo William Ricciuti, *New Orleans and its Environs,* William Helburn, New York, 1938.

J. Frazer Smith, *White Pillars, Early Life and Architecture of the Lower Mississippi Valley Country,* William Helburn, New York, 1941.

William P. Spratling and Natalie Scott: *Old Plantation Houses in Louisiana,* William Helburn, New York, 1927.

Part Three

GEORGIAN ARCHITECTURE

1700–1780

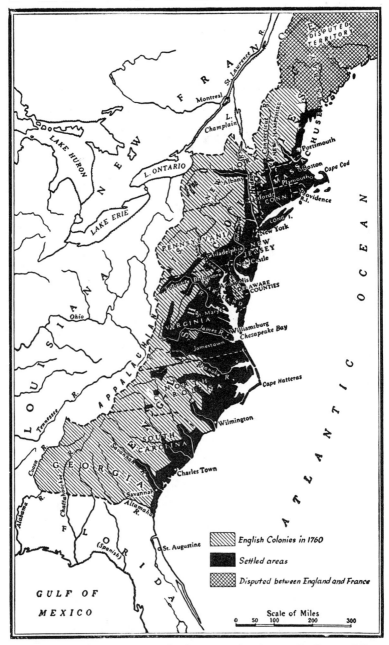

English Colonies in 1760

Settled areas

Disputed between England and France

Scale of Miles
0   50   100   200   300

232. The English colonies in 1760, showing extent of settlement (Faulkner and Kepner, *America: Its History and People*, Harper and Brothers)

9

The Emergence of Georgian

IN JANUARY of the year 1700, when William Penn made his second visit to Philadelphia, he found a thriving city of 14,000 persons. Merchants, laborers, ship owners, landlords, and the artisans and craftsmen of a score of trades mingled on the busy streets he had laid out a short generation before in a well-ordered gridiron pattern. Many were men of wealth, devoted not only to the pursuits of government and commerce but also to the arts of cultured living. Two-thirds of the houses were of brick, and as Gabriel Thomas had reported two years before, they were ' generally three stories high after the mode in London.'

Penn occupied a fine brick house with a slate roof built a few years before at the corner of Second Street and Norris Alley. Designed by James Porteus, a trained British architect, the Slate House was one of the earliest Georgian buildings. Formally arranged on an H-shaped plan, like some of the greater English houses, its level lines of belt course and cornice emphasized the reposeful horizontals of the classical taste. Steep Gothic roof and cross gables had given way here to an elegant hipped roof with Georgian dormers. Classic decorative detail made a timid appearance: modillions enriched the cornice, a pediment topped the front door, and in the great room the fireplace was framed by elaborate moldings and crowned by classic frieze and cornice.

No style changes overnight, and it would be false to suggest that Colonial was abruptly transformed into Georgian precisely in the year 1700. More than a decade earlier the formal composition and classic detail of Boston's Foster-Hutchinson House had decisively announced it as the first Georgian building in America. But it is equally true that the whole generation after 1700 was an era of transition, and it was not until 1720 that a majority of the finer houses, even in the cities of the eastern seaboard, were built in the Georgian style. Nonetheless, the College of William and Mary (begun in 1695), Stoughton Hall at Harvard (1699), the first New York City Hall (1699), the Slate House, and the Capitol and Governor's Palace at Williamsburg all demonstrated that around the beginning of the eighteenth century America was entering a new architectural era.

By 1700 the colonies of the eastern seaboard had been settled for three-quarters of a century, more or less (see map, fig. 232). They were united under English rule. The Swedes and the Dutch had been vanquished; the Indians and their French allies had been pushed back along the northern frontier, and assaults against the Spanish had been carried to the very gates of St. Augustine. The population was about 275,000, and was to double itself with almost mathematical regularity every twenty-three years up to 1790.[1] Not only Englishmen, but large numbers of Scotch-Irish, French, and Germans immigrated in an augmenting tide, until by 1763 two-thirds of the American population had been born overseas.

It was a population in which class distinctions were increasingly important. Wealth unimagined in the pioneer days was pouring into the eastern cities. Boston, Newport, New York, Philadelphia, and Charleston were the metropolises of the eighteenth century, and in them ship owners, merchants, and plantation owners formed the nucleus of a new leisure class. Together with manorial lords and royal governors and their circles, they constituted a society that looked increasingly to England: to the manners, the costume, the culture, and the architecture of the aristocratic world of Queen Anne and the three Georges.

English architecture in 1700 was borne on the full tide of the Renaissance, a major cultural and architectural epoch that had begun almost 300 years earlier in Italy and manifested itself in a succession of national and period styles in all the countries of western Europe. Since the Georgian style was the last, and in some ways the luckiest, inheritor of the Renaissance tradition, it is necessary to know something of the character and doctrine — for there was a doctrine — of the architecture of the Renaissance in Europe. This is particularly true because of the misleading similarity between the Renaissance styles, such as the Georgian, and the Neoclassic styles, such as the Federal, which followed in the late eighteenth and early nineteenth century. Both eras confess allegiance to the classic; both use classical forms in what seems at first glance similar ways. But they are far apart in essence, and the fact that Jefferson could assail his Georgian predecessors as ignorant of the first principles of architecture is only one of the important and sometimes baffling symptoms that ' classicism ' meant different things to the different ages.

RENAISSANCE ARCHITECTURE

All Renaissance styles made use of the vocabulary of ancient Roman architectural forms. This language of architecture was revived after a thousand years of disuse with as much enthusiasm and reverence on the part of architects as the classical scholars displayed in the study of Cicero, Plautus, and Virgil. This revival of a past style differed in three important respects from the style revivals of nineteenth- and twentieth-century eclectic architecture. It was in the first place truly expressive of a broad philosophy or point of view widely prevalent in the Renaissance period. After several generations of medievalism, the man of the Renaissance found in classical literature, philosophy, and art valid and useful solutions to the problems of a humanistic mode of life. Classical culture was not merely exhumed, it was in a true sense revived: it was brought to life again; it was believed in; it was creatively used as a guide to a present life, not, as in the nineteenth century, as an escape to an idealized past.

The Renaissance revival of the classical style in architecture was thus a valid expression of contemporary life.

In the second place, the architects of the Renaissance made use of only one past style, not many. This gave a unity that was in marked contrast to the multiplicity of discordant styles used by the eclectic architects of the nineteenth and twentieth centuries. And in the third place, the architects of the Renaissance never resorted to the slavish imitation of specific buildings of the past. They used Roman forms, but they composed and balanced them in new ways; they used an old vocabulary, but they spoke a new language and expressed new ideas. The East Front of the Louvre, for example, uses Roman forms but says something specifically French and seventeenth-century: grand in scale, integrated to its smallest detail, imposing and unified in composition, it proclaims with superb force all of the arrogant power, the regal grandeur of Le Roi Soleil, Louis XIV, monarch of the most powerful and civilized country in Europe. Here is no timid and sterile imitation of the Romans.

But the Renaissance revival of the Roman style was not uniformly successful. Not always did architects succeed in achieving the creative classicism of the great masterpieces. Many of the less gifted architects followed the new style in a conventional and uncreative way, and as time passed the gradual formulation — in the writings of critics and theorists — of a doctrine of design made it easy to substitute a mechanical manipulation of classical forms for expressive creation in the classical spirit. The development in the sixteenth and seventeenth centuries of absolutist forms of government called for absolutist forms of cultural expressions, and it was only too easy to reduce the apparent simplicity and regularity of the classic mode to inflexible rules of design. There was inherent in the very nature of the aesthetic ideal of the Renaissance the canker of academicism: an inevitable urge toward codification and 'correctness.' This was to have its effect on the Georgian architecture of America.

Renaissance architects naturally sought to base their rules of design on the practices of the Romans, and for these they found a ready-made codification in the Ten Books of Architecture, written by that pedantic architect and engineer of the first century B.C., Marcus Vitruvius Pollio. Vitruvius has had a greater influence on architecture than any other single man. So far as we know he was not a brilliant architect; he seems rather to have been a methodical, thorough scholar, with a great urge to reduce the disturbing richness of classical architecture to a textbook standard. He did not know Greece, but he must have seen a great deal of Roman architecture. Despite the fact that Roman architects themselves adhered to no set standards — they invented at least a couple of dozen versions of their favorite Corinthian capital — Vitruvius, in his effort to define convenient norms, made it seem that there was only one proper Doric order, only one Ionic, only one standard Corinthian, and so on through the Roman vocabulary of forms. He little knew that the power of his written word would prevail so completely that when a Roman building was uncovered 1500 years later and its measurements were found not to correspond with the Vitruvian standard, the architects of the Renaissance would blandly assume that the building must be wrong, not Vitruvius.

For Vitruvius was a made-to-order source for that authority which the Renaissance architects so keenly sought. His work became the architectural Bible of the Renaissance. It was edited, rewritten, and its basic content repeated by every great Renaissance writer on architecture from the gifted Italian Alberti, in the fifteenth century, down to Leoni in the eighteenth — a long line whose names formed a brilliant roster of authority

233. Columns of the five classic orders according to Palladio (Leoni edition, Book 1, Plate 8)

familiar to every gentleman-builder and amateur architect of the eighteenth century in America. Among the galaxy of names — Vignola, Serlio, Palladio, Scamozzi, Blondel — we may select for particular attention that of Andrea Palladio (1518–80) of Vicenza, in northern Italy.

Palladio, one of the greatest architects of the Renaissance, published his *Four Books of Architecture* in 1570. Its importance to later English and American architecture can hardly be overestimated. It contained chapters on construction and beautiful engraved plates of ancient Roman buildings, together with a large number of Palladio's own designs. Many plates were devoted to the proper form and use of the classic orders. Figure 233, taken from Palladio's book, illustrates, for example, the details of base and capital and the proper proportions of the five Roman orders: Tuscan, Doric, Ionic, Corinthian, and Composite. Figure 234, also reproduced from Palladio's plate, shows the façade and section of the Villa Rotonda, a country residence by Palladio near Vicenza; a square mass enclosing a circular domed rotunda and fronted by classic porticoes on four sides, this was to become a favorite model for Jefferson and for several English architects. Figure 235 shows Palladio's Villa Trissina, similar to the Villa Rotonda but extended by curved corridors to colonnaded buildings flanking a great forecourt, another motive to be followed later.

Palladio's influence might have been fruitful, but to an age that sought authority rather than freedom, it was well nigh disastrous. In codifying

234. Palladio's Villa Rotonda, Vicenza, Italy (Leoni edition, Book II, Plate 15)

the proportions and details of the classic orders, he rigidified what the Romans themselves — and still more the Greeks — had used freely, and by successfully establishing an arbitrary standard of ' correctness ' in design, he set the stage for the sterile rules of the seventeenth-century Academies.

In some countries, notably Italy and Spain, architects soon chafed at the bonds of such cold correctness and burst out in a riot of color and movement and extravagant ornament, breaking every rule of classical architecture and using its broken and tortured forms in novel and wilful ways. It was ' incorrect,' and it was ornate, but it was often exciting and expressive. This phase of the Renaissance style is known as the Baroque, and in Italy it flourished from about 1550 to 1780. But France, ' the country of order by reason,' was not greatly affected by it, and England, except for a few extravagances, remained faithful, by and large, to strict Palladian classicism. A few wayward details — an occasional broken pediment or scroll pediment — found their way into English architecture of the seventeenth century, and thence to a number of delightful doorways in our own Georgian.

The general chronology of the Renaissance period is graphically illustrated in figure 2. The Renaissance style, started in Italy as early as 1420, had come to maturity in the 'High Renaissance' in the first half of the sixteenth century, and by 1550 had developed (or degenerated, depending on the point of view) into the Baroque, which lasted longer and reigned more powerfully in Italy than it did in any other country.

France took over the style from Italy after 1500, in the delightful half-Gothic, half-Renaissance chateaux of Louis XII and Francis I in the

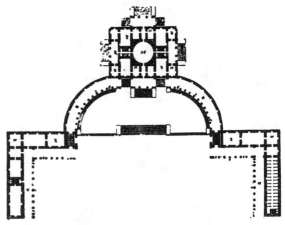

235. Palladio's Villa Trissina, Vicenza (Leoni edition, Book II, Plate 45)

Loire valley, and developed it steadily and logically through the subperiods named after its leading Renaissance monarchs. That oft-cited and delightful style, the Rococo, which was to exert some influence on American architecture during the later eighteenth century, was primarily a style of interior decoration, employing intricate curvilinear patterns, pastel colors, and fragile moldings in a delicately ornate fashion. It flourished from 1715 to 1745, in the first half of the reign of Louis XV. It was in France that the Renaissance achieved, in such superb masterpieces as the Louvre and the Petit Trianon at Versailles, its finest examples of creative classical architecture.

Spain took over the Renaissance style from Italy about 1500 and, as we have seen, progressed through its own peculiarly national variants of the cycle, the Plateresque, Griego-Romano, and Churrigueresque. Holland never did move completely within the Renaissance orbit. Classical details began to creep into Dutch architecture by about 1590 and were extensively used in the 1600's, but the spirit and composition of Dutch buildings always remained individual and free rather than correct and prescribed. The Renaissance styles were royalist fashions, an architectural absolutism the Dutch instinctively disliked, just as they hated the political yoke of absolutist Spain, a fact that explains why, when the Dutch builders came to America, the houses they built showed hardly a trace of classical influence.

It must be re-emphasized that the Renaissance style as a whole was an absolutist style, in its very nature and in the uses to which it was put. It reached its highest development in those countries most absolutely governed: Italy, France, Spain, and to a lesser extent England under the Stuarts and the four Georges. With all its emphasis on formality and correctness, its opulent ornament and calculated grandeur, it was the perfect architectural expression of royalty and aristocracy, of a limited and privileged social class and a fashionable and worldly church. Its characteristic monument is the palace, not the house or office or farm. It is an architecture of elegance and impressiveness, not of comfort or utility.

The Renaissance era, as a broad architectural and cultural epoch, came to a rather abrupt end in most of the countries of western Europe in the last part of the eighteenth century. The political and social order of the *ancien régime* was undergoing revolutionary developments; the system of production was being profoundly changed by the Industrial Revolution; and the established architectural doctrine of many generations' standing was being overthrown by the discoveries of scientific archaeology. The period around the year 1780 marks a Revolution of Architecture no less significant than the American and French revolutions in politics, and it inaugurates the modern era.

THE RENAISSANCE IN ENGLAND

The Renaissance in England was belated. England was somewhat remote from the fountainhead of the Renaissance in Italy, and Englishmen, besides, were naturally conservative. The Tudor Gothic, the last phase of England's medieval style, persisted with an extraordinary tenacity. It was a beautiful style, native, natural, and charmingly picturesque. Henry VIII saw little reason for abandoning it, though he did import some Italian craftsmen to add touches of Renaissance decoration to his palace at Hampton Court. It was not until Elizabeth's day that Renaissance architecture entered England.

The Elizabethan style, 1570–1620

These fifty years, embracing most of the reigns of Elizabeth (1558–1603) and James I (1603–25), comprise the early Renaissance in England. Characteristically, the opening wedge of the new style was a book, not a building. Throughout the Renaissance, theory and practice marched hand in hand, the theory being highly impractical, and the practice highly theoretical. In 1563, John Shute, ' Paynter and Archytecte,' published his *First & Chief Groundes of Architecture*. Antedating Palladio's book, this brought to the attention of the English public, for the first time, a knowledge of the ancient Roman orders and rules for their proper employment in design. Shute had visited Italy in 1550, seen buildings by Palladio, Vignola, and Michelangelo, and he based his book largely on Vitruvius' and Serlio's.* In it he stressed that an architect (the supplanting of the unpretentious ' master builder ' of the medieval period by the Latin title is significant of the new learning) should be not a mere builder but a man of education in the arts and sciences.

John Thorpe, one of the first professional architects in England, built Kirby Hall, Northamptonshire, in 1570. It was a rambling country house, basically Gothic in plan, structure, and mass, but with undeniable Renaissance intentions as revealed by pilastered doorways, pedimented windows, and other crudely applied details. It was an awkward building compared with the consummately graceful chateaux the French were building at a comparable stage of development, but it nevertheless marks the beginning of the architectural Renaissance in England.

But the Elizabethan style proved to be a ghastly *mésalliance* between Gothic fact and classic theory. John Thorpe and an associate, Robert Smithson, built a few other big mansions in the new fashion: Burghley House, Hardwicke Hall with its factory windows (' Hardwicke Hall, more glass than wall '), Wollaton, and one or two other monstrous and inept stone piles. They had lost the virtue of Gothic genuineness and not yet achieved the refined polish of Renaissance artifice. Boasting of a new learning that was only half-learned, these Elizabethan mansions achieved not grandeur or distinction but merely a formidable vulgarity.

Buildings erected during the reign of James I are often classified as Jacobean in style. The distinction seems unnecessary: the mansions of that era, such as Knole House, Hatfield House, and Aston Hall, betray little advance in style: they still represent an incomplete transition from Gothic to Renaissance. But during this period the ordinary city or country dweller continued to build in the medieval tradition, and undoubtedly the vast majority of all the buildings in the England of Shakespeare's day were Gothic in style.

The early Stuart style, 1620–60

The mature phase of England's architectural Renaissance may be said to have begun in 1620, and its protagonist was Inigo Jones (1573–1652), a name well known to eighteenth-century Americans. The style he inaugurated prevailed during the reign of Charles I (1625–49) and in the small amount of building that was done during the Cromwellian era (1649–60).

Before he was 30, Jones had visited Italy to learn at the source what proper classical design should be, and he made another visit in 1613–15, particularly to Vicenza, where he became an ardent admirer of Palladio's buildings. He returned with a copy of Palladio's book, which in later years he thoroughly studied and annotated. For some years Jones designed stage scenery for masques and balls at court (over 450 of his drawings of scenery have been preserved) , and it was doubtless his scenic presentations of Italian architecture that popularized the new mode at court.

James I commissioned Jones to design the Queen's House at Green-

* Sebastiano Serlio, *Five Books of Architecture*, Venice, 1537–75.

wich Palace in 1618 and the Banqueting House at Whitehall Palace in 1619. Though the rest of the projected vast Whitehall Palace was never built, the Banqueting House (fig. 236) stands as the first example of 'correct' classical design in England. Though undeniably Palladian in style, it is an original composition, not a copy. Particularly noteworthy are the flat roof, as in Italian palaces, the regularly spaced pilasters, Ionic below and Corinthian above, coupled at the corners to delimit the composition. Four engaged columns on each story emphasize the central axis. Masonry

236. Banqueting House, Whitehall Palace, London, 1619–22, by Inigo Jones (British Information Services)

joints of the wall are drafted to gain texture interest. Windows are topped by small cornices in the upper story, and by alternating angular and segmental pediments below. A garlanded frieze, classic cornice, and balustrade complete the façade.

It is clear that Jones could use the classic vocabulary with assurance to compose a beautifully modulated design, but in common with most Renaissance buildings, the building's 'architecture' is rather a frontispiece than a volume — a façade for its own sake rather than as an expression of the whole mass, structure, and plan of the building. The fact that the interior is one great hall, rising the whole height of the building, is nowhere expressed in the exterior design.

This building reveals the great difference between Gothic and Renaissance architecture. A Gothic building evolved out of the plan, which was controlled by needs, and out of the varied materials employed, which were developed into decorative forms almost adventitiously by the many craftsmen who worked with them. It was not planned, so to speak — it just grew. In Renaissance architecture, on the other hand, a building was created as a work of abstract art. One man designed its total form and every detail in advance, working from preconceived canons of order and proportion. These had little or nothing to do with the requirements of use or the peculiarities of the materials to be employed. Such practical matters were subject to the strict control of an ideal aesthetic form. The great difference between Gothic and Renaissance architecture is not merely a matter of stylistic details, but an essential difference in basic methods and philosophies of building. The one is expressional, the other

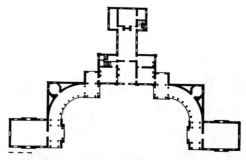

237. Plan of Stoke-Bruerne, Northamptonshire, England, 1641, by Inigo Jones (Thomas T. Waterman, *The Mansions of Virginia*, University of North Carolina Press)

abstract; the one is organic, the other geometric; Gothic architecture was evolutionary, Renaissance architecture was created.

Inigo Jones's devotion to Palladianism is revealed not only by the Banqueting House but by his plan for Stoke-Bruerne (1641) in Northamptonshire (fig. 237), where he echoes Palladio's favorite villa arrangement (cf. fig. 235), a scheme which is to crop up in the colonies later. We need devote little attention to other architects of the early Stuart period. Such men as John Webb (1611–72), Sir Roger Pratt (1620–84), and Hugh May (1622–84) contributed to the rising tide of formal design, but they were far less well known in the colonies than Inigo Jones.

The late Stuart style, 1660–1714

Three events conspired to effect a change in English architecture in the last third of the seventeenth century. One was the restoration of the Stuart monarchy in 1660; a second was the Great Fire of London in 1666, which destroyed the medieval city and necessitated much rebuilding; the third was the career of Sir Christopher Wren, generally considered the greatest of English architects.

When the Stuart dynasty, in the person of Charles II (1660–85), was restored to the throne, there was a general relaxation from the Puritan strictness of the Cromwellian era. Court and aristocracy indulged themselves in the entertainment of the Restoration drama, the enjoyment of the arts, and a general luxuriance and richness of architecture and interior decoration which was England's closest approach to a baroque style. At the same time, since the Royalists had sojourned in Holland during the revolution, they brought back with them many Dutch architects and craftsmen, so that Dutch influence is strong in the post-Restoration period.

These influences are apparent in the architecture of Christopher Wren (1632–1723). Wren was an infant prodigy, and in his youth developed wide-ranging interests. His early career was devoted largely to mathematics, astronomy, and engineering. When Charles II gained the throne he appointed Wren Assistant Surveyor General and, two years after the fire, Surveyor General.

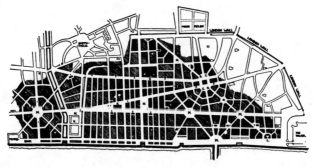

238. Christopher Wren's plan for rebuilding London after the fire of 1666 (Thomas H. Mawson, *Civic Art*, B. T. Batsford, Ltd.)

Wren was given the task of creating a new city plan for London. He had visited the French court, and his plan (fig. 238) bore many resemblances to the magnificent scheme that LeNôtre had prepared for the gardens of Versailles. Wide streets surrounded large rectangular blocks and at intervals formed radiating stars or *rond-points* from central plazas surrounded by important public buildings. Great diagonal avenues connected important points. A forked *patte d'oie* of streets converged on the focal point where the new St. Paul's Cathedral was to arise. Wren's plan, obviously the prototype of that of Washington, D.C., was a magnificent example of Renaissance city planning, and it is a pity that its adoption was defeated by landowners and businessmen who wanted the old medieval streets rebuilt just as they had been.

William and Mary commissioned Wren to do large additions to Hampton Court Palace in 1682. In the new Garden Front (fig. 239) he produced one of the masterpieces of the English Renaissance. The palace is imposing in its breadth, the even rhythm of its windows, and the stable horizontals of cornice and balustrade. Yet what might have been an undue severity is given gaiety by the color combination of warm red brick and white Portland stone trim, and the monotony of a four-story building is relieved by the varied scale and shapes of the windows — even by the size of their panes. There are not too many pilasters and pediments: an over-all simplicity is enlivened by a few touches of baroque decoration. It is both majestic and graceful, as a palace should be.

Wren is most famous for his London city churches. Between 1670 and 1711 he designed 52 of them. From the time of Henry VIII's separation of the Anglican and Catholic churches in 1534 until the fire of 1666, there had been almost no church building in England, so Wren virtually created a new type of English Protestant architecture, which was to set the pattern for Georgian churches in the colonies. Many of his churches are on small, irregular sites, hemmed in by surrounding buildings, and there-

239. The Garden Front, Hampton Court Palace, England, 1682–94, by Sir Christopher Wren (University Prints)

fore Wren gave particular emphasis to their towers. Wren's church towers are, so to speak, Gothic cathedral spires done with Roman forms. Though extremely varied in shape and detail, the general pattern involves a lofty square tower, surmounted by upper stories of diminishing size, and topped by a needle-like spire. Typical is the tower of St. Mary-le-Bow (fig. 240), with its arched and pilastered main story topped by balustrade and ornamental supports for classic urns, two smaller circular stories surrounded by classic columns, and the topmost spire. The tower of St. Bride's, Fleet Street (fig. 241), has a telescope of diminishing octagons with an arch on each face. Wren was skilful in introducing just enough of the curvilinear and opulent detail of the baroque to enliven Jones's propriety and yet preserve an Anglican reticence: fragile, nervous, and precise, these towers pierce London's sky with infinitely varied aspiration.

Though William Talman and Nicholas Hawksmoor were his disciples, Wren had no real 'school,' and no other architect of the late Stuart period equaled his genius. Sir John Vanbrugh (1664–1726), a Dutchman and dramatist, designed buildings during the reign of Queen Anne, somewhat as he designed stage scenery. Gargantuan piles such as Castle Howard, for the Earl of Carlisle, and Blenheim, for the Duke of Marlborough, have a certain elephantine majesty, but they were vastly expen-

sive and inconvenient, and well merited the spiteful epitaph proposed by
a protégé of the disgusted Duchess for Vanbrugh's tomb:

> Lie heavy on him earth, for he
> Laid many a heavy load on thee.

Fortunately the heavy-handed and clumsy work of Wren's followers had
little influence in the American colonies, chiefly because there wasn't
enough money to build anything approaching those massive structures.

240, 241. The steeples of St. Mary-le-Bow in Cheapside (1680) and St. Bride's, Fleet
Street (1700) in London, by Sir Christopher Wren (engraving by T. Malton, 1798,
and photo from George H. Birch, *London Churches of the Seventeenth and Eighteenth Centuries*, B. T. Batsford, Ltd.)

But if Wren had no school, he did have many anonymous followers in
the late seventeenth century. Skilled masons and carpenters, building
smaller manors and country houses, learned enough from Wren's example
to endow their modest buildings with a singular grace of form and detail.
In some of these unpretentious buildings of the late Stuart period is the
best architecture produced in the entire English Renaissance, and by
exceptional good fortune, its modesty and economy precisely matched the
needs of the American colonists in the early eighteenth century. Thus
the American Georgian style was the inheritor, almost by accident, of the
best rather than the worst that the English Renaissance produced.

Take for example Honington Hall in Warwickshire (1685, fig. 242). It
is formal in layout, with its symmetrical façade, hipped roof, and balanced chimneys. It has the classical decorative detail demanded by the
new taste: modillioned cornice, stone quoins at the angles, and a delightful baroque doorway flanked by Corinthian columns and topped by

a segmental pediment broken in the middle to admit a large cartouche or shield. Yet it lacks the pretenses of pilasters, pedimented windows, or other burdensome paraphernalia. And its red brick with white painted sash windows and details contribute to a sprightly and cheerful effect. The busts between the windows, fortunately, are an uncommon embellishment.

242. Honington Hall, Warwickshire, England, 1685 (*Country Life*, London)

Not less fine is Aspley House in Bedfordshire (1695, fig. 243). The projecting central pavilion topped by a pediment was to become a favorite feature in the colonies after 1750, and other details such as the low-pitch hipped hoof, sash windows, framed entrance door, and modillioned

243. Aspley House, Bedfordshire, England, 1695 (J. H. Thurston)

cornice are very familiar in the American Georgian. Rampyndene at Burwash in Sussex (1699), with its steep pitched roof, heavy chimneys, and burly mass, is strikingly similar to William Byrd's Westover, built in Virginia a generation later.

Interiors show a marked change from the Tudor Gothic. Fine paneling sheaths the walls, richly carved woodwork with fruits and garlands frames the fireplace, and the front hall is enlarged to a grandiose room (fig. 244), often spanned by an elliptical arch that separates the reception hall from

244. Entrance hall, Rutland Lodge, Petersham, Surrey, England (*Country Life*, London)

the cascading stairway, elaborate with turned balusters, carved step ends, and mahogany handrail. It is abundantly clear that the American Georgian style comes directly from such houses as these built in the late Stuart period in England.

The early Georgian style, 1714–60

The eighteenth century has been described as England's Era of Power, Prestige, and Prosperity. Architecturally, if we may match the alliteration, it was an era of pompous Palladian palaces. An age of military force, colonial expansion, and commercial prosperity often expresses itself architecturally by timid, though large-scaled, academicism.

The revival of Palladianism was sponsored largely by that munificent patron Richard Boyle, Earl of Burlington (1695–1753). Lord Burlington, an amateur architect, was an ardent disciple of Palladio. He sponsored an English publication of Palladio's book in 1715, and in Burlington House, London, designed about 1716 by Colen Campbell, he built what was intended to be a model of Palladian design (fig. 245). Learned and 'correct,' it was hopelessly dull. That Burlington devoted himself to formal façade design, with little concern for interior functions, is illustrated by the house he made for General Wade, which Lord Hervey described as:

> Possessed of one great hal! of state
> Without a room to sleep or eat.

Burlington gathered about him several protégés, among whom were Colen Campbell, author of *Vitruvius Britannicus;* Giacomo Leoni, a Venetian who did the drawings for Burlington's edition of Palladio; and

245. Burlington House, London, *c.*1716, by Colen Campbell (*Vitruvius Britannicus,* III, 23–4)

William Kent, who published the *Designs of Inigo Jones.* Campbell, in his Mereworth Castle, made a direct copy of Palladio's Villa Rotonda; Burlington used the same model for his villa at Chiswick; and at least two other copies of this building were made, despite its complete unsuitability to the English climate and to English domestic requirements. The Palladian school was not only completely uncreative but wholly unintelligent.

One wonders whether by 1731 Lord Burlington himself had realized its follies, or whether Alexander Pope, by praising his patron for the very qualities he lacked, was attempting by subtle indirection to instruct him in common sense. At any rate, one of Pope's *Moral Essays,* addressed to his noble patron, reveals not only the follies of the Palladians, but a dawning appreciation of Nature and 'natural' design that was to characterize the later Romantic movement:

> Shall call the winds thro' long arcades to roar,
> Proud to catch cold at a Venetian door:
> Conscious they act a true Palladian part,
> And if they starve, they starve by rules of Art . . .
> Something there is more needful than expense,
> And something previous ev'n to Taste — 'tis Sense.
> Good Sense, which only is the gift of Heav'n,
> And tho' no science, fairly worth the sev'n . . .
> To build, to plant, whatever you intend,

> To rear the column, or the arch to bend,
> To swell the terrace, or to sink the grot,
> In all, let Nature never be forgot . . .
> 'Tis use alone that sanctifies expense,
> And splendor borrows all her rays from sense.
> *Epistle* IV, *Moral Essays* (1731)

The same common-sense criticism came from Isaac Ware, a chimney sweep's apprentice who was sent to Italy and educated as an architect, perhaps with Lord Burlington's aid. In *A Complete Body of Architecture*

246, 247. St. Martin's-in-the-Fields, Trafalgar Square, London, 1721–6, by James Gibbs (George H. Birch, *London Churches of the Seventeenth and Eighteenth Centuries*, B. T. Batsford, Ltd.)

(1756), Ware says that it is stupid 'to transfer the buildings of Italy right or wrong, suited or unsuited to the purpose, into England'; and that 'the art of building cannot be more grand than it is useful; nor its dignity a greater praise than its convenience.' [2]

Not all English architects of the early Georgian period were so academic and impractical as the Palladians. James Gibbs (1682–1754) ably continued the tradition of Wren's church architecture. He is best known for St. Martin's-in-the-Fields, on Trafalgar Square, London. Built in 1721–6, this was the direct inspiration for several American Georgian churches. The exterior (fig. 246) approaches the ideal of the classical temple shape, with a full portico of columns rising from steps to a pediment fronting the main roof slope. The tower is similar to Wren's, with a square story embellished by arches and pilasters, classic urns, clock faces under curved cornices, and a small octagonal story carrying the spire. The interior (fig. 247) illustrates the new type of Protestant church plan that Wren had introduced. A central aisle separates built-in box pews, and the side and rear balconies are carried halfway up giant columns, each bearing a small square of entablature. A segmental-arched vault, framed in timber and adorned with molded plaster reliefs, spans the nave.

Gibbs was of very great influence in the colonies through his *Book of Architecture*, first published in 1728 (fig. 248). He explained his hope

that such a Work as this would be of use to such Gentlemen as might be concerned in building, especially in the remote parts of the Country, where little or no assistance for Design can be procured. Such may here be furnished with

B O O K

OF

ARCHITECTURE,

CONTAINING

D E S I G N S

OF

B U I L D I N G S

AND

O R N A M E N T S.

By JAMES GIBBS.

LONDON:

Printed M DCC XXVIII.

The CITY and COUNTRY

BUILDER's and *WORKMAN's*

TREASURY of DESIGNS:

Or the ART of

DRAWING and WORKING

The Ornamental PARTS of

A R C H I T E C T U R E.

Illustrated by upwards of *Four Hundred* Grand Designs, neatly engraved on One Hundred and Eighty-fix COPPER-PLATES, for

Piers,	Pavements,	Obelisques,
Gates,	Fretts,	Pedestals, for
Doors,	Guloch's,	Sun-Dials,
Windows,	Pulpits,	Bufto's, and
Niches,	Types,	Stone Tables,
Buffets,	Altar-Pieces,	Book-Cafes,
Cisterns,	Monuments,	Cielings, and
Chimney-Pieces,	Fonts,	Iron Works.
Tabernacle-Frames,		

Proportioned by ALIQUOT PARTS.

With an *APPENDIX* of Fourteen PLATES of Truffes for Girders and Beams, different Sorts of Rafters, and a Variety of Roofs, &c.

To which are prefixed,

The Five Orders of Columns, according to ANDREA PALLADIO; whose Members are proportioned by ALIQUOT PARTS, in a more easy Manner than has yet been done.

The WHOLE interfperfed

With fure RULES for working all the Varieties of Raking Members in Pediments, Modillions, &c.

The &c. for the immediate Ufe of WORKMEN, never published before, in any Language.

By B. L.

LONDON, Printed for S. HARDING:

And fold by B. DOD, in Ave-Mary-Lane; and J. MARKS, on the Pavement in St. Martin's-Lane. 1756.

248, 249. The title pages of James Gibbs's *Book of Architecture* and Batty Langley's *Treasury of Designs*

Draughts of useful and convenient Buildings and proper Ornaments which may be executed by any Workman who understands Lines, either as here Design'd, or with some Alteration, which may be easily made by a person of Judgment . . .[3]

Gibbs's hopes were amply justified, for the book was so successful as to earn him a profit of £1,900.

Another, and more prolific, author of this period was Batty Langley (1696–1751). The son of a gardener and a self-made ' architect and surveyor,' the industrious Batty was derided by his polite contemporaries, but he had a sure sense for that blend of useful facts about building with a practical presentation of the mysteries of geometry, the classic orders, Good Taste, the work of the Antients, and the like, which would appeal to the average carpenter-builder. And despite his lowly origin and repute, Batty Langley's architectural handbooks were the most widely used of all in the eighteenth century, both in England and America.

He wrote over twenty of them, and many went into multiple editions.

Perhaps most famous was *The City and Country Builder's and Workman's Treasury of Designs,* first published in 1740 (fig. 249). It contained plates showing details — over 400 of them — for every part of a house. Simple and practical, they were suited to houses of modest cost and pretensions. *The Builder's Jewel* was first published in 1741 and ran through eleven editions by 1787. Shrewdly, Batty Langley foresaw the decline of Palladianism before many of his gentlemen rivals and, with a sure sense for the swing of the pendulum toward the picturesque and romantic, had his books on Gothic architecture in print before the Gothic Revival began. Though at first he compromised with classic respectability in *Ancient Architecture, Restored, & Improv'd by a Great Variety of Grand & Usefull Designs, Entirely New in the Gothick Mode, for the Ornamenting of Buildings and Gardens* (1742), soon he was not only offering 'Gothick' unashamedly, but venturing to correct it: in 1747 he published *Gothick Architecture, Improved by Rules & Proportions.*

Dawning romanticism brought with it an interest not only in the Gothic, but in anything remote or exotic. Oriental decorative motives had already appeared in the rococo style in France: Chinese summer houses, mandarins and peacocks, or apes and monkeys disporting themselves in parody of Louis XV's courtiers. When the taste for these 'Chinoiseries' reached London, author William Halfpenny was ready to cater to it with his fantastic *New Designs for Chinese Temples, Triumphal Arches, Gardens, Seats, & Palings* (1752). And in the 1750's Thomas Chippendale, the famous furniture maker, became so enamored of the quaint possibilities of Oriental motives that he produced a style now called 'Chinese Chippendale.' These English architectural handbooks of the eighteenth century were to prove particularly useful in the colonies, as will be seen.

The history of English architecture in the late Georgian period (after 1760) is largely a history of revivals — the Gothic Revival, the Greek Revival, and others — but these had little influence on American Georgian architecture, and consideration of them may be reserved until later.

BUILDING PRACTICES IN THE COLONIES

The origin of the Georgian style in America was in the English architecture of the late Stuart period; its development during the eighteenth century was influenced by the academic Palladianism of England's early Georgian period. The means of transmitting these styles to the colonies were several.

There was an increasing stream of immigration to the colonies. Among the new arrivals were gentlemen whose education might have included the Grand Tour on the Continent, and who certainly were conversant with matters of architectural style and taste. More numerous were men of the building trades — carpenters, masons, joiners, plasterers — who brought with them knowledge of the new practices and the inevitable handbooks of design.

A very few of the immigrants were men of some professional training. Among these were James Porteus, whom William Penn brought to Philadelphia to 'design and execute his Proprietary buildings'; John James, who worked in Boston in the 1730's; Peter Harrison, who became Rhode Island's most distinguished architect; John Hawks, whose palace for Governor Tryon of North Carolina reveals a thorough knowledge of English academic design; James McBean of New York, a pupil of James Gibbs; and William Buckland, foremost architect of Maryland. Such men as these were leaders in introducing the new English fashions to the colonies.

John Ariss, designer of several of the great Georgian houses of Virginia, emerges through recent studies as ' certainly the most distinguished American architect of his period.' [4] It is of interest to read his advertisement in the *Maryland Gazette* for 22 May 1751:

By the Subscriber (lately from Great Britain) Buildings of all Sorts and Dimensions are undertaken and performed in the neatest Manner, (and at cheaper rates) either of the Ancient or Modern Order of Gibbs' Architect and if any Gentleman should want plans, Bills of Scantling or bill of Charges, for any Fabric, or Public Edefice, may have them by applying to the Subscriber at Major John Bushrods at Westmoreland County, Va., where may be seen a great variety and sundry Draughts of Buildings in Miniature, and some buildings near finished after the Modern Taste.

English architecture also came to be better known through visits of Americans to London. The greatly increased trade between the two countries resulted in more frequent sailings, and it was common for men of position to go across on business, politics, or family matters, just as they sent their sons to England to be educated. Thus Andrew Hamilton, Philadelphia jurist, while receiving his legal training at the Inns of Court, may have acquired the architectural background that enabled him to design so fine a building as Independence Hall. The quality of Westover may owe much to William Byrd's education in London and his occasional later visits as representative of the Virginia Assembly.

The use of architectural books

But doubtless the most important means of transmitting English architectural influences were the architectural books produced in such quantity during the eighteenth century. These seem to fall into two general categories: the large and expensive volumes, which gave primary emphasis to Renaissance architectural theory and composition and to the works of acknowledged masters; and the smaller, cheaper handbooks, which emphasized details of practical building for carpenter-builders. To be sure, there was no sharp distinction between the two, and both types were widely circulated. But in general, men of position in the colonies expected to own the more important volumes and left standing orders with their London booksellers to send the new publications. Of these the most widely used in the colonies were:

Palladio, *Four Books of Architecture*. Of the fourteen editions between 1663 and 1738, the most splendid was the two-volume folio edited by Giacomo Leoni and issued under the patronage of Lord Burlington in 1715.

Vignola, *Rule of the Five Orders of Architecture*. Six editions appeared between
   1665 and 1729.
Colen Campbell, *Vitruvius Britannicus*, issued under the patronage of Lord Bur-
   lington, 1715–25.
William Kent, *Designs of Inigo Jones*, issued under the patronage of Lord Bur-
   lington, 1727.
James Gibbs, *A Book of Architecture*, 1728.
Isaac Ware, *Designs of Inigo Jones*, 1735.
William Adam, *Vitruvius Scoticus*. Edinburgh, 1750.
Isaac Ware, *A Complete Body of Architecture*, 1756.

The more popular carpenter's handbooks appeared in several editions.
Of those which first appeared before 1760, perhaps the most widely used
in the colonies were:

William Salmon, *Palladio Londinensis*, 1734.
Batty Langley, *The City & Country Builder's and Workman's Treasury of De-
   signs*, 1740 (usually referred to as ' Langley's *Treasury* ').
Batty Langley, *The Builder's Jewel*, 1741.
William Halfpenny, *The Modern Builder's Assistant*, 1742.
Abraham Swan, *British Architect*, 1745. (An edition was published in Philadel-
   phia in 1775.)
Robert Morris: *Rural Architecture*, 1750.
Robert Morris: *Select Architecture*, 1757 (used extensively by Thomas Jefferson).

These carpenter's handbooks were particularly important in America.
Since there were few professional architects, most buildings in the colonies were designed by owners assisted by carpenter-builders, who together
would lay out the chief elements of the plan and structure. The handbooks were used less for plans of buildings or elevations of whole façades
than they were for details, particularly such features as doorways, mantelpieces, cornices, windows, and cabinetwork. Comparison of such features
in existing houses with the engraved plates of the handbooks leaves little
doubt about the specific source of many Georgian details. Yet it also reveals that the carpenters and joiners of the colonies departed freely — and
usually intelligently — from their sources, altering a detail here or a dimension there in accordance with necessity, invention, or taste. Though
the impact of Lord Burlington's academicism was felt increasingly as the
century progressed, Georgian architecture in America was singularly free
from either the practice or the doctrine of exact imitation.

Amateur architects

Besides the few ' professional ' architects with English training mentioned above, there was a larger number of Americans whose untutored
skill in design and building caused them to be in demand in their communities. The backgrounds and occupations of these amateur architects
varied widely. Richard Munday of Newport, for example, was an innkeeper who turned house carpenter and proved so successful that he was
asked to design important public buildings such as Trinity Church and
the Colony House. Joseph Brown of Providence was a successful manu-
facturer whose interest in mechanics, electricity, and astronomy led to a

professorship and trusteeship of Brown University; as an amateur architect he designed several houses and the First Baptist Church in Providence.

Three noteworthy amateurs were responsible for some of Philadelphia's finest buildings. Dr. John Kearsley, designer of Christ Church, was by profession a physician and by avocation a civic and provincial leader. Andrew Hamilton, a lawyer who became Attorney General of Pennsylvania and Speaker of the Provincial Assembly, was a man of catholic knowledge and of versatile talent, as Independence Hall attests. Samuel Rhoads was more nearly a professional, for he was brought up to be a builder and became a leading member of the famous ' Carpenters' Company,' a Philadelphia society founded in 1724 on the model of the medieval carpenters' guild in London; but he was also a member of Franklin's American Philosophical Society, served for many years on the Provincial Assembly, and became Mayor of Philadelphia and a delegate to the first Continental Congress.

In Virginia the most noteworthy architect, after John Ariss, was Richard Taliaferro of Williamsburg. Referred to in 1749 as ' our most skillful architect,' he worked on the Governor's Palace and the president's house at William and Mary, and he probably designed several other Virginia houses. He was appointed Justice of the Peace and later Sheriff of James City County, and served as senator in the Virginia Assembly.

Both John Smibert and John Trumbull, famous as painters, occasionally turned to architecture, designing Faneuil Hall, Boston, and the early buildings at Yale. Through scanty references a few other amateur architects are slightly known — such men as Caleb Ormsbee of Providence, Henry Caner of New Haven, Governor Francis Bernard of Massachusetts, Samuel Blodget and Robert Smith of Philadelphia — and it seems likely that further research will discover other vanished personalities who may be definitely connected with Georgian buildings in America. But the total number now known, including both professional and amateur architects, totals only about a score — nowhere near enough to have directed the expanding building program of a population that grew about fifteenfold during the course of the eighteenth century.

Because of the shortage of architects, the vast majority of Georgian houses were planned by their owners, assisted by the master carpenters. We are fortunate that both groups were so able. Knowledge of architecture and some talent in drawing were esteemed polite accomplishments in the eighteenth century, with the result that the average gentleman was far better equipped to build a house than is the average college graduate today. It is undoubtedly true, too, that men of the building trades were more competent to execute work without close supervision, and were more conscientious about their craftsmanship, than are their modern successors. Actual drawings and specifications for buildings were amazingly elementary, not to say childish. Witness, for example, the second oldest domestic design preserved today: Richard Munday's plan for the Ayrault House at Newport, done in 1739 (fig. 250). A rough plan, a traditional structural system that did not have to be explained, and reference to the desired details in handbooks — to be modified on the job as necessary — were all that was needed. Great faith was placed in clauses in the building contract requiring ' the said (carpenter) to provide sound materials and to carry through the work to the best of his ability,' or stipulating that the job ' be finished well and workmanlike.'

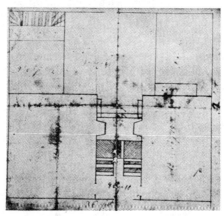

250. Richard Munday's drawing, 1739, for the Daniel Ayrault House, Newport, R.I. (Fiske Kimball, *Domestic Architecture of the American Colonies and of the Early Republic*, Charles Scribner's Sons)

Materials of construction

Materials of construction were the same in kind in the eighteenth century as they had been in the seventeenth but, as might be expected, improved in quality and increased in quantity. Frame construction with clapboard siding remained common in all the colonies, especially in the smaller and less pretentious buildings. In New England the wood-building tradition was stronger than in the other colonies, so that even the finer Georgian mansions were often clapboarded. The heavy hand-hewn frame with notched and pegged joints continued in use, and perhaps the only important change in the structural system was the general adoption, after 1700, of a layer of sheathing boards under the exterior siding — whether the latter was of clapboards or shingles. This double layer was warmer and more weather-tight, and it permitted the gradual abandonment of the interior filling of clay or brick insulation.

But the great building material of Georgian architecture was brick. Brick manufacture had become common almost everywhere, the quality of hard-burned face brick had improved, and from the kilns came a great variety of colors and glazes, ranging from warm roses and salmon pinks through darker reds to purples and blue-blacks. The latter were bricks from the arched vault of the kiln itself, where being laid radially the inner ends were burned in successive firings to a glass-like surface and deep color; when a new kiln was built, these were saved and used to enliven surfaces with patterns of glazed headers.

Brick shared honors with wood in New England and with stone in Pennsylvania, but it was all but universal in the other colonies, and it was almost invariably laid in Flemish bond. Molded bricks were produced in curved shapes for use in water tables, belt courses, chimney caps, or the trim of doorways. Bricks were scoured with a rubbing stone to produce a smooth surface which reflected light almost as well as did the glazed bricks, but were a lighter vermilion in color. These ' rubbed ' or ' gauged ' bricks were sometimes used to accentuate jambs, corners, or other architectural trim.

Stone construction, however, remained extremely uncommon in the eighteenth century, even in public edifices. Outside of Pennsylvania and the former Dutch Colonial region, the number of stone houses in the colonies was very small. But these few were mostly large and expensive houses of advanced academic design, and the architectural importance of such buildings as the Hancock House in Boston and Mount Airy in Virginia will be referred to later. In Pennsylvania, of course, stone building was the common vernacular. It was used not only in the fine houses of Philadelphia and Germantown but in farmhouses and even barns of the eastern counties. In general the stone masonry improved from rough rubble walls in the early period to hewn blocks laid in level courses of random heights and then to the final perfection of even-coursed smooth-finished ashlar masonry.

Stone trim was so expensive to carve that it was little used, but there was an occasional pilaster, capital, column, or belt course made of stone. For the most part the rich classical trim of Georgian houses was made of wood. Easy to shape and carve into the intricate moldings and details of the new classic vocabulary, it could be more lavishly used than either brick or stone, and, when it faded, a coat of paint restored it to pristine whiteness.

Perhaps the most important ' new ' materials were paint and plaster. Plaster, to be sure, had been used extensively in the seventeenth century but it was mostly poor stuff: clay bound with hay or hair, or sand and shell lime mixed to a brown- or gray-white. With increased quarrying of limestone, the building of lime kilns, and improved transportation by sea and road, fine white lime plaster was available to most Georgian builders. Ceiling timbers, previously left exposed, were covered by hung ceilings of plaster, often with molded or precast ornamental patterns and cornices. Plaster or stucco was frequently used as an exterior coat over brick or stone, especially in Philadelphia and Charleston.

So far as we know, paint was very little used in the seventeenth century, though interiors were quite generally whitewashed — including not only exposed plaster walls but wooden wainscot and ceilings. But in Virginia in the early years of the eighteenth century, paint mixed with white lead and oil was being applied to exterior clapboards,[5] and apparently paint was used for both exteriors and interiors of Pennsylvania houses from the foundation of the colony.[6]

Researches for the Williamsburg Restoration, pursued in documents and in old houses, have given ample evidence of the variety and richness of colors used in Georgian interiors. A number of invoices of paints ordered from England have been found; William Beverley, for example, requested on 24 July 1739:

10 gals. Linseed Oyl in a jarr
½ Qt. Wte Lead
¼ Qt. Red Lead
½ Qt. Spa Blue
As much paint of a deep olive col^r ready ground with linseed oyl as will paint 200 yds. wainscott.[7]

Other inventories reveal ' Spanish brown ' paint, lampblack, indigo, light blue, ' red paint from Maryland,' yellow ochre, Venetian red, and Prussian blue. As early as 1705 the Virginia House of Burgesses

Resolved that the wanscote and other Wooden Work on the first and second ffloor in that part of the Building [the Capitol] where the General Court is, be painted Like Marble and the wanscote and other wooden work on the two first floors in the other part of the Building shall be painted like Wanscote, and the Doors and other wooden work in the roof shall be painted white . . .[8]

The dining room of the Governor's Palace was painted a pearl color, and the adjoining parlor a cream color, according to an order-in-council of 2 May 1727. Ochres, greens, and blues were used, but the favorite colors were a blue-gray, now widely known as ' Williamsburg blue,' a warm buff, and a rich red-brown. Colors were ground and mixed by hand, and often applied in successive coats, each one carefully rubbed. ' The salient characteristic of the earlier colors,' wrote Mrs. Nash, ' is the intensity of tone. They were often used in their pure form (especially the ochres and reds), but a great variety of colors resulted from the mixture of the pigments and the use of lampblack.' [9]

The woodwork of the Capitol ' painted Like Marble ' was by no means unique, for this grained or marbleized treatment was also used at Marmion and Argyle in Virginia, and in the dining room of the McPhedris House at Portsmouth, New Hampshire. The fashion probably passed from Holland to England after the Restoration, and thence to the colonies. In 1760 the *Maryland Gazette* (26 June) carried an advertisement: ' House Painter . . . can imitate marble or mahogany very exactly. . .' The famous drawing room of Marmion, set up in the Metropolitan Museum, has a marbleized dado and panels above painted with garlands, vases, cornucopias, and landscape scenes — though to be sure these were not added to the old woodwork until about 1781. In general, however, the vigorous, solid Williamsburg colors prevailed during the first half of the century, gradually yielding to the more classical whites and creams as the academic influence strengthened in the latter half of the period.

Georgian plans

Georgian house plans reveal the greater wealth of the period by the larger number and greater size of the rooms, compared with those of the seventeenth century. Plans were almost universally two rooms deep — a double file of rooms separated by a central hall running from front to back. The triple function of the old Colonial ' hall ' was now divided into three specialized rooms: a kitchen, a separate dining room, and a ' library ' or ' sitting room ' or ' drawing room ' serving as a family living room. The parlor was preserved as a formal room, unless perhaps its functions were served, in big houses, by a very large banquet hall or ball room. The kitchen, with servants' rooms, in New England was placed in a separate ell at the back, with its own stairs, and in the South was housed in a separate building at some distance from the main house. Ceiling heights increased to an average of about 11 feet for the main floor and 9 for the chamber floor.

In the South separate outbuildings housed kitchen, laundry, offices, and servants' rooms, these buildings flanking the main house in a symmetrical relationship. In a few of the greatest houses of the late Georgian period, outbuildings were connected to the main house by curved passageways, forming the full Palladian villa scheme. Though the corners of rooms might be beveled on a diagonal, to accommodate a fireplace or cupboard, room shapes were otherwise rectangular. In Georgian houses, according to Kimball, ' no single instance of a circular or elliptical room, or of a curved projection on the exterior, is attested before the Revolution,' [10] and even in public buildings the only known examples of these forms are in the Capitol at Williamsburg.*

Sanitation

Eighteenth-century sanitation was incredibly backward in the colonies, as it was in England. Almost universally, houses lacked running water; all water used was brought in pails from springs or wells. The ' great spring ' that supplied Thomas Lee's grandiose mansion Stratford, in Virginia, was located at a considerable distance from the house and all water toted by Negro slaves. City houses were, however, generally supplied from public or private wells equipped with pumps. Boston, Newport, and Philadelphia had public pumps along the city streets; indeed in 1744 Philadelphia had ' plenty of excellent water,' Dr. Hamilton reported, ' there being a pump at almost every fifty paces in the streets.' [11] New York was less well off, having few public wells, and those with no pumps until after 1741. There is always the exception that proves the rule, for we read that in 1723 one John Headly of Newport piped water ' underground from the Spring ' and thus enjoyed running water in his house.[12]

We have record of only one interior bathroom in colonial days — that at Whitehall, Maryland. The medieval vapor or steam bath had gone out of fashion, and bathing in portable tubs and with pitcher and basin served for ordinary ablutions. Outdoor privies were quite general; as early as 1652 Boston had prohibited the building of a ' house of office ' within 12 feet of a street or house. On the other hand, many New York houses lacked privies even as late as the mid-eighteenth century, and excrement was carried in ' ordure tubs ' to the East River at night.[13] Southern man-

---

* The curved ends of the Council Chamber and Representatives' Hall in the Old State House at Boston date from a remodeling of 1830. They were wrongly assumed, in the restoration of 1882, to have been part of the original plan.

sions had outdoor privies for the use of the young men and for white servants. These 'necessaries' were often octagonal structures made of brick,
with multiple accommodations, such as those at Cleve and Brandon in
Virginia. Sometimes they served the Palladian passion for symmetry, as
at Mount Vernon, where twin octagonal structures flanked the forecourt
leading to the main entrance. But most members of the family made use
in their own rooms of commode chairs equipped with pottery receptacles,
which were cleaned by the servants. This was one reason for the adoption,
in the better houses, of service stairs separate from the main stairs.

Heating, cooking, and illumination

There was a fireplace for heating in every important room in a Georgian house, and of course the big kitchen fireplace with its crane and
bake-oven was used for cooking as it had been in the preceding century.
But during the course of the century men discovered the use of the iron
grate, the tile stove, Franklin's ingenious iron fireplace, and the box stove
for both heating and cooking. The chronology of these improvements is
not certainly known, nor indeed how extensively they were in use at various times and in various places.

Cast-iron fire-backs had been used in the seventeenth century, to protect
the bricks at the back of the fireplace. But the first improvement over the
open fire remains a puzzle. It has always been supposed that Franklin's
fireplace (1742) or the nearly contemporary Pennsylvania 'five-plater'
was the first iron stove. Yet in the diary of Boston's Judge Sewall we read
under the date of 16 January 1702: 'Comfortable, moderat wether; and
with a good fire in the stove worm'd the Room.' And again, on 27 February 1706: 'Passed out of the Stove Room into the Kitchen.' What kind
of stove did the Judge have? Perhaps it was merely a cast-iron hearth, such
as was used on shipboard. Possibly it was a coal grate; we know that such
existed, for the *Boston News-Letter* of 1732 advertised a fine 'chamber
grate,' and again a large grate for coal, fit for a kitchen.[14] More likely it
was a large tile heating stove, such as had been used in Germany and
Holland for generations. That these were known in Boston is evident
from advertisements in 1723* and 1731. If it was, there is still room to
puzzle about the sale of 'a good *iron stove* and a chamber table, at auc-
tion' in 1740. Franklin's stove, invented two years later, must be the type
referred to as 'a very good Philadelphia stove or fireplace' offered for
sale in Boston in 1747.[15]

Certain it is that Benjamin Franklin's stove was invented in 1742 and
cast at the Warwick blast furnace in Chester County, Pennsylvania. As is
well known, it was a sort of open fireplace made of iron, set on low legs
and provided with a smoke pipe to the fireplace flue; less well known,
however, is the fact that it had a built-in 'cold air box' and a baffled flue
designed to heat air in a chamber at the back of the fireplace, exactly on
the principle of the modern Heatilator fireplace. Franklin's fireplace was
immensely superior to any type of open fire as a heating device; it was

* Grafton Feveryeare offered 'Holland stoves' for sale at The Black Wigg in North
Boston in 1723.

widely adopted in all parts of the north, and as the century developed was cast in all manner of decorative forms.

Various kinds of Pennsylvania box stoves were made during the mid-century, and since they had been known in Europe for a long time, it is quite possible that they antedated — and even suggested — Franklin's invention. The earliest type was a ' five-plate ' stove, built of five cast-iron pieces forming the four sides and back, and open at the front. It stood on legs, free from the wall, and had a stovepipe. Sometimes such stoves were built into a chimney, the open front being in the rear of an open fireplace, and the back extending into the room behind the chimney, so that the stove heated two rooms. The six-plate stove was similar except that the front was closed in. The ten-plate stove, which appeared about 1765, was the first iron stove used for baking. It was a six-plate box with a large door on each side, opening to a small four-plate baking oven within. But while such stoves served as auxiliaries for small-scale cooking, they did not entirely replace the big open fireplace and brick bake-oven for half a century. They were small and, with no cement at the joints, must have leaked smoke. The first wholly satisfactory cooking stove was not invented until 1815: the James stove, patented by William T. James of Union Village, New York, was first made and sold in Troy, and later in many other New York and New England towns.

The advertisement quoted above indicates that coal was in use as a fuel for domestic heating as early as 1732, and probably earlier. The steadily increasing use of timber for firewood meant higher costs, and as time went on inhabitants of the larger coastal cities burned ' sea-coal,' brought from England and Nova Scotia, though inland towns still depended on the forests. Bridenbaugh states that after 1730 the use of imported coal by wealthy Bostonians became general.[16] One traveler reports her arrival in Brunswick, North Carolina, on 31 January 1775. Received into the house of a wealthy merchant, she found the hall ' had a cheerful look, to which a large carron stove * filled with Scotch coals not a little contributed. The night was bitterly cold, and we gathered around the hearth with great satisfaction.' [17] As early as 1752 round cast-iron stoves — a form made particularly for coal rather than wood fuel — were used in New York, and in the nineteenth century, as anthracite came into general use for heating stoves, round stoves were designed in an endless variety of awkward forms.

Domestic illumination improved markedly during the course of the eighteenth century. Whale oil came into use as a fuel and afforded a much brighter and more even flame in lamps than did the sputtering grease of the old Betty lamps. Candles were improved and used more lavishly, especially in chandeliers whose cut-glass crystals, imported from Europe, multiplied their soft light into hundreds of glittering points. One had only to beware the dripping of wax or tallow into one's hair. Branch chandeliers made of iron or wood were locally produced, but brass chandeliers were imported. Local resources of copper were either unknown or inac-

---

* The Carron ironworks, near Glasgow, began production on 1 January 1760 and specialized in domestic stoves and grates, ordnance, and architectural ironwork, much of the latter in the style of the brothers Adam.

cessible, so brass door hardware, fire irons, chandeliers, or furniture fittings were almost invariably of European manufacture. Wall sconces for candles were widely used, and mirrors often had candle brackets at the base, the reflected wavering flames affording a moving decoration. Candlesticks — mostly of imported brass — were of varied and beautiful forms; set upon side tables and lowboys, their candle flames were often shielded by gracefully shaped ' hurricane glass ' globes.

The first tentative efforts at lighting city streets at night were made during the eighteenth century.[18] At least one lantern was used in Boston as early as 1719, for that which Eliakim Hutchinson presented to the town was accepted by the selectmen and ordered ' well fixed with Lights on all dark or Stormy Nights ' by a lamplighter. The first street lights in Philadelphia were installed shortly after 1757; Benjamin Franklin devised for them a ' long funnel above to draw up the smoke,' an improvement over London lamps, which were soon smoked up. In Boston a committee under John Hancock undertook the first large-scale scheme: in 1773, 310 street lamps were installed. Apparently these had a square glass lantern topped by tin funnels or ventilating hoods. They burned whale oil and, after a few years' experience, were kept lighted during evenings from October first to May first. No improvement over whale oil was devised until 1840, when a ' burning fluid ' compounded of alcohol and turpentine was used; this fluid remained in use until the advent of kerosene.

READING SUGGESTIONS

Nathaniel Lloyd's *History of the English House* (William Helburn, New York, 1931) is the most comprehensive and best-illustrated one-volume history of English architecture.

Houses of the Wren and Early Georgian Periods, by Tunstall Small and Christopher Woodbridge (William Helburn, New York, 1928) affords convincing pictorial evidence of the close relationship between the English architecture of these periods and American Georgian.

Harold Donaldson Eberlein's *Architecture of Colonial America* (Little, Brown and Co., Boston, 1927) deals briefly with materials and structure (Ch. 13) and with early American architects (Ch. 14).

Fiske Kimball's *Domestic Architecture of the American Colonies and of the Early Republic* (Scribner's, New York, 1922) has much valuable material on the architectural books, materials, structure, and plans used in eighteenth-century American building.

10

The Georgian Style

IN THE Colonial house, need shaped structure and structure *was* style. In the Georgian house, need itself was shaped by form, and structure and style were — if not incompatible — irrelevant to each other. In a wealthy society the complicated and beautiful employment of leisure demands a certain ritual: life itself must become an art. If parson Capen had to stoop to enter his low-beamed rooms, it was merely becoming to one whose cares were spiritual, and if his wife appeared a little awkward climbing down the steep and tortuous stair, no harm was done. But a few miles away and fifty years later, Isaac Royall needed a room befitting his name for the expansive and graceful gestures of the minuet, and a wide and easy flight of steps for the gracious descent of a wife who brought her own twenty-seven slaves from Antigua. Thus art shaped needs and needs shaped forms in Georgian architecture.

It was essentially a formal style. House shapes themselves became simple and regular geometric figures, no longer expressive of the accidents of internal asymmetries or of evolutionary growth. The ordered rhythm of windows could brook no interference from internal necessities: if the central hall at Westover needed a front window it must borrow one at the expense of a neighboring room; and when in the Jeremiah Lee House a partition abutted against a window (fig. 422) the conflict did not budge the window from its axial position. The Colonial saltbox with its sag-backed roof seemed only a poor relation to the regular perfection of the elegant Georgian hipped roof. Houses were more pretentious in their posture: they were superior to the ground rather than a part of it, and a flight of steps often enhanced the hauteur of the front door. The unkempt lilacs and rambling roses of a careless Colonial gave way to the clipped box and yew of the Georgian formal garden.

But the compositions of Georgian houses were never stereotyped. Within the rule of symmetry there was ample play for variety of spacing and choice of detail. Proportions could be studied with differing combinations of elements, and decorative highlights and accents could be selected from the rich vocabularies of the handbooks. Georgian design became a sort of game; played according to strict rules, it nonetheless afforded the endless richness of the theme and variations of classical music.

Georgian doorways

The front door was the first feature to betray the onset of the new style, and a great variety of doors and doorway compositions may be found in

Georgian houses (fig. 251). The door itself was paneled in many ways and was usually of generous width. A small rectangular transom above it lighted the hall, though frequently glazed lights in the upper panels of the door itself took the place of a transom. If the hall was wide enough, separate windows on one or both sides of the door were used, but these

251. Types of Georgian doorways (Philip White)

windows were rarely included within the exterior doorway composition until after the Revolution.

Flanking the door at the sides, classic orders were used in a variety of ways. Pilasters, plain or fluted, and either full height or raised on pedestals, were most common, though from the mid-century engaged columns (projecting about a half of their diameter) rivaled them in popularity. These members carried cornices or pediments crowning the doorway composition.

The four most common types of overdoor features are shown in figure 251. Simplest was a flat section of classic entablature. The frieze sometimes bulged out as a curved molding (spoken of as a ' pulvinated ' frieze) and was topped by a row of small blocks (dentils) and a molded cornice. In the example illustrated (fig. 251A) the place of an architrave is taken by a transom window and small stilt blocks over the pilasters, in order to avoid a top-heavy effect. The simple angular pediment (B) was the most common type throughout the Georgian period; to avoid undue heaviness the frieze rather than the architrave has been omitted in this case. The curved or segmental pediment (C) was also popular; this example possesses all three elements of the classic entablature: architrave, thin frieze, and a dentiled cornice.

Both angular and segmental pediments were sometimes ' broken ' by omitting the top central section (fig. 260) or by recessing the central portion (fig. 271). Such broken pediments were usually a sign of the baroque influence of Wren's style. The most elaborate type was the scroll or ' swan's neck ' pediment (D). Its reverse-curve cornices terminated in patterned rosettes. A pedestal motive occupied the center of the pediment and was echoed in the entablature below. Such a pedestal, in any form of broken pediment, often carried an ornamental feature, usually a carved pineapple, symbol of hospitality.

The variety and freedom of Georgian design may be seen in the many variations of these four types of door enframement. The classic entablature was sometimes fully equipped, in the more academic examples, with triglyphs and metopes, mutules and their small peg-like guttae, as at Cliveden (fig. 254). Or the doorway was treated simply with a pediment carried by projecting consoles or brackets. In general, Georgian doorways had a masculine quality, with vigorous moldings and burly forms, in contrast to the more fragile detail of the Federal period. After the mid-century there were a few examples of doorways with a semicircular lunette or fanlight over the door; the motive became popular on the eve of the Revolution. But the door flanked by two narrow windows or ' sidelights,' all three elements topped by a graceful elliptical arched fanlight, was definitely a Federal type; that of the Miles Brewton House in Charleston is the only authenticated example in pre-Revolutionary domestic architecture.

The small projecting portico was uncommon in Georgian houses, as was the larger two-story portico used only in the South. The ' giant portico,' with columns rising through two or more stories to the full height of the building, was a Federal or Greek Revival, not a Georgian feature.

The only authentic examples among Georgian houses were those of Whitehall, Maryland, and the Roger Morris House in New York.

Georgian windows

The sliding-sash window with pulleys, cords, and counterweights was universal in Georgian architecture. The date of its origin is not certain, but it was used in English houses of the last half of the seventeenth century, and possibly earlier. Wren used sash windows in Hampton Court Palace (1689) and also in the College of William and Mary at Williamsburg (completed 1702) — the latter probably the first examples in this

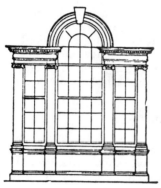

252. Palladian window (Norman M. Isham, *A Glossary of Colonial Architectural Terms*, The Walpole Society)

country. They were also used in the Capitol and the Governor's Palace at Williamsburg, in the early eighteenth century.

Leaded casements of the medieval type were advertised in the Boston papers as late as 1713, but from then on the offers were of sash windows with pulleys and counterweights.[1] Early Georgian windows had many small panes — 18 or 24 per window. There was a general increase in size of panes as the century progressed, to a standard of 12 panes per window in the later and finer houses.

Throughout the Georgian period window glass was imported from England. In 1738, for example, we find Thomas Hancock ordering from his London agent 380 panes of the best crown glass, cut $11\frac{1}{2}$ by 18 inches for his main windows, and 100 smaller panes for the attic dormers. There were, however, attempts to establish glass factories in the colonies. We read in the *Boston Gazette* of 26 September 1752 that

Tuesday last a ship arrived here from Holland, with about 300 Germans . . . Among the Artificers come over in this ship, there are Numbers of Men skilled in making of Glass, of various sorts, and a House proper for carrying on that useful manufacture, will be erected at Germantown [Braintree] as soon as possible.

But that the process was semi-secret and aroused great curiosity is attested by a notice from this factory about a year later:

Notice is hereby given, That for the future none will be admitted to see the new manufactory at Germantown, unless they pay at least one shilling lawfull money; and they are desired not to ask above three or four Questions, and not to be offended if they have not a satisfactory answer to all or any of them. *Note.* — The manufactory has received considerable Damage, and been very much retarded by the great Number of People which are constantly resorting to the House. [*Boston Gazette,* 4 September 1753.]

Windows generally were framed by an architrave,* and sometimes topped by a small flat cornice; a few of the more pretentious houses had small angular pediments over the windows. Blinds with the familiar slanted slats or louvers were rare until late in the century; the paneled shutter was almost peculiar to the middle colonies. Windows also had paneled interior shutters which folded back into the reveals when open. All windows were rectangular in shape or topped by a low segmental arch, except that a tall round-arch window often lighted the stair landing. This was elaborated, after about 1750, into the Palladian window or ' Venetian window ' as it was then called, a favorite accent for the middle of a façade (fig. 252).

Exterior wall treatments

Renaissance architects generally devoted considerable attention to the textures of wall surfaces, often treating them ' artificially ' (from the standpoint of the material employed) to gain desired effects of pattern or composition. Fortunately, Georgian builders in America did not usually go to extremes of artificiality in this respect. The laying of brick masonry in Flemish bond with patterns of glazed headers, or the graduation of wooden clapboards from a wide weather at the bottom of the wall to a narrow one at the top, to enhance the perspective illusion of height, were perhaps permissible compromises between the natural or simplest use of materials and a contrived formation of these for aesthetic purposes. Similarly, the use of angle quoins, the staggered blocks laid either flush with the wall surface or projecting from it in rusticated form, was an appropriate aesthetic expression of the needed structural strength at corners.

But Georgian architecture was not without examples of arbitrary and deceptive treatment of materials for an aesthetic end. For example, stucco over brick was perhaps legitimately used in Philadelphia and Charleston houses to make walls warmer and more weatherproof; but when, as in the formal Mount Pleasant (fig. 445), this stucco was incised with lines to make it resemble grooved ashlar masonry, a problem of aesthetic propriety was approached. Similarly, a small group of New England Georgian houses and Mount Vernon have walls made of wooden planks grooved to simulate rusticated stone masonry. In general, history seems to show that the treatment of one material to imitate another and more expensive material is aesthetically unsuccessful. Whether deception in architecture, either palpable or implicit, is to be condemned on moral grounds need not here be argued; the important fact is that these ' rus-

* This term applies not only to the ' master beam ' or main lower member of a classic entablature but also to a molded face frame of door or window.

ticated wood' houses do not look as well as their more honest contemporaries, especially in close-up actuality. Flattering photographs blur the deception.

The walls of Georgian houses usually had moldings that served to emphasize horizontals and to mark floor levels. If there was a visible basement, for example, it was usually set forward a few inches and topped by

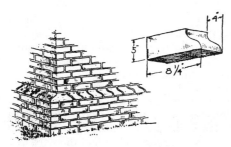

253. Water table of molded bricks (J. Frederick Kelly, *The Early Domestic Architecture of Connecticut*, Yale University Press)

a course of molded bricks, called the 'water table' (fig. 253). The division between first and second stories was commonly marked by a belt course (fig. 254). This usually consisted of three or four brick courses slightly projected and often differentiated from the wall by the use of bricks of a different color; sometimes a stone belt course was set in a brick

254. Cliveden, Germantown, Pa., 1763-4 (*The Georgian Period*)

wall. Belt courses were used only in brick and stone houses * and originated as an exterior expression of the level at which floor joists were carried on the inner face of the masonry wall. In common with many other
decorative features that had a structural origin, they seem aesthetically
most effective when used with close reference to their original structural
significance. Only rarely in Georgian was a belt course used without any
reference to interior floor division, as in the Walnut Street façade of Independence Hall, and the effect seems forced and arbitrary.

But the Georgian architect's chief motives in composing a façade, apart
from windows and doorway, were pavilions and applied pilasters. Until
about 1750, façades were ' flat,' but after that date it was common to introduce a projecting central pavilion, topped by a gable treated as a classic pediment (fig. 254). In a few late Georgian examples, such as the west
façade of Mount Vernon and the Gibbes House in Charleston, a pedimented gable was used without a projecting pavilion, a treatment that
lacks structural plausibility and therefore aesthetic identity.

From about the mid-century on, giant pilasters, extending the full
height of the façade, were used on the more pretentious houses. At the
bottom, they started from the main-floor level or were elevated on low
pedestals; at the top, each pilaster usually had, over its capital, an individual fragment of architrave and frieze, the main cornice of the house completing the order. This scheme, which was used in England and figured in
many of the architectural handbooks, had the practical advantage of permitting full height windows in the second story. The alternative scheme
of permitting the full classic entablature to encircle the building is found
in only one Georgian house (fig. 481), where it necessitated small square
windows in the second story.

Pilasters were usually placed at or near the corners of the house, and
on the central pavilion. The Doric and Ionic were the favorite orders; the
Corinthian was more common in small entrance porticoes. The proportions were fairly solid and sturdy; the very slender pilaster became popular with the influence of Robert Adam after the Revolution.

Roof treatments

Georgian roofs, of whatever shape, were usually lower pitched than
Colonial ones: 30° or less was much more common than the 45° standard
of late Colonial. A low-pitched roof brought out to the end permitted a
gable closely approaching the broad, low shape of a classic pediment (fig.
254), and, though gable ends were not immediately detailed in this fashion, the classical influence was doubtless responsible for the generally
lowered roof pitches. The classic cornice, with modillions and moldings,
and sometimes a row of dentils, replaced the simple eaves of Colonial
houses. The gabled roof continued much in use, and the gambrel became more popular, especially in New England, but the hipped roof was
the favorite Georgian type and was used on a majority of the finer houses.

Though many roofs continued up to a sharp ridge, it was more usual

* Their appearance in frame houses such as Tuckahoe. Virginia, and the Randolph-
Peachy House at Williamsburg is decidedly exceptional.

to cut the ridge off at the top to form a nearly flat roof-deck. This was enclosed with balustrades to form a ' captain's walk.' Balusters of the common profile and taller posts topped by knobs formed the usual balustrade, but after 1750 railings of ' Chinese lattice ' occasionally appeared. Roof-decks became almost universal in the larger Georgian houses after 1750. In the Federal period, the roof balustrade migrated from its deck position at the top to the outer perimeter of the roof, over the eaves, so that it surrounded the entire roof and in large measure concealed it. Such ' eaves balustrades ' appeared only three or four times in the Georgian period.

Dormer windows of many shapes were used in Georgian architecture, appearing on gabled, gambrel, or hipped roofs wherever these were of sufficient pitch to permit attic rooms. There seems to have been no objection to dormers on aesthetic grounds. The standard dormer was narrow, and topped by a low-pitched gable treated on the front as a small pediment, but in certain southern houses of the early Georgian period, small hipped-roof dormers were used. Sometimes in the more academic houses alternating angular and segmental pediments were used on dormers, and toward the end of the period, semicircular-headed dormer windows appeared.

Cupolas or ' lanthornes ' are generally thought to have been common features of Georgian houses, yet only half a dozen examples can with certainty be placed before the Revolution. Needless to say, the supposition that either the roof-deck or the cupola was invented in Salem or some other seaport, so that the resident sea captain could go to the roof to watch for his returning ships, is a legend. Though they may have been used on occasion for such a purpose, cupolas had appeared long before on English houses of the Stuart period, some scores of miles from the sea.

Georgian chimneys abandoned the elaborate pilastered shapes of the Colonial period; they were usually rectangular in shape with a simple plinth or small molded cornice at the top. When end chimneys occurred in pairs, as in the Foster and Royall Houses in Boston, they were sometimes connected by brick parapets rising above the roof surface (figs. 396 and 405).

Georgian interiors

In general Georgian interiors progress from the frank structural revelation and functional character of the Colonial period to sheathed and highly finished surfaces and formal division and composition of wall and ceiling. This is evident in Colonial houses, which during the course of the eighteenth century had their exposed posts, girts, and summers boxed in by smooth, painted boards, their walls paneled or papered, and their ceilings plastered under the old joists.

Builders' handbooks were very influential in the design of interior details. They were richly illustrated with designs for mantelpieces, stairways, door and window enframements, cornices, paneling, and the like, and it is often possible to identify the particular book from which such details were taken. While exterior design tended toward a more strict Palladianism as the period progressed, interiors often remained free and

florid, employing some of the baroque scrolls and broken pediments Wren
had used in his interiors, and even some of the elaborate rococo ornament
of French Louis XV interiors.

Materials for interior finish do not seem to have been imported from
England, as is sometimes alleged. Flooring, wall paneling, stair balustrades, chimneypieces, and the like were made on the job. A few exceptions prove the rule: domestic marble was not used until after the Revolution, and marble fireplace facings and carved mantels were imported;
brass hardware and iron locks were likewise imported, and so was wallpaper.

255, 256. Georgian stairways, showing paneled and scrolled step ends, swash-turned
balusters (*The Georgian Period*)

The entrance hall and stairway

Perhaps the most marked contrast between Colonial and Georgian
houses was in the treatment of the entrance hall. Wide, well-lighted, high-
ceilinged, with paneled or papered walls and a handsome staircase, the
Georgian hall extended through the house from front to back and was
often subdivided into reception hall in front and stair hall behind by a
graceful elliptical arch.

The stairway itself (fig. 255) was wider and had a more gradual ascent
than did its Colonial predecessor. A straight flight at one side of the hall
reached a spacious landing across the end, then doubled back for a few
steps to reach the upper hall. Frequently there were three 'runs,' with
two landings. The 'open-string' staircase, with visible step ends, was
universal. The ends of the steps were variously ornamented: paneled, or
carved with naturalistic foliage and flowers in the tradition of Grinling
Gibbons (fig. 257), carved more formally like an academic modillion, or
fitted with a flat block sawn to a complex scroll profile. In a few of the
most elaborate houses carved scrolls were used in combination with paneled step ends (fig. 256). The soffit of the stairway was ordinarily a pan-

eled slanting surface, though occasionally the profile of the step ends was carried the full width of the under surface.

Lathe-turned balusters, generally three to each step, carried the handrail; they were taller and more slender than their Colonial prototypes. From about 1730 appeared the spirally twisted or 'swash-turned' balusters, later developed into such a rich variety of forms, especially in New England. Joseph Moxon's *Mechanick Exercises,* published in London in 1694, described the technique 'Of Turning Swash-Work.' Since the three balusters on each step were of different lengths, they were often treated with different spiral patterns. The heavier newel posts at corners and ends of balustrades were of great variety: square, circular, spirally twisted, or

257. Carved step end, Carter's Grove, Va. (*The Georgian Period*)

even with double spirals, one inside the other, turning in opposite directions.

The molded and polished handrail, generally of mahogany, became increasingly graceful. At first it ran directly into the newel post at an awkward angle (fig. 256). Later it was brought into the newel at a right angle, with a curved 'easing' at the bottom and an upward-curving 'ramp' at the top to effect graceful transitions (fig. 255). After 1730, the newel was set out of line and the handrail curved out to meet it, and after the mid-century it was common to use a plain newel with balusters and handrail winding themselves into a spiral around it. The wall paneling opposite the balustrade echoed every detail of its vertical contour, including the curved ramp at the top of the straight flight. There were a very few examples, dating in the 1760's, of stair rails supported by Chinese lattices or trellises, instead of the customary balustrade.

Floor and wall treatments

The wide boards of oak or hard pine of the Colonial period were supplanted in Georgian houses by finished and polished hardwood floors of narrow matched boards. More elaborate floor treatments were used occasionally; there is record of a house in Boston with a parquet floor 'laid in diamond-shaped figures' and a central inlaid coat of arms. Floors were often painted with decorative borders and centerpieces.

Walls were sheathed with finer materials and were more formally com-

posed than in the Colonial period. Of chief importance was the fine
wood paneling that began to supplant the simple Colonial wainscot
around 1700. Georgian paneling is of such immense variety in the size,
shape, and arrangement of panels, their projection or recession from the
surface of stiles and rails, and the bevelings and moldings of the borders
that a detailed analysis would require a monograph.

The quantity and location of paneling employed depended partly on
the period, partly on the means available. In general, floor to ceiling paneling (fig. 258) was most common in the early Georgian period, but even
then paneling was confined to the chimney wall, or to the two interior
walls, if means were lacking for a fully paneled room. After 1750, pan-

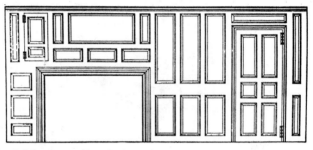

258. Paneled fireplace wall, early Georgian style (J. Frederick Kelly, *The Early Domestic Architecture of Connecticut*, Yale University Press)

eling was usually restricted to the dado, a treatment that first occurred,
naturally enough, in stair halls because of the great height and awkward
shapes of the spaces to be covered. In the main rooms, paneled dadoes accompanied the increasing use of wallpapers.

As far back as the late seventeenth century, numerous newspaper items
indicate the use of ' paper hangings,' and the fact that these were imported from England. Michael Perry, Boston bookseller and stationer,
died in 1700, and in the inventory of his stock we find ' 7 quires of
painted paper and three reams of painted paper.' [2] At first, eighteenth-
century paper hangings were sold in large sheets, 22 by 32 inches, and the
designs were colored by hand. These might be repeated patterns made
with pasteboard stencils, or continuous pictorial patterns of great diversity, such as those mentioned by Thomas Hancock as containing (about
1734) ' different Sorts of Birds, Peacocks, Macoys, Squirril, Monkys, Fruit
and Flowers.'

In the latter half of the eighteenth century, pictorial papers printed
from wood blocks were imported from both England and France, the designs ranging from Chinese scenes, such as those of the Supper Room in
the Governor's Palace at Williamsburg, to the classical ruins in rococo
frames ordered by Jeremiah Lee of Marblehead in 1768. By 1765 wallpapers were being made in the colonies, for several patterns produced by
John Rugar of New York were displayed at a meeting of the ' Society for

promoting Arts, etc. in this Province' in that year. Just after the Revolution, wallpapers were being manufactured in Pennsylvania, New Jersey, and Massachusetts.[3] But even after local manufacture was established, the finest rolls were still imported. The use of wallpapers increased steadily after 1750, but the plain plastered and painted walls of the Chase House at Annapolis (1769–71) are indicative of a growing severity of taste which appeared on the eve of the Revolution.

Though tall narrow wood panels often gave a room sufficient vertical membering, pilasters appeared on Georgian walls from the second quarter of the century. They were usually confined to positions of particular importance, such as flanking chimney-breasts (fig. 259) or doors. Sometimes they rose from the floor, sometimes from pedestals of dado height. In very

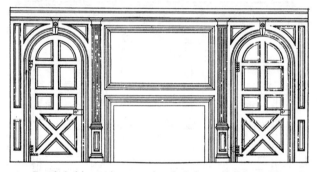

259. Paneled chimney-breast and arched doors (Stevenson Flemer)

few Georgian rooms, however, was there a consistent scheme of pilasters rising to a full classic entablature; of these, the great hall at Stratford and the entrance hall at Carter's Grove were the most imposing examples. Free-standing classic columns appeared in only a few late Georgian interiors.

Door and window treatments

Interior doors, like exterior ones, were invariably paneled. In the early Georgian period they were framed by a simple architrave, often as not accented by projecting 'ears' (crossettes) at the top corners. But after the mid-century a more pretentious treatment prevailed: the top was burdened by a frieze-and-cornice treatment and, in 'important' doors, by a pediment (fig. 261). Arched doors occurred occasionally throughout the Georgian period, most commonly on cupboards flanking the fireplace (fig. 259). Frequently there was an arched niche or buffet without a door in the dining room, the open shelves displaying fine china or glassware.

Window casings were usually simple architraves, often eared at the top like door casings. Paneled shutters folding into the window jambs were common. Rarely, windows were topped by a small cornice, and in one example (Gunston Hall, Virginia) they had flanking pilasters and a full entablature across the top.

Fireplaces and chimneypieces

Georgian fireplaces, being used for heating rather than cooking, were smaller in size, shallower, and had smaller flues than their Colonial predecessors. The opening was almost invariably rectangular (a low segmental arch was occasionally used) and was usually faced by flat marble slabs or a series of Dutch tiles, the latter particularly in New England and New York.

The enframement of fireplaces and the treatment of the chimney-breast were extraordinarily varied. The early Georgian fireplace (to about 1750) was usually framed by a molded architrave, with or without 'ears,'

260. Late Georgian fireplace and overmantel, Steadman-Powel House, Philadelphia (Metropolitan Museum of Art)

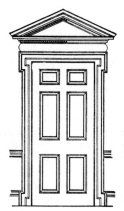

261. Georgian doorway with 'eared' architrave and triangular pediment, Mount Pleasant, Philadelphia (*The Georgian Period*)

had no mantel shelf, and had a chimney-breast above, paneled in the style of the adjoining walls (fig. 258).

The late Georgian fireplace (fig. 260), more ornately treated, had an elaborately carved frame around the fireplace opening, with a garlanded frieze over it; a projecting mantel shelf, often supported by consoles; and a unified overmantel treatment. This usually consisted of a single large panel, framed by an eared architrave. The latter was variously elaborated and adorned: by carved spiral motives at the sides, and at the top by either carving, a broken angular pediment, or a scroll pediment. In a few examples the overmantel was flanked by small pilasters, but in general pilasters or colonets were used very rarely in locally made fireplace compositions. Local designs reveal a particularly strong influence from Swan's *British Architect,* which contained plates of ' a great Variety of New and curious Chimneypieces.'

Several of the finer houses boasted imported fireplaces of carved marble. These made more frequent use of pilasters flanking the overmantel, and even of colonets flanking the fireplace opening to support the mantel. The latter do not otherwise appear in the colonies before the Revolution.

Ceilings

Ceiling cornices were generally of wood, and occasionally of plaster as at Kenmore and Mount Vernon. They ranged from simple cornice moldings to full classic entablatures, richly detailed with dentils or carved modillions; the degree of elaboration depended largely on the cost of the house but tended to increase as the period advanced.

Ornamental-stucco workers were rare in the colonies, and most plastered walls and ceilings were left plain. A few ceilings from about 1745 on, however, were lavishly ornamented with rococo reliefs. Those at Westover, the Miles Brewton House at Charleston, and the Philipse Manor at Yonkers are particularly noteworthy. The rococo motives are rambling, curvilinear, and non-architectonic, with birds, animals, and pastoral figures in rather high relief.

On the eve of the Revolution, the ornamental plaster ceilings of the Chase House at Annapolis, Kenmore near Fredericksburg, and two rooms at Mount Vernon heralded the stricter classicism of the Federal period. Composed more geometrically, with circles, quatrefoils, and octagonal coffers, the delicate low-relief ornament had a profusion of husks, flutings, rosettes, festoons, and garlands such as the brothers Adam had popularized in London. The ceilings at Kenmore were the richest in the country, as were the stucco cornices and overmantels of the fireplaces.

Georgian furniture

The furniture of the eighteenth century was more varied in type than that of the seventeenth, made of finer materials, and more richly ornamented. Around 1700 walnut came into favor for all the finer furniture pieces, and after 1750, mahogany. Maple and pine continued in use for the simpler, utilitarian pieces, usually painted as in the seventeenth century.

The backless benches and stools, the simple stretcher tables and low heavy chests of the seventeenth century gave way to settees, sofas and love seats, graceful side chairs, comfortably upholstered wing chairs, side tables and lowboys, desks and secretaries of all kinds, carved four-poster and canopied beds, and all manner of gracefully shaped mirrors, footstools, firescreens, and the like.

The seventeenth-century chest with a hinged top was found less convenient and elegant than the ' lowboy,' which had a few sliding drawers raised to convenient height by graceful cabriole legs. For added storage space, the lowboy was surmounted by a chest of drawers to become a ' highboy.' Even more space was afforded by two chests of drawers superimposed, a form known as a double chest of drawers or — often — a ' chest-on-chest.' Other impressive pieces were the slant-topped desks, sometimes with bowed fronts, accidentally associated with Governor Winthrop and given his name; and the desk with a case-top, containing bookshelves and pigeon holes, which formed the high secretary. The tops of these lofty pieces were usually shaped as broken swan's neck pediments, carved with fluted shells, and crowned by turned vases and urns.

Of particular importance was the tall-case clock or ' grandfather ' clock, which despite a great variety of decorative detail, became highly standardized in shape and proportion. Tea tables, with pie-crust or raised edges to protect their dainty cargoes of China ' table setts,' Derby or Lowestoft porcelain, and Stiegel glass, revealed the growth of the amenities of wealth and leisure. Card tables, tiptop or stationary, had curved corner projections for the brass candle sticks that lighted a game of whist or piquet. Upholstery materials and hangings were of silk damasks and brocades imported from England or France, or of linens and woolens in humbler rooms. Homemade braided and hooked rugs were still the standard floor covering, but English needlework rugs and the luxurious imported orientals were used by the wealthy.

Many paintings and prints hung on the walls. Among oil paintings, family portraits were most numerous, but a copy — and sometimes even an original — of an Italian or Flemish Old Master might be found. The Byrd family boasted no less than forty portraits on the walls of Westover, as well as a reputed Rubens and a Titian. Engravings of famous paintings, especially portraits of the reigning King and Queen, were also popular. During the eighteenth century, America's first important portrait painters began to produce work worth hanging. Smibert, Hesselius, and Pelham, during the early part of the century, put their talents to good use in portraying the important men and women of their day, and in the late Georgian period men such as Copley and Stuart produced work almost as accomplished as that of the great English portraitists.

The furniture style of the early Georgian period was the English ' Queen Anne,' which though graceful in its continuous curved lines, appears sturdy and sober compared to the exotic details of the later Chippendale. Most characteristic were the splat-backed side chairs, with smooth stiles curved to a ' round-shouldered ' top (the lathe-turned spindles of the seventeenth century had entirely disappeared), and with the reverse-curve cabriole leg terminating in a 'slipper' foot like the head of a wooden golf club. Indeed the cabriole leg, drawn to various smooth reverse-curve profiles, was found on almost all pieces. Queen Anne furniture was generally smooth-surfaced, though a few of the more monumental pieces were richly carved.

The great style of the late Georgian period was Chippendale, which entirely dominated a period of extensive American furniture production in the 1760's and 1770's. Thomas Chippendale (1718–79), most famous of English cabinetmakers, first published his trade catalogue *The Gentleman and Cabinetmaker's Directory* in 1754. His graceful and playful forms were soon followed by a number of American craftsmen, including Rivington in New York, Gillingham in Philadelphia, and others of note in Boston, Newport, and Charleston.

The Chippendale style was by no means light or fragile; of about the same weight as the Queen Anne, and continuing many of its forms, it was distinguished chiefly by the inspiration of French rococo, Chinese, and 'Gothick' motives. The material was dark-finished mahogany, always without inlays. Side chairs were made with cabriole legs (which often terminated in the claw-and-ball foot), but the straight, square, front leg gradually surpassed the cabriole in popularity. Back splats were pierced and soon supplanted by more elaborate and frivolous motives: dainty ladder backs, interlaced openwork of Gothic inspiration, Chinese lattice, and other forms, often sumptuously carved. Graceful long settees and lofty secretaries and china cabinets, often with latticed glazed doors, were among the most successful pieces, and the well-upholstered love seats, wing chairs, and couches with their brocade coverings were both comfortable and elegant.

The Windsor chair was an especially successful type. Of English origin, it was in common use in the colonies by 1760, and proved highly practical. Simply produced, the solid, saddle-shaped seat housed the legs from below and the back spindles from above. No mortise-and-tenon joints were necessary, and with stretchers to brace the legs and the back spindles held in place by a hooped top rail, the chair was extraordinarily firm, light, and cheap. Varieties included a horizontal rail, which braced the back spindles and curved forward to form arms; an upward extension of the back spindles to form a high headrest (called the 'comb-back' type); and even a widened right arm to form a writing chair. The Windsor chair became a 'folk' type; mass-produced in the nineteenth century, it became the most standardized, the most practical, and the most successful single piece in the history of American furniture.

The Chippendale style lived a few years after the Revolution but was soon succeeded by the Hepplewhite and Sheraton styles. Hepplewhite's *Cabinet-Maker and Upholsterer's Guide* was published in 1788, and Thomas Sheraton's catalogues appeared from 1791 to 1804. Both styles, or perhaps we should say *the* style, for the two are practically indistinguishable,[4] reveal Neoclassic inspiration from the French Louis XVI and English Adam styles. Far lighter than Chippendale, with emphasis on the straight line, fine moldings, and ornament, this was to become, in the Federal period, one of the finest furniture styles produced in this country.

Development of the Georgian style

The course of development of the Georgian style within the eighty years after 1700 was one of gradual evolution rather than sudden change. The appearance of certain features in isolated examples long before they were commonly adopted and the retention of early forms in the smaller and less pretentious houses up to and even after the Revolution underline the fact that it would be erroneous to present too hard and fast a picture of Georgian stylistic development.

But it does seem possible to make a broad distinction between early Georgian and late Georgian style, the dividing band occurring about 1745–50. The early Georgian style was, in general, the simpler of the two. It was robust and vigorous, in the burly shapes of its houses and the boldness of its moldings. It had many of the baroque details of English late Stuart architecture: broken and scroll pediments, eared architraves, et cetera. In the shapes of its windows and in its steeper roof pitches, it betrayed a lingering Gothic verticality, whereas the late Georgian style was more completely horizontal in emphasis.

The late Georgian style was more complex and more formal in composition. Its detail was less vigorous, but richer and more highly ornamented. It was influenced less and less by the baroque school of Christopher Wren, more and more by the academic Palladianism of the English early Georgian period. But French rococo influences appeared, and Chinese motives became more popular.

The difference between early Georgian and late Georgian houses may be seen more clearly by a tabular comparison of specific features. The details listed in each column below indicate common use in that period, though it is understood that there are exceptions.

Before 1750	After 1750
Wood houses: plain clapboards	Wood houses: sometimes rusticated treatment
Unbroken façade usual	Projecting central pavilion common
Corners marked by angle quoins	Corners often marked by giant pilasters
No entrance portico	Small entrance portico or, in South, two-story portico
Front door with rectangular transom window	Front door with semicircular arched fanlight occurs
Angular or scroll pediment over door	Segmental pediment over door also used
Windows with many small panes	Windows with fewer and larger panes
Plain or corniced windows	Pedimented windows often occur
Single arched window on stair landing	Palladian window more popular for stair landing
Steeper roof pitches	Lower roof pitches
Balustraded roof-decks uncommon	Balustraded roof-decks common

Before 1750	*After* 1750
Dormers have rectangular windows	Dormers sometimes have arched windows
Interiors with full-height wall paneling	Interiors with paneled dado and wallpaper above
Several panels in chimney-breast, no mantel shelf	One large panel, elaborately framed, over a mantel shelf
Plain or scrolled step ends on stairs	Paneled step ends on stairs
Classical and baroque decorative motives	Rococo and Chinese decorative motives also occur

Regional differences in style in the Georgian period were far less marked than in the Colonial period. This was owing primarily, of course, to the fact that all of the colonies were united under English rule and were more closely and constantly in touch with the mother country than they had been in the seventeenth century. The common dependence of all colonists on English architectural books also served as a unifying factor. But regional differences did exist, based partly on the earlier Colonial traditions, partly on differences in climate and materials, and partly on differences in economic and social conditions, as will be brought out in the following chapters dealing with the Georgian architecture of the South, of New England, and of the middle colonies.

READING SUGGESTIONS

Fiske Kimball's *Domestic Architecture of the American Colonies and of the Early Republic* (Scribner's, New York, 1922) affords the most complete and authoritative analysis of the development of style.

J. Frederick Kelly's *Early Domestic Architecture of Connecticut* (Yale University Press, New Haven, 1924) and Thomas T. Waterman's *Mansions of Virginia, 1706–1776* (University of North Carolina Press, Chapel Hill, 1946), though restricted to the domestic architecture of these two states, contain much valuable material on the nature and development of the Georgian style.

The two folio volumes of *Great Georgian Houses of America* (Architects' Emergency Committee, New York, 1933, 1937) comprise a fine collection of illustrations of houses of the Georgian, Federal, and Greek Revival styles.

11

Early Georgian Architecture in Virginia

VIRGINIA WAS the largest, wealthiest, and most populous of the American colonies in the eighteenth century. In 1699 its capital was transferred from Jamestown to Williamsburg, and here in the early years of the new century appeared the first important group of buildings in the American Georgian style of architecture. The College of William and Mary, the Capitol, the Governor's Palace, and Bruton Parish Church formed an impressive array, and it was inevitable that the wealthy plantation owners who visited the capital should seek to emulate this formal and courtly elegance in the new mansions they built throughout Virginia's Tidewater.

Williamsburg itself was small in comparison to other colonial capitals; its population never exceeded 2000 resident citizens. But at 'Public Times,' when the Provincial Assembly, the Governor's Council, and the courts were in session, it became a brisk metropolis of 5000 or 6000 persons, with a brilliant social season of formal balls, theatrical performances, horse races, and other entertainments. As the social, political, economic, and educational center of a large and prosperous colony, its influence was very great.

The architectural splendors of the great Georgian houses of Virginia were firmly based on a slave economy. Slave trading, hitherto the monopoly of certain companies, was thrown open to all British subjects in 1697 and further encouraged by the Treaty of Utrecht in 1714. The growth of this hideous traffic may be gauged by the population increase from an estimated 20,000 slaves in 1703 to 120,000 in 1755 — about 40 per cent of the total population. Slave competition drove out paid labor, and, as the small independent planters were driven to the wall, their farms were absorbed by the big holders, who thus amassed great estates. William Byrd of Westover owned 179,440 acres, or about 218 square miles, in 1744. Robert ('King') Carter, reputedly the wealthiest proprietor in Virginia, was in 1732 the owner of about 1,000 slaves and 300,000 acres of land.

Though George Washington's Mount Vernon, with its 125 slaves and 8,000 acres, was relatively small, it presents a good picture of the Virginia plantation economy. The architecture of the Mansion House itself, being late Georgian in style, is reserved for discussion in the following chapter. Mount Vernon consisted of five separate farms, each with its own buildings, livestock, slaves, and equipment, supervised by its own overseer. Four of the farms were intensively cultivated and showed considerable profit.

The fifth was the Mansion House Farm, with the main house and its numerous dependencies and some 500 acres laid out in gardens and parks. The Mansion House, with its fine scale of living and hospitable treatment of guests, absorbed most of the profits of the producing farms; for example in 1798, a typical year, the balance after expenses was less than $2,700.

A large Virginia estate was a self-contained community. At Mount Vernon 90 of the 240 people worked on the Mansion House Farm and lived in an orderly village. 'It's astonishing,' wrote Robert Hunter in 1785, 'what a number of small houses the General has upon his estate for his different workmen and Negroes to live in. He has everything within himself — carpenters, bricklayers, brewers, blacksmiths, bakers, etc., etc.' Among the separate buildings at Mount Vernon were the office, kitchen, butler's house, gardener's house, smokehouse, washhouse, coach house, stable, carpenter shop, spinning house, storehouse, dairy, seed house, schoolhouse, two small 'necessaries,' and the large servants' quarters.

Adjacent to the buildings were the areas reserved for the lawns, flower garden, kitchen garden, orchard, 'bowling green,' and a park-like expanse between the mansion and the Potomac River. ' I do not hesitate to confess,' wrote Washington to his manager, ' that reclaiming and laying the grounds down handsomely to grass, and in woods thinned, or in clumps, about the Mansion House is among my first objects and wishes.' At another time he described to his manager his plan for ' groves of Trees at each end of the dwelling House . . . these Trees to be Planted without any order or regularity . . . and to consist that at the North end, of locusts altogether, and that at the South, of all the clever kind of Trees (especially flowering ones) that can be got.'

Washington was particularly interested in his gardens, formally laid out with brick walls and paths, flower beds and boxwood hedges. He took pleasure in showing them to guests and one of these, a Polish gentleman who visited Mount Vernon in the June of 1798, wrote in his diary:

In the evening General Washington showed us round his garden. It is well cultivated, perfectly kept, and is quite in English style. All the vegetables indispensable for the kitchen were found there. Different kinds of berries, — currants, raspberries, strawberries, gooseberries, — a great quantity of peaches and cherries, but much inferior to ours; they are destroyed by robins, blackbirds, and negroes before they are ripe. There were very many beautiful trees: the tulip-tree with flowers like the tulips, white with an orange touch at the base; magnolias with flowers whose scent is almost as strong as the smell of an orange-tree, but not so pleasant; . . . the splendid catalpa is not yet in flower; the New Scotland spruce of beautiful dark green, and many other trees and shrubs, covered with flowers of different hues, planted so as to produce the best of color-effects . . .

The whole plantation, the garden, and the rest prove well that a man born with natural taste may guess a beauty without ever having seen its model. The General has never left America; but when one sees his home and his garden it seems as if he had copied the best samples of the grand old homesteads of England.[1]

Gardens, shops, stables, and service quarters were commanded by the mansion itself, which at Mount Vernon, as at other Virginia estates, formed the focus of the grand composition of the grounds. Most of the big plantation houses were substantially built of brick, two stories high with a hipped roof and balanced chimneys. Symmetrically placed dependencies, on a smaller scale, emphasized the dominance of the main house. Taken as a group, the great Georgian houses of Virginia surpass in architectural quality those of any other colony. The exteriors in particular have a grand simplicity, unspoiled by an excess of applied decorative features.

Perhaps this quality of well-measured and simple dignity was due to professional architectural talent. Waterman, in his important book *The Mansions of Virginia*,[2] argues the probability that most of the 'great houses' fall into three stylistic groups and were designed by Richard Taliaferro (1705–79), John Ariss (c.1725–99), and Thomas Jefferson (1743–1826). Though evidence to date is not conclusive, the limited number of houses (there are fewer than three dozen 'great' mansions), the intimate relationships between the families that built them, and the stylistic character of the houses themselves seem to support the theory that a very few professional architects may have designed the majority of them. But their fine quality may also be due in large measure to the example of the buildings at Williamsburg, which inaugurated the new century and the new style.

GEORGIAN WILLIAMSBURG

Williamsburg was the capital of Virginia from 1699 to 1779, a span of years almost identical to the period in which the Georgian style flourished in America. First known as Middle Plantation, it was settled in 1633 on a rise of land halfway between the James and York Rivers, only five miles from Jamestown. When the State House at Jamestown was burned in Bacon's Rebellion of 1676, the Assembly met temporarily at Middle Plantation, and with the building of the second Bruton Parish Church (1683) and the foundation of the College of William and Mary (1693) the village grew in importance. After the State House at Jamestown burned again, the Assembly passed an act in 1699 directing the transfer of the colonial capital to Middle Plantation and the building of a new city there to be called Williamsburg in honor of his majesty William III.

Williamsburg was the fourth 'planned town' in the American colonies.* Surveyed and laid out by Theodorick Bland in accordance with the detailed instructions of the Assembly, it reveals the gridiron plan and the attention to major and minor axes and 'reciprocal vistas' common to many European town-planning enterprises of the Renaissance (fig. 262). The major axis is the Duke of Gloucester Street, a 'noble great street' 99 feet wide and seven-eighths of a mile long, terminated at the west by the College and at the east by the Capitol. The minor axis, about midway, is a wide boulevard whose two roadways enclose the Palace Green and join in a sweeping curve at the gateway of the palace, which forms the terminus of the northern vista. Bruton Parish Church occupies

* Charleston (1680), Philadelphia (1682), and Annapolis (1694) preceded it.

the northwest corner of the main intersection, and a block east of it the Court House faces the head of England Street. Open spaces were preserved in Court House Green, Market Square, and the area surrounding the Capitol, and building restrictions governed the type of structure that could be built on the half-acre lots. The Duke of Gloucester Street near the Capitol was lined by taverns, inns, and ordinaries which did a roaring business during ' Public Times.' Indeed the Raleigh Tavern became almost as important as the Capitol and the palace itself, for it was not only the center of business transactions, dances, and balls, but a hive of political activity; more than once when royal governors dissolved the rebellious

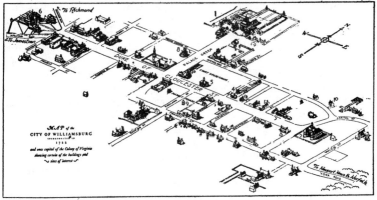

262. Bird's-eye view of the restoration area, Williamsburg, Va. (Colonial Williamsburg)

House of Burgesses at the Capitol, during the stormy years preceding the Revolution, it continued business down the street at the Raleigh.

In 1776 the Convention of Delegates adopted the first constitution of a free and independent state, and Patrick Henry, first Governor of the Commonwealth of Virginia, took up residence in the palace. He was succeeded there by Thomas Jefferson in 1779. But Jefferson had already prepared an act for the transfer of the capital to Richmond. This was passed in 1779 and the government was actually transferred in 1780. From then on Williamsburg declined in importance; many of its buildings burned or fell into disrepair and its population declined. But since it did not become a flourishing modern city, it has preserved the essentials of its city plan practically unchanged, and a substantial proportion of its old Georgian houses.

At the instigation of Dr. W. A. R. Goodwin, of Bruton Parish Church, and with the munificent support of Mr. John D. Rockefeller, Jr., the restoration of Williamsburg as a complete eighteenth-century colonial capital was begun in 1927. Only salient details of the most remarkable job of preserving, restoring, and rebuilding in American architectural history need be given here. The architectural work, involving detailed historical and technical research, was directed by the firm of Perry, Shaw and Hepburn of Boston; the landscape design, which was based on authentic eighteenth-century practices and has contributed so greatly to the setting of the buildings, was directed by Arthur A. Shurcliff of Boston. Some 600 inappropriate buildings have been torn down or removed from the restoration area; 80 have been carefully repaired and restored; nearly 300 have been reproduced on their original sites; and some 50 gardens have been made. In eighteen years nearly $28 million was spent on an enterprise governed by a scrupulous concern for historical accuracy and completeness in the re-creation of a setting and way of life that flourished two centuries ago.

Williamsburg is the largest, most nearly perfect, and most vital ' museum piece ' in America. If during the twentieth century it has unfortunately encouraged widespread and sterile imitation of the Georgian style, the fault lies with those who imitate, not with what was imitated. The last lesson to be learned from Williamsburg is the imitation of a two-centuries-old style, for the men who created it were building in the most modern way that they knew and were imitating nothing. To be sure they were influenced by the tradition of the immediately preceding generation in England, but they were building, as in all sound periods of architecture, out of the past into a new present; tradition was behind them, pushing forward.

More than 300 buildings at Williamsburg present a rich and varied picture of eighteenth-century architecture, ranging from important public buildings and residences to humble cottages, smokehouses, and fowl houses. It is not possible within the space at our command to treat more than half a dozen of the most important ones.

The College of William and Mary. 1695–1702

The whole colony was excited when word came in 1693 that a royal charter had been granted for Virginia's first college, with permission to name it after the reigning sovereigns. The Reverend James Blair returned from London with an order for some £2,000, an English master builder, Thomas Hadley, and, it is said, plans drawn by the Surveyor General, Sir Christopher Wren. The Assembly decided that ' Middle Plantation be the place for erecting the said college,' the cornerstone was laid in 1695, and two sides of a proposed quadrangle of buildings were completed by 1702. It was first called simply ' The College.'

The building faces east, directly down the long vista of the Duke of Gloucester Street toward the Capitol (fig. 263). Four stories high (counting the attic and English basement) and 136 feet long, it was the largest building yet erected in Virginia and probably in any of the colonies. Except for the Foster-Hutchinson House in Boston, it was also the first example of mature Renaissance design in the colonies. Gone are Gothic gables, steep-pitched roof, leaded casement windows, and picturesque asymmetries; in their place reigns a formal symmetry, with round-arch portal, balcony, gable, and cupola accenting the central axis, and windows disposed in uniform rhythm on either side. Windows are omitted at the ends to 'strengthen the corners,' the outside rooms taking their light from north and south sides.

Classical decorative details are used with restraint: a balustrade for the balcony and wooden brackets under the cornice — but there are no exterior columns or pilasters. The roof is hipped, and bristles with narrow Georgian dormers. A pavilion juts forward in the center of the facade to accent the middle, but Christopher Wren's scorn of academicism is shown

263. The College of William and Mary, Williamsburg, 1695–1702 (Colonial Williamsburg)

in the gable over it: where the Palladians would have placed a low-pitched classic pediment, Wren used a sharp-pitched gable to give greater emphasis and continuity to his vertical axis. Other features reveal Wren's signature: the round windows on front and back, such as those at Hampton Court; the arcaded piazza at the back, reminiscent of his Royal Hospital at Kilmainham, Dublin; the lofty cupola; but most of all a bold and large simplicity combining classical breadth and repose with a suspicion of the nervous angularity, the sharp and brittle aspiration of his church steeples.

The plan (fig. 264) shows a U-shaped court at the west connected by five bold arches to an open, brick-paved piazza, and low wings containing the great dining hall and the chapel. The building housed all the faculty, students, and Indian scholars, as well as the President of the College and his wife. Only the main block and the Hall wing were initially completed in 1702. The structure burned in 1705, but was rebuilt, and the Chapel wing added in 1732. Hugh Jones reported in 1722:

The Building is beautiful and commodious, being first modelled by Sir *Christopher Wren*, adapted to the Nature of the Country by the *Gentlemen* there; and since it was burnt down, it has been rebuilt, and nicely contrived, altered and adorned by the ingenious Direction of *Governor Spotswood;* and is not altogether unlike *Chelsea Hospital* . . . At the *North* End runs back a large *Wing*, which is a handsome *Hall,* answerable to which the *Chapel* is to be built; and there is a spacious *Piazza* on the *West* Side, from one *Wing* to the other.[3]

The Wren Building was again damaged by fires in 1859 and 1862. Only two-thirds of the height of the original walls was left, and the interior

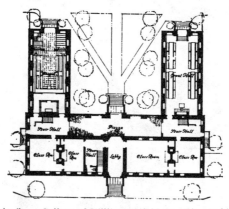

264. Plan of main floor, College of William and Mary (*The Architectural Record*)

woodwork was completely burned out, so that the modern restoration had to be based largely on old documents and prints.

The Capitol at Williamsburg. 1701–5

The act of 1699 directing the transfer of the capital included meticulous specifications for the new Capitol to be erected at Williamsburg. This was built 1701–5 under the direction of Henry Cary as master builder or ' overseer.' Pending its completion, Assembly meetings were held in the College.

The plan of the Capitol (fig. 266) shows a lucid and convenient organization of the several governmental functions served. The building is in two wings, connected by an open arcaded piazza at the ground level, with rooms above this space. The east wing contains the large round-ended hall for the House of Burgesses on the ground floor, and their committee rooms above. The west wing houses the General Court below and the Governor's Council in an oval chamber above.

The interior of the House of Burgesses is rather severe, with wood-paneled dado and plastered wall above, paneled window reveals, two rows of straight-backed benches on either side of the room, and a canopied armchair at the curved end for the speaker of the House. But the

Governor's Council Chamber (fig. 267) is more magnificently adorned
with full-height paneling framed by Doric pilasters carrying a continuous
mo!ded wood cornice around the room. Rectangular windows around the
curved end wall lighted the room, supplemented by chandelier and candlesticks for late sessions. The furniture, as specified in an act of the burgesses in 1703, was to consist of ' one Oval table fourteen foot long and six
foot broad with two doz: arm'd Cain Chairs one larger ditto, twenty-five
green Cushions for the said Chairs stuft with hair, and a large turkey
work Carpet for the table.'

265. The Capitol at Williamsburg from the southwest (Thomas L. Williams photo,
Colonial Williamsburg)

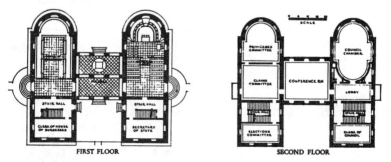

266. Plans of the first and second floors of the Capitol (*The Architectural Record*)

The exterior (fig. 265) is a simple and direct expression: the chief features of the south side are the bold semicircular projections called for by the plan. The main roof masses are hipped and carry a tall octagonal cupola, which, as the burgesses decreed in 1705, ' shall have a clock placed in it; and on the top of the said cupola shall be put a flag upon occasion. . .' The west façade, with its arched door leading directly into the

267. The Council Chamber in the Capitol (Richard Garrison photo, Colonial Williamsburg)

Court Room, balcony above, and four arched windows, was evidently felt insufficient to command the long vista of the Duke of Gloucester Street, for a two-storied classic portico was added as a frontispiece in 1753.

The original building was without any fireplaces or chimneys whatever and has been so restored. The burgesses must have been much afraid of a conflagration, for they forbade the use of fire, candles, or tobacco within the building. But these rigors were abandoned in 1723, when fireplaces and two chimneys were added at the north side. Unhappily the fears were justified, for the building was destroyed by fire in 1747; on 30 January ' a most extraordinary Misfortune befel this Place, by the Destruction of our fine Capitol.' The attic and roof ' soon burnt thro', and descended to the second Floor, and so to the Bottom, till the whole Timber and Woodwork was destroyed; and the naked Brick Walls only left standing.' [4] The Capitol was rebuilt 1751–3 and became the scene of dramatic events prior to the Revolution. But after 1780, when the government removed to Richmond, the fabric deteriorated to such an extent that in 1793 the east wing was sold to raise funds for the repair of the west wing, and even that fell victim to a fire in 1832. Nothing but foundations remained at the time of the restoration in 1928–34.

268. The Governor's Palace, Williamsburg, from the southeast (Thomas L. Williams photo, Colonial Williamsburg)

The Governor's Palace. 1706–20

Climaxing the vista at the north end of the Palace Green the palace built for the royal governors of Virginia was without doubt the finest residence of its day in the colonies. The Assembly in 1706 appropriated £3,000 for its construction and named Henry Cary, who had just finished his work at the Capitol, as the supervisor of construction. There is no mention of an architect in the documents concerning the palace, but the design was very probably made in London, and extensive researches by Waterman point to the possibility that the designer was Sir Christopher

Wren.[5] Work on the palace proceeded slowly; there is record of the receipt of imported slate for the roof in 1709, so we may assume that the exterior was virtually complete by that time, but renewed appropriations were made in 1710 and 1713 for finishing and beautifying the house, and it was not formally completed until about 1720.

The palace is singularly handsome in its setting (fig. 268). Facing south toward the Palace Green, it is preceded by a forecourt enclosed by twin service dependencies connected by a curved wall thrusting out to the arrogant entrance gates (fig. 269). Tall brick piers surmounted by

269. Through the gateway to the Palace Green, Williamsburg (Wendell MacRae photo, Colonial Williamsburg)
270. The formal garden of the Governor's Palace (F. S. Lincoln)

the heraldic Lion and Unicorn, carved of English Portland stone, carry the painted and gilded wrought-iron gates with their intricate overthrow centered on the royal crown and topped by a gilded finial. The story-and-a-half service buildings, simply treated, probably first housed a kitchen and stable, but perhaps the noise and odors in the narrow court (it is only a hundred feet wide) proved offensive; they seem later to have been used for office and guardhouse purposes.

The façade of the main building has a precise clarity of composition, classic only in its symmetry and in certain minor decorative details, but pure Christopher Wren in the narrow verticals of its ranges of windows, its steep roof, and slender two-story cupola, nervous and fragile against the sky. There are certain irregularities of accent, a *tempo rubato,* that a Palladian designer would not have permitted: the irregular spacing of the windows and dormers; the cantilevered balcony, more dynamic than a columned portico; the accented width of the balcony window; and the dormers hipped to the slope of the main roof rather than lidded with pediments. Glazed headers lighten the fine brick masonry with glancing highlights, set off by the belt course of smooth rubbed brick. A subtle diminution in the height of windows, from 8 to 7 to 5 lights, leads the eye upward to the light forms of the roof-deck balustrade — a very unusual feature in Virginia — and the pilastered chimneys culminate the upward movement. Regularity of form, symmetry, details — all bespeak a classical influence, but one that has not yet fully triumphed over the vertical aspirations of the Gothic tradition.

271. Ball Room Wing added to the Governor's Palace, c.1749–51 (Richard Garrison photo, Colonial Williamsburg)

One enters, up a pyramidal flight of stone steps, to the reception hall, lighted by two windows as well as the transom over the door (plan, fig. 272). The restored walnut paneling follows that of Carter's Grove, and the black-and-white marble floor is based on ruined fragments found in

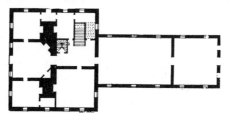

272. Plan of the first floor, Governor's Palace (Thomas T. Waterman, *Mansions of Virginia*, University of North Carolina Press)

the excavations. There is an angle fireplace here, and a closet to balance it; the fireplace is faced by white and gray-green marble, with a simply paneled overmantel bearing the royal coat of arms.

To the right of the entrance hall is a reception room, 16 feet square, and balancing it on the left a small family dining room. Both have fireplaces with marble mantels and little service closets. The state dining room, largest room in the main block, is paneled from floor to ceiling and the marble fireplace is flanked by full-height Corinthian pilasters. The stair hall at the back has a coved ceiling ornamented by an oval frame enclosing the cypher of George I. The stairs, with spirally twisted balusters, rise under an elliptical arch to a landing.

The second story contains family bedrooms and, over the entrance hall,

273. The Supper Room, Governor's Palace (Thomas L. Williams photo, Colonial Williamsburg)

a sitting room with walls paneled to a chair rail and above that hung with tooled and gilded leather. The chief feature of the third story is a long central hall covered by an elliptical barrel vault penetrated by a circular stair to the cupola, whose eight windows afford fine views of the gardens, lagoon, and Palace Green.

At the north end of the palace is a long one-story addition called the Ball Room Wing; this was designed by Richard Taliaferro and built c.1749–51 (fig. 271). The Ball Room, 26 by 47 feet, must have been one of the most magnificent rooms in Georgian architecture. With coved ceiling rising to a height of 18 feet, walls hung with gold-edged blue wallpaper, two great crystal chandeliers, and featured portraits of King George and Queen Charlotte attired in robes of state, it must have been a fit setting for the spectacular formal balls of the colony.

Behind it is the Supper Room (fig. 273), 26 feet square, rising to a lofty coved ceiling with central Waterford chandelier. Though the decoration of this room is entirely conjectural, the Chinese Chippendale style was coming into popularity elsewhere in the 1750's, and the room has been restored in this taste. Fantastic concave-curved pediments over the doors suggest pagoda roofs, and the walls are hung with a superb eighteenth-century Chinese wallpaper of stylized trees in gray against a soft blue ground, with sparkling flowers and birds in bright colors. The window casings are carved and their reveals paneled. Paneled dado and modillioned cornice complete a brilliant room.

Through the double walnut doors of the Supper Room is the formal garden with its geometric beds and trimmed box hedges (fig. 270). This portion of the gardens is enclosed by brick walls punctuated by diagonally set brick piers bearing ball finials of stone. The wide gravel path on the main axis leads to great iron gates piercing the *clairvoyée,* an ' open fence,' through which in colonial days could be seen an extended vista cut through the adjoining woods. The *clairvoyée* piers are topped by varied urns executed in stone and lead. The two small square buildings set diagonally at the corners served as ' necessaries.'

The whole extent of the palace grounds included at least a dozen subsidiary service buildings, a kitchen garden, orchard, the terraced water garden overlooking the lagoon, and probably also a maze and bowling green. The restored gardens undoubtedly suggest the authentic and magnificent setting of this viceregal palace, in which lived a remarkable succession of able governors: Alexander Spotswood; William Gooch; Francis Fauquier; Norborne Berkeley, Baron de Botetourt; John Murray, Earl of Dunmore; and at the end, the first governors of the Commonwealth of Virginia, Patrick Henry and Thomas Jefferson. Through these fine rooms moved also the Carters, the Burwells, the Byrds, the Lees, the Washingtons, and other distinguished families of Virginia.

Balls and ' illuminations ' were held on royal birthdays, and lavish entertainments lightened the duties of ' Public Times.' Governor Spotswood once entertained 200 guests at an official supper, and Lord Botetourt was so accustomed to large-scale hospitality that he mentions only casually in a letter that ' fifty-two dined with me yesterday, and I expect at least that number today.' The Revolutionary War was in progress when Jefferson transferred the capital to Richmond, and the palace was used as a hospital for American soldiers wounded at the siege of Yorktown in the autumn of 1781. In December of that year it was completely destroyed by fire.

Bruton Parish Church. 1710–15

Within a decade after the transfer of the capital to Williamsburg, the small seventeenth-century church of Bruton Parish proved inadequate to serve as the court church of the colony. The present church was begun in 1711 and completed in 1715. Of its designer we have no certain information, though it is said that Alexander Spotswood, then Governor, made the drawings. Here for the first time in Virginia appeared a church built on a cruciform plan, a feature usually associated with Gothic churches,

but all other details of the architecture are characteristic of the early
Georgian style.

The exterior (fig. 274) has plain walls laid in Flemish-bond brickwork,
pierced by tall round-arch windows and topped by a simple modillioned
cornice. The steep-pitched roof recalls the Gothic, but the projecting wall
buttresses and traceried windows of the seventeenth-century churches have
disappeared. Circular windows, which may reflect the influence of Wren's
round windows in the College of William and Mary, pierce the end walls
of the chancel and two transepts. The square tower at the west end, sur-

274, 275. Bruton Parish Church, Williamsburg, 1711–15 (photos by Thomas L.
Williams and Richard Garrison, Colonial Williamsburg)

mounted by a wooden octagonal spire in two stages, seems rather of the
Gibbs tradition. It was not built until 1769 and is a simplified version of
the heavy octagonal tower of St. Michael's, Charleston, completed at the
beginning of that decade.

The interior (fig. 275) is one of the simplest among major Georgian
churches. Flat ceiling and white plastered walls afford an effective contrast to the rich colors of the woodwork and hangings. Projecting transepts and choir add variety to the space composition. The cost of the edifice was shared by the colony and the parish. Governor Spotswood had
arranged that if the vestry would pay for the two ends of the building, the
General Assembly would appropriate funds for the transepts and crossing and for the building of pews for the governor, members of the Council, and burgesses; and the Governor himself paid for 22 feet of the nave.

As the court church of the colony, Bruton Parish was a theater for the
display of pomp and circumstance of rank and position. The royal governor and his family occupied the most prominent pew, to the northeast
of the crossing, and over his chair was a silk canopy with a valance; a cur-

tain could be drawn around to shield him from the gaze of the vulgar. Directly across was the high pulpit with its sounding board. The square pews in the transepts seated members of the House of Burgesses, while the rector and the surveyor general occupied pews in the choir. The commonalty sat in the nave, men on the north and women on the south. Students of the College, including some Indians, were herded into the west gallery and part of the south gallery; servants of parishioners were permitted to stand in the north gallery.

While church-going was a regular habit for all proper members of society, it was regarded as a somewhat tiresome duty, and members of the landed gentry were only too glad to combine with religious routine an opportunity to see and be seen in their finest clothes, and particularly to gossip and talk politics in the churchyard before and after services.

In 1839 the interior of the church was much altered: partitions were inserted, the pulpit removed, pews rearranged, and even some of the graves in the chancel were disturbed. But in 1905–7, under the initiative of the rector, Dr. Goodwin, these ravages were repaired, and the building was eventually returned to its eighteenth-century condition in the Williamsburg Restoration.

Other buildings at Williamsburg

Only brief mention may be made of a few of the less important buildings at Williamsburg. The majority of the houses were white painted clapboarded structures, a story and a half high, with steep-gabled roofs and end chimneys. Small and simple, they were essentially a continuation of the seventeenth-century Colonial style, modified by the use of Georgian sliding-sash windows, paneled front doors, plastered interiors, and an occasional molded cornice. Such were to be found all over Virginia in the eighteenth century. Jefferson, with his prejudice in favor of masonry construction and his formal Palladian taste, viewed them unsympathetically. ' The private buildings,' he wrote in his *Notes on the State of Virginia,* ' are rarely constructed of stone or brick; much the greatest portion being of scantling and boards, plaistered with lime. It is impossible to devise things more ugly, uncomfortable, and happily more perishable.' [6]

There were a few more substantial residences, built of brick, or at the least equipped with interior paneling. Of these the Brafferton, at the College of William and Mary, illustrates the immediate influence that the Governor's Palace had on smaller Virginia houses of any architectural pretensions (fig. 276). Built in 1723, its façade composition, window treatment, and cornice betray a marked similarity to those at the palace. A small pediment over the door takes the place of a balcony, and the hipped roof rises to a sharp ridge instead of a balustraded deck. The building was erected for an Indian school and was supported by the income from Brafferton Manor in England; after the Revolution it was used for College purposes. The President's House, a twin building erected in 1732, faces the Brafferton and the two together make a formal approach to the main college building.

The two finest private houses in Williamsburg are Wythe House and the James Semple House. The former was built in 1755 by the architect Richard Taliaferro for his daughter Elizabeth and son-in-law George Wythe. Architecturally, the house belongs with the group of great plantation houses discussed below. Wythe became famous as the first professor of a college law course in America, a signer of the Declaration, and Chancellor of Virginia. The house served as Washington's headquarters before the siege of Yorktown.

The James Semple House, probably built about 1780, represents a late

276. Brafferton Hall, College of William and Mary, 1723 (Thomas L. Williams photo, Colonial Williamsburg)

Georgian 'Roman House' type, now attributed to Jefferson, and discussed in the following chapter. Another fine house of similar type was built about 1788 by St. George Tucker, Wythe's successor as professor of Law at the College and a distinguished jurist. All of these houses have been restored.

Of the many inns and taverns, which did such a flourishing business when the town was crowded for meetings of the Court and Assembly, the most noteworthy were the Raleigh Tavern, built before 1742, and the Market Square Tavern, built about 1749. The town at such times was alive with gaming, cock fights, horse races, lotteries, slave auctions, and dances, and there were also theatrical performances, for the first theater in America was erected, facing the Palace Green, in 1716. The manager, William Levingston, built a ' good, substantial house, commodious for acting,' and his partners, Charles and Mary Stegg, dancing teachers just arrived from London, produced ' comedies, drolls or other kinds of stage plays.' It is hoped that this theater will shortly be rebuilt in the continuing program of restoration. A second theater was built on Waller Street, back of the Capitol, in 1751, and opened with a performance of *The Merchant of Venice* by Lewis Hallam's London company. The theater was very popular with members of the Assembly.

Williamsburg also had its necessary civic buildings: a public jail which housed, at one time or another, a motley assortment of debtors, criminals, pirates, and lunatics; the Court House, built in 1770; and the fine octagonal brick Powder Magazine built in 1714 to house 'All the Arms, Gun-Powder, and Ammunition, now in the Colony, belonging to the King.'

GREAT GEORGIAN HOUSES OF VIRGINIA

Williamsburg presents today the most authentic picture of an eighteenth-century town, but to complete the picture of Georgian architecture in Virginia it is necessary to include some of the great plantation houses, isolated in their immense estates along the shores of the four great Tidewater rivers: the Potomac, the Rappahannock, the York, and the James. There are perhaps three dozen 'great houses,' and as a group they represent the finest Georgian domestic architecture in the colonies. A few of the outstanding mansions, considered in two groups, may illustrate the character of the style and its development during the Georgian period:

Early Georgian: 1700–1750
Stratford, Westmoreland County, c.1725–30.
Westover, Charles City County, c.1730–34.
Carter's Grove, James City County, 1750–53.

Late Georgian: 1750–1780
Mount Airy, Richmond County, 1758–62.
Mount Vernon, Fairfax County, 1757–87.
Brandon, Prince George County, c.1765.
James Semple House, Williamsburg, c.1780.
Monticello, Albemarle County, 1771–8.

Stratford, Westmoreland County. c.1725–30

A mile away from Lee's Landing below the 80-foot cliffs of the Potomac, Thomas Lee, one-time explorer, merchant-fleet owner, and Governor of Virginia built his great house on its 16,000-acre plantation. The construction is believed to have occupied the five years from 1725 to 1730. House and dependencies are built of bricks fired on the premises; their variety of color and texture somewhat softens the austerity of the impressive mass, which is unique in Georgian architecture (fig. 277). The house has a raised basement, so that the main-floor level is almost 10 feet above the ground. Though such a scheme had been used in Palladian buildings in England, it was usually accompanied by extensive use of pilasters and other academic forms; Stratford's nude, bold masses have far more vigor and force. The bricks of the lower wall are of extra large size, laid in Flemish bond with glazed headers; the masonry above is of smaller bricks of a uniform pink-red color, with fine gauged-brick dressings. The molded water table, the great flight of steps at the west end (fig. 278), and even the rudimentary pediments over the main doors are all of brick; wood trim is used only in the windows, cornice, and chimney balustrades.

The 90-foot façade has uniformly spaced windows, those below with segmental-arch heads, those above with flat arches. An awkwardly vigorous flight of stone steps, diminishing in width and framed by ponderous balustrades, leads to the main door. The roof is low-pitched and hipped, but accented by twin sets of four great chimney stacks, connected by arches

277. Stratford, the Lee mansion, Westmoreland County, Va., c.1725–30, from the southeast (Robert E. Lee Memorial Foundation)

and enclosing balustraded roof-decks from which, according to tradition, Thomas Lee could see his ships on the Potomac. Sir John Vanbrugh had used such a motive in England, and indeed Stratford seems to share the ponderous vigor of Vanbrugh's style rather than the light precision of Wren's, yet it remains quite unlike anything in England, or in the colonies. It used to be said in Virginia that whereas the Carters cherished good living and social prestige, the Lees stood for plain living and intellectual integrity. Perhaps that is what makes Thomas Lee's house so full of character.

The plan (fig. 279) is also unusual for the colonies. It consists of two four-room formations connected by a central hall, forming a wide H. Such plans had been used in England, particularly in Shropshire, and had been recommended in Stephen Primatt's *City and Country Purchaser and Builder*, published in London in 1667. The H-shaped plan had already appeared also in the colonies in the Slate House at Philadelphia, the New

York City Hall, the Capitol at Williamsburg, and Tuckahoe in Virginia, but it was by no means common. On the lower floor were the service quarters and some bedrooms; the upper floor was devoted to main living rooms and master bedrooms. These are not small: the 'library closet' in the west wing, for example, measures 12 by 21 feet. The dining room in the east wing had a service alcove, as was common in Virginia houses. From this through the passageway, out the east door, down a flight of steps, and across to the kitchen outbuilding was no short trip, but this mattered little

278. View of Stratford from the west (Thomas F. Scott photo, Robert E. Lee Memorial Foundation)

in a household with dozens of servants. Unlike most Virginia mansions, there was no main stairway; a small stair in the east wing, with steep risers and many winders, was the only connection between floors.

The Great Hall between the two wings is the most formal and monumental room of its period (fig. 280). More than 28 feet square, its windows and double doors command fine vistas to north and south. Tall Corinthian pilasters, set on projecting pedestals, flank all doors and windows, and they carry a full entablature around the room, broken out *en ressaut* over each pilaster. Very few Georgian rooms have more than a pair or so of pilasters adorning a chimney-breast, and still fewer have anything more than a cornice at the ceiling line; the complete academic formality of this room is indeed exceptional in the early Georgian period. The full-height paneling of walls, window recesses, and interior shutters is entirely original. After the purchase of Stratford by the Robert E. Lee Memorial Foundation in 1929, the woodwork of this room was restored to its early gray-blue color and the windows hung with crimson damask. The unusual 'tray' ceiling has four slanting panels converging to a flat panel at a height of 18 feet, with a multi-armed chandelier in the center.

The main house is surrounded by four service dependencies. Flanking the entrance forecourt are the kitchen at the southeast and library at the southwest. These are story-and-a-half brick buildings with jerkin-head

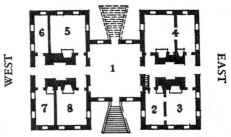

279. Plan of main floor, Stratford (Robert E. Lee Memorial Foundation)

roofs; the kitchen contains a fireplace 4 feet deep, 12 feet wide, and 7 feet high to the crown of the arch which spans it. Outside of these are balanced buildings for the stable and smokehouse. At the northwest is an office and at the northeast a school; both of these have hipped roofs. The formal gardens at Stratford, to the east of the main house, have been restored within their old brick walls, the gravel walks, wooden gateways,

280. The Great Hall at Stratford (Thomas F. Scott photo, Robert E. Lee Memorial Foundation)

and boxwood hedges defining a series of fine terraces connected by brick steps. In one of these a box border is quartered in the pattern of the Lee coat of arms. The profusion of damask and moss roses, snowballs, periwinkle, holly and lilac trees, fig, pomegranate, and dwarf apple once more bring to life the beautiful and dignified setting of the house.

Stratford has perhaps given to the nation more famous men than any other house in America. It was the home of four members of the Governor's Council, twelve burgesses, four members of the Convention in 1776, and two of the signers of the Declaration of Independence. From it came governors of Virginia, members of the Continental Congress, diplomats, and, of course, Robert E. Lee, one of America's greatest military geniuses and one of her noblest men.

Westover, Charles City County. c.1730–34

Westover, 25 miles up the James River from Williamsburg, is perhaps the most famous Georgian house in America. Distinguished in quality, unusually complete in its architecture, interiors, and setting, it is the first of a large group of Virginia houses of similar cast. Its owner-builder was also in many respects a typical Virginia gentleman of the eighteenth century.

William Byrd II (1674–1744) was born to wealth and position. He was educated in London, inherited a large estate, and turned as naturally to its supervision as he did to directing public affairs in the colony. Holder of many offices, he was thirty-seven years a member of the Governor's Council and ultimately its president. He surveyed lands to the west and founded Richmond and Petersburg. He read Greek, Latin, and Hebrew at sight and had the largest library in colonial Virginia, catalogued at over 3600 volumes.

Essentially an extrovert, whose chief enjoyments were dancing, hunting, and fencing, his intellectual interests were in reality limited. His ' secret diary ' is as devoid of ideas as it is of perceptions. Morning after morning, with monotonous regularity, he arose at six, took a dose of Latin and Greek before breakfast, with considerable less interest than he reveals in his bowels, prayed or did not pray (he never omits to say which) , ' did my dance ' (a calisthenic routine) , and breakfasted. After the day's routine of duties around the plantation, or on horseback to Williamsburg, he dined well, ' talked with my people,' danced or conversed with guests, drank milk, and went to bed. Though he could connive at immorality or improvidence, he could not tolerate social heresy. Of a well-born girl who married the plantation overseer he remarked:

Had she run away with a gentleman or a pretty Fellow, there might have been some Excuse for her, tho' he were of inferior Fortune; but to stoop to a dirty Plebian, without any kind of merit, is the lowest Prostitution.

Yet he bought books and oil paintings from England, and he certainly had a gentleman's taste in architecture. At first he lived in a smaller house — perhaps one of the old service dependencies — which he soon started to improve, for his diaries of 1709–11 contain references to men at work on brick masonry, woodwork, sash windows, and hanging gates. On 3 June 1712, he wrote: ' The stonecutter came from Williamsburg to put up my marble chimney piece,' and on the next day a workman ' began to work in the library chimney.' But in 1729 he wrote to a friend in London that ' in a year or two I intend to set about building a very good house.' The present Westover was accordingly started about 1730, and probably took three or four years to build. The contractor-builder is not known.

The mansion is approached from the north, or inland, side through the finest old wrought-iron gates in America, probably made in the shop of the distinguished London smith, Thomas Robinson (fig. 281). Each leaf

281. The entrance gate at Westover, Va. (E. F. O'Dwyer drawing. *Great Georgian Houses*, 1)

is 5 feet wide and 10 feet high, hinged to a large brick post with cut-stone base and cap, surmounted by a large bird as a rebus for the owner's name. A magnificent scrolled overthrow, enriched with acanthus leaves and finials, and centered on a panel bearing an initialed cypher, spans the hinged leaves. The gates were probably originally painted blue or green, with gilt finials. On either side a *clairvoyée* of thirteen bays stretches across the forecourt. Its square brick piers, now plastered, are topped by cut-stone caps and finials in a variety of shapes; the original wrought-iron railings, lost long since, have been replaced by modern cast-iron fencing.

The entrance façade (fig. 282) and garden façade (fig. 283), looking south to the James River, are almost identical except for the doorways. The north door, with an entablature and segmental pediment resting on Corinthian pilasters, has the finer detail; the south door, with its baroque swan's neck pediment resting on Composite pilasters, is more florid but a little clumsy in execution. Both doors seem to have been derived from Plates xxv and xxvi of William Salmon's *Palladio Londinensis,* a builder's guide first published in London in 1734, the very year when the doorways may have been installed. But — quite exceptionally in the colonies — they are made of Portland stone and may have been imported from London, as were the gates and several of the mantelpieces. Both façades are raised three feet above grade on an English basement, and the doors approached by pyramidal flights of steps.

The main windows are spanned by segmental brick arches but — uniquely — instead of being leveled to a wooden lintel, the windows are cut to fit the arches. The belt course, at one time painted white, has an undue prominence, but the detail of the main cornice, with its rows of dentils and modillions, is good. The roof is steep and lofty, rising to a

282. Westover, the Byrd mansion, Charles City County, Va., c.1730–34. The entrance (north) façade (Wayne Andrews)

sharp ridge instead of a deck; there are very tall chimneys and rows of hipped dormers, as at the Governor's Palace.

The façade composition has such an easy simplicity that it appears almost tame, yet details such as the three tiers of windows, diminishing not only in height and in width but in the size of the glass panes, and the graduated weather of the fine roof slates, contribute to an illusion of enhanced height and an interplay of verticals with horizontals that recalls the subtleties of the Governor's Palace.

The plan (fig. 284) shows an off-center hall which, though it preserves the axial position of the main doors, borrows one of the regularly spaced façade windows for purposes of light. This has an advantage in giving a useful variety of size to the rooms. One enters from the north door under the stair landing into an ample hall, 14 feet in width. The two rooms at the left are rather narrow for their length of almost 25 feet, and the chimney-breasts, which might better have been suppressed, project awkwardly between the two pairs of end windows. The first of these was the music room, while the wider room with its three windows looking out to the south lawn and the river served as the drawing room (fig. 286). Its large marble mantlepiece was probably derived from Plate LXXI of Gibbs's book, and the wall, fully paneled from floor to ceiling, is accented by pairs of Doric pilasters flanking the two doors. The ceiling of this room is rich in cast plaster ornament, but it is composed in a dispersed and spotty fashion.

On the other side of the hall were two small rooms, one used as a dining room, the other perhaps as William Byrd's library; these have since been thrown together to form one large dining room, with two chimney-pieces and a service alcove between them. An outside door led to the

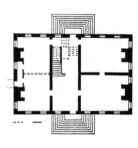

283. The garden (south) façade of Westover (HABS)
284. Plan of first floor, Westover (Thomas T. Waterman, *The Mansions of Virginia*, University of North Carolina Press)

kitchen. The original dependencies at Westover were separate from the house, flanking it symmetrically on the line of the south façade, and were small story-and-a-half brick buildings in the seventeenth-century style. The one at the west contained kitchens and servants' rooms, that at the east perhaps served for offices. These were connected to the central block by brick passages in 1901 and have since been remodeled.

The spacious entrance hall (fig. 285) has a wide staircase, ascending in three runs, with richly turned mahogany balustrade. Walls are paneled full-height and topped by full cornice moldings. The most unusual feature is the enriched plaster ceiling, unique for its early period. Plaster ornaments were often precast in the eighteenth century, and set in plaster. These 'compo' ornaments at Westover are very early examples of a rococo style, derived ultimately from France but doubtless immediately from some English handbook. The ceiling is framed by a rod-and-ribbon border with corner motives of scrolled leafage, masks, and vases. The central feature has curvilinear scrolls of flowers and leaves and fruit. Though fine and rich in detail, the whole is not well composed. All told, the interiors at Westover do not match the architectural assurance of those at Stratford and Carter's Grove. In the second-floor bedrooms are four notable

mantels, however, three in painted wood and one in stone, all probably
made in London.

One room seems to be lacking at Westover. William Byrd makes frequent mention in his diary of promenading in his ' gallery ' on rainy days.
It sounds like a long room, light and airy. None of the main rooms, it
seems, fits this description. A painting of Westover made in Civil War
days [7] shows a passage connecting dining room and kitchen, with an open
colonnaded piazza on the south front; the detail is hazy and looks early

285, 286. The entrance hall and southeast drawing room at Westover (HABS)

nineteenth century, but it is barely possible that Byrd's lost ' gallery ' was
this piazza or an earlier predecessor. In fair weather, however, he prome-
naded in the formal gardens, which were laid out to the northwest of the
house, or under the fine trees shading the lawn between house and river.

Carter's Grove, James City County. 1750–53

Six miles below Williamsburg, and about half a mile north of the James
River, stands the house built by Carter Burwell, grandson of the fabu-
lously wealthy ' King ' Carter. Framed by giant tulip poplars, it commands an impressive series of terraces and fields toward the river. The
house was constructed in 1750–53 by David Minitree, a contractor-builder
from Williamsburg, and probably designed by Richard Taliaferro. The
superb woodwork of the interior, the finest in Virginia, may be credited to
Richard Bayliss, an English carpenter who came to Virginia for this purpose. Even in the mid-century oyster-shell lime was still being used, for
we find Carter Burwell announcing in the *Virginia Gazette* of 21 February
1751, that ' being in Want of Oyster Shells, will give at the Rate of Three

287. Carter's Grove, Carter Burwell's mansion, James City County, Va., 1750–53. Entrance (north) façade before the remodeling of 1928 (Metropolitan Engraving)

288. The south façade of Carter's Grove after the remodeling of 1928 (Wayne Andrews)

Shillings per Hogshead for any Quantity that can be delivered at [my] Landing by the last of March.'

Carter's Grove, culmination of Virginia's early Georgian style, shows greater breadth and repose than Westover, yet remains extremely simple compared to its Palladian successors. The original appearance may be seen in an old photograph of the north side of the house (fig. 287). Balanced dependencies were completely detached, and the roof was of low pitch, unbroken by dormers. The nine windows of this façade leave substantial areas of solid wall. The brick masonry is plainer than that at Stratford; bricks are of a uniform dark red color laid in Flemish bond. During extensive alterations in 1927–9 the roof-tree was raised 11 feet in order to accommodate attic rooms lighted by dormers, and the dependencies were

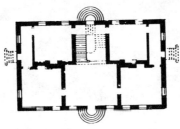

289. Plan of first floor, Carter's Grove (Thomas T. Waterman, *The Mansions of Virginia*, University of North Carolina Press)

rebuilt and connected to the main house. As may be seen from the south (fig. 288), the house lost something of its reposeful simplicity by these changes, but it gained in the fine restoration of its interiors.

The south façade, facing the sun and the river, has thirteen windows, four more than the north façade. A high basement is topped by the molded water table, and this is echoed by the strong horizontal of the rubbed-brick belt course between stories. Nine-over-nine light windows in both stories have flat-arch lintels. Many moldings and heavy modillions form a bold cornice. The original roof had a slight flare at the eaves; this is enhanced by the raised roof pitch to a very graceful feature. The doorways at Carter's Grove are much simpler than those at Westover; they are executed entirely of brick, with simple crowning pediments.

The plan (fig. 289) shows one marked advance: the front hall is widened to a spacious room and separated from the narrower stair hall by an elliptical arch. This permits a window on either side of the south door and a location on the central axis. Another difference from Westover is the use of two interior chimneys instead of four end chimneys, permitting fireplaces on the long sides of the rooms, with much better architectural effect.

The great entrance hall is superb (figs. 290, 291). The details by which Richard Bayliss achieved his effect are not in themselves unique. There is a simple unpaneled dado topped by a chair rail, forming a pedestal for the upper-wall treatment of finely proportioned panels. Openings are flanked by Ionic pilasters and topped by sections of full entablature *en*

290. North side of the entrance hall, Carter's Grove (Robert W. Tebbs)

291. South side of the entrance hall, Carter's Grove (Robert W. Tebbs)

ressaut. The doorways are topped by restful horizontal panels rather than scrolled or broken pediments. The elliptical arch to the stair hall has a magnificent weight and sweep. The fine stair has round-shaft balusters, all of the same pattern, rather than the varied swash-turned balusters of more ornate houses. The handrail runs into a scroll around the newel post, which is itself spirally turned. The woodwork was probably originally painted, but during the modern restoration it was cleaned, stained, and waxed, and in this darker form it undoubtedly accords better with the weighty dignity of the room.

This room is a masterpiece — early Georgian brought to its finest maturity. Spaces are certainly shaped and well related, details are chosen with unerring taste, and the whole composed with the sure touch of a master architect. To the writer it is the finest room in all Georgian architecture.

The early Georgian style

Carter's Grove is only the culmination of a group of houses of similar style and quality built during the second quarter of the eighteenth century. With few exceptions, these houses lack such academic motives as pavilions, angle quoins, rusticated masonry, or Palladian windows; they adhere rather to a straightforward masculine simplicity. In details, all of them show derivation from one book: William Salmon's *Palladio Londinensis, or the London Art of Building,* a book otherwise rarely used in America. This was first published in 1734; thus it may have been available for the completion of Westover, but not for any earlier houses. The houses in this group are:

Westover, built about 1730–34.
Nelson Hall, Yorktown, built about 1740 for Thomas Nelson, a grandson of Robert Carter.
Carter's Grove, built in 1750–53 for Carter Burwell, a nephew of Charles Carter.
Cleve, built about 1750 for Charles Carter. The plan is almost an exact counterpart of that of Carter's Grove.
Wilton, built in 1753 for William Randolph III, practically identical in plan to Westover.
George Wythe House in Williamsburg, built in 1755 by the architect Richard Taliaferro.
Elsing Green, built for Carter Braxton, a grandson of Robert Carter, in 1758. The plan shows certain similarities to that of Westover.

In view of the close family ties and the stylistic similarities between the houses within this group, it seems entirely probable that they were designed by one architect, and that he was Richard Taliaferro.

Richard Taliaferro (1705–79) was the grandson of Robert Taliaferro who came to Virginia as early as 1655 and received a grant of land (in which his name was spelled Toliver, as it is pronounced) in Gloucester County. His father Francis was a resident of York County. Nothing is known of Richard's childhood and training. At the age of 32 he emerges in a document of 1737 as a justice of the peace at Williamsburg; in 1740 he was appointed Sheriff. The Acting Governor, Thomas Lee, referred to

him in 1749 as ' our most skillful architect,' and he was in charge of the
' Ball Room Wing ' at the palace in 1749–51. In 1756 he made some repairs on the President's House at William and Mary. In the previous year
he had built the George Wythe House at Williamsburg as his town residence, and he also owned an out-of-town plantation, Powhatan. He was
appointed to the Committee of Safety in 1774, and became a senator in
the Assembly before his death in 1779. These are all the facts known
about Richard Taliaferro's life.

His career as an architect must be based on circumstantial evidence and
surmise. But since the qualities of the George Wythe House are shared by
the other houses in this group, and since Taliaferro, as a citizen and prop-
erty-owner of Williamsburg doubtless knew personally the owners of
these houses, and since furthermore he was regarded as a distinguished
architect, it seems a reasonable hypothesis that he may have been the designer of all of them.

It is unlikely that Taliaferro received his architectural training in England. There must have been, however, some English-trained architect
working in Virginia in the early eighteenth century. Such evidence as we
can get of Robert (' King ') Carter's grandiose Corotoman, built perhaps as early as 1715; Rosewell, a great pavilioned mansion three stories
high built by Carter's son-in-law Mann Page in 1726–30; Sabine Hall,
built for Landon Carter about 1730, with a rusticated stone pavilion and
a plan like that of the much later Mount Airy; and Nomini Hall, built by
Robert Carter II about 1730, with its two Palladian windows unique for
this early date, suggests that some or all of these buildings may have been
designed by a professional architect of advanced academic training, such
as could have been obtained only in England at that time.

Waterman suggests the possibility that Taliaferro himself may have
designed these early mansions for the Carter family. This does not seem
probable. ' King ' Carter evidently wished to rival, or surpass, the Governor's Palace in the mansions he built for himself and his children. It is
not likely that he would have chosen an unknown architect still in his
'teens or early twenties. And if Taliaferro was capable of the academic
sophistication revealed by these early houses, would he have reverted to
the provincial simplicity of the later ones?

It seems more probable that Taliaferro learned his trade from this unknown English architect working in Virginia, developed his own individual style, better suited to the Virginia society and economy, and relied
heavily for details on his favorite *Palladio Londinensis*. Westover may
have been his first big house, begun when he was 25 years old. It shows
many stylisms that became characteristic of his later houses, but it also reveals a clumsy inexperience in details such as the south doorway, the awkward placement of fireplaces in the two east rooms, and the inexpert composition of the two ornamented plaster ceilings. That he overcame these
deficiencies is indicated by his selection as architect for the Ball Room Wing
in the mid-century, and by the assured mastery of houses such as Carter's
Grove, Cleve, and Wilton. That his own house in Williamsburg lacked
some of the resplendent interior detail of these great mansions is not sur-

prising: an architect in the eighteenth century was a 'hired man,' and he presumably gained no great wealth from his calling.

Christ Church, Lancaster County. 1732

One other Virginia building of the early Georgian period is particularly noteworthy, and it takes us again to 'King' Carter and the problem of who designed his buildings. This building is Christ Church in Lancaster

292. Christ Church, Lancaster County, Va., 1732 (Wayne Andrews)

County, without question the finest and best-preserved Georgian church in Virginia (fig. 292). 'King' Carter bore the entire cost of its construction, stipulating in his will that 'always the chancel be preserved as a burial place for my family . . . and that there be preserved for my family a commodious pew in the chancel.' According to tradition, the congregation awaited the arrival of the 'King' before entering church for services. He died in 1732, only shortly after the completion of the building.[8]

The cruciform plan of the church, with a nave only slightly longer than the equilateral transepts and chancel, was not unusual among Virginia Georgian churches, but the architectural style, with its fine and sophisticated detail, was entirely exceptional. The high walls and steep roof give the church a more vertical character than is usual, and the rich wood entablature at the eaves is of unusual fineness and elaboration. The tall arched windows, with rubbed brick dressings and cut-stone sills, imposts, and keystones, are remarkably similar to the fine stair windows of Rosewell, begun six years earlier. The two transept doors, with their Doric pilasters and angular pediments, are executed with remarkable skill in molded and gauged bricks, with some stone trim, while the main entrance door at the west is more imposing with its arched lunette and high segmental pediment. All three doors are made of walnut, finely paneled, and are preceded by stepping-stones of Portland stone, cut to an elliptical curve. The workmanship in brick masonry, woodwork, and stone trim is unrivaled in American architecture of this period. The small oval windows over the doors and especially the splayed eaves of the roof, almost reminiscent of a Chinese pagoda, add a touch of playful grace to an otherwise dignified exterior.

Interior details match the exterior in quality of design and execution and are unique in their completeness and excellent state of preservation. High box pews, paneled dadoes, a tall pulpit with curved stair, hexagonal sounding board with ogee dome and finial, paneled gallery in the south transept, communion rail, altar, and reredos are all superb examples of craftsmanship. Most of the interior woodwork is in black walnut, contrasting effectively with the white plaster walls, which rise to a curved vault. Aisles are paved with dark blocks of Purbeck marble, and the graceful baptismal font, made of marble carved with acanthus leaves and cherubs' heads, was undoubtedly imported from England. The body of Robert Carter lies under a superb marble tomb against the chancel wall. All told, Christ Church is a surpassing example of Georgian design and workmanship, and it inevitably arouses speculation about who the architect could have been.

Waterman found in the details of the church an ' all-prevailing ' influence from William Salmon's *Palladio Londinensis* and, because this was Richard Taliaferro's favorite design book, suggested that he may have been the architect of Christ Church.[9] But details of the church and of the book are by no means identical, and even though allowances are made for the freedom with which the design books were then used, there is room for supposing that not this, but some other book or some unknown architect determined the details of Christ Church. This supposition is confirmed by the fact that the first edition of *Palladio Londinensis* appeared in London in 1734, while the date of completion of Christ Church seems well attested as 1732. The similarity of certain details in the church and in the early group of Carter houses, as well as the personal interest of Robert Carter in the church, lead us again to the hypothesis — and it is purely an hypothesis — that some architect as yet unknown to us, a man of English architectural training and high repute in the colony, designed some of its most notable buildings in the early eighteenth century. Perhaps some day his name will be discovered, just as patient study of the ruined remnants of Corotoman, Rosewell, and Nomini Hall has recovered for us some conception of the vanished splendors of these great houses.

Reading Suggestions

Thomas Tileston Waterman's *The Mansions of Virginia, 1706–1776* (University of North Carolina Press, Chapel Hill, 1946) is the acknowledged authority on the great Georgian houses of Virginia. Comprehensive, scholarly, excellently illustrated with photographs and plans, it is one of the outstanding books in the literature of American architectural history.

Earlier books on this field include: Edith Tunis Sale's *Manors of Virginia in Colonial Times* (J. B. Lippincott, Philadelphia, 1909) and *Interiors of Virginia Houses of Colonial Times* (William Byrd Press, Richmond, 1927); Robert A. Lancaster's *Historic Virginia Homes and Churches* (J. B. Lippincott, Philadelphia, 1915); T. T. Waterman and J. A. Barrows, *Domestic Colonial Architecture of Tidewater Virginia* (Scribner's, New York, 1932).

Virginia Georgian churches are discussed and illustrated in: Henry Irving Brock's *Colonial Churches in Virginia,* with photographs by Frances Benjamin Johnston (Dale Press, Richmond, 1930); Edward F. Rines, *Old Historic Churches of America* (Macmillan, New York, 1936); George Carrington Mason, *Colonial Churches of Tidewater Virginia* (Whittet and Shepperson, Richmond, 1945).

For additional references pertaining especially to the late Georgian period in Virginia, see bibliography, Chapter 12.

12

Late Georgian Architecture in Virginia

THE PERSONALITIES and achievements of three men, John Ariss, George Washington, and Thomas Jefferson, dominate the architecture of the late Georgian period in Virginia. Ariss was a professional architect, Washington a gentleman amateur, Jefferson an amateur with professional knowledge and standards. Of the three, Ariss produced by far the greatest quantity of buildings: during the twenty-five year period from 1750 to 1775 he designed a large group of important houses. These are more properly Palladian than their early Georgian predecessors. Their lines are more horizontal, their roof pitches lower, and they make more prominent use of ' texture ' motives such as quoins and rustication. They introduce the Palladian window more frequently. Most of all they strive for greater axial emphasis by a central pavilion with its crowning classic pediment, visible on the main façade.

This style, a belated Burlingtonian phenomenon, was less pretentious than its English counterpart — fortunately the Virginia houses were smaller than the English ' great houses,' they made less use of stone, and they avoided exterior pilasters — but nonetheless the style probably could have been learned nowhere else. Thus it is not surprising to find John Ariss, who was born at Albany, Virginia, about 1725, traveling to England during his early twenties. He doubtless wandered and observed; he may even have served an architectural apprenticeship. Thus he was equipped to advertise, after his return to Virginia, the performance of architectural work ' in the neatest Manner (and at cheaper rates) either of the Ancient or Modern Order of Gibbs' Architect ' as we have seen in the *Maryland Gazette* of 1751.

He settled first in Westmoreland County until about 1755, moved to Richmond County until 1762, and is later recorded as a resident of Berkeley County from about 1770 to his death in 1799. His architectural career must have begun in his mid-twenties. He is recorded as having done commissions for churches, but his chief work was undoubtedly domestic.

Ariss's two chief architectural sources were James Gibbs's *Book of Architecture* and, especially, William Adam's *Vitruvius Scoticus*. William Adam was the father of the more famous Robert Adam; he practiced in Scotland in the second quarter of the eighteenth century and was on occasion associated with Gibbs. His book, published in Edinburgh in 1750, was ' a Collection of Plans, Elevations and Sections of Public Buildings, Noblemen's and Gentlemen's Houses in Scotland. . .' It was particularly

useful to a builder in the colonies because it contained a good deal of
bread mixed with the cake; even Virginia planters did not have noblemen's incomes, and Adam's smaller house designs were suited to the market. Ariss used these plates freely, modifying details, combining elements
from different designs, or devising substitutes for unsuitable features. He
remained singularly faithful to this source book during a practice of more
than twenty-five years; even his latest work shows no sign of the newer
English style led by William Adam's sons Robert and James.

293. Mount Airy, built by John Tayloe, Richmond County, Va., 1758–62. Entrance
(north) façade and dependency (HABS)

The modern discovery (in 1946) of John Ariss's life and probable
works, hitherto unknown, is one of Waterman's most important contributions to American architectural history.[1] On the basis of all available
documentary and stylistic evidence, Waterman attributes to Ariss a group
of 14 houses, of which at least 8 may be assigned with considerable certainty; 7 were 'important' formal houses in the Palladian manner, including the Carlyle House at Alexandria (1751), Mount Airy (1758–62),
the now-destroyed Mannsfield (c.1760–70), Harewood (c.1769), Bland-
field (1770), Fairfield (c.1770), and Elmwood (c.1774). For our purposes,
Mount Airy, one of the finest formal mansions of the late Georgian period, may represent this group.

Mount Airy, Richmond County. 1758–62

This is one of the few stone houses built in Virginia during the eighteenth century. The walls are made of a local dark-brown sandstone, carefully hewn and laid in courses of random heights, with architectural trim
in a light-colored limestone. It is possible that the exterior may originally

have been plastered, though no trace remains. The house was begun by Colonel John Tayloe in 1758, on a ridge commanding a wide view of the valley of the Rappahannock.

The north or entrance façade (fig. 293) is approached by a flight of steps leading to a recessed loggia, whose square piers, composed of four Roman Doric pilasters, define three rectilinear openings. The projecting pavilion is of rusticated limestone, with three windows in the second story and a crowning pediment. The south façade (fig. 294) is identical in com-

294. The south façade of Mount Airy (Wayne Andrews)

position except that the three entrances are spanned by round arches with heavily marked voussoirs and keystones, and the upper windows of the pavilion are unframed. The other windows are framed by stone architraves and sills, and the limestone belt course and rusticated angle quoins are very prominent. The original roof has been remodeled. This façade was undoubtedly taken from Plate LVIII of Gibbs's *Book of Architecture* (fig. 295); indeed, for a whole façade composition, it is the closest known approach to direct imitation in American Georgian architecture. The north façade was less directly derived from a plate of Haddo House, Scotland, in *Vitruvius Scoticus.*

Unfortunately the probably fine interiors were destroyed by fire in 1844, but the plan remains of great interest (fig. 296). This has a magnificent central hall, 20 by 30 feet, extending clear through the house between the loggias. A spiral stairway was later inserted in the northwest corner room, but the original stair was probably in a separate hall between the two east rooms, lighted by the central arch of a Palladian window. The plan is very similar to that of Sabine Hall, built almost thirty years before, and only a few miles away. But the location of fireplaces on interior partition walls, accounting for the two pairs of chimneys so prominent on the exterior, was unprecedented in Virginia. Of greatest interest are the quadrant passages connecting the main house with the two square dependencies that flank the forecourt: Mount Airy was the first house in the colonies to achieve the ideal scheme of the full Palladian villa, so much admired by Inigo Jones and later English architects.*

Yet if we can recognize John Ariss's advance in academic formality, we cannot as readily approve of the result. Mount Airy may be ' correct,' but

295. Design by James Gibbs which served as a model for the south façade of Mount Airy (James Gibbs, *Book of Architecture*)

it is hardly as native or as vigorous as the early Georgian houses; their warmth of color and grace of detail are more agreeable than the heavy architectural pretensions of this cold composition.

Mount Vernon, Fairfax County. 1757–87

Mount Vernon also boasts a Palladian-villa plan and other academic pretensions, but the architect is not certainly known. It has always been supposed, in the words of Custis's *Memoirs* (1859) that ' Washington was his own architect and builder, laying off everything himself.' [2] There is no evidence in Washington's accounts, domestic records, or published writings that he ever hired an architect; indeed there is ample evidence that he directed and supervised most of the work, and that he preferred to do so personally. At one time he desired a London merchant to send him ' a marble chimney piece, cost not to exceed fifteen guineas, paper mâché for the ceiling of the two rooms, 250 panes of window glass, a dozen fashionable locks for partition doors, fashionable hinges '; at another he wrote ' I am very much engaged in raising one of the additions to my house, which I think (perhaps it is fancy) goes on better whilst I am present, than in my absence from the workmen '; or we find a note in his diary that ' Mr. Saunders not coming according to expectation I began

---

* Rosewell may have had quadrant passages; Waterman has so indicated in a restored perspective (p. 106), but in the text he says, ' it is not sure the connecting passageways were ever built ' (p. 111).

with my own people to shingle that part of the Roof of the House wch. was stripped yesterday. . .' [3]

There is, however, a possibility that John Ariss designed the remodelings of 1757–8 and 1773–9. Ariss's grandfather on his mother's side was John Spencer, a man of considerable wealth, who had held property jointly with both John and Lawrence Washington. Throughout John Ariss's life many records indicate a close association with the Washington family, and Waterman states that there is evidence, ' in a literary reference not now available for quotation,' that Ariss provided the drawings for the alterations of Mount Vernon.[4] But the architectural evidence is far from conclusive, and the authorship of the Mount Vernon designs must remain an open question until further evidence is discovered.

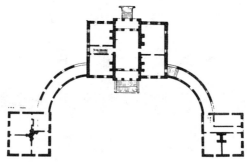

296. Plan of first floor, Mount Airy (Thomas T. Waterman *The Mansions of Virginia,* University of North Carolina Press)

Mount Vernon has so many associations and has become so rich a part of our living past that there has been a tendency to overvalue its intrinsic architectural merit. Certain details, both of exterior and interior, are indeed of fine quality, but as a whole this product of the accidents of thirty years' growth has many imperfections. It warrants our attention not as a masterpiece but as an intimate and very human record of the architectural ideals, problems, and solicitudes of a Virginia gentleman building a much-loved home.

The history of Mount Vernon is complex indeed. The name of the estate was given by its former owner, Major Lawrence Washington, in honor of Admiral Vernon of the British Navy, under whom he had served. Lawrence Washington lived on the property from 1740 until his death in 1752. The house at that time was a small story-and-a-half cottage with end chimneys, four rooms, and a central hall — the part now lying between the two chimneys (plan, fig. 297). This farmhouse may have been built in the seventeenth century or perhaps by Augustine Washington, George's father, between 1726 and 1735. In any event, George Washington acquired it in 1754.

During the 1750's his duties as aide to General Braddock and as commander of the Virginia militia permitted few visits to his new home. But becoming engaged to Martha Custis in 1758, he foresaw the need for a larger and finer mansion and set under way an extensive remodeling, which he found time to direct by correspondence between battles and marches. From 1757 on, for thirty years, Mount Vernon was almost constantly being extended and improved, but we shall not be far wrong in picturing its growth as concentrated in three ' campaigns ' of remodeling: in 1757-8, 1773-9, and 1784-7.

The first remodeling. 1757-8

In these years Washington thoroughly rebuilt the old farmhouse and remodeled it to a more impressive architectural form. The brick founda-

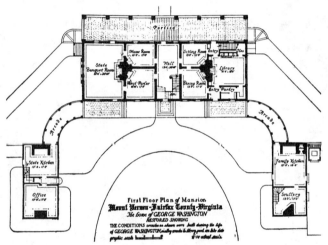

297. Plan of first floor, Mount Vernon, Fairfax County, Va. (*Great Georgian Houses*, I)

tions were reconstructed, the house virtually stripped to its old frame of hand-hewn oak timbers, new siding put on the walls, the height raised from one and a half to two and a half stories, a new roof built, and the interiors thoroughly renovated by new paneling, plastering, painting, and architectural trim. Four outer dependencies (not in the locations of the present ones) were also built at this time, or slightly later, and connected to the main house by ' pallisades ' or fences. The work of construction was supervised in Washington's absence by William Fairfax, of neighboring Belvoir. Washington was mustered out of service after the fall of Fort Duquesne in November 1758; he and Martha Custis were married on 6 January 1759; and they moved into their new home that spring.

The new walls were covered by what Washington called ' rusticated boards,' planks of long-leaf pine beveled in a fashion to resemble blocks of stone masonry, and painted with a sand finish to enhance the illusion. Though such ' faking ' had earlier been used in New England, it was unexampled in Virginia. The new roof had a modillioned cornice and was probably hipped; the chimneys, probably projecting from the end walls of the house, bounded the composition. But retention of the old plan made all sorts of difficulties in achieving a formal façade composition. The north (left) rooms were two feet wider than the south rooms; this brought the hall off center. The front door was moved off-center in the hall so that it might appear in the middle of the façade, but this in turn brought it off-center of the façade window pattern. This compositional enigma must have bothered Washington a good deal. He never resolved it successfully. For the next fifteen years there were no further changes of consequence at Mount Vernon.

298. West (entrance) façade of Mount Vernon (Mount Vernon Ladies Association of the Union)

The additions of 1773–9

With an increasing number of guests it became imperative to enlarge the house and especially to provide a large room for formal entertaining. So the building was lengthened at each end by about 20 feet. The Library at the south was added first, a spacious room with built-in bookcases and a fireplace. Above it was a new master bedroom, and a separate entrance and stair made this a private suite for the master and mistress of the house. The great Banquet Room at the north end of the house was next completed, except for certain details of its interior decoration. The hipped roof was lengthened to cover the extensions (fig. 298).

This gave a very long, featureless façade. We may imagine that John Ariss (if he was indeed the architect of these additions) wished he could build a projecting central pavilion and relocate all the old asymmetric windows. But a pavilion the full width of the original house would have been too wide, and one only as wide as the hall would have been too narrow — and off-center to boot. As a compromise the roof, at least, was remodeled to provide an axial pediment of suitable width; this was completed in 1778. The lack of a supporting pavilion below, and even worse, the location of one corner of the pediment directly over a window-void, must have seemed appalling solecisms. Partly to distract attention from these imperfections, Ariss may at this time have added to the front door its heavy frame of Tuscan columns and pediment, with a large winged

299, 300. The Palladian window of the Banquet Room and its prototype in Batty Langley's *Treasury of Designs*, Plate 52 (photo courtesy Mount Vernon Ladies Association of the Union)

keystone in the entablature. The detail of the door was probably taken from Plate 33 of Batty Langley's *Treasury*, and the rusticated elliptical window in the main pediment from Plate 54.

But further problems arose in treating the wall of the Banquet Room addition. The Banquet Room was two stories high and consequently had no second-story bedrooms over it. Yet to express this fact on the façade by a blank wall would have occasioned an embarrassing lack of symmetry. The solution was the insertion of two false windows, with sashes and blinds but a blank wall immediately behind them, at the second-story level on both east and west façades. Such false windows have frequently been used in twentieth-century buildings but only one other instance is known in Georgian architecture in this country. Nothing could better illustrate the extremes of artificiality that a rigid doctrine of formal symmetry imposes on architectural design.

It was usually possible, in Georgian houses, to shape both plan and exterior so that a formal pattern could be achieved without losing integrity of relation between interior and exterior. This was not possible at Mount Vernon because of the manner in which the additions were made; but it would have been better, it seems, to make the addition in some entirely different manner, just as it would have been better to avoid the use of one material to imitate another and more expensive material in the exterior siding. We have no way of knowing who insisted on such features, but the discovery of John Ariss is perhaps very helpful; we may, if we like, make him a scapegoat and credit him with the defects and Washington with the virtues of Mount Vernon. Perhaps some of these infelicities were in the mind of Benjamin Henry Latrobe, one of the greatest architects of the Federal period, who wrote in his *Journal* after visiting Mount Vernon:

> The approach is not very well managed but leads you into the area between the stables . . . It is a wooden building, painted to represent chamfered rustic and sanded . . . The whole of this part of the building is in very indifferent taste . . . Everything else is extremely good and neat, but by no means above what would be expected in a plain English Country gentleman's house of £500 or £600 a year.

The present office and kitchen dependencies, with their front walls of rusticated wood, were added at this time. Symmetrically flanking the forecourt, they were connected to the main house by light arcades in quadrant curves, thus completing a Palladian-villa scheme of unusual attractiveness.

Washington had to leave Mount Vernon in May 1775 to assume command of the Continental Army. He was away for eight years, and much of the building of the years 1775–9 was supervised by his distant cousin Lund Washington, who managed the estate during his absence.

The completion of Mount Vernon. 1784–7

After Washington's return from the war, he added the great two-story portico along the entire east side of the house, overlooking the Potomac River (fig. 301). This is one of the most striking and successful features of the mansion. Measuring some 14 by 94 feet, its lofty shelter was an excellent adaptation to the climate and site, and it gave unity and dignity to the east façade. Many old photographs of this east portico reveal a fine Chinese lattice balustrade over the eaves; this feature was added by Bushrod Washington in the early 1800's but was removed in a recent restoration. The paving stones, foot-square blocks of gray and red sandstone, were imported from England. The lofty square piers, simply paneled, may have been inspired by plates in Langley's *Treasury*. No such long giant portico is known to have existed in the colonies before this one at Mount Vernon; the innovation was a bold one and proved highly influential in later periods.

Some of the interiors had their decorations completed at this time, and the final touch was the addition of a large octagonal cupola on the roof ridge, bearing at its apex a weathervane modeled in accordance with Washington's wish: 'I should like to have a bird . . . with an olive branch in its Mouth.'

Mount Vernon was thus finally completed in 1787, the very year that Washington left for Philadelphia to preside over the Constitutional Convention. After two terms of the presidency, he retired to his home in March 1797. 'I can truly say,' he had earlier remarked, 'I had rather be at Mount Vernon with a friend or two about me, than to be attended at

301, 302. The east portico, and stairway in the main entrance hall, Mount Vernon (Mount Vernon Ladies Association of the Union)

the seat of government by the officers of state and the representatives of every power in Europe.' He lived here until his death on 14 December 1799.

The interiors of Mount Vernon

Though the interiors of Mount Vernon lack the opulent grandeur of those at Carter's Grove, they are for the most part well designed and executed. There are several notable mantelpieces and three fine plaster ceilings, but many of the rooms — especially Washington's own bedroom — have a homely simplicity. Indeed when Samuel Vaughn sent from London an exceptionally fine and elaborate marble mantelpiece for the Banquet Hall, Washington wrote: 'I have the honor to inform you that the chimneypiece is arrived, and, by the number of cases [ten] too elegant and costly by far, I fear, for my own room and republican style of living.'

The entrance hall (fig. 302) is a spacious room, 13 feet wide and 31 feet long, and its cross-ventilation made it the most comfortable room in the house during warm weather, when it was much used for informal social life. It was decorated during the 1757–8 remodeling. The walls have a series of tall panels above the chair rail, and a modillioned cornice. The four doors to the flanking rooms are topped by broken pediments. The stairway is simple, but of very good quality. The walnut handrail, winding in a large spiral at the newel, is supported by very plain balusters — three to a step — with long round shafts. The walnut string piece is adorned by flat step ends sawed to a scrolled profile but not carved or paneled. Graceful ramps and easings carry the handrail over the intermediate posts at

503. The Dining Room fireplace at Mount Vernon (Mount Vernon Ladies Association of the Union)

the corners, and their profile is echoed by the dado cap on the wall, which is plastered rather than paneled.

The two east rooms are rather small. One was used as a family sitting room, or, in other years, as a downstairs bedroom. Its extremely simple paneling is of a style that suggests the early farmhouse of the first half of the century, and it may never have been remodeled. The Music Room, however, has the plain plastered walls that became popular late in the century, and its wooden chair rail, cornice, and mantel, though simple, are of the style of the Banquet Room; it was probably retrimmed when the latter was finished, just before or just after the Revolution. Though Washington himself, as he said, could ' neither sing one of the songs, nor raise a single note on any instrument,' music played an important part at Mount Vernon as at other Virginia houses. Washington ordered ' 1 Very good Spinit ' in 1760, and imported from London in 1793 the fine harpsichord that now stands in this room. Itinerant music-masters taught his stepchildren, and music and dancing were frequent recreations.

The two west rooms are larger and have more architectural pretensions. To the left or north of the entrance hall is the West Parlor, redecorated in 1757–8. Like most of the early rooms it has full-paneled walls; the chair

304. Model for the Dining Room fireplace in Abraham Swan's *British Architect*, Plate 50 (courtesy Avery Library, Columbia University)

rail is ornamented by a Greek fret pattern and the cornice by a row of dentils. The two doors are framed by Ionic pilasters bearing entablatures and angular pediments, copied exactly from Plate 349 of Batty Langley's *Ancient Masonry* (1734). The chief feature of the room is a fine mantelpiece set on a diagonal chimney-breast, as are the mantelpieces in all four of the smaller rooms. The design was taken from Plate 51 of Swan's *British Architect*, but with several improvements, including a crowning swan's neck pediment enclosing a cartouche bearing the Washington arms. The overmantel frames a painting that may be original, for its dimensions coincide exactly with those of a ' neat landskip ' that Washington ordered from an English agent at this time. The ceiling was done over during the second remodeling and has a fine pattern of rayed husks emanating from a central sunburst and enclosed by an eight-lobed frame of festoons and oval medallions. This is an early example in the colonies of the delicate low-relief style of plaster ornament created in England by Robert Adam.

The Dining Room, to the right of the entrance hall, is the finest and most elaborate room at Mount Vernon (fig. 303). Its decoration was completed in the autumn of 1775 by two craftsmen named Lamphier and Sears; it is possible that the latter was from Philadelphia, for the unusually rich plaster ornament of the room is matched in certain houses there. Above the paneled dado the smooth plaster walls serve as a foil to the ornate detail of chimneypiece, cornice, and ceiling.

The chimneypiece is modeled after Plate 50 of Swan's book (fig. 304), and is representative of the highly developed late Georgian type. The fireplace opening is framed by mottled blue marble, and this in turn by a richly carved backband, eared at the upper corners and flanked at the sides by baroque acanthus-leaf consoles, modified from Swan's pattern. A frieze over the facing is rich with rococo foliage, bounded at the sides by heavy curved brackets ornamented with acanthus leaves. Every part of the much-molded mantel shelf is carved, with rows of leaf-and-tongue, dentil, and egg-and-dart ornament. The eared frame of the overmantel is enriched by rope molding, ribbon-and-reel ornament, and rococo motives at top and bottom. A detailed comparison with Swan's plate will demonstrate the similarity of the two compositions and yet will show how freely the craftsman changed individual motives.

While the fireplace is the center of attraction of the room, it is superbly complemented by the rich plaster frieze at the top of the wall and the exceptionally fine ceiling (fig. 305). A central rosette is enclosed by a wheel of husks and, outside this, more husks formed in graceful festoons. The outer pattern of delicate foliage is skilfully adapted to the irregular shape of the room. The set of nine ladder-backed Chippendale chairs in the dining room was owned by Washington, and must seldom have stood idle: some months after his retirement from the presidency Washington wrote to a friend that he and Mrs. Washington were having dinner alone for the first time in twenty years!

The large Banquet Room, 23 by 31 feet, occupies the north end of the house and is two stories high with a coved ceiling. The construction and decoration of this room occupied the ten years from 1776 to 1786. With plain plastered walls and delicate plaster ornament, it represents a transition from Georgian to the Adam style of the post-Revolutionary period. The room's chief features are the fireplace, the Palladian window on the north wall, and the fine plaster ceiling.

The fireplace (fig. 306), sent by Samuel Vaughn from London as a gift to Washington, is of a type not made in the colonies until the Federal period. Noteworthy are the two free-standing Ionic colonets and the absence of an overmantel; this relative simplicity heralds the growing severity of taste of the Classic Revival. But in detail, the mantel is very rich with its carved marble frieze panels and its hearth inlaid with colored stones.

Opposite it is the great Palladian window, an interesting fusion of

Georgian form with Adam decorative detail. The pattern was taken from Langley's *Treasury,* but while the exterior face of Langley's design (Langley's Plate 52, see fig. 300) was followed precisely — at least above the line of the window sill — the interior face was adorned with the thin, delicate, low-relief ornament of the Adam style — a far cry from the bold relief and robust vigor of early Georgian carved ornament.

The ceiling of the Banquet Room, with its central sunburst, its wreathed and entwined foliage, has been called ' the outstanding example

305. Detail of the Dining Room ceiling, Mount Vernon (Mount Vernon Ladies Association of the Union)

of its period in this country.' [5] Of particular interest are the wreathed panels enclosing dainty reliefs of spades, pickaxes, sickles, and other agricultural implements (fig. 307). Such bucolic felicities had originated in the fragile panels of rococo *salons* and *boudoirs,* when Louis XV's courtiers, stimulated by Diderot's moralistic sermons, took up rusticity and the Simple Life — at least as novel and morally commendable subjects for conversation and art. A little later Marie Antoinette built her Rustic Hamlet at Versailles, and the English ' naturalistic garden ' came into its own. All of these were evidences of a dawning romanticism, which was later to destroy the entire Renaissance tradition of classical form in the arts, but which in the late eighteenth century was still merely a matter for dainty decoration. When Washington requested groves of trees at each end of the house ' to be Planted without any order or regularity,' he was reflecting the current taste for the natural rather than the perfect geometric artifice of the governor's gardens at Williamsburg. But Romanticism was still only a vague taste, its murky power but a slight cloud on the clear classic horizon.

Mount Vernon's plastered ceilings suggest brief mention of those at contemporary Kenmore, near Fredericksburg, Virginia. All but one of the lower rooms in this house have plastered ceilings of the most extraordinary richness; as a group they are unrivaled in America. Presumably done about 1770 by itinerant French craftsmen, their motives are derived from plates in Langley's *Treasury,* and the workmanship is unsurpassed. But they represent a heavier and more geometric mid-Georgian style than the rambling, attenuated delicacies of Mount Vernon's Adamesque ceilings. Kenmore was owned by Fielding Lewis, whose wife was Betty Wash-

306, 307. The Banquet Room, Mount Vernon (Mount Vernon Ladies Association of the Union)

ington; when Lund Washington wrote to George in 1775, he boasted that the new dining room ceiling at Mount Vernon was ' a handsomer one than any of Colonel Lewis's although not half the work on it.' [6]

The Library at the south end of Mount Vernon was Washington's favorite workroom but is rather plainly treated. The plaster walls are broken by many doors to cupboards and bookcases, and the mantelpiece is unimpressive. Over the Library was the master bedroom, and there were five other bedrooms on the second floor. The third floor contained three bedrooms, three storage or ' lumber ' rooms, and a hall from which a spiral staircase gave access to the cupola.

The chief charm of Mount Vernon is in its orderly setting of gardens and trees and the little village of plantation dependencies. Washington was an enthusiastic gardener, and his diary is full of such notes as: ' Enjoyed myself the greatest part of the day in pruning . . . my trees and shrubs. . . Took up the clump of lilacs which stood at the corner of the south garden plot and transplanted them.' The gardens have been splendidly restored and the house kept up and properly furnished by the

Mount Vernon Ladies' Association of the Union, which maintains the estate as a national shrine.

Pohick Church, Fairfax County. 1771–2

Pohick Church is almost as closely associated with the memory of Washington as is Mount Vernon. His father, Augustine Washington, was a vestryman of the first church of Truro Parish, built about 1732. George Washington attended the church as a young man and was appointed a warden in 1752. Later, as master of near-by Mount Vernon, it was natural that he should be actively interested in the construction of a new church for the parish. There was some discussion whether the site of the old frame building should be retained. Washington, with his surveyor's instincts, drew a map of the parish, showing where each member lived, and suggested a new location in the center of population. The recommendation was adopted and incidentally brought the new church two miles closer to Mount Vernon.

Washington served on the building committee and is reported to have made the design himself, drawing it on white paper with India ink.[7] It seems more likely that he copied the plans of Christ Church, Alexandria, making the necessary reduction in size, for the two churches were originally very similar. As a vestryman in both churches, Washington could have had access to these plans, which had been drawn up in 1767 by James Wren. The builder of Pohick Church was one Daniel French, and the cost was £887. When the vestrymen accepted the new building, in 1772, and auctioned off its pews, Washington purchased pew number 28 for his own use and pew number 30 for the guests who invariably accompanied him to service. The receipt of £23/10 was duly recorded.[8]

Pohick Church is fairly typical of the small Virginia churches of the late eighteenth century (fig. 308) . The cruciform plan has been abandoned in favor of a simple rectangle, and there is no tower.* But the façades are symmetrically composed, with rectilinear windows below and arched windows above. The low-pitch hipped roof has a modillioned cornice. The angle quoins and trim of the doorways are in a light sandstone. Two doors at the west end, framed by rusticated masonry, Ionic pilasters, and pediments, lead into the two aisles of the interior. A third door, on the south side, faces the high pulpit on the middle of the north wall. The interior woodwork was badly damaged during the Civil War, but the box pews, gallery, and other features have been restored. The Washington coach-and-four, with its liveried riders, was a familiar sight at Old Pohick, and the rectors of the church were frequent guests at Mount Vernon.

Late Georgian tendencies

Three tendencies mark the architecture of the last years of the Georgian period in Virginia: (1) the adoption of the decorative style of Robert Adam, as we have seen in the ceilings at Mount Vernon; (2) a growing severity of form and color, with a greater dependence on Palladio; and

* The tower of Christ Church, Alexandria, otherwise very similar to Pohick Church, was an awkward addition made in 1818.

(3) a new type of strung-out house plan, based on Palladio's 'Roman Country House' style. Washington was the leader in the first of these trends, Jefferson in the second two.

Though Palladio's *Four Books* had undoubtedly been regarded by earlier Virginia gentlemen as a sort of architectural Bible, its gospel, like the religious one, was often interpreted with a certain freedom. Palladio's designs were severe and academic and the early Georgian builders preferred the pictorial warmth and color of the Wren-Williamsburg tradition. But Mount Airy and Mount Vernon had already led the way to the

308. Pohick Church, Fairfax County, Va., 1771-2 (Frances Benjamin Johnston)

complete Palladian-villa plan, and Jefferson was to go even further in the return to strict Palladianism.

Jefferson, in the first place, was a scholar and not afraid of source books; he was, in the second place, an architect in his blood and bones: if he was not a professional in the sense of practicing for pay, he was a professional in his enthusiasm for the art, in his technical knowledge, and in his aesthetic standards. The splendid Leoni edition of Palladio first came to his attention about 1769; from then on, Jefferson remained faithful to Palladio for fifty-five years.

One favorite Palladian motive of these years was the two-story classic portico. Jefferson evidently felt that the ordinary Georgian doorway was too insignificant an accent and that a more imposing frontispiece would give a building that classical unity which was one of the 'first principles of the art.' At his own home Monticello, as it was first designed in 1771-2, he used a two-story portico, not dissimilar to the Palladio design shown in fig. 309. Two other examples in Virginia, which probably cannot be attributed to Jefferson, were at Shirley and the Capitol at Williamsburg.

Shirley, in Charles City County, was built about 1769 by Charles Carter, a former student at William and Mary and a frequent visitor at Williamsburg. There are two-story classic porticoes at both north and south sides, topped by pediments (fig. 310). Some confusion has arisen because these were renewed in 1831 and doubtless changed somewhat at that time; the upper order, for example, was probably changed from Ionic, which would have been in conformity with the Palladian precedent, to Doric. But evidence indicates that the original porticoes were of the same general form as the present ones.

309. Design for a two-story portico by Palladio (Leoni edition, Book II, Plate 61)

The similar two-tiered portico on the Capitol at Williamsburg was added in 1751–3 to the middle of the west façade, commanding the long vista of the Duke of Gloucester Street. Jefferson disapproved of Georgian, and this portico was the only thing that seems to have interested him in the architecture of the building. His whole description of it, in the *Notes on Virginia* (1781) was as follows:

The capitol is a light and airy structure, with a portico in front of two orders, the lower of which, being Doric, is tolerably just in its proportions and ornaments, save only that the inter-columniations are too large. The upper is Ionic, much too small for that on which it is mounted, its ornaments not proper to the order, nor proportioned within themselves. It is crowned with a pediment, which is too high for its span. Yet, on the whole, it is the most pleasing piece of architecture we have.[9]

Waterman suggests that the Capitol portico was designed by Jefferson,[10] but this seems unlikely in the light of such faint praise.

The ' Roman Country House ' style of Palladio is exemplified in several houses of the late Georgian period. The plan layout is completely different from that of early and middle Georgian houses. In place of a large central block, two and a half or three stories high, with detached dependencies, the ' country house ' had a long series of connected units, two stories high in the middle, decreasing to low one-story wings and passages, and sometimes accented by two-story terminal pavilions at the ends. This type of plan had many advantages: most rooms were on the ground floor, and the main

310. Shirley, Charles City County, Va. (HABS)

stair and its wasteful hall could be minimized; all rooms had cross-ventilation; and the kitchen, though located in an end pavilion, was at least under the same roof and not too far distant from the dining room.

Brandon, Prince George County

A fine example is Brandon, in Prince George County. Probably built about 1765 for Nathaniel Harrison, family tradition attributes it to the young Jefferson (22 at the time) who was best man at his friend's wedding that year. The source of the plan was undoubtedly a plate in Robert Morris's *Select Architecture* (London, 1757) , a book little used in the colonies but a favorite possession of Jefferson's. The plan of Brandon (fig. 312) shows a central block of three rooms, only the middle one rising to a second story, the others being covered by low hipped roofs. Small low passages connect with two-story terminal buildings housing chambers and service quarters. The original arrangement of the central ' living hall,' with a stair partitioned off at one end, is shown in the plan. Main interior rooms have very tall narrow panels and fully membered cornices. One of the small stairs, in the west pavilion, has a Chinese-lattice rail, instead of the familiar Georgian balustrade; such are occasionally found in late Georgian houses.

Brandon's exterior presents a totally different architectural effect from the traditional Georgian mansion (fig. 311). Low, strung out, its structure divided into small-scale units, it has a refreshing variety and an expression of welcome rather than of aristocratic hauteur. The house is interestingly composed, with its repeated hipped roofs — the central one

311. Brandon, Prince George County, Va., c.1765 (John O. Brostrup)

dominating — its receding and diminishing shapes, and its almost musical *reprise* in the strong simple masses of the end pavilions.

This is a large house, finely designed and well built, but it has an intimate, human scale and the kind of 'American freedom' that Patrick Henry in that very year defended so eloquently in the House of Burgesses

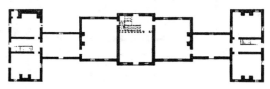

312. Plan of first floor, Brandon (Thomas T. Waterman, *The Mansions of Virginia*, University of North Carolina Press)

against the tyranny of the Stamp Act. It also has many practical functional advantages. It is Palladian only by courtesy, for Robert Morris in his prototype design had departed far from the usual Palladian *grandezza*, and Brandon went even further in the direction of simplicity and practicality.

It seems very probable that Jefferson designed this house, for Morris's *Select Architecture* was one of his favorite books in the early years. If indeed it was built in 1765 or shortly after, Brandon has a particular importance in revealing to us Jefferson's architectural genius as a young man in his early twenties. It would seem that he was well on the way toward creating a free, simple, practical, and indigenous American architecture. We can only regret that this early genius was so stiffened and formalized

313. James Semple House, Williamsburg, Va., c.1780 (Thomas T. Waterman, **HABS**)

by his discovery of Palladio's book, only a few years later, and his subsequent lifelong devotion to the great Italian classicist.

James Semple House, Williamsburg

Jefferson was perhaps the designer also of the Semple House at Williamsburg (fig. 313). It is believed to have been built about 1780 and was bought in 1799 by Judge James Semple, member of the House of Dele-

314. Plan of the Semple House (Thomas T. Waterman, *The Mansions of Virginia,* University of North Carolina Press)

gates and General Court of Virginia and a professor of Law at the College. It is a small house, with only five rooms; three of these on the ground floor are strung out in a line (plan, fig. 314). The end rooms, containing dining room and drawing room, form one-story wings, their roofs of such low pitch that the gable ends can be treated as perfectly proportioned classic pediments.

The central block contains a salon, with a fireplace at one end. Above it are two small chambers reached by a winding staircase behind the chimney in the east wing — reminiscent of the small ' concealed ' stairs at Monticello. Indeed Jefferson's first drawing for Monticello, in Waterman's view ' parallels the design of the Randolph-Semple house to such a degree that there can be no doubt that they are by the same author.' [11] Of chief interest is the handling of the exterior of the central unit: though considerably wider than it is deep, it is treated as a classical temple motive. The roof forms a wide low-pitched gable which is brought out to the main façade as a smooth-boarded pediment. Here, then, the pediment is not merely an applied decorative element on a roof of greater size and different axial direction, but an architectonic feature integral with the mass behind it.

Jefferson and the first Monticello

Thomas Jefferson was born in 1743 at Shadwell, near Charlottesville, where his father Peter Jefferson owned a 1900-acre plantation and 130 slaves. His early childhood was spent at Tuckahoe, near Richmond, and his early teens at Shadwell or at school. In 1760 he went to Williamsburg to attend the College of William and Mary. It was his first opportunity to see any considerable amount of Georgian architecture, and the orderly town plan and formal buildings doubtless impressed him. At Williamsburg three men influenced him greatly: Dr. William Small, professor of Mathematics; George Wythe, the great professor of Law; and Francis Fauquier, one of the finest of the royal governors of Virginia. Jefferson became close friends with these men, ate dinners at Wythe House and at the palace, and enjoyed ' more good sense, more rational and philosophical conversation, than in all my life beside ' — a fact that doubtless influenced his later educational and architectural plans for the University of Virginia.

At this time Richard Taliaferro was probably living at Wythe House with his daughter and son-in-law, and it seems entirely likely that Jefferson came to know him and to acquire a serious interest in architecture. We have no certain means of knowing whether he actually began to practice, about 1765, with Brandon and Battersea, but his earliest preserved drawings of about 1768 show such professional quality that they suggest considerable previous experience.

The site of Jefferson's future home was a considerable hill, not far from Shadwell; Jefferson called it his ' little mountain ' and long dreamed of building on the summit, with its splendid views in all directions. This in itself was a romantic taste, but his first operations were eminently classical rather than romantic: as early as 1768 he began shaving off the picturesque hilltop by extensive grading operations to prepare a level site of almost three acres.

Work proceeded slowly, and Jefferson evolved several preliminary studies of the plan, presumably in the years 1768–71. These show influences from Robert Morris's *Select Architecture,* but after about 1769, when Leoni's *Palladio* came to hand, that book exerted a controlling influence. The beautifully drawn elevation of the façade is not a copy of any single

Palladian design, but practically every one of its elements occurs in Palladio's work, and the full-size details of the orders are taken line for line from Palladio's plates of the Doric and the Ionic. His many drawings and notes — unexampled at that time for precision and professional quality — are covered with figures. With his methodical mind, trained to mathematics, he predetermined all his proportions and dimensions by calculation. If using a detail from Gibbs, he would 'correct' it by reference to

315. Jefferson's Monticello as it was first built, 1770–75. Conjectural restoration by Waterman, rendered by R. E. Collins (Thomas T. Waterman, *The Mansions of Virginia*, University of North Carolina Press)

Palladio, whose figures he believed more authoritative. By totting figures he would arrive at the proportions of a column or the height of an entablature before he started to draw them. This was, to be sure, partly because he was unskilled at freehand and did his drawing mechanically in ink on large sheets of paper, which was laborious and expensive. But it nonetheless reveals a markedly academic method of design.

The first Monticello was begun in 1770 and probably completed in 1775. The house built in these years was later (1796–1809) so completely altered and enlarged that its first appearance must be reconstructed chiefly on the basis of Jefferson's drawings, though its rooms actually form the back part of the present house. The exterior, as originally designed (fig. 315), consisted of a central two-story unit with a pedimented roof running from front to back, somewhat like the scheme of the James Semple House. At the sides were lower wings, with one main story and an attic.

The building was of red brick with cut-stone trim. Brick was made and lumber sawed on the site, and for much of the building Jefferson was his own contractor and foreman of construction; skilled labor was scarce in near-by Charlottesville, and Jefferson trained and supervised his masons, carpenters, joiners, and ironworkers.

The chief architectural accent was the two-story portico, Doric below and Ionic above, all correct in accordance with Palladio. The full entablature of the Doric order, as well as a podium or base for the Ionic, was carried around the wings, forming an unusually heavy band as if to emphasize a one-story composition. The attic above this, in the wings, was a feature also to be found in Palladio. But Jefferson's enthusiasm for a

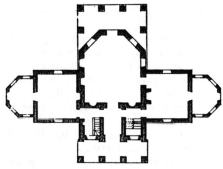

316. Plan of the first Monticello, Albemarle County, Va., by Thomas Jefferson (Thomas T. Waterman, *The Mansions of Virginia*, University of North Carolina Press)

display of Palladian erudition ran away with his sense of proportion: the portico, proper enough on an Italian villa big enough to carry it, was too large for so small a house. The building was all frontispiece and no volume, like a six-shooter with a shotgun barrel.

The original design was not precisely carried out. It would appear that the upper porticoes were never completed, though the walls behind them were built. As late as April in '75 Jefferson was refiguring the order for the Ionic columns, and it is probable that the Revolution prevented their execution. On the other hand, he added small polygonal projections to the ends of the wings.

The plan (fig. 316) shows a small entrance hall flanked by inconspicuous stair halls. The main room was a drawing room with a polygonal bay projecting under the rear portico. This feature, which does not appear in Palladio, was derived from Morris's book; it was unprecedented in Virginia though a few houses with polygonal projecting bays had been built in Philadelphia and Annapolis. Measuring more than 24 by 28 feet, and with an 18-foot ceiling, the drawing room was an impressive salon for so small a house. The wing at the right, or north, contained a dining room, and there was a tea room in the polygonal addition. The rooms at the left served for Jefferson's bedroom and study. All of these rooms had very lofty ceilings. A corridor connected the two ends of the house. The second story contained a large library, in the central block, and attic sleeping rooms in the two wings. Service rooms were located in the cellar.

Even as early as 1772 Jefferson prepared a grandiose plan for the location of service rooms in two great L-shaped wings, below ground level (as seen from the west lawn) but taking advantage of the sloping site to gain windows in the outer walls. This also was a skilfully adapted Palladian scheme. It was the basis of the later dependencies but none of these was executed before 1796, except for the small southwest pavilion. This, actually, was the first building at Monticello, for Jefferson had started it as a *pied-à-terre* before the fire at Shadwell in February 1770. He moved in the same month and occupied it as bachelor quarters. And it was to this building that he brought his bride, Martha Wales, during a heavy blizzard on New Year's Day, 1772; it is still referred to as ' Honeymoon Cottage.'

Jefferson's early plans for the terraces and gardens are of extraordinary interest. Though a Palladian at heart, he was not unaware of English romantic landscape design, with its little ' temples ' and ' summer houses ' and other architectural surprises scattered about the ' naturalistic ' gardens. He possessed, as early as 1771, Sir William Chambers' *Designs of Chinese Buildings. . .* (London, 1757). His drawings and notes of 1771 and the years immediately following show schemes for Chinese pavilions at the corners of his terraces, for little Greek buildings, for fantastic ' classic ' towers of superposed orders, and even for a Roman triumphal column to surpass that of Trajan's Forum! In 1778 he made a drawing for a medieval tower, with four telescoped stories and a battlemented top.

To Jefferson, as to his English predecessors, these bits of architectural scenery were play architecture: fantasies and surprises, not to be taken seriously. But these little caprices in the ' Gothick ' or ' Greek ' or ' Chinese ' taste were portentous omens of that romantic eclecticism which was to sweep England and America in the nineteenth century. Jefferson doubtless had no idea that he was responding to an inner and unconscious romantic rebellion against the strait jacket of Palladianism, nor least of all that he was setting a precedent for later widespread attacks on it. In any event the Revolution and subsequent events prevented the erection of these fantastic pavilions.

Jefferson at Williamsburg

During the very years that Monticello was being planned and built, Jefferson served in the House of Burgesses at Williamsburg (1769–75). Governor Dunmore requested him to plan a great enlargement of the College of William and Mary, and his drawing of 1771 or 1772 shows the old U-shaped plan doubled by an equal addition to the west, forming a large arcaded court. It would have made an impressive building. The foundations were built (and have recently been uncovered in new researches at Williamsburg), but the project was abandoned during the Revolutionary War.

For Dunmore also, probably about 1772, Jefferson made several studies for remodeling the Governor's Palace.[12] The most interesting of these (fig. 317) involved a complete alteration of the exterior to resemble a classical temple. The Ball Room Wing at the rear was to be demolished, and the entrance hall lengthened by a polygonal projection similar to that planned for the drawing room at Monticello, thus forming an octagonal room. Temple façades of eight columns, carrying pediments, were planned for both ends of the building, and presumably the entire roof was to be remodeled to fit them. This was the closest approach to the complete classical temple form proposed in America to that time. The ideal had been approached in Whitehall, Maryland, a few years earlier,

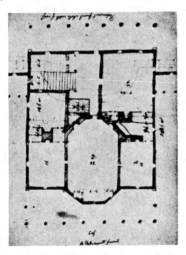

317. Jefferson's plan for remodeling the Governor's Palace at Williamsburg to a classical temple form, c.1772 (drawing in Coolidge Collection, Massachusetts Historical Society)

but the central temple motive was there embedded between one-story side wings. But Jefferson's temple proposal for the Governor's Palace was evidently discarded as too radical, or too expensive, for nothing was done about it.

In 1776 he drew up the act calling for the transfer of the capital from Williamsburg; it was passed in 1779, and the transfer made in 1780. It seems likely that even in 1776 Jefferson was contemplating new classical splendors for Richmond, as his act specified in some detail the reservation of six blocks for the construction of the new public buildings of the Commonwealth, ' to be built in a handsome manner with walls of brick or stone, and Porticos where the same may be convenient or ornamental, and with pillars and pavements of stone.' [13]

Jefferson's taste had certainly progressed away from the Georgian style in the direction of the Classic Revival of the post-Revolutionary period. In 1781 he wrote scathingly of the state of architecture in Virginia. Of the buildings at Williamsburg, he described the palace as ' not handsome without.' and the College and Hospital as ' rude, misshapen piles, which, but that they have roofs, would be taken for brick-kilns.' There were in the whole colony, he said, ' no other public buildings but churches and court-houses, in which no attempts are made at elegance.'

Indeed [he added], it would not be easy to execute such an attempt, as a workman could scarcely be found here capable of drawing an order. The genius of architecture seems to have shed its maledictions over this land. Buildings are often erected, by individuals, of considerable expence. To give these symmetry and taste would not increase their cost. It would only change the arrangement of the materials, the form and combination of the members. This would often cost less than the burthen of barbarous ornaments with which these buildings are sometimes charged. But the first principles of the art are unknown, and there exists scarcely a model among us sufficiently chaste to give an idea of them.[14]

What these ' first principles ' were, in Jefferson's thought, we may guess from his next executed work. In 1785, while American Ambassador to Versailles, Jefferson designed the new Capitol for Richmond in the form of a complete Roman temple, based very directly on the old Maison Carrée at Nîmes. This was not only the pioneer work of the Classic Revival in America, but it antedated by many years the first adoption of the complete temple form in Europe.

Equally significant is the catalogue of his library, which Jefferson drew up just before his departure for Europe. In addition to the books already owned, he listed the books he desired to acquire. Among these were White's publication of the Greek ruins at Paestum; Wood and Dawkins' works on the Roman cities of Baalbek and Palmyra; the full publication on the Palace of Diocletian at Spalato, by Robert Adam and Clérisseau; and, most important of all, the epoch-making publication – for the first time to the Western world – of the great masterpieces of Greek architecture in Stuart and Revett's *Antiquities of Athens*. These were pioneer publications in the new science of classical archaeology. During the coming generation, in both Europe and America, they were destined to exert a decisive influence on architecture. But the story of the nature and significance of these books, and of their influence on American architecture, may be reserved for a final chapter.

It is impossible to leave the early Jefferson without some attempt at an explanation of the curious discrepancy between the man as an architect and as a political leader. Jefferson's passion for Palladio seems paradoxical in so famous an apostle of individualism. Kimball, in his definitive work,[15] explains it as an outgrowth of Jefferson's legal ability, his constant search for fundamentals based on natural law, and his respect for precedent. To him, Palladio's work had the quality of ' law derived by a process of reasoning,' and it impressed because of its appeal to the authority of Roman sources.

While this is doubtless true, it does not fully explain the paradox. Palladio's architecture and his doctrine about architecture are not really ' natural ' or ' reasonable.' They doubtless seemed so to their own age, but that age was a singularly limited one. Its ideals and its methods of thought, as discussed in Chapter 9, were quite circumscribed: in order to achieve a desired unity of thought or of form, it restricted experience to congruities; its artists and philosophers 'created out of the world as it was a world as they would have it.' Though Palladio grubbed diligently in the ruins of ancient Rome, he did so not to find what was there, but to find what he sought. Every age seeks in history evidence to support its own predilections and conclusions. Palladio sought authority rather than freedom, a manageable ideal rather than the myriad confusion of living actualities, a crystal form rather than an evolving process. The Renaissance considered this method 'reasonable,' and it bore its full fruit in seventeenth-century rationalism and the so-called ' Age of Reason ' in the eighteenth.

But the late eighteenth century was just as much an ' Age of Feeling.' Already men were beginning to realize the superiority of direct experience over purely rational insights. They were discovering that human behavior is not eternally noble and measured and fine, in the manner of Poussin's shepherds, but infinitely varied and unpredictable, ruled often more strongly by passion than by intellect. They found that Nature, rather than being a humanized and serene and ordered background for man's life, was beyond human control, awesome and tempestuous, alien and inhuman. They found that the comfortable and established absolutism of state, church, and society was not the best of all possible worlds, and they launched a violent critical attack, from all sides, against these citadels of authority. In the realm of human fears and mysteries and emotions, they explored new avenues to aesthetic and spiritual satisfaction.

Science, social revolution, and romanticism were triple spear points against the easy certitudes of the established order, and by the mid-nineteenth century it had completely disintegrated. Jefferson, in the late eighteenth century, felt these things — keenly — but he did not yet *think* them. Consciously, he sought in Palladian architecture lawful and ordered form; unconsciously, he sought freedom from this stringent authority in the ' play ' architecture of the pavilions at Monticello. He copied the Maison Carrée at Nîmes in order, as he thought, to arrive at ' first principles ' in architecture. But in utilizing the new science of archaeology for his basic data, his method was of the new age rather than of the old, and his aim was compounded more of revolutionary political ideology and romantic idealization than he knew. Though he wrote whimsically from Nîmes to the Comtesse de Tesse of ' gazing whole hours at the Maison Quarré, like a lover at his mistress,' he seems not to have realized that his passion for Roman classicism was more romantic than rational, more political than architectural.

Precisely this same blend of scientific method, democratic idealism, and emotional perception was to animate a whole generation of Americans in the early nineteenth century, and the architecture of the Greek Revival, though classic in form, was essentially romantic in spirit.

If Jefferson had lived until the era of Darwin, he would have had a totally different concept of what constitutes natural law, just as mastery of Gothic architecture would have taught him a new concept of organic rather than geometric form, or as the achieved Industrial Revolution would have completely altered his notion of what was 'reasonable' in architecture.

Jefferson lived between two ages. He experienced the passions, the intensities, the novelties of the new; yet his keen mind perceived the rational clarities of the old. As is so often true of really great men, he was most radical in his vocation, most conservative in his avocations. The mind that played — with cool intelligence — at Palladian architecture was not the mind that worked — with passionate ardor — on the Declaration of Independence. In architecture he revered an authority that was not yet dead; in politics he sought a freedom that was yet to be born.

READING SUGGESTIONS

A general bibliography on Georgian architecture in Virginia is given at the end of Chapter 11.

The complete history of Mount Vernon is given in Paul Wilstach's *Mount Vernon, Washington's Home and the Nation's Shrine* (Doubleday, Page and Co., New York, 1916) and H. H. Dodge's *Mount Vernon, its Owner and its Story* (J. B. Lippincott Co., Philadelphia, 1932). The most complete and up-to-date account of the architecture of Mount Vernon is contained in Waterman's *Mansions of Virginia*, pp. 268–98.

The bibliography on the architecture of Thomas Jefferson is very extensive. Of those items pertaining to his work up to 1785, the following are salient:

Fiske Kimball, 'Thomas Jefferson as Architect of Monticello and Shadwell,' *Harvard Architectural Quarterly*, vol. 2, pp. 89–137 (June 1914).

Fiske Kimball, *Thomas Jefferson, Architect: original designs in the possession of Thomas Jefferson Coolidge, Jr.*, Riverside Press, Cambridge, Massachusetts, 1916.

Fiske Kimball, 'Thomas Jefferson and the First Monument of the Classic Revival in America,' *Journal of the American Institute of Architects*, Part 1, 3:371–81 (September 1915); Part 2, 3:421–33 (October 1915); Part 3, 3:473–91 (November 1915).

Fiske Kimball, 'Jefferson and the Public Buildings of Virginia,' *Huntington Library Quarterly*, I, 'Williamsburg, 1770–1776,' vol. 12, no. 2 (February 1949), pp. 115–20; II, 'Richmond, 1779–1780,' vol. 12, no. 3 (May 1949), pp. 303–10.

Eleanor Davidson Berman: *Thomas Jefferson Among the Arts, an Essay in Early American Esthetics*. Philosophical Library, New York, 1947.

13

Georgian Architecture in Maryland and the Carolinas

OUTSIDE OF VIRGINIA, the finest examples of Southern Georgian architecture are to be found in Annapolis, Charleston, and the river plantations of South Carolina. These can hardly be said to constitute separate regional styles — indeed the dependence of all the colonists on English architectural books and the improved communications between South and North meant a general unity of style from New Hampshire to Georgia. Yet just as there were differences in temperament and manners between New Englanders and Southerners, there were subtle variations between the crisp and prim precision of northern houses and churches and the rather careless grandeur of the southern plantations. Each region had its individual architectural quality, just as it had its own fashions and manners.

Eighteenth-century Annapolis

In Maryland, architectural fashions were set in Annapolis. Georgian architecture throughout the colonies was essentially an urban fashion, just as the Colonial style had been an expression of farm and small village. Annapolis was founded in 1694, five years before Williamsburg became the new capital of Virginia. On his arrival in the colony Sir Francis Nicholson, the second Royal Governor, moved the Maryland capital from old St. Mary's City to the small village of Anne Arundel Town, on the peninsula between the Severn River and Carrol's Creek where the two enter the broad waters of Chesapeake Bay, and renamed it in honor of Princess Anne. Throughout the century Annapolis and Williamsburg were rivals in social and cultural activity, but the former developed as the more prosperous commercial center because of its shipping. By the time of the Revolution it had grown to a city of 3000 persons and boasted 450 houses and several public buildings.

Annapolis was one of America's first planned towns. Charleston and Philadelphia had been laid out on well-ordered gridiron plans in 1680 and 1682, and modified gridiron plans were later chosen for Williamsburg, New Orleans, and Savannah. But Governor Nicholson chose a new type: undoubtedly influenced by the imposing schemes of Wren and Evelyn for the rebuilding of London after the fire of 1666, he adopted a modified radial type of plan. The twin foci were circles, the larger one containing the Capitol, the other the Anglican church. From these radi-

ated diagonal arteries intersecting a more conventional rectilinear grid
of streets (fig. 318), as in Major L'Enfant's plan for Washington of a century later. In the northwest quarter was the fine large Bloomsbury Square,
and in other quarters street names such as 'King George,' 'Prince
George,' and 'Duke of Gloucester' betrayed English loyalties while 'Calvert' and 'Bladen' reflected Maryland's own history. 'Market' and
'Ship-wright' Streets marked the more plebeian quarter of town near the
docks.

Several public buildings were erected within Nicholson's term of office
(1693–9). Earliest was the small Council Chamber, erected to house the

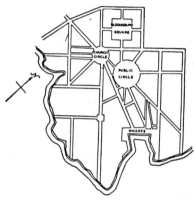

318. Plan of Annapolis, Md. (founded 1694) (Philip White, after Deering Davis)

Governor's Council and still standing within the shadow of the State
House. Probably built within the year of Annapolis' foundation, 1694–5,
it followed the cross plan used in the more elaborate seventeenth-century
Virginia farmhouses and in the Old State House at St. Mary's City, but
interior changes and paint on the old brick masonry have altered its orig-
inal appearance. The building was for a time used as a provincial courthouse, and from 1837 to 1903 as the State Treasury. Within the Church
Circle, old brick St. Anne's was erected at an early period, but it was entirely rebuilt in the Gothic style in the mid-nineteenth century. The first
State House was built in 1697, and King William's School (now Kentish
House) was begun in the preceding year. The school was incorporated in
St. John's College when the latter was founded in 1784, and the original
building has been much remodeled. Thus even before 1700 Annapolis
presented a flourishing appearance, and a visitor in Nicholson's day
wrote:

Col. Nicholson has done his endeavor to make a town of the place. There are
about forty dwellings in it, seven or eight of which can afford a good lodging
and accommodations for strangers. There are also a State House and Free School,
built with brick, which make a great show among a parcel of wooden houses, and
the foundation of a church is laid, the only brick church in Maryland.[1]

Toward the middle of the century a more ambitious edifice was started. Governor Thomas Bladen, seeking to emulate the splendors of Williamsburg, prevailed upon the Assembly in 1742 to grant £4,000 for the building of a 'Dwelling House and other Conveniences for the Residence of the Governor of Maryland.' [2] Simon Duff, a Scotch builder, worked on the building for two years, completing 'the Brick Work and Joists two Stories High,' but the Assembly refused further funds for the extravagant enterprise, and for forty years it stood unfinished as 'Bladen's Folly.' When St. John's College was founded, after the Revolution, it acquired the edifice, completed a third story with hipped roof, and named it McDowell Hall. Extremely simple, the building barely avoided monotony by its projecting pavilion and pediment and the diminution of window sizes from 12 to 9 to 6 lights. If the projecting pavilion was indeed a part of the original structure of 1742–4, it was an early instance of this academic motive; only Rosewell (1726-30) and Sabine Hall (c.1730) in Virginia seem to have anticipated it. The porch was a later addition, and the interiors were entirely rebuilt after a fire in 1909 which destroyed all but the walls.

The first State House, rebuilt after a fire in 1706, soon became so completely dilapidated as to be 'an emblem of public poverty,' and the present State House was built in 1772, under the direction of one Joseph Clarke. It was a long two-story building, with central pavilion and hipped roof, much like the abortive Governor's Palace, but with a more richly detailed cornice, and arched door and flanking windows in the central pavilion. William Buckland was working in Annapolis at the time, and there is written evidence to show that he contributed his talents to the beautiful Senate Chamber.[3] In this room was held the first meeting of the Continental Congress; here Washington tendered his resignation as Commander in Chief of the Continental Army in 1783; and here also the peace treaty with Great Britain was ratified by the new Congress in 1784. A ponderous wood-and-plaster dome was added in the latter year,[4] but later remodelings and a large nineteenth-century addition at the rear have impaired the colonial character of the building.

Annapolis was, like Williamsburg, the center of a brilliant social life, and many diversions enlivened the 'season' from November through April when the plantation owners came to enjoy their fine town houses and the life of the capital. There is record of the building of at least three theaters (in 1752, 1760, and 1771), the first of which was one of the earliest in the colonies. An English visitor reported his pleasure and surprise at 'finding performers in this country equal at least to those . . . at home.' [5] Dancing was also a favorite entertainment, and the public Ball Room built on Duke of Gloucester Street in 1764, from the proceeds of a lottery, provided not only a fine dance floor but also a card room and supper room.

Horse racing was a favorite sport, and the Jockey Club numbered many principal gentlemen of this and . . . adjacent provinces,' according to the *Maryland Gazette*. During the race meets in spring and fall, courts were adjourned and schools dismissed in order that everyone might enjoy a full week of festivities. Washington frequently rode over from Mount Vernon in his post chaise with four horses and a retinue of servants, and when he went to town he evidently had a gay week. His accounts reveal expenditures for tickets to 'the play' and 'the Ball,' £25 for claret, £50 for a horse, £4/4 for a new hat for Miss Custis, as well as a scrupulous entry of £13 'won at cards.'

Annapolis boasts an exceptional number of fine Georgian town houses. Originally they were surrounded with large grounds, extending in many cases from the street to the shore of river or bay, and their gardens included formally planted terraces descending to the water, orchards of fruit trees, flower and vegetable gardens, as well as stables and slaves'

319. Montpelier, Prince George's County, Md., c.1751, wings added c.1770 (*Great Georgian Houses,* 1)

quarters. Most of the finest surviving examples date from the decade immediately prior to the Revolution, and it is necessary to explore the county plantations to see some of the better Maryland houses of the mid-eighteenth century.

County houses and manor houses

Scattered along Maryland's three-thousand mile coastline on Chesapeake Bay, in Anne Arundel, Calvert, Queen Anne's, Talbot, and other counties are many plantation houses of the eighteenth century. Some were merely large farms; others were true feudal manors, boasting the rights and privileges of manorial lords, like the great estates up the Hudson. Forman, in his *Early Manor Houses and Plantation Houses of Maryland,* estimates that as many as 5000 pre-Revolutionary houses survive. Among the finest and most interesting are three mansions of the mid-century: Montpelier, in Prince George's County, and Tulip Hill and Whitehall, both in Anne Arundel County.

Montpelier was built about 1751 for Nicholas Snowden. The original central block (fig. 319) has a fine early Georgian dignity: raised on an English basement and with a steep hipped roof rising to a sharp ridge, it resembles Westover and Carter's Grove in Virginia. But the façade is broken by a projecting pavilion and pediment, more in the mid-Georgian manner of John Ariss's Virginia houses, and the front doorway is of a type we have not yet encountered: a half-round transom over the door rises through the broken horizontal cornice of an angular pediment. Flanking pilasters complete the enframement. Such arched doorways had been pictured in the English architectural books, but they were definitely a late Georgian preference in the colonies. The earliest instance of certain date is at Gunston Hall, Virginia (1755–8), and, although others followed in the late 1750's,* this, if original, is a very early example.

The end wings and connecting passages which give Montpelier its impressive length were added about 1770 by Nicholas Snowden's son Thomas. The five-part composition was a late Georgian development,

320. Tulip Hill, Anne Arundel County, Md., c.1756 (Wayne Andrews)

and particularly so were the polygonal ends of the two wings. The latter motive had been published in English architectural books around 1750 but did not appear in the colonies until 1765.† As it was used in the Hammond House at Annapolis, on the eve of the Revolution, it has been assumed that William Buckland may have designed the wings at Montpelier; the interior detail gives some support to this hypothesis, but no documentary confirmation has been found.

Tulip Hill, in Anne Arundel County, was built by Samuel Galloway about 1756. Though the original front door has been removed and the slender-columned entrance portico may be a later addition, the central block of the house is typical of the finer Georgian mansions of the mid-century (fig. 320). Of interest is the somewhat experimental approach toward late Georgian formality: there is a central pediment, but no projecting pavilion beneath it. A round window and unusual decorative panels adorn the pediment. The roof is of the double-hipped type fre-

* In the Izard House at Charleston (before 1757), and a side doorway at Woodford, Philadelphia (after 1756).

† The rear wing of the Roger Morris (Jumel) House in New York was the earliest instance of certain date.

quently encountered in Southern Georgian houses, and the arched and vaulted chimneys are reminiscent of the more massive stacks at Stratford, Virginia. The main cornice is modillioned in front only. Over the rear door is an interesting cantilevered hood carried on boldly projecting carved consoles; plastered inside its arched head and adorned by curious crockets on its raking cornices, it suggests the Oriental flavor of Chinese Chippendale.

The plan and interior woodwork of Tulip Hill are typical of the mid-Georgian period. A wide front hall borrows light from the window to the

321. Whitehall, Anne Arundel County, 1764–5, south façade (Wayne Andrews)

right of the front door, but the stair hall at the rear is narrower and on axis; in it arises a beautiful carved walnut staircase, with scrolled step ends and handrail winding around an offset newel post at the bottom. Paneling on the wall echoes the contour of its gracefully curved ramps and easings. A visual separation between front and rear halls is achieved by an unusual double arch without a supporting post in the middle; the free-hanging impost of the arches is adorned by a lotus ornament and hanging candle light, not unlike the carved pendant in a similar position at Gunston Hall, Virginia, built at this same time. Though the pedimented end blocks and connecting passages greatly enhance the impressiveness of the five-part composition, they were not added until after the Revolution, probably about 1810.

Whitehall in Anne Arundel County is one of the most interesting and important houses of the eighteenth century. With its broad two-story mass and giant portico looking southward over the gardens and broad estuary of the Severn, the house is imposing in its present form (fig. 321). But abundant evidence of changes and additions since its first construction challenges speculation as to its original appearance. Was it initially two stories high? Was the giant portico — so rare a feature in Georgian archi-

tecture — a part of the original house? Only recently, through the discovery of old drawings and specifications in a dusty roll in the attic, has
it become possible to reconstruct its history, and, though some details
must remain conjectural, it now appears that Whitehall is of salient importance in the history of American architecture.[6]

The house was built for Governor Horatio Sharpe on a thousand-acre
estate. The central block, begun in the fall of 1764 and doubtless completed the following year, was at first only a pavilion used by the Governor as a retreat and for the entertainment of guests making excursions
down the river from Annapolis. In the basement were the Governor's
office and dining room, and cellars under the central hall. On the main

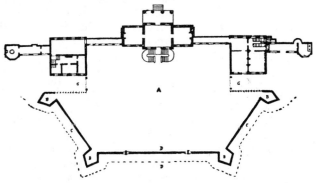

322. Original plan for Whitehall (courtesy Charles Scarlett, Jr.)

floor (see plan traced from original drawing, fig. 322) were a Great Hall,
fronted on the south by a portico of four columns, and two withdrawing
rooms. The central room was 20 feet in height, its coved ceiling actually
projecting upward into the roof space. The smaller parlors had lower
ceilings, and the one to the west was connected by a small circular stairway to the office below it. Bedrooms were located at first in an earlier
plantation house and later in the west wing, while a kitchen wing was
added at the east.

It is not known when these wings, with the connecting passageways to
the central block, were built, but that they were a part of the original
plan is shown by the drawing entitled ' A general plan of the House and
Offices, with a semi-octagon fortification with bastions, formed by a Ha'a,
vid. plans etc.' Though the drawing is torn through the ' A ' in the court
and the lower half lost, it has been possible to reconstruct from the specifications the probable layout of the courtyard terrace, facing the park,
with its sunken ditch or haha and its projecting bastions.

This strung-out plan, based on Palladio's ' Roman Country House '
type, was shown in plates of Robert Morris's *Select Architecture*, published in London in 1757 and used in a group of Virginia houses of the
1760's.* As we have seen at Brandon, the type was both convenient and

* Chatham, Brandon, Battersea, Belle Isle, the Semple House, and Monticello. See
Waterman, *Mansions of Virginia*, pp. 360–98.

architecturally interesting. None of the Virginia houses, however, boasted a two-story salon or a giant portico.

The portico itself is superbly executed. The opulent Corinthian columns, resting on bases of sandstone and molded brick, are made of white-cedar logs with a five-inch hole bored from end to end, presumably to prevent splitting. Every detail of the richly carved entablature follows the pattern of a Corinthian model shown in Plate XVIII of *The Modern Builder's Assistant,* by Halfpenny, Morris, and Lightoler.[7] The interiors of the main rooms are extraordinarily rich in carved decoration. Modillions, egg-and-dart ornament, window casings with lateral consoles, and especially the four satyr-like masks at the corners of the great coved ceiling, all bear a strong resemblance to similar details at Honington Hall, England, and the Chase and Hammond Houses at Annapolis.

All three of these houses have been associated with William Buckland, and the finding at Whitehall of several fragments of drawings for ornamental details which seem to be by his hand leaves little doubt that Buckland did the interior trim. It is much less certain, however, that he was the original architect. When Whitehall was planned, Buckland was residing in Richmond County, Virginia. The inventory of his library makes no mention of either of the books on which the plan and the giant portico appear to have been based, and nothing he did before or after bears any similarity to the general scheme of Whitehall. Presumably he moved to Annapolis about 1770, and he died there a decade after the house was started. Since a document cited below indicates that Whitehall was not fully completed late in 1769, it seems reasonable to assume that Buckland completed the decorating after his arrival at Annapolis. The only clue to the identity of the original architect is that the name of one Joseph Horatio Anderson, Architect, appears in the plantation accounts for the year 1773 — but this was nine years after the house was started, and he may have been working on additions to the estate.

Of particular interest are the extensions shown at the extreme ends of Whitehall. That at the east was a well house, connected by a semi-underground passage to the kitchen; that at the west was a water closet with a passage to the bedroom wing. The latter was of the ' water seal ' type, fed by a cistern, with a pair of marble seal troughs, a wooden seat pierced by two holes, and a cesspool below; this convenience was demolished about 1793, but the seal troughs are extant. So far as is known today, it was the only interior water closet of colonial times in America, but the type undoubtedly came from England. Celia Fiennes's travel diary of the late seventeenth century describes the Prince of Wales' dressing room in Windsor Castle as equipped with ' a seate of Easement of Marble wth sluices of water to wash all down.' [8]

Construction of the outbuildings and gardens of the estate was probably not completed for some time. After Governor Sharpe's retirement in 1769 a visitor to Whitehall wrote to a friend in England on October first of that year:

Colonel Sharpe, the late governor, possesses a most delightful retirement . . . his house is on a large scale, the design is excellent, the apartments well fitted up and perfectly convenient. The adjacent grounds are so judiciously disposed that utility and taste are everywhere united; and when the worthy owner has completed his extensive plan, Whitehall will be one of the most desirable situations in this, or in any of the neighboring provinces.[9]

But as early as 1773 Sharpe revisited England, never to return. Upon his death in London in 1790 he willed Whitehall to his one-time secretary and friend, John Ridout. It is apparent that the Ridouts altered the house about 1793, and at this time the second story was added to the cen-

323. Whitehall as it originally appeared, with temple-form central block. Conjectural restoration by Waterman, rendered by R. E. Collins (Thomas T. Waterman, *The Dwellings of Colonial America*, University of North Carolina Press)

tral block. Bedrooms were built over the two drawing rooms, staircases to reach them were built in added end pieces with hipped roofs, and the present gabled roof was constructed over the whole central block. The brick masonry of the façades clearly indicates how the walls were heightened. The profile of the new main cornice was different from the old one on the giant portico, and the levels of the two do not quite match; it was this circumstance which for many years led to the supposition that the giant portico had been added at a still later date.

But study of the attic of the house reveals that underneath the present roof may be found, nearly intact, an older roof covered by slates, running from front to back and lined up with the slope of the front pediment. This seems conclusive evidence that the giant portico of Whitehall was indeed a part of the original house built in 1764–5. As such, it is a milestone in American architectural history, for it was the first built on a house and was paralleled by only one other example — that of the Roger Morris House in New York, built a year later — in American domestic architecture before the Revolution. But the first giant portico on any type of building in the American colonies was that of the Redwood Library in Newport, as will be seen in the following chapter.

Waterman made a restoration of the original appearance of Whitehall, showing the portico and one-story wings (fig. 323). Fragments of a great seal of the province have been found, and it is likely that this emblem adorned the pediment in the days of Governor Sharpe's administration. It is probable that the wings were terminated by hipped roofs, as at Brandon, rather than by pedimented gables, and that a balustrade surrounded the eaves, but otherwise the drawing conveys a good impression of the original appearance of America's first temple-form dwelling.

The architecture of William Buckland

At Annapolis in the six years 1768–74 were built six houses of unusual architectural sophistication. Three were of the five-part type, rarely found in the colonies before the Revolution, and all were graced by lavish interior detail. One of the six, the Hammond House, can quite certainly be credited to William Buckland. It is perhaps natural that all of the others should be associated with his name, yet attribution of these to Buckland on the basis of style raises many questions. There is an almost complete dearth of reliable documentary evidence concerning Buckland's Annapolis work — indeed the work of no other colonial architect of such apparent importance is so uncertainly known. There is need for further research on his life and work.*

William Buckland was born at Oxford, England, on 14 August 1734. At the age of thirteen he was apprenticed to his uncle James Buckland in London. The uncle was not only a master joiner but proprietor of a bookstore in Paternoster Row that specialized in architectural books, and these undoubtedly played an important part in Buckland's professional training. He possessed Thomas Chippendale's *The Gentleman and Cabinet Maker's Directory* and is believed to have made furniture, though no surviving examples are known. Chippendale's undoubted influence on Buckland is attested by the beautiful Chinese Chippendale room at Gunston Hall, as well as by a certain playful eclecticism of taste. It seems very probable that he worked on the remodeling of Honington Hall, 22 miles from Oxford, just before 1750, for innumerable details of its lavish interior are reflected in Maryland houses attributed to Buckland.

Buckland was brought to Virginia by Thompson Mason in 1755, and was indentured for four years to serve as a carpenter and joiner in the building of George Mason's Gunston Hall in Fairfax County. On its completion in 1758, Mason endorsed the indenture paper with a statement that Buckland had done all the carving and joining in the house. It is perhaps significant that he was not mentioned as the architect. Of Buckland's other work in Virginia we know very little. After completing Gunston Hall he moved, in 1762, to the vicinity of Mount Airy in Richmond

---

* The late R. T. H. Halsey made a considerable study of Buckland, but it was not published before his death. Deering Davis has made use of this, and other sources of information, in his essay on Buckland, the most complete account published to date, in *Annapolis Houses* (1947).

County. Woodwork at Pohick Church and at Mount Airy, which was designed by John Ariss, has been ascribed to Buckland on the basis of style, and documents reveal that he did a mantelpiece for Robert Carter at Nomini Hall and a jail in Richmond County. He is also documented as serving on juries, marrying one Mary Moore, advertising for several runaway indentured carvers or joiners, and owning three horses. These items suggest that he operated a fairly large workshop and attained a reasonable affluence.

It has been assumed that Buckland moved to Annapolis about 1770 (no certain date is documented), that he designed several of the city's fine houses, and that he died there in 1774.[10] There is written evidence that he worked on the Senate Chamber in the State House, but no other Maryland documents have been found — which seems strange considering his apparent importance and alleged activity. Did he actually reside at Annapolis, or did he merely accept commissions there and make visits from Virginia? Was he really an architect, or did he run a sort of interior-decorating workshop? Though he apparently designed the Hammond House, is it safe to assume that similar decorations in other houses indicate his authorship, or were they products of other local craftsmen using the same bookish sources as did Buckland? There seems to be no answer to these questions at present, and the puzzle is not made easier by the diversity of architectural styles in the houses attributed to him.

Of his work at Gunston Hall in Virginia, however, there can be no doubt. The plan and exterior were probably designed by the owner, George Mason. It is a modest story-and-a-half brick house of almost seventeenth-century simplicity, with only angle quoins and a modillioned cornice to betray Georgian aspirations. It has, however, two elaborate projecting porches. One has four columns and a central arch, reminiscent of the Palladian motive; the other is a demi-octagon quite like a similar porch at Honington Hall.

We have George Mason's statement that Buckland did all the carving and joining of the interiors. They are extraordinarily rich. The central hall, with a curious double arch, is quietest, while the Chinese Chippendale room (the only original one of its type in Virginia) is graceful and somewhat fantastic with its scalloped reliefs and crestings (fig. 324). The Palladian drawing room, however, suffers from an elephantine profligacy (fig. 325). Buckland, who was only in his early twenties, wielded his undoubted skill as a woodcarver with uncritical abandon. Doors and windows are framed by pilasters and entablatures of extravagant weight; friezes and moldings are carved with lavish ornament; the highly enriched cornice is too large; the broken pediments of the corner cupboards are bizarre pretensions indeed. Only the natural pine sheathing of the walls, probably intended for toile or damask covering, gives rest to the eye.

In over-scaling and over-ornamenting his details, Buckland was not decorating a room but was making a museum of decorations. It would be easy to guess that he was trained as a joiner rather than as an architect; he saw details rather than totalities. And with a mixture of naïve respect for English models and technical virtuosity in emulating them, he fell

324. The Chinese Chippendale room at Gunston Hall, Fairfax County, Va., 1755-8, by William Buckland (Metropolitan Engraving)

325. The Palladian room at Gunston Hall, by William Buckland (Alfred Eisenstaedt photo, courtesy Life © Time, Inc.)

victim to that disintegration which so often results when interior deco-
rators attempt to make use of architectural vocabularies whose original
integrities they fail to perceive. The youthful Samuel McIntire of Salem
was another example of the woodcarver-turned-architect whose lavish detail became architecturally acceptable only from the accidents of its more
fragile post-Revolutionary style and the strong architectonic influence exerted on him by the great Bulfinch. The extreme contrast between this

326. Brice House, Annapolis, Md., *c.*1740? (Kosti Ruohomaa photo from Black Star,
© Time, Inc.)

ornate room and the fine reserve of Carter's Grove, completed only a few
years before, illustrates the damage that English Palladianism could do
when transported to the colonies.

Deering Davis attributes to Buckland, on the basis of ' very positive de-
ductive and circumstantial evidence,' the following Annapolis houses: the
Scott House (*c.*1768), the Chase House (1769–74), the Ridout and Paca
Houses (both *c.*1770), and the Brice House. He adds to Buckland's possible *œuvre* the wings at Montpelier, Whitehall, both already discussed,
and the octagonal wings of Ogle Hall and the Governor's House. Space
does not permit discussion of all these houses; it is suggested, however,
that attribution of the Scott, Ridout, and Paca Houses to Buckland be
viewed with caution until further evidence is forthcoming. The three
finest, architecturally, are the Brice House, Chase House, and, of course,
the Hammond House. Not even these afford a history of unmixed cer-
tainties.

The Brice House is the most impressive of the three (fig. 326). It has been traditionally dated *c.*1740, Thomas Jennings having given it to his daughter Juliana upon her marriage in 1742* to Colonel James Brice, Acting Governor.[11] But perhaps this first house was torn down and replaced by a second one in the early 1770's; an advertisement of 1773 refers to 'Mr. James Brice's new house' on East Street, and Buckland is

327. Living-room chimneypiece, Brice House (HABS)

known to have worked on it, for a bill he left at his death was sent to Mr. Brice by the estate.

But it seems unlikely that Buckland could have designed this fine and impressive exterior. The boldness and simplicity of the masses, the plain walls in a sturdy all-header bond of large bricks, the steep roof, the wide, thin chimneys rising high above the roof, the domination of the arrogant central mass over the side wings and passages — all reveal the hand of an unlettered but instinctive master builder, a man who knew nothing of Palladian pavilions and classic pediments but who had a sure sense for impressive form. No pediment mars the pure rectangle of the door, nor cornices the simple windows whose bold flush woodwork maintains a wall plane unbroken except by a telling belt course. And yet instinctively he felt the need for some enrichment, and in the central window over the door and in a deep wood cornice he has carved an array of naïve detail the like of which will not be seen in any Palladian source book; it is all

* Scarborough dates the marriage 1745. See p. 177.

'incorrect' but completely charming. This is one of the most truly imposing buildings in all Georgian architecture. Its quality is much more early than late Georgian, and one wonders whether it was not built about 1740 and its interior trim added later.

Certainly most of the interior details are 'late' in character. Walls are plastered, not paneled in wood, though the plaster is molded in the form of panels. The carved wood fireplace of the living room (fig. 327), with its exceptionally ornate lateral consoles flanking the opening, its ornamented frieze and eared overmantel panel, comes straight from the plates

328, 329. Chase House, Annapolis, 1769–71. Exterior and entrance hall (HABS)

of Swan's *British Architect,* and the elaborate plaster cornices, rich with oak leaves, dentils, and modillions, are of a Buckland stamp. The stairway, too, of Santo Domingo mahogany, has scrolled step ends and a band of Greek fret ornament such as are found in the Hammond House. We may never know who designed the fine exterior; whoever it was, he was an architect in his blood and bones. The house is today maintained by St. John's College for faculty residences.

The Chase House (fig. 328) reveals all the sophistication which the Brice House lacks, though even here we have no positive knowledge that Buckland was the architect. The house was begun in 1769 by Samuel Chase, one of the signers of the Declaration, but he sold it in July 1771 to Colonel Edward Lloyd IV for nearly £3,000, including all 'buildings, improvements, waters, easements, privileges, commodities and advantages whatsoever.' [12] Since Chase had purchased the land for only £100, the price paid suggests that the house must have been nearly complete on transfer of the property, though Davis believes it was only partly finished and was completed in 1774: 'credit for its unusual and magnificent in-

terior should go to Mr. Lloyd who presumably employed Buckland to
add the superb finishing touches which make the mansion so outstanding.' [13]

It is the only three-story house in Annapolis built before the Revolution, and its every detail reveals an effort for the ultimate in magnificence.
The lofty walls, 18 inches thick, are adorned by belt courses and enriched
cornice, and the axial line emphasized by the tall, narrow, projecting
pavilion with its doorway, arched window on the third story, and crowning pediment. The doorway deserves particular attention. The half-moon
transom with its fan of slender muntins was a late Georgian motive favored by Buckland in Gunston Hall and the Hammond House, but here

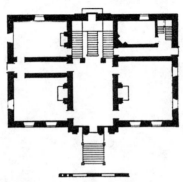

330. Plan of the Chase House (courtesy Fiske Kimball)

the composition is enlarged to include flanking windows lighting the hall.
This expanded doorway motive was rarely used before the Revolution:
it occurs in the Schuyler House at Albany (1761–2) and the William
Gibbes House at Charleston, built on the eve of the Revolution, but in
few other Georgian houses.

The plan (fig. 330) is of unusual monumentality, dominated by an immense central hall, about 16 by 40 feet. The rear portion of this (fig. 329)
is screened from the front by a pair of free-standing Ionic columns bearing a full entablature; the use of free-standing columns is paralleled elsewhere in Georgian house interiors only at Cliveden in Germantown. The
stair rises to a wide landing, lighted by an immense Palladian window,
and continues in parallel flights to the second floor. In these upper flights,
it can be seen that the usual supporting string pieces have been omitted,
and the scrolled step ends are echoed in the molded profile of the soffit
across the full width of the stairway. This was a *tour de force* of construction, and in recent years supporting posts have been inserted to reinforce
the sagging flights. The stair is also unusual in the simplicity of its rail:
plain uncarved spindles supplant the twisted balusters of early Georgian,
and even newel posts are here omitted — for the first time — as the rail
curves around the landing in an uninterrupted sweep.

The upper hall also reveals the trend, on the eve of the Revolution,
toward an austere classical simplicity: pictorial wallpaper is supplanted

by plain painted plaster (as at Monticello), and the arched niches of the upper hall frame classical pieces of imported European statuary. The ceiling of the hall is of molded plaster, but the central rococo motive is framed by a severe circle, and the thin delicacy of the relief heralds the light Adam style of the postwar era. The ceiling of the parlor, to the left of the hall, has an even more geometric composition of shallow octagons.

The dining room to the right of the hall is the richest room in the

331. Hammond House, Annapolis, 1773-4, by William Buckland (Wayne Andrews)

house. Entered by mahogany doors with wrought-silver handles, it is dominated by an imported Italian marble mantelpiece, and every detail is rich with ornament. Cornice, window frames, door casings and chair rail overflow with carving. Windows are adorned by rope ornament, foliage, bead-and-reel, and the recessed panels underneath them are festooned with ribbons and clusters of roses and grapes. Lateral consoles adorn the sides, as at Whitehall, and the shutters are adorned by octagons and rosettes. On the whole, the room is too rich: like the Palladian room at Gunston Hall, it is a somewhat meretricious display of the decorator's art, though here the large and ornate details are more successfully accommodated because of the sheer size of the room.

The Hammond House, last of the fine Georgian houses of Annapolis, may be attributed to William Buckland with reasonable certainty, for Charles Willson Peale's portrait of Buckland shows him with a paper bearing the plan and elevation of the house. The portrait was begun in

1773, and presumably the house was started in that year and completed in 1774, the year of Buckland's death. It was built by Matthias Hammond, an elegant young lawyer who derived a large income from his fifty-four tobacco plantations and who never sallied forth without donning his lace cuffs and rapier. Legend has it that he built the house for a Philadelphia fiancée who, on its completion, eloped with another man.

The exterior (fig. 331) is more modest than that of the three-story

332. Doorway of the Hammond House (HABS)

Chase House across the street, but it achieves a more interesting effect through its five-part composition. The polygonal bays of the end wings, we have already seen, were extremely rare before the Revolution. The wing at the left, shut off from the main house, was used by Hammond as a law office, while kitchen and service rooms were located in the right wing. The central block, laid up in Flemish bond with rubbed brick dressings in window lintels and belt course, has the low-pitch hipped roof and central pavilion favored in the late Georgian period. The central window in the second story is enriched, and an unusually elaborate bull's eye window marks the pediment.

The doorway (fig. 332) is one of the most admired in Georgian architecture. Of the arched fanlight type, it is unusually rich with its carved ornament of festooned roses, ribboned laurel on the pulvinated frieze, and other classical details. The two chief rooms, architecturally, are the large dining room (fig. 333) on the first floor and the ball room over it. The three windows of the dining room overlook the garden. They are uniformly treated — as are the three doors on other sides of the room — with rich enframements. The shutters are carved with octagons bearing rosettes, alternating with plain elongated octagons, a motive perhaps suggested by Honington Hall and used elsewhere by Buckland. These windows illustrate his passion for academic symmetry. The right-hand one, though treated inside like the others, can be raised and its dado panels hinged open to serve as a door. Outside it is indeed treated like a door, being on the central axis of the house and serving as the focus of the rear

333. Corner of the dining room, Hammond House (J. H. Schaefer and Son)

pavilion with its four giant pilasters in brick and its rich pediment; the
other windows, however, are bricked up to sill level.

Despite its rich decoration, the dining room of the Hammond House
has an over-all simplicity. The plain plastered walls and ceiling afford
the necessary foil to the elaborate detail, and the ornament is far more
successfully scaled to the size of the room (which is large and has a high
ceiling) than in any other work attributed to Buckland. Here at last, it
seems, he merits the appellation of 'architect' rather than 'decorator,'
and it is a pity that his death at the early age of 40 interrupted the de-

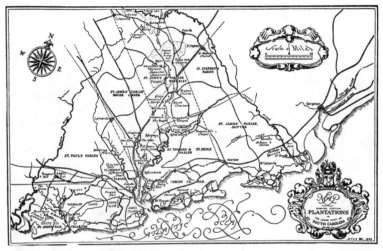

334. Map of the South Carolina Low Country (courtesy Carolina Art Association)

velopment of a remarkably gifted talent just as it reached maturity. The
house, which was occupied by the Harwood family in the last half of the
nineteenth century, is now restored and maintained as a public monument by the Hammond-Harwood House Association.

South Carolina in the eighteenth century

By the dawn of the eighteenth century South Carolina was ready to
enter its great era of plantation building. The developing rice trade
brought undreamed-of wealth to a rising aristocracy of planters, and
merchants profited greatly from the export of meat, lumber, tar, and
deerskins to the West Indies. In a short generation Charleston had grown
to a population of 2000, and plantations such as Middleburg and Mulberry had carried the area of settlement 30 miles inland, up the east and
west branches of the Ashley River (see map, fig. 334). Rivers and creeks
formed the natural avenues of transportation to the interior, for roads
were difficult to build across the mucky swamps and deep river marshes.
After the temporary setback of the Yemassee Indian War in 1715, settlement proceeded farther inland. Large numbers of Scotch-Irish, Swiss, and
German settlers pushed the frontier into the Piedmont and southward

through Georgia nearly to Spanish Florida. South Carolina became a Crown colony in 1719, and the generation from 1720 to 1740 was the first Augustan Age of the South Carolina plantations. An interlude of depression came at the time of the intercolonial wars of the mid-century, but by 1760 the indigo crop was established, and it brought new wealth and another great era of building, which lasted until the Revolution.

335. Drayton Hall, S.C., 1738–42, west façade (Frances Benjamin Johnston)

The river plantations

The ravages of two wars, fires, hurricanes, earthquakes, and economic decline have played havoc with the once magnificent houses that faced the rivers, but within the last generation many have been bought by wealthy northerners and their moldering ruins restored. Such, for example, has been the history of Fenwick Hall, on the Stono River. One of the finest Georgian mansions, built by John Fenwick in 1730, the house received a large addition at the north end, about 1787, which reveals the octagonal ends popularized by Jefferson and Buckland just before the Revolution. In 1928 this magnificent house was a seemingly hopeless ruin, but since that day it has been purchased and splendidly restored.

More remarkable architecturally is Drayton Hall, outstanding surviving example of South Carolina's plantation houses (fig. 335). It must have been built between 1738 and 1742, for John Drayton, member of the King's Council, bought the land on the Ashley River, about ten miles from town, in 1738, and four years later a son, William Henry Drayton, was born in the house. The early date seems remarkable, for Drayton Hall is far in advance, architecturally, of contemporary great houses in Virginia. The west or 'land' façade is dominated by a projecting two-

336. East façade of Drayton Hall (Samuel G. Stoney, *Plantations of the Carolina Low Country*, Carolina Art Association)

story portico, with superposed Doric and Ionic orders. This feature, which stemmed directly from Palladio, was apparently not employed elsewhere in the colonies until the 1750's.* The plan, too, has a monumentality not found elsewhere at this early period (fig. 337). As in Palladio's own

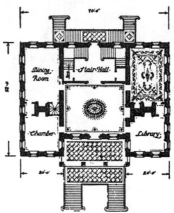

337. Plan of main floor, Drayton Hall (*Great Georgian Houses,* I)

scheme, the projecting portico fronts a recessed central bay, permitting a sheltered porch to the main entrance and above it a balcony for the second floor drawing room. The high basement and parallel flights of steps enhance the dignity of this impressive façade.

The east or 'river' façade (fig. 336) lacks a projecting portico, or even

---

* Palladio, Book II, Plate 61 (see fig. 309). Two-story porticoes were used in the Capitol at Williamsburg (1751-3), the Miles Brewton House, Charleston (1765-9), Shirley, Virginia (c.1769), and Monticello (1771-2).

a pavilion, but it has a classic pediment to emphasize the main axis. The
roof is of the double-hipped type frequently found in Southern Georgian
houses. The entrance door and three windows above it are framed by
pilasters and pediments, executed like the front portico in finely carved
Portland stone imported from England. From England, too, came the motive of the double flight of steps meeting at the main entrance; a motive
echoed, as one passes through the door, by the magnificent stairs in the
great hall (fig. 338). Nothing like this had yet been seen in the colonies;

338. Stair hall, Drayton Hall (Frances Benjamin Johnston)

it calls to mind the entrance hall of Sir Roger Pratt's Coleshill, in England, and the whole academic tradition of Inigo Jones.

The entrance hall, with its majestic dimensions, full-paneled walls, and
ornamented ceiling, also recalls Inigo Jones, for the mantelpiece at one
end came from a plate in William Kent's *Designs of Inigo Jones,* and the
eight fluted pilasters bearing an entablature with triglyphs and rosetted
metopes reflect the English Palladian revival in full swing when this house
was built. Other rooms are almost equally fine: the library and small
drawing room adjacent to it, with richly plastered ceiling; the dining
room and downstairs chamber; the great drawing room and four chambers on the second floor. All have full-paneled walls, rich cornices, and
elaborate fireplaces — though two of the latter were replaced in 1800 by
mantels in the then-popular Adam style. Service quarters are in the high
basement; there were originally two symmetrically placed dependencies,
but only the foundations of these remain today.

The grandeur of the plan, with its monumental effects and excellent circulation between rooms and porches, and the advanced character of the architectural details point to something more than an amateur designer using architectural books; they suggest a professional architect, perhaps one of English training. But as to who he may have been there is no hint.

Hampton, on Wambaw Creek near the Santee, though less imposing

339. South façade of Hampton, S.C. (Wayne Andrews)

than Drayton Hall, is of interest because of its step-by-step growth, very similar to that of Mount Vernon. In the plan and elevation (fig. 339) can be read the history of the house. Originally it was a small four-room and central-hall structure, built by the Huguenot Noë Serré in 1735. After 1757, when Daniel Horry came into possession of the house by marriage, he added extensions to both ends, much as Washington did twenty years later at Mount Vernon. One end contained a large two-story ball room, the other a lofty bedchamber. Rather than leave the second-story wall of these extensions blank, Horry inserted false windows (in the guise of closed shutters paneled like those below), a device similar to Mount Vernon's false windows. Obviously it would have been better, architecturally, to use large Palladian windows, as did Governor Shirley at Roxbury, Massachusetts, a decade earlier, to express on the exterior a lofty interior space. The shutters of the great chamber (visible at the left end of the façade) had primitive slat blinds, a device previously used in Charleston.

But the long façade must have seemed rather featureless, and after the Revolution Horry's descendants added a six-column giant portico and pediment. According to tradition the first guest to cross its red-tiled floor, in 1791, was George Washington; if true, he must have felt quite at home in Hampton. He had completed his great East Portico, overlooking the Potomac, only five years before. This giant portico, one of the earliest in American domestic architecture, is of particular interest because it reveals the slender columns, the paterae and dainty flutings of the Adam style of the Federal era. Its prototype was probably the great portico of David Garrick's villa at Hampton, England, designed by Robert Adam himself.

Nationally famous for its beautiful gardens is Middleton Place on the Ashley, a dozen miles above Charleston. The present buildings are not in the Georgian style. The original ones, begun in 1755 by John Williams, and later extended by his son-in-law Henry Middleton, were burned during the Civil War. One flanker was rebuilt in 1868, with anachronistic Flemish gables, and the other more recent structures have been built to match it. But the gardens, developed by the Middleton family for the most part during post-Revolutionary days, are the finest in South Carolina. Here, it is said, Louis XVI's botanist André Michaux first introduced *Camellia japonica*. Other exotics such as azaleas, poinsettias, and gardenias mingle with a profusion of oleanders and myrtles, wild roses and magnolias, and the great live oaks festooned with Spanish moss endow the fine formalities of geometric walks and terraced flower beds with a romantic picturesqueness.

But the Revolution brought an end to the first Golden Age of the plantations. Great areas had been fought over or despoiled, herds of cattle and horses dispersed, and many mansions destroyed. Moreover, the loss of some 25,000 Negro slaves to the British and the lifting of the royal bounty on indigo removed the economic bases by which they might have been rebuilt. For years the Carolina Low Country was blighted. But the invention of a rice-husking mill by Jonathan Lucas in 1790 and the development of tidal rice culture inaugurated a revival that was vastly augmented by the new crop of 'black seed' cotton planted on the sea islands. Tidal rice and sea-island cotton brought a new wave of prosperity after 1800, and for another half century the South Carolina plantations prospered — but under a different government and in the new styles of the Federal and Greek Revival periods.

Carolina churches

Scattered through the Carolina Low Country are ten or a dozen survivors of the many churches and tributary chapels of ease to which the plantation folk came from miles around in their dugout canoes, hollowed from giant cypresses and paddled along quiet rivers and creeks by slaves chanting ancient African songs. The churches are small, somewhat quaint in their architecture, battered by age, and among the most completely charming of all colonial buildings.

In the earliest days one parish — that of St. Philip's, Charleston — embraced the entire colony. But in 1706 the Church of England became the established church of South Carolina, and the Low Country was divided up into several parishes to serve the plantation people. There were also many Huguenot and Presbyterian congregations, and some Baptists, Quakers, and Sephardic Jews. But gradually the Anglican Church pre-

340. St. Andrew's Church, Ashley River, S.C., 1706 (Wayne Andrews)

vailed, especially among the Huguenots, and as the Presbyterian and Quaker meeting-houses were rather plain and flimsy structures, only the solidly built masonry structures of the Anglicans have endured to the present.

Oldest is St. Andrew's, along the lower Ashley River (fig. 340). Begun in 1706, the year the parish was established, the church at first was simply the rectangle which is now the nave, with stucco-covered brick walls and arched windows. In 1723 the addition of transepts and a choir brought it

341. St. James' Church, Goose Creek, S.C., 1711 (HABS)

to a cruciform plan. But lacking tower, spire, or indeed any ornament save the angle quoins, the building remained extremely simple. It was burned in 1764 but rebuilt within the original walls.

Little St. James' Church, on Goose Creek, was more richly adorned by the wealthy Barbadian planters who formed the colony's first aristocracy. The exterior (fig. 341) has the same one-story modesty as St. Andrew's; indeed it is nought but a rectangular box topped by a low-gabled roof whose corners, clipped off to form jerkin-heads, give it a snub-nosed com-

342. Interior of St. James' Church, Goose Creek (HABS)

pactness. But round-arch windows are framed by plaster architraves adorned with cherubs' heads as keystones, and the front door is quite elaborate: a frieze carried by flanking pilasters is adorned by triglyphs, and metope reliefs show flaming hearts. Above this an angular pediment bears a stucco relief of a pelican piercing her breast with her own beak to nourish her young. This was, of course, the medieval theme of the Eucharist; it was also the symbol of the Society for the Propagation of the Gospel, which had sent both money and clergymen hither from London.

The interior (fig. 342) has a High Church mood as one faces the raised pulpit, with its little spiral stair and suspended sounding board, for back of this is an enormous baroque reredos of painted plaster. Two pairs of Composite pilasters carry the broken ends of a heavily enriched scroll pediment, and between these ends are the Royal Arms, modeled in high relief and painted in full color. Turning back toward the entrance door one encounters an almost pathetic quaintness and simplicity. The stone-paved floor and box pews are neat and tidy, but the four columns and their engaged responds on the end walls, carrying planks cut to low arches, are obviously an attempt by some unlettered but earnest carpenter to achieve the effect of elliptically arched vaults over side-aisle gallery bays, such as may be seen in Boston's Old North Church or the Wren prototypes that inspired it. He even simulated blocks of entablature over the capitals (if such they may be called) and keystones for his arches. The rear gallery, which was provided for those unable to afford pews on the

343. St. Michael's Church, Charleston, S.C., 1752–61 (Carolina Art Association)

floor, appears almost an afterthought. Supported on dwarf columns with naïve Ionic capitals, it had to be 'jerried' over the front door for lack of headroom. But seldom in Georgian architecture have imperfections been so endearing, for they are of the childhood of the style. St. James', the first really Georgian church in the colonies, was built as early as 1711.

The immense advance in wealth and style during the next forty years is illustrated by St. Michael's, Charleston, one of the great Georgian churches of the colonies (fig. 343). The South Carolina Assembly authorized its erection in 1751, the cornerstone was laid on 17 February 1752, and the church was virtually completed by 1753, though the final dedication and distribution of the pews did not occur, for some unknown reason, until 1761. Reporting on the cornerstone ceremony, the *South-Carolina Gazette* stated, ' This Church will be built on the Plan of one of Mr. Gibson's Designs; and 'tis tho't, will exhibit a fine Piece of Architecture when compleated: The Steeple being designed much larger than that of St. Philip's, will have a fine Set of Bells.' [14]

The brick for the edifice was supplied by one Zachariah Villepontoux, renowned for the fine quality of his product; it is covered by a hard stucco. The façade is dominated by a Roman Doric portico reaching the full height of the two stories. This was the first giant portico built on a Georgian church in the colonies and calls to mind James Gibbs's St. Mar-

344. Interior of St. Michael's Church (Carolina Art Association)

tin's-in-the-Fields on Trafalgar Square. The idea, however, was not entirely new in the colonies: Peter Harrison had built a giant portico on the Redwood Library in Newport (1748–50) and had intended one for King's Chapel, Boston (1749–54), though the latter was not erected until later.

The spire of St. Michael's is unusually solid in its proportions. Rising on a square base (the lower part of which has been smoothed over), it consists of a series of three diminishing octagons adorned by various arched openings, pilasters, and cornices, and a terminal spire rising to a height of 185 feet. No baroque ' surprise ' offends its easy flight, nor does it have the sharp and brittle obelisks or bulging urns of Wren's nervous designs. The pattern is perhaps to be sought in Plate 14 of James Gibbs's *Book of Architecture,* though the design as a whole can be traced to no single source. The building was evidently designed by an architect sophisticated enough to be able to depart successfully from the book.

The interior (fig. 344) is rectangular except for a shallow projection at the end to house the semi-dome of the apse. A coved ceiling converges on all four sides to a lofty flat, bordered by a large band of Greek fret ornament and a modillioned cornice. Relatively low side galleries are carried by fluted columns with extravagant Ionic volutes and an appearance of being stunted, owing to their partial concealment by the pews. The conventional stenciled ornament in the half-dome was applied by a New York firm in 1905. After the tornado of 1938, the cedar woodwork was cleaned of its many layers of paint, waxed and polished, and the plaster pilasters of the apse were painted to match.[15]

The architect of St. Michael's remains unknown. For a time it was supposed that the builder Samuel Cardy (who received £8,000 for the completion of his work) had designed the building, making use of one of James Gibbs's published plans, the latter's name being misrendered by the *South-Carolina Gazette's* passage quoted above. Since no Charleston architect or builder of this period by the name of Gibson is known, the supposition has seemed plausible.[16] But evidence has now come to light that Samuel Cardy was definitely not the designer of the church. Bridenbaugh, in his recent book on Peter Harrison, suggests that Harrison may have been the architect; he had made frequent business trips to Charleston, was acquainted with some of its most prominent men, was an ardent Anglican, and had already had experience in designing Boston's most important church.[17] Though the interior of St. Michael's is unlike Harrison's other churches, he was an adaptable designer, and since certain exterior details seem to give stylistic support, it is quite possible that the attribution to Harrison may someday be confirmed.

It is natural that the churches and chapels of the plantation parishes should have followed, with diminished glory, the example set by so fashionable an edifice as St. Michael's. Indeed Prince William's Church at Sheldon, built in 1753, must have been quite impressive. But it stood in the way of both British and Union armies in 1779 and 1865, and nothing is left of it but a vine-covered skeleton of brick walls, whose lofty arches and engaged columns have a ghostly grandeur.

Little Pompion Hill Chapel, however, still stands pert and neat. It was built in 1763 on ' Punkin' Hill,' and wealthy Gabriel Manigault subscribed £50. Zachariah Villepontoux provided the brick — at least his initials are carved on the north and south doors. The fine red and white exterior is compact and well ordered (fig. 345). Jerkin-head roof, arched windows with solid woodwork and paneled shutters, and heavy entablature all contribute to an unusually vigorous effect. At one end a shallow projection houses a small chancel below a Palladian window; at the other a vestry opens near the steps to the pulpit. Doors enter at the middle of both sides.

The interior (fig. 346) is one of the most thoroughly charming of all the small country parish churches. The herringbone brick floor has crossaisles of red tiles, for which Gabriel Manigault contributed an extra £10. The floor is raised a step at one end, and the red-cedar pulpit is styled after that of St. Michael's. The arrangement of pulpit at one end and chancel at the other must have kept the minister busy as he walked back and forth between the neat rows of benches, their end pieces so cheerfully scrolled — those at the far side painted white, those near the chancel painted light brown, to distinguish the occupants for whom they were reserved. Embracing all are the white plastered walls, the coved ceiling rising to a flat panel, and the pleasant woodwork of the windows and doors. Cool and serene, this little chapel is a miniature masterpiece.

St. James' Church, Santee, was originally very similar to Pompion Hill

345. Pompion Hill Chapel, S.C., 1763 (Frances Benjamin Johnston)

Chapel in its interior arrangements, but these have been altered since its construction in 1768. The exterior, however, has a new impressiveness (fig. 347). The hipped-roof body of the church is preceded, both front and back, by classic porticoes. A provincial reflection of St. Michael's, Charleston, these of course lack the full vocabulary of Roman Doric details but are nonetheless remarkably complete. The brick columns have molded bases and capitals, and the shafts, built up in perfect circles, display both diminution and entasis — 'taper' and 'swelling,' to put it in non-technical terms. The rear portico has been walled in between the columns to form a vestry.

Many of these backwoods churches suffered during the Revolution — Biggin Church, for example, was used by the British as a munitions depot and was burned in 1781 — and others were destroyed by forest fires or simply allowed to decay. Disestablishment of the Anglican Church after the war meant loss of financial support, and eventually, of parishioners. And as in Virginia, there was never again a period of comparable architectural excellence in small rural churches.

Urban Charleston

Charleston has always been a center of fine architecture. No other large American city possesses so many first-rate buildings representing every major style over a period of two and a half centuries. Fourth among

346. Interior of Pompion Hill Chapel (Frances Benjamin Johnston)

American colonial cities,* it may well claim today to be the first, architecturally.

Founded in 1670, the city was moved to its present location at the confluence of the Ashley and Cooper Rivers in 1680. At this time it was laid out in a gridiron plan, the first American town in which an orderly laying out of streets preceded the erection of dwellings. This was in accordance with Lord Ashley's instructions to Sir John Yeamans to divide the town ' into regular streets, for be the buildings never so mean and thin at first, yet as the town increases in riches and people, the void places will be filled up and the buildings will grow more beautiful.' [18] By 1704 the town formed a trapezoid (fig. 348), guarded on all sides by fortifications, with wide streets dividing large and regularly formed blocks. There were four churches within the walls, a Quaker meeting-house outside, and

* In the mid-eighteenth century the rank in population was: (1) Boston, (2) Philadelphia, (3) New York, (4) Charleston.

several fine houses as well as many modest dwellings and a few shops and
warehouses.

Fires in 1698 and 1704 led the Assembly to stipulate that all chimneys
be constructed of stone or brick, and that wooden ones be forthwith
demolished. A disastrous hurricane in 1713 brought a ruling that houses

347. St. James' Church, Santee, S.C., 1768 (Wayne Andrews)

too should be built of brick, but it was impossible to enforce, and most
dwellings continued for a time to be built of mahogany and cypress,
though with an increasing number of red-tiled roofs. In November 1740,
Charleston suffered a conflagration that destroyed 334 dwellings and un-
counted shops and warehouses. This led to further action by the Assembly, requiring all new buildings to be made of brick or stone, and old

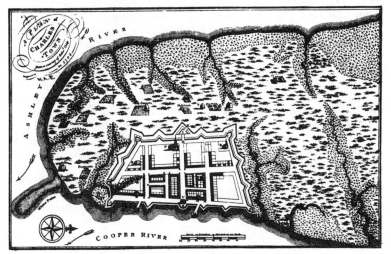

348. Plan of Charleston, in 1704 (New York Public Library)

frame ones to be torn down within five years. From this time on Charleston became a city of brick, stone, stucco, and tile.

Although Charleston had a flourishing commerce with the West Indies, her staple exports, of rice, deerskins, meat, and lumber, in exchange for molasses, sugar, rum, tortoise shell, and Negro slaves, were carried in Yankee bottoms. The town never developed docking or shipbuilding facilities to compare with those of the northern ports, and as late as the Revolution there were scarcely a dozen Carolina-built vessels in the transatlantic trade. After a storm in 1700 two landing places were built, but sizeable ships had to be unloaded by lighters. At this same time the Assembly ordered all owners of land fronting the Cooper River to build brick retaining walls — the beginning of Charleston's famous sea wall. Owners with two-story brick houses were permitted to abut their piazzas to the sea wall and build steps up to their doors.

Between 1700 and 1740 the city more than doubled in area and tripled in population. The first walls were demolished in 1717 as the town grew beyond them. The three main streets were extended westward straight across the peninsula to the Ashley; others grew to the south, and the whole peninsula began to fill up with hundreds of houses, warehouses, stables, and kitchens, all disposed on streets and alleys conforming more or less to the original gridiron plan.

Among the many churches were St. Michael's, already discussed, and fashionable St. Philip's, for which a new edifice, ' spacious and executed in very handsome taste,' was erected in 1727. This building was supplanted in 1835 by the present St. Philip's. Much of Charleston's public architecture was military, for work on watch houses, barracks, powder magazines, and the ever-expanding lines of fortifications went on throughout the eighteenth century. As the city advanced in wealth, it built one of the most elaborate of all Georgian civic buildings: the Exchange and Customs House on East Bay Street at the foot of Broad. This was built in 1767–71 by Peter and John Adam Horlbeck, two brothers of wide European travel and experience, on designs by an unknown architect. It was richly adorned, with a classic portico facing the Cooper River, ' Four Columns and Twenty-four Pilasters of the Ionick Order . . . An Ionick Modillion Entablature round the Building with four Venetian Windows and eight Columns of the Ionick Order,' according to the lengthy contract signed by the brothers Horlbeck on 1 December 1767.[19]

Robert Mills described the Exchange in 1826 as ' opened all round . . . with an arcade, forming a spacious, airy walk or 'change within for the merchants,' but unfortunately the arcades have been walled in, wings, portico, and cupola removed, the ' Ionick ' pilasters of the second story stripped off, and the urns of ' Solid Portland Stone,' which formerly adorned a parapet over the eaves, scattered through sundry Charleston gardens. Even today the Exchange is solid and imposing; originally it must have been very elaborate indeed.

Charleston was no less a cultural and recreational center than Annapolis. Its race track, called York Course, was laid out in 1735. There were many taverns, inns, and ordinaries: that of best repute for cooking and

good Madeira was owned by Peter Poinsett, member of a Charleston family now better known for the flower named after it. Famous Dock Street
Theatre* was built in 1735, and during the following winter a series of
ten popular London plays was produced by the aid of subscriptions from
planters and merchants. The museum and the library society were among
the earliest such institutions in the colonies.

We have an unusually rich picture of the early builders, engineers, and
architects of the town in the pages of Ravenel's *Architects of Charleston*.
One of the earliest, for example, was Samuel Holmes. According to his
announcement in the *Gazette* of 1734, ' Samuel Holmes of Charlestown
Bricklayer undertakes and performes in workmanlike manner all sorts of
Brickworck and Plastering at reasonable Rates: He likewise if required
draws Draughts of Houses, and measures and values all sorts of Workmanship in Houses or Buildings.' [20] Professional lines were but poorly
drawn in those days; indeed there was no profession as we know it today.
An architect was a jack-of-all-trades, distinguished from a carpenter-
builder only by his more thorough knowledge of English books, usually
by a mastery of surveying and military architecture, and sometimes by a
talent at landscaping. Witness, for example, the versatility of one whose
self-styled ' Mr.' proclaims his professional pride:

Mr. Peter Chassereau, newly come from *London,* surveys Lands, and makes neat
maps thereof, draws Plans and Elevations of all kinds of Buildings whatsoever,
both Civil and Military, likewise perspective Views or prospects of Towns or
Gentlemens Houses or Plantations, he calculates Estimates for Buildings or Repairs, inspects and measures Artificers Work, sets out ground for Gardens or
Parks, in a grand and Rural manner, and takes Levels; young Gentlemen and
Ladies will be attended at their own Houses to be taught Drawing. To be heard
of at Mr. *Shepherd's* in Broad Street . . .[21]

Charleston houses

Charleston houses of the eighteenth century were Georgian in style —
but Georgian with a special southern flavor. Old brick and worn stucco,
tinted in faded pastels, combined with red-tiled roofs and the fine
wrought-ironwork of balconies and gates to give a Mediterranean richness
of color and detail. Lots were often narrow and deep, and the houses with
their kitchens, servants' quarters, and stables were enclosed in walled
gardens with a tropical profusion of fig trees, pomegranates, peaches,
oranges, acacias, roses, oleanders, and yellow jessamine, the whole shaded
by giant live oaks and magnolias.

The long and narrow ' single house,' with its shadowed piazzas, vied
with the more fashionable ' double house ' of typical Georgian plan. Ex-

---

* Properly ' Queen Street,' as the Assembly changed the name of old Dock Street in
1734. The *South-Carolina Gazette* referred to it as ' the New Theatre in Queen Street '
in describing the opening. Often called the oldest theater in America, it was preceded,
as we have seen, by that at Williamsburg (1716) . Later burned and rebuilt, it was supplanted by a group of residences which, about 1835, were thrown together to form the
Planters Hotel. In the 1937 restoration of the theater, mantelpieces and door enframements from the demolished Ratcliffe House (1802) were used, and the façade and interiors were variously designed in Georgian, Federal, and Greek Revival styles.

amples of the two may be seen in the Robert Pringle and Daniel Horry Houses, standing side by side (fig. 349). The 'single house' stood narrow end to the street, with a door at one side entering a long piazza. A stair hall in the center separated front and back rooms, but the plan was only one room deep. Service dependencies extended to the back. The 'double house,' on the other hand, had its entrance in the middle of the main façade (facing to the right in the Horry House), with a central hall and double file of rooms. The two-tiered classic porticoes, at front and back of the Horry House, were added in the nineteenth century. In both types

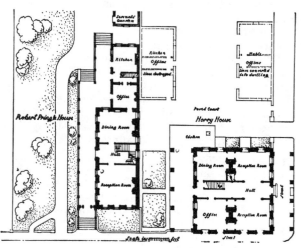

349. Plans of the Pringle and Horry Houses, Charleston (Carolina Art Association)

of house the first story was usually raised well above grade, giving an opportunity for fine flights of steps from the street to the front door. Together with lofty ceiling heights, this lifted the second story high enough to benefit from the fresh sea breezes that swept across the peninsula, and it was customary to place an important drawing room or parlor on this upper floor.

Finest of Charleston double houses was that built by Miles Brewton in 1765-9 (fig. 350). The almost-square mass, covered by a sharply ridged, hipped roof, is dominated on the street façade by a magnificent two-story portico with Doric and Ionic orders executed in carved stone. Both architrave and frieze of the upper order have a rich incised ornamental pattern which is carried around three sides of the house in the main cornice. The first story is raised several feet above grade and approached by fine flights of steps on both street and garden façades. The entrance door is topped by an elliptically arched fanlight: the only undoubtedly authentic example of this motive in a pre-Revolutionary house.

The marble-paved central hall, wider at the back than in front (fig. 351), is divided midway by a crossbeam, which is ornamented by triglyphs. The mahogany stair rises to a landing lighted by a large Palladian window in the middle of the garden façade. Step ends are adorned by rocaille scrolls, and the handrail turns in a smooth curve between the newel posts of the landing. The main rooms are very richly adorned, revealing many details characteristic of the late Georgian period. Mantels flanked by

350. Miles Brewton House, Charleston, 1765-9 (Wayne Andrews)

lateral scrolls, such as Abraham Swan had so often illustrated, doorways with an entablature supported by projecting consoles, molded plaster ceilings in rococo style, and a wealth of Gothic and Chinese detail such as Chippendale had popularized in the 1750's in England — all contribute to the rich and varied ornamentation. The finest and largest room in the house is the second-floor drawing room, with its coved ceiling 17 feet

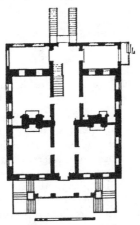

351. Plan of the Miles Brewton House (courtesy Fiske Kimball)

high, its full-paneled walls, and the rich overmantel of the fireplace flanked by Ionic pilasters and topped by a scroll pediment.

Ezra Waite was the joiner and carver, as we know from his advertisement in the *Gazette* on completion of the house in 1769:

Ezra Waite, Civil Architect, House-builder in general, and Carver, from London, Has finished the Architecture, conducted the execution thereof, viz: in the joiner way . . . and carved all the said work in the four principal rooms; and also cal-

352. William Gibbes House, Charleston, *c.*1779 (Wayne Johnston)

culated, adjusted, and draw'd at large for to work by, the Ionick entablature, and carved the same in the front and round the eaves, of Miles Brewton, Esquire's House on White Point . . . he flatters himself to give satisfaction to any gentleman, either by plans, sections, elevations, or executions, at his house in King Street, next door to Mr. Wainwright's where architecture is taught by a peculiar method never published in any book extant.[22]

Though 'architecture' in the eighteenth century often meant only decorative details, it is possible that Ezra Waite planned and designed the house as a whole, though of this we have no evidence. Like William Buckland at Annapolis, he may have been merely a decorator or perhaps an architect in the more modern sense. Waite died in November 1769, and six years later Miles Brewton, his wife, and all his children were drowned at sea. The house, being the most splendid in Charleston, was spared damage in two wars by serving as British headquarters during the Revolution and as Federal headquarters in 1865.

Another notable town house is that of William Gibbes, built about 1779 (fig. 352). Characteristically Charlestonian is the high basement, with service door at the sidewalk level, and the twin flights of steps with fine iron rails. The entrance door, with sidelights enclosed in one architectural composition of pilasters, entablature, and pediment, is all but unique in Georgian domestic architecture. Pedimented windows and a large classic pediment in the roof also reveal sophisticated architectural pretensions, though the house is of clapboards rather than brick.

Urban congestion soon led to multiple dwellings in Charleston. As early as 1735 a house ' divided into four commodious Tenements ' was advertised,[23] and at some time between 1760 and 1772 was erected the impressive three-story building known as Daniel Blake's Tenements, on Court House Square.

Many of Charleston's finest residences date from the postwar era, when polygonal and oval plan-motives gave new interest to exterior forms, and the delicate decoration of Robert Adam set a new interior style. Leader in this development was Gabriel Manigault (1758–1809), a rice planter of Huguenot stock. His interest in architecture was perhaps aroused by a visit to Rhode Island in 1774, and a few years later he studied in Geneva and in London. After his return, he was the first to introduce to the city the grand scale and sophisticated decoration of the Federal style.

The expanding frontier: Georgia and North Carolina

The architectural development of Georgia, like that of many other frontier regions, was belated. From the colonization of Carolina until well into the eighteenth century the district between the Savannah and Altamaha Rivers was the most dangerous region in British North America. Warfare between the Spanish and the British was perennial, and incursions by French fur traders from Louisiana who incited the dangerous Cherokees of Appalachia and the Creeks of the southern swamplands did not contribute to a peaceful and stable society. James Oglethorpe's colony, founded in 1732 and named after George II, was settled by a mixture of Englishmen — many released from debtors' prisons — Moravian Germans, Swiss, and Scotch. He founded his capital at Savannah in 1733, laying out the town on a gridiron plan. A view of 1734 (fig. 353) shows the straight streets, regular blocks, and numerous public squares that still dominate the appearance of the modern city.

But the colony did not flourish economically until it became a royal province in 1753, when the burdensome restrictions against slavery and the sale of rum or land were removed and more settlers were induced to immigrate. But even in the late eighteenth century the Georgian style of architecture gained little foothold: town houses and farmhouses were belated Colonial in style, like those of Virginia in the seventeenth century. Simplified Georgian houses appeared just before and after the Revolution, but it was not until the era of the Greek Revival that the state achieved buildings of first-rate architectural quality.

North Carolina was also in a sense a frontier region during the eighteenth century, for the line of settlement extended deep into the Piedmont

and the Great Valley. The state is interesting architecturally for its mé-
lange of styles imported from various older and better-established colonies. From South Carolina came the long sheltering piazzas that may be
seen at Beaufort; in the Tidewater, Virginia influences naturally prevailed; Moravians moving down the Great Valley brought the Pennsylvania-German style to the religious colonies at Bethlehem, Salem, and
Bethania; from Maryland and New Jersey came the diaper-patterned
brickwork that may be seen in scattered communities; certain houses at
New Bern look like Hudson River mansions, while others have elaborate

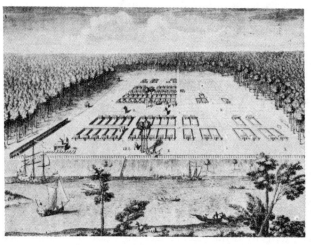

353. View of Savannah, Ga., in 1734 (Phelps Stokes Collection in the New York
Public Library)

parlors of a Philadelphia cast; there are even strong influences from faraway Connecticut, for New Bern was frequently visited by Yankee ships.
All through the state may be seen houses that reveal the crossing and re-
crossing of lines of communication between south and north, between
Tidewater and mountains. It may fairly be said that never in the colonial
period did North Carolina develop a regional style of its own, and the
rapid nationalization of post-Revolutionary architectural styles in the
Federal, Greek Revival, and Gothic Revival eras prevented the development of a distinctive local idiom.

It is unnecessary to examine more than a few representative examples
of North Carolina architecture; its complete story, with superb illustrations, has been told in the best of all state architectural studies published
to date, to which the reader is referred.*

The Cupola House at Edenton (fig. 354) is of particular interest, for
it is the only surviving house in the entire South that carries a second-

* Thomas Tileston Waterman (text) and Frances Benjamin Johnston (photographs), *The Early Architecture of North Carolina*, University of North Carolina Press,
Chapel Hill, 1941.

story ' jetty ' or overhang. The overhang, with its four scrolled brackets, the beaded clapboards, and the steep roof pitch suggest a New England Colonial ancestry, while the great end chimneys with sloping offsets and the rare oval window in the cross gable seem to stem from Virginia. Carved on one of the gable finials appear the initials of Lord Granville's agent, Francis Corbin, and the date 1758, but the architectural evidence points to a much earlier origin: Waterman believes the house must have

354. Cupola House, Edenton, N.C., c.1715 (Frances Benjamin Johnston)

been built about 1715.[24] The porch was probably a later addition, but the cupola ' bears every evidence of being original,'[25] as do the paneled shutters of the lower story. The cupola, of course, is a feature of the Georgian style, as are the sliding-sash windows and the fine paneling of the interior rooms,* so the house seems an almost perfect example of the transition from Colonial to Georgian.

South Carolinian or West Indian influence may account for the form of the MacMillan House at Sloop Point (fig. 355), a type found widely in the Tidewater area. An ample ' shed porch,' covered by the main roof, is balanced by shed rooms in the rear. Detail of the house, which was

---

* The woodwork of first-story rooms has been removed to the Brooklyn Museum; that of the second-story rooms, still in place, is of exceptionally fine quality for the early date.

built about 1728, is square and simple, essentially Colonial rather than
Georgian in spirit. The massive end chimneys and the broad sweep of
the low-pitched roof give the house an unusually satisfying quality of
solidity and repose.

The most interesting architecture of the Piedmont is in the Moravian
German settlements of Bethlehem, Salem, and Bethania. Bishop Spangen-
burg, from Bethlehem, Pennsylvania, chose a large tract of land (100,000
acres) as the site for a religious colony in 1752. He called it Wachovia.
The first pioneers came down the valley of Virginia in 1753, and gradu-

355. MacMillan House, Sloop Point, N.C., c.1728 (Frances Benjamin Johnston)

ally there grew up communities which are today remarkable survivals
of Moravian German building. Most of the surviving houses and churches
date from the post-Revolutionary period, and they reveal a mixture of
belated Georgian and Federal motives with Germanic details, to be paralleled only in the Pennsylvania religious communities.

No notable Georgian churches survive in North Carolina, but there is
one fine public building: the Chowan County Courthouse at Edenton
(fig. 356). It was built in 1767, perhaps by one Gilbert Leigh who is believed to have come from Williamsburg in Virginia. The two-story façade
with projecting pavilion and pediment reveals its late Georgian date, but
the detail of doorway, windows, and cornices is of the simplest. A two-
story cupola topped by an ogival roof provides an admirable focal feature.
The interior (fig. 357) is dominated by a central courtroom with a semicircular apse holding a high-backed judge's chair, like that of the House
of Burgesses in the Capitol at Williamsburg. The plan, with its flanking
offices, is closely paralleled by that of the old Isle of Wight Courthouse
at Smithfield in Virginia. On the second floor is a very large room, 30 by
45 feet with a 13-foot ceiling, containing full-height wall paneling and a
complete entablature.

Beyond question the finest house in North Carolina, and perhaps in any of the colonies, was Governor Tryon's Palace at New Bern. An act providing for the construction of a Capitol and Governor's Palace was passed by the North Carolina Assembly on 1 December 1766. Governor

356. Chowan County Courthouse, Edenton, 1767 (Frances Benjamin Johnston)

Tryon evidently desired no colonial amateur to design his residence and brought over an English architect, John Hawks. On 31 January 1767, he wrote to the Earl of Shelburn in part as follows:

I have employed Mr. Hawks, who came with me out of England, to superintend this work in all its branches. He was in the service of Mr. Leadbeater. Mr. Hawks

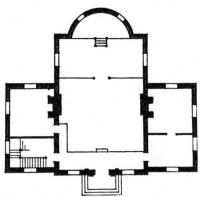

357. Plan of the Chowan County Courthouse (Thomas T. Waterman, *The Early Architecture of North Carolina*, University of North Carolina Press)

has contracted to finish the whole in three years . . . He goes soon to Philadelphia to hire able workmen, as this province affords none capable of such an undertaking. I shall send as soon as possible the plan and elevation of this house and offices for his Majesty's approbation.[26]

The ' plan and elevation ' of the palace show John Hawks to have been a professional in matters of draughtsmanship as well as design. Actually, two sheets of drawings exist: one, at present in the New York Historical Society, shows a preliminary design with a central block three stories in

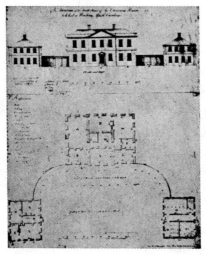

358. John Hawks' plan and elevation for Governor Tryon's Palace, New Bern, N.C., 1767 (British Public Record Office)

height; the other, in the Public Record Office in London (fig. 358), with a two-story central block, was the one actually built. The central block, 59 by 82 feet, had a hipped roof and eaves parapet (rare before the Revolution) and a central pedimented pavilion. Dependencies 39 by 49 feet were connected by curved colonnades to the central block — one of the few instances in Georgian architecture of the complete Palladian-villa plan.* The forecourt between the dependencies was screened by a wrought-iron fence. This façade was probably based, in part, on Plate 10 of Morris's Select Architecture, and in part on Hawks's recollections of Lord Harcourt's estate, Newnham in England.

The central building contained a large entrance hall on one face and a balancing drawing room at the rear. Between them was a stair hall lighted by a cupola. At the left was a large room for meetings of the Assembly. Seven chambers for the governor and his family were contained in the second story. The splendor of the interiors is suggested by fragmentary

---

* Other examples were Mount Airy, Virginia (1758–60) ; Mount Vernon, as added to between 1773 and 1779; and Mannsfield, Virginia, built between 1760 and 1770 and unfortunately destroyed during the Civil War.

records. Window sashes and lead for the roof were imported from England, and likewise ' hinges, locks, and other articles for the finishing this much admired structure.' Of especial elaboration, we may imagine, were the four chimneypieces which ' are arrived also from London,' the one for the Governor's Council Chamber being:

A large statuary Ionic chimney piece, the shafts of the columns sienna and the frett on the Frieze inlaid with the same. A rich edge and Foliage on the Tablet; medals of the King & Queen on the Frieze over the Columns, the mouldings enriched, a large statuary marble slab and black marble covings.[27]

The palace was roofed by 12 January 1769, so we may conclude that the interiors were finally completed in that or the following year, and the splendid gardens that were so impressive a sight to visitors were doubtless developed in the remaining years before the Revolution. But after the war, when the capital of the state was moved away from New Bern, the building was not used, and on 27 February 1798, it was destroyed by fire. Only one of the dependencies remains today, but announcement has recently been made that this great Georgian house will be entirely reconstructed as a memorial of North Carolina's colonial history.

READING SUGGESTIONS

Maryland:

Henry Chandlee Forman, *Early Manor and Plantation Houses of Maryland, 1634–1800,* Easton, Maryland, 1934.

Katherine Scarborough, *Homes of the Cavaliers,* Macmillan, New York, 1930.

Deering Davis, *Annapolis Houses, 1700–1775,* Architectural Book Publishing Co., New York, 1947.

Lewis A. Coffin and A. C. Holden, *Brick Architecture of the Colonial Period in Maryland & Virginia,* Architectural Book Publishing Co., New York, 1919.

South Carolina:

Samuel Gaillard Stoney, *Plantations of the Carolina Low Country,* Carolina Art Association, Charleston, 1938.

Beatrice St. Julien Ravenel, *Architects of Charleston,* Carolina Art Association, Charleston, 1945.

Albert Simons and Samuel Lapham, *Charleston, South Carolina,* American Institute of Architects, Washington, 1927.

North Carolina:

T. T. Waterman (text) and Frances Benjamin Johnston (photographs), *The Early Architecture of North Carolina,* University of North Carolina Press, Chapel Hill, 1941.

14

Georgian Public Buildings in New England

THE FOCAL centers of Georgian architecture in New England were the seaports. With the gradual shift of the economic basis of colonial life from agriculture to manufactures and shipping, the coastal communities grew from villages to towns and then to bustling cities, cobblestoned streets noisy with the rumble of drays running to and from the docks, and harbors skylined with masts and rigging. From Portsmouth came the tall pines reserved for His Majesty's ships of war, Salem's harbor was busy with shipbuilding and fisheries, Newport and New Haven were prosperous commercial centers, and Boston in the early eighteenth century was not only the largest city and busiest port in all the American colonies, but fourth largest city in the British Empire.*

Settlement proceeded inland — up the valleys of the Saco and the Salmon Falls, the Merrimack and Connecticut Rivers — but New England's poor land and stone-strewn fields produced a meager agriculture compared to the fertile plantations of the South. And from the time of King William's War in the late seventeenth century, raids by French and Indians plagued the frontier settlements. Within a dozen miles of prosperous Portsmouth, Dover and Durham were villages of garrisons and blockhouses, and for years old 'fort no. 4' at Charlestown, New Hampshire, marked the northern outpost of a precarious safety in the Connecticut valley. It was not until the Treaty of Paris in 1763 that northern portions of Maine, New Hampshire, and Vermont were opened to pioneer farmers. As they pushed the frontier north and west they built in the simple fashion of the seventeenth-century tradition, which was better suited to pioneer conditions than the new Georgian. Thus in northern New England may still be seen 'Colonial' houses built after the Revolution.

In the South, the Georgian style was adopted first in the great plantation houses of a primarily rural economy. In New England, it flourished first in the cities, where the wealth of the Yankee traders was concentrated, and where the commercial and cultural ties with England were strongest. And though New England boasted many elaborate Georgian residences, as will be seen in the following chapter, it was her fine public buildings and churches, her commercial and educational edifices, which were of primary architectural importance and which revealed an awakened civic consciousness unparalleled anywhere in the South.

* In the 1740's only London, Bristol, and Norwich were larger than Boston.

Eighteenth-century Boston

In the fifty years following 1690 Boston more than doubled in population, and by the mid-eighteenth century it had become not only one of the largest but one of the cleanest and best-managed cities in the Empire. An English visitor reported in 1740 that the city contained 'a great many good houses, and several fine streets, little inferior to some of our best in London.' [1] By 1742, according to the *Boston News-Letter*, the city had a

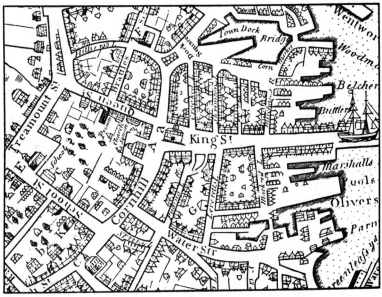

359. Downtown Loston, a detail from Captain John Bonner's map of 1722 (*Old Time New England*)

population of 16,382 persons, including 1,374 Negroes.[2] There were 166 warehouses and 1,719 houses, a large proportion of them built of brick. The city had many public and institutional buildings: 17 churches, the Province House, a new Town-House, Faneuil Hall, an almshouse, workhouse, 5 public schools (the best in the colonies), and a good college in near-by Cambridge.

Boston filled in its tangled medieval street pattern with a typically urban congestion. A detail from Captain John Bonner's map of 1722 (fig. 359) shows a downtown section with narrow streets lined by rows of steep-gabled houses. The main traffic artery from the narrow 'Neck' was named, in different portions, Orange, Newbury, and Marlbrough Streets, in true English fashion. It emerged through Cornhill to the new Town-House, which separated King Street and Queen Street. The center of the commercial district was at Dock Square, site of the later Faneuil Hall. During the early years of the eighteenth century, old streets were widened and extended (particularly after the fires of 1690, 1691, and

1711), and many new ones were built. By 1708 Boston, uniquely among colonial cities, had officially assigned names to all streets, lanes, and alleys.

There was an extensive campaign of street-paving: in the main streets, the town paved a center strip 24 feet in width, while the sides were improved by abutting property owners. Streets were graded for proper drainage, crowned in the middle and with gutters at the sides, along which ran waste water from the numerous pumps beside the street. A sub-surface sewer was laid on Orange Street in 1704, built of stone (some earlier ones had been made of wood), and this drained not only the street but the cellars of abutting houses. Between 1708 and 1720 some 420 sections of sewer with connecting house drains were laid, and during the next sixteen years permits were granted for 234 additional drainage constructions. By 1720 Boston had the finest street system in the colonies — and one which greatly surpassed that of most English cities.[3]

Streets were cleaned by scavengers hired by the town — unique in the colonies — but there was still difficulty caused by the practice of throwing slops out of windows and the presence of large numbers of ' noisome swine ' and hordes of ' curst & unruly doggs and bitches.'[4] Streets were increasingly jammed by carts, drays, hackney coaches, and horsemen — especially the bottleneck road along the narrow Neck, with its heavy wintertime traffic of sleds bringing loads of firewood. The noise went on into the night, and one Jonathan Willis protested bitterly at town meeting in 1742 about ' the great Disturbances Occasioned by Horses and Chaise in great Numbers Crouding into Town and also out . . . till Nine, Ten, and sometimes Eleven a clock.'[5] Though carters were required to lead their teams through the streets and galloping of horses was forbidden, accidents to persons and property occurred, and after 1717 the selectmen granted rights to individuals to set up rows of protecting posts eight feet from the building line, thus forming rudimentary sidewalks such as were used also at Newport and Philadelphia. The number of shop signs hanging out over the street increased to such an extent that after 1736 their use had to be curbed.

As a busy seaport, Boston built many wharves, both private and public. Outstanding was the famous Long Wharf, a great public pier built in 1710–13, projecting so far out into the harbor that 30 vessels could berth along its south side at once; the north side was covered by a row of great warehouses. By 1742, the town's waterfront was crowded with 166 wharves and docks jutting into the bay.

Of the scores of warehouses, not one that can be dated with certainty in the seventeenth or eighteenth century survives today. Still recalled as one of Boston's curiosities, however, was the Triangular Warehouse, which formerly stood at the head of North Market Street between Clinton Street and Merchants' Row. Supposedly built by Richard Wharton about 1680, the building was demolished in 1824.[6] As pictured in Shaw's *History of Boston* (1817), it was indeed a curious structure (fig. 360). Triangular in plan, with sides measuring 48, 51, and 55 feet, the two-story walls built of brick of a larger than usual size were topped by a steep slated roof. Three large octagonal towers marked the corners.

Though it is impossible to say how nearly authentic the architectural details are in this picture, the style appears to have been more Tudor than Georgian; such details as the brick relieving arches, the apparent overhang of the second story, the embattled motive over the central window, the shelf dormers and steep-pitched roof topped by stone ball finials are distinctly of the medieval tradition.

Both commercial and residential structures were built increasingly of brick in the early eighteenth century. After the great fire of 1691 the General Court decreed that all new buildings should be constructed of brick or stone, and roofed with slate. Only by special permission from the governor and Council might a frame structure be built, and such was given

360. Triangular Warehouse, Boston, 1680? (from Shaw's *History of Boston*, 1817)

usually only for stables and sheds. There were difficulties in enforcing this law, but the fire of 1711 gave it added justification, and by 1716 Boston had virtually succeeded in preventing the erection of frame buildings within the town.[7] The danger from fires was also countered by a successfully operated municipal chimney-sweeping monopoly, and eight trained fire-engine companies with wooden and copper 'water engines' and all manner of buckets, axes, hooks, ropes, and ladders.

Boston licensed more taverns, inns, alehouses, and ordinaries than did any other colonial town. The best and most fashionable were the Blue Anchor, frequented by aristocratic and official circles, the Rose & Crown and the Royal Exchange, both on King Street (now State), the Green Dragon, and the Bunch of Grapes. Mariners and 'the poorer sort' frequented the rougher dives of the waterfront such as the Dog & Pot near Bartlett's Wharf, or the Crown Tavern. All Boston inns and taverns were carefully regulated by the town, and despite an amount of drinking that alarmed worthies such as Cotton Mather, they were usually respectable. The tavern was an important focus of business and social life, and increasingly it robbed the church of its social and recreational functions. Entertainments by itinerant showmen, exhibitions, and meetings of private clubs of all sorts made it a headquarters of social life, as well as a place where food and drink of increasingly better quality and service of considerable elegance might be obtained. News of the world emanated from the inns, too, for many of them had post boxes for the collection and delivery of the letters and newspapers of the weekly postal route which by 1698 connected Portsmouth, Boston, Newport, New York, Philadelphia, and New Castle, Delaware.* Coffeehouses had become increasingly popular in London in the early eighteenth century, and by 1720 Boston had four of them, frequented by merchants, ships' captains, and officials; they were frequently the scene of ' vendues ' or auctions.

Nowhere else in the colonies, and probably even in Europe, did free public education approach the high standard set in Boston. Pioneered by famous ' Boston Latin ' (founded in 1643), the five public schools established before 1720 maintained such excellent instruction that they enrolled children from as far afield as the West Indies. Buildings were spacious and well kept, masters and ushers well paid, and the conduct of the schools supervised annually by a committee of important citizens. By 1738 the town-supported schools enrolled nearly 600 pupils. Unfortunately we know nothing of the architectural character of the school buildings, but in the sphere of ecclesiastical and public architecture many surviving buildings contribute to our knowledge of the Georgian style.

Early Georgian churches in Boston

The tradition of the seventeenth-century ' four-square ' meeting-house lingered into the eighteenth century. Indeed plain, barn-like clapboard structures with the side-entrance type of plan and no tower or spire were built in small New England towns until nearly 1800. But the congregations of wealthier towns such as Boston and Newport were ready in the early eighteenth century for a more formal architecture, and the inspiration for this was ready to hand in the London churches of Sir Christopher Wren. This more elaborate type of structure, with a front tower topped by a lofty spire, a main entrance at one end of an oblong plan, and longitudinal aisles separating the box pews, was first adopted in New England by Anglican (Episcopal) congregations.

At first the older type of Congregational house of worship was called a ' meeting-house,' and the rarer word ' church ' was applied only to the newer architectural form. But as the century progressed both the architectural type and the name of the Anglican ' church ' were adopted by Congregationalists, Presbyterians, and Baptists; thus Place's phrase ' from meeting-house to church ' aptly summarizes the development of New England ecclesiastical architecture in the eighteenth century.[8]

This development may be seen in five Boston churches built during the first two-thirds of the century; each was of outstanding architectural quality in its day and served as a model for later churches in the smaller towns of New England. Earliest was the Old Brick Meeting-House (fig. 361), built in 1713 and demolished in 1808.† This was essentially seventeenth

---

* The route was extended by 1732 to Annapolis and Williamsburg, and by 1740 to Charleston.

† Not to be confused with the New Brick Meeting-House on Hanover Street at the head of Prince Street, a structure erected in 1721 and demolished in 1844.

century in type, like the Old Ship Meeting-House in Hingham (see figs.
61–3), but of larger size, made of masonry, and with some Georgian architectural detail. Like the Hingham Meeting-House, it was almost
square in plan, with a two-story entrance porch in the middle of the long
side, a hipped roof with a railed deck, and a light arcaded cupola. But
the entrance porch was adorned by classic orders of pilasters and entablatures in two stories; the walls were three stories in height and adorned by
occasional round windows such as Wren had used in Hampton Court
Palace; there was a modillioned cornice, and probably sash windows in-

361. Old Brick Meeting-House, Boston, 1713 (courtesy The Bostonian Society)

stead of medieval casements. The most costly meeting-house built in the
colonies to that time, Old Brick set a new standard of architectural elaboration, but one which was to be surpassed within a decade by the first
Georgian ' church ' in New England.[9]

This was Christ Church (Old North) on Salem Street in North Boston,
the oldest Anglican church still standing in Boston. There was an Anglican congregation in Portsmouth as early as 1640, but the earliest important one was King's Chapel, Boston, organized in 1686. Though the first
wooden edifice of King's Chapel was doubled in size in 1710 to take care
of a growing congregation representing much of the wealth and fashion of
the town, this proved inadequate and a new church was planned for the
North End in 1723. The cornerstone of Christ Church was laid in April
of that year by the Reverend Samuel Myles, rector of King's Chapel. The
designer was William Price, a Boston print seller who is alleged to have
made a study of Wren's London churches, and indeed the exterior is a
simplified adaptation of Wren's forms and the interior is markedly similar
to that of St. James's, Piccadilly.

The body of Old North (fig. 362) is a simple rectangular mass, 51 feet wide and 70 long, with two tiers of arched windows, the walls laid in English-bond brickwork.[10] This is preceded by a square brick tower, nearly a hundred feet high, surmounted by a wooden spire whose set-back stages, classical decorative detail, and fragile, nervous lines are strongly reminiscent of Wren's churches. The original spire, more lofty

362. Christ Church (Old North), Boston, 1723 (HABS)

than this, has long been famous because of its connection with Paul Revere's ride, for it was in the 'upper window' of the belfry chamber that the sexton Robert Newman flashed the two signal lanterns to the horseman waiting on the Charlestown shore. The original spire, 191 feet high, was blown down in a gale in 1804 and replaced in 1807 by one of similar design and a height of 175 feet; this reconstruction was supervised by the famous architect Charles Bulfinch.* The belfry contains a peal of eight bells, one of which was cast by Paul Revere in 1816.

The interior of Old North (fig. 363) reveals the new 'church' plan, with longitudinal aisles separating the groups of square box pews. The

---

* Bulfinch's spire was rebuilt along the same lines, in 1847, and strengthened in the restoration of 1912.

two-story architectural scheme, with square paneled pillars below and fluted ones above, is echoed in this country only in Trinity Church, Newport, but Wren had employed a similar arrangement in three London churches. The arched bays of the galleries and the elliptically vaulted plaster ceiling of the nave follow Wren's St. James's, Piccadilly. The total effect is somewhat amateurish compared with Peter Harrison's superb interior at King's Chapel, built a generation later, but the intimate scale

363. Interior of the Old North Church (Detroit Publishing Company)

and the old woodwork have much charm. The church was thoroughly restored in 1912.*

Even more famous for the part it played in Boston's turbulent pre-Revolutionary history is the Old South Meeting-House (fig. 364). The first edifice on this site was a modest two-story frame structure built in 1669; in it Judge Sewall stood up in his pew while public confession was read of his unsavory activities in the witchcraft persecutions of 1692, and in it Benjamin Franklin was baptized on 17 January 1706. The present large structure was built in 1729–30, designed by one Robert Twelves, and built by Joshua Blanchard, a master mason who later built the Han-

* By the architects R. Clipston Sturgis and Henry C. Ross. Exterior masonry was sand-blasted, woodwork repainted its original white, floor timbers and gallery stair replaced, the original arched window at the east end reinserted, and the old box pews reproduced. The pulpit was modeled after that of Trinity Church, Newport. The Massachusetts Society of Colonial Dames has placed name plates on the 65 pew doors, bearing the names of the original owners. See ' The Restoration of Christ Church, Boston,' *Old Time New England*, vol. 3, no. 3 (February 1913) , pp. 2, 5–8.

cock House and Faneuil Hall. Though retaining the side-entrance ' auditorium plan ' of the seventeenth-century meeting-house, the building was undoubtedly influenced by new Christ Church, for it had two tiers of arched windows and a projecting tower in front. The brick masonry was laid in Flemish bond. The spire differed from that of Old North in having octagonal rather than square stages; less brittle and fussy, it was copied in no less than six other New England churches, notably that at Farmington, Connecticut (1771). A clock by the famous **Gawen Brown**

364. Old South Meeting-House, Boston, 1729–30, from a photo made about 1890 (Halliday Historic Photograph Co.)

was set in the tower in 1770 and, according to the *Boston Gazette* of that year, ran ' with great regularity and exactness.' [11]

The interior of Old South was arranged, like the earlier meeting-houses, with a high pulpit and suspended sounding board on the middle of the long side, and a gallery around the other three sides. Because of its great size, the building was often used for mass meetings too large for Faneuil Hall, including protest meetings after the Boston Massacre in 1770 and a stormy session on 16 December 1773, which ended up after candlelight in the Boston Tea Party. Such rebellious incidents were not forgotten when British regiments occupied Boston in 1775, and at General Burgoyne's order the pulpit, pews, and other interior furnishings were torn out and destroyed and the building was used as a riding school for the King's cavalry. The interior was restored in 1783, and a lofty second gallery added at some time subsequent to this. Partly damaged in the great fire of 1872, the building was abandoned as a church and for a time served as a post office. A threatened demolition in 1876 resulted in the formation of the Old South Association, which has since preserved the building as a historical museum.

The finest achievements in New England church architecture were the new King's Chapel (1749–54) in Boston and Christ Church, Cambridge (1759–61). Both of these were designed by the distinguished architect, Peter Harrison of Newport, and are discussed with his other work later in this chapter.

The second Town-House, Boston. 1712–13

If we except the reconstructed buildings at Williamsburg, the Old State House at Boston is the oldest extant public building of the Georgian period. Few other buildings, and none so famous, have been so inaccurately dated, erroneously named, or wrongly restored.* The historic structure, which dominated the half-mile vista down King Street to the end of Long Wharf, was the successor of Boston's first Town-House (see fig. 70). The half-century-old wooden building was destroyed in the great fire of the night of the second and third of October 1711. This most destructive fire in Boston's colonial history laid waste all buildings on both sides of Cornhill between School Street and Dock Square, and on both sides of King Street, including the historic First Church and the Town-House.[12]

A new building for the town and province was started in 1712 and completed in time for the town meeting of 13 May 1713. A legislative order of 17 November 1712 required that the builders ' fit the East Chamber for the Use of His Excellency the Governor and the Honorable the Council, the Middle Chamber for the House, the West Chamber for the Superior and Inferior Courts,' and it was likewise provided that the ground story should contain small offices for the Secretary, the Suffolk County Register of Deeds, and a ' Walk for the Merchants.'[13] Though used (and paid for) jointly by province, county, and town and referred to occasionally as the ' Court House' or ' Province Court House,' it is clear that the building was commonly called the ' Town-House ' throughout the colonial period.

We cannot be certain about the plan and architectural details of the original building, for a fire on 9 December 1747 destroyed all but the walls, including a great quantity of valuable papers and records. Five years earlier than this town meetings had been removed to the more capacious Faneuil Hall, so that the structure which was rebuilt in 1748, after the fire, was devoted entirely to province, county, and local mercantile affairs, but it continued to be called the Town-House, as many documents written at the time of the Boston Massacre reveal.

The second Town-House, as rebuilt in 1748, was a handsome edifice of full-blown Georgian style. Free-standing in the middle of King Street, the

* The date of construction has been given as 1728 by Eberlein and Tallmadge, as 1748 by Baedecker and the Encyclopædia Britannica. The building was actually used as a state house only from 1776 to 1797. The 1882 restoration of the building, with a central spiral stair and second-floor rooms of post-Revolutionary architectural style, was wrong.

west end (fig. 365) faced Cornhill. The main entrance at this end was at street level. Framed by engaged colonets bearing scrolled brackets, like the front door of the Hancock House (1737–40), the door was topped by an angular pediment. Round windows adorned the gable ends, and ' steps ' in the parapet of the gable were filled with baroque scrolls. There were doors at the middle of both long sides, and the interior of the ground story was one large hall (except for the two small offices at the north side and the two staircases which led to the second floor) ; this hall served as a merchants' exchange. The second story was supported by a row of ten Doric columns, presumably on the long axis.

365. Second Town-House (Old State House), Boston, 1712–13. View from southwest in 1793 (engraving by S. Hill in *Massachusetts Magazine,* July 1793)

Shortly after its reconstruction in 1748, Captain Francis Goelet described the structure as ' a very Grand Brick Building, Arch'd all Round, and Two Stories Heigh, Sash'd above; its Lower Part is always Open, design'd as a Change.' [14] This description is particularly interesting, for it suggests a ground story with open arcades, like English market halls. It is possible that such existed until the Revolution or after. A newspaper description of 1794 stated that ' the lower floor of the building serves as a covered walk for any of the inhabitants '; on the other hand the careful engraving made for the *Massachusetts Magazine* in 1793 (fig. 365) shows the lower story with conventional wall and windows. The center of the roof was topped by a tower or cupola, considerably less lofty than those of churches, with its three stories finished ' according to the Tuscan, Dorick and Ionick orders complete. . .'

The east end of the Town-House (fig. 366) faced King Street as it sloped down to the waterfront. The façade was dominated by a fine doorway framed by Corinthian pilasters and topped by a segmental pediment. This led from the Governor's Council Chamber, on the second floor, to the small balcony from which the laws were customarily proclaimed to the sound of trumpet and beat of drum. The gable at this end was more

ornately treated than that at the west end, with ornamental scrollwork and
leafage, and the steps in the parapet filled by vigorously carved figures of
the British Lion and Unicorn. The central circular panel was evidently
filled by a sun dial from the first construction of the building, for there
is record that its face was repainted in 1736; the clock that superseded it
first appeared in a view of 1826.

366. East end of the second Town-House, Boston, after the restoration of 1882 (The
Bostonian Society)

Access to the second floor was by two staircases leading to hallways between the three main rooms. Of these, the easternmost, a room 32 feet
square serving as the Council Chamber, was the most ornately furnished
and decorated. In the middle of the building was the Representatives'
Chamber, measuring about 32 by 38 feet, with small lobbies in the stair
halls at either side. The speaker's chair was on the south side, and wooden
seats for the members were arranged around the other sides of the room.
On the clerk's table stood a large branched candlestick, of brass, given by
Colonel Isaac Royall in 1748, and over one door were the arms of the
colony, carved, painted, and gilded by Moses Deshon in 1750. Hanging
from the ceiling in the middle of the room was a large wooden codfish,
' Emblem of the staple of Commodities of the Province'; this figure must
have been in the first building, for there is mention of repainting it in a

bill of 1733. In 1766 a gallery for visitors was provided by utilizing space over the west lobby. The westernmost room, measuring about 22 by 32 feet, was the Court Chamber. This housed the superior and inferior courts until a new courthouse building was erected in 1769. The third floor, under the roof, was occupied in colonial times by a number of offices and committee rooms.

The history of the Town-House during Revolutionary times and afterward accounts in some measure for the confusion that has arisen concerning its original form. The building became the State House of the new Commonwealth of Massachusetts in 1776; ' Saturday last, the General Assembly of this State adjourn'd from Watertown, to meet at the State House in this Town,' reported the *Boston Gazette* of 11 November in that year. The large size of the new legislature necessitated an enlargement of the Representatives' Chamber, and since the former Court Chamber was not being used, the stairway and lobby between the two rooms were removed and they were thrown together, making a hall 57½ feet in length. These alterations were ordered on 18 October 1776. A new stairway and lobby, 11 feet wide, were constructed at the west end of the building, and a visitors' gallery built over it. The old Council Chamber at the east was used for the State Senate. Revolutionary animosities led to the removal of the lion and unicorn on the east gable, and they were not replaced until the restoration of 1882.

But the building served as a State House for only twenty-one years. Bulfinch's new State House was built in 1795–7, and the House of Representatives first met in it on 11 January 1798. The old building fell into almost complete disuse. The town bought out the Commonwealth and county interests in 1803, and for a generation leased it to miscellaneous tenants. From 1830 to 1840 it served as the Boston City Hall, and for this use it was remodeled by a famous architect of the Greek Revival period, Isaiah Rogers. The interiors were completely replanned, the principal new feature being a spiral staircase in the center of the building. To install this, old transverse floor girders were cut out in the center section, their ends being carried by iron rods to the roof trusses in the third floor. Classical porticoes were added at east and west ends of the building. But the building was abandoned as a city hall in 1840, and for the next four decades was rented to a number of commercial firms. The spiral staircase was removed, interiors again remodeled several times, and by 1876 the building had become defaced by an ugly mansard roof and a plethora of advertising signs.

By 1881 the building had deteriorated into a ramshackle and ugly rabbit warren of shabby commercial premises. The City Council determined that it should be demolished. But this was the building in which James Otis had delivered his eloquent plea against writs of assistance; from its balcony George II had been proclaimed King in 1760 and the Declaration of Independence had been read in 1776; Washington had been fêted here before the throngs of people in State Street on his triumphal visit in 1789. Demolition seemed unthinkable, and it was the offer of the city of Chicago to transfer the building to Lincoln Park, paying all expenses of removal and reassembly, that stung the Boston City Council into preserving the edifice on its original site.

The building was accordingly restored to its 'pre-Revolutionary condition' in 1881–2. At this juncture a plan found in Cincinnati was identified as pertaining to the Town-House, and was followed in the rebuilding: it showed a spiral stair, and sure enough, an examination of the old timbers revealed that there once had been a spiral stair in the middle of the building. In actual fact, the City Architect, George A. Clough, had stumbled upon the Isaiah Rogers remodeling plan of 1830. It seems incredible today, but in 1881 so little was known of the history of American architecture — the methods of draughtsmanship and planning of the different eras — that this plan of 1830 was naïvely assumed to be the plan for the rebuilding of 1748! The spiral stair was rebuilt, equipped with Georgian detail copied from Governor Shirley's house at Roxbury (c.1747). Thus Boston's old Town-House was 'restored,' its lion and unicorn sitting in uneasy propinquity with stairs and rooms that would have seemed strange indeed to His Excellency the Governor and the Honorable the Council in the halcyon days of George II.

Faneuil Hall, Boston. 1740–42

Less confusing is the architectural history of Faneuil Hall, even more renowned than the Town-House and the Old South Church as the 'Cradle of Liberty' in colonial Boston. Even its inception was fraught with civic turbulence. For years, Boston merchants and men of property had wanted a civic market hall, with conditions of sale and prices properly regulated. Farmers and their artisan and laborer allies in town preferred a free 'black market' system, by which goods and provisions were bought up by fast-operating hucksters and resold to city dwellers at exorbitant prices. So determined was the 'free trade' faction that civic markets opened at Eliot's Wharf, the Dock, and the Old North Church were demolished by mobs in 1737, despite warnings and threats by the Lieutenant Governor. When, in 1740, wealthy Peter Faneuil offered to build a market house as a gift to the town, his proffer was indeed looked in the teeth. The town meeting of 14 July was so jammed that it had to be moved to the Brattle Street Church, and after a maneuver that kept non-taxpayers from voting, the meeting, amid 'Heat and Vehemence on both Sides,' accepted Peter Faneuil's offer by the slender margin of 367 to 360.[15]

The building was promptly begun and was opened with proper ceremonies on 24 September 1742. Samuel Ruggles was the carpenter and Joshua Blanchard the master mason. The building was designed by the famous painter John Smibert, turned amateur architect for this one occasion. Smibert, a native of Edinburgh, had come to Boston in 1729 and set up a studio to paint portraits and teach students. He was about sixty years old when Faneuil Hall was designed.[16]

The market hall stood between Dock Square and the waterfront, just near the entrance to Damnation Alley. Two stories high and 40 by 100 feet when first built (fig. 367), Faneuil Hall displayed unusual architec-

367. Faneuil Hall, Boston, 1740–42, from an engraving of 1780 (Harvard University Department of Architecture)

368. Shem Drowne's grasshopper weathervane on Faneuil Hall, 1742 (National Gallery of Art, *Index of American Design*)

tural pretensions. Both stories had an applied order of Doric pilasters, executed in brick, and the second story was crowned by a fully membered Roman Doric entablature of stone. Open arcades to the public market on the ground floor were echoed by round-arch windows above, and the roof was crowned by a large central cupola. At the apex of the latter was a delightful weathervane (fig. 368) completed by Deacon Shem Drowne on 25 May 1742, in his shop on Ann Street. It was a gargantuan grasshopper

369. Faneuil Hall after Bulfinch's enlargement of 1805–6 (Arthur C. Haskell)

of hammered copper, with green glass eyes and long antennae questing the wind. Often supposed to be a good-luck symbol or a product of Shem Drowne's fancy, like the cockerels, fish, horses, and cows which perched on many a New England house and barn, the grasshopper was in reality a copy of the one atop the Royal Exchange in London, whose founder Sir Thomas Gresham owned it as a family crest.[17] On the second floor were certain offices for town business, and a hall large enough to accommodate a thousand persons. Town meetings were usually held here, except when overflow crowds forced a removal to the Old South Meeting-House.

On Tuesday, 13 January 1761, during a spell of extremely cold weather, a fire broke out in the vicinity, and ' communicated itself to that stately edifice, Faneuil Hall Market, the whole of which was entirely consumed, except the brick walls, which are left standing.'[18] The building was promptly rebuilt, with minor changes, by aid of a public lottery, and the town meeting of 14 March 1763 was held in it, as well as many mass meetings in the stormy years before the Revolution.

In 1805–6 Faneuil Hall was tripled in size, by dint of doubling its width (to 80 feet) and adding a third story (fig. 369). The architect of the re-modeling, Charles Bulfinch, retained the original architectural scheme except for moving the cupola to the Dock Square end of the building and adding a series of barrel-shaped dormer windows in the new roof. He employed an order of Ionic pilasters for the high third story. The Town Hall in the second story was widened and its ceiling raised, permitting galleries supported by superposed Doric and Ionic orders; the result was rather like an enlarged church interior. The distinction between the original building and Bulfinch's addition may be observed in the brick masonry: the old work has rather large bricks ($2 \times 3\frac{3}{8} \times 7\frac{1}{8}$ inches) laid in Flemish bond with dark headers; the later brickwork is smoother and lighter in color, and lacks the dark headers. The building as it stands today has a breadth, vigor, and scale that make it far more imposing than its Georgian prototype.

Newport, Rhode Island

In New England, only Newport ranked with Boston as a center of commerce, wealth, and fine architecture in the eighteenth century. Though its population, which grew from 2600 in 1700 to 7000 in 1760, seems small in today's terms, it was exceeded in the colonies only by Boston, Philadelphia, New York, and — after 1730 — Charleston. Most of Newport's banking and foreign exchange were handled through Boston, with which it was connected by fast post service, but it was a big mercantile center in its own right, boasting 4000 tons of shipping and 439 warehouses, shops, and auxiliary buildings. Though provided with many privately owned docks and wharves, the ambitious citizenry planned a great town dock. Long Wharf, which Newport built in 1739–41, was 50 feet wide and over 2000 feet long — large enough to berth a multitude of the biggest ships. There were 27 shops and warehouses lining the dock, and from its western end, along the straight line of the dock and Queen Street, extended a magnificent vista of one mile, terminated by the fine new Colony House. The enterprising merchants justly predicted a ' beauty and grandeur . . . which will appear the greatest perhaps in New England.' [19]

Richard Munday, amateur architect

The name of Richard Munday is associated with many buildings of Newport in the early eighteenth century. Little is known of his life. He married a Newport girl in 1713 and by 1719 appeared in the civic records as an innkeeper and house carpenter. He built Trinity Church, the fine Colony House, the Daniel Ayrault House, and very probably the Sabbatarian Meeting-House and several Newport residences.[20]

Trinity Church, built in 1725–6, might be termed a copy in wood of Boston's Old North. The Boston print dealer, William Price, was one of the founders of the church, and, as the designer of Old North, it seems entirely probable that he either made or procured the designs for Trinity;

both churches show the strong influence of Sir Christopher Wren. But it is clear from the records that Richard Munday was the builder, and he proved himself an able one. The exterior of Trinity, like Old North, has a rectangular body with arched windows in two tiers and a projecting front tower and spire. The east doors have curiously awkward overdoor features: deep segmental pediments broken at the top by inverted semicircles, as though the joiner had misunderstood some drawing in an ar-

370. Interior of Trinity Church, Newport, R.I., 1725–6 (Robert Meservey photo, courtesy Preservation Society of Newport County)

chitectural handbook.[21] The church was lengthened two bays (30 feet) about 1762, by sawing the body in two, moving back the rear portion, and filling in the gap to match the old work. Very likely it was at this time that the spire was built. Except for the double-arch openings in the second stage, the spire is very similar to that of Boston's Old North, which was erected in 1741. Trinity's spire had to be rebuilt after a gale in 1768.

The interior of Trinity (fig. 370), with its superposed orders of square pillars, paneled below and fluted above, again resembles the scheme of the Old North Church. But added depth to the gallery fronts, which have fine raised panels framed by bolection moldings, gives a more dignified architectural effect, and the projection of the arched vaults over the gallery bays into the nave to form a kind of groined vaulting contributes to a more monumental interior unity. Noteworthy features are the fine raised pulpit and sounding board, the clerk's desk, branched candelabra, old box pews, and the arched east window with clear, small panes and draped red curtain.[22]

Richard Munday was probably the builder of the small meeting-house built by the Seventh Day Baptists in Newport in 1729. Externally an extremely simple clapboard building with gabled roof, it followed the meeting-house pattern, with entrance on the long side and no tower or spire. But the interior is adorned by some of the most exquisite and elaborate

371. Old Colony House, Newport, 1739–41, by Richard Munday (Wayne Andrews)

carving and paneling of the eighteenth century, much of it very similar to that of Trinity Church. The gallery extending around three sides is particularly fine, and the wine-glass pulpit topped by a cantilevered sounding board is reached by an unusually beautiful flight of stairs, rich in spirally twisted balusters and newel posts.

Munday's best-known work is the Colony House in Newport (fig. 371). Fronting the mile-long vista of Queen Street and the Long Wharf, this was a worthy rival, among civic buildings, of Boston's Town-House and the old Philadelphia State House. Built in 1739–41, the design is more domestic than monumental; like most Georgian public buildings it resembles an enlarged private dwelling rather than a state house. Indeed, its prototypes are to be sought in English manor houses of the late Stuart period rather than in the Palladian monuments of the early eighteenth century. The main (west) façade is elevated on a basement of drafted granite masonry, and the door approached by a flight of granite steps.

Above this base, walls are made of red brick with rusticated sandstone trim surrounding the windows and emphasizing the corners. The belt course between stories, composed of three courses of stone, is of unusual depth.

The gabled roof is cut off at the top to form a flat deck, and this shape is echoed in the truncated gable on the main façade, a novel but clumsy feature. The small-paned windows are topped by segmental arches with prominent sandstone keystones, a shape echoed in the subtle upward curves of the pedimented dormer windows. But the dominant feature of the façade is the central unit combining doorway and balcony, a motive strongly reminiscent of the Hancock House in Boston, begun two years earlier than this building. The balcony doors are topped by a broken segmental pediment whose carved scrolls effloresce into swept-back foliage; between the scrolls a pedestal carries a carved and gilded pineapple. A large octagonal cupola in two stories crowns the roof deck with its Chinese Chippendale rail.

The interior of the first story is one large room, 40 by 80 feet, with a row of square Doric pillars running down the middle, each with pedestal and segment of entablature. The second story contains three rooms, originally designed to house the Governor's Council (at the south), the Chamber of Deputies (at the north), and a large lobby or hallway between them. Walls with tall narrow panels are featured by pedestaled pilasters in the Ionic and Corinthian orders. The Colony House was used not only for legislative and administrative purposes, but for public meetings and religious and social functions. From its balcony were proclaimed the death of George II, the ascendancy of George III, the repeal of the Stamp Act, and the adoption of the Declaration of Independence. Washington attended a banquet in the great hall when he came to visit his French allies. The building has been carefully restored under the direction of Norman M. Isham and stands today as a public monument.[23]

Richard Munday undoubtedly designed and built some houses. One of them, according to legend, was the great stone country house of Captain Godfrey Malbone, alleged to have resembled the Colony House; but it burned in 1764 and little is known of it. Just before his death, Munday designed a house for the Newport merchant Daniel Ayrault; a crudely drawn plan of this house survives (see fig. 250), and the contract and specifications drawn up in May 1739, between Ayrault and Richard Munday and Benjamin Wyatt, 'housewrights,' is an interesting document of eighteenth-century building practices.[24] But Munday died in 1739, before the Colony House was completed; in that same year Peter Harrison, his talented successor, made his first voyage to Newport as a young man of 23.

The architecture of Peter Harrison

During the fifteen years of his architectural activity (1748–63) Peter Harrison was the most distinguished architect of colonial America. Shipowner and merchant of Newport, and in later years collector of His Majesty's customs at New Haven, Harrison, like many educated gentlemen of the day, practiced architecture as an amateur, without pay. Yet by training, talent, and standards he perhaps deserves the appellation — so frequently given — of 'America's first professional architect.' Earlier in the century, only Richard Taliaferro of Virginia had rivaled him in talent, and of his own generation John Ariss was his only compeer in architectural sophistication. As the first American architect to adopt in thorough and rigorous fashion the formal Palladianism of contemporary English architecture, and the first (in the Redwood Library at Newport) to utilize

372. The architect Peter Harrison, from a portrait by Nathaniel Smibert about 1756 (courtesy Maurice P. Van Buren)

a nearly complete classical temple form, Peter Harrison was the most significant architect of his age. He brought the Georgian style to full maturity in New England, and he anticipated by almost forty years the scholarly classicism of Thomas Jefferson.

As portrayed by Nathaniel Smibert (fig. 372), Harrison appeared a mild and sensitive person, the primness of his Quaker origin overlaid with the pride of an adopted Anglicanism. Born of modest family in York, England, in 1716, he had a natural and gentlemanly dignity. 'Peter's instincts were aristocratic,' writes Bridenbaugh. 'Conservative in politics as in temperament, an admirer of all things British, he mightily respected property with all its appurtenances, its duties and its rights. . .' [25] In his youth he acquired knowledge of shipbuilding and some skill in wood carving; he also seems to have been particularly impressed by the newer Palladian school of architecture, which he saw exemplified in the Assembly Rooms at York, designed by Lord Burlington and William Kent in 1735. Possibly he even met Kent, who also was a Yorkshireman.

Peter's first visit to Newport was in 1739, when he shipped as a steward on his brother Joseph's ship the *Sheffield;* on this visit he met his future wife, Elizabeth Pelham. For the next five years he was at sea, becoming captain of one of the largest ships in the American trade at the age of 23, and the next year he commanded the *Leathley,* whose completion and fitting at Providence he personally supervised. Coursing the Atlantic on several trips between Newport, Charleston, and the English ports, his ship was seized by a French privateer in 1744 and taken as a prize into Louisburg. Though imprisoned for some months, Harrison learned all details of the coast and harbor of Cape Breton and of its weak defenses. This information he recorded on a carefully drawn map, which Governor Shirley of Massachusetts used in planning the attack on Louisburg. The next year he drew plans for strengthening Fort George on Goat Island in Newport Harbor. Later (in 1755) he designed a new lighthouse for Conanicut Island, and made a very well drawn ' Plan of the Town and Harbour of Newport on Rhode Island,' which is still preserved in the Public Record Office in London.

In these and other activities, in his career as a merchant and as a farmer, Harrison became unusually proficient in a diversity of fields. ' Not a jack of all trades,' as Bridenbaugh writes, but ' rather a master of *ten* – ship-handling, navigation, shipbuilding, woodcarving, drafting, cartography, surveying, military engineering and construction, commerce, and the new agriculture,' [26] Harrison equaled Benjamin Franklin in versatility of talent, if not in the former's curiosity and shrewd wisdom.

In 1746, Harrison married Elizabeth Pelham of Newport, a young lady of unrivaled social position and owner of property worth £20,000. In that year he and his brother Joseph set up their own shipping firm, with a warehouse and retail store on Thames Street, down by the busy docks. Peter himself continued traveling, with trips to Liverpool, Hull, Charleston, and other ports. His frequent trips to England must have kept him *au courant* with the newer English architecture, and on his return to Newport in 1748 he brought a large box of books – the nucleus of what was to become the largest and best-selected architectural library of colonial America.[27] In that same year his architectural career began.

The Redwood Library, Newport. 1748–50

In 1747 Abraham Redwood contributed £500 to a Newport philosophical society for the purchase of books, and other Newport citizens subscribed £5,000 for construction of a library building. Joseph Harrison was a member of the original corporation, and during the initial stages, at least, he collaborated with his brother Peter on the design. A contract for construction was signed on 9 August 1748, when Peter was in England. Probably based on a preliminary sketch that Peter sent over, the design was materially changed after his return, in February 1749, and the building was completed about a year later (fig. 373).

We may assume that Peter Harrison was dissatisfied with the traditional style and domestic aspect of public buildings in the provinces, and that he aspired to the greater severity and monumentality of the English Palladian mode. He was already well versed in the newer fashion, and from his books he could seek proper models. For the façade he chose a temple portico with side wings forming the ends of a larger and lower pediment — a motive, descended from Palladio, which he found in a book by Edward Hoppus (fig. 374).[28] Certain details of the façade and many elements of the plan evidently came from a garden pavilion designed by William Kent for Sir Charles Hotham, also published in one of his

373. The Redwood Library, Newport, 1748–50, by Peter Harrison (Wayne Andrews)

books.[29] The rear façade, especially its three Venetian windows (now moved to form a side wing, visible in fig. 373), came from a garden temple at Chiswick designed by Lord Burlington.[30] For the elaborate bookcases inside the library, he probably relied on a plate in Batty Langley's *Treasury of Designs*.[31]

All of this dependence on books, and particularly on the cold and,

374. Design for a Palladian façade from the *Fourth Book of Andrea Palladio*, by Edward Hoppus, London, 1756 (courtesy Avery Library, Columbia University)

formal classical tradition of Palladio — Inigo Jones — Lord Burlington, was characteristic of advanced work in the late Georgian period in the colonies. It was extremely academic in method, and the results were not always happy. The Redwood Library is devoid of the color and feeling, the occasional delightful bits of baroque ornament, with which Sir Christopher Wren had endowed the early Georgian style. It is faulty as a formal design, for the projecting ' half-pediments ' of the wings, in their original state (fig. 375), were excrescences essentially unrelated to the main mass. Even the main mass may be criticized: it lacks the sheer size that warrants

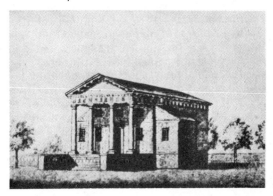

375. The Redwood Library in 1767, from a drawing by Pierre Eugène du Simitière (HABS)

the grand-scale treatment of the Roman classical temple, for the columns are only 17 feet high. True grandeur in a big building may be mere grandiosity in a little one.

Criticism may also be made of the exterior siding. Seeking the impressiveness of classical stone masonry with the inexpensiveness of wood, the specifications called for an exterior surface of ' Pine Plank worked in imitation of Rustick.' The imitation in one material of another and more expensive material smacks of snobbishness in any age; we see no more reason for condoning it in the Georgian period than we do of applauding the imitation of brick masonry in asphalt composition siding or of manufacturing ' quarry-faced stone masonry ' out of concrete in the twentieth century. The history of the use of rusticated wood siding in Georgian architecture has never been thoroughly explored, but it seems possible that Peter Harrison may have been the one primarily responsible for its adoption. The Redwood Library is the earliest building in the colonies of definite date to employ the motive, though Shirley Place at Roxbury may antedate it. Harrison used the same treatment in a small octagonal summer house erected on Abraham Redwood's estate about 1748–9 (since removed to the grounds of the Library), and it was also used on three Newport houses that have been attributed to him.* The motive became

---

* Isham attributed the Bull House (now destroyed), the Banister House (before 1765), and the Bowler-Vernon House (1758) to Harrison on stylistic grounds.

fairly popular in New England, being used on the west façade of the Royall House at Medford (1747–50), the Matthew Cozzens (Dudley) House at Middletown, Rhode Island (c.1750), The Lindens at Danvers, Massachusetts (1754), the Wentworth-Gardner House at Portsmouth (1760), the Sir William Johnson House at Johnstown, New York (1762), the Jeremiah Lee House at Marblehead (1768), and probably on several others; it ultimately received the sanction of Washington at Mount Vernon, as we have seen.

Immediately after its completion, the Library became one of the show places of Newport. Dr. William Douglass commended it in his *Summary of the British Settlements in North America* (Boston, vol. II, 1752, p. 101); it was noted by the Englishman Andrew Burnaby in his *Travels;* and the Frenchman Pierre Eugène du Simitière made a watercolor of it in his sketchbook (fig. 375) when he visited Newport in 1767.

All told, the Redwood Library may be accounted the least successful and the most significant of Peter Harrison's buildings. It was important because it was a unique exemplar in America of the newest English mode, and it pointed the direction of evolution of architectural style. With its Roman Doric temple façade, approached by steps between parotids, and with its pedimented gable carried back to form the main roof slope, it was the first approximation in America of the classical temple form. In the post-Revolutionary years, of course, this form became increasingly popular and culminated in the ubiquitous classical temples of the Greek Revival period.

Except for the side wings, the faults of the Redwood Library were the faults of an age rather than of an individual. As a beginning amateur, Peter Harrison is perhaps to be forgiven for his failure to perceive that the English models he followed were themselves at fault: their classicism was a spurious one, for they reduced the grandeur that was Rome to the scale of toy temples in villa gardens; they treated architecture as playful scenery, an impertinence to the mistress art if not to their own sense of the trivial. Fortunately, Peter Harrison was never again so naïve.

The library seems to have served its purpose fairly well. There was one large room, 26 feet wide by 36 long, which served for the stacks, and the projecting wings served for small offices. On its completion the library was well stocked with an excellent collection of books, and it has continued to grow and serve the original society, which exists to this day. Additions to the sides and rear were made in 1858, and the building was restored in 1928. It was prophetic of his whole architectural career that Peter Harrison asked for no reward for designing the building and received none.

King's Chapel, Boston. 1749–54

King's Chapel was the first important Anglican congregation in New England. When the congregation was first founded in 1686, services were held (by order of Governor Andros) in the Old South Meeting-House. A small edifice was erected in 1688–9, and this was doubled in size in 1710–13. But by 1741 this was once again too small and a building committee, with Peter Faneuil as treasurer, was appointed to raise funds for a new church.³² The committee, having stipulated the dimensions of the proposed edifice and that 'rough stone' should be used for the walls, sought the advice of 'Mr. Harrison, of Rhode Island, a gentleman of good judgment in architecture,' who on 5 April 1749 was requested for 'a drawing of a handsome church agreeable to the limits set forth.' ³³ Harrison worked on the drawings steadily throughout the spring and summer, and on 15 September 1749 posted to Boston a plan, elevations of east and west fa-

376. King's Chapel, Boston, 1749–54, by Peter Harrison (Detroit Publishing Company)

çades, a cross section, and designs for a steeple and the pews — an unusually detailed set of drawings for that day. Construction began in 1749 and the building opened for services on 21 August 1754.

The exterior of King's Chapel (fig. 376) as first completed, without the portico, was extremely simple. The stone walls (which made the first recorded use of Quincy granite) enclosed a rectangle of about 65 by 100 feet, topped by a hipped roof. The two tiers of arched windows on the long sides, the lower ones opening underneath the galleries, were probably derived from a plate in James Gibbs's *Book of Architecture,* and many details of the interior, such as the Corinthian order, the Palladian window at the east end, and the balustrade for the altar rail, came from Gibbs's *Rules for Drawing.*

Harrison planned a front porch of Ionic columns, 25 feet in height, topped by a balustrade; this was not built until 1785–7 (by Thomas Clem-

ent, following Harrison's design except for the balustrade), when it was
executed in wood rather than stone. This portico, and those of St.
Michael's, Charleston, and St. James', Santee, South Carolina, were the
only full-height classical porticoes designed for churches in the colonies.
The projecting stone tower, 26 feet square and with 4-foot-thick walls, was

377. Interior of King's Chapel (Detroit Publishing Company)

intended to carry a lofty spire, more elaborate than any in London. Harrison's design (which was still in existence in 1784) called for

an elegant and lofty steeple of two square stories and an octagonal spire. The
first story is to be of the Ionick order, with sixteen fluted coupled columns and
pilasters, nineteen inches in diameter. The second story, of the Corinthian order,
formed of eight fluted single columns, fourteen inches in diameter. The spire
rising above, to be finished in the richest manner. The columns with their entablature, which projects from the body of the steeple, to support highly finished and
ornamental urns.[34]

Though wealthy Ralph Allen, the 'Squire Allworthy' of Bath, England,
offered to send Bath stone and trained workers for its construction, the
spire was never built — a pity, for the exterior might then have matched
the sophisticated grace of the interior.

The interior of King's Chapel (fig. 377) is without question the finest
of Georgian church architecture in the colonies. The plan and nave were
strongly influenced by Gibbs's Marylebone Chapel in London, published
in Plate 24 of his *Book of Architecture* but Harrison was working with

more freedom and assurance than he had in the Redwood Library. There is an easy mastery of space composition, a sophisticated handling of the fine carved details of the Georgian vocabulary, and, particularly, a sure sense for true grandeur of scale, which had been lacking in his first work.

The general arrangement is not dissimilar to that of Old North Church, but a far greater unity of effect is achieved by the use of giant Corinthian columns, projecting in front of the gallery fronts. Their arrangement in pairs gives a more varied and powerful rhythm than the uniform spacing of single columns used in every other major Georgian church in the colonies. The order is fully displayed: molded bases, fluted shafts, opulent capitals, and fully membered blocks of entablature over each pair of columns form a complete and logical structural statement, brought up into full view by the square pedestals below pew level. Gallery fronts are beautifully paneled, and a fine Palladian window floods the sanctuary with light. The raised pulpit, saved from the earlier church, dates from 1717.

Being an Anglican church, King's Chapel received many royal favors. James II had given the first pulpit; Queen Anne, a red silk damask cushion for it as well as surplices and altar linen; and George III, a silver communion service. The church of course suffered no damage when the British occupied Boston during the Revolution, but afterward the crown and miter were removed from the organ, the governor's pew was torn out, and the name 'King's Chapel' was for a time abandoned in favor of 'Stone Chapel.' In 1785, it became the first Unitarian church in the United States, and since that time the royal appurtenances of the Church of England have been gradually restored, so that the building today presents very nearly its original superb architectural appearance as Peter Harrison's masterpiece.

It is possible, as discussed in the preceding chapter, that Harrison designed St. Michael's, in Charleston, South Carolina. It was begun in 1751, while King's Chapel was under construction. But for the next eight years, Harrison devoted himself to commercial and agricultural affairs, and it was not until 1759–60 that he engaged in another burst of architectural activity, producing in rapid succession the designs for Christ Church, Cambridge, and for the Jewish Synagogue and the Brick Market in Newport.

Christ Church, Cambridge. 1759–61

Harrison's increasing freedom in his use of bookish sources is illustrated in Christ Church, a building that shows many unusual features. It was a small and inexpensive church. The building committee wrote to Harrison in 1759 for ' a Plan and Elevation of the Outside and Inside, and of the Pulpit and Vestry ' but stipulated that ' the Building be of wood, and covered on the outside with Rough-cast; that there be only one tier of Windows; and no Galleries, except an organ Loft . . . and that, if Mr. Harrison approves of it, there be no steeple, only a Tower with a Belfry. . .' [35] They also limited the cost to the impossibly low figure of £500. Harrison posted a complete set of drawings in March 1760, and the building was completed and opened for services in 1761. The cost, to be sure, mounted to £1,300, but even that was only about a sixth of the cost of King's Chapel, without its spire and portico.

The exterior (fig. 378) is pleasantly unconventional. There is a simple tower in front, topped by a smaller cruciform belfry. The low side walls (there being no interior galleries) are treated with a row of arched windows connected by continuous archivolt and impost moldings and topped by a vigorous Roman Doric cornice. These exterior details, to be sure, may have been derived from plates in Gibbs's *Rules for Drawing,* but the over-

378. Christ Church, Cambridge, Mass., 1759–61, by Peter Harrison (HABS)

all design came from no single prototype. The exterior walls are made of a sort of rusticated planking; although the original intention was to cover this with rough-cast to resemble a stone finish, it must be the cost of even this cheap substitute for masonry was regarded as too high.

The interior (fig. 379) lacks the grandeur of King's Chapel, but it is one of great charm. Originally it was almost square; the nave was lengthened by the insertion of two additional bays in 1857. The single Ionic columns are raised on pedestals; it seems probable that they would have been fluted except for the cost. The ceiling over the nave rises in curved coves to a flat panel, the whole being quite separate from the aisle ceilings, which are flat. The absence of a gallery gives the church an unusual sense of spaciousness and light for so small a structure. There is a small balcony over the entrance doors, and a deep semicircular chancel lighted by a Palladian window at the opposite end. Rarely in the history of American architecture has so successful a church been achieved with so little expenditure of money. The parsimony of the congregation, however, did not extend to the architect; though he asked no pay, a gift of £45 (about 3 per cent of the cost) was sent to him.

Touro Synagogue, Newport. 1759–63

The synagogue on Touro Street in Newport, which Peter Harrison designed for Congregation Jeshuat Israel, has the distinction of being the oldest synagogue in the United States; since 1946 it has been preserved as a national historic monument.

The small congregation of fifteen or twenty families of Sephardic Jews, under the leadership of the Rabbi Isaac Touro, broke ground for its

379. Interior of Christ Church (HABS)

synagogue on 1 August 1759. Financial support for the work was given by Portuguese Jewish groups in New York, Jamaica, Curaçao, Surinam, London, and Amsterdam. Peter Harrison gave his services as architect, and Isaac Touro, who had only recently come from the Rabbinical Academy in Amsterdam, instructed him in the traditional Sephardic layout. The interior had to be small, with seats only around the perimeter; on three sides above was to be a gallery reserved for the women; there must be twelve columns representing the twelve tribes of Israel, a pulpit for reading the Law, and on the east wall the Ark of the Covenant.

The completed building was dedicated 2 December 1763. The brick exterior is plain to the point of barrenness. Only round-arch windows, a belt course, and a small Ionic porch relieve the severity of the box-like mass. The building had to be canted at an angle on the small lot in order to bring the Ark to the east, as demanded by ritual. A plain two-story school building was attached at the north side.

After this Spartan exterior, the extraordinary richness and delicacy of the interior (fig. 380) come as an astonishing contrast. Indeed, for its relatively small size, the interior is overrich in its display of every device and detail of the joiner's and carver's arts. Peter Harrison followed the instructions of the rabbi in the main plan and layout, but there the distinc-

380. Touro Synagogue, Newport, 1759–63, by Peter Harrison (HABS)

tively Jewish character of the design ceases entirely. Every detail of this brilliant interior stems from the English academic architectural books with which he was accustomed to work; indeed in this unfamiliar commission, with no precedent to guide him, he leaned more heavily than ever before on English sources, and though he did so with remarkable taste and skill, the total effect is far removed from the profound emotional content of the Hebrew service and tradition.

The general scheme of the interior he took from a two-story galleried hall in Whitehall Palace, which he found in William Kent's *Designs of Inigo Jones* [36] — a hall with Corinthian columns superposed on Ionic, and an arched ceiling above. This he adapted to the ritual requirement, there being twelve columns below and above. The gallery for the women, reached by a stairway in a small exterior addition, he adorned with a rich balustrade taken from Gibbs's *Rules for Drawing*. The ornate pulpit for reading the Law stands in the center of the floor, nearer the west than the east end; reached by three steps, it is surrounded by a heavy balustrade. A wainscoted seat runs along the sides of the hall, and there is another in the gallery. In the middle of the north side, this is raised to afford a throne for the ruler and elders, the breast and back inlaid with mosaic. The east wall is dominated by a two-story composition of great richness, to house the Ark of the Covenant. The lower part Harrison derived from a ' Tuscan altarpiece ' in the pages of Batty Langley [37]; it frames four narrow doors opening into a shallow closet containing three copies of the Pentateuch, written on vellum. The upper part combines motives from two chimneypieces published in books by Kent and Ware.[38]

Touro Synagogue has often been regarded as Harrison's masterpiece. It is indeed a brilliant display of virtuosity in adapting the novelties and details of the English fashion, but it expresses nothing of the sombre and tragic intensities of the service it was designed to house, and in this it fails of being great architecture. On the contrary, it is aggressively cheerful, sprightly, elegant, and as English eighteenth century as it could possibly be. It calls to mind not the profundities of the service of Atonement, but rather a Boston shopkeeper's advertisement of 1725: ' Just imported from London . . . all sorts of Womans Shoes, and Pattoons, fine Macklins, & English Laces & Edgings, Mantua Silks, Paderina, fine Cambricks, Lawns, Hollands, Muslins, Gold & Silver Stomachers, Ribbons, Gloves, &c.' [39]

The Brick Market, Newport. 1761–72

Harrison's last architectural work was the old Brick Market in Newport. In 1760 the proprietors of the Long Wharf deeded waterfront land to the town, on which they proposed to erect, by aid of a public lottery,

a handsome brick building, to be thirty-three feet in front . . . and about sixty-six feet in length. The lower part thereof for a Market House, and for no other use whatsoever . . . the upper part [shall] be divided into stores for dry-goods, and let out to the best advantage; and all the rents thereof, together with all the profits that shall arise on said building, shall be lodged in the Town Treasury of said town of Newport, towards a stock for purchasing grain, for supplying a Public Granary forever.[40]

This public-spirited enterprise was begun in September 1762 and roofed about a year later, but not all details were completed until July 1772. Peter Harrison, of course, was chosen as architect for such a civic project. He turned again to his English books, selecting as a model the

great gallery at Somerset House in London (fig. 382), designed by Inigo
Jones and John Webb and published by Colen Campbell in *Vitruvius
Britannicus*.[41] As applied to the market, the design was modified for brick
rather than stone construction, the rustication of the base omitted, the
giant pilasters changed from Corinthian to Ionic, and the urns over the
cornice omitted (fig. 381). Nonetheless the design was unusually close to
the original.

381. Brick Market, Newport, 1761–72, by Peter Harrison (Wayne Andrews)

The market was built with open arcades on the ground floor — seven
arches on the long side, three on the short — and the two upper stories,
whose windows had alternating angular and segmental pediments, were
devoted to retail dry-goods shops and offices. The exterior design was
completely formal, and one of the most academic in the colonies; it is
believed to be the earliest instance of the favorite academic composition
of arcaded base with an order of giant pilasters above — familiar in Renaissance design from the time of Palladio down. The building was later
put to a variety of uses: it served as a theater in 1793, and from 1842 to
1900 as a Town and City Hall. Finally, it was thoroughly restored in
1928–30 and is maintained as a public monument by the Newport Chamber of Commerce.

In 1766 Peter Harrison was awarded the post of Collector of Customs in

New Haven, and went there with his family to live. It proved an ill-advised move. A Tory and an Anglican, Harrison was soon subject to the abuses and hostilities suffered by all who stood for the Royalist cause. For a time, he escaped on a visit to Governor John Wentworth of New Hampshire, and while at Portsmouth in 1769 he may have had some hand in designing the Governor's summer estate on Lake Wentworth, near Wolfeboro. Wentworth also recommended Harrison to President Eleazar Wheelock of Dartmouth for 'the Building of a great College' in 1773. Wheelock, who disapproved of Wentworth's and Harrison's Anglicanism and in general thought he knew what was what, preferred his own choice of a

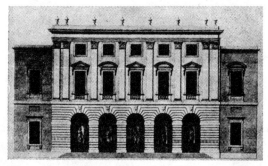

382. Model for the Brick Market design: gallery at Somerset House, London, by Inigo Jones and John Webb (Colen Campbell, *Vitruvius Britannicus,* I, Plate 16)

house carpenter from Stillwater, New York, and nothing came of the suggestion.

Back in New Haven during the early 1770's, Peter Harrison was subject to all manner of insults and abuse from the Patriots (or 'rebels' as he called them), which he received with increasing alarm and tension. The battles of Lexington and Concord in April of 1775 seemed to tumble his entire Royalist world about his ears, and on 30 April he died of a stroke. That autumn a New Haven mob destroyed his extensive library and records.

Later Georgian churches

Of a large number of Georgian churches in New England, three may be selected as representing types common in the late eighteenth century.

Simplest was the old-fashioned meeting-house, exemplified in the Rocky Hill Meeting-House at Amesbury, Massachusetts (fig. 383). Built as late as 1785, it represents a type that had been common throughout the eighteenth century and remained popular in small towns until about 1800. These churches had box-like masses topped by gabled roofs, and two rows of windows indicating the main and gallery levels within. There was no tower or spire, but frequently a two-story porch on the middle of the long side permitted a stair to the gallery outside of the main auditorium. Georgian decorative detail was used most sparingly: the front door always received some treatment, such as flanking pilasters and a cornice or pediment above; windows were sometimes corniced; the eaves were often adorned with modillions; but the total effect was very plain. The meeting-houses at Amesbury and Sandown, New Hampshire (1774), are the two best of this type, but there are good examples at Rockingham, Vermont (1787), and in Maine at Waldoboro (the Old German Church, c.1770), Bristol (Walpole Church, 1772), and Alna (1789).

Towns with somewhat more wealth usually voted for the 'spired meeting-house' type, a combination of the old side-entrance meeting-house plan with a tower and spire at one end, after the model of the Old South

383. Rocky Hill Meeting-House, Amesbury, Mass., 1785 (HABS)

at Boston. Representative are the meeting-houses at Dedham, Massachusetts (1763), Wethersfield, Connecticut (1761), and Farmington, Connecticut (1771). The Farmington church (fig. 384) is the best of these. The Greek Revival porch in front of the side entrance door is a later addition, and the gallery posts, 'slip' pews, and organ were inserted about 1836, but otherwise the church is unchanged. The tower and spire at the end are modeled after Boston's Old South. The church was designed, and very soundly built, by one Captain Judah Woodruff, who is said to have traveled over New England looking at other churches, to have selected the wood for the building with unusual care, and to have calculated its unusually sturdy and durable structure. The eight posts that give the spire such an airy support are carried 25 feet down into the body of the tower and securely fastened by hand-wrought bolts. The transverse roof trusses have cross girts a foot square and 53 feet long; each truss, made of white oak, has been estimated to weigh almost $4\frac{1}{2}$ tons. So strong was the roof construction that the ridgepole has sagged only an inch and a half during the past 175 years, and it is said that the original white-cedar shingles of the roof needed no replacement for 128 years.[42]

The Farmington church proved influential in the early nineteenth century, for some of its details were published in Asher Benjamin's architectural handbooks, which had a wide circulation in New England.

The third and most elaborate type of late Georgian church was based on the sophisticated work of Peter Harrison, or even more directly on English sources. One of the largest and finest examples is the First Baptist Meeting-House in Providence.[43] This was built in 1774–5, for the most part under the direction of Joseph Brown. A successful merchant, Brown

384. Congregational Meeting-House, Farmington, Conn., 1771. Judah Woodruff (Wayne Andrews)

was also a student of astronomy and mechanics, a faculty member and trustee of Rhode Island College (later Brown University), and the designer of several buildings. Brown, in company with two other men, journeyed to Boston to look at churches before undertaking this house 'for the Publick Worship of Almighty God, and also for holding Commencement in.' But like many gentleman amateurs of the eighteenth century, he owned his own copy of James Gibbs's *Book of Architecture* and relied more directly on it than on any Boston edifice.

The church was originally 80 feet square, with doors on all four sides, the main entrance being at the west end under the tower. A gabled projection contained the necessary stairs, and above this rose the tower and spire to a height of 185 feet (fig. 385). Based directly on an unexecuted design for St. Martin's-in-the-Fields in London, published in Plate 30 of Gibbs's book, the spire was almost too elaborate. Its features were detailed

by the master carpenter, James Sumner of Boston, and it was originally
'painted with different colors,' probably marbleizing.

The interior (fig. 386), which was lengthened during the nineteenth
century, bears a strong resemblance to two of James Gibbs's churches,
Marylebone Chapel and St. Martin's-in-the-Fields (fig. 247). Giant Doric
columns are cut midway by the galleries. A shallow plaster vault over the

385. First Baptist Meeting-House, Providence, R.I., 1774-5 (George B. Brayton)

nave meets groined vaults over the gallery bays. The east end was originally flat, with a fine Palladian window set with clear glass; this was
moved backward by the later addition of a small chancel. Despite the
loss of original pews and pulpit and an interesting second gallery at the
west end, where Negro slaves used to sit, the interior preserves most of its
fine detail in windows, doors, cornices, and the like, carefully transcribed
by Joseph Brown from the pages of Gibbs, and over the nave hangs a
beautiful cut-glass chandelier, brought from England in 1792. On the
whole, the church has justified the hope of the *Providence Gazette* on
10 June 1775 that 'it will be a most elegant Piece of Architecture.' A
descendant of the first Baptist congregation in America, led by Roger
Williams in 1638, this is now the oldest Baptist church edifice in the
country.

New England colleges in the eighteenth century

Harvard, Yale, Brown, and Dartmouth were founded before the Revolution; of these only Harvard dates back to the seventeenth century, but its seventeenth-century buildings (figs. 65–9) have entirely disappeared. Thus Massachusetts Hall, built 1718–20, is the oldest Harvard building now standing (fig. 387). The province granted £3,500 for construction, and the building was designed by President John Leverett and Benjamin

386. Interior of First Baptist Meeting-House, Providence (George B. Brayton)

Wadsworth. It was a dormitory containing 32 chambers and a small private study for each of the 64 students.

Three stories high, and with a fourth under the broad gambrel roof, the building has an air of solidity and permanence. The six chimneys, arranged in pairs, are massive stacks, those at the ends being connected by parapets and shaped by recessed channels on the outer faces. The break of the gambrel is marked by a balustrade on either side of the roof. The west gable originally carried a large clock. The walls are plainly treated, marked only by brick belt courses between stories; the brick masonry is laid in English bond below the water table and in Flemish bond above, except at the ends where there is a mixture of English and common bonds. The simple mass and heavy woodwork of the windows give a very satisfactory effect of solidity, and it is this effect — an early Georgian simplicity and weight — which has been sought (not always successfully) in the recent buildings of Harvard.

387. Massachusetts Hall, Harvard University, 1718–20 (Arthur C. Haskell)

388. Holden Chapel, Harvard University, 1742–4 (HABS)

Quite the richest Georgian building at Harvard was the miniature Holden Chapel (fig. 388), built in 1742–4. The initial gift of £400 for its construction came from the widow of Samuel Holden, a director of the Bank of England, and her arms were emblazoned on the west pediment (and now duplicated on the east one). The round-arch windows, classic pilasters, and entablature gave the building a sophisticated architectural dress. It was built as a chapel, but instead of box pews it had a central aisle paralleled by longitudinal rows of seats rising in successive tiers to

389. Harvard Hall, Cambridge, as rebuilt in 1764–6 (drawing by A. J. Davis, engraved by James Archer)

the side walls. The president's desk was at the east end, and the ceiling rose in a gently curved vault. Morning and evening prayers were held here until after the Revolution, when the building became the first home of the Harvard Medical School, its rising tiers of seats serving well for a dissecting amphitheatre. Later it was used for lectures and debates; in 1880 the building was restored to its original chapel form.

Old Harvard Hall (see figs. 67–9) was burned in January 1764, and in 1764–6 was replaced by 'New' Harvard Hall, which still stands. Additions in 1842 and 1870 have changed its appearance, but as originally built (fig. 389) it was the first major Harvard building to attempt a non-domestic architectural effect. With hipped roof, classic cornice, pedimented gables, and a large cupola, it had something of the 'public' quality of Faneuil Hall. Built with money donated by the province, the building provided, in its western half, a chapel (with round-arch windows) and above it the Library; in the eastern half were kitchen and buttery in the basement, a dining hall on the main floor, and a ' philosophical chamber ' (meaning a rudimentary scientific laboratory) in the second story.

Hollis Hall, Harvard's only other eighteenth-century building, was built just to the north of Harvard Hall in 1762–3 (fig. 390). Four stories high, with a hipped roof and many chimneys, a central pavilion topped by a pediment, and three entrance doors (originally on the west side), the structure was very similar to the then recently completed Nassau Hall at Princeton, and to the later college edifices at Brown and Dartmouth.

Bare, forthright, and simple, these Georgian buildings at Harvard had

390. Hollis Hall, Harvard University, 1762–3 (HABS)

vigor and honesty, but they did not suit the romantic tastes of the later nineteenth century. President Lowell, in an address marking Harvard's 250th anniversary, deplored their plainness:

> There in red brick, which softening Time defies,
> Stand square and stiff the Muses' factories.

He complained that ' We have none or next to none of those coigns of vantage for the tendrils of memory or affection, built into English universities. . . Not one of our older buildings is venerable or will ever become so. Time refuses to console them. They look as if they meant business and nothing more.' Unfortunately, his sentimental tastes were met by the Gothic and Romanesque edifices of Bond and Schulze, and by the Victorian glitter of Memorial Hall and other buildings of the 1870's. Oliver Wendell Holmes, writing a generation earlier, had shown a truer appreciation of Harvard's ivy-covered old red-brick buildings:

> We find her at her ancient door, and in her stately chair,
> Dressed in the robes of red and green she always loved to wear.
> (*Autocrat of the Breakfast Table*, 1857)

Almost lost amid the gorgeous Gothic of Yale's twentieth-century architectural scenery stands Old South Middle, only relic today of the sound and simple architectural tradition of the eighteenth century. Yale was founded in 1701 and for some years was operated on slender means as a Collegiate School at Saybrook, Connecticut. Induced by ' the amenity and salubrity of the air, and the cheapness and abundance of victuals ' at New Haven, the infant College moved thither in 1716 and proceeded to erect the first large college edifice. Many records of its construction survive, though the building itself was demolished more than 160 years ago.[44] Work at cutting and squaring the framing timbers was begun on 8 January 1717. They were of majestic size: 20 posts, 10 × 10 inches and 27 feet long; 3 huge sills, 8 × 10 inches and 54 feet long; 3 plates almost as large; 2 girts for ' ye Hall,' 8 × 10 inches and 31 feet long; as well as some 90 other heavy timbers. The frame was raised on 8 October, and the building was substantially complete for the Commencement of 10 September 1718. In August of that year Elihu Yale, a native of Boston then resident in England, had sent a cargo of books and goods to the value of £562, and thus achieved an immortality that perhaps exceeded the proportions of his gift.

The master builder of Yale College was Henry Caner, an Englishman born near Bristol about 1680 and a resident of Boston as early as 1710. His architectural work began in Boston with the enlargement of the old wooden structure of the first King's Chapel; this doubtless brought him to the attention of Connecticut's Governor Saltonstall, and he probably went to New Haven in the autumn of 1717. Caner designed the college edifice, the first Rector's House (1722), and possibly the first State House, which was built in 1719 on the northwest corner of the Green. He died in 1731; his gravestone may still be seen in the Grove Street cemetery.

The new college edifice (fig. 391) was three stories and garret in height, very long and narrow in plan (about 22 by 170 feet), with a steep roof, many dormer windows, six chimneys, and a central cupola. The exterior walls were of wood. Three entrances on each side were connected by halls across the building. The largest rooms were the Hall, used for commons and chapel, on the ground floor at the south end, and the Library directly over it. There were in addition 22 suites of chambers and studies to accommodate 66 students, a sanguine provision for an institution that hitherto had not had more than 30 persons in attendance at any one time. A separate one-story kitchen was attached to the dining hall. The College records show no disbursement for paint until 1734, so it is possible that the building remained unpainted for its first sixteen years. It is clear that there were sash windows, for only five years after the building's completion the trustees ' Agreed that the Schollars shall be obliged to repair the Damages by breaking the Glass Weights to draw up the Windows. . .'

The only detailed representation of the old building is engraved from a drawing made by J. Greenwood between 1742 and 1745. Possibly Greenwood drew the building only from descriptions, for the engraving has many errors. The great length of the building in proportion to its width is not suggested, the windows of the north end are omitted, and we know

that there was a hipped roof rather than a gabled one. The squat, heavy
cupola shown does not answer to other evidence of a light and lofty belfry,
and the great clock concealing the central dormer window may be purely
imaginary, for there is no documentary evidence of any clock whatsoever.
The college edifice, like Harvard's first building, was short-lived. It may
not have been too soundly constructed, and it certainly received rough
treatment. The building was razed — in stages — between 1775 and 1782;

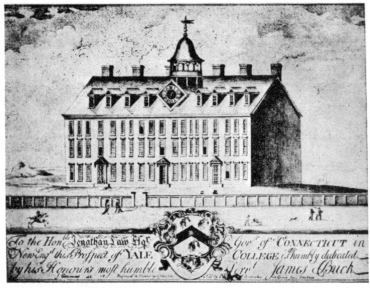

391. First Yale College edifice, New Haven, built 1717–18, demolished 1775–82, by
Henry Caner. From an engraving by James Buck, c.1745 (Yale University News
Bureau)

by this time Connecticut Hall, first of the historic Brick Row, had been
erected.

Connecticut Hall, called Old South Middle, was built in 1750–52 for
the sum of £1,660, about half of which was raised by a lottery. The only
pre-Revolutionary building left, it is Yale's equivalent of Massachusetts
Hall at Harvard (fig. 392). Indeed in size and arrangement it is a close
parallel to the latter, the chief difference being that the interior chimneys
permit the profile of the gambrel roof to be seen at the ends. Dormer windows and a fourth story were added under this roof in 1796–7. It is one of
the most satisfactory of Yale's buildings.

Rhode Island College, which became Brown University in 1804, was
founded at Warren, Rhode Island, in 1764, but was soon moved to Providence when a fine new brick building, the present University Hall, was
built there in 1770–71 (fig. 393). Joseph Brown was a member of the
building committee which drew up plans based on old Nassau Hall at
Princeton. Somewhat smaller than its model, University Hall lacks the

fine proportions that Nassau originally had, the increase in height to four stories being the most damaging difference. The gaunt walls, relieved only by belt courses and the slightly arched heads of doors and windows, give this a better claim to Lowell's appellation of 'Muses' factory' than had Harvard's Massachusetts Hall. The exterior was plastered in 1835, but this coat was happily removed in 1905, and the building has recently been restored by the Williamsburg architects.

392. Connecticut Hall, Yale University, 1750–52 (Yale University News Bureau)

By 1770 college edifices in America had crystallized into a more or less standard pattern: a long building mass three or four stories high, covered by a hipped roof and topped by a belfry, with a pedimented pavilion breaking the middle of the long side, and three entrance doors. Such were Nassau Hall, Hollis at Harvard, and University Hall at Brown. Since decorative details were sparingly used (the four pedimented pavilions on King's College, New York, built in 1760, were exceptional), the architectural effect depended almost solely on such fundamentals as proportion, fenestration, and the relation of pavilion to wings. Both Nassau and Hollis had five-window pavilions, a little oversized in relation to the total mass; the three-window pavilion on University Hall appeared too tall and narrow for its four-story height and excessive projection. The cupolas on both Nassau and University Halls were of insufficient size to dominate such large building masses.

The happiest solution of shape and proportion within this collegiate type was achieved in Dartmouth Hall, built after the Revolution (fig. 394). The College was founded in 1769, and, as we have seen, a proposal in 1773 that Peter Harrison design its first permanent edifice came to nought. The war intervened, and construction was not undertaken until 1784–91. Great difficulties were encountered in raising the necessary funds,

393. University Hall, Brown University, Providence, R.I., 1770–71 (courtesy Antoinette F. Downing)

394. Dartmouth Hall, Hanover, N.H., 1784–91, as rebuilt in 1935 (Adrian Bouchard)

subscriptions being encouraged in 'lawful money, beef, pork, grain, or boards to be delivered at the College, or in glass, nails, or merchandise. . .'[45] During the heavy work of raising the great frame, which required ten days, the workmen's spirits were refreshed by prayer and their bodies refreshed by spirits, as was then customary. Main framing timbers were 15 inches square, sills and plates 75 feet long, and cross girts over 50 feet long. Stone and brick were used only in the foundations, the walls being covered by clapboards for reasons of economy.*

The architect of Dartmouth Hall is not known. Designs had been submitted by William Gamble in the early 1770's, but these were rejected, and the drawings still preserved in the College archives do not resemble the executed building. Comfort Sever, a carpenter from Stillwater, New York, had settled in Hanover in 1773 under Wheelock's patronage, and drew plans at that time. Possibly the eventual design was arrived at by the contractor, Bezaleel Woodward, on the basis of Gamble's and Sever's drawings.[46]

Three stories high and 175 feet long, the building was covered by a low-pitch hipped roof with four pairs of massive chimneys. The graceful cupola, 'with proper ornaments agreeable to the rules of architecture,' was completed by the joiner Israel Parsons, of Hatfield, Massachusetts, and the clapper of the College bell housed therein was periodically removed by later generations of spirited 'young schollars' to be deposited in the Connecticut River. The relationship of the three-window central pavilion to the flanking wings was happier than in either Nassau Hall, Hollis at Harvard, University Hall at Brown, or the rejected Gamble design. With perfect repose and integrity, Dartmouth Hall achieved an architectural distinction unmatched in its group. It is particularly fortunate in its setting and in the harmonious grouping of its near neighbors, Wentworth and Thornton Halls, built in 1828, the three making Dartmouth Row perhaps the finest group of early college buildings in the country outside of Charlottesville, Virginia.

READING SUGGESTIONS

The history of Boston to 1742 is well treated in Carl Bridenbaugh's *Cities in the Wilderness* (Ronald Press Co., New York, 1938).

For the architecture of New England meeting-houses and churches, see: Edward F. Rines, *Old Historic Churches of America* (Macmillan, New York, 1936); Aymar Embury II, *Early American Churches* (Doubleday Page and Co., New York, 1914); Elise Lathrop, *Old New England Churches* (Tuttle Publishing Co., Rutland, Vermont, 1938); J. Frederick Kelly, *Early Connecticut Meetinghouses* (Columbia University Press, New York, 1948); George Franklin Marlowe, *Churches of Old New England* (Macmillan, New York, 1947); Eva A. Speare, *Colonial Meeting-Houses of New Hampshire* (Courier Co., Littleton, New Hampshire, 1938).

* Burned in 1904, the building was rebuilt in brick with different interior arrangements, but the original exterior was followed in all but a few details. Another rebuilding of the interior occurred after a fire in 1935.

For New England inns and taverns, see Elise Lathrop's *Early American Inns and Taverns* (Tudor Publishing Co., New York, 1935).

For the early architecture of New England colleges, see Charles Z. Klauder and Herbert C. Wise's *College Architecture in America* (Scribner's, New York, 1929), Chapter 1.

Some Rhode Island public buildings are discussed in Antoinette Downing's *Early Homes of Rhode Island* (Garrett and Massie, Richmond, 1937); and the authoritative work on Peter Harrison is Carl Bridenbaugh's *Peter Harrison, First American Architect* (University of North Carolina Press, Chapel Hill, 1949).

15

Georgian Houses in New England

SINCE THE Georgian style was pre-eminently an expression of wealth, it first evolved in the larger and finer mansions of the coastal and inland towns of New England. It is inevitable that these should claim major attention in any history of architectural style. But it is worth remarking that in New England there was a large group of middle-class houses, quite in contrast to the South, where there was almost no middle ground, architecturally, between the mansions of the wealthy and the miserable cabins of the slaves.

These middle-class houses were, at first, either seventeenth-century constructions or new edifices built in that traditional style. As the eighteenth century progressed, the houses of the middle class became smaller and simplified versions of the Georgian mansions the wealthy had built a generation earlier. We can see this in the gradual evolution of eighteenth-century house plans (fig. 395).

At the beginning of the century the typical New England house had a central-chimney plan with small entry or porch in front of the chimney, a big room on either side, and three smaller rooms at the back. This was a belated Colonial-type plan — on the ground story, at least — identical to the lean-to plan of the late seventeenth century (cf. fig. 12). Except for sliding-sash windows and a pilastered and pedimented doorway, the architectural style was also traditional. But these houses differed from their seventeenth-century prototypes in having two full stories: the rear wall rose to two-story height and the early lean-to chambers were replaced by full-size rooms, as big as the hall and parlor chambers. At the same time the roof ridge migrated backward from its axis over the front rooms to the axis of the whole house, creating a symmetrical gabled roof with equal front and rear slopes; the old saltbox roof became a thing of the past.

By the end of the first generation the example already set by a few of the finest houses was widely followed, and the second plan-type became almost universal. This had a central hall running through the house from front to back, not usually very spacious, but with a Georgian-type stairway. The pairs of rooms on either side were separated by interior chimneys with fireplaces front and back, and were often connected by passages or closets beside the chimneys. The kitchen was usually located in an ell at the back, with its own large fireplace and service stair to the garret rooms. The ell was usually prolonged in a straggling series of connected woodsheds and carriage houses, which permitted protected access to the

stable, the barn, and the chicken house during the cold winters — a striking contrast to the completely detached outbuildings found in the
South.

As brick construction became increasingly common, it was found eco-
nomical to abandon the two large interior chimneys in favor of end chimneys built into the walls. The flues of the two fireplaces at each end might
merge into a single chimney stack or be carried up as twin chimneys at
each end, connected above the roof slope by a brick parapet. This latter
end-chimney type of plan remained popular into the Federal period. Occasionally one finds the logical economy of brick end walls, incorporating
the chimneys, combined with clapboarded front and rear walls — but almost never, in the eighteenth century, the illogical converse of frame end
walls and brick front and rear.

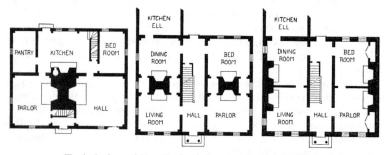

395. Typical plans of New England Georgian houses (Philip White)

Certain predilections in materials or stylistic forms distinguish New
England Georgian houses from those of other regions. Frame construction
always remained more popular than in the other colonies; the vast majority of ordinary houses were clapboarded or shingled, and even the fine
mansions were usually of wood rather than brick. Among these, a sizeable minority made use of rusticated wood siding, simulating masonry.
The hipped roof occurred, but not so universally as in the South; the
gabled roof continued in use, and the gambrel roof gained steadily in
popularity. But as if to offset these homely simplicities, New England
houses made more extensive use of applied pilasters, roof-decks, and cupolas than did those of other regions. The elaborate swan's neck pediment
atop the entrance door was also favored, particularly in the Connecticut
valley. Yankee carpenters and shipwrights were especially skilful in woodcarving, and their mantelpieces, step ends, and stair rails were often very
elaborate. The spirally twisted baluster and newel post received particular emphasis in New England.

The character and development of the Georgian style in New England
may be traced in a series of a dozen houses of outstanding architectural
interest, half of them built before the mid-century, half between then and
the outbreak of the Revolution. Some of the earliest ones in Boston,
though long since demolished, are worthy of inclusion because of their
historical importance in the development of the style.

Foster-Hutchinson House, Boston. c.1688

Though we must depend on some conjecture, it seems almost certain that this mansion of the late seventeenth century was the first Georgian building in the American colonies. Since it was demolished in 1833, we know its exterior appearance only through a view (fig. 396) published in 1836.[1] Some details of its history are gleaned from various documents, and

396. Foster-Hutchinson House, Boston *c.*1688 (*American Magazine of Useful Knowledge*, 1836)

descriptions of the house are given in Lydia Maria Child's novel *The Rebels* (1825).[2] The cardinal question is whether the remarkably advanced architectural style of the house as pictured in 1836 dates from its original construction or was the product of extensive remodeling during the eighteenth century.

The house was built by Colonel John Foster, from Ayelsboro in Buckinghamshire, England. Foster came to Boston in 1675 and became a rich merchant, a member of the Provincial Council, and Judge of the Court of Common Pleas. He purchased land in 1686 on the northwest side of North Square, the desirable residential section at that time, and built his house shortly after; we may presume that it was completed about 1688.[3] After Foster's death in 1711, his widow bequeathed it in the same year to her nephew Colonel Thomas Hutchinson, who lived in it until his death in

1739. His son Thomas, who was to become Royal Governor,* was born in the house in 1711 and continued to live in it until his departure for England in 1774. Hutchinson was the only governor of the colony who did not reside in the Province House — because, as he said, he had a better one of his own.

Certain eighteenth-century events give clues to the history of the house. It evidently had a cupola, for it is recorded that this and the roof were damaged by a fire in 1748. The cupola must have been rebuilt, for it was again destroyed and the interiors of the house were looted by an angry mob, protesting the Stamp Act, on 26 August 1765. Mrs. Child, doubtless using poetic license, recounts how

the Governor watched the movements of the rabble; — saw crow-bars and axes busy on the roof of his magnificent dwelling . . . the noise of shattered glass and falling timber was mingled with horrid imprecations, in the midst of which, down fell the magnificent cupola, crushed to a thousand atoms.

But a British officer, present at the time of the riot, wrote to London more soberly:

As for the house, which from the structure and inside finishing seemed to be from a design of Inigo Jones or his successor, it appears they were a long time resolved to level it to the ground. They worked three hours at the cupola before they could get it down, and they uncovered part of the roof; but I suppose, that the thickness of the walls, which were of very fine brick-work, adorned with Ionic pilasters worked into the wall, prevented their completing their purpose.[4]

The roof was evidently repaired, minus the cupola. The interiors may have been either repaired or completely renewed to form the basis for Mrs. Child's glowing descriptions. She speaks of the hall with its ' spacious arch,' richly carved and gilded, the parlor paneling ' of the dark, richly-shaded mahogany of St. Domingo, ornamented with the same elaborate skill as the hall,' and two arched alcoves in the parlor looking out upon the garden. But most of the furniture, portraits, and tapestries that she mentions date from the reigns of George I and II, and it may be assumed that the description of the interiors after the riot of 1765 gives no certain evidence of their original appearance.

The same cannot be said for the exterior. This presents the incredible features — for a house built so early — of five chimneys built into the brick end walls; carved stone trim of remarkably fine quality †; a balustrade over the eaves, forty years earlier than the next instance of this feature in the colonies; a roof of considerably lower pitch than the seventeenth-century standard; giant pilasters in the Ionic order, made of stone set two inches deep in the brick wall; not to mention an array of minor details such as balustraded balcony, segmental pediment, mutuled cornice, and a formal composition of unparalleled sophistication for that time. Indeed the giant pilasters, used some sixty years before they appeared elsewhere

* He served as Lieutenant Governor for many years, finally succeeding Bernard as Governor in 1769.
† One of the Ionic capitals is preserved in the Massachusetts Historical Society.

in the colonies, and the detail of the Ionic capitals were such that it seemed 'almost inconceivable' to Kimball that these could date from the original construction of the house, and he suggested that they might have been added in a remodeling after the fire which damaged the cupola in 1748.[5]

The roof was rebuilt after this fire, and its pitch could have been changed. It is possible that details such as the balcony and balustrade could have been products of an eighteenth-century remodeling, but it seems highly improbable that the giant pilasters were. The sheer labor of chiseling two-inch deep channels into the 'very fine brickwork' to receive the wide pilasters; the fact that the window spacing was so opportune to receive them; the location of the chimneys and the nature of the heavy stone cornice — all these seem to belie the theory of a remodeling. Certainly one would have expected any such major building operation to receive mention in Governor Hutchinson's diary. The conclusion seems inescapable that the exterior of the Hutchinson House was substantially the same when it was built as it appears in the engraving of 1836.

Despite a proper skepticism of the many claims of 'designs sent over from England,' one is tempted here to think that the British captain who saw this house and its interiors in 1765 was guessing correctly. The three-story composition, with small square windows at the top, the Ionic pilasters set on low pedestals, the segmental pediment, and the eaves balustrade are all features to be found on Lindsay House in Lincoln's Inn Fields, built about 1640 by Inigo Jones or a follower. It is interesting that the garlanded type of Ionic capital is used in both buildings and that Lindsay House is also made of brick, though it is stuccoed. If Wren could send designs for the College of William and Mary in 1693, some other English architect might well have forwarded designs for the finest private house in Boston in the preceding decade.

If so, it was not only the earliest Georgian building in the American colonies but, being in the Jones-Palladian tradition, was an example, more than half a century in advance, of the formal style of the late Georgian period of the 1750's and 1760's.

Thomas Savage House, Boston. 1706–7

One of the three-story residences of the early eighteenth century on Dock Square, heart of Boston's commercial district, survived until 1926. When it was demolished, the brick walls were found sufficiently intact to make a conjectural restoration (fig. 397).[6] The house was built in 1706–7 by Thomas Savage, a lieutenant colonel of the Suffolk regiment, merchant, selectman for several years, and owner of several downtown properties. The arrangement of the interior is unknown, except that the ground floor was occupied by a counting house and storerooms, and that the second and third floors were residential. Probably there was on each floor a central hall with two rooms on each side.

The façade was symmetrically composed, accented by a pilastered doorway topped by a narrow pavilion bearing a round arch; the brickwork of the latter being rough, it may have been filled by molded plaster ornament. The other brickwork was of very fine quality. Walls were laid in Flemish bond, the string courses in molded brick, and the flat window arches in gauged brick. The side walls had segmental-arched windows, and they rose as parapets to conceal the gambrel roof. Twin chimneys at each end were simply paneled. This house was of the general type of middle-class residence built by the street-full in London in the 1680's by the rapacious real-estate developer Nicholas Barbon. But since Barbon's houses still used transomed casements and Boston newspapers do not advertise double-hung sash until 1712–13, the windows of the Savage House were probably of the medieval type.

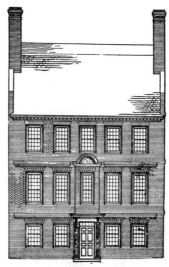

397. Restored front elevation of the Thomas Savage House, Dock Square, Boston, 1706–7 (Thomas T. Waterman, *Old Time New England*)

McPhedris-Warner House, Portsmouth, New Hampshire. 1718–23

The most typical of the better kind of early Georgian residence in New England was built at Portsmouth by Captain Archibald McPhedris. Mc-Phedris came from Scotland to become a prosperous fur trader and member of the Governor's Council; he married Sarah, one of the sixteen children of Governor John Wentworth, who gave the land. The house, of large scale, solidly built with 18-inch brick walls, and adorned within by many imported niceties, is reported to have cost £6,000, a fabulous sum for those days.

The façade (fig. 398), composed with dignity, has a brick belt course separating the floors, and windows topped by segmental arches below and flat arches above. The doorway, with broken segmental pediment, flanking pilasters, and twelve-panel door with the top panels supplanted by glazed lights, is especially fine. The gambrel roof with its balustrades and cupola is not original, for underneath it have been found the shingled surfaces of two parallel gabled roofs with a deep valley between. Such double gables had been used in England — they were common in medieval times — but it may be supposed that snow and ice proved the arrangement impracticable in New England. At some later date, accordingly, the valley between the old gables was covered by a low-pitched roof, making the whole a gambrel shape. Balustrades at the break of the gambrel were presumably added at this time, and also the octagonal cupola.

398. McPhedris-Warner House, Portsmouth, N.H., 1718–23 (Frank Cousins, The Essex Institute)

The brick end wall at the north is carried up as a parapet between the two end chimneys. The other end wall, curiously enough, is clapboarded and its windows topped by angular pediments — if original, a very early instance of this motive. The dormer windows are topped by alternating angular and segmental pediments. In 1762 the house was equipped with a lightning rod, probably the first in New Hampshire, said to have been installed under the personal direction of the ubiquitous Benjamin Franklin.

The plan (fig. 399) is of the central-hall type with end chimneys and a wing with a scullery back of the kitchen. The parlor and a small downstairs chamber have diagonal corner fireplaces, sharing one chimney, which is honestly carried up as such despite its off-center position and lack of symmetry with the north chimneys. The service stair taken out of the small chamber does not seem to be original. The parlor is paneled from

floor to ceiling, with round bolection moldings which project the panels
in front of the surface of the rails. Fireplaces in both parlor and dining
room are faced by Dutch tiles, and the house contains many fine pieces
of Chippendale and Sheraton furniture, some of them formerly owned by
Captain McPhedris.

The hall is divided by an elliptical arch resting on projecting pilasters,
a motive perhaps inspired by the earlier Hutchinson and Clark-Frankland
Houses in Boston. The stairway betrays an early Georgian simplicity, with
square newels and plain block step ends; the contour of the balustrade is
echoed by the paneled dado on the wall. Above this, and on the stair

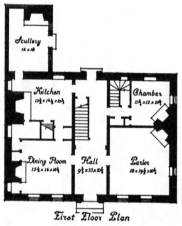

399. Plan of the McPhedris-Warner House (*Great Georgian Houses*, 1)

landing, the walls are adorned by curious and rather primitive mural
paintings, reputedly the work of Langdon Towne, hero of Kenneth Rob-
erts' novel, *Northwest Passage*. Life-sized Indians flank the arched window
of the landing, and other paintings, uncovered under four layers of wallpaper, show Sir William Pepperrell riding to victory at Louisburg, a
scripture scene, a lady at her spinning wheel, and a hawk after chickens.

The house passed to McPhedris's daughter Mary, who married Jonathan Warner, and it remained in the Warner family for generations. It is
now well maintained by the Warner House Association.

Hancock House, Boston. 1737–40

The stone house that Thomas Hancock built on Beacon Hill (fig. 400)
set a standard of elegance and architectural sophistication which was
widely emulated elsewhere in New England. A successful bookseller and
stationer, owner of a Boston paper factory, and importer of fine English
wallpapers, Hancock bought his land on the south slope of Beacon Hill
in 1735. He straightway laid ambitious plans for gardens, terraces, hedges,
walks, trees, and flowers. Writing to his London agent for plum and tulip
trees, holly, jasmine, ' Dwarf Trees and Espaliers,' he boasted that

the Kingdom of England don't afford so Fine a Prospect as I have both of land and water. Neither do I intend to Spare any Cost or pains in making my Gardens Beautifull or Profitable . . . Let me know also what you'll take for 100 small Yew Trees in the rough which I'd Frame up here to my own fancy.[7]

The granite blocks for his house he obtained from Braintree, and the sandstone trim, quarried in Middletown, Connecticut, was guaranteed ' well cut, fitted and polished, workmanlike and According to the Rules of Art every way Agreeable.' Window glass to the number of 480 panes, cut to size, came from London, and there also he ordered ' twenty dozen blue

400. Hancock House, Boston, 1737–40 (drawing by J. Davis, engraved by T. Illman, c.1850)

and white Dutch tiles with handsome figures,' a magnificent tall clock, fine looking-glasses, and the Hancock crest and arms ' in Silver and fixt to Ivory.' As an importer of paper hangings, he was particularly interested in some ' painted papers ' for the house and wrote to his London agent:

Inclosed you have the Dimensions of a Room for a shaded Hanging to be Done after the same Pattern I have sent per Capt. Tanner . . . If they can make it more beautiful by adding more Birds flying here and there, with some Landskips at the Bottom, Should like it well . . . In other of these Hangings are great variety of different Sorts of Birds, Peacocks, Macoys, Squirril, Monkys, Fruit and Flowers, etc. — I think they are handsomer and better than Painted hangings done in Oyle . . .[8]

The construction and decoration of the house required three years. The master mason was Joshua Blanchard, well known for his work on the Old South Meeting-House and Faneuil Hall. Documents also tell us the names of the stone cutter, glazier, and painter, as well as of the joiner, William More, who added the paneling and trim of the parlor and great chamber in 1745–6, and who was hired, probably the next year, to do the magnificent woodwork of Isaac Royall's house at near-by Medford.

The fine masonry of the walls was laid in even courses of granite ashlar, and the trim of windows, corners, doorway, and cornice executed in Connecticut sandstone. Though the original house was demolished in 1863, we can gain an excellent idea of its appearance from the replica built in 1925–6 at Ticonderoga to house the New York State Historical Association (fig. 401).[9] The doorway with engaged columns against a rusticated

401. Entrance and balcony of the Hancock House, as reproduced in the New York State Historical Association headquarters at Ticonderoga, N.Y., in 1926 (New York State Historical Association)

wall was unprecedented in the colonies, and the balcony, carried on great projecting brackets, a most unusual feature. The balcony window, framed by pilasters set against a rusticated wall and topped by a swan's neck pediment, was detailed in Middletown and probably set the fashion for this type of doorway, which later became so popular in the Connecticut valley. Wrought-iron brackets supported two lanterns over this balcony. One of the modillions from the main cornice, now preserved in the Massachusetts Historical Society, reveals fine carving of scrolls and acanthus leaves. The gambrel roof, with its dormers of alternating shapes, was topped by a balustraded deck.

The main entrance hall was unusually spacious, and it is fortunate that the stairway was removed, at the time of the demolition, to a house in

Manchester, Massachusetts. This stairway established a new standard of elaboration: it was the first in the colonies to employ a double newel post, spiraled in one direction outside and with an inner post twisted in the opposite direction; the first to use three spirally twisted balusters, each of a different profile, on each step *; the first to employ a combination of paneled step ends and scrolled blocks; and the first to reveal the profile of the steps on the soffit of the upper run. A masterpiece of the woodcarver's art, the stairway set a fashion for similar elaboration in later New England mansions.

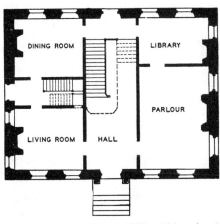

402. Plan of the Hancock House (Philip White, after Sturgis)

The stair landing, with its great arched window, paneled reveals, and flanking pilasters, was also of unusual quality. At the back of the hall, on the main floor, a door led to the gardens behind the house and to a hilltop summer house commanding a view of all Boston and its environs.

The plan of the house (fig. 402), with its thick granite walls, shows nothing unusual except for the separate service stair, between the living room and dining room. The large parlor to the right of the hall must have been an impressive room, with its big fireplace, paneled walls, mahogany chairs, and damask curtains and cushions. The small room back of this was a library or study. There were four chambers on the second floor and four more rooms in the garret.

The house passed in 1764 from Thomas Hancock to his more famous nephew, John Hancock, Revolutionary patriot, President of the Continental Congress, and first signer of the Declaration of Independence. During the war, occupation of the house as British headquarters by Lord Percy and General Clinton probably saved it from spoliation. Hancock was chosen first Governor of Massachusetts in 1780 and served all but two years until his death in 1793. In this house he received Washington, Lafayette,

* Priority in these first two respects may be claimed for the pulpit stairway in the Sabbatarian Meeting-House at Newport, Rhode Island, if this can be shown to date as early as the main structure (1729).

d'Estaing, and many other distinguished visitors. The unnecessary demolition of the house in 1863 might not have occurred but for the confusion of the Civil War. For many years a proposal was before the legislature to rebuild the famous mansion as a residence for the governors of Massachusetts, but nothing was done about it, and it remained for New York to memorialize one of Massachusetts's outstanding architectural and historical monuments.

Shirley Place, Roxbury, Massachusetts. c.1747

One of the most formal and imposing houses of the eighteenth century was built by William Shirley, Royal Governor from 1741 to 1756.[10] The

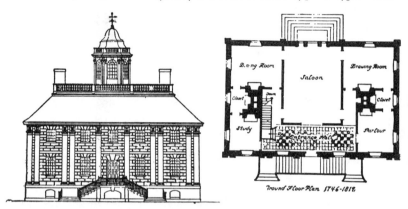

403, 404. Entrance (west) façade and plan of Shirley Place, Roxbury, Mass., c.1747 (W. W. Cordingley, *Old Time New England*)

tract of 33 acres of land in Roxbury was purchased on 22 November 1746, and the house was probably begun the next year. Standing 200 yards from the street, it was approached by a drive leading to the entrance (west) façade (fig. 403). The first floor was raised on a high stone basement which contained kitchens and offices; an imposing double flight of steps led up to the main entrance. The entrance façade was treated with two single and eight paired pilasters, the garden façade with four single pilasters; all of these were executed in wood. Except for the Hutchinson House in Boston, this was the first use of giant pilasters in New England, but the precedent established by so distinguished a gentleman was soon followed elsewhere.

The wall, though later covered by clapboards, was originally faced by boards grooved to simulate rusticated masonry, perhaps the first use of this questionable motive in the colonies. Curiously enough, the walls had nearly a foot of air space between the outer wall of brick-filled framing timbers and an inner wall of studs and plaster. The steep-pitch hipped roof was surmounted by a balustraded deck with an ornate and somewhat gargantuan cupola.

The original plan (fig. 404) suggests an unrivaled magnificence for large social gatherings. One entered a hall extending across the front of the house, with paneled walls, two large windows, and a floor paved with dark blue and white marble blocks. Double doors to the salon were on the main axis; at the north end was the main stair. The very large salon served for receptions and state banquets; it was two stories high, with coved ceiling and a musicians' gallery over the entrance. Woodwork and the plaster of the walls were painted a pale greenish-gray and the floor painted — tradition says 'like a carpet' — with enriched borders and a central ornament. In the middle of the east wall was a great Palladian window, its central arch a story and a half high, and its piers and jambs faced by Corinthian pilasters inside and Doric outside. From this window one looked out over a pyramidal flight of steps, across the formal garden with its maze, and down a hillside to the distant waters of the Old Harbor. The smaller family rooms at the corners of the house must have emphasized the great scale of the salon.

A house of such academic pretensions as this would probably have been designed by a professional architect. The monumentality of the plan, the sophistication of the details, and the use of rusticated wood siding all suggest Peter Harrison of Newport. Mrs. Shirley and Mrs. Harrison were related, and Harrison and the Governor may have come to know each other in connection with the work on King's Chapel, Boston, to which the one contributed talent, the other money. Shirley Place was considerably remodeled by Dr. William Eustis when he bought it in 1819. It was sold by the Eustis family in 1867 and gradually deteriorated after that date.

Royall House, Medford, Massachusetts

The nucleus of the large Royall mansion was a seventeenth-century brick house, two and a half stories high but only one room in depth, long owned by John Usher.[11] This was bought in 1732 by Isaac Royall and remodeled 1733–7; the height was raised to a full three stories and the present east façade completed at this time. The plans for the remodeling are said to have been drawn in Antigua from a nobleman's house which Royall admired. Evidently desiring the profuse architectural detail which is possible in wood more economically than in stone or brick, he recased the old brick surface with a wall of clapboards (fig. 405), treating it with wooden angle quoins, elaborately molded window frames connected by spandrel panels to form continuous vertical strips, a modillioned cornice, and a central doorway of pilasters against rusticated wood. At this same time a separate brick building for slaves' quarters — one of the few in New England — and other outbuildings for coach, horses, et cetera were erected.

Royall's son Isaac Jr. (1719–81) inherited the house on his father's death in 1739. In the estate appraisal of 1740, the house was valued at £50,000 and the land at £37,000, phenomenal sums for those days. Between 1747 and 1750 Colonel Royall undertook a great enlargement. He more than doubled the depth of the house, extended the end walls correspondingly, and built twin chimneys at both ends, with parapets connecting them. The present west façade is thus dated 1747–50, and the house as it stands consists of a great three-story mass with low-pitch gabled roof, three wood façades, and one brick end wall.

The west façade (fig. 406) has rusticated wood siding and giant pilasters at the corners, a treatment that may have been suggested by Shirley Place, built just at this time only six miles away. Isaac Royall evidently desired even greater architectural richness, for he added pediments over his windows and an elaborate doorway.

405. Royall House, Medford, Mass., east façade, 1733–7 (HABS)

The chief interior rooms of the Royall House were either built anew or redecorated at the time of the second enlargement, giving Isaac Royall a chance to emulate the standard set by Thomas Hancock in Boston only a few years before. The entrance hall (fig. 407) was divided midway by a paneled elliptical arch resting on scrolled capitals — all the detail being richer than in the McPhedris House arch. The stair, with its double-spiraled newel, twisted balusters, and paneled and scrolled step ends, followed the Hancock example, and in the two main rooms the detail of the woodwork is so nearly identical to that of Hancock's two main rooms, completed by William More in 1745–6, that we may conclude they were by the same hand.

Both the living room of the Royall House and the great chamber above it (fig. 408) are marked by full-height paneling and numerous pilasters — Doric below, Corinthian in the bedroom — and the carved detail of capitals, keystones, and ornamented moldings is fine and precise. Both rooms have interior end fireplaces, but an appearance of awkward projec-

tion into the room is avoided by the use of alcoves on either side of the
fireplace, with elliptical arches, window seats, and paneled folding shutters. From literary descriptions of their vanished glories, we might suppose
that similar alcoves were to be found in the earlier Hutchinson and Clark-
Frankland Houses in Boston. The bedroom fireplace is framed by an
eared architrave, with a single panel of unusual size above, but lacks a
mantel shelf. Three rows of Dutch tiles adorn the sides of the fireplace
recess; the living-room fireplace has not only these but an additional row

406. Royall House, west façade, 1747-50 (Wayne Andrews)

framing the opening. This abundance may give a clue to the use of the
inordinate number of tiles which Hancock had ordered for his house.

Appointed a brigadier general in 1761, Royall was of course a staunch
Loyalist and fled the country at the outbreak of the Revolution. He died
in England in 1781. But he left permanent memorials of himself in the
Royall Professorship of Law at Harvard University, and in his great house,
which since 1905 has been maintained as a public monument by the Royall House Association.

The Lindens, Danvers, Massachusetts (now Washington, D.C.). 1754

The academic formalism that prevailed in Virginia after the mid-
eighteenth century is evident at the same time, or perhaps somewhat earlier, in New England. The grandiose pretensions of Shirley Place were
soon echoed, though on a reduced scale, in other New England houses of
the late Georgian period. An axial pediment on the main façade, either

with or without a projecting pavilion below it, giant pilasters, and hipped roofs, are found with increasing frequency on the finer houses.

One of these is The Lindens, originally built in Danvers, Massachusetts, in 1754 by wealthy Robert ('King') Hooper of Marblehead.* The house fell on evil days in the twentieth century, and after the removal of its living-room woodwork to the William Rockhill Nelson Gallery in Kansas

407. Entrance hall of the Royall House (Mary H. Northend)

City and the threatened piecemeal sale of the remaining features, it was fortunately purchased, dismantled, moved to Washington, D.C., in 1937, and reassembled. The living room has been reproduced and the whole house superbly restored and furnished.[12]

Three sides of the exterior are clapboarded, but the entrance façade is faced with rusticated wood, sanded and painted as at Mount Vernon (fig. 409). Angle quoins, window lintels, and door enframement are emphasized by a contrasting color. Balustrades at the curbs conceal the upper

* Hooper bought the land in 1753, and, as a traveler on that road reported seeing 'the country-seat of "King" Hooper of Marblehead' in June 1754, the house was evidently built immediately. Indeed, circumstances of the title transfer suggest that an earlier purchase contract permitted the start of building before the deed was actually delivered.

slopes of the gambrel roof, and the chimneys are asymmetrically arranged, as may be seen in the plan (fig. 410). The steep-pitched pediment suggests a pavilion, but there is actually no projection of the wall below it, the central bay being emphasized only by giant Corinthian columns engaged against the wall. Though engaged columns differ little as a design feature from giant pilasters, they were rarely used in Georgian houses; Corinthian capitals are also unusual in the giant order. The treatment of

408. Great chamber in the second story, Royall House (Samuel Chamberlain)

the front door, with quoins rather than the usual architectural enframement, is less successful than the somewhat similar motive at Shirley Place. On the whole, the somewhat heavy exterior betrays little of the suavity of the superb interiors.

Of these the entrance hall, 12 feet in width and 42 in length, is one of the finest rooms of the Georgian period (fig. 411). The staircase is of the Hancock type, with both paneled and scrolled step ends, and the profile of the steps is echoed underneath these by projecting corners in the lower run and across the full width of the soffit of the upper run. The wide landing is dominated by a great arched window flanked by Corinthian pilasters (fig. 412).

The hall of The Lindens has magnificent scenic wallpapers of three series printed in France: Dufour's *Voyages d'Antenor* (c.1814); Dufour's *Télémaque dans l'Ile de Calypso* (c.1825); and *Les Incas,* inspired by Marmontel's eighteenth-century novel of that name and printed by Dufour's successor Leroy in 1832. Gray, vermilion, deep blue, and a vivid green predominate in the color scheme. A former owner of the house acquired these papers in the 1860's from a factory in Mülhausen, Alsace; their comparatively recent application accounts for the fine condition in which they are found today. The task of removing and re-applying them when the house was moved was expertly done. The door openings in the hall, framed by simple architraves, are far more effective in combination with the wallpaper than more elaborate pedimented treatments would have been.

409. The Lindens, built in Danvers, Mass., by Robert Hooper in 1754. Re-erected in Washington, D.C., in 1937 (Arthur C. Haskell. HABS)

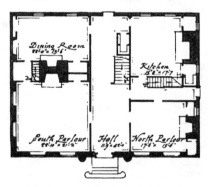

410. Plan of The Lindens (*Great Georgian Houses,* II)

411. Entrance hall of The Lindens (John O. Brostrup)

412. Upstairs hall of The Lindens (John O. Brostrup)

The wide pine boards of several of the rooms still reveal painted borders and centerpieces of scrolls, fruit, and leafage, in stenciled patterns. The painting of the upper hall is most elaborate, but that of the lower hall (fig. 413) is historically more important, for it is believed to have been done when the house was built, making it the oldest known example of this treatment. The master bedroom has a large circular composition, possibly of some symbolic significance.

The parlor is a superb room (fig. 414). Pilasters on pedestals flank the fireplace, their fine carving enhanced by the simple narrow panels arranged in pairs between the windows of the outer walls. The fireplace

413. Painted floor, downstairs hall of The Lindens (John O. Brostrup)

lacks mantel shelf, and the conservative two-panel treatment of the chimney-breast is very satisfactory. Eight-paneled doors beside the fireplace lead into chimney closets. The walls are painted a delicate gray-green, and the window drapes are of gold brocatelle hung under Chippendale cornices. The woodwork in other rooms, in pale yellow, gray, dull red, and blue-green, illustrates the positive character of Georgian color schemes.

The house contains one of the most remarkable furniture collections in America. Every piece is an original of a style that might have been used in the house when it was built in 1754. The superb Queen Anne and Chippendale sofas, wing chairs, highboys, serving tables, side chairs, et cetera, seen in their architectural settings, re-create an authentic picture of a fine Georgian mansion such as is to be equaled only in a few museum rooms, and in no other house.

All told, the interiors of The Lindens are among the very finest in Georgian architecture. The style is essentially one of refined artifice rather than of simple or natural treatment of materials and structure. As such it depends on formalities of arrangement and graceful enrichments of detail, pattern, and color, which had descended to eighteenth-century America from the long tradition of Renaissance classicism. Only too often — it must be said — the colonists and their designers and craftsmen were so eager to display their English culture that they not only went too much by the book, but threw its whole content on their walls. The results were vulgar. In an artificial style it is always hard to mark the line between elegance and opulence, but that distinction seems worth remarking in connection with rooms such as these, which combine richness with restraint, which

414. Parlor of The Lindens as reconstructed in Washington (Harris and Ewing)

merge sophistication with fine simplicity, and which so perfectly balance beautifully calculated surfaces with the volumes of space they compose.

John Vassall (Longfellow) House, Cambridge. 1759

The house that dominates Tory Row on Brattle Street in Cambridge was built by Major John Vassall in 1759. He was driven out on the eve of the Revolution, and for nine months in 1775–6 the house served as headquarters for General Washington. It was later occupied by Henry Wadsworth Longfellow from 1837 until his death in 1882, a period unfortunately honored in the present furnishings and interior decorations of the mansion.

The exterior is typical of the better New England house of the late Georgian period (fig. 415). Balustrades, steps, and terraces enhance the posture of the house, and the façade is adorned by a central pavilion and pediment, rather prominent modillioned cornice, and four giant pilasters.

The windows, however, are simple openings, equipped with both interior shutters and exterior blinds. The house is almost square and has a double-hipped roof, with four lower slopes crowned by balustrades which conceal four upper slopes of very low pitch. The plan is of the central-hall type with interior chimneys, differing from the norm only in the depth of the hall, which permits a partitioned back hall with separate servants' staircase.

The end piazzas of the Vassall House were added later, but they are of a type first discussed in Boston not long after the house was built, in a

415. Vassall (Longfellow) House, Cambridge, 1759 (HABS)

correspondence between the painter John Singleton Copley, who at the time was in New York, and his half-brother Henry Pelham of Boston. Copley had seen some piazzas, perhaps on Dutch Colonial houses, and fancied one for the house he was building on Beacon Hill. The letters manifest the customary eighteenth-century *insouciance* in spelling.

Copley: I shall add a peazer when I return, which is much practiced here, and is very beautiful and convenient . . . [14 July 1771.]
Pelham: I don't comprehend what you mean by a Peazer. [28 July.]
Copley: You say you don't know what I mean by a Peaza. I will tell you than. [Here he describes a piazza of the Vassall House type, but adorned with a rail of Chinese lattice.] . . . these Peazas are so cool in sumer and Winter break off the storms so much that I think I should not be able to like an house without. [3 August; Copley enclosed a sketch with this letter, showing piazzas at the ends of a house.]
Pelham: I have talked to Capt Joy about the Peazas. he says that he could not possably do them a farthing under 63£ and at that is afraid he shall not be able to make days Wages. I am drawing an Elivation of the House with the Peazzas. it will (if possable) have the advantage of the first most Beautiful Plan. The Peazzas extend the Front and by their being open make it appear higher. [24 September.]

Henry Pelham's carefree spelling 'Peazza' came much closer to the Italian original of this word than did his tutor's 'peazer.' Its use in the modern sense dates back to a seventeenth-century English corruption. Inigo Jones, as we have seen, was a devoted apostle of things Italian. When in 1630 the fourth Earl of Bedford asked him (mayhap with some prompting from Charles I) to design the Covent Garden housing development, Jones laid out a fine rectangular plaza, faced on two sides by row dwellings fronted by lofty arcaded corridors, within which were the entrances to the individual houses. Jones called the whole square, like its Italian

416. Wentworth-Gardner House, Portsmouth, N.H., 1760 (Samuel Chamberlain)

prototypes, a 'piazza,' but its denizens soon called the arcaded corridors themselves 'piazzas,' and it was but a short step from this to the use of the word for any covered place before a house. A rival term 'veranda,' apparently derived from the Sanskrit, became current in England after the penetration of India but was not commonly used in America until the advent of romantic tastes in the early nineteenth century.

Wentworth-Gardner House, Portsmouth, New Hampshire. 1760

The house built for Thomas Wentworth in 1760 faces the quiet waters of a tidal bay, the South Mill Pond, at Portsmouth (fig. 416). Smaller in size but more elaborate than its neighboring McPhedris House, it shows how far the Georgian style had developed in forty years — from the robust and simple vigor of the early years to a thin and academic refinement. Like The Lindens it is a clapboard house boasting a rusticated wood façade with over-prominent angle quoins, but it approaches closer to the late Georgian ideal in its use of the hipped roof, pediments over windows, and a particularly ornate doorway with a swan's neck pediment.

Carpenters, joiners, and ship carvers are said to have devoted fourteen months to the elaborate interiors, of which the entrance hall is the most striking: the stair has alternating plain and twisted balusters turned in black cherry, a painted pine handrail, and paneled and scrolled step ends. Above the elliptical arch that divides the hall is a particularly rich cornice, carved with many moldings, dentil blocks, leaf-and-tongue ornament, and modillions. The upper hall (fig. 417) is almost unique in Georgian architecture in the completeness of its academic treatment, with an order of fluted Ionic pilasters bearing molded architrave, pulvinated frieze, modillioned cornice, and a plastered cove.

417. Upstairs hall of the Wentworth-Gardner House (Samuel Chamberlain)

The plan is the standard four-room type with interior chimneys and a kitchen ell at the back. The kitchen fireplace is of the early type, with lug pole and trammels, and the flue has a chimney-jack, a sort of windmill rigged to turn a roasting spit.[13] The house was purchased by the Gardner family in 1796. It has in recent years been owned by the Metropolitan Museum.

Lady Pepperrell House, Kittery Point, Maine. c.1760

Overlooking Portsmouth harbor from the Maine side of the Piscataqua River stands the fine late Georgian house built for Lady Pepperrell. Sir William Pepperrell, the only American baronet, had raised and financed a regiment which he led to victory at Louisburg in 1745; received in London by the King, he was awarded a baronetcy in recognition of this service. Successful business ventures brought him a fortune estimated at a quarter of a million pounds, and he owned vast tracts of land between the Saco and Piscataqua Rivers. After his death in 1759, Lady Pepperrell built this house, where she lived for nearly thirty years (fig. 418).

The façade, with its hipped roof rising to a sharp ridge and untroubled by dormers, most nearly approaches the simplicity of the Georgian mansions of Virginia. The projecting pavilion is distinguished from the clapboarded walls by smooth white boarding approximating the effect of ashlar masonry. Giant Ionic pilasters raised on pedestals frame the entrance door. The molded window frames are set well forward of the wall, and rusticated quoins emphasize the corners. The doorway, topped by a cornice carried on curved brackets, is of a type more often found in the early Georgian period.

Though of frame construction throughout, the house has two pairs of end chimneys. The interiors are generally simpler than those of the Went-

418. Lady Pepperrell House, Kittery Point, Me., c.1760 (John Mead Howells, *Great Georgian Houses*, I)

worth-Gardner House, though the stair rail might have been carved by the same craftsmen. The house contains paintings by Smibert, Copley, and Hopner, fine mirrors, clocks, and rugs; furniture by Chippendale, Hepplewhite, Sheraton, and Duncan Phyfe; fine Waterford glass and Lowestoft china. It is now owned by the Society for the Preservation of New England Antiquities.

Jeremiah Lee House, Marblehead, Massachusetts. 1768

Portsmouth, Marblehead, and Salem still boast many massive three-story houses of the period of their greatest prosperity just before and after the Revolution. One of the largest is the mansion built by Colonel Jeremiah Lee, reputedly at a cost of £10,000 (fig. 419). Façades are of rusticated wood, and the pretense of masonry forms is carried out in angle quoins and keystone window lintels. A projecting pavilion breaks the entrance façade, but giant pilasters and window pediments are fortunately lacking. A small entrance portico in the Ionic order heralds the many graceful variations of this theme that were to become so popular in the Federal period. The hipped roof is dominated by a cupola and two chimneys of immense girth.

419. Jeremiah Lee House, Marblehead, Mass., 1768 (Arthur C. Haskell)

420. Entrance hall of the Lee House (Arthur C. Haskell)

The grandiose scale of the house is manifest in the entrance hall (fig. 420). The stairway, with its unusually gradual ascent, is a majestic 8 feet in width. Adorned by every device of the turner's and carver's art, it is one of the richest in New England. To the left of the hall is the Banquet Room, 21 by 25 feet (fig. 421). The focal feature is an ornate fireplace, carved in oak with the high-relief garlands and swags favored by Grinling Gibbons in England. The design was taken from Plate 51 of Swan's

421. Banquet Room of the Lee House (Arthur C. Haskell)

British Architect. It should be noticed in the plan (fig. 422) how this room is paneled to the corner, at the left of the fireplace, despite the presence of a window which was required only by the rigid symmetry of the façade pattern.

The great drawing room on the second floor is still adorned with the original wallpapers imported from England. The subjects are taken from Piranesi's views of Roman ruins and framed by wide borders of rococo scrolls. 'Newly invented' and printed in oils with a roller, these magnificent papers were obtained from Jackson of London. The house, maintained by the Marblehead Historical Society, is furnished in the styles of the Georgian and Federal periods.

Richard Derby House, Salem. 1762

Grandiose mansions such as the Lee House were of course the exception rather than the rule, and the house that Richard Derby built in 1762, though it is the oldest brick house in Salem, more nearly typifies the Georgian house of smaller scale and lesser extravagance (fig. 423). Every detail of the brick exterior — the paired end chimneys, the gambrel roof with its three dormers, the five-window façade, the simple classical doorway — bespeaks the typical Georgian house of good quality. The interiors, too, are less pretentious than those of the great houses. Old-fashioned early Georgian paneling, shaped by fine deep-cut moldings, suffices for the fireplace, and, though legend has it that Derby brought his intricate stair balusters from abroad, they were certainly not beyond the skill of Salem's carpenters and ship carvers. The paneling is painted a dark olive green;

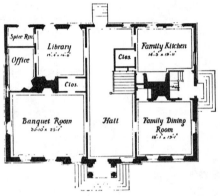

422. Plan of the Lee House (*Great Georgian Houses,* I)

other rooms have elusive shades of maroon and gray-blue. Richard Derby may have built this house as a wedding present on the occasion of his son Elias Hasket Derby's marriage to Elizabeth Crowninshield.[14] Standing at the head of Derby Wharf, now a national historic site, it heralded the days of Salem's greatest maritime glories.

The Federal style in New England

Elias Hasket Derby was to become ship captain and merchant prince of legendary wealth and frame. It was his *Grand Turk* which, after capturing sixteen prizes as a privateer in the Revolution, opened the Cape of Good Hope trade in 1784. The next year she was the first American ship to make the round trip to China, just as Derby's *Atlantic* was the first to reach Calcutta and Bombay. Thus Salem's fortunes boomed. Spice from Mocha, ivory from Calcutta, pepper from Sumatra, silk and jade from China, monkeys and parrots from the Indies built the great houses on Washington Square and on Federal and Chestnut Streets. And it was Elias Hasket Derby who hired the superb artist-carver Samuel McIntire, near the end of the century, to build the finest of the great Salem houses.

These houses of the post-Revolutionary period, in Salem and Portsmouth, in Bulfinch's Boston, in Providence and New Haven, in the quiet Connecticut-valley towns which fell under Asher Benjamin's widespread influence, betray a new character. The world-wide wave of renewed and more intense classicism, which arose from eighteenth-century archaeological discoveries in Europe and the Near East, was felt in New England as it was in Virginia, Washington, and Philadelphia. Yet in New England there were never, until the time of the much later Greek Revival, the grand scale and academic correctness of a Jefferson. The New Englanders sought less to imitate classical forms than to achieve classical qualities. Walls made of boards laid flush, or of painted or stuccoed brick, had the abstract smoothness of classical masonry. Masses became more geometric

423. Richard Derby House, Salem, Mass., 1762 (Wayne Andrews)

in effect, with low-pitched roofs virtually concealed by eaves balustrades or parapets, and often with bold curvilinear projecting bays.

This accent on curved forms introduced a new grace of movement. The beautiful Federal doorway, with its elliptical fanlight spanning the narrow sidelights, was a theme played with many variations. The columns of its projecting portico became slender under Adam influence. Dynamic, too, were the graceful sweep of the spiral stair and the rooms shaped to an oval plan or with curved ends or projecting bays. Decorative motives of door casings, mantelpieces, and ceilings became more slender, more delicate, of lower relief and finer detail than in Georgian architecture. Though often of extraordinary richness, they were better subordinated to the architectonic governance of the larger forms and spaces, and were more universally painted a chaste white, in keeping with the new spirit of classical simplicity.

In the Federal period America achieved one of its greatest architectural styles. Compared with it, Georgian seems at times merely naïve — charming in its warmth of color, its richly carved detail, its youthful robustness and vigor, but lacking in the subtle unity of part and whole that is the mark of architectural maturity. Against the assured mastery of space composition, the extraordinary restraint in surface and color, the refinement and grace of detail of a Bulfinch masterpiece of the next generation, Georgian houses seem merely pictorially pleasant, not architecturally great.

To be sure, the Georgian style continued after the Revolution, with minor changes. For a half-generation, houses continued to be built in the Georgian mode; indeed for a time they perhaps outnumbered the exemplars of the newer style. But from the time that Bulfinch returned to Boston in 1786, fresh from the London of the brothers Adam, new influences were at work and the Federal style was in the ascendant. To it belonged the generation following the Revolutionary War.

READING SUGGESTIONS

Samuel Chamberlain's many picture books, especially *Open House in New England* (Stephen Daye Press, Brattleboro, Vermont, 1937) and *Beyond New England Thresholds* (Hastings House, New York, 1938) have the finest photographs yet taken of New England Georgian houses.

Mary H. Northend's *Historic Homes of New England* (Little, Brown and Co., Boston, 1914), though outdated in details, is a useful general account.

The files of *Old Time New England,* journal of the Society for the Preservation of New England Antiquities, are invaluable.

For state and regional fields the best books are J. Frederick Kelly's *Early Domestic Architecture of Connecticut* (Yale University Press, New Haven, 1924); Antoinette Downing's *Early Homes of Rhode Island* (Garrett and Massie, Richmond, 1937); Herbert Wheaton Congdon's *Old Vermont Houses* (Stephen Daye Press, Brattleboro, Vermont, 1940); and three beautifully illustrated books by John Mead Howells: *The Architectural Heritage of the Piscataqua* (Architectural Book Publishing Co., New York, 1938); *The Architectural Heritage of the Merrimack* (Architectural Book Publishing Co., New York, 1941); and *Lost Examples of Colonial Architecture* (William Helburn, New York, 1931).

16

Georgian Architecture of the Middle Colonies

THOUGH THE region of the lower Delaware River had scattered settlements of Swedes and Dutch before the mid-seventeenth century, it
boasted no distinctive architectural style until after the founding of Pennsylvania in 1681. The extraordinary success of Penn's ' Holy Experiment '
led to a great outburst of building activity in the last decades of the seventeenth century and the first decades of the eighteenth. But almost from
the very first the architecture of Philadelphia and its surrounding region
was Georgian rather than Colonial in style. Fresh from a London rebuilt
after the fire of 1666, the Quaker settlers brought the new style of the
Renaissance: symmetrical façades, classical decorative detail, molded cornices, sliding-sash windows, and painted woodwork took the place of the
medieval architectural forms that still prevailed in the older colonies of
New England and the South.

Utilizing the rich building resources of the region – the ledge stone,
clay, and lime which made possible an architecture of stone and brick –
and influenced partly by the austere simplicity of early Quaker life, partly
by the German tradition imported by hordes of emigrés from Moravia
and the Rhenish Palatinate, the Pennsylvania colonists soon evolved a
distinctive architectural style of great vigor. From Philadelphia and
Germantown it spread to the Pennsylvania hinterland, to West Jersey,
to Delaware, and even to northern Maryland, and the entire region of
the middle colonies still bears the imprint of this strong architectural
tradition.

By the middle of the eighteenth century increasing wealth and a relaxation of Quaker austerity brought a richer and more luxurious architectural style: the late Georgian houses of the region – and especially of
Philadelphia – are among the most elaborate in the colonies, but by the
same token they differ little in style from the fine mansions of the late
Georgian period in New England, Virginia, and South Carolina. In all
the colonies, the passing of pioneer conditions – the gradual winning of
the battle against poverty, climate, and lack of materials and building
skills – led to the gradual decline of the vigorous and individual regional
styles these conditions had produced, and the concurrent development of
something closely approaching a national architectural style.

This development occurred also in New York and northern New Jersey.
The Dutch Colonial style, strongly formed in the seventeenth century,
continued as the basic tradition of the eighteenth – especially in the

houses and outbuildings of farmers and the ' poorer sort.' But by the mid-eighteenth century, as will be seen in the public buildings of New York and the mansions of the Hudson valley, it had given place to the refinements of the late Georgian mode.

New Sweden

Following the example of England, France, and Holland, the Swedish court chartered ' New Sweden ' in 1638, and during the following decade five or six Swedish trading posts were set up near the mouth of the Delaware River. But the colony was short-lived. With little support from home

424. John Morton Birthplace, Prospect Park (near Chester), Pa. Oldest portion dates from 1654 (Department of Art, Dartmouth College)

and no provision for defense, it was taken without a struggle by New Netherland in 1655. The region fell in turn to the English in 1664, but Swedish traders and farmers continued to live there. As early as 1643 they had established a village at the mouth of the Schuylkill, near the site of Philadelphia. When Penn's first contingent arrived, there were several hundred people of Swedish stock within 25 miles of his new capital.

Only two or three structures erected by Swedish colonists are thought to survive, and there is such scanty documentary evidence about their now-vanished buildings that we are hardly justified in speaking of a ' Swedish Colonial style.' Certain architectural features of later houses built by the English, however, appear to have been Swedish in origin.

It seems evident, as pointed out in Chapter 1, that Swedes introduced the log cabin to America — meaning a type of construction employing round logs, notched at the corners and with protruding ends. No seventeenth-century example of such construction is known to survive today, but a description by the Dutch traveler, Jasper Danckaerts, leaves no doubt that he stayed overnight in a true log cabin in 1679, and he refers to it as ' made according to the Swedish mode.' [1] There is also mention in a letter of 1645 of the house of John Printz on Tinicum Island as ' a pretty strong fort constructed by laying very heavy hemlock logs the one on the other.' [2]

The Swedish settlers also used the superior form of hewn-log construction with fitted corner joints, and two such buildings survive today on Darby Creek, Pennsylvania. One of them, the Lower Log House at Darby, is thought to have been built in 1640; this would make it the oldest log structure in the country. Another early example is the John Morton Birthplace at Prospect Park, near Chester, Pennsylvania (fig. 424). The house as it stands consists of three units or ' pens '; one was built in 1654, a second standing a few feet distant was built in 1698, and in 1806 the two units were connected. The logs are hewn square and the dovetailed corners cut so carefully that the close fit between logs requires no chinking.

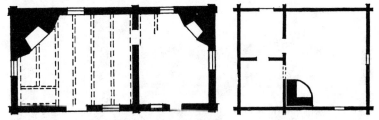

425, 426. Plan of the Lower Log House, Darby, Pa., 1640?, and typical Swedish three-room house plan (Thomas T. Waterman, *The Dwellings of Colonial America*, University of North Carolina Press)

Many hewn-log houses were built by German settlers in Pennsylvania in the eighteenth century. They may have acquired the technique from the Swedes, since most of them entered by way of the Delaware valley, but they may have introduced it independently, for hewn-log construction was known in Germany as well as in Sweden.

The plan of the Lower Log House at Darby (fig. 425) illustrates certain features that were to recur in many later houses of the region. It is a Swedish-type plan, with two rooms of unequal size, chimneys built within the corners at both ends of the house, and corner fireplaces. We know that the corner fireplace was common in the region from the travel journals of Jasper Danckaerts and Peter Kalm. In the days of clay-daubed wooden chimneys it was an economy, since two sides of a triangular flue were formed by the building itself.

A common three-room plan found in Sweden is illustrated in figure 426. This has a great room, or *stuga*, with a two-sided fireplace built within a corner and a projecting hood over it. One small room served as an entry or *förstuga*, and the other usually as a bedroom or *kammara*. Swedish settlers on the Delaware built such houses, and they must have appealed to William Penn as practical pioneer dwellings, for in 1684 he recommended that his immigrants '. . . build then, a House of thirty foot long and eighteen broad, with a partition neer the middle, and an other to divide one end of the House into two small Rooms.' [3] The plan became fairly common in Pennsylvania and spread from there along the migration route to North Carolina. It is sometimes called the ' Quaker plan.'

Many houses in New Jersey, Pennsylvania, Delaware, and near-by Mary-land have gambrel roofs of a distinctive profile (fig. 95c). Upper and lower slopes are of about equal length, but the lower is of unusually steep pitch. Less attractive than the Dutch gambrel, it affords more useful space in the garret. Though it remains to be conclusively demonstrated, this type of roof was probably of Swedish origin and came to the middle colo-nies with Swedish settlers.[4]

Thus if we cannot reconstruct a complete picture of the Swedish Colo-

427. Holy Trinity (Old Swedes) Church, Wilmington, Del., 1698–9 (Sanborn Studio, courtesy H. Edgar Hammond)

nial style in domestic architecture, we can at least identify four contribu-tions that it made to American architecture: the log cabin, the corner fire-place, the ' Quaker plan,' and the ' Swedish gambrel ' roof.

Two surviving churches — the Old Swedes churches at Wilmington and Philadelphia — though largely English in form, were built by Swedish congregations and have a certain Scandinavian flavor. Holy Trinity was built at Christina (Wilmington), Delaware, in 1698–9 (fig. 427). The young pastor Eric Bjork, sent from Sweden as a missionary-priest of the Lutheran Church in the summer of 1697, immediately pressed his congre-gation to build a new edifice. The cornerstone was laid on 28 May 1698. It was contracted that the Philadelphia mason Joseph Yard and his three sons should

lay all the stone and Brick worck . . . from ye foundation to the lower ends of the windows 3 foot thick, and then afterwards 2 foot thick upwards, and all ye Windows and doors upon the Church shall be Arched, and the doors and Win-dows Arched and Quined with Bricks . . .[5]

John Smart, carpenter, and John Harrison, joiner, of Philadelphia, pushed ahead the woodwork of doors, windows, 'four pewess Enclosed,' benches, and the 'pulpit and Canape.' The phrase 'Casements to the windows' suggests that sliding sash had not yet appeared in this region. Eric Bjork, for his part, had to

find all Timber and Boards and Iron worck and all Ready Sawyed and brought to place and also to finde and allow ye said Carpenters, Meat, Drink, Washing and Lodging duering ye said worck.

Originally, the church had no tower or side porches, and it was evidently intended to have a hipped roof. But as the work progressed, the carpenters suggested that its appearance would be improved by building up the gable ends. Pastor Bjork, who had already battled with his congregation for increased size, felt it necessary to compromise, and 'finally, as I thought it would be difficult to get them all the way up, I would have them half way, and then it would look more like a church building.' The resultant shingled roof was thus clipped at the gables 'half way' to form jerkin-heads at both ends — as it still is at the east end.

So expeditiously was the work pushed, 'some of the congregation taking hold and happily finishing by the blessing of God without any accident,' that the building was roofed by Christmas, and the completed church was consecrated on Trinity Sunday, 1699. The exterior was a plain rectangular structure, with stone walls in length ' 66 foot from out to out ' and in breadth ' 36 foot from out to out.' The 20-foot walls were pierced by ' one large and four smaller ' arched windows, which were glazed by a Hollander named Lenard Osterson, and by doors at the middle of each side. All four sides were adorned by inscriptions, in queer Latin abbreviations, set in letters of iron made by one Matthias de Foss. That on the west end read:

If God be for us who can be against us? In the reign of William III, by the Grace of God, King of England, William Penn, Proprietor, Vice-Governor William [Markham], the Most Illustrious King of the Swedes, Charles XI, now of most glorious memory, having sent here Ericus Tobias Biork of Westmania, Pastor Loci . . .

The steep-gabled roof, 'framed with Nealing Principles,' was concealed inside by a hung ceiling of ' Ovale ' (more properly low segmental) shape, with ' laths nailed to the arch of the roof '; and a smooth coat of plaster covered both walls and vault. In this it differed from a near contemporary, for ancient Prince George's Chapel at Dagsboro Hundred, Delaware, probably built in 1717, still has walls and semicircular vault sheathed only in broad unpainted boards. John Harrison, the joiner, was assigned

all ye Inside work . . . that is all ye pews and Windows, shot work and the Pulpit with a canape over it and a pew of each side of ye communion Table and also with Reals and Banisters about ye church . . . and finish all the Sealing Joice which is to doe and fitt In ye ceiling of ye Roof . . .

Box pews and a red-brick floor, herringboned to form a central aisle, completed this simple but charming interior. The church served in this form for half a century. A new pastor, Isaac Acrelius, arriving from Sweden in 1749, found not only that the Swedish language was 'very much fallen out of use,' but that the church needed several minor repairs — in particular that the stone walls, despite their thickness, were spreading from

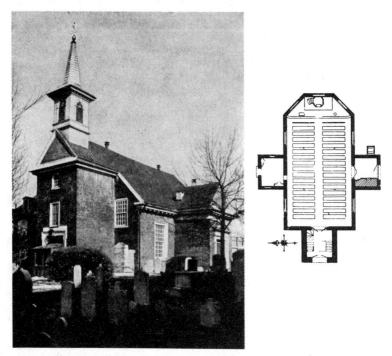

428, 429. Exterior and plan of 'Gloria Dei' (Old Swedes) Church, Philadelphia, 1698–1700 (HABS photo, plan from *The Georgian Period*)

the outward thrust of the roof ' so that the arch in the church is in danger of breaking. . .' To buttress the walls, a large arched porch of stone and brick was added at the south side. In 1774, 'there being great want of seats in the church,' a gallery holding 25 additional pews was added at the west end, attained by a delightful exterior staircase built within the south porch. It was not until 1802 that the vestrymen decided to add at the west end a tower and belfry, ' twelve by fourteen feet, and thirty-four feet high, of stone and brick, with a sufficient cupola to swing the bell in above the roof . . .' thus completing the church in the form that we see it today.

Swedes probably helped build the first Anglican church in Philadelphia, described as of ' typically Swedish lines.' [6] But erected of timber, in 1695, it has long since disappeared, and its nearest contemporary survivor is Old

Swedes church in that city. ' Gloria Dei,' as it is properly called, was built
on the site of an old Swedish blockhouse of 1677, and the quaint steep
roofed structure with its peaked gable and brittle belfry has more than
a suggestion of its Swedish origin (fig. 428). The church was begun in
1698 and dedicated on 2 July 1700. Roofed by a steep ' A ' truss, with a
high collar in order to accommodate the vaulted ceiling within, the walls
almost immediately began to spread, and as early as 1703 it was necessary
to buttress them by the addition of an entrance porch on the south side

430. Interior of ' Gloria Dei ' Church (Detroit Publishing Company)

and a small vestry on the north (see plan, fig. 429). The wooden trim of
cornice and windows is English in character, but the moldings are heavy
and bold — almost crude — and the naïve modillion blocks under the cornice have an inordinate projection. Quite in contrast is the woodwork of
the south doorway, where paneled doors, eared architrave, and pulvinated
frieze suggest the sophistication of a later date.

The brick masonry, too, suggests various building periods. Main walls
and porches have Flemish bond with glazed headers, but the tower is of
English bond and, in its top third, common bond. Flanking the entrance
door are decorative lozenges in glazed brick. The small entrance vestibule
in the tower barely permits a stair winding up to the gallery, and one
enters the simple nave (fig. 430) to a central aisle flanked by ' slip ' pews,
doubtless of a later period. The unpaneled galleries are supported by the
slenderest of posts, and on the gallery at the west end, below the organ
loft, are two big-eyed winged cherubim suggestive of Swedish wood-

carving. The baptismal font was brought from Sweden, and perhaps to Swedish influence is due the unusual shape of the ceiling. Polygonal in plan at the east end, the hung ceiling of the nave is vaulted in plaster to an irregular curve, steeper than that at the Wilmington church, and covers the whole like some quaint parabolic saucer. Fine and spacious for their early date, the two Old Swedes churches could be spoken of by Pastor Eric Bjork with justifiable pride:

Thus, with God's blessing we have completed the great work, and built two fine churches superior to any built in this country . . . so that the English themselves, who now govern this province and are richer than we, wonder at what we have done.[7]

The founding of Philadelphia

But except for its earliest Swedish origins, Philadelphia was entirely an English town. When Charles II granted to William Penn the entire tract west of the Delaware River between the provinces of New York and Maryland, Penn became the proprietor of an immense and fertile domain. At that time the 'Three Lower Counties' remained nominally a part of New York, but being separated by New Jersey from the parent colony, Penn easily persuaded the Duke of York in the following year (1682) to grant them to him, and he thus gained an extensive coastline on the Delaware Bay. Though these counties were given a separate government in 1702 as the colony of Delaware, they remained part of the proprietary domain of the Penn family until the Revolution.

Envisioning his 'Sylvania' as an asylum for persecuted Quakers, Penn insisted on religious toleration and welcomed all races and creeds. Shrewdly foreseeing the economic possibilities of the immense region which extended inland to the Alleghenies, he offered attractive terms to settlers and soon large numbers of immigrants came. To the original Swedes, Dutch, and English were added Welsh, Irish, and Swiss; Germans from the oppressed Rhineland, from the Black Forest, upper Bavaria, and Saxony began pouring into the colony in large numbers from about 1710; Scotch-Irish from Ulster escaped from laws and landlords at home to advance into the Pennsylvania hinterland. The population leapt from 2,000 in 1682 to about 20,000 in 1700, and to 200,000 by 1750. By 1740 only Virginia, Massachusetts, and Maryland exceeded Pennsylvania in size, and Philadelphia, second city in the colonies, was soon to outstrip Boston and become the greatest center of population, wealth, and culture in the American colonies in the second half of the eighteenth century.

Penn planned his capital city well. He appointed a commission to choose the site, and in the summer of 1682 its Surveyor General, Captain Thomas Holme, laid out a regular gridiron pattern of streets (fig. 431), extending some two miles east and west, between the Delaware and Schuylkill, and about one mile north and south. There were 9 broad streets between the rivers, and these were crossed by 21 shorter streets to divide the town into rectangular blocks. According to Penn's wish, north-south streets were numbered, east-west streets were named after various native trees and fruits, as is recalled in the old rhyme:

> High, Mulberry, Sassafras, Vine;
> Chestnut, Walnut, Spruce, and Pine.

Five areas of about two blocks each were set aside as public squares, and in time these were planted to English grass, so that townsmen might graze their cattle for the modest annual fee of twelvepence. Penn desired that each house be placed in the middle of its lot and surrounded by gar-

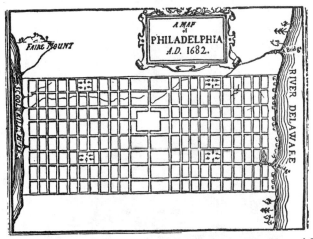

431. Plan of Philadelphia as laid out by Thomas Holme in 1682 (Harvard University Department of Landscape Architecture)

dens, ' so that it may be a greene country towne which may never be burnt.' [8] And in 1700 the town ordered that each inhabitant plant one or more ' shady and wholesome trees ' in order that it might be ' well shaded from the violence of the sun in the heat of the summer and thereby be rendered more healthy.' [9] This is not a far cry from Frank Lloyd Wright's conception of ' Broadacre City'; present-day Philadelphians, as well as New Yorkers, might well reflect on the fact that a bad city plan is not made but develops through misuse.

But not all was idyllic, even in the early days of the City of Brotherly Love. The town government took no responsibility for paving streets, and for years the mud, filth, and mire were a civic disgrace. Traffic was dense and disorderly, making it necessary finally to prohibit ' Galloping Horses, & also Carters Riding in their Carts and Drays, and excessive . . . driving in any of the Streets.' [10] The first fines for speeding were levied in 1712. By 1720, private citizens, banding together, cobblestoned several streets, and a few years later an effort was made to pitch them to the center, so that waste water from street-side pumps might drain into water courses in the middle of the streets. Soon brick sidewalks, the only ones in the colonies,

were laid, and posts set to guard them from the street traffic. Underground
brick sewers were also laid, as in Boston.

Commercial activities were well provided for. As early as 1684 Penn
granted to merchant Samuel Carpenter land at the foot of Walnut Street
for the construction of a wharf, and by the next year a pier 'to which a

432 Second Street Market, Philadelphia, 1745 (Frank Cousins, The Essex Institute)

ship of five hundred Tuns may lay her broadside' extended 200 feet into
the river and supported several warehouses and a flour mill. By the mid-
century many other docks and quays lined the waterfront, but Carpenter's Great Wharf continued to be the busiest. Certain streets contained
orderly rows of market sheds, for the sale of the great quantities of produce
that came in from the agricultural hinterland. A combination market-
and-court house was built in the center of High Street (between Second
and Third) in 1710, and in 1745 the market sheds of South Second Street
were terminated at Pine by a 'head house' (fig. 432) built of red brick
with white stone trim. The ten-foot central archway lined up with the
central aisle of the market sheds, and small flanking rooms housed fire

engines kept in constant readiness. For years the large rooms above housed the volunteer Hope Engine Company, and it may be assumed that the neat cupola served as a fire lookout post.

Philadelphia's first shelters were mere dugouts or caves along the banks of the Delaware, much like those at New Amsterdam. But frame houses must have been built almost immediately, for by 1684 the town boasted 357 dwellings. William Penn in one of his informative tracts for prospective immigrants, issued in that same year, included full instructions for building a frame house 18 by 30 feet, containing three rooms, and added that such a house could be built in less than forty days. Framing timbers, of course, were hand-hewn; laths and shingles were split; clapboards were split and shaved; and joists, floor boards, wainscot, and roofers were sawed. Apparently from the first, laborious pit-sawing was supplanted by power-sawing. The early Dutch and Swedish settlers had built sawmills, both wind- and water-powered; there is record that an Englishman named William Hampton built a sawmill at Salem, New Jersey, in 1683. By 1760 there were forty sawmills in Philadelphia County. According to Eberlein,[11] paint was used both inside and out from the earliest days of the colony.

But brick soon became the favored material for Philadelphia houses. Clay was in ample supply, and lime was at first obtained from sea shells. But the presence of ample deposits of limestone was soon discovered, and 'stone lime' came to be preferred because of its better quality. When wealthy Robert Turner, with his daughter and seventeen indentured servants, arrived in Philadelphia in 1683, he lived in what has been called the first brick house in the town. Writing home to London in 1685, he reported:

Bricks are exceedingly good, and cheaper than they were, say at 16 shillings per thousand, and brick houses are now as cheap to build as wood. Many brave brick houses are going up with good cellars . . . We build most houses with balconies.[12]

The housing supply was soon so good that the Provincial Council was enabled, by April 1687, to order those who still dwelt in the dismal caves on the Delaware 'to provide for themselves other habitations, in order to have the said Caves Distroy'd.'[13] A decade later, Gabriel Thomas described Philadelphia's houses as 'most of them stately, and of brick, generally three stories high, after the mode in London, and as many [as] several families in each.'[14] The three-story tenement house had thus put in an appearance before 1700. Others followed as the town became more densely populated; there is record of the construction of four tenement houses on Front Street in 1722.

The appearance of most of these early city houses is a matter of conjecture. That most of them were of brick, three stories high, and with balconies, 'after the mode in London,' suggests that they were probably like the row houses the real-estate developer Nicholas Barbon was putting up in London in the 1680's: rather plain brick houses, with stone and wood trim, regularly spaced windows, sparing classical decorative detail, and casements rather than sliding sash. It would be natural for the colonists to follow the post-fire mode in London.

The most important — though hardly the most typical — of early Philadelphia houses was the Slate Roof House, which stood at the corner of Second Street and Norris Alley until its demolition in 1867. Its appearance is known to us from a drawing of 1830 (fig. 433). This belonged to the wealthy merchant Samuel Carpenter and was built on land purchased by him at the founding of the colony. It was certainly completed by 1699, for William Penn occupied it in January 1700 on his second visit to the

433. Slate Roof House (Samuel Carpenter House), Philadelphia, 1687? (Watson's *Annals of Philadelphia*, 1830)

city, and it may have been finished by 1687.* The Slate Roof House was one of the earliest Georgian buildings in the colonies. It was built on an H-shaped plan, such as had been used in some of the English manor houses of Elizabethan and Jacobean times. The formal composition, horizontal emphasis, hipped roof, modillioned cornice, and pedimented doorway all reveal the advent of Renaissance architectural influences. The windows, however, were still filled by the medieval type of diamond-shaped panes; these remained in place through the eighteenth century [15] but had evidently been replaced by sliding sash at the time this picture was made. Such a house, though far less elaborate than its near contemporary, the Foster-Hutchinson House in Boston, bears the stamp of a professional designer, and it is not surprising, considering the personal friendship between Carpenter and Penn, to find that it was planned by James Porteus, a trained British architect brought over by Penn to 'design and execute his Proprietary buildings.' [16]

Undoubtedly more typical of the early houses of small merchants and skilled artisans is the Letitia Street House (fig. 434), a small dwelling orig-

---

* 'By 1687 Samuel Carpenter's " Slate Roof House " was the show place of the village.' (Bridenbaugh: *Cities in the Wilderness*, p. 99.) It is logical to suppose that a man of Carpenter's means would have built a large house soon after he obtained the land for it.

inally built on Letitia Street, but moved to Fairmount Park in 1883 and recently restored. Long supposed to have been the house Penn occupied on his first visit to the colony in 1682, the house is now thought to have been built at some time between 1703 and 1715.[17] Laid in Flemish-bond brickwork, with heavily vitrified headers, the modest façade has regularly spaced openings; the windows have sliding sash and paneled shutters. Over the door is a pent-roofed hood supported by bold scrolled brackets. The coved cornice, executed in neatly fitted boards, is of a type more often found in this region surfaced by stucco. It is carried across the gable ends, with little pent roofs over it. The low-pitched roof is pierced by a later

434. Letitia Street House, Fairmount Park, Philadelphia, 1703–15 (Philadelphia Museum of Art)

shed dormer. Despite the fact that the house is twice as deep as it is wide, the ridge is parallel to the short sides; this permitted a larger garret and incidentally set the pattern for the later continuous row houses of urban Philadelphia.

The plan of the Letitia Street House (fig. 435) is clearly based on a Swedish type such as that of the Lower Log House at Darby, with a large front room and smaller back room. The two corner fireplaces are arranged back to back (unlike the Log House, but also echoing Swedish precedent), and the chimney inside the wall is carried up back of the roof ridge. The partly sheathed stair at the partition rises to a second floor much like the first. This is a basic plan-type, repeated in scores of houses in the region of the middle colonies.

With its rapid growth and great building activity, Philadelphia had an unusually large number of men engaged in the building trades. Penn reported the presence, in 1685, of 'most sorts of useful Tradesmen,' including carpenters, 'Joyners,' bricklayers, masons, 'Plumers,' smiths, and glaziers. In 1724, the master carpenters banded themselves together in America's first builders' guild, modeled after the Worshipful Company of Carpenters founded in London in 1477. Among the original members of the Carpenters' Company were James Porteus, John Harrison, Samuel Powell, Jacob Usher, Ebenezer Thompson, Joseph Henmarsh, Edmund

Woolley, and Isaac Zane. It was their purpose to 'obtain instruction in the science of architecture, and to assist such of the members as should by accident be in need of support, and of the widows and minor children of such members.' By exchange of ideas, study of the best models, and the assembly of an architectural library — to which Porteus, on his death in

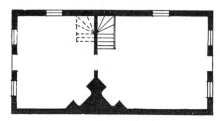

435. Plan of first floor, Letitia Street House (Thomas T. Waterman, *The Dwellings of Colonial America*, University of North Carolina Press)

1736, gave his valuable collection of books — they hoped to improve quality of design and workmanship. To this end they also issued a small *Manual* of design, containing house plans, elevations, frames, and details of roof trusses, doorways, windows, dormers, mantels, and the like, a veritable *vade mecum* which must have become the standard work for carpenters in the entire region.

Nor did they neglect the financial side of their profession. In attempting

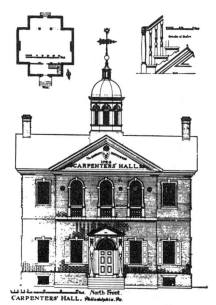

436. Carpenters' Hall, Philadelphia, 1770–71, by Robert Smith (*The Georgian Period*)

to set standards of measurement and quality, they issued a *Book of Prices* to each member, in order that ' everyone concerned in building may have the value of his money and every workman the worth of his labor.' Herein they pointed out that ' plain simple buildings ' and those involving ' many elegancies ' demanded differing rates of pay per square. They also made some complaint of the high cost of living, pointing out that ' men could live thirty years ago with two thirds of the expense that they can at present, and journeymen's wages were at one fourth less than is now given.' In establishing standards of quality as well as of pay, the Carpenters' Company did much to develop a group of master builders probably unrivaled elsewhere in the colonies.

The Company built its own guild hall in 1770–71, with the aid of subscriptions from members. Facing north on Chestnut Street, Carpenters' Hall (fig. 436) was designed by Robert Smith, a member also known for his design of Nassau Hall at Princeton. A rectangular building with projecting pedimented pavilions at north and south, the walls were laid in Flemish bond with dark greenish-gray headers. Paneled shutters adorned the first-story windows, and pedimented doorways, arched windows on the second story, and a crowning cupola revealed somewhat elaborate pretensions. But the false balustrade motive of the upper windows was inept, and the proportions of the whole somewhat heavy and clumsy. The building is perhaps justifiably more famed as the meeting place of the First Continental Congress in 1774 than as an architectural masterpiece.

Early Georgian houses of Philadelphia and its vicinity

The detached ' country houses ' of the late seventeenth century and the first half of the eighteenth reveal more clearly than do the city houses the qualities and details that mark the early Georgian architecture of Pennsylvania as a distinctive regional style.

The finer houses were almost universally built of stone or brick. The choice depended largely on availability. Wertenbaker points out [18] that east of a line drawn from Princeton to Wilmington brick was generally used; west of it houses were almost invariably built of stone. A stratified gneiss, particularly suitable for building, was abundant in the neighborhood of Germantown and Chestnut Hill, and good building stone was available over most of Chester, Berks, and Bucks Counties. The masonry varied from a crude rubble in the early period to even-coursed ashlar after the mid-century, but random-coursed and somewhat rough-surfaced stonework prevailed. Stone walls were often covered by a coat of smooth stucco, depending on the quality of the masonry; brick walls almost never were. In certain localities, brick masonry was enlivened by ' black-diapering,' as in Maryland. The houses of Salem County, Delaware, and the southern counties of New Jersey were particularly rich in glazed-brick patterns of zigzags, diamonds, checkerboards, dates, and initials. Stone walls would have been a stubborn material in which to work the elaborate decorative details of the Georgian mode, but until the mid-century walls were devoid of such architectural pretensions as giant pilasters, pedimented windows, projecting pavilions, and the like.

As if to offset the severity of bare stone walls, wood trim was particularly heavy. Door and window frames, paneled shutters, and richly molded cornices, all painted a gleaming white, afforded a telling contrast to dark gray masonry. Paneled exterior shutters were particularly a feature of the Georgian style in the middle colonies; usually they were employed only on first-story windows, while louvered blinds were often used on the second story. Very characteristic, also, was the 'skirt roof' or pent house projecting over first-story windows (fig. 443). Found widely in houses of the Rhine valley, where it was originally used to help protect half-timbered walls, it of course remained popular with German settlers in Pennsylvania even when not functionally necessary. The English also adopted it *con amore;* old prints show Philadelphia streets lined with pent-roofed buildings, and such were almost typical of the lower counties of New Jersey. Another favorite motive was the door hood, which might project as a separate feature (see fig. 442) or emerge as a pediment from a skirt roof (fig. 443). Main cornices were usually deep and richly molded, though they generally lacked architrave and frieze members. Frequently cornices crossed gable ends (figs. 437, 442).

Roofs were almost always of gentle pitch and gabled. The hipped roof occurred on the more formal mansions, such as Stenton. The gambrel roof was rarely employed in Pennsylvania but, when used, was of the Swedish profile, with very steep lower slopes (figs. 440, 442). Round-arch dormers and cupolas were late Georgian features.

The impressive three-part composition of main building and service dependencies so often found in southern Georgian mansions was not used in the middle colonies. The single exception today is Mount Pleasant in Philadelphia, built in 1761. Elsewhere service wings projected at the rear of houses and did not form a part of the main composition. They were often, however, attached at a corner, in order to leave an open vista from the central hall and back door to the garden.

Interiors were, in general, less distinctively regional in character. The same types of doorways, paneled walls, mantelpieces, and cornices may be seen in all the colonies. There was somewhat greater use in the middle colonies, however, of bare plastered walls. The plaster was applied direct to the brick or stone masonry, a bad practice because of damp-penetration and the poor insulating qualities of such construction. By the late Georgian period, an interior plaster wall was 'furred out' on strapping and hand-split laths, to leave an air space. Since rabbit fur, feathers, cotton, and wool were sometimes used in the eighteenth century to stop drafts at doors and windows, such air spaces may have been filled with fur, and it may be surmised that this practice gave rise to the modern term 'furring.' [19] Main interior partitions were of masonry, but thin ones consisted merely of rough boards, overlapped at the joints, the whole plastered on both sides.

As previously remarked, interior woodwork was painted from the earliest days, though the vigorous colors we have seen at Williamsburg probably prevailed over the whites that have since become so universal. Wrought-iron hardware was extensively used, for soon after Penn's ar-

rival the rich iron-ore resources of the region were exploited in the manufacture of nails, hinges, beam anchors, shutter catches, and the like. Iron
was not used structurally in building, but as early as 1787 Thomas Paine
proposed the construction of an iron bridge over the Schuylkill. The fame
of Baron Stiegel's glassworks has led some people to suppose that window
glass was being manufactured, so it is perhaps worth remarking that
eighteenth-century factories produced little more than green bottle glass
and glass trinkets for the Indian trade; window glass was still imported
from England, and it was not until 1792 that it was manufactured on a
successful commercial basis in this country.

437. Wynnestay, West Philadelphia, 1689 (Cortlandt V. D. Hubbard)

Half a dozen mansions of the Philadelphia region may illustrate the
distinctive qualities of the Pennsylvania style in the early Georgian period.
Oldest is Wynnestay in West Philadelphia, built by the Wynne family in
1689, and very little altered except for the raising of the main roof to
meet the level of an addition made in 1700 (fig. 437). With thick rubble-
masonry walls, massive stone lintels over doors and windows, and a vigorous main cornice of wood, the house has an appearance of rugged strength
and solidity. Skirt roof and door hood are characteristic of the style,
though it is unusual to find paneled shutters, with their crescent cuts, on
second-story windows.

Wyck, in Germantown, conceals beneath its long, uniform façade a succession of buildings. The first unit (at the top in the plan, fig. 439) was
built about 1690 by Hans Millan. A small, separate house was built to the
northeast about 1720, and a brick-paved carriage drive ran between the
two. At some later date the two units were connected by an overhead link.
In 1824 the architect William Strickland closed in the wagon way to form
a living room or conservatory, with wide double doors on each side of

the room. This succession of additions helps to explain the irregular placement of doors and windows on the 80-foot façade which fronts the southeast lawn (fig. 438). The rough stone wall is covered by a smooth coat of whitewashed stucco, and this in turn by a trellis for climbing vines. The windows, 24 light below and 20 above, have paneled shutters. The gable roof above the richly molded cornice is of lower pitch than that at Wynnestay. The northeast end of the building, toward the street, is stuccoed,

438. Wyck, Germantown, Pa., c.1690, 1720, southeast façade (HABS)

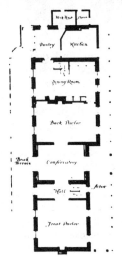

439. Plan of Wyck, after alterations by William Strickland in 1824 (*Great Georgian Houses*, II)

440. Graeme Park, Horsham, Pa., 1721–2 (Frank Cousins, The Essex Institute)

441. Drawing room, Graeme Park (Philip B. Wallace, Historical Society of Pennsylvania)

but the southeast or service end is of bare stone masonry and the cornice is not carried across the gable end, as it is at Wynnestay.

Somewhat the same type of one-room-deep plan is evident in the remarkable house that Sir William Keith, Governor of Pennsylvania, built at Horsham in Montgomery County, in 1721–2. Graeme Park (fig. 440) is so utterly devoid of exterior embellishment that it appears truly Colonial, yet its interiors are rich in Georgian woodwork. The contract for the house was signed with the mason John Kirk on 12 December 1721. Neither doors nor windows, which are of extraordinarily tall and narrow proportions, have classic enframements, and the cornices are little more than boxed eaves. Both the plan, which resembles the Swedish *parstuga* type, and the high gambrel roof betray the long-persistent influence of the Swedish Colonial tradition.

Within this rugged and severe shell are rooms with paneling, mantelpieces, and door enframements of very advanced Georgian style for their early date. One enters the front door to a large square hall with a fireplace, lighted by the one window to the left of the door. Back of it a small stair hall contains a steep winding staircase of almost seventeenth-century aspect, with square solid newel posts, simply turned balusters, and a closed string. There are only two other main rooms on the ground floor, and of these the large east drawing room (fig. 441) is the most remarkable. Over 20 feet square, its walls are paneled from floor to ceiling in gray-painted yellow pine, with a simple sheathed dado and molded chair rail, and above this broad panels extending to the fully membered entablature. The white plastered ceiling is 14 feet high. The deep window embrasures have interior paneled shutters.

The fireplace on the west wall is the focal point of the room. Remarkable for this early date are the mantel shelf and the single-panel overmantel composition, more usually found in the late Georgian period. The panel is surrounded by an eared architrave and topped by a pediment. The fireplace wall of the second-floor parlor has a similar composition, but this time with no mantel shelf, and with flanking doors topped by semicircular arched lunettes rather than pediments. All the moldings at Graeme Park have an unusually bold projection and vigorous contour.

Kitchens and service quarters at Graeme Park were in detached buildings, now disappeared. Sir William must have lived in considerable style in his six-room mansion. His inventory reveals a silver punch bowl and ladle, 70 large pewter plates, miscellaneous basins, pots, and bowls of pewter and brass, 6 china tea sets and 6 more in white stone, 2 dozen chocolate cups, a dozen venison pots, 6 dozen plates, a dozen wine decanters, 44 sheets, 50 tablecloths, 12 dozen napkins, 10 dozen knives and forks, and other such household utensils. Of furniture, he owned 60 beds, 144 chairs, 32 tables, 3 clocks, and 15 mirrors. His stables boasted 4 coach horses, 7 saddle horses, 6 work horses, a 'large glass coach,' 2 chaises, 2 wagons, 1 wain, and herds of cattle, sheep, and hogs.[20] He was wont to ride to church, over the special road built for him, in his emblazoned coach with four horses, liveried footmen, and outriders.

Moore Hall, in Chester County, built by Judge William Moore somewhat after 1722, with later additions, is more typical of the early Pennsylvania style in plan and exterior appearance (fig. 442). With central hall and double file of rooms, it has a depth that contributes to the quality of ample solidity so characteristic of the region. The walls exhibit three different types of masonry: the front is built of hewn blocks in courses of even heights, the end walls have courses of random heights, and the small wing is of uncoursed rubble. Noteworthy details are the broad, low-pitched roof, the molded cornice carried across the gable end, the projecting door hood, and the gambrel roof of characteristic profile on the wing. The small Doric entrance portico was doubtless a later addition.

442. Moore Hall, Chester County, Pa., after 1722 (Cortlandt V. D. Hubbard)

The Green Tree Inn at Germantown is also typically Pennsylvanian (fig. 443). A stone bears the date 1748 and the initials of Daniel and Sarah Pastorius. Very little changed since its construction, the building reveals most of the architectural features peculiar to the region: paneled shutters on the lower story, a skirt roof broken by a pediment over the door, a deep cove under the cornice, and a low-pitch gabled roof. Masonry work was becoming more regular by the mid-century, and the stones of the façade are well-hewn rectangles — some of unusual length — laid in regular courses. Segmental-arched basement windows are found elsewhere, but the segmental-topped windows of the dormers are unusual. Standing on the main thoroughfare, Germantown Avenue, this house served as an inn for driving parties from the city and has gone under a succession of names: 'Sadler's Arms,' 'Hornets' Nest,' and 'Widow Mackenet's Tavern,' as well as the name familiar today.

Stone houses abound in the Philadelphia region. Space does not permit description or illustration of other notable examples such as Waynesboro in Chester County (1724), the unusual Bartram House in West

Philadelphia, begun in 1730–31, Grumblethorpe in Germantown (1744), now-destroyed Whitby Hall (1754), or the Johnson House in Germantown (1765–8).

In Philadelphia and to the east of it, however, brick houses rivaled stone in popularity. Hope Lodge in the Whitemarsh valley was one of the finest; built by Samuel Morris in 1724, some of its splendid interior woodwork seems hard to credit as of this period. Another fine example is Stenton, in Germantown. It was built in 1728 by James Logan, scholar and

443. Green Tree Inn (Pastorius House), Germantown, Pa., 1748 (Frank Cousins, The Essex Institute)

man of affairs, and sometime Secretary of the province, Chief Justice, and President of the Council.

The façade of Stenton (fig. 444) has an early Georgian simplicity but, unlike Graeme Park, is completely regular in composition. Semicircular soapstone steps approach the doorway, unframed by classic pilasters. Flanking it are two narrow sidelights, perhaps the earliest instance of this motive in Georgian architecture. The rectangular transom over the door, giving additional light to the entrance hall, is, however, of common occurrence at this period. The interruption of the brick belt course over these central openings suggests that there may originally have been a sheltering porch of some kind — perhaps a projecting hood. Rudimentary brick pilasters or piers flank the entrance-hall unit and mark the corners of the house. Twenty-four-light windows divide the façade in regular bays, topped by segmental arches of gauged brick, as in early Virginia mansions. Unshaped blocks at the cornice take the place of academic modillions. The hipped roof with flat deck is more characteristic of a later period. A covered porch at the back of the house connects to a long story-and-a-half service wing extending to the rear.

It is worth remarking that neither side nor rear façades at Stenton are symmetrically composed; doors and windows occur where demanded by the plan, and even at the odd level of the stair landing in the rear. The interiors are in the main, however, formal. The staircase, like that at Graeme Park, has the handrail meeting square newel posts at acute angles

444. Stenton, Germantown, 1728 (Frank Cousins, The Essex Institute)

rather than at right angles by means of curved ramps and easings, as in a later era. Quite unusual was the long library extending across the entire front of the second story. Since subdivided, it must originally have been a splendid room, with its many windows, for James Logan's fine library, reputedly one of the best in the colonies.

Somewhat comparable to Stenton, though less formal in character, was the fine Ridgeley House in Dover, Delaware, also built in 1728. The similarity of both these brick houses to Brafferton Hall and the President's House at Williamsburg is worthy of note.

Late Georgian houses

As the eighteenth century wore on, houses became more elaborate but less authentically regional in character. Exterior giant pilasters never became as popular as they did in New England, but the same pavilions breaking façades, the same classic door enframements, the same balustraded roof-decks, and the same Palladian windows that may be seen from Massachusetts to South Carolina appeared also in the middle colonies. There was, perhaps, a particular emphasis on a rich façade treatment, even if this necessitated a more plebeian simplicity elsewhere, like the houses of a later era with a ' Queen Anne front and Mary Anne behind.' More noticeable, too, is the tendency of the late Georgian designer, pas-

445. Mount Pleasant, Fairmount Park, Philadelphia, 1761–2 (Wayne Andrews)

sionately bent on external symmetry, to ignore the relationship of windows to necessary internal features such as partitions and stair landings, so that flights or landings may be found crossing windows at curious angles or levels. The Philadelphia late Georgian style is most distinguished, perhaps, by the extraordinary richness of interior woodwork and plasterwork in the finer houses; surpassing even the ornateness of Buckland's Annapolis houses, this opulence may be traced partly to the growing wealth of the city, partly to the professional competence of its craftsmen. It was not for nothing that George Washington, when he wanted to redecorate his dining room at Mount Vernon in 1775, sent for a Philadelphia man to do it.

If the first of these late Georgian mansions, chronologically, was Woodford, built by William Coleman in 1756 in what is now Fairmount Park; the most pretentious was Mount Pleasant, also a present-day ornament of the park. Mount Pleasant was built in 1761–2 by John Macpherson, a Scotch sea captain who had amassed a fortune at privateering and evi-

dently desired to set himself up in manorial splendor. A lavish display
of almost every device of late Georgian design, the house has a somewhat
nouveau-riche character (fig. 445) .

Raised on a hewn-stone basement 6 feet high and with 12-foot ceilings
and a lofty roof, the sheer height of the house is emphasized by its position on a hilltop overlooking the Schuylkill River to the west. Commanding broad views up and down stream, it takes no advantage of them,
for both north and south walls are devoid of windows — indeed they are
blank areas of stucco broken only by the brick belt course which circles
the house. In a building so obviously designed to stand in splendid isolation, this failure to take advantage of view and, especially, the south sun-

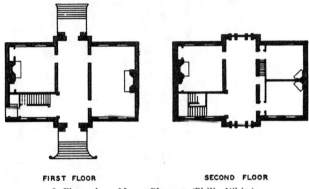

FIRST FLOOR   **SECOND FLOOR**
446. Floor plans, Mount Pleasant (Philip White)

light, seems curious. All architectural emphasis is on the west and east
façades. The latter was the main entrance from the city, and the approach
was flanked by outriding barns (now destroyed) and twin service dependencies whose modest size emphasized the grandeur of the main mansion. This is the only surviving example in the middle colonies of a symmetrical composition of three units, such as was common in southern
Georgian architecture.

Walls of the house are of rubble masonry 18 inches thick, surfaced by
a salmon-tinted coat of stucco lightly scored to simulate the joints of ashlar masonry. Another trick is the use of stone lintels, over the windows, incised in imitation of flat keyed arches. Pavilions break both east and west
façades, and all eight corners of the building are emphasized by prominent brick angle quoins. The two entrance doorways with Doric enframements and round-arch lunettes with heavy fluted muntins are similar in
design, the west one lacking triglyphs and mutules. Over each is a Palladian window. The hipped roof is topped by a balustraded roof-deck, and
arched quadruple chimneys add weight to the perfectly symmetrical composition. Round-arch dormer windows, such as had appeared in the Carpenters' Company *Manual,* were very common in late Georgian houses of
the region, but the inept flanking consoles used here are fortunately a
rarity.

The plans (fig. 446) show a main entrance hall unbroken by a stairway, a feature found in the equally formal Mount Airy, Virginia. The stairway is in a small separate hall at the southeast corner. Under its main landing, an outside door and small corridor connected dining room with kitchen in the southeast dependency. Woodwork of the hall has fluted pilasters and a full Doric entablature similar to that of Independence Hall. The large drawing room extends across the whole north end of the house. Dominated by a great chimneypiece almost 8 feet wide, in the middle of

447. Second-floor hall, Mount Pleasant (Philip B. Wallace, Historical Society of Pennsylvania)

the north wall, the blank spaces to right and left are featured by elaborate pedimented doors that lead nowhere, for there is a solid wall behind them. The upstairs hall (fig. 447) also extends clear through the house. Decorated in the Ionic order and lighted by the Palladian windows at the ends, it is as formal as the lower rooms. Indeed all of the upstairs rooms, and particularly the great chamber with its scrolled overmantel and flanking arched cupboard doors, reveal features of advanced academic design and superb workmanship.

Mount Pleasant was sold in 1779 to General Benedict Arnold, whose occupancy, due to unfortunate circumstances, lasted only two years; in 1868 it became the property of the city.

Cliveden in Germantown is another notable late Georgian mansion (fig. 254). It exhibits a characteristic 'façade emphasis,' the front wall being built of regular ashlar masonry, the others of rubble masonry stuccoed and grooved to simulate ashlar. The central pavilion is so narrow

(12 feet) that it appears pinched. Belt course, window sills, and lintels are made of dressed sandstone, the lintels grooved to simulate flat keyed arches as at Mount Pleasant. The big 24-light windows and the arched dormers with flanking scrolls are also like those at Mount Pleasant. An otherwise reposeful roof is cluttered by five gargantuan stone urns, all visible from the front. Paneled shutters adorn the lower-floor windows.

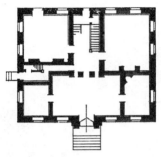

448. Plan of Cliveden, Germantown (courtesy Fiske Kimball)

The plan of Cliveden (fig. 448) has the unusual monumentality to be gained by an imposing entrance hall, 16 by 27 feet, well lighted by façade windows, and the whole separated from the stair hall by a screen of columns (fig. 449). The latter feature, as we have seen, is paralleled elsewhere in Georgian domestic architecture only at the Chase House in An-

449. Entrance hall of Cliveden, 1763–4 (Philip B. Wallace, Historical Society of Pennsylvania)

napolis. The treatment of the Doric order, with triglyphs and recessed panels in the metopes, is similar to that in the hall at Mount Pleasant. Small offices flank the entrance hall, and the two main rooms at the back are dining room (at left) and drawing room (at right). Cliveden, like some other Georgian houses, has a secondary stair and service hall. Kitchen and service rooms were originally in detached wings at the rear.

450. Parlor from the Steadman-Powel House, Philadelphia, in the Metropolitan Museum of Art, 1768 (Metropolitan Museum of Art)

Cliveden was built in 1763–4 * by Benjamin Chew, at that time Attorney General of the province, later Chief Justice of Pennsylvania. The British took refuge within its solid stone walls during the Battle of Germantown in 1777, and it took nearly a year to repair the damage done by the cannon fire of the American forces.

Among the finest interiors in Philadelphia were those of the house on South Third Street built in 1768 by Charles Steadman and sold a year later to Samuel Powel. The plain brick façade, with its arched entrance door at one side, gave little hint of the graceful refinements of the interior. Its beautiful music room and parlor were veritable museum pieces; since the abandonment of the house, the former has been removed to the Philadelphia Museum, the latter to New York's Metropolitan (fig. 450). Crisply cut white paneling set off the fine carving of a mantelpiece that might have come from Abraham Swan's book, while superb Chippendale furni-

---

* Not 1761 as frequently stated. The land was not purchased until 17 July, 1763.

ture, including two gilded Chinese mirrors, reflected a European vogue echoed in the Oriental details of the magnificent imported wallpaper. The white plaster ceiling was adorned by plaster arabesques of rococo intricacy and featured by a glittering cut-glass chandelier. The room, extending the full width of the house, must have been a graceful setting for the social occasions which it frequently saw after Samuel Powel became Philadelphia's Mayor in 1770.

Of the many other notable city residences in Philadelphia, perhaps the

451. William Corbit House, Odessa, Del., 1772–4 (Wayne Andrews)

finest was the Reynolds-Morris House on South Eighth Street. Three stories high and of ' double ' width, the house had paneled shutters, arched entrance door, keyed window lintels, and many other features of the Georgian style. It was built by John Reynolds after the Revolution — in 1786–7 as shown by two marble date stones. In 1817 it came into the possession of the Morris family.

No other city in the middle colonies, of course, rivaled Philadelphia's architectural richness, but mention should be made of New Castle, Delaware, a miniature Philadelphia of great charm. Many of the old buildings bordering The Strand are of pre-Revolutionary date, and perhaps nowhere else today except at Williamsburg can one better savor the atmosphere and character of a mid-eighteenth-century town. Its one really notable house, however, often described as Georgian, is in reality Federal in both date and style; this famous house built by George Read II in 1791–1801, though with many belated Georgian features, has a round-arch entrance embracing both door and sidelights, intricate interior decoration in the Adam style, and other features never seen before the Revolution.

The town of Odessa, Delaware, boasts several very good Georgian houses, of which the finest is the William Corbit House built in 1772–4 (fig. 451). Fine brick masonry, stone belt course and window lintels, paneled shutters, arched doorway, and dormer windows of the arched and consoled type are all typical of the regional style. Perhaps the reason for the exceptionally satisfying quality of the façade is the reposeful horizontality which the omission of a central pavilion permits – a quality enhanced by the broad 20-light windows and gently sloped hipped roof. The cornice is unusual in having flat mutule blocks rather than modillions; the Chinese lattice rail around the flat roof-deck may be of later date, for such features were more common after the Revolution.

Complete memoranda of materials and costs for this house have been preserved, and they form an interesting picture of contemporary building practices.[21] As the mason carried on his work (he used some 90,000 bricks), and the carpenter proceeded with the rough framing and roof, a contract was entered into with Robert May and Company to do the joinery. Their bill for the finished woodwork came to £563. This firm also did the joinery for the near-by David Wilson residence (1769) and the Old Drawyers' Church at Odessa (1773), and their finish in the Corbit House is of a richness scarcely surpassed in the finest Philadelphia houses. Especially splendid is the big drawing room on the second floor, where fine Greek fret, guilloche, and interlaced diamonds adorn the subtly curved moldings of baseboard, chair rail, pilaster caps, and the broken pediments of doors and overmantel.

Public and institutional buildings

Philadelphia ranked second only to Boston in the number and architectural quality of its churches and public and institutional buildings. Outstanding among these, of course, was the Old State House, better known as Independence Hall. Viewed from the south, the group of buildings forms an impressive whole (fig. 452). The repose of a dominantly horizontal composition is set off by the aspiring tower, and its dignified symmetry is enlivened by the warmth of sunlit reds and whites. In its complete form, this most beautiful of Georgian public buildings gives little hint of the conflicts, delays, and difficulties of its building history.

In 1730 the Provincial Assembly determined on the construction of a State House (as it was called from the start) and purchased land in October of that year. Thomas Lawrence, Andrew Hamilton (the Speaker of the Assembly), and Dr. John Kearsley were members of the committee appointed to undertake the work. Both of the latter submitted designs. Kearsley, an eminent physician and member of the Assembly, had recently directed – with marked success – the building of near-by Christ Church. Hamilton was inexperienced in architecture but perhaps had absorbed with his legal training at the Inns of Court in London some familiarity with Georgian design. When the two designs were submitted to the Assembly, Hamilton's was chosen.

The foundations were started in 1731. Among the men at work on the project, at one time or another, were the brickmasons Joseph Hitchcock and Thomas Bonde; the marble worker William Holland; Edmund Woolley, Ebenezer Tomlinson, Thomas Shoemaker, and two other carpenters; John Harrison, joiner; Thomas Kerr, plasterer; Thomas Ellis, glazier; Brian Wilkinson, woodcarver; and Gustave Hesselius, woodcarver and painter. Hesselius, the most notable of these craftsmen, was a man of versatile talent. Known primarily as painter and portraitist, he advertised in 1740 to do painting ' in the Best Manner . . . viz. Coats of Arms

452. South front, Independence Hall, Philadelphia, 1731–6 and later. Andrew Hamilton (Frank Cousins, The Essex Institute)

drawn on Coaches, Chaises, &c, or any other kinds of Ornaments, Landskips, Signs, Showboards, Ship or House Painting, Gilding of all Sorts, Writing in Gold or Colour, old Pictures clean'd and Mended.' [22] To him are attributed much of the interior carving and painting.

But despite this roster of craftsmen, work went slowly, impeded by conflicts about the site and the design, building obstructions, lack of labor, and insufficient money. By the time the Assembly first met in its great room in October 1736, windows were still unglazed, plastering had not been done, and even some of the masonry was incomplete. The roof and the second-floor rooms were completed by 1741, the year Judge Hamilton died after a decade of — we may imagine — frustration and disappointment at the slow progress of the work to which he had contributed so generously of both time and money. The Assembly Hall was finally finished and decorated by 1745.

Hamilton never saw the great tower and steeple which now dominate the building. The tower was built in 1750 and the steeple finished in 1753. But a generation saw it in such rickety condition that it had to be removed in 1781, and the building stood for nearly fifty years without any steeple. Finally, in 1828, it was rebuilt, along the old lines, under the direction of the architect William Strickland, who reinforced the construction by various diagonal girders and iron clamps. Curved ships' knees were extensively used as braces, and the work is said to have been done by marine engineers from the South Philadelphia Arsenal. This construction remains in excellent condition today.

The two-story wings which flank the building to east and west have also seen a complex history. First built in 1736 and 1739, they were then connected to the main building by brick arcades with solid curtain walls on the south side. Rebuilt in 1813 by Robert Mills, they were finally reconverted to their original form in the restoration of 1897-8, but with the lofty connecting arcades open to both north and south.

The larger two-story buildings which now terminate the composition of this seven-unit façade were completed after the Revolution. Congress Hall, built as a County Court House in 1789 at the west end of the group, was occupied by the United States Congress from 1790 to 1800; in it Washington was inaugurated for his second term, and Adams was inaugurated in 1797. The City Hall, at the east end of the group, was completed in 1791. Together with the near-by Episcopal Academy, Philosophical Hall, Philadelphia Library, and Carpenters' Hall, the group constituted a civic center unrivaled elsewhere in the colonies.

The north, or Chestnut Street, façade of the building (fig. 453), is the least satisfactory of the two main faces. The uniform rhythm of its nine bays becomes a little monotonous over so great a length, and the simple and effective color contrast of red brick and white wood windows is unduly complicated by a profusion of decorative trim in bluish-white marble. The introduction of two marble belt courses with a series of nine oblong marble panels between them creates a spotty effect. The belt course as an architectural feature, we have seen, originated as an exterior indication of a floor level inside, and though by this time it had become a purely decorative feature, the history of architectural styles seems to show that decorative features of structural origin are most effective when used with fairly close reference to their original structural meaning. Thus employed, they serve the dual purpose of clarifying the unity of interior and exterior by symbolizing the structural form of the building and at the same time enhancing that basic integrity by graceful refinements in form and color.

It is possible, too, that a further architectural expression of the functional importance of the main doorway, by means of enframing motives with which Georgian designers were so familiar, might have relieved the façade of that flat featurelessness which characterizes it.

The end walls of the main building are blank, and the four interior chimneys at each end are linked by arches at the top. The end walls also express the shape of the roof, with its low pitches at each side and the flat balustraded deck on top. Round windows in the gable ends were originally clock faces; the hands were actuated by a mechanism in the middle of the attic and long shafts extending to the ends. For a time stone piers and enframements built outside the wall made these look like gigantic grandfather clocks; parts of the stone piers remain.

The south façade is more pleasing because of the utter simplicity of the ranges of rectangular windows, with their fine frames and boldly sized muntins, and the warmth of red brick and white trim. Almost all decorative detail is concentrated in the tower, certainly one of the finest in Georgian architecture. Descended from Christopher Wren's church towers, but not a copy of any one of them, it is of massive proportions and construction. With walls ranging in thickness from 3 feet at the base to 18 inches at the top, the progressive lightening of the construction is symbolized by

453. North (Chestnut Street) front, Independence Hall (Frank Cousins, the Essex Institute)

the slight setbacks of the upper two brick stories and the further setbacks and increasing openness of the light wood steeple. Evolving from the weight and solidity of the lower walls to the open arches of the cupola, the tower affords a perfect transition from reposeful stability to aspiring loftiness. Noteworthy details are the Doric doorway and fine Ionic Palladian window over it, the brick pilasters in Doric and Ionic in successive higher stories, and the wooden Corinthian pilasters of the clock story. Setbacks are adorned by urns and balustrades. The windows of the uppermost brick story have keystones with carved grotesque faces, an unusual motive in Georgian architecture.

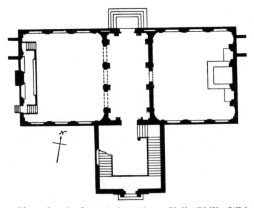

454. Plan of main floor, Independence Hall (Philip White)

When the new tower was built (in 1828), clock faces were installed in it, and as these were deemed adequate for civic promptitude, the old ones at the gable ends were removed. The famed Liberty Bell, cast in England in 1752, never did hang in a proper belfry. The first steeple, completed in 1753, was so flimsy that the bell was hung on two beams in the lower brick portion of the tower. Removed in 1781 when the tower was taken down, it was replaced by a new bell in the steeple of 1828. The old bell, hung in a lower story, was rung only on occasions of great importance. On one of these — the death of Chief Justice John Marshall on 8 July 1835 — it was cracked, and in 1843 this crack was so widened that the sound of the bell was destroyed.

The plan of Independence Hall (fig. 454) is simple in form and its interiors majestic in scale. The tower contains a magnificent stairway winding around three sides to the balcony of the second floor. Adorned with carved scroll step ends, heavy balusters, and gracefully ramped mahogany handrail, it is well lighted by the great Palladian window over the south landing. The main oblong of the building, 44 by 107 feet, has only three rooms. The central hallway is richly adorned by a Roman Doric order of columns and entablature, fully membered, and from it an arch order of three openings leads to the Supreme Court Chamber (originally the Court of Common Pleas), while a single door opens to the great square chamber at the east side originally occupied by the Pennsylvania Assembly. About 40 feet square and 20 feet high, this great room in which the Declaration of Independence was signed was one of the most impressive in the colonies. Twin segmental-arched fireplaces flanked the speaker's dais at the east end, walls were adorned by massive fluted pilasters raised on pedestals, and a heavy Roman Doric entablature bordered the white plaster ceiling with its central chandelier of myriad lights and crystals. The second floor had a ' long room ' or Banquet Hall on the Chestnut Street side, and smaller rooms for antechamber and Council Hall. The Old State House was purchased by the City of Philadelphia in 1816 to serve as a historical museum.

The first Anglican church in Philadelphia, built in 1695, was rebuilt and enlarged in 1710–11, but so rapid was the growth of the town that the congregation needed a large new edifice in less than a generation. Generous contributions from the parishioners, who numbered many of the politically and socially prominent persons of Philadelphia, financed the construction of new Christ Church. Work was begun as an enlargement of the old church, at the west end, in 1727; the decade of the 'thirties saw the replacement of the eastern two-thirds of the old church by the present structure, which was completed in 1744. The work was under the direction of Dr. John Kearsley. Though he is generally credited with the design, the original drawings are lost, and there is no certain evidence whether he made them himself or merely superintended the construction of a design drawn by someone else. The steeple was not completed until a decade later (1754), and though Dr. Kearsley may have submitted several alternative ' drafts,' it is quite clear from the records of the vestry that the one selected was ' the draft which Mr. Harrison drew,' and that construction was directed by Robert Smith of the Carpenters' Company.* A famous peal of eight bells, which ' rang out a merry chime ' on 4 July 1776, was obtained in London for £500 by the aid of a lottery Benjamin Franklin helped to manage in 1753.

Christ Church is one of the largest, and is certainly the most ornate, of Georgian churches in the colonies (fig. 455). With numerous details taken from English architectural books, the general design is closest to that of St. Andrew-by-the-Wardrobe, in London, though details of the spire may come from Gibbs's St. Martin's-in-the-Fields. The 28-foot square tower at the west end has stone walls 4 feet thick, faced by brick, and the octagonal wooden spire surmounting it rises to the great height of 196 feet. The body of the church is elaborate with Georgian architectural dress. Superposed orders of pilasters and entablatures adorn the sides, and the heavy wooden balustrade crowning the eaves is topped by pedestaled urns emitting carved flames.† The commanding feature of the exterior is the great

* Peter Harrison of Newport immediately comes to mind, but since the Carpenters' Company numbered both a Joseph Harrison and a John Harrison at this time, and a certain Henry Harrison was a vestryman and warden active in the affairs of the church, the identity of the designer of the steeple remains uncertain. The steeple was repaired in 1771 and rebuilt in original form after a fire in 1908.

† Originally of wood, now of cast iron filled with concrete.

Palladian window lighting the chancel, topped by carved keystone and medallion and a rich Ionic entablature. Great spiral scrolls flank a crowning pediment well laden with bulbous urns. On the whole, the exterior, with its false front at the east, its balustrades concealing the separate slope of gallery roofs, and its many blind windows, niches, and panels, seems arbitrary and overburdened in comparison with the simple grandeur of St. Michael's, Charleston.

455, 456. Christ Church, Philadelphia, 1727–54 (Frank Cousins, The Essex Institute)

The interior, too, suffers by comparison with superb King's Chapel, Boston, but it is somewhat hard to visualize its original appearance. The three widely spaced columns on each side rise to nave arches that carry an elliptical plaster ceiling (fig. 456). Blocks of entablature separating columns and arches, though of unassailable Renaissance heritage from Brunelleschi's time down, are no more successful here than they were in San Lorenzo. Apparently these columns were originally engaged against the gallery fronts, as at King's Chapel and the First Baptist Church in Providence, for, when Thomas U. Walter remodeled the galleries in 1834, ' the parapets at the front were made to recede so as not to interrupt or encumber the shafts of the beautiful Doric columns.' [23] The old-fashioned wine-glass pulpit, reading desk, and font were made in 1770, but the organ over the rear gallery dates from 1837, and the stained glass in the chancel window from an even more unfortunate period.

St. Peter's, the second Anglican congregation founded in Philadelphia, built a large Georgian church in 1758–61, under the direction of Robert Smith. Considerably less pretentious than Christ Church, the interior has a Colonial simplicity and the exterior is marked by a tower of Gothic lines, added by Strickland in the nineteenth century.

The Quaker meeting-houses of Pennsylvania were extremely simple in form and almost devoid of ornament. Built of frame construction in the early years of the province, they most nearly resembled the barn-like meeting-houses of small New England towns but were marked by twin entrance doors on the long sides. Soon they were built of brick or stone — like the houses of the surrounding region. Minor embellishments were permitted, such as the paneled shutters or projecting door hoods of the regional style, but they always remained domestic in character rather than ecclesiastical. As Wertenbaker remarks, it would have seemed as im-

457. Old Drawyers' Church, St. George's Hundred (near Odessa), Del., 1773 (Wayne Andrews)

proper to adorn the meeting-house with tower, spire, altar, or candelabrum as it would for the Quaker gentleman to attend meeting in a velvet coat and ruffled shirt, or his lady in silks and jewelry. The plain two-storied rectangular edifices with gentle gabled roofs formed a type that changed little from the time of the Radnor meeting-house of 1713 to that at Media built a century later, and almost none of them had the pilasters or pediments, the elaborate moldings or carved ornament of the Georgian style. Typical among many examples are the Buckingham Meeting-House at Lahaska, Pennsylvania, built of random-coursed ashlar masonry, and the brick structure of Crosswicks Meeting-House.

The Quaker style is echoed in the simple and extremely satisfying form of Presbyterian Old Drawyers' Church, at St. George's Hundred (near Odessa), Delaware (fig. 457). Built by a Scotch-Irish congregation in 1773, no tower or transept mars the simple rectangle of the plan, nor spire the simple low-pitched gable of the roof. To be sure, the vestry did contract with Robert May and Company, of London, to do the joinery, and there is a columned and pedimented entrance which no Quaker meeting would have permitted, despite its reticence. Graceful segmental arches, and paneled shutters shaped to fit, top the lower range of windows, and the gable ends, with the main cornice carried across, are featured by round windows.

The main door faces the pulpit on the middle of the long opposite wall, and galleries on the three other sides complete the parallel to the New England meeting-house. Raised pulpit and carved sounding board, paneled box pews and gallery fronts, though quiet and unpretentious, reveal the same superb craftsmanship that the joiners displayed in their more elaborate work at the Corbit House in Odessa. On a rise amidst lonely fields, Old Drawyers is a fine and beautifully preserved example of the eighteenth-century meeting-house.

Though the University of Pennsylvania, founded in 1740 as Franklin Academy, is the fourth oldest college in the country, none of its original

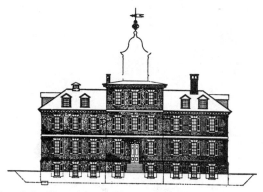

458. East wing of the Pennsylvania Hospital, Philadelphia, 1755–6. Samuel Rhoads (*The Georgian Period*)

structures remains standing. The most notable Georgian institutional building surviving today, accordingly, is the Pennsylvania Hospital at Philadelphia (fig. 458). The city was indebted to Franklin's vision and initiative for both College and Hospital, the latter the first public hospital in the colonies. Funds were raised by individual subscriptions as well as by benefit exhibitions and plays, and the first unit of the present large complex of buildings was erected in 1755–6. Facing eastward on Eighth Street, between Pine and Spruce, the 110-foot façade was, in effect, four stories high, for it included a story in an 'English basement' and another under the hipped roof with its several narrow dormer windows. Reddish-brown bricks were laid in Flemish bond with such heavily glazed headers that the masonry has a very brilliant texture. A central pavilion, three full stories high, was later topped by a cupola. Decorative details were otherwise confined to stone belt courses, window sills, and lintels — the latter grooved in the Pennsylvania manner to simulate flat keyed arches — and a modillioned cornice. The paneled doors were unframed by architectural motives.

This building was designed by Samuel Rhoads (1711–84), another of Philadelphia's distinguished amateur architects. Brought up in accordance with the Quaker theory that every boy should learn a trade, Rhoads learned carpentry; and though his principal activities were later mercantile, he became an early member of the Carpenters' Company. An officer of the American Philosophical Society from 1743, he also sat in the Provincial Assembly, became Mayor of Philadelphia in 1774, and a delegate to the First Continental Congress. Chosen one of the managers of the hospital enterprise, Rhoads consulted physicians concerning the desirable location and equipment of rooms, and presented the plan not only for this first wing, but for a second, almost exactly matching it, which was built facing westward on Ninth Street in 1796. At the same time was erected the main building, facing south on Pine Street and connecting the east and west wings, but many of its architectural motives reveal the sophisticated style of the Federal era.

Pennsylvania Dutch architecture

In the regions where the German dialect called ' Pennsylvania Dutch ' is spoken today may be found an equally unique and interesting architectural dialect in the houses and barns which remind us so forcefully of the medieval architecture of the Rhine valley.[24] The Pennsylvania Dutch consisted chiefly of Germans from the Rhenish Palatinate, which William Penn had visited in 1677, pamphleteering to encourage emigration to his New World haven. His success was almost overwhelming. From 1710 on German settlers began arriving in large numbers, and in 1738 alone about 9000 passed through the port of Philadelphia.[25] They planted themselves in York and Lancaster Counties, spread into Berks, Dauphin, and Bucks, and advanced up the Lehigh valley and as far north as the Delaware Water Gap.

With them the Germans brought their crafts and their mode of building. Hewn-log houses sprang up in the Pennsylvania wilderness and for decades served as the homes of the first pioneer farmers; many eighteenth-century examples survive today. Of particular interest were the half-timber houses which newly arrived German settlers built. Half-timber construction was a familiar tradition of the medieval period in Germany, and until a few generations ago a few ancient structures of this type might still be seen in York and Lancaster, their stout corner posts and heavy girts securely tied by a profusion of diagonal braces. The brick nogging, laid horizontally or in diagonal or herringbone patterns, was either exposed on the exterior or covered by a layer of plaster. Only one such example remains today, an old Moravian Meeting-House in the Oley valley, built between 1743 and 1745 (fig. 459). Between the whitewashed plaster panels covering the wall filling may still be seen the aged framing timbers, which have carried the heavy walls for more than two centuries. Later used as a schoolhouse and more recently as a residence, this building is almost unique and of great historic importance. With the exception of a nineteenth-century half-timber house at Kimswick, Missouri, it is, so far as is known, the sole surviving example in the United States of a mode of construction that may also have been used by the earliest English colonists.

But by the eighteenth century, the Pennsylvania Germans naturally turned to the solid stone walls which the abundant resources of the region permitted. An excellent example of the style is the Georg Müller House at Milbach, Pennsylvania, built in 1752 (fig. 460). Rough stone walls, featured by dressed brownstone quoins at the corners, rise two full stories to the picturesque roof. This is a gambrel of a distinctive German type, with a 'bell-cast' at the eaves formed by adding 'lookouts' or false rafters to the main rafters to produce a flared projecting eave, and with

459. Moravian Meeting-House, Oley valley, Pa., 1743–5 (Berks County Historical Society)

460. Georg Müller House, Milbach, Pa., 1752 (Philadelphia Museum of Art)

the upper slope of the gambrel slightly overlapping the lower one. Two pent roofs cross the end of the house, and there was originally a third, around three sides of the house, as the line below the second-story windows indicates. The house has lost its original small-pane sash windows, but their appearance may be seen in the restored interiors (fig. 462).

The plan of the Georg Müller House (fig. 461) repeats faithfully a Rhine valley type, with a three-room arrangement not unlike the 'Quaker plan,' but with a central chimney. The main room was the *küche*, a combined kitchen-dining room of ample size, with a winding stair in the corner near the door. The rest of the house was divided into *stube* (living room) and *kammer* (bedroom). Noteworthy is the wide fireplace, with an

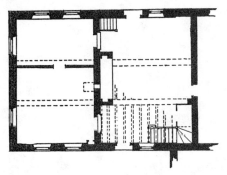

461. Plan of the Müller House (Thomas T. Waterman, *The Dwellings of Colonial America,* University of North Carolina Press)

aperture at the back through which was fed a five-plate iron stove that heated the living room.

The typically German interiors of the Müller House have been removed to the Philadelphia Museum. One end of the main room is shown in figure 462. The wide, low door, paneled and hung on long iron hinges, was divided in halves, like the Dutch doors of New Netherland, and the stair was adorned by the curiously awkward flat balusters of the German baroque style. Small-pane windows had splayed reveals in the thick walls, and the clean plastered wall surfaces served as a foil to the carved and painted chests and cupboards, laden with their homemade pottery. So large a room needed two heavy summer beams, but unlike New England framing, the joists of the second floor rested on top of these beams rather than being let into them by notches. Both summer beams and floor joists were molded, to give a ceiling of unusual richness and vigor. In such a room could be seen

the big fire hearth, in which was the iron crane and tripod with the steaming kettles hanging on them . . . In one corner . . . stood the table with the benches running along its sides, and on it zinc dishes, pewter spoons and tin cups. In another corner stood the spinning wheel with bundles of flax, tow or wool. On the other side of the hall was the best room with plain but neat furniture, and back of it the *Kammer,* with the bed and crib . . . In the attic were several beds for the boys, and hanging along the rafters were rows of smoked sausages and hams with bundles of flax and wool.[26]

For generations, the interiors of Pennsylvania Dutch houses, with their furniture, utensils, and varied articles of *Volkskunst*, remained unchanged, just as the language persisted. But exteriors soon tended to follow the English forms of the early Georgian stone houses of Philadelphia and Germantown, and the landscape of eastern Pennsylvania was dotted

462. Hall of the Müller House, as re-erected in the Philadelphia Museum of Art (Philadelphia Museum of Art)

with the ample, solid, and comfortable houses that have made the regional style so clearly marked.

But the Pennsylvania barns always retained a certain German flavor. Immense, capacious, solid — eloquent of the fertile fields and bumper crops of a rich agricultural region — these barns are magnificent. Wertenbaker sees in them the heritage of the great house-barns of Upper Bavaria, the Black Forest, and Switzerland, but a heritage modified by local climate and conditions.[27] Materials at hand were used; some barns are all of stone, others all of wood, a very few of brick. But most characteristic is a combination of stone and wood, the ground story of stone topped by lofty walls of vertical boarding, and the whole secured at the ends by massive stone walls of full height.

One of the finest is a great barn at Friedensburg, in the Oley valley, in Berks County (fig. 463). A typical feature is the overhanging upper story or forebay. This projection, ranging from 5 to 10 feet, formed a covered 'aisle' to shelter buckets, tools, wagons, and farm implements. Back of it, a series of doors and windows in the stone wall opened to the stalls of the livestock. The great threshing floor and hay loft above were usually approached by a ramp at the rear, leading to great doors through which a heavily loaded hayrick could be driven up onto the threshing floor. Three or four ranges of windows in the gable ends lighted the hayloft, with its forest of framing timbers and dim heights under the ample roof. Some of these barns were huge: dimensions of 40 by 100 feet and a height of 45 feet to the ridge were not uncommon.

463. 'Hex' barn, Friedensburg, Oley valley (Eleanor Raymond)

Very often the settlers decorated their barns with the painted symbols called *hexenfoos* (fig. 464). Modern Pennsylvania farmers often deny that these have any other than a decorative function, but it seems probable that they were originally made as signs to keep away the lightning or to preserve the animals from being bewitched or *ferhexed*. Certain it is that in South Germany and Switzerland these same symbols may be seen today, and they can be matched on Pennsylvania furniture, utensils, and pottery. In Germany, the symbols were supposed to protect against evil spirits; it may be that in Pennsylvania their original significance has been forgotten, but tradition keeps the forms alive, as so often happens in folk art. Barns are decorated by a variety of patterns (fig. 465); most popular is the star within a circle, but various forms of rosettes, whirls, and quatrefoils are also used.

Most markedly German and medieval of all the Pennsylvania Dutch architecture is the group of buildings known as The Cloister, at Ephrata, a dozen miles northeast of Lancaster. This monastic community was

founded by Johann Konrad Beissel, a German mystic who settled on Co-
calico Creek in 1732. In 1735 he organized the Society of the Solitary, a
sect practicing a strange mixture of mystic religious observances, handi-
crafts, and practical social and economic activities. Chastity, poverty, and
obedience were among the ideals of the order, as well as the doctrines of

464. 'Hex' barn, Berks County, Pa. (Department of Art, Dartmouth College)

total immersion and the Seventh-day Sabbath. At its peak, this colony of
'Seventh Day Dunkers' numbered some 300 members and was a prosperous and self-sufficient community with its own gristmill, bakery, pottery, barns, and stables. It manufactured paper and had one of the earliest printing presses in America, on which it issued a German version of
Bunyan's *Pilgrim's Progress* and a flood of pamphlets and tracts.

The three main buildings of The Cloister were the *Saal*, a great hall or

465. Decorative patterns from (A) Pennsylvania barns; (B) upper Bavarian peasant houses (Thomas Jefferson Wertenbaker, *The Founding of American Civilization; The Middle Colonies,* Charles Scribner's Sons)

community house, built in 1740; the *Saron* or Sister House, built in 1742–3; and *Bethania*, the Brother House, built about 1746. The Society continued to occupy The Cloister until about 1925, when the buildings were abandoned. In 1941 the State of Pennsylvania obtained the site and is now undertaking a praiseworthy job of restoration.

The *Saal* (fig. 466), now completely restored, recalls the steep-roofed houses of medieval Germany. The frame of hewn-oak timbers has a filling

466. The *Saal* (1740) at The Cloister, Ephrata, Pa. (courtesy G. Edwin Brumbaugh)

of stones and clay, protected outside by split and shaved red-oak clapboards. Rows of shed dormers light the two stories within the capacious roof, and the east side has a still higher dormer near the ridge. Of particular interest are the shingles: oak shakes, side-lapped as well as end-lapped, in the manner of certain parts of the Rhine valley and Bavaria. A small hood shelters the entrance door on the west, and at the east side (left in photo) is a small stone kitchen, added about 1780.

The *Saron* (fig. 467) was originally built as a sort of double convent, for a celibate brotherhood and a celibate sisterhood of voluntarily divorced couples, but the idea did not seem to work out successfully, and within a year it was reserved for the Sisters, while a separate Brother House was added shortly afterward. The construction is even more primitive than that of the *Saal*, with walls of oak logs dovetailed at the corners, chinked with wood splints and clay. The poplar clapboards, which once covered most of the walls, deteriorated badly and in some areas were

later replaced by shingles and other clapboards. Small windows, steep roof,
and shed dormers contribute to the medieval appearance. A nineteenth-
century entrance porch and an added bell cupola astride the roof will
shortly be removed and the chimneys restored to their original wood-and-
clay form, like that of the *Saal*. *Bethania*, which was demolished about
1900, will eventually be reconstructed in the continuing program of the

467. The *Saron* or Sister House at The Cloister, 1743 (Wayne Andrews)

restoration, with all materials made by hand — even to hand-forged nails
— in a scrupulous attempt to reproduce the form and nature of surviving
original fragments.

Inside the *Saal*, heavy ceiling beams, great fireplaces, and winding stairs
are eloquent of the medieval tradition. Typical is the chapel (fig. 468)
with its white plastered walls and its plain and simple furniture.

Equally German are the buildings of the Moravian Seminary at Bethlehem, such as the Sisters' House (fig. 469) built in 1773. Persecuted in faraway Bohemia and Moravia, the 'United Brothers,' under the leadership
of Count Zinzendorf, fled to Pennsylvania to found communities at Bethlehem and Nazareth. The buildings they erected have heavy stone walls
and great steep roofs lined with rows of small dormer windows. One of
them, Nazareth Hall, at Nazareth, was intended as a manor house for
Count Zinzendorf; of great size and with formal composition, German
gambrel roof, and crowning cupola, it is clearly Renaissance in spirit.
From Pennsylvania, as we have seen, the United Brothers migrated to

North Carolina in 1753 to found the Moravian communities at Bethlehem, Salem, and Bethania.

Eighteenth-century New York

Considering the wealth and importance of the province of New York in the eighteenth century, it may seem surprising that the state today has a great dearth of fine Georgian buildings as compared with New England,

468. Old Chapel in the *Saal,* Ephrata (courtesy G. Edwin Brumbaugh)

Pennsylvania, and the South. Four reasons may account for this deficiency. First and most obviously, the Georgian was primarily an urban style that flourished in the big cities. Doubtless New York City had a large number of splendid Georgian houses, but they have all but vanished today. Secondly, the very wealth of the region proved ruinous to its Georgian heri-

469. Moravian Seminary, Bethlehem, Pa., 1773 (Wayne Andrews)

tage, for the fine country houses of the eighteenth century usually remained in possession of wealthy families who, in the nineteenth century,
felt it necessary to keep in fashion by adding Gothic towers, mansard roofs,
rambling porches, bay windows, and the like, completely destroying their
Georgian character. This, for example, was the fate of most of the great
houses of the nine English manors that bordered the Hudson River.
Thirdly and most important, in the ordinary farm and village houses of
the Hudson valley, the Dutch Colonial tradition remained singularly
strong, persisting well through the eighteenth century. Instead of a gradual process of transition from the Colonial to the Georgian style, such as
occurred in New England, in New York the Dutch Colonial style resisted
the entrance of all but a few decorative details of the new style. And
fourthly, the regions to the west of the Hudson valley — the valley of the
Mohawk and the agricultural lands of southern New York — did not develop prosperous communities until after the Revolution, and with rare
exceptions the earliest ' fine houses ' of these regions are Federal or Greek
Revival in style, not Georgian.

The city of New York developed rapidly after the English captured it
in 1664. The population had doubled, to about 5000, by 1700; 40 years
later, with 11,000 persons, New York was the third city of the colonies. In
general it remained, however, more carefree and addicted to social pleas-
ures and amusements than Quaker Philadelphia or Puritan Boston. By
the same token, it was insouciant regarding civic improvements. At a time
when both the other cities had paved streets and underground drainage,
New York's streets were of dirt; since there were no street-side pumps, the
matter of drainage was not pressing, except for animal offal and after
heavy rains. To be sure, civic authorities had already forbidden the throwing of ' any rubbish, filth, oyster shells, dead animal or anything like it '
into the streets, and by 1675 the filthy waters of the Heeregraft or Great
Inlet from the East River were filled in and paved to form Broad Street.[28]
The English built a Great Dock for shipping in 1676, but it remained the
only public dock in the city until 1750, a poor provision for commerce
compared to Philadelphia's 8 public wharves and Boston's 166 wharves
and docks, public and private, at a comparable period. There was no
city plan,* as there was at Philadelphia, and the tangled pattern of streets
and alleys of old New Amsterdam was simply projected haphazardly beyond the wall. Streets were not built into the ' Outer Ward ' until 1707.
New York's first public park was laid out in 1733, when a tract on lower
Broadway near the fort was ' Inclosed to make a Bowling Green . . . with
Walks therein, for the Beauty & Ornament of the said Street as well as for
the Recreation & delight of the inhabitants.' [29]

There was considerable congestion in the city. The 1703 census listed
only 750 houses, for a population of over 5000 persons; most of the houses
were packed closely behind the wall, since the city government discour-
aged the sale of land beyond it. Throughout the eighteenth century, hous-

---

* The famous Commissioners' Plan, which marked the present city off into a gridiron of rectangular blocks, was not adopted until 1811, and Central Park was not laid
out until 1857.

ing conditions in New York remained inadequate as compared with Boston and Philadelphia. The majority of the houses, however, were of brick or stone, as they had been in Dutch days, and this prevented such a series of disastrous conflagrations as plagued Boston and Charleston. In style, the Dutch tradition persisted for a long time. As late as 1744, Dr. Alexander Hamilton described the houses as 'a few built of wood, but the greatest number of brick, and a great many covered with pantile and glazed tile with the year of God when built figured out with plates of iron upon the fronts of several of them.' [30]

The most notable of the early public buildings were the City Hall and

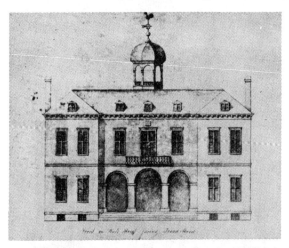

470. Old City Hall, New York City, 1699–1700. Drawing by David Grim (1818) of the building as it appeared in 1745–7 (New-York Historical Society)

Trinity Church. The half-century-old Dutch *Stadthuys* was sold by the city in 1699, and its successor the City Hall was built in 1699–1700 at the corner of Broad and Wall Streets where the Sub-Treasury now stands. Built of brick and amply planned to house the Assembly and Council, the structure was an interesting halfway step in the evolution of style from Colonial to Georgian (fig. 470). The windows, with their cross mullions dividing the areas into four, had leaded diamond-pane sash (presumably fixed) in the upper lights, and casements, which were apparently hinged, with rectangular panes in the lower lights. But the main lines of the building were Georgian. With symmetrical façade, three round arches sheltering an entrance vestibule, a 'state' balcony approached by double doors from a second-floor chamber, modillioned cornice, hipped roof, and crowning cupola, the building owed allegiance to English manor houses of the Stuart period rather than to the high-gabled structures of old Amsterdam. Within were the chambers for the Common Council and court, a jury room, debtors' prison, and a dungeon for criminals. The building became the official residence of the Mayor, John Cruger, in 1740. It was extensively remodeled and enlarged after the Revolution, and, under the name of Federal Hall, saw the inauguration of Washington as first President.

The first Trinity Church also betrayed the last lingering traces of the Gothic (fig. 471). When the English took Manhattan, the Church of England superseded the Dutch Reformed, and this first important Angli-

471. The first Trinity Church, New York City, 1698. Woodcut from **Valentine's** *Manual*, 1859 (New-York Historical Society)

can parish was chartered by William III in 1697. The first church, a small, almost square, stone structure with gabled roof, was built in the following year. It stood on the site of the present Trinity Church, on the west side of Broadway, with a green meadow back of it sloping down to the Hudson River, for it was then ' without the north gate of the city.' The tall windows were round-arched, but were divided by mullions interlaced (perhaps of brick, like those of Old Brick at Smithfield, Virginia) to form pointed arches in the tracery. The tower, too, rose in a lofty square, with projecting corner buttresses, to support a Gothic spire flanked by corner pinnacles — a far cry from the telescoped boxes and octagons of Christopher Wren. First Trinity was destroyed in the great fire that broke out four days after the British, under General Howe, took the city in 1776. A second church, also of stone and with a certain Gothic flavor, was built on the site in 1788, to be replaced little more than half a century later by the present structure, a masterpiece of the nineteenth-century Gothic Revival.

A child of Trinity, St. Paul's, has outlasted its parent and is now the

472. St. Paul's Chapel, New York City, 1764–6, spire and portico 1794–6, by Thomas McBean (James Ellery Marble photo, courtesy Robert C. Hunsicker)

sole surviving religious edifice of pre-Revolutionary New York. St. Paul's, properly called Chapel, for it was established as a chapel of Trinity, was built in 1764–6. Facing Broadway, between Fulton and Vesey Streets, the site was then a relative wilderness, and there was some criticism of the vestry for planning ' so large and ornate a building in a place so remote and sequestered, so difficult of access, and to which the population could never extend.' [31] The chapel was indeed an ambitious architectural monument (fig. 472). Planned by the Scotchman Thomas McBean, it closely echoed James Gibbs's splendid St. Martin's-in-the-Fields in London, and the body of the church, with its two tiers of arched windows, was similar to those of St. Michael's, Charleston, and King's Chapel, Boston.

The spire, so similar to that of St. Martin's in London, and the giant portico of Ionic columns on the Broadway side were added between 1794 and 1796, at a time when the chancel was deepened, and it is probable that Major L'Enfant was in charge of this work. But since St. Paul's was one of the major churches of the colonies, it seems entirely probable that the portico and spire were part of the original design, as they were with Peter Harrison's King's Chapel in Boston. For so important a building, it would seem that original drawings of these features, or at least evidence

473. Interior of St. Paul's Chapel (Frank Cleveland)

that such existed, might someday be found. The fact remains, however, that only five buildings in the colonies, so far as we know today, were equipped with giant porticoes before the Revolution.*

St. Paul's was a viceregal chapel, for the governor of the colony had his pew here, and the interior (fig. 473) was truly royal in effect. Surpassed architecturally in the colonies only by King's Chapel, Boston, the nave shows much the same superb mastery of scale and space composition. The single columns at the sides are raised on pedestals and engaged against the gallery fronts, as in other churches, but the Corinthian order is treated with splendid opulence, and the fully vaulted ceiling flowing from central elliptical arch to the graceful interpenetrations of gallery vaults

* In chronological order, the Redwood Library at Newport (1748–50); St. Michael's, Charleston (1752–61); Whitehall, Maryland (1764–5); the Roger Morris House, New York (1765); and St. James', Santee, S.C. (1768).

unites the whole interior space. The Palladian window of the chancel faces the Broadway side. In front of it, over the altar, is a 'Glory' executed by Major L'Enfant. Over the top of the high sounding board are the feathers of the Prince of Wales, and there are other reminders of colonial days in the tomb of General Montgomery, killed at Quebec, and pews reserved for Lord Howe, Major André, and Sir Guy Carleton during the time of the British occupation. Washington also attended services here, including a special celebration after his first inauguration on 30 April 1789.

474. Nassau Hall, Princeton, 1754–6, by Robert Smith and William Shippen. From the Henry Dawkins engraving of 1764 (courtesy Princeton University)

The first important college edifice in this vicinity was not in New York but in New Jersey. Princeton was founded in 1746 and Nassau Hall, its first permanent college building, was erected in 1754–6. Old Nassau (fig. 474) was designed by Robert Smith, of the Carpenters' Company in Philadelphia, who was working at the same time on the spire of Christ Church, and who was later the architect of St. Peter's Church and Carpenters' Hall, as we have seen. He was assisted by Dr. William Shippen.

The façade, 170 feet in length, was broken by a central pavilion topped by a pediment, and three doors led to corridors separating the various classrooms and offices. Walls were built of brownstone dug from a near-by quarry and were left unadorned except for the quoined and corniced entrances and the keyed flat-arch lintels of the windows on the first two stories. A low-pitch hipped roof, crowned by a cupola and many chimneys, covered the dominantly horizontal mass. Simple, solid, and reposeful, it was an impressive building and seems to have set the pattern for later college buildings such as Harvard's Hollis Hall (1762–3), University Hall

at Brown (1770–71), and Dartmouth Hall (1784–91). Nassau Hall suffered some damage during the Battle of Princeton, and again in fires of
1802 and 1855. After the latter, the building was remodeled and its fine
horizontal lines destroyed by an excessively lofty cupola.

Rutgers University, at near-by New Brunswick, was founded in 1766 as
Queens College, but lack of funds prevented the construction of any major
building until after the Revolution.

What is now Columbia University was founded in 1754 as King's College under Anglican auspices. Its first building in New York was a small
schoolhouse adjoining Trinity Church, but within half a dozen years the

475. King's College (Columbia University), New York City, 1760. From the Tiebout
engraving, *New York Magazine*, May 1790 (New-York Historical Society)

College moved to the outskirts of the city, at Park Place. Here was erected
in 1760 the first large college building (fig. 475). Considerably more elaborate than Nassau Hall, its façade was broken by four pedimented pavilions, each with a pilastered and pedimented entrance door. Paneled shutters adorned the first-story windows, the main cornice was modillioned,
and a balustrade topped the hipped roof. The cupola also was more pretentious than that of Old Nassau; raised on a square base with round windows, its cornice carried four classical urns and was topped by a dome
carried on eight arches. The repetition of pavilions made the façade appear longer than that of Nassau Hall, though actually it was somewhat
shorter, and the total effect was both heavy and rather monotonous. King's
College was used as a barracks and hospital during the Revolution but
continued to serve the institution, renamed Columbia College at this
time, until 1857, when it was again moved to the outskirts at Madison
Avenue and 49th Street.

Georgian houses in New York

As previously indicated, Georgian houses in New York have suffered
heavily through inept additions and remodelings and the process of urban

growth. Comparatively few first-rate examples remain, but of these the Philipse Manor Hall at Yonkers was one of the most notable houses in the colonies.

Philipseborough Manor occupied much of the land of the earlier and ill-fated patroonship of Colen Donck, which had been founded in 1646 by the Jonkheer ('Youncker') Adriaen van der Donck. No manor house was built, the patroonship was dissolved in 1666, and its unfortunate found-

476. South front, Philipse Manor Hall, Yonkers, N.Y., c.1720 (Cortlandt V. D. Hubbard)

er's name is recalled today only by the town of Yonkers. Frederick Philipse, the former official carpenter of the Dutch West India Company, had in the meantime built a fortune by trade in New Amsterdam, and in 1672 he bought a large tract of the Colen Donck property. Known as the richest man in the colony, he acquired over the next twenty years a princely estate extending some 22 miles along the east bank of the Hudson from Spuyten Duyvil Creek to the Croton River. In 1693 he received the royal charter granting him manorial privileges and responsibilities and thus became the first Lord of Philipseborough Manor.

The present Philipse Manor Hall is an imposing building of L-shaped plan. The long north arm of the L was built of brick, about 1745. The base of the L, an older structure of stone, is widely believed to have been built in 1682. If this were true, the south wing would have the distinction of being — by a margin of several years — the first Georgian building in

America, for its general style and its details are indubitably Georgian. The south façade (fig. 476), solidly built of a rough gneiss rubble, has large sliding-sash windows (unknown elsewhere in the country until about 1700), spaced somewhat irregularly but in approximate symmetry. Paneled door and classical entrance porch, modillioned cornice, hipped roof, and balustraded deck are definitive marks of the Georgian style. But an examination of details raises questions. The divided Dutch door, sometimes claimed to have been brought over from Holland in 1681 by the wife of the first Lord, is richly paneled. Over it is an arched lunette, oc-

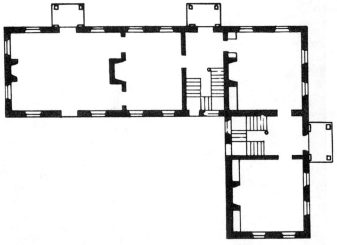

477. Plan of first floor, Philipse Manor Hall (Philip White, after Edward Hagaman Hall)

curring in no other authenticated example before 1755, with the same kind of lobed periphery found at Mount Pleasant, Philadelphia, as late as 1761. The classical entrance porch, a distinctly late Georgian feature elsewhere in the colonies, has Roman Doric detail almost identical to that of Cliveden (after 1763). Doorway, porch, and the paneled window shutters might easily be later additions to an early structure, and since all the window openings are squared up with brick, the windows, too, may have been replacements of earlier ones. The cornice and roof, however, are more likely to be original; the former is adorned by squared blocks rather than academically shaped modillions, and seems to be of early Georgian date. The interior trim of the south entrance hall and west parlor (see plan, fig. 477) appears early: the stairway has a closed string and lathe-turned pine balusters, and the parlor trim is simple. But the east parlor (fig. 478), in which Mary Philipse was married to Major Roger Morris in 1758, has full-blown Georgian detail: engaged Ionic columns on the fireplace wall, paneled walls and window seats, a consoled overmantel with a scroll pediment, and an intricately molded plaster ceiling of rococo style are all of late Georgian character, and since there is ample structural evidence of a remodeling, it might well have been done at about this time.

The long north wing is of brick, regularly composed, and, with its paneled shutters, skirt roof, and twin entrance porches, suggests the Pennsylvania style. The southeast porch leads into an entrance hall with an open-string staircase and twisted mahogany balusters; to the north of it is the paneled dining room, and beyond this were originally the kitchen and

478. The southeast parlor, Philipse Manor Hall (Cortlandt V. D. Hubbard)

pantry, and probably a back hall and service stair. These latter rooms were later replaced by a single large hall which served as a court room during the nineteenth century.

Despite the number of historians who have asserted that the south wing of Philipse Manor was built in 1682,* we must conclude that this date is wholly erroneous. The building's most scrupulous historian,[32] as early as 1912, after careful study of all the evidence, concluded that although the foundations of the southwestern portion of the building might date back to an early structure erected by Frederick Philipse between 1682 and 1694, the present south wing was perhaps built in 1719 when the second

---

* First published in 1866 by Lossing (*The Hudson from the Wilderness to the Sea*), who cited no primary authority. Subsequent writers, though introducing no new documentary or architectural evidence, have clung more or less tenaciously to the 1682 date: Lamb (1874), Bolton (1881), Scharf (1886), Allison (1896), Eberlein (1924), Reynolds (1929), Bolton (1933), Torrey (1935), Gloag (1940), and Eberlein (1942).

Frederick Philipse was married, or more probably, on architectural evidence, between 1725 and 1730. The north wing was probably built in 1745, as usuaily claimed, the southeast parlor redecorated about 1758, and, we might add, the south porch and entrance very likely added at this same time. But although Philipse Manor, it seems, can claim no priority in the evolution of the Georgian style in America, it remains, of course, one of the distinguished examples of the style and a building with notable historical associations.

479. Van Cortlandt House, Van Cortlandt Park, New York City, 1748–9 (Wayne Andrews)

The Van Cortlandt Mansion in Van Cortlandt Park, New York, was built in 1748–9. A heavy-looking, oblong house built of stone, it is marked by the almost rude simplicity of the earliest phase of the style (fig. 479). The main stairway has a closed string and square newel post of seventeenth-century stamp, and the arched cupboard doors flanking a fireplace are of an early eighteenth-century form. The roof is of the double-hipped or mansard type, with no deck or balustrade, and walls are unadorned except by grotesque masks carved on the keystones of the window heads.

The Roger Morris or Jumel Mansion, overlooking the Harlem River, is the only important pre-Revolutionary house still standing in Manhattan. Built in 1765 by Major Roger Morris, Washington's fellow aide on Braddock's staff, and later husband of wealthy Mary Philipse, the house reveals many advanced stylistic motives (fig. 480). It is built of rusticated wood planks, with quoins at the four corners. The hipped roof has a deck surrounded by a Chinese lattice rail — somewhat of a rarity among late Georgian houses. At the back is a projecting octagonal wing, known before this only in one porch of Gunston Hall, Virginia, but used occasionally at Annapolis in the following decade.

Of outstanding interest is the giant entrance portico. From early descriptions of the house, this seems to be an original feature. Though common in the Federal and Greek Revival styles, the giant portico can be

480. Roger Morris (Jumel) Mansion, Harlem River, New York City, 1765 (Wayne Andrews)

found elsewhere in Georgian houses only at Whitehall, Maryland, begun the year before the Morris House. But the column proportions are very different. Thirteen diameters high, these Doric columns herald the post-Revolutionary attenuation of proportions that entered with the Adam influence. The elliptically arched entrance door was inserted at a later date. During the Revolution the house served for a time as military headquarters; Washington used a room in the octagonal rear wing as his study. The house is frequently known as the Jumel Mansion, from a wealthy French merchant whose widow lived there at a later period.[33]

Another remarkable late Georgian mansion in New York City was the Apthorp House, which formerly stood at West End Avenue and 90th Street. Built of cut-stone ashlar, about 1767, it was unusually architectonic in its treatment of the classical order (fig. 481). Giant Ionic pilasters marked the bays of both ends of the house and turned the corners to frame the façade. The treatment of the central pavilion was also unusual:

projecting only slightly from the façade, it framed a recessed entrance porch with engaged piers at the corners. The entrance door was unique in almost every feature; it consisted of a Palladian motive, the central arch with a lunette over a rectangular door, and the flanking units filled by sidelights to illuminate the hall. Even the door was glazed in its upper portion, to match the flanking windows. Also unique in Georgian domestic architecture was the use of a full classic entablature over giant pilasters. Usually the architrave and/or frieze motives were omitted, but here was a full Ionic entablature: architrave in three fascia, molded taenia, pulvinated frieze, dentil course, and a modillioned cornice. The depth of the entablature necessitated reduction of the second-story windows to small

481. Apthorp House, New York City, c.1767 (The Georgian Period)

squares, forming an interesting grouping with the tall pedimented windows of the main floor. It seems likely that the Apthorp House was designed by a professional architect; approaching the temple form, it was classical not only in its decorative vocabulary (as all other Georgian houses were) but in its entire mode of composition. Not even Jefferson, in his first Monticello, was to approach so closely the classical ideal.

The fine house that Philip Schuyler built near the center of present-day Albany in 1761-2 is also one of the distinguished late Georgian houses of New York (fig. 482). The hexagonal porch, which one notices first on approaching the house, was an addition of the late eighteenth century, but other exterior features are original: the fifteen pairs of shutters that adorn the lower range of windows were charged for in bills of 1761, and there seems no reason to doubt the authenticity of the light Chinese lattice rail that surrounds the roof. This was the earliest appearance in Georgian architecture of such a feature (either rail or balustrade) over the eaves of a house; almost always it served to surround a roof-deck at the top. The eaves balustrade was to become a common and delightful feature of the Federal style.

The interiors of The Pastures, which saw the marriage of Elizabeth Schuyler to Alexander Hamilton in December 1780, were of considerable splendor. Like the New England nabobs, Schuyler had his stairway decorated with spirally twisted balusters of three different profiles on each step; the walls of his spacious rooms were adorned with broad panels reaching from dado to dentiled and modillioned cornices, and he procured four marble chimneypieces for his fireplaces. The house has been

482. Schuyler House (The Pastures), Albany, N.Y., 1761–2 (John J. Vrooman)

maintained by the state as a public monument since 1911, and in 1948 was thoroughly redecorated with the rich-colored paints — Prussian blues, Venetian reds, greens, yellows, and white — which removal of some fourteen later layers revealed on the old woodwork.

Even more splendid, when originally built, was the second Van Rensselaer Manor Hall at Albany, built by Stephen Van Rensselaer in 1765–8. It had the great central-hall plan (fig. 483) of the most impressive houses in the colonies, with a separate stair hall at the side and four large corner rooms The four separate fireplaces called for two chimneys built within each end wall. Mantelpieces of the most elaborate sort, with scrolled pediments and even with overmantels flanked by small pilasters — a rare feature in Georgian design — framed the fireplaces, and the walls were either full-paneled in wood or covered with the splendid made-to-order wallpapers which Van Rensselaer ordered from Jackson of London in 1768. But the house was so drastically remodeled in 1840–43, by the famous architect Richard Upjohn, that it entirely lost its Georgian character. Dismantled in 1893, it was removed to Williamstown, Massachusetts, to serve as a fraternity house.

These great Georgian mansions, however, were the homes of the elite — the Philipses, the Sir William Johnsons, the Schuylers, and Van Rensselaers — and were correspondingly few in number. The small villages and farms of the Hudson valley were still Dutch Colonial in appearance — and were to remain so for some time yet. It is striking in turning once again to the Dyckman House (fig. 103) to realize that such a house was built

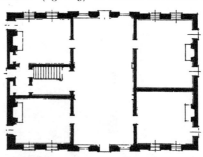

483. Plan of the Van Rensselaer Manor House, Albany, 1765–8 (courtesy Fiske Kimball)

fifteen years after Stephen Van Rensselaer assembled his imported splendors at Albany, half a dozen years after Lord Howe's redcoats had marched in triumph down Broadway, and only a scant two years before the cold majesty of Thomas Jefferson's Capitol at Richmond announced the birth of a new architectural style in a new republic.

READING SUGGESTIONS

General:

> Thomas Jefferson Wertenbaker's *The Founding of American Civilization: the Middle Colonies* (Scribner's, New York, 1938) has the best general account of the architecture of the middle colonies before the Revolution.
>
> Carl Bridenbaugh's *Cities in the Wilderness* (Ronald Press Company, New York, 1938) gives the urban scene in New York and Philadelphia to 1742.

Pennsylvania, Delaware, New Jersey:

> George Fletcher Bennett, *Early Architecture of Delaware,* Historical Press, Wilmington, 1932.
>
> Frank Cousins and Philip M. Riley, *Colonial Architecture of Philadelphia,* Little, Brown and Company, Boston, 1920.
>
> H. D. Eberlein and Cortlandt Van Dyke Hubbard, *Portrait of a Colonial City, Philadelphia 1670–1838,* J. B. Lippincott, Philadelphia, 1939.
>
> — and Horace Mather Lippincott, *Colonial Homes of Philadelphia and its Neighborhood,* J. B. Lippincott Company, Philadelphia, 1912.

John T. Faris, *Old Churches and Meeting-Houses in and around Philadelphia*, J. B. Lippincott, Philadelphia, 1926.

Eleanor Raymond, *Early Domestic Architecture of Pennsylvania*, William Helburn, New York, 1931.

Philip B. Wallace and William Allen Dunn, *Colonial Churches and Meeting-Houses, Pennsylvania, New Jersey and Delaware*, Architectural Book Publishing Company, New York, 1931.

— and M. Luther Miller, *Colonial Houses, Philadelphia, Pre-Revolutionary Period*, Architectural Book Publishing Company, New York, 1931.

Herbert Clifton Wise and Ferdinand H. Beidleman, *Colonial Architecture for Those About to Build*, J. B. Lippincott Company, Philadelphia, 1913.

New York:

H. D. Eberlein, *Manors and Historic Homes of the Hudson Valley*, J. B. Lippincott Company, Philadelphia, 1924.

—, *Manor Houses and Historic Homes of Long Island and Staten Island*, Lippincott, Philadelphia, 1928.

— and Cortlandt Van Dyke Hubbard, *Historic Houses of the Hudson Valley*, Architectural Book Publishing Company, New York, 1942.

17

Toward a National Style

IT IS NOT within the proper scope of this volume on the American colonies to give an extended account of the architecture of the early Republic: of the Federal style, without doubt one of the most sophisticated and most nearly perfect of American architectural achievements; of the classic temple façades of the later Greek Revival; or of the Gothic castles, Egyptian gateways, and Italian villas which now evoke a blended amusement and nostalgia for the most romantic period in America's architectural history. Yet it may round out our view of the architecture of the colonial period if we survey the main trends of the era up to the Civil War, for within that period are revealed the culmination of the ideals exemplified by Peter Harrison and Thomas Jefferson before the Revolution, and the dawn of sentiments and sciences of which they never dreamed. The world was entering a critical new era, and architecture advanced with it.

The decade that followed the Revolution saw the growth of the first of the post-colonial styles. If its birth was announced in the Capitol at Richmond, fully conceived in Jefferson's mind by 1780, its maturity was signaled by the laying of the cornerstone of the national Capitol in September 1793. During that period new men and new influences emerged in the American architectural scene. Charles Bulfinch returned from Europe to Boston in 1786; Major L'Enfant and Stephen Hallet came from France to work on the plan of Washington and the design of the Capitol; James Hoban, architect of the White House, came from Ireland in 1789; in the same year the Englishman William Thornton arrived in Philadelphia, and Jefferson returned from the court of Louis XVI at Versailles, confirmed in his vision of a new architecture for the new Republic.

The Federal style, which emerged in the four decades from 1780 to 1820, revealed three chief influences: a revived Roman classicism, which Jefferson and many others believed to be a suitable ' Republican style ' for the new nation; French architecture of the period of Louis XVI, a style brought over by several French architects and engineers in the train of war-bred Franco-American friendship; and the continuing tradition of the American Georgian style, reinforced by importation of the latest English fashion set by the brothers Adam. At first glance, there may appear no striking difference between the Georgian and Federal styles; both used the classical vocabulary of columns, pilasters, pediments, and the like, in somewhat similar ways. The gradual approach in the Federal pe-

riod toward the ideal of the complete classical temple form seems only a
logical continuation of Harrison's and Jefferson's earlier ventures in that
direction. Indeed many historians have considered the Greek Revival of
the forty years preceding the Civil War to be merely the last phase, the
glorious sunset, of that evolution of Renaissance classicism which had
begun four centuries earlier in Italy.

Neoclassicism

Actually, a revolution in architecture had occurred in the decades of
the 1780's and 1790's — a revolution less sudden and dramatic than the

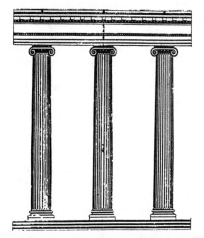

484. The Ionic Order according to Palladio (Leoni edition, Book I, Plate 17)
485. The Ionic Order of the Erechtheum at Athens (Stuart and Revett, *Antiquities
of Athens*, 1762)

storming of the Bastille in 1789 but no less significant of a profound
change from one era to another. Not only in America but in the countries
of western Europe, these decades marked the birth of the modern period.
And the first of the modern styles — the Neoclassic vogue which swept over
the Western world — was profoundly different in underlying principle
from the Renaissance classicism of the preceding centuries. The architectural revolution did not occur overnight, it did not manifest itself in everything being built at the time, and it is safe to assume that most of the
very architects who participated in it failed to realize its meaning. We
might say that people who lived through it were unaware of its existence, as
were those who lived through the Industrial Revolution, yet both movements, seen in historical perspective, had immense consequences.

The contrast between Renaissance classicism and Neoclassicism is typi-
fied in a seemingly trivial detail: the difference between two Ionic capitals, the one from the pages of Palladio, the other from Stuart and
Revett's *Antiquities of Athens* (figs. 484, 485). The Palladian capital had
served more than ten generations of Renaissance architects as the stand-

ard model of what an Ionic capital should be. Echoed, with very minor variations, in dozens of Renaissance architectural books by many authors in different countries, it may be found on thousands of buildings of the Renaissance era. Palladio's Ionic was accepted as an authentic version of that described by Vitruvius and thus as having the infallibility of that supreme authority of all Renaissance architecture. It was regarded, so to speak, as an absolute architectural fact.

The Ionic capital was of course only one of the many details of classical architecture, all of which were presented in the pages of Palladio and the many other architectural writers who followed him. Together with these models of form, the books presented rules of proportion and design. Thus over the generations, Renaissance architects worked with an established vocabulary of forms and according to authoritative canons of design. These conformed with the nature and suited the purposes of an absolutist society. If they tended on the one hand to encourage a narrow academicism, they permitted on the other certain creative variations, so long as these were regarded as trifling departures from an established norm rather than a serious and fundamental challenge to it. By and large they promoted that unity of creative expression, in any given country and period, which we call style.

The rise of scientific archaeology

But the second half of the eighteenth century saw the collapse of absolute architectural authority. The attack had its source in the rise of classical archaeology. The long-lost sites of two Roman cities buried by the eruption of Vesuvius A.D. 79 came to light: Herculaneum was accidentally discovered in 1719, and Pompeii in 1748. Excavations of the two cities began in 1735 and 1755, respectively, and continued for several generations. As buildings, works of art, furniture, and household utensils were uncovered from layers of cinders and lava, they revealed in striking intimacy the everyday life of the Romans of the first century. Though only comparatively little was discovered that was not already known in a general way, the clarity and completeness of this new picture of the past had a great impact: all over Europe a wave of popular interest in Roman antiquity sprang up, much as the discovery of Tutankhamen's tomb in 1922 excited the modern world about the field of Egyptology.

There followed a generation of archaeological study and publication, far more exact and scientific than earlier studies of the classic past had been. Charles-Nicolas Cochin published a study of the antiquities of Herculaneum in 1754, and the German scholar Winckelmann gave further information on the discoveries at Herculaneum and Pompeii in 1762 and 1764.[1] The Englishman Robert Wood published monographs on the Roman ruins at Palmyra and Baalbek, in the Syrian desert, in 1753 and 1757.[2] Most important was the work of James Stuart and Nicholas Revett at Athens. Supported by funds from the London Society of Dilettanti, they went in 1751 to what was then a squalid Turkish town. Making exhaustive studies and measurements, particularly of the buildings on the Athenian Acropolis, they brought to the Western world, for the first time, detailed and accurate knowledge of the great Greek masterpieces of the fifth century b.c. Stuart and Revett's *Antiquities of Athens,* the first volume of which was published in 1762, was destined to take its place along with Vitruvius and Palladio as one of the three most influential books in the history of architecture.

Other important books followed. The famous English architect Robert Adam published the *Ruins of the Palace of the Emperor Diocletian,* at Spalato on the Dalmatian coast, in 1764. Winckelmann included mention of the Greek temples at Paestum in his *Observations on the Architecture of the Ancients* in 1760, and these were more fully described in 1768 by Thomas Major in his *Ruines de Paestum.* The Dilettanti Society supported an elaborate publication of the *Antiquities of Ionia,* the first volume of which appeared in 1769; and Charles-Louis Clérisseau published in 1774 his *Antiquités de la France,* the first volume of which, *Les Monuments de Nîmes,* included the famous temple that Jefferson, in collaboration with Clérisseau, was to imitate in the Richmond Capitol a decade later.

Specific imitation

These pioneer publications in the science of classical archaeology were to become the new source books for architectural design. They soon revealed that the Ionic capital according to Palladio was not an ' absolute architectural fact'; there were other Ionic capitals used by the Greeks and the Romans, and who should say which one out of many was the authoritative standard? James Stuart himself used the Ionic order of the Erechtheum at Athens (fig. 485) for Lord Anson's house at 15 St. James's Square in London; built in 1760, this has been called the first residence in the Greek Revival style. Other architects followed suit: they supplanted their copy of Palladio by Stuart and Revett and others of the new books. Instead of using *the* Ionic order, they used the Ionic order of the Erechtheum, or of the Temple of Athena Polias at Priene, or of Fortuna Virilis in Rome, or any other specific Ionic order detailed in the archaeologies as a true fact.

It was easy to extend the practice of imitating specific prototypes from details of the orders to entire buildings. In Nancy, as early as 1751, the architect Héré de Corny built a complete Roman triumphal triple arch, modified in only minor details from the Arch of Constantine at Rome. This structure was especially significant for it may be considered the first building of the Classic Revival; it marks the dividing line between the Renaissance and the modern architectural eras. ' Athenian ' Stuart built a little garden temple for Lord Lyttleton's estate, Hagley Park, near Birmingham, in 1758, which was virtually a copy of the façade of the Theseum at Athens.

Significant theoretical support for this practice came from the German scholar Johann Joachim Winckelmann (1717–68). In 1755 he published a little book entitled *Thoughts on the Imitation of Greek Works in Painting and Sculpture.* Winckelmann departed from the age-old classical and Renaissance arguments about the method and degree of art's imitation of

Nature and proposed instead the imitation of previous art, specifically the Greek. His text was followed by a pretended attack, nominally by an impartial critic, on the argument of the book, that concluded with a defense of its principles. This was the first serious attempt to advocate the direct imitation of a previous artistic style.

Winckelmann's doctrine was not long in finding followers. In the great church of Ste. Geneviève in Paris (renamed the Panthéon at the time of the Revolution), Jacques-Germain Soufflot used for his monumental portico the Corinthian order of the Pantheon at Rome, and Jefferson's Richmond Capitol was, in intent at least, a copy of the Maison Carrée at Nîmes, as we have seen. In the years following 1800 there were many instances of imitation, *in toto,* of classical prototypes, such as Napoleon's Arc du Carrousel in the Tuileries Gardens, the Roman column of the Place Vendôme, John Nash's Marble Arch in Hyde Park, London, and the Walhalla at Regensburg, a Teutonic Parthenon.

The revolution in architecture

The rise of scientific archaeology, then, had a profound impact. The new books destroyed the fundamental postulates of Renaissance architectural doctrine: they challenged the infallibility of Vitruvius and of the whole structure of forms and rules based on Vitruvius, much as divine right was being challenged in political thought. They overthrew one god and supplanted him by many. The old books were humanistic, the new ones scientific; the old ones were rational, the new ones empirical; the old ones were authoritarian, the new ones libertarian — in the sense that they permitted complete freedom of individual choice from a diversity of models. In short, the old books belonged to the *ancien régime,* the new ones to the modern world. This was the revolution in architectural doctrine.

But in practice, the revolution was not very radical. Architects thought they had gained a new freedom, but they took it only as freedom to select which classic orders, out of many, they wished to follow; few of them sought to free themselves from the classic orders entirely. Liberated from the bonds of Palladianism, architecture was in principle free to work from new needs to new forms and eventually to evolve a new style expressive of the new age. The forces of science, industrialism, and democracy, which so greatly affected the ideals and achievements of the modern period, would have been cardinal qualities in its aesthetic expression.

But a sudden freedom rarely gains its intended ends, and in any age of extremely rapid change creative interpretation is likely to fall behind material development. The Classic Revival in architecture represents a curious kind of cultural lag. Its method was inherited from the worst phase of Renaissance architecture — that academicism which upheld the absolute authority of books. Its materials were derived from the new publications of classical archaeology. Its goal, divorced from the creative humanism of the Renaissance, became spuriously scientific. The controlled freedom of the Renaissance was supplanted by the self-imposed slavery of nineteenth-century imitation; thus the potentialities of the new freedom were lost in a new and different kind of authoritarianism. Somewhat analogously, we may suppose, the freedom augured in the French Revolution was lost in Napoleonic despotism.

The difference between Renaissance classicism and Neoclassicism, though not striking in form, was of profound significance. For when the eighteenth-century revolution destroyed Renaissance architectural theory, it set up no new one in its place; architecture was left prey to an anarchical proliferation of new facts and new techniques. The archaeologists soon discovered the facts about medieval architecture. If it was permissible to imitate several different kinds of Greek and Roman models, why not Gothic? And as the science of the history of art grew, augmented by the formation of museums of art-historical facts, and soon by photography, which widened the range of the museums, it became not only possible but laudable to imitate all past styles. Thus we may say that when Palladio's Ionic capital was supplanted by that of the Erechtheum, this seemingly trivial change led straight — almost inevitably — to nineteenth-century eclecticism, which was plainly and simply a lack of style rather than the presence of one. The old order was dead; no new order had yet come to take its place.

The impetus of social change

The phenomenal popularity of the Neoclassic movement in the late eighteenth and early nineteenth centuries was not caused solely, however, by the rise of classical archaeology and the attendant collapse of Renaissance architectural theory. These were, after all, matters for scholars and savants; and while changes in theoretical principles underlie revolutions, they are rarely immediate causes. The Neoclassic movement owed its success in larger measure to the climate of opinion that preceded the French Revolution.

The earlier part of the reign of Louis XV had seen the apogee of the frivolity and the flippant immorality of the *ancien régime*. Released from the tedious conventionalities of the aged Louis XIV, the era sought novelty, gaiety, and spice. Sophisticated, artificial, witty, the court life was perfectly expressed by the brilliant painting of the *Ecole Galante* and the dainty decoration in ivory and gold on the walls of many a rococo boudoir. But already the more serious note had been struck. Voltaire had attacked with barbed wit the political and social follies of the age; Diderot had called for a return to morality; Rousseau had begun to preach the Simple Life. From about 1750, these preachments found favor with the aristocracy, less from a serious desire to correct the condition of society than from the novel entertainment that the new sentiments afforded. ' Morality,' Diderot had announced sententiously, ' dwells only in the cottage '; so it became fashionable for the ladies to masquerade as shepherdesses rather than Dianas, or for love to be played in the mood of Strephon and Phyllis rather than of Eros and Psyche. A little later Marie Antoinette was to don calico dress and straw hat to play at milking cows and picking berries in her rustic hamlet at Trianon. This sophisticated rusticity, this orgy of virtue, was perfectly expressed in the paintings of Greuze — a long series of luscious portraits of yearning girls, celebrating with maudlin morality the felicity of virtue or the tragedy of its departure.

Yet the moralistic vogue, spurious as it was, added impetus to the Neoclassic fashion. Winckelmann was not merely a scholar; he was also a preacher. He saw in the 'noble simplicity and tranquil greatness' of Greek art an antidote to the sophistication and corruption of his own age; his call for the imitation of Greek work was moral as well as aesthetic. In his greatest book, the *History of Ancient Art* (1764), he gave the story not only of Greek art but of the political, social, and intellectual conditions that produced it, and held the whole up as a lesson to the eighteenth century. Here was a made-to-order expression for the moralistic fashion.

Its adoption was made easier by the dawning spirit of Romanticism, which was to exert so great an influence on nineteenth-century culture. Romanticism, diligently in search of emotion rather than reason as an avenue to reality, most typically sought inspiration in the remote or the exotic rather than in the here-and-now. It idealized the distant, either of time or of place, and as Geoffrey Scott has said, cast upon the screen of an imaginary past the vision of its unfulfilled desires.' What better screen than that of ancient Hellas — the world of gods and heroes, of noble men and virtuous women, living in tranquillity against a backdrop of white columns, gnarled cedars, and the blue Aegean?

The antique became surrounded by a golden aura of perfection. Ancient Greece seemed the lost epoch of an ideal life, and men turned for lessons in morality to the austere simplicity of the Republican Romans. ' Be stern, like the grand old Romans,' adjured Jacques Louis David, as he painted the declamatory tableau of his ' Oath of the Horatii.' Thus even before the Revolution, the Neoclassic movement was well under way. But it could serve the new ideologies equally well. David himself became the foremost painter of the Revolution, and as the political pendulum swung again, he apotheosized Napoleon. Napoleon was himself a great enthusiast for the new Roman discoveries; he conceived his conquests as establishing a new kind of Roman Empire, and he not only built triumphal arches and memorial columns and temples, but had Canova carve portraits of himself in the guise of the Caesars. Each new age rewrites history in terms of its own ideals; the classic past became all things to all men. It was the Simple Life of Rousseau, the Upright Life of Diderot; to the Revolutionists it was Democracy, and to Napoleon Empire.

Thus the Neoclassic movement accumulated force and breadth over two generations. Enthusiasm for the antique became the ideology of all kinds and conditions of men, and imitation of classical styles extended from architecture, sculpture, and painting to many other activities. Neoclassic interiors were adorned by all manner of candelabra, urns, lamps, grape vines, and cupids; Pompeiian models were popular in furniture, and the artist Mme Vigée LeBrun gave Roman banquets, to which guests wore togas and, reclining on low couches, ate supposedly Roman foods brought by pages in the garb of slaves. Early steam engines, even, were often housed in little Doric temples. Perhaps the extreme of translating everything into classical terms occurred in 1827, when, shortly after the

discovery of the use of vaccines in medicine, the painter Gautherot celebrated current progress by a picture entitled ' Venus Vaccinated by Aescu-
lapius.'

Romanticism and the Gothic Revival

But if the Classic Revival dominated the century from 1750 to 1850, it
was rivaled — increasingly as time went on — by the Gothic Revival. In
the same year that Héré de Corny built his Roman triumphal arch at
Nancy, the English novelist Horace Walpole started his Gothic work on
Strawberry Hill near London. The year 1751 thus saw the first monuments of both Classic and Gothic Revivals. Even before this, in England,
the ' Gothick taste ' had been revealed in the plates of Batty Langley's
architectural handbooks and in the quaint ' umbrellos ' and ' terminaries '
of the gardens. Though Walpole would not advocate the brittle and in-
accurate Gothic of his picturesque mansion as a matter of serious aesthetic doctrine against the entrenched Palladians (' I do not mean to de-
fend by argument a small, capricious house,' he said, ' it was built to
please my own taste — and in some degree to realize my own visions '),
the example he set proved alarmingly popular with his week-end guests.
Before long, many other ' Gothick ' mansions raised their donjon towers,
notched battlements, and spiky spires to the skies of rural England.

The popularity of the Gothic was undoubtedly due to the rising tide
of romantic sentiment. Romanticism, as we have seen, idealized the past,
and though this nostalgia might fasten itself to ancient Greece and Rome,
it most typically sought the more murky mysteries of the medieval past.
The Middle Ages were not at all well known to the late eighteenth century, but they appealed for several reasons. For one thing, Gothic art
afforded a pleasing novelty to an age becoming slightly bored with the
ordered classicism of the Palladians and the ' rule of reason ' which that
expressed. Walpole, in a letter of 1750, admired the ' whimsical air of
novelty ' that Gothic motives achieved. Romanticists had — or thought
they had — much in common with the medieval point of view: its concern
with the infinite and the immaterial rather than the finite and material,
its emphasis on emotional and intuitive rather than rational realities.
Furthermore, the medieval had the enchantment of the mysterious; Gothic
art was so little known that it could be invented to taste.

Most of all, Gothic had the attraction of antiquity; ' charming venerable Gothic,' Walpole called it. Battlemented towers and vine-covered
walls were hallowed by history; great men and great events had marched
beneath them. Many medieval buildings were in ruins, and their crumbled
vaults afforded secluded nooks, to which the Georgian gentleman might
retire to reflect on the vanished glories of the past. The contemplation of
ancient ruins, Vanbrugh had found, ' moves lively and pleasing reflections
. . . on the persons who have inhabited them [and] on the remarkable
things which have been transacted in them.' If no genuine ruins were
convenient to hand, it was easy to build new ones, and all over England
crumbled walls and broken towers were added to the classical architectural
scenery of the great gardens. The novelist William Beckford, in erecting

his vast mansion Fonthill Abbey, instructed architect James Wyatt to design for him 'an ornamental building which should have the appearance of a convent, be partly in ruins, and yet contain some weatherproof apartments.'

Romanticism was primarily a literary movement, and its architectural values were more often associative than direct. People admired not so much the actual style of Gothic buildings as their literary and historical overtones; to many visitors, for example, Anne Hathaway's cottage was beautiful not for its architecture but for the sentiments that it brought to mind.

Romanticism brought with it not only the revival of Gothic, but an interest in anything remote or exotic. We have already commented on Oriental decorative motives in the eighteenth century, and on 'Chinese Chippendale' furniture. In 1761 the normally Palladian architect, Sir William Chambers, adorned Kew Gardens with a full-sized 'replica' of a Chinese pagoda, and before long Hindu, Turkish, and other motives were imported from the 'Mysterious East.' Kew Gardens eventually boasted, in addition to its pagoda, an Alhambra, a mosque, a 'house of Confucius,' several classical templets, a Gothic cathedral, and a medieval ruin. Thus before the end of the eighteenth century there was in Europe an extensive romantic eclecticism, well summed up in the amazing title of a book published by William Wrighte in 1790:

Grotesque Architecture, or Rural Amusement; Consisting of Plans, Elevations, and Sections, for Huts, Retreats, Summer & Winter Hermitages, Terminaries, Chinese, Gothic, and Natural Grottos, Cascades, Baths, Mosques, Moresque Pavilions, Grotesque & Rustic Seats, Green Houses, &c., Many of Which May be Executed with Flints, Irregular Stones, Rude Branches, and Roots of Trees.

The Federal style in America

All of these confusing currents of doctrine and taste — scientific archaeology, the collapse of Palladianism, the rise of Neoclassicism, the revival of Gothic and other romantic styles — had their impact on the new American republic. The results were not fully apparent at once; not until the period from 1820 to the Civil War did the flood of romantic eclecticism finally burst the gates of the Georgian academic tradition.

Yet it is a mistake to see in the quiet and dignified façades and the delicate decorative detail of the Federal period no important change from the Georgian style. An increased desire for classical qualities and for classical correctness manifested itself: in the nature and use of the orders; in the abstract, white smoothness of flush-boarded walls or of painted brick or stucco; in the geometric motives of circular, oval, or octagonal rooms; and in the bare simplicity of painted plaster walls. Certain motives distinguish these houses sharply from the Georgian: the giant portico; the almost universal 'Federal doorway,' with its narrow flanking sidelights and an embracing elliptical fanlight; the projecting curved or polygonal bay on an exterior wall; the balustrade or parapet placed over the eaves rather than higher up the roof; the graceful spiral stairway of the front hall; and most of all the fragile and attenuated but very rich ornament executed in carved wood or molded plaster, inspired by the brothers Adam, who in turn had learned from the decorated walls and ceilings of Pompeii and Herculaneum.

An even more complete classicism marked the larger public and institutional buildings of the Federal period. Jefferson inaugurated it with the Richmond Capitol, and continued it in the scholarly Romanism of the rotunda and pavilions at the University of Virginia. Benjamin Henry Latrobe as early as 1799 earned his title ' father of the Greek Revival ' by his use of the Erechtheum-Ionic in the beautiful Bank of Pennsylvania at Philadelphia, and later proposed a Greek Doric portico for the Capitol at Washington. William Strickland brought the classical trend to its culmination in the old Customs House, a Philadelphia Parthenon.

The Greek Revival and other romantic styles

From 1820 on, the Greek temple became the highest architectural ideal for a generation of Americans. They were animated not merely by a taste for the style, but perhaps more importantly by its romantic associations, for the ancient Greeks were by now endowed with a halo of political, moral, and cultural perfection, and the modern Greeks were earning the sympathy of the new nation by their struggle for independence against Turkey in the war of 1821-7.

The Greek Revival became the most universal and widespread style of the generation before the Civil War. Ranging from Maine to Georgia and from the Atlantic coast to the Old Northwest and the lower Mississippi valley, the style was adapted to public buildings, churches, commercial structures, small story-and-a-half houses, the great houses of the southern plantations — indeed to almost all types of buildings except factories, barns, and privies. Everywhere the white classic portico, usually Doric or Ionic, was the hallmark of the style, and in a few outstanding examples the complete classical temple form, with surrounding peristyle of columns, was achieved. Yet these chaste serenities, these strong but nonetheless refined forms that had arisen from an aristocracy of intellect and culture in Athens of the fifth century B.C., were in reality little expressive of the energetic materialism of our economy, the homely crudity of the Jacksonian ' common man,' or the ruggedness and friendliness of American democratic ideals.

Though it dominated the era from 1820 to 1860, the Greek was of course by no means the only style; our American architects, no less than those of Europe, felt the wider influences of Romanticism. Even Jefferson, scholarly classicist though he was, as early as 1771 designed garden pavilions for Monticello in quaint versions of the Gothic and Chinese as well as in the more familiar Roman and Greek. Latrobe did Sedgeley, a Gothic country house near Philadelphia, in 1800, and five years later submitted a Gothic design for the Cathedral of Baltimore. That Strickland, known primarily as an exponent of the Greek Revival, was an accomplished eclecticist is demonstrated by his Gothic Masonic Temple at Philadelphia (1809), the quaintly Oriental Pagoda and Labyrinth Garden at Philadelphia (1827), and the Egyptian style of his First Presbyterian

Church at Nashville (1848). Almost every important architect worked in Greek and Gothic, and some purveyed also the Romanesque, Egyptian, Islamic, or Italian Villa. Alexander Jackson Davis, one of the most prolific and important architects of the era, noted in a diary his repertory of styles for suburban and country houses:

American Log Cabin, Frame House, English cottage, Collegiate Gothic Manor House, French suburban, Switz cottage, Lombard Italian, Tuscan from Pliny's villa at Ostia, Ancient Etruscan, Suburban Greek, Oriental, Moorish, and Castellated.

Within half a century, the architectural revolution had taken place. Scientific archaeology had destroyed the theoretical bases of Renaissance architecture, while Romanticism had destroyed its taste. The old order was dead. In place of the single architectural language, the broad unity of creative expression of the eighteenth century, there was a heterogeneous collection of borrowed forms. There was no *style,* only a collection of quotations. Lewis Mumford cites the perfect parallel from an oration delivered in 1846:

I thank you for the patience you have manifested on this occasion, and promise never more to offend in like manner, so long. I have now, as Cowper observes —
                    ' Roved for fruit,
                        Roved far, and gathered much . . .'
And can, I think with Scott, surely say that —
                    ' To his promise just
                        Vich-Alpine has discharged his trust.'
I propose now, gentlemen, to leave you at Carlangtoghford,
                    ' And thou must keep thee with thy sword.'
Let me say to you on this occasion, as Campbell does on another:
                    ' Wave, Munich! all your banners wave!
                        And charge with all your chivalry.'
And should you in the contest fall, remember with old Homer —
                    ' Such honours Ilion to her hero paid,
                        And peaceful slept the mighty Hector's shade.'
Allow me now to close in one of Scott's beautiful strains:
                    ' Charge, Chester, charge! On, Stanley, on!
                        Were the last words of Marmion.' [3]

Advances in building technology

Some of the fundamental technical developments that were to lay the basis for a modern architecture occurred in the era between the Revolution and the Civil War. Two key inventions led to the abandonment of the age-old hand-hewn and wood-pegged frame. The circular saw, far faster than the old reciprocating saw, was first used in England in 1773 and in the United States in 1814. A nail-cutting machine produced in the United States in 1777 manufactured nails and spikes, and successive improvements over half a century reduced their price to one-fifth that of wrought nails. As far as is known, the first modern ' balloon frame,' made of light machine-sawed lumber in standard sizes, and with overlapped spiked joints instead of notched and pegged joints, was used for a building in Chicago in 1833.* During the ensuing generation, it was called simply ' Chicago construction,' just as was the skyscraper technique after its invention there half a century later. A true product of the machine age, the balloon frame soon became — and has remained ever since — standard for wood construction.

The oldest cotton textile factory in the United States, the Slater Mill at Pawtucket, Rhode Island, was built in 1793 of conventional wood construction. But the new factories, with their large floor areas and batteries of heavy machines, needed a stronger and less inflammable structural system. The salient advances were made in England. The first factory with an interior framework of iron columns and beams for the support of floors was probably the Calico Mill at Derby, built in 1792–3 by William Strutt.[4] This type of construction soon became standard for factories and warehouses. An improvement was achieved by embedding iron columns within exterior walls, to carry the outer ends of iron floor beams, thus completely removing floor weights from exterior masonry walls. The date of this step is not known, but it was the last important advance in iron framing before the invention of the skyscraper in 1883.

Iron was increasingly used in other structural and decorative ways. As early as 1786 Thomas Paine, the famous pamphleteer of the American Revolution, had proposed an iron arched bridge of 400-foot span to cross the Schuylkill at Philadephia. The Greek Revival architect Robert Mills used structural elements of iron in his Fireproof Record Office at Charleston (1822–3) and in the Patent Office at Washington (1839). So likewise did Thomas U. Walter in the great Greek temple he designed for Girard College, Philadelphia, in 1833; and, as is well known, Walter's dome for the Capitol at Washington, built in 1860–65, is largely of cast iron. Another cast-iron dome was designed in the 'sixties by William Rumbold for the St. Louis Courthouse.

The ' cast-iron front ' made its first appearance in a building at Pottsville, Pennsylvania, designed by John Haviland in 1830. James Bogardus of New York attached the cast plates of an iron façade to an iron frame in his building in New York (1847–8), and this construction became common in commercial buildings of the 'fifties and 'sixties. Under the Treasury Department, post offices and customs houses of the 'fifties used a standardized structural system of cast-iron columns with wrought-iron floor beams carrying brick floor arches, and this fire-resistant construction was supplemented by the use of iron stairs, balconies, window sash and frames, doors and door frames.

Perhaps the most dramatic use of iron construction before the Civil War was to be found in the Crystal Palace, built at Sixth Avenue and 42nd Street in New York to house the 1853 Exhibition. The building designed by Carstensen and Gildemeister was of octagonal ground plan, rose to a cruciform plan at gallery level, and was climaxed by a central dome 100 feet in diameter and 150 feet high. This was the largest dome

---

* The invention is attributed to George Washington Snow (1797–1870) of Keene, New Hampshire, by Siegfried Giedion in *Space, Time, and Architecture* (pp. 269–76). But other claimants have been named, and the matter is still controversial.

erected in the United States to that time. The building employed 1800 tons of cast- and wrought-iron in a structural system of standard 27-foot square bays, and the 55,000 square feet of glass which made the exterior seem like a gigantic greenhouse was coated with a translucent enamel to produce a cool, diffused light inside — a great improvement over the sunlit glare of the Crystal Palace in London built two years before.

Even bolder than its construction was the idea behind its ornament: the plan of the decoration has been to bring out the beautiful construction of the building — to decorate construction rather than to construct decoration. . . . The result is surprisingly beautiful.' [5] The Crystal Palace heralded that reintegration of engineering and architecture which was to underlie the development of the modern style.

Other advances, too numerous to mention here, were being made in the fields of fireproofing, concrete construction, interior plumbing, and the development of the elevator. But in general the new materials and structural techniques were hidden behind Greek, Gothic, or Italian façades.

Rebellion against eclecticism

A few prophetic minds, animated partly by the progress of industry and technology and partly by national pride, called for a declaration of independence from borrowed styles. At a time when Jefferson was calling for a return to the ' correctness ' of the Roman temple as a source for a new Republican style, the rebellious Tom Paine was expressing the very opposite idea — that an American style should have nothing whatever to do with the Greeks and the Romans. As he put it, ' I have no notion of yielding the palm of the United States to any Grecians or Romans that were ever born.' [6]

Paine's was a lone voice in the late eighteenth century, but it was soon joined by others. Though Robert Mills favored the Greek in his practice, he wrote before his death:

. . . I say to our artists: Study your country's tastes and requirements, and make classic ground *here* for your art. Go not to the old world for your examples. We have entered a new era in the history of the world; it is our destiny to lead, not to be led.[7]

Ralph Waldo Emerson likewise spoke against eclecticism in architecture and criticized its tendency ' to detach the beautiful from the useful.' Like Mills, he saw the possibility of a truly American style:

And why need we copy the Doric or Gothic model? Beauty, convenience, grandeur of thought, and quaint expression are as near to us as to any, and if the American artist will study with hope and love the precise thing to be done by him, considering the climate, the soil, the length of the day, the wants of the people, the habit and form of the government, he will create a house in which all there will find themselves fitted . . .[8]

But it was Emerson's friend and artistic mentor Horatio Greenough (1805–52) who became the most trenchant critic of the old and the most perceptive prophet of the new. With his eloquent call for a functional and organic architecture, an architecture created out of the climate and circumstances of American life, he anticipated Louis Sullivan by some fifty years in ' functionalist ' architectural thinking. Greenough's most important writings on architecture are three essays: *American Architecture,* first published in 1843; *Aesthetics at Washington,* 1851; and *Structure and Organization,* 1852.[9]

Greenough attacked eclecticism fearlessly. In the Washington essay, he criticized the landscaping and certain details of the Capitol, attacked Robert Mills's design for the Washington Monument, and deplored the ' tower and battlement, and all that medieval confusion ' of Renwick's pseudo-Romanesque Smithsonian Institution. He dared to criticize Jefferson for following the Maison Carrée in the Richmond Capitol and lamented that ' like the captive king . . . the Greek temple, as seen among us, claims pity for its degraded majesty, and attests the barbarian force which has abused its nature and been blind to its qualities.'

The quality of Greenough's architectural thinking may be suggested by the following quotations, taken from his several essays:

. . . if we have yet to fight for sound doctrine in all structure, it is only because a doctrine which has possession must be expelled, inch by inch . . . I maintain that the first downward step was *the introduction of the first inorganic, nonfunctional element, whether of shape or color.*

The men who have reduced locomotion to its simplest elements, in the trotting wagon and the yacht *America,* are nearer to Athens at this moment than they who would bend the Greek temple to every use. I contend for Greek principles, not Greek things . . . the American builder by a truly philosophic investigation of ancient art will learn of the Greeks to be American.

The law of adaptation is the fundamental law of nature in all structure . . . If we compare the form of a newly invented machine with the perfected type of the same instrument, we observe, as we trace it through the phases of improvement, how weight is shaken off where strength is less needed, how functions are made to approach without impeding each other, how straight becomes curved, and the curve is straightened, till the straggling and cumbersome machine becomes the compact, effective, and beautiful engine.

The puny cathedral of Broadway,* like an elephant dwindled to the size of a dog, measures her yearning for Gothic sublimity, while the roar of the Astor House, and the mammoth vase of the great reservoir, show how [America] works when she feels at home and is in earnest.

Observe a ship at sea! Mark the majestic form of her hull as she rushes through the water, observe the graceful bend of her body, the gentle transitions from round to flat, the grasp of her keel, the leap of her bows, the symmetry and rich tracery of her spars and rigging, and those grand wind muscles, her sails . . . What academy of design, what research of connoisseurship, what imitation of the Greeks produced this marvel of construction? . . . Could we but carry into our civil architecture the responsibilities that weigh upon our shipbuilding, we

* In this passage Greenough refers to Richard Upjohn's Trinity Church (1839-46), Isaiah Rogers' impressive Astor House (1834-6), and Renwick's great Croton Reservoir, built in 1842 on the site of the present New York Public Library.

should ere long have edifices as superior to the Parthenon, for the purposes we require, as the *Constitution* or the *Pennsylvania* is to the galley of the Argonauts.

To conclude: The fundamental laws of building found at the basis of every style of architecture must be the basis of ours . . . No longer could the mere tyro huddle together a crowd of ill-arranged, ill-lighted, and stifled rooms and, masking the chaos with the sneaking copy of a Greek façade, usurp the name of architect.

The redundant must be pared down, the superfluous dropped, the necessary itself reduced to its simplest expression, and then we shall find, whatever the organization may be, that beauty was waiting for us . . .

Greenough's thinking did not lead at once to a modern American architectural style, as the riot of ill-formed fashions of the post-Civil War period attests, but in a generation the ' roar of the Astor House ' had grown to the many-voiced chorus of America at work, at home and in earnest, and the great factories, the impressive office buildings of the ' Commercial style,' and the free and natural forms of the brown-stained shingled houses of the 'eighties were sure indications that American life was at last finding its own architectural expression. And curiously enough, those honest shingled houses, partaking of the colors and quality of the landscape, owed more to the tradition of the Colonial houses of the seventeenth century than to any of the styles that had since intervened.

About a century had passed since the building of the Richmond Capitol. A revolution in architecture had occurred. The old order, expressed so beautifully in the ordered unity, the aristocratic temper, the measured decoration of the Georgian style, had given way to the stirring confusion of a new era in civilization. Scientific archaeology, Neoclassicism, Romanticism, industrial and technological advance were all more or less unrelated forces in an era that did not yet understand itself. But by the end of that century, these various trends were beginning to draw together to form an integrated and characteristically American culture, out of which might emerge a genuine architectural style such as had belonged to the thirteen colonies in the eighteenth century.

Reference Notes

Chapter 1 THE COLONIAL STYLES

1. Bradford, *History of Plymouth Plantation* (ed. W. C. Ford; Mass. Hist. Soc., 1912), I, 192–3.
2. John Smith, *True Relation* . . . (London, 1608), publ. in *Works*, Arber edition, 1884, p. 9.
3. *A Breife Declaration of the Plantation of Virginia* (London, 1623), reprinted in *Journals of the House of Burgesses of Virginia, 1619–58/9* (ed. H. R. McIlwaine, Richmond, 1915), p. 28.
4. Quoted in Helen Reynolds, *Dutch Houses in the Hudson Valley before 1776* (New York, Payson and Clarke, for the Holland Society of New York, 1929), p. 16.
5. Bradford, op. cit. I, 275.
6. Harold R. Shurtleff, *The Log Cabin Myth* (Cambridge, Harvard University Press, 1939).
7. Robert Johnson, *The New Life of Virginia* (London, 1612), reprinted in Peter Force, 'Tracts . . . ,' I, no. 7, p. 14.
8. Edward Johnson, *Wonder-Working Providence of Sions Saviour in New-England* (1654), p. 211 of the 1910 edition.

Chapter 2 THE COLONIAL HOUSE IN NEW ENGLAND

1. J. Frederick Kelly, *The Early Domestic Architecture of Connecticut* (New Haven, Yale Univ. Press, 1924), ch. 2.
2. Thomas Jefferson Wertenbaker, *The Founding of American Civilization: The Middle Colonies* (New York, Charles Scribner's Sons, 1938), p. 150.
3. Norman M. Isham, *Early American Houses* (Boston, The Walpole Society, 1928), p. 28.
4. *Journal of Jasper Danckaerts* (1913 edition), p. 275.
5. *Old Time New England*, XXVII, no. 1 (July 1936), p. 36.
6. *Records of the Governor and Company of the Massachusetts Bay* (ed. N. B. Shurtleff, Boston, 1853–4), I, 74.
7. James E. Defebaugh, *History of the Lumber Industry of America* (Chicago, 1907), II, 9.
8. Albert S. Bolles, *Industrial History of the United States* (Norwich, Conn., 1878), p. 498.
9. Quoted in Isham, op. cit. p. 53.
10. *Boston Gazette*, 21/28 Nov. 1737.
11. Martin Shaw Briggs, *Homes of the Pilgrim Fathers in England and America, 1620–1685* (New York, Oxford Univ. Press, 1932), p. 81.
12. Fiske Kimball, *Domestic Architecture of the American Colonies and of the Early Republic* (New York, Charles Scribner's Sons, 1922), p. 46.
13. Briggs, op. cit. p. 177.
14. Meyric R. Rogers, *American Interior Design* (New York, W. W. Norton and Co., 1947), pp. 30, 33.
15. Harold Donaldson Eberlein, *The Architecture of Colonial America* (Boston, Little, Brown and Co., 1927), p. 45.

Chapter 3   NEW ENGLAND COLONIAL ARCHITECTURE

1. From the 1665 *Report of His Majestie's Commissioners* concerning Massachusetts, in H.M. Public Records Office, quoted in Russell Hawes Kettell, *Early American Rooms, 1650–1858* (Portland, Southworth-Anthoensen Press, 1936), p. 18.

2. Quoted in Briggs, *Homes of the Pilgrim Fathers* . . . , pp. 145–6.

3. *Old Time New England*, XXIX, no. 4 (April 1939), p. 131.

4. Date based on Kelly, *Early Domestic Architecture of Connecticut*, p. 89. Undocumented.

5. See Donald Millar, 'A Seventeenth Century New England House,' *The Architectural Record*, XXXVIII, no. 3 (Sept. 1915).

6. Caroline O. Emmerton, *The Chronicles of Three Old Houses* (Salem, published by the author, 1935).

7. There is no documentary proof of this, but historical and structural arguments concerning the secret staircase are given in Emmerton, op. cit. pp. 13–19, 26, 33.

8. Hubert G. Ripley, 'The Jethro Coffin House,' *Journal of the American Institute of Architects*, XVI, no. 6 (June 1928), p. 219.

9. Quoted in Kimball, *Domestic Architecture of the American Colonies,* . . . p. 35.

10. J. Frederick Kelly, 'Restoration of the Henry Whitfield House, Guilford, Connecticut,' *Old Time New England*, XXIX, no. 3 (Jan. 1939), pp. 75–89.

11. Edward Johnson, *Historie of New England* (1654), quoted in Briggs, op. cit. p. 145.

12. Title to the land was passed in 1677, 'but by some special arrangement, Mr. Tufts was in possession at an earlier date,' according to Ruth Dame Coolidge, 'The "Cradock" House, Past and Future,' *Medford Historical Register*, XXIX, no. 3 (Sept. 1926), p. 50. The evidence concerning the mechanic is cited in *Old Time New England*, XXVIII, no. 1 (July 1937), p. 17.

13. Coolidge, op. cit. p. 54.

14. Mann, 'The Renovation of Peter Tufts' House,' *Medford Historical Register*, XXIX, no. 4 (Dec. 1926), pp. 70–75.

15. See *Old Time New England*, XI, no. 4 (April 1921), p. 178, and XIII, no. 4 (April 1923), pp. 190–91; Edward B. Allen, 'Tudor Homes of Colonial Days,' *International Studio*, vol. 77, no. 314 (July 1923), pp. 345–8; Thomas T. Waterman, *The Dwellings of Colonial America* (Chapel Hill, Univ. of North Carolina Press, 1950), pp. 256, 261.

16. R. A. Douglas-Lithgow, 'The Province House, Boston,' *Massachusetts Magazine*, III, 199–203, based on *Journals of the House of Representatives* (Mass. Hist. Soc., 1919), vol. I (1715–17).

17. *Journals of the House* . . . , vol. VIII (1727–9), pp. 63–4.

18. Ibid. p. 387. Waterman believed the sash windows were installed in 1725; see *Old Time New England*, XXIII, no. 1 (July 1932), p. 22.

19. *Journals of the House* . . . , vol. XII (1734–5), p. 14.

20. Published in S. A. Drake, *Old Landmarks and Historic Personages of Boston* (1873), p. 235.

21. Carl Bridenbaugh, *Cities in the Wilderness* (New York, The Ronald Press, 1938), p. 56.

22. For New England garrisons, see Waterman, *Dwellings* . . . , pp. 239–43.

23. These dates from Henry Chapman Mercer, 'The Origin of Log Houses in the United States,' *Old Time New England*, XVIII, no. 1 (July 1927), p. 9. HABS, however, dates the building between 1660 and 1692, and Waterman (op. cit. p. 243) calls it about 1670.

24. Murray P. Corse, 'The Old Ship Meeting-House in Hingham, Massachusetts,' *Old Time New England*, XXI, no. 1 (July 1930).

25. Thomas Jefferson Wertenbaker, *The Puritan Oligarchy: The Founding of American Civilization* (New York, Charles Scribner's Sons, 1947), p. 111.

26. Samuel Eliot Morison, 'A Conjectural Restoration of the "Old College" at Harvard,' *Old Time New England*, XXIII, no. 4 (April 1933), pp. 131–58.

27. Restorations by Harold R. Shurtleff in Samuel Eliot Morison, *Harvard College in the Seventeenth Century* (Cambridge, Harvard University Press, 1936), II, 423–30.

28. Quoted in *Harvard University Handbook* (Cambridge, Harvard University Press, 1936), p. 16.
29. See Morison, *Harvard College in the Seventeenth Century*, I, 342–4.
30. The complete contract and other papers relative to the first Town-House are published in *Rededication of the Old State House, Boston, July 11, 1882* (Boston City Council, 3rd ed., 1885), Appendix A.
31. E. M. Avery, *A History of the United States and its People* (Cleveland, 1904–10), II, 371–2.
32. Bradford, *History of Plymouth Plantation* (New York, 1908), p. 105.
33. Percival H. Lombard, 'The Aptucxet Trading Post,' *Old Time New England*, XXIII, no. 4 (April 1933), pp. 159–74.
34. Bradford, op. cit. p. 301.
35. Russell Hawes Kettell, op. cit. p. 79. See also Elise Lathrop, *Early American Inns and Taverns*, pp. 77–8.
36. Kettell, loc. cit.
37. Bridenbaugh, op. cit. p. 109.
38. Alfred Elden, 'Tide-Mills in New England,' *Old Time New England*, XXV, no. 4 (April 1935), pp. 117–27.
39. *New Hampshire Provincial Papers*, I, 45.
40. Bolles, *Industrial History* . . . , pp. 499–500; Defebaugh, *History of the Lumber Industry* . . . , II, pp. 8, 50, 51, 184–203, 271–8.
41. Rex Wales, 'Notes on Some Windmills in New England,' *Old Time New England*, XXI, no. 3 (Jan. 1931), pp. 99–128.
42. William Wood, *New Englands Prospect: a true, lively, and experimentall description* . . . (London, 1634), p. 41.
43. Philip Ainsworth Means, *Newport Tower* (New York, Henry Holt and Co., 1942); Hjalmar R. Holand, *America, 1355–1364* (New York, Duell, Sloan and Pearce, 1946).
44. Antoinette Forrester Downing, *Early Homes of Rhode Island* (Richmond, Garrett and Massie, 1937), p. 55.
45. Holand, op. cit. chs. 3–11.

Chapter 4 DUTCH COLONIAL ARCHITECTURE, 1624–1820

1. Letter in the library of Colin Johnston Robb, of Loughgall, County Armach, Ireland. Reprinted in *The Architectural Record*, vol. 98, no. 2 (August 1945), p. 146.
2. A. J. Barnouw, *History of New York*, I, ch. 7.
3. Quoted in Reynolds, *Dutch Houses in the Hudson Valley* . . . , p. 16.
4. Thomas Jefferson Wertenbaker, *The Founding of American Civilization: The Middle Colonies*, p. 47.
5. Quoted in Harold Donaldson Eberlein, *The Manors and Historic Houses of the Hudson Valley* (Philadelphia, J. B. Lippincott, 1924), p. 52.
6. Rosalie Fellows Bailey, *Pre-Revolutionary Dutch Houses and Families in Northern New Jersey and Southern New York* (New York, William Morrow and Co. for the Holland Society of New York, 1936), p. 23.
7. Wertenbaker, op. cit. p. 47.
8. J. Leander Bishop, *History of American Manufactures*, I, 216–31.
9. Reynolds, op. cit. p. 21.
10. Quoted in Alice Morse Earle, 'The Stadt Huys of New Amsterdam,' *Historic New York* (New York, G. P. Putnam's Sons, 1897), p. 70.
11. Wertenbaker, op. cit. pp. 40–81.
12. Bailey, op. cit. p. 20.
13. Muzzey, *American History*, p. 64.
14. Wertenbaker, op. cit. p. 40.
15. Eberlein, op. cit. p. 6.
16. Dr. Alexander Hamilton's *Itinerarium*, p. 87, quoted in Wertenbaker, op. cit., p. 53.
17. Eberlein, op. cit. p. 218. Dilliard, *Old Dutch Houses of Brooklyn* (New York, Richard R. Smith, 1945) gives the builder's name as Klaes Arents Vecht, ch. 28.
18. Eberlein, loc. cit.

19. Wertenbaker, op. cit. p. 79.
20. F. N. Zabriskie, *History of the Reformed Church at Claverack*, p. 12.
21. Bailey, op. cit. p. 20.
22. Wertenbaker, op. cit. p. 70.
23. William E. Griffis, *The Story of the Walloons*, p. 8.
24. Bailey, op. cit. p. 24.
25. Ibid. p. 141.
26. Henry Chandlee Forman, *The Architecture of the Old South: The Medieval Style,*
    1585–1850 (Cambridge, Harvard University Press, 1948), p. 21.
27. Bailey, op. cit. p. 21.
28. Waterman, *The Dwellings of Colonial America*, p. 201.
29. Bailey, op. cit. p. 33.
30. Ibid. p. 20.
31. Ibid. p. 33.
32. Ibid. p. 15.
33. Ibid. p. 33.

Chapter 5 SOUTHERN COLONIAL ARCHITECTURE

1. Shurtleff, *The Log Cabin Myth*, p. 59.
2. Ralph Hamor, *True Discourse of the Present Estate of Virginia* (London, 1615),
   1860 reprint, p. 33.
3. Ibid. pp. 30–31.
4. Robert Johnson, *The New Life of Virginia*, reprinted in Peter Force ' Tracts . . . ,'
   I, no. 7, p. 14.
5. Henry Chandlee Forman, *Jamestown and St. Mary's: Buried Cities of Romance*
   (Baltimore, The Johns Hopkins Press, 1938).
6. For restored plans and elevations see Forman, *The Architecture of the Old South,*
   figs. 23, 32.
7. Illustrated in Shurtleff, op. cit. opposite p. 156.
8. Shurtleff, op. cit. p. 19, footnote.
9. Wertenbaker, *The Old South: The Foundation of American Civilization* (New York,
   Charles Scribner's Sons, 1942), p. 74; Forman, *Architecture of the Old South*, p. 17
   and fig. 7.
10. Hugh Jones, *Present State of Virginia* (written in 1722, published in 1724), p. 32.
11. *Henrico County Records*, 1677–92, no. 1.
12. Eberlein, *The Architecture of Colonial America*, p. 84.
13. Prices given, ibid. p. 86.
14. Forman, *Architecture of the Old South*, p. 90.
15. Waterman and Barrows, *Domestic Colonial Architecture of Tidewater Virginia*
    (New York, Charles Scribner's Sons, 1932), pp. 1–7; Forman, *Architecture of the
    Old South,* fig. 54.
16. Waterman and Barrows, op. cit. p. 12.
17. Waterman, *The Mansions of Virginia*, 1706–1776 (Chapel Hill, Univ. of North
    Carolina Press, 1946), pp. 21–2.
18. Quoted in Waterman and Barrows, op. cit. p. 13.
19. Forman, *Architecture of the Old South*, p. 58.
20. Ibid. p. 59.
21. Wertenbaker, op. cit. p. 86.
22. Waterman, *Mansions of Virginia* . . . , p. 26.
23. George Carrington Mason, *Colonial Churches of Tidewater Virginia* (Richmond,
    Whittet and Shepperson, 1945).
24. Quoted in Shurtleff, op. cit. p. 136.
25. *Purchas his Pilgrimes* (Glasgow, 1905), XIX, 56.
26. Archives of Maryland: *Proceedings and Acts of the General Assembly* (ed. W. H.
    Browne, Baltimore, 1884), II, 224.
27. Downing, *Early Homes of Rhode Island*, p. 14.
28. Forman, *Architecture of the Old South*, p. 128, figs. 157, 168.
29. Archives, *Proceedings of the Council*, 1667–87/8.

30. Forman, *Architecture of the Old South*, p. 139.
31. Ibid. fig. 182 and p. 135.
32. Thomas Tileston Waterman (text) and Frances Benjamin Johnston (photos), *The Early Architecture of North Carolina* (Chapel Hill, Univ. of North Carolina Press, 1941).
33. Quoted, ibid. pp. 3–4.
34. Beatrice St. Julien Ravenel, *Architects of Charleston* (Charleston, Carolina Art Association, 1945), p. 1.
35. Samuel Gaillard Stoney, *Plantations of the Carolina Low Country* (Charleston, Carolina Art Association, 1938), p. 23.
36. Ravenel, op. cit. pp. 4–5.
37. Waterman, *Dwellings of Colonial America*, pp. 32, 35.

Chapter 6 FLORIDA AND THE SPANISH SOUTHWEST

1. Quoted in Albert C. Manucy, ed., *The History of Castillo de San Marcos and Fort Matanzas* (Washington, Government Printing Office, 1945), p. 8.
2. George Kubler, *The Religious Architecture of New Mexico* (Colorado Springs, The Taylor Museum, 1940), pp. 7–8.
3. Ibid. p. 73.
4. Ibid. p. 140.
5. Cleve Hallenbeck, *Spanish Missions of the Old Southwest* (New York, Doubleday, Page and Co., 1926), p. 57.
6. Ibid. p. 47.

Chapter 7 MISSIONS AND RANCH HOUSES OF ALTA CALIFORNIA

1. George Vancouver, *A Voyage of Discovery*, II, p. 31.
2. John A. Berger, *The Franciscan Missions of California* (New York, G. P. Putnam's Sons, 1941), p. 276. Berger also says (p. 278) that 'in 1852 the roof collapsed'; this may refer to a wooden roof built after 1813. From 1852 to 1884 the church remained unroofed.
3. Ibid. p. 344.

Chapter 8 FRENCH COLONIAL ARCHITECTURE OF THE MISSISSIPPI VALLEY

1. Charles E. Peterson, 'French Houses of the Illinois Country,' *Missouriana*, I, no. 4 (Aug.–Sept. 1938), pp. 9–12.
2. Charles E. Peterson, 'Old Ste. Geneviève and its Architecture,' *Missouri Historical Review* XXXV, no. 2 (Jan. 1941), pp. 207–32.
3. The second building, known today as the Archbishopric, was measured and drawn by the Historic American Buildings Survey in 1934. The complete history of the convent, its attached hospital, and many subsidiary structures is given in the valuable article by Samuel Wilson, 'An Architectural History of the Royal Hospital and the Ursuline Convent of New Orleans' *The Louisiana Historical Quarterly*, XXIX, no. 3 (July 1946), pp. 559–659, with 33 plates.
4. Letter of 24 April 1728, quoted in Wilson, op. cit. p. 569.
5. J. Frazer Smith, *White Pillars, Early Life and Architecture of the Lower Mississippi Valley Country* (New York, William Helburn, 1941), p. 186. The date of this house is given in HABS as 'between 1830 and 1840' but this is based on interior trim, which was doubtless the result of a remodeling.
6. Talbot Hamlin, *Greek Revival Architecture in America* (New York, Oxford Univ. Press, 1944), p. 215 and pl. LVIII.

Chapter 9 THE EMERGENCE OF GEORGIAN

1. Franklin Bowditch Dexter, *Estimates of Population in the American Colonies* (Worcester, American Antiquarian Society, 1887).
2. Isaac Ware, *A Complete Body of Architecture* (London, 1756), pp. 694, 695.
3. James Gibbs, *A Book of Architecture* (London, 1728), Introduction.
4. Waterman, *Mansions of Virginia*, pp. 243–6, 408.
5. Jones, *Present State of Virginia*, p. 32.

6. Eberlein, *Architecture of Colonial America*, p. 250.
7. Manuscript Division, New York Public Library.
8. Quoted in Susan Higginson Nash, ' Paints, Furniture and Furnishings ' (The Restoration of Colonial Williamsburg), *The Architectural Record*, vol. 78, no. 6 (Dec. 1935), p. 458.
9. Ibid. p. 448.
10. Kimball, *Domestic Architecture of the American Colonies* . . . , p. 81.
11. Bridenbaugh, *Cities in the Wilderness*, p. 373.
12. Ibid. p. 373.
13. Ibid. p. 312.
14. *Boston News-Letter*, issues of 23/30 March and 23/30 November 1732.
15. For the early history of stoves in New England, see *Old Time New England*, XXVI, no. 2 (Oct. 1935), p. 74; also Edwin Jackson, ' New England Stoves,' ibid. pp. 55–64.
16. Bridenbaugh, op. cit. p. 319.
17. Janet Schaw, *Journal of a Lady of Quality* (New Haven, 1921).
18. Leroy L. Thwing, ' Boston Street Lighting in the Eighteenth Century,' *Old Time New England*, XXVIII, no. 2 (Oct. 1937), pp. 72–8.

Chapter 10   THE GEORGIAN STYLE

1. *Old Time New England*, XIV, no. 4 (Apr. 1924), pp. 193–4.
2. Walter Kendall Watkins, ' The Early Use and Manufacture of Paper-Hangings in Boston,' *Old Time New England*, XII, no. 3 (Jan. 1922), p. 109.
3. Ibid. p. 114.
4. See Rogers, *American Interior Design*, p. 292.

Chapter 11   EARLY GEORGIAN ARCHITECTURE IN VIRGINIA

1. Diary of Julian U. Niemcewicz, quoted in *Mount Vernon, an Illustrated Handbook* (Mount Vernon Ladies Association of the Union, 1947), pp. 29–30.
2. Waterman, *Mansions of Virginia*.
3. Jones, *Present State of Virginia*, p. 26.
4. *Pennsylvania Gazette*, 5 Feb. 1747.
5. Waterman, op. cit. pp. 31–41.
6. Thomas Jefferson, *Notes on the State of Virginia* (1781; 2nd ed., Philadelphia, 1794), p. 221.
7. Painted by E. L. Henry in 1863, reproduced in Waterman and Barrows, *Domestic Colonial Architecture of Tidewater Virginia*, p. 77.
8. Henry Irving Brock, *Colonial Churches in Virginia* (Richmond, Dale Press, 1930), p. 46. The date of 1732 for the church is also attested by Aymar Embury, *Early American Churches* (New York, Doubleday, Page and Co., 1914), p. 186; Edward F. Rines, *Old Historic Churches of America* (New York, Macmillan, 1936), p. 16; and Waterman, op. cit. p. 123.
9. Waterman, op. cit. pp. 124–5, 218.

Chapter 12   LATE GEORGIAN ARCHITECTURE IN VIRGINIA

1. Waterman, *Mansions of Virginia*, pp. 243–337.
2. G. W. P. Custis, *Memoirs of Washington* (New York, 1859), p. 371.
3. *Mount Vernon, an Illustrated Handbook, passim*.
4. Waterman, op. cit. p. 271.
5. Ibid. p. 295.
6. P. Wilstach, *Mount Vernon, Washington's Home* (1916), p. 140.
7. Embury, *Early American Churches*, p. 82.
8. Rines, *Old Historic Churches of America*, p. 34.
9. Jefferson, *Notes on the State of Virginia*, p. 222.
10. Waterman, op. cit. p. 397.
11. Ibid. p. 343.
12. Kimball's date of c.1779 for these studies, published in *Thomas Jefferson, Architect* (1916), is now revised. See Fiske Kimball, ' Jefferson and the Public Buildings of

Virginia: I. Williamsburg, 1770-1776,' *The Huntington Library Quarterly*, XII, no. 2 (Feb. 1949) , p. 120.

13. Quoted in Kimball, *Thomas Jefferson, Architect*, p. 31.
14. Jefferson. op. cit. pp. 222-3.
15. Kimball, *Thomas Jefferson, Architect*, p. 23.

Chapter 13 GEORGIAN ARCHITECTURE IN MARYLAND AND THE CAROLINAS

1. Katherine Scarborough, *Homes of the Cavaliers* (New York, Macmillan, 1930) , pp 188-9.
2. Deering Davis, *Annapolis Houses, 1700-1775* (New York, Architectural Book Publishing Co., 1947) , p. 106.
3. Ibid. p. 19.
4. Coffin and Holden, *Brick Architecture of the Colonial Period in Maryland and Virginia* (New York, Architectural Book Publishing Co., 1919) , p. 11.
5. William Eddis, *Letters from America* (1792) , quoted in Scarborough, op. cit. p. 175.
6. The following account is based largely on the researches of the present owner, Mr. Charles Scarlett, Jr., who generously shared the results of his investigations before publication of his article on ' Whitehall' in the *Maryland Historical Magazine*, XLVI, no. 1 (Mar. 1951) .
7. I am indebted to Fiske Kimball for bringing this prototype to my attention.
8. Celia Fiennes, *Through England on a Side Saddle, in the Time of William & Mary*, p. 304.
9. William Eddis, *Letters from America* (1792) , quoted in Kimball, *Domestic Architecture of the American Colonies* . . . , p. 300; and Scarborough, op. cit. p. 172.
10. Waterman, *Mansions of Virginia*, p. 230; Davis, op. cit pp. 22-3.
11. T. H. Randall, ' Colonial Annapolis,' *The Architectural Record*, I (1892) , p. 335; Davis, op. cit. p. 22; Scarborough, op. cit. p. 177.
12. Scarborough, op. cit. p. 211.
13. Davis, op. cit. p. 84.
14. *South-Carolina Gazette*, 22 Feb. 1752.
15. Ravenel, *Architects of Charleston*, p. 33.
16. Ibid. p. 27.
17. Carl Bridenbaugh, *Peter Harrison, First American Architect* (Chapel Hill, Univ. of North Carolina Press, for the Institute of Early American History and Culture, Williamsburg, 1949) , pp. 63-6.
18. Bridenbaugh, *Cities in the Wilderness*, p. 12.
19. Ravenel, op. cit. p. 40.
20. *South-Carolina Gazette*, 2-9 Feb. 1733/4.
21. Ibid. 4-11 Jan. 1734/5.
22. Ibid. 22 Aug. 1769.
23. Bridenbaugh, *Cities in the Wilderness*, p. 310.
24. Waterman and Johnston, *The Early Architecture of North Carolina*, p. 29.
25. Ibid. p. 30.
26. *Colonial Records of North Carolina*, vol. 7 (1890) , p. 431.
27. Ibid. vol. 8, p. 8.

Chapter 14 GEORGIAN PUBLIC BUILDINGS IN NEW ENGLAND

1. Bridenbaugh, *Cities in the Wilderness*, p. 308.
2. *Boston News-Letter*, 23 Dec. 1742.
3. Bridenbaugh, op. cit. pp. 155-60, 318.
4. Ibid. p. 167.
5. Ibid. p. 324.
6. Dated 1680 by I. A. Chisholm in his *Map of Boston, Ancient and Modern* (1929) , and ' about 1700 ' by James H. Stark, *Antique Views of Ye Towne of Boston* (1882, revised ed. 1901) , p. 79. See also *American Magazine of Useful Knowledge*, II, 80 (Oct. 1835) .
7. Bridenbaugh, op. cit. pp. 146, 206, 364.

8. Charles A. Place, ' From Meeting House to Church in New England,' *Old Time New England*, XIII, no. 2 (Oct. 1922), pp. 69–77; no. 3 (Jan. 1923), pp. 111–23; no. 4 (Apr. 1923), pp. 149–64.

9. Frank Chouteau Brown, ' Early Brickwork in New England,' *Pencil Points*, XV, no. 4 (Apr. 1934), p. 168. See also Stark, op. cit. p. 297.

10. Brown, op. cit.; Place, op. cit. XIII, pp. 149–64; Edward F. Rines, *Old Historic Churches of America*, pp. 57–61.

11. *Boston Gazette*, 16 Apr. 1770.

12. Bridenbaugh, op. cit. p. 210.

13. The following sources on the history of the Old State House in Boston have been consulted:

   (1) *Rededication of the Old State House, Boston, July* 11, 1882 (Boston City Council, 3rd ed. 1885).

   (2) George H. Moore, *Prytaneum Bostoniense: Notes on the History of the Old State House . . . a paper read before the Bostonian Society, May 12*, 1885 (Boston, Cupples, Upham and Co., 1885).

   (3) George H. Moore, same title, 2nd paper read before the Bostonian Society, 9 Feb. 1886 (Boston, Cupples, Upham and Co., 1886).

   (4) William H. Whitmore, *The Old State House Defended from Unfounded Attacks upon Its Integrity, Being a Reply to Dr. George H. Moore's Second Paper* (Boston, 1886).

   (5) George H. Moore, *Prytaneum Bostoniense: Examination of Mr. William H. Whitmore's Old State House Memorial and Reply to His Appendix N* (Boston, Cupples, Upham and Co., 1887).

   (6) James H. Stark, *Antique Views of Ye Towne of Boston*, pp. 83–4.

   (7) Charles F. Read, ' The Old State House and its Predecessor the First Town House,' *Proceedings of the Bostonian Society*, 1908, pp. 32–50.

   (8) ' Boston's New Old State House,' *Magazine of History*, XIII (June 1911), pp. 305–10.

   (9) Hubert G. Ripley, ' Boston Dry Points, Part I, Old State House,' *Architectural Record*, vol. 58 (Dec. 1925), pp. 542–8.

   All important facts and documents concerning the history of the building are given in the first five sources cited. In the voluminous and bitter controversy of 1885–7 between Messrs Whitmore and Moore, the point of view of Dr. Moore seems beyond all doubt the correct one, and is followed throughout in the text discussion.

14. See reference 13 (1), p. 61.

15. Bridenbaugh, op. cit. p. 353.

16. Frank Chouteau Brown, ' John Smibert, Artist, and the First Faneuil Hall,' *Old Time New England*, XXXVI, no. 3 (Jan. 1946), pp. 61–3.

17. J. Rayner Whipple, ' Old New England Weather Vanes,' *Old Time New England*, XXXI, no. 2 (Oct. 1940), pp. 45–51; Richard W. Hale, note in *OTNE*, XXXI, no. 3, p. 70.

18. See reference 13 (1), p. 151.

19. Bridenbaugh, op. cit. p. 326.

20. Antoinette Forrester Downing, *Early Homes of Rhode Island*, pp. 109–25, 129.

21. Ibid. drawing 25.

22. Embury, *Early American Churches*, pp. 50–54; Rines, op. cit. pp. 76–7; Downing, op. cit. pp. 107–13; Place, op. cit. *Old Time New England*, XIII, no. 4 (Apr. 1923), p. 154.

23. Norman M. Isham, ' The Colony House at Newport, Rhode Island,' *Old Time New England*, VIII, no. 2 (Dec. 1917), pp. 3–20; Downing, op. cit. pp. 116–23.

24. Quoted in full in Downing, op. cit. footnote 8, p. 213.

25. Bridenbaugh, *Peter Harrison*, p. 74.

26. Ibid. pp. 44–5.

27. Ibid. p. 43.

28. Edward Hoppus, *Andrea Palladio's Architecture in Four Books, . . . revis'd . . . by E. Hoppus* (2 vols., London, 1735, 1736), headpiece to Book IV.

29. Isaac Ware, *Designs from Inigo Jones and others* (London, 1735), pl. 43.

30. William Kent, *Designs of Inigo Jones* (London, 1727), I, pl. 73.
31. Batty Langley, *Treasury of Designs . . .* (London, 1745), pl. 35.
32. Rines, op. cit. pp. 52–3.
33. Embury, op. cit. p. 61.
34. *Geographical Gazetteer of 1784*, quoted in Bridenbaugh, *Peter Harrison*, p. 59.
35. Records of Christ Church, Cambridge, quoted in Bridenbaugh, *Peter Harrison*, pp. 112, 113.
36. William Kent, *Designs of Inigo Jones* (1833 reprint), I, pl. 50.
37. Langley, *Treasury of Designs . . .* (1740), pl. 108.
38. Kent, op. cit. I, pl. 63; Ware, op. cit. pl. 53.
39. Bridenbaugh, *Cities in the Wilderness*, p. 341.
40. Newport Historical Society, *The Story of the Old City Hall* (Newport Chamber of Commerce, pamphlet, undated).
41. Colen Campbell, *Vitruvius Britannicus*, I, pl. 16.
42. Rines, op. cit. pp. 87–8; J. Frederick Kelly, 'Raising Connecticut Meeting-Houses,' *Old Time New England*, XXVII, no. 1 (July 1936), pp. 3–9; Place, op. cit. *OTNE*, XIII, pp. 121–2.
43. Downing, op. cit. pp. 271–80; Henry M. King, 'The First Baptist Church, Providence, Rhode Island,' *Old Time New England*, XXXIV, no. 3 (Jan. 1944), pp. 39–43; Norman M. Isham, *The Meeting House of the First Baptist Church in Providence* (Providence, Akerman-Standard Co., 1925).
44. George Dudley Seymour, 'Henry Caner, 1680–1731, Master Carpenter, Builder of the First Yale College Building, 1718, and of the Rector's House, 1722,' *Old Time New England*, XV, no. 3 (Jan. 1925), pp. 99–124.
45 Minutes of Trustees' Meeting, 31 March 1784.
46. For a full account, see Henry F. Lenning, *A History of Dartmouth Hall*, 1937, thesis in Archives Room, Baker Library, Dartmouth College.

Chapter 15 GEORGIAN HOUSES IN NEW ENGLAND

1. *American Magazine of Useful & Entertaining Knowledge*, Feb. 1836.
2. Lydia Maria (Francis) Child, *The Rebels, or Boston Before the Revolution* (Boston, Cummings, Hilliard and Co., 1825).
3. Stark, *Antique Views of Ye Towne of Boston*, p. 53. Colonel Thomas Hutchinson, who was born in the house in 1711 and later inherited it, placed its construction between 1681 and 1691. See P. O. Hutchinson, *Diary of Thomas Hutchinson* (Boston, 1884), I, pp. 46–7.
4. C. H. Snow, *History of Boston* (1828), quoted in Fiske Kimball, *Domestic Architecture of the American Colonies . . .* , p. 275.
5. Kimball, op. cit. p. 65.
6. Thomas T. Waterman, 'The Thomas Savage House, Dock Square, Boston,' *Old Time New England*, XVII, no. 3 (Jan. 1927), pp. 107–10.
7. Letter of 20 Dec. 1736, quoted in Walter Kendall Watkins, 'The Hancock House and its Builder,' *Old Time New England*, XVII, no. 1 (July 1926), p. 7.
8. Letter from Thomas Hancock to John Rowe, 23 Jan. 1738, quoted in Walter Kendall Watkins, 'The Early Use and Manufacture of Paper-Hangings in Boston,' *Old Time New England*, XII, no. 3, p. 112.
9. *New York State Historical Quarterly*, VII, 291–3 (Oct. 1926).
10. W. W. Cordingley, 'Shirley Place, Roxbury, Massachusetts, and its Builder, Governor William Shirley,' *Old Time New England*, XII, no. 2 (Oct. 1921), pp. 51–63.
11. George S. T. Fuller, 'The History of the Royall House and its Occupants,' *Medford Historical Register*, XXIX, no. 1 (Mar. 1926), pp. 1–11.
12. Under the direction of Walter Mayo Macomber and the owner, Mrs. George Maurice Morris. See *Antiques*, vol. 33, pp. 67, 76–9 (Feb. 1938). A history and description of the house is given in Winifred Fales, 'The Lindens — a House with a History,' *Country Life*, XXXIII, 46–9 (Mar. 1918).
13. John Mead Howells, *The Architectural Heritage of the Piscataqua* (New York, Architectural Book Publishing Co., 1937), p. 72.
14. Felt, *Annals of Salem*, I, 415.

Chapter 16 GEORGIAN ARCHITECTURE IN THE MIDDLE COLONIES

1. Shurtleff, *The Log Cabin Myth*, p. 124.
2. *Pennsylvania Archives*, quoted in Waterman, *The Dwellings of Colonial America*, p. 119.
3. Quoted in Waterman, op. cit. p. 125.
4. Ibid. p. 126.
5. This and following details of the construction of Old Swedes at Wilmington quoted in George Fletcher Bennett, *Early Architecture of Delaware* (Wilmington, Historical Press, 1932) , pp. 19–25.
6. H. M. Lippincott, *Early Philadelphia* (1917) , pp. 68–9.
7. J. Thomas Scharf and Westcott, *History of Philadelphia* (Philadelphia, 1884) , II, 1234.
8. Bridenbaugh, *Cities in the Wilderness*, p. 57.
9. Ibid. p. 169.
10. Ibid. p. 169.
11. Eberlein, *Architecture of Colonial America*, p. 250.
12. Robert Turner to William Penn, 3 June 1685, quoted in Wise and Beidleman, *Colonial Architecture for Those About to Build* (Philadelphia, J. B. Lippincott, 1913) , p. 16.
13. Bridenbaugh, op. cit. p. 10.
14. Wise and Beidleman, op. cit. p. 17.
15. Kimball, *Domestic Architecture of the American Colonies . . .* , p. 290.
16. Wertenbaker, *The Founding of American Civilization: The Middle Colonies*, p. 235.
17. Fiske Kimball, *Pennsylvania Museum Bulletin*, XXVII, no. 149 (May 1932) .
18. Wertenbaker, op. cit. p. 236.
19. Wise and Beidleman, op. cit. p. 216.
20. Eberlein, *Architecture of Colonial America*, pp. 126–7.
21. Quoted in Wise and Beidleman, op. cit. pp. 130–34.
22. Bridenbaugh, op. cit. p. 458.
23. Wise and Beidleman, op. cit. p. 170.
24. The text discussion owes much to Wertenbaker's excellent account of Pennsylvania German architecture and folk art. See *The Middle Colonies*, chs. 8, 9.
25. Bridenbaugh, op. cit. p. 409.
26. *The Pennsylvania-German*, VII, 388.
27. Wertenbaker, op. cit. pp. 321–5.
28. Bridenbaugh, op. cit. pp. 18, 20.
29. Ibid. p. 325.
30. Ibid. p. 308.
31. Rines, *Old Historic Churches of America*, p. 139.
32. Edward Hagaman Hall, *Philipse Manor Hall, Yonkers, New York* (New York American Scenic and Historic Preservation Society, 1912) .
33. William Henry Shelton, *The Jumel Mansion* (Boston, Houghton Mifflin, 1916) .

Chapter 17 TOWARD A NATIONAL STYLE

1. Charles Nicolas Cochin and Bellicard, *Observations sur les antiquités de la ville d'Herculaneum . . .* (Paris, 1754) .
2. Robert Wood, *The Ruins of Palmyra, otherwise Tedmor in the Desert* (London, 1753) ; *The Ruins of Balbec, otherwise Heliopolis in Coelosyria* (London, 1757) .
3. Lewis Mumford, *Sticks and Stones* (New York, Boni and Liveright, 1924) , pp. 92–3.
4. Turpin Bannister, ' The First Iron-Framed Buildings,' *Architectural Review*, vol. 107, no. 640 (Apr. 1950) , pp. 231ff.
5. B. Silliman and C. R. Goodrich, *The World of Science, Art, and Industry . . . in the New-York Exhibition* (1854) , p. 4.
6. Quoted in Oliver Larkin, *Art and Life in America* (New York, Rinehart, 1950) , p. 80.
7. H. M. Pierce Gallagher, *Robert Mills . . .* (New York, Columbia Univ. Press, 1935) , p. 156.

8. Ralph Waldo Emerson, 'The American Scholar,' address delivered at Harvard, 31 Aug. 1837, in *The Complete Essays and Other Writings* (New York, Modern Library, 1940), pp. 165–6.

9. Republished with other writings, in *Form and Function, Remarks on Art by Horatio Greenough*, edited by Harold A. Small (Berkeley, Univ. of California Press 1947).

Index of Sources of Illustrations

Individuals, firms, and institutions from whom photographs and permissions were obtained are listed alphabetically, with addresses at time of publication. The credit line in the caption indicates the source of each picture.

Index

A CATALOG OF SELECTED
DOVER BOOKS
IN ALL FIELDS OF INTEREST

A CATALOG OF SELECTED DOVER
BOOKS IN ALL FIELDS OF INTEREST

CONCERNING THE SPIRITUAL IN ART, Wassily Kandinsky. Pioneering work by father of abstract art. Thoughts on color theory, nature of art. Analysis of earlier masters. 12 illustrations. 80pp. of text. 5⅜ × 8½.   23411-8 Pa. $3.95

ANIMALS: 1,419 Copyright-Free Illustrations of Mammals, Birds, Fish, Insects, etc., Jim Harter (ed.). Clear wood engravings present, in extremely lifelike poses, over 1,000 species of animals. One of the most extensive pictorial sourcebooks of its kind. Captions. Index. 284pp. 9 × 12.   23766-4 Pa. $11.95

CELTIC ART: The Methods of Construction, George Bain. Simple geometric techniques for making Celtic interlacements, spirals, Kells-type initials, animals, humans, etc. Over 500 illustrations. 160pp. 9 × 12. (USO)   22923-8 Pa. $9.95

AN ATLAS OF ANATOMY FOR ARTISTS, Fritz Schider. Most thorough reference work on art anatomy in the world. Hundreds of illustrations, including selections from works by Vesalius, Leonardo, Goya, Ingres, Michelangelo, others. 593 illustrations. 192pp. 7⅛ × 10¼.   20241-0 Pa. $8.95

CELTIC HAND STROKE-BY-STROKE (Irish Half-Uncial from "The Book of Kells"): An Arthur Baker Calligraphy Manual, Arthur Baker. Complete guide to creating each letter of the alphabet in distinctive Celtic manner. Covers hand position, strokes, pens, inks, paper, more. Illustrated. 48pp. 8¼ × 11.
    24336-2 Pa. $3.95

EASY ORIGAMI, John Montroll. Charming collection of 32 projects (hat, cup, pelican, piano, swan, many more) specially designed for the novice origami hobbyist. Clearly illustrated easy-to-follow instructions insure that even beginning papercrafters will achieve successful results. 48pp. 8¼ × 11.   27298-2 Pa. $2.95

THE COMPLETE BOOK OF BIRDHOUSE CONSTRUCTION FOR WOOD-WORKERS, Scott D. Campbell. Detailed instructions, illustrations, tables. Also data on bird habitat and instinct patterns. Bibliography. 3 tables. 63 illustrations in 15 figures. 48pp. 5¼ × 8½.   24407-5 Pa. $1.95

BLOOMINGDALE'S ILLUSTRATED 1886 CATALOG: Fashions, Dry Goods and Housewares, Bloomingdale Brothers. Famed merchants' extremely rare catalog depicting about 1,700 products: clothing, housewares, firearms, dry goods, jewelry, more. Invaluable for dating, identifying vintage items. Also, copyright-free graphics for artists, designers. Co-published with Henry Ford Museum & Greenfield Village. 160pp. 8¼ × 11.   25780-0 Pa. $9.95

HISTORIC COSTUME IN PICTURES, Braun & Schneider. Over 1,450 costumed figures in clearly detailed engravings—from dawn of civilization to end of 19th century. Captions. Many folk costumes. 256pp. 8⅜ × 11¾.   23150-X Pa. $11.95

THE INFLUENCE OF SEA POWER UPON HISTORY, 1660-1783, A. T. Mahan. Influential classic of naval history and tactics still used as text in war colleges. First paperback edition. 4 maps. 24 battle plans. 640pp. 5⅜ × 8½.

25509-3 Pa. $12.95

THE STORY OF THE TITANIC AS TOLD BY ITS SURVIVORS, Jack Winocour (ed.). What it was really like. Panic, despair, shocking inefficiency, and a little heroism. More thrilling than any fictional account. 26 illustrations. 320pp. 5⅜ × 8½.   20610-6 Pa. $7.95

FAIRY AND FOLK TALES OF THE IRISH PEASANTRY, William Butler Yeats (ed.). Treasury of 64 tales from the twilight world of Celtic myth and legend: "The Soul Cages," "The Kildare Pooka," "King O'Toole and his Goose," many more. Introduction and Notes by W. B. Yeats. 352pp. 5⅜ × 8½.   26941-8 Pa. $8.95

BUDDHIST MAHAYANA TEXTS, E. B. Cowell and Others (eds.). Superb, accurate translations of basic documents in Mahayana Buddhism, highly important in history of religions. The Buddha-karita of Asvaghosha, Larger Sukhavativyuha, more. 448pp. 5⅜ × 8½. ,   25552-2 Pa. $9.95

ONE TWO THREE . . . INFINITY: Facts and Speculations of Science, George Gamow. Great physicist's fascinating, readable overview of contemporary science: number theory, relativity, fourth dimension, entropy, genes, atomic structure, much more. 128 illustrations. Index. 352pp. 5⅜ × 8½.   25664-2 Pa. $8.95

ENGINEERING IN HISTORY, Richard Shelton Kirby, et al. Broad, nontechnical survey of history's major technological advances: birth of Greek science, industrial revolution, electricity and applied science, 20th-century automation, much more. 181 illustrations. ". . . excellent . . ."—Isis. Bibliography. vii + 530pp. 5⅜ × 8¼.

26412-2 Pa. $14.95